STAR WARS®
OMNIBUS
AT WAR WITH THE EMPIRE

STAR WARS

OMNIBUS

AT WAR WITH THE EMPIRE

VOLUME 1

DARK HORSE BOOKS®

cover illustration Brian Horton
president and publisher Mike Richardson
series editors Randy Stradley and Scott Allie, with assistance from Jeremy Barlow and Dave Marshall
collection editor Randy Stradley
assistant editor Freddye Lins
collection designer Kat Larson

special thanks to Jann Moorhead, David Anderman, Troy Alders, Leland Chee, Sue Rostoni, and Carol Roeder at Lucas Licensing

Star Wars® Omnibus: At War with the Empire Volume 1

This volume collects Star Wars: Empire #1–#6, #9 (partial), #10–#11, #13–#14, #20–#21, #19, #22, #24–#25, and #31.

Published by Dark Horse Books
A division of Dark Horse Comics, Inc.
10956 SE Main Street
Milwaukie, OR 97222

darkhorse.com | starwars.com

To find a comics shop in your area, call the Comic Shop Locator Service toll-free at 1-888-266-4226

Library of Congress Cataloging-in-Publication Data

Allie, Scott.
Star wars omnibus : at war with the empire volume one : betrayal / script by Scott Allie ; pencils by Ryan Benjamin ; inks by Curtis Arnold ; colors by Dave Stewart ; lettering by Michelle Madsen. -- 1st ed.
     p. cm.
ISBN 978-1-59582-699-2
1. Star Wars fiction--Comic books, strips, etc. 2. Graphic novels. I. Benjamin, Ryan. II. Arnold, Curtis. III. Title.
PN6728.S73A533 2011
741.5'973--dc22
                            2010043488

First edition: April 2011
ISBN 978-1-59582-699-2

10 9 8 7 6 5 4 3 2 1

Printed at 1010 Printing International, Ltd., Guangdong Province, China

All-out war is coming to the galaxy. The Sith Empire is not yet aware of the seriousness of the rebels that have formed an alliance, but they soon will be . . .

CONTENTS

Betrayal | Illustration by Brian Horton

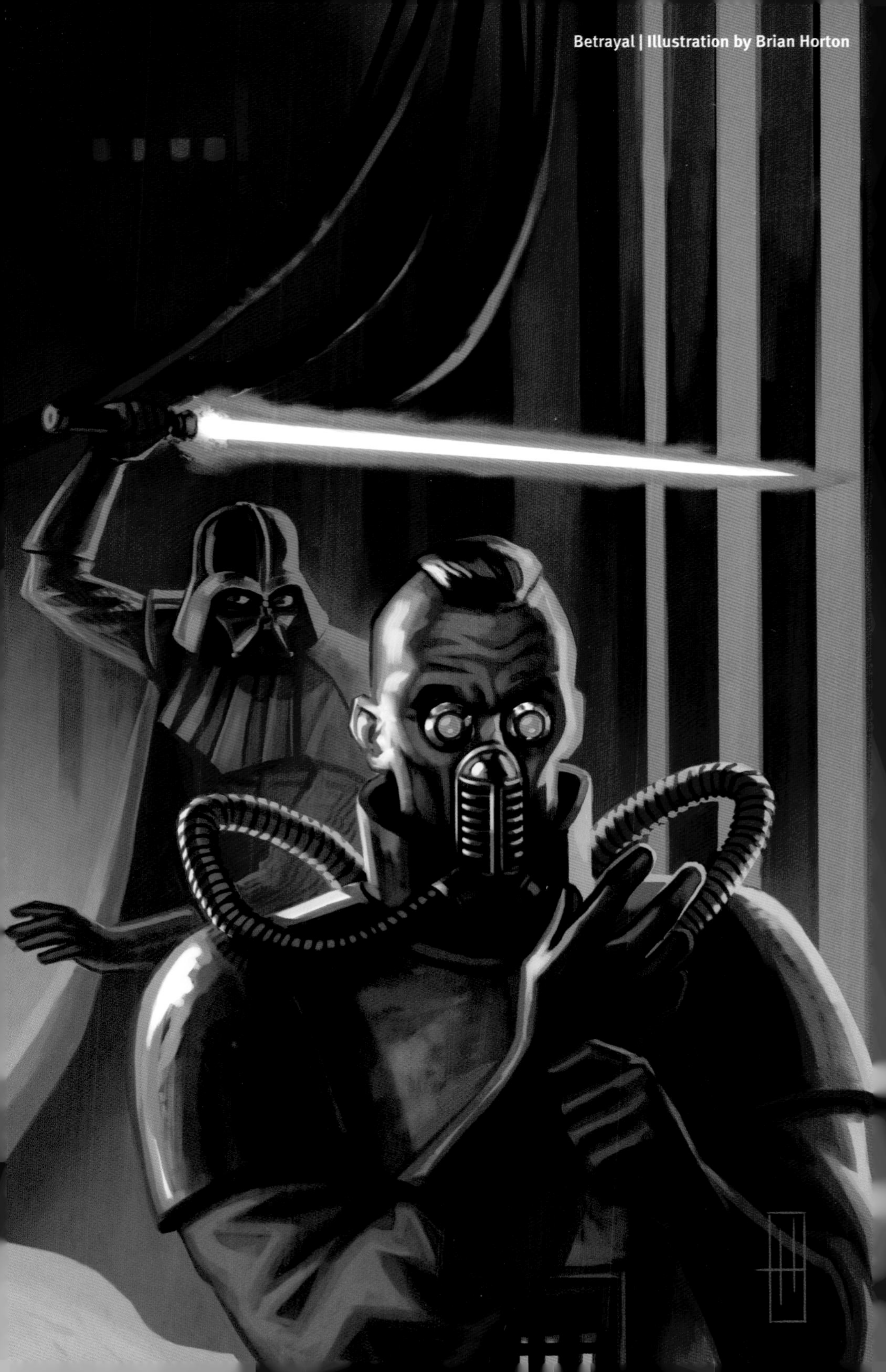

A FEW WEEKS PRIOR TO THE BATTLE OF YAVIN . . .

script by Scott Allie
pencils by Ryan Benjamin
inks by Curtis Arnold
colors by Dave Stewart
lettering by Michelle Madsen

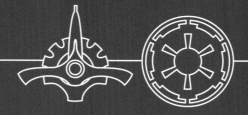

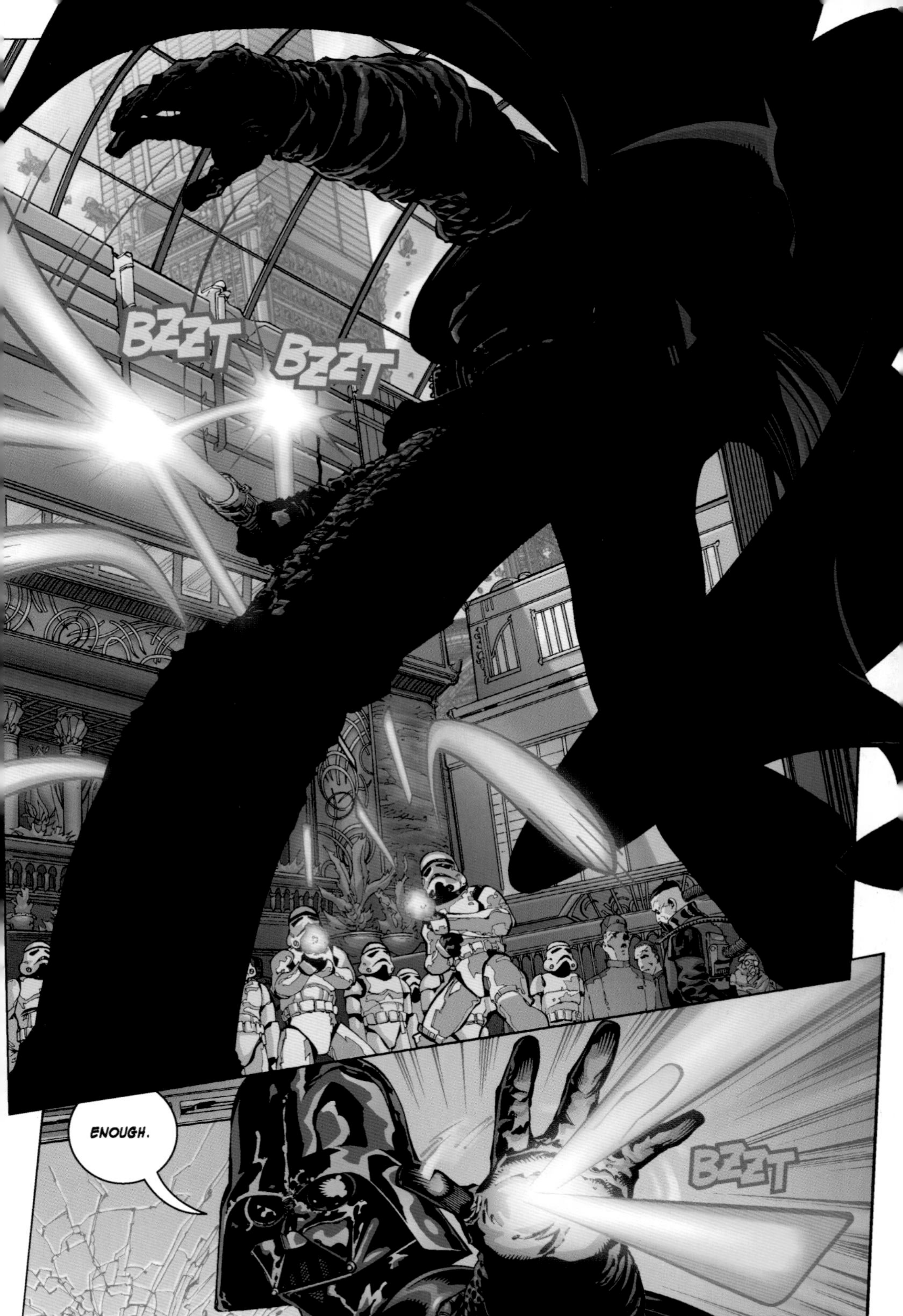
BZZT
BZZT
ENOUGH.
BZZT

BZ-TZ ZKANK

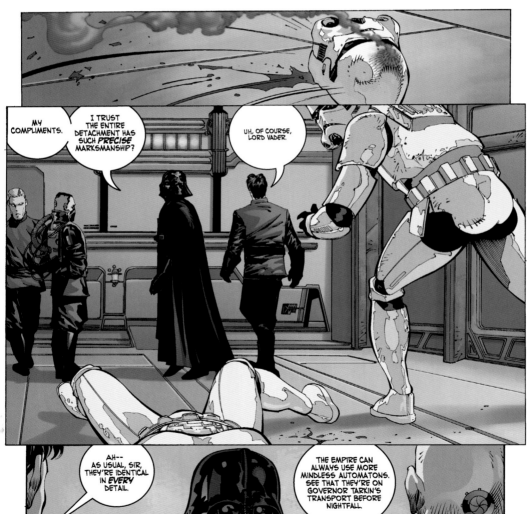

MY COMPLIMENTS.

I TRUST THE ENTIRE DETACHMENT HAS SUCH *PRECISE* MARKSMANSHIP?

UH, OF COURSE, LORD VADER.

AH-- AS USUAL, SIR, THEY'RE IDENTICAL IN *EVERY* DETAIL.

THE EMPIRE CAN ALWAYS USE MORE MINDLESS AUTOMATONS. SEE THAT THEY'RE ON GOVERNOR TARKIN'S TRANSPORT BEFORE NIGHTFALL.

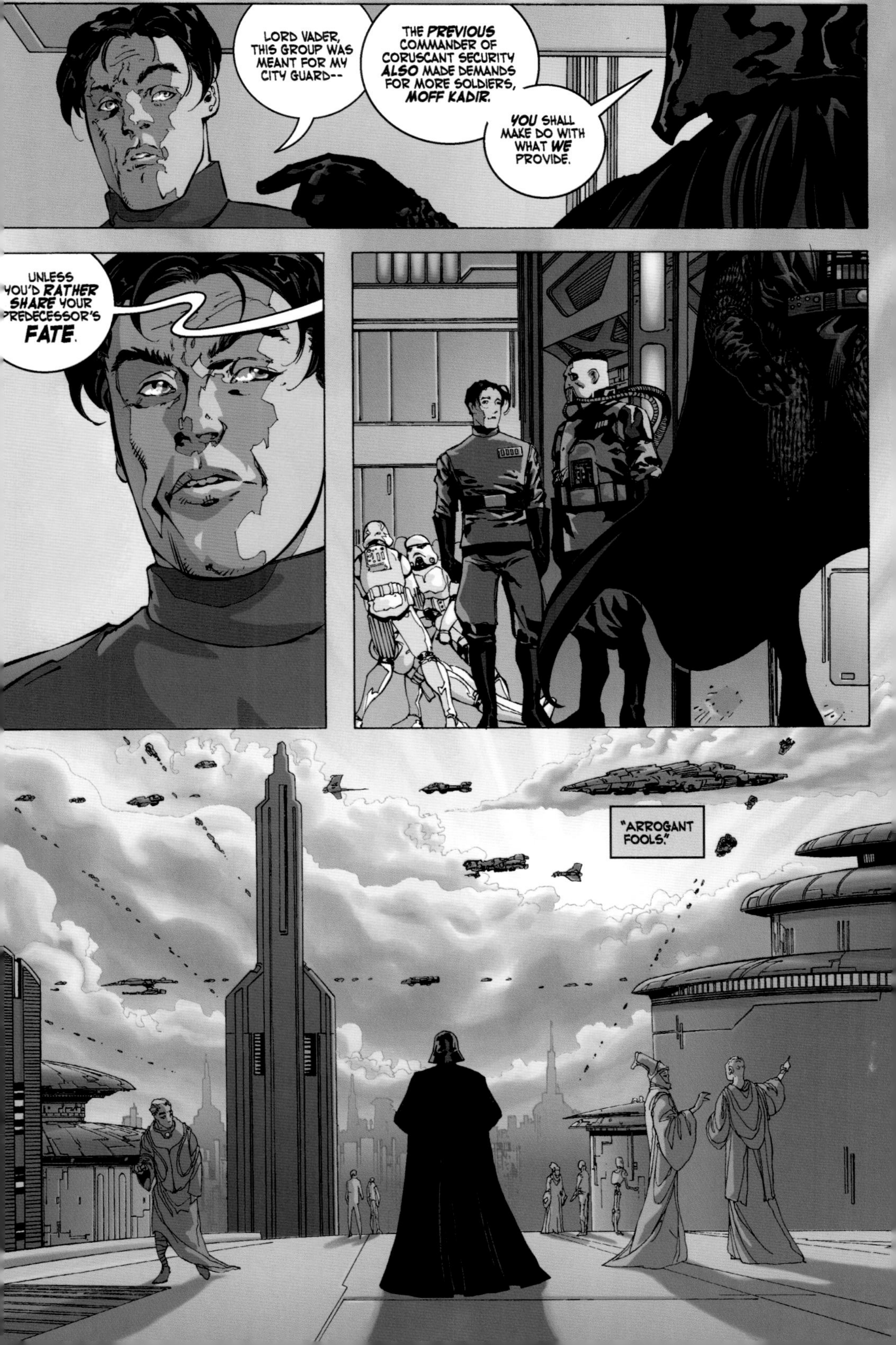
LORD VADER, THIS GROUP WAS MEANT FOR MY CITY GUARD--
THE PREVIOUS COMMANDER OF CORUSCANT SECURITY ALSO MADE DEMANDS FOR MORE SOLDIERS, MOFF KADIR.
YOU SHALL MAKE DO WITH WHAT WE PROVIDE.
UNLESS YOU'D RATHER SHARE YOUR PREDECESSOR'S FATE.
"ARROGANT FOOLS."

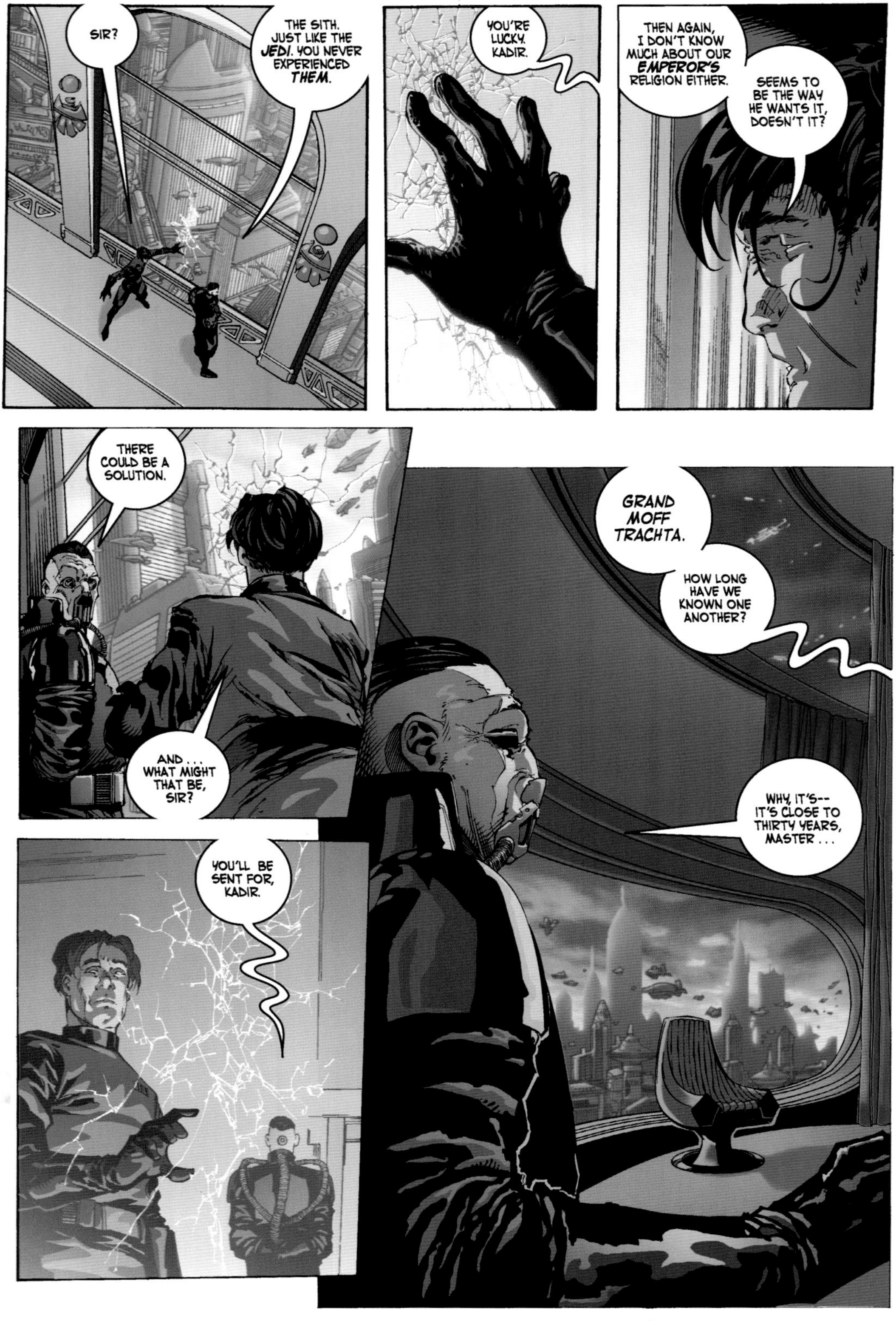
SIR?
THE SITH. JUST LIKE THE JEDI. YOU NEVER EXPERIENCED THEM.
YOU'RE LUCKY, KADIR.
THEN AGAIN, I DON'T KNOW MUCH ABOUT OUR EMPEROR'S RELIGION EITHER.
SEEMS TO BE THE WAY HE WANTS IT, DOESN'T IT?
THERE COULD BE A SOLUTION.
AND . . . WHAT MIGHT THAT BE, SIR?
YOU'LL BE SENT FOR, KADIR.
GRAND MOFF TRACHTA.
HOW LONG HAVE WE KNOWN ONE ANOTHER?
WHY, IT'S-- IT'S CLOSE TO THIRTY YEARS, MASTER . . .

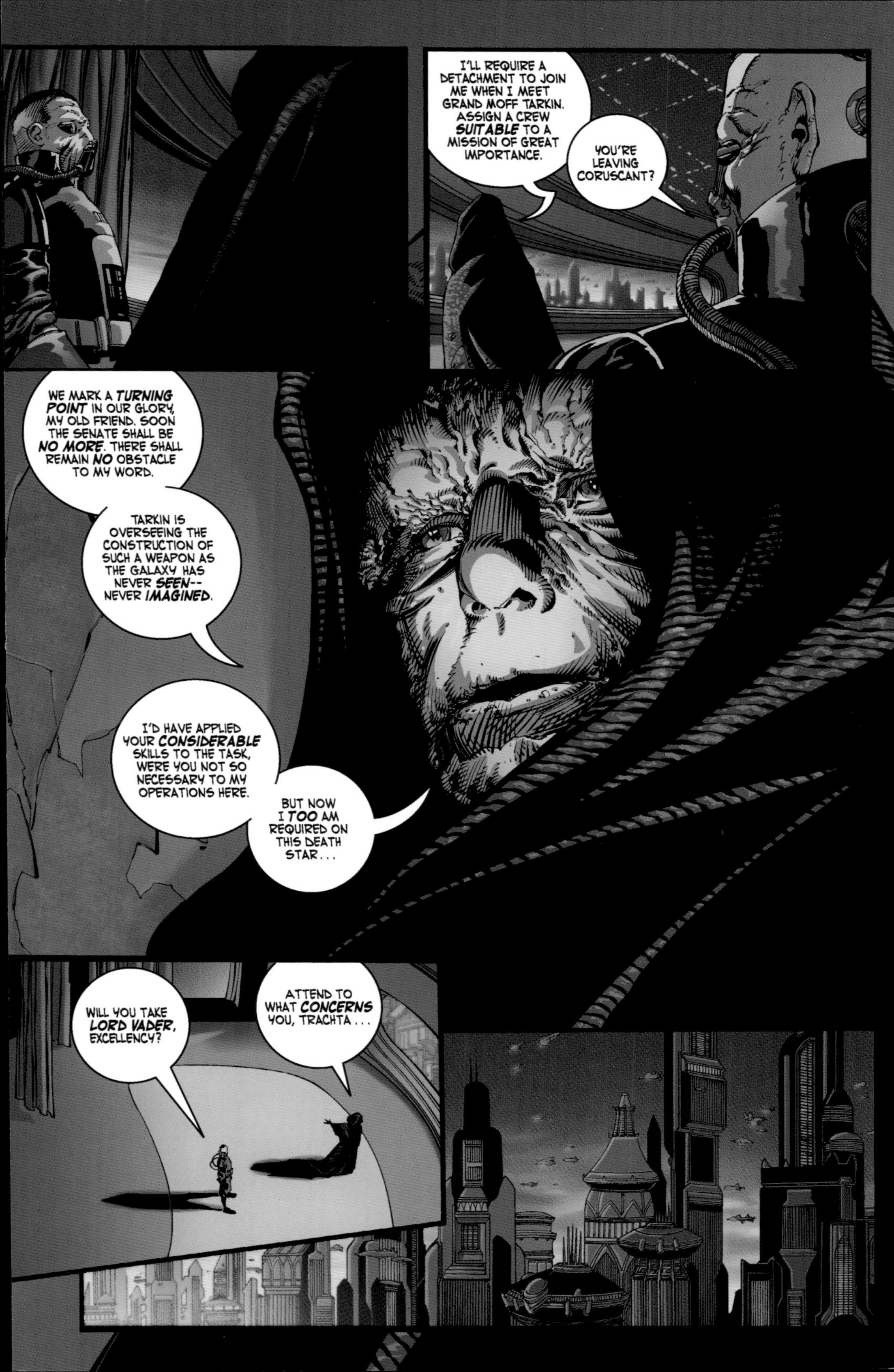

I'LL REQUIRE A DETACHMENT TO JOIN ME WHEN I MEET GRAND MOFF TARKIN. ASSIGN A CREW SUITABLE TO A MISSION OF GREAT IMPORTANCE.
YOU'RE LEAVING CORUSCANT?
WE MARK A TURNING POINT IN OUR GLORY, MY OLD FRIEND. SOON THE SENATE SHALL BE NO MORE. THERE SHALL REMAIN NO OBSTACLE TO MY WORD.
TARKIN IS OVERSEEING THE CONSTRUCTION OF SUCH A WEAPON AS THE GALAXY HAS NEVER SEEN--NEVER IMAGINED.
I'D HAVE APPLIED YOUR CONSIDERABLE SKILLS TO THE TASK, WERE YOU NOT SO NECESSARY TO MY OPERATIONS HERE.
BUT NOW I TOO AM REQUIRED ON THIS DEATH STAR . . .
WILL YOU TAKE LORD VADER, EXCELLENCY?
ATTEND TO WHAT CONCERNS YOU, TRACHTA . . .

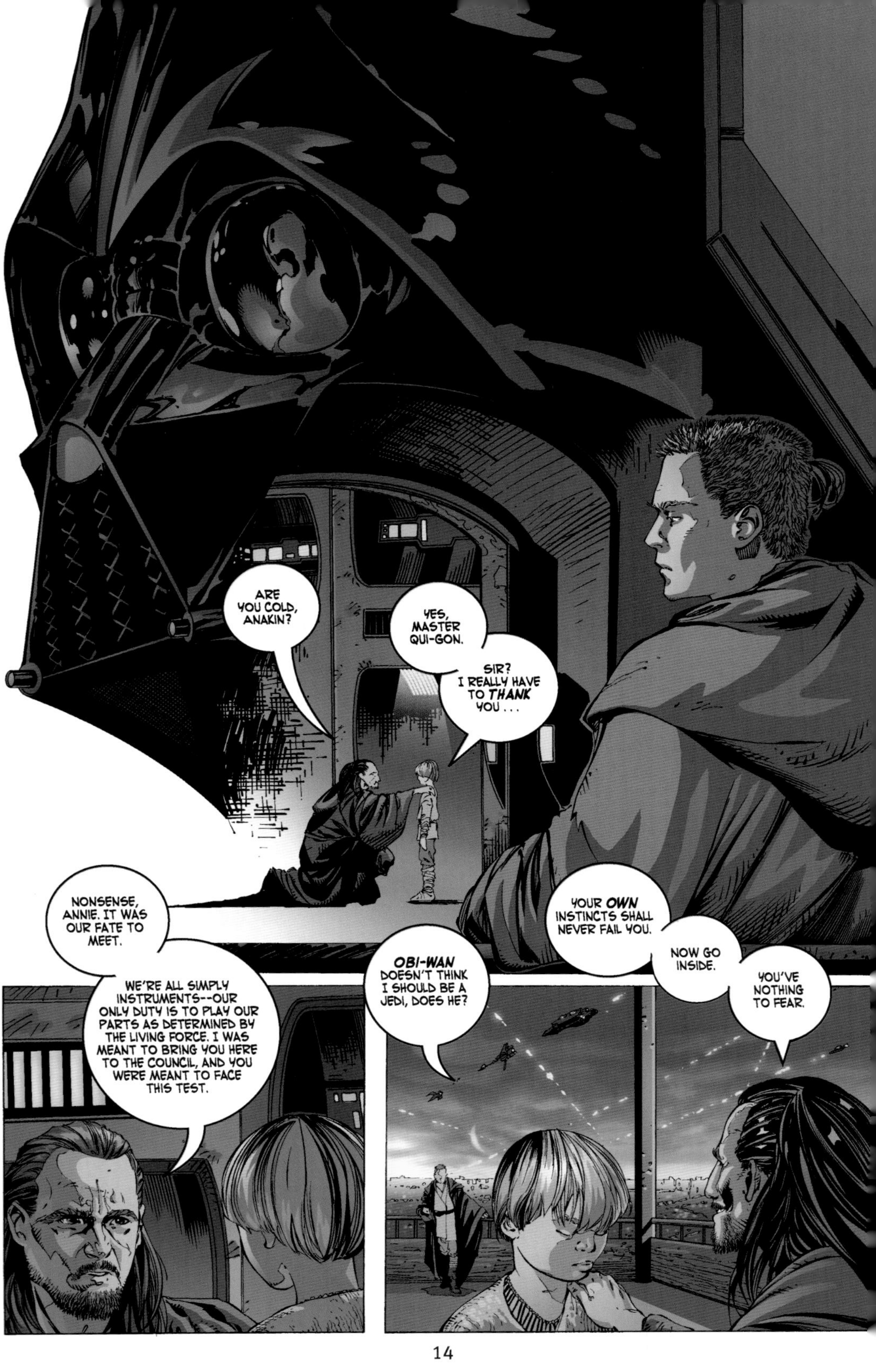
ARE YOU COLD, ANAKIN?
YES, MASTER QUI-GON.
SIR? I REALLY HAVE TO *THANK* YOU . . .
NONSENSE, ANNIE. IT WAS OUR FATE TO MEET.
WE'RE ALL SIMPLY INSTRUMENTS--OUR ONLY DUTY IS TO PLAY OUR PARTS AS DETERMINED BY THE LIVING FORCE. I WAS MEANT TO BRING YOU HERE TO THE COUNCIL, AND YOU WERE MEANT TO FACE THIS TEST.
OBI-WAN DOESN'T THINK I SHOULD BE A JEDI, DOES HE?
YOUR *OWN* INSTINCTS SHALL NEVER FAIL YOU.
NOW GO INSIDE.
YOU'VE NOTHING TO FEAR.

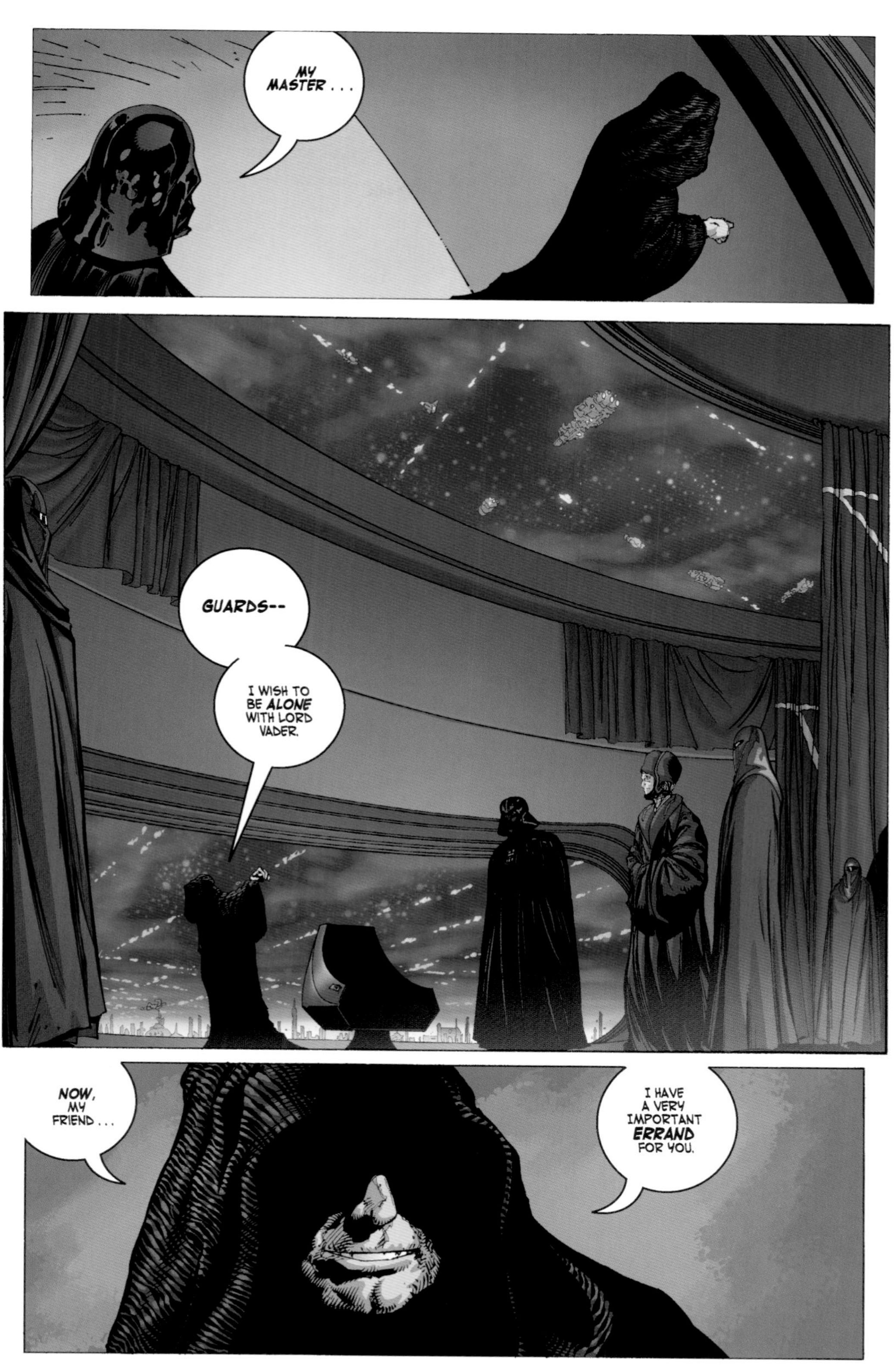
MY MASTER . . .
GUARDS--
I WISH TO BE ALONE WITH LORD VADER.
NOW, MY FRIEND . . .
I HAVE A VERY IMPORTANT ERRAND FOR YOU.

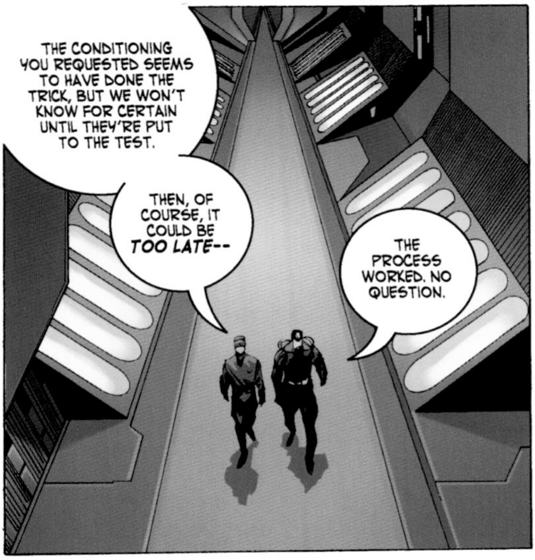
THE CONDITIONING YOU REQUESTED SEEMS TO HAVE DONE THE TRICK, BUT WE WON'T KNOW FOR CERTAIN UNTIL THEY'RE PUT TO THE TEST.
THEN, OF COURSE, IT COULD BE *TOO LATE--*
THE PROCESS WORKED. NO QUESTION.

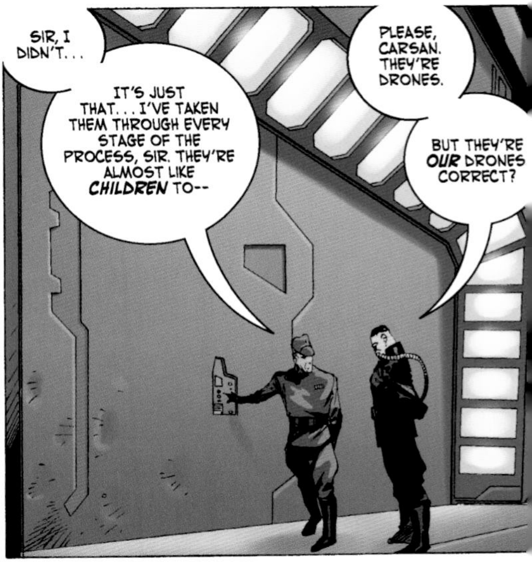
SIR, I DIDN'T. . .
IT'S JUST THAT. . . I'VE TAKEN THEM THROUGH EVERY STAGE OF THE PROCESS, SIR. THEY'RE ALMOST LIKE *CHILDREN* TO--
PLEASE, CARSAN. THEY'RE DRONES.
BUT THEY'RE *OUR* DRONES CORRECT?

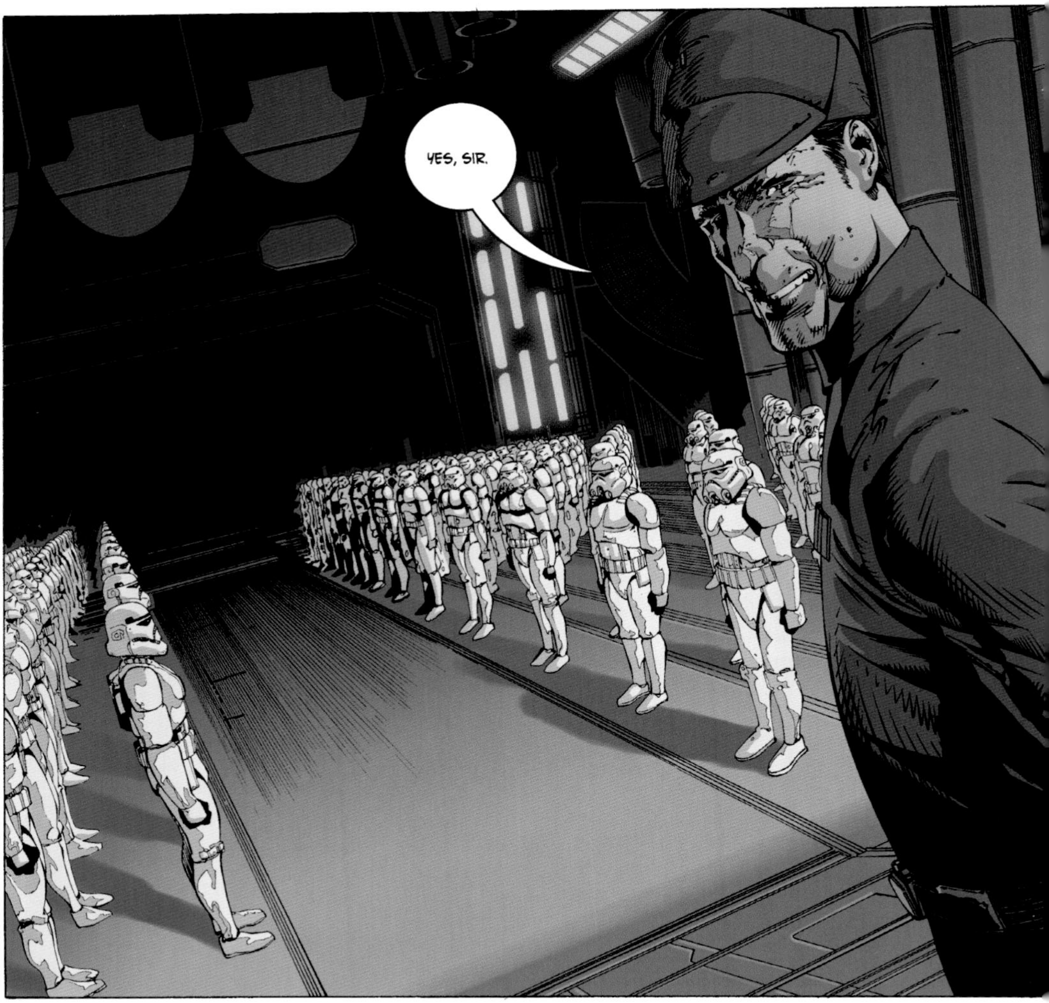
YES, SIR.

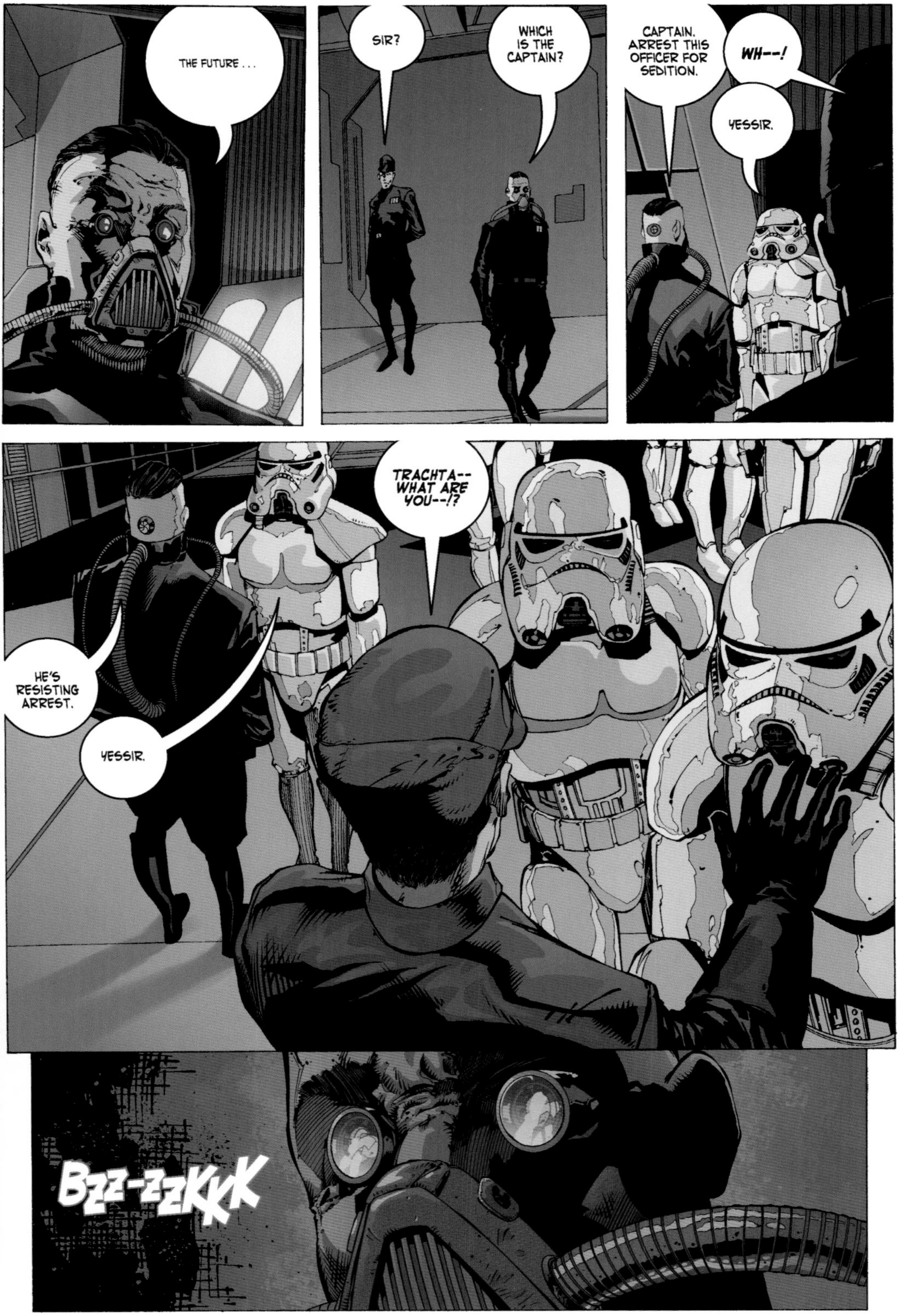
THE FUTURE . . .
SIR?
WHICH IS THE CAPTAIN?
CAPTAIN. ARREST THIS OFFICER FOR SEDITION.
WH--!
YESSIR.
TRACHTA-- WHAT ARE YOU--!?
HE'S RESISTING ARREST.
YESSIR.
BZZ-ZZKKK

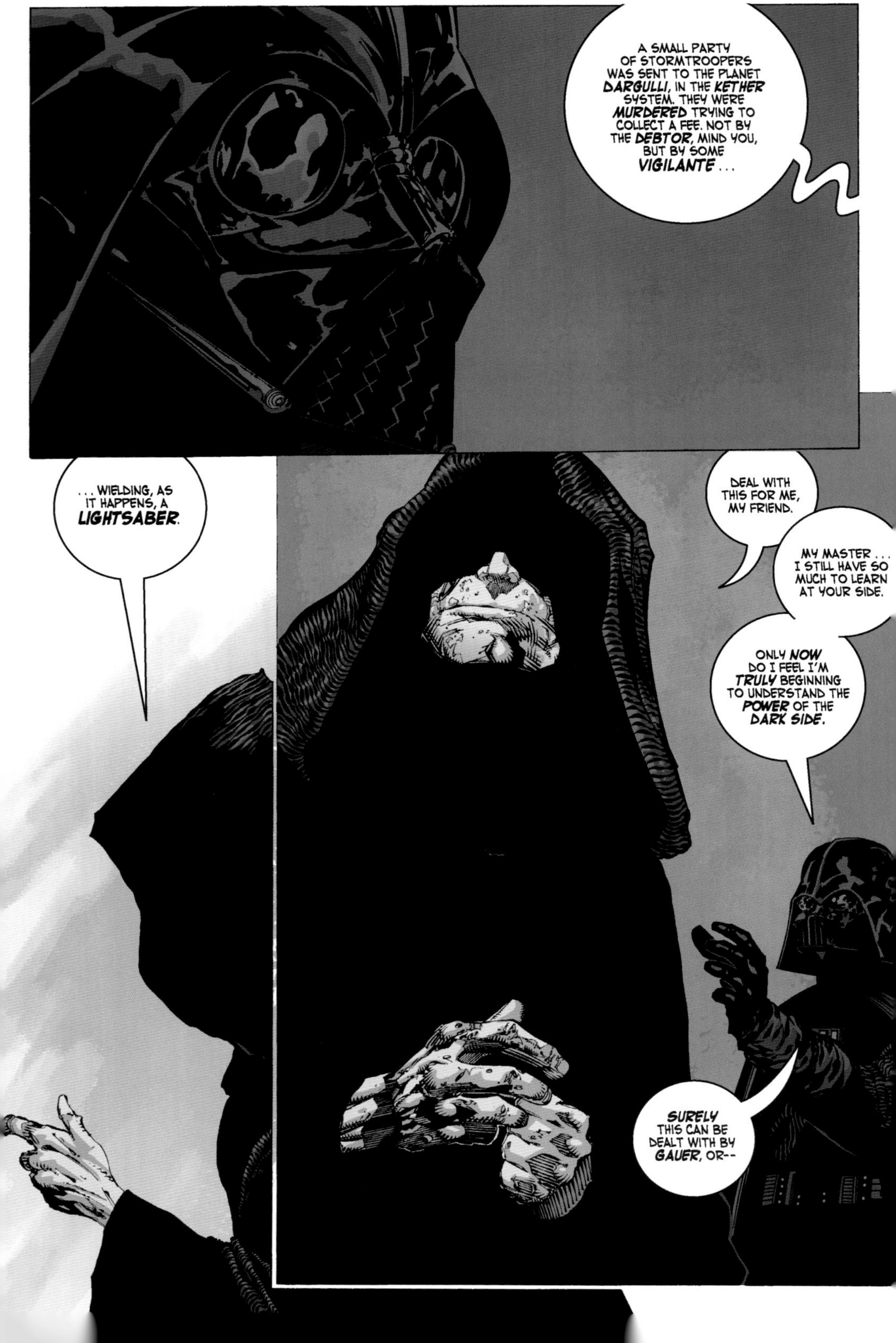
A SMALL PARTY OF STORMTROOPERS WAS SENT TO THE PLANET DARGULLI, IN THE KETHER SYSTEM. THEY WERE MURDERED TRYING TO COLLECT A FEE. NOT BY THE DEBTOR, MIND YOU, BUT BY SOME VIGILANTE . . .
. . . WIELDING, AS IT HAPPENS, A LIGHTSABER.
DEAL WITH THIS FOR ME, MY FRIEND.
MY MASTER . . . I STILL HAVE SO MUCH TO LEARN AT YOUR SIDE.
ONLY NOW DO I FEEL I'M TRULY BEGINNING TO UNDERSTAND THE POWER OF THE DARK SIDE.
SURELY THIS CAN BE DEALT WITH BY GAUER, OR--

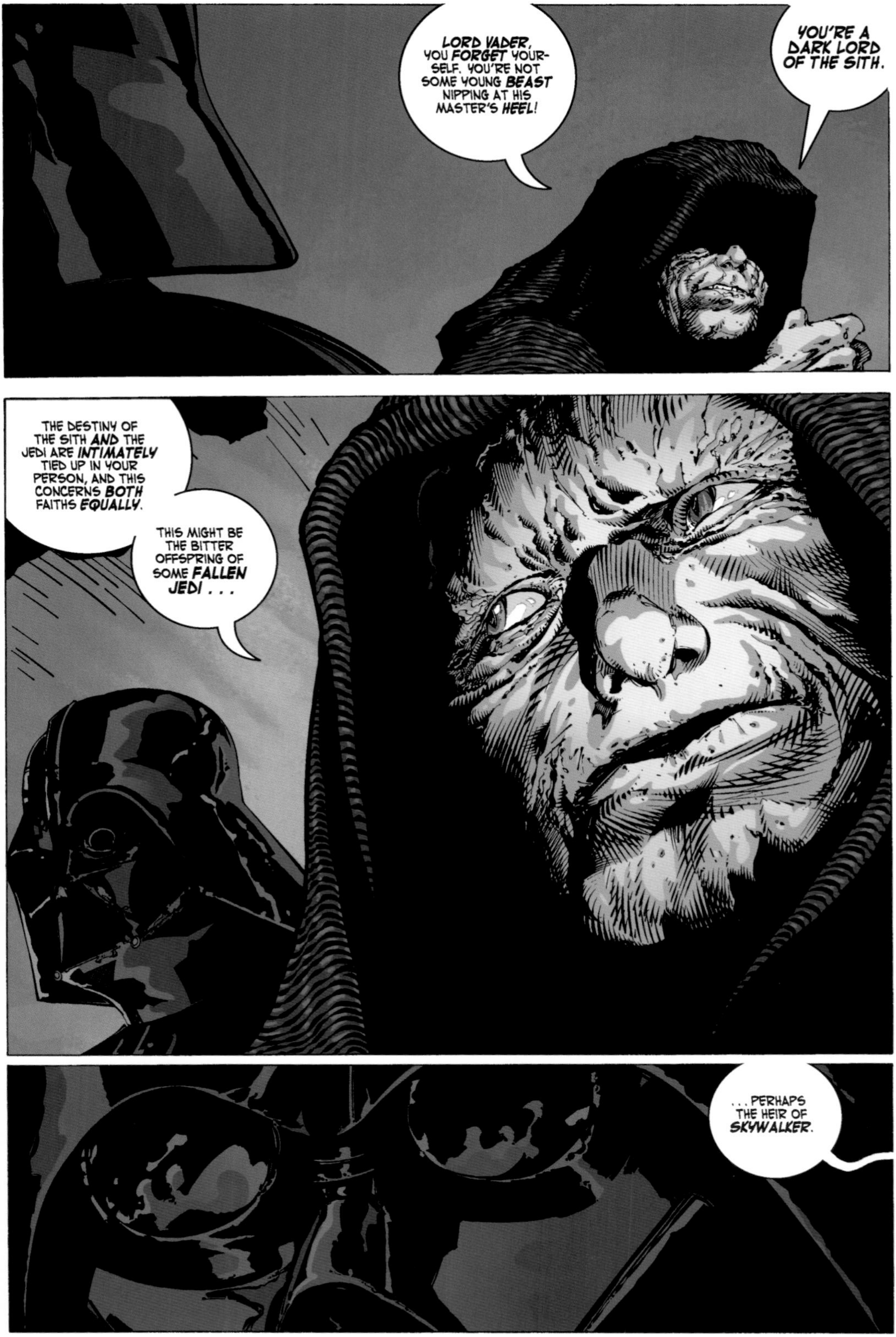
LORD VADER, YOU FORGET YOURSELF. YOU'RE NOT SOME YOUNG BEAST NIPPING AT HIS MASTER'S HEEL!
YOU'RE A DARK LORD OF THE SITH.
THE DESTINY OF THE SITH AND THE JEDI ARE INTIMATELY TIED UP IN YOUR PERSON, AND THIS CONCERNS BOTH FAITHS EQUALLY.
THIS MIGHT BE THE BITTER OFFSPRING OF SOME FALLEN JEDI . . .
. . . PERHAPS THE HEIR OF SKYWALKER.

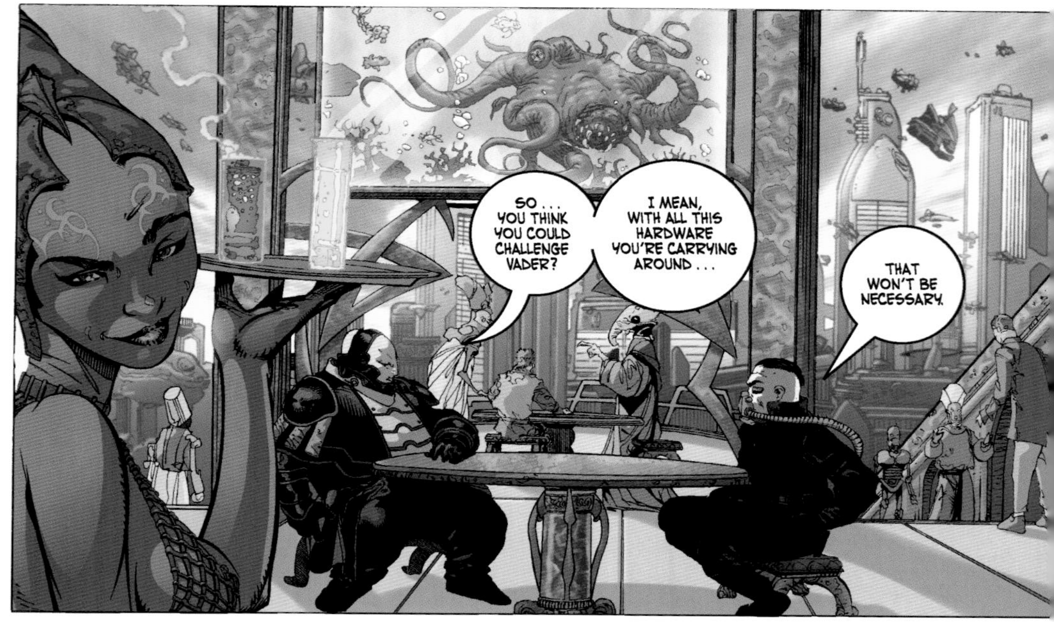
SO . . . YOU THINK YOU COULD CHALLENGE VADER?
I MEAN, WITH ALL THIS HARDWARE YOU'RE CARRYING AROUND . . .
THAT WON'T BE NECESSARY.

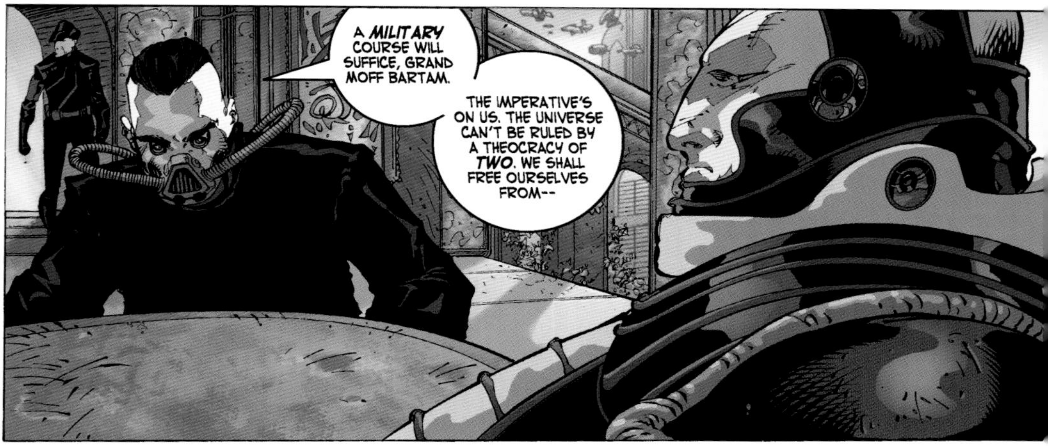
A MILITARY COURSE WILL SUFFICE, GRAND MOFF BARTAM.
THE IMPERATIVE'S ON US. THE UNIVERSE CAN'T BE RULED BY A THEOCRACY OF TWO. WE SHALL FREE OURSELVES FROM--

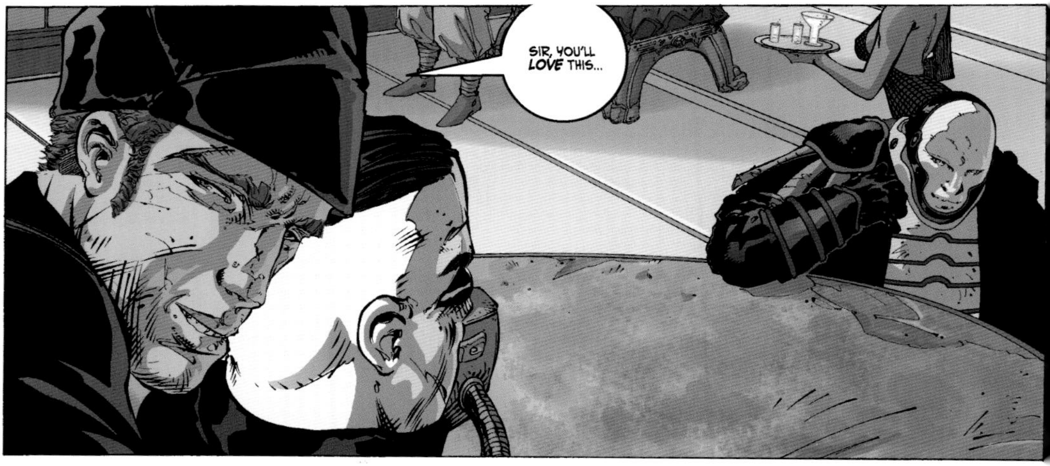
SIR, YOU'LL LOVE THIS...

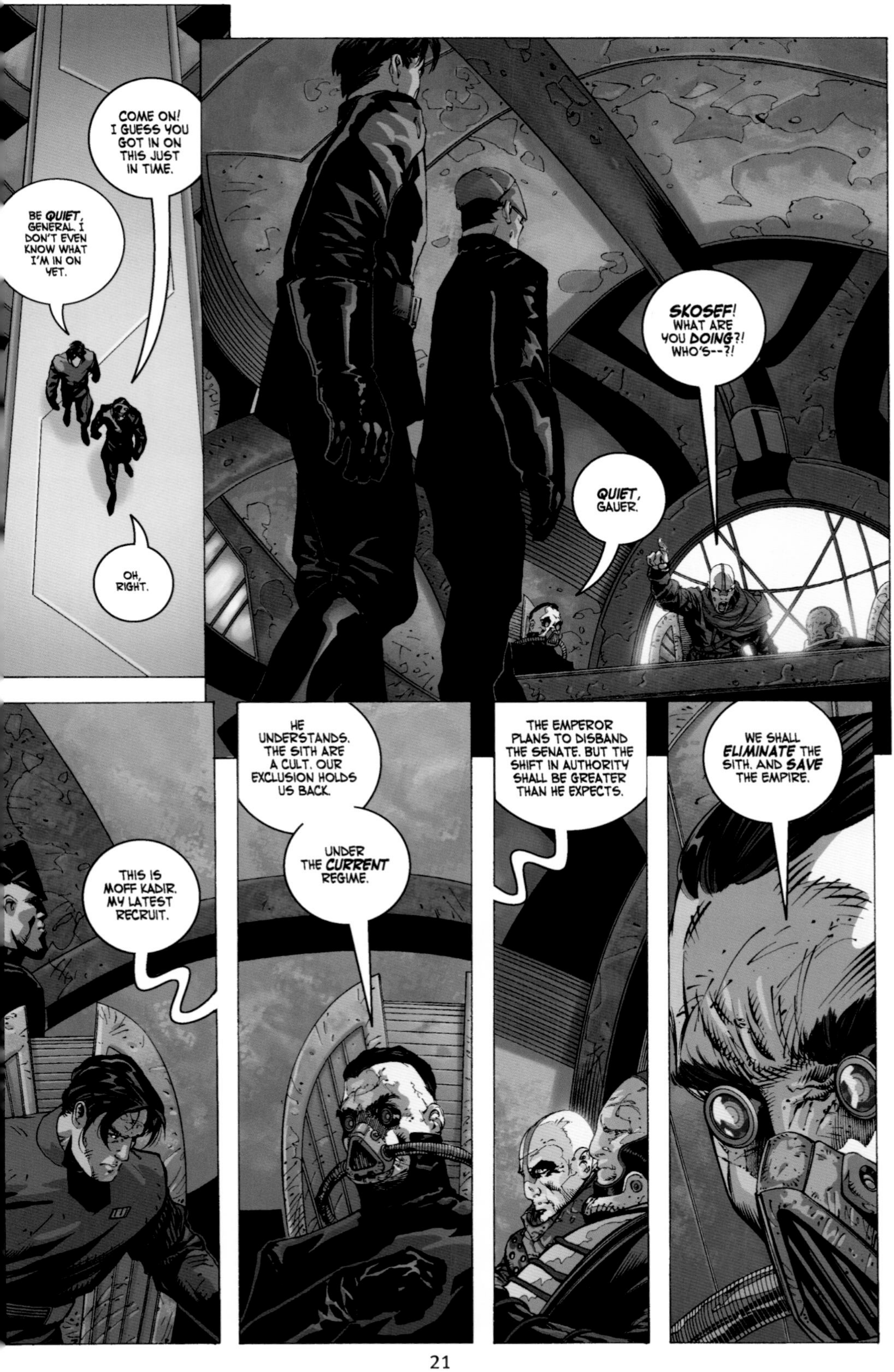

COME ON! I GUESS YOU GOT IN ON THIS JUST IN TIME.
BE QUIET, GENERAL. I DON'T EVEN KNOW WHAT I'M IN ON YET.
OH, RIGHT.
SKOSEF! WHAT ARE YOU DOING?! WHO'S--?!
QUIET, GAUER.
THIS IS MOFF KADIR. MY LATEST RECRUIT.
HE UNDERSTANDS. THE SITH ARE A CULT. OUR EXCLUSION HOLDS US BACK.
UNDER THE CURRENT REGIME.
THE EMPEROR PLANS TO DISBAND THE SENATE. BUT THE SHIFT IN AUTHORITY SHALL BE GREATER THAN HE EXPECTS.
WE SHALL ELIMINATE THE SITH. AND SAVE THE EMPIRE.

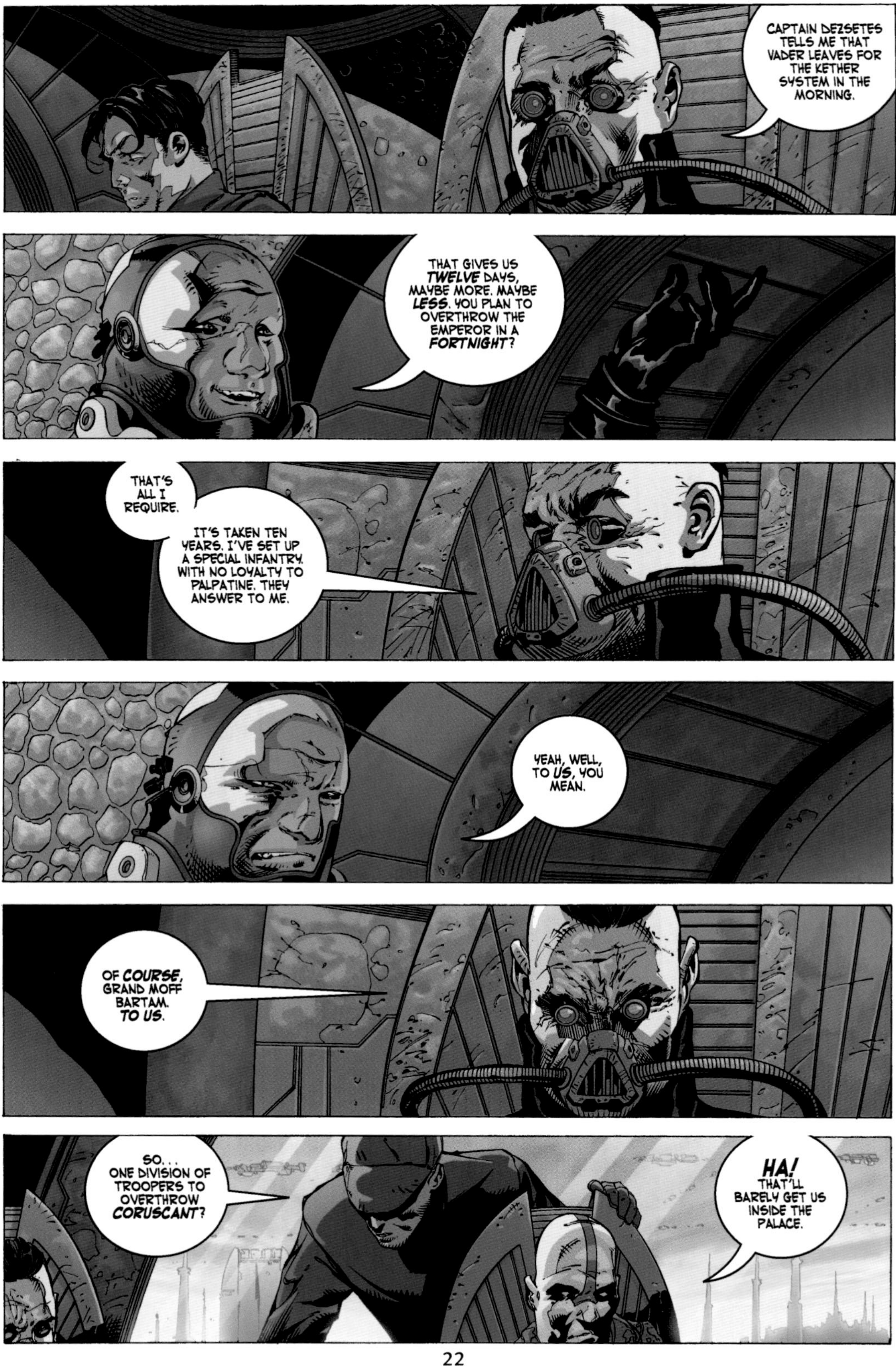
CAPTAIN DEZSETES TELLS ME THAT VADER LEAVES FOR THE KETHER SYSTEM IN THE MORNING.
THAT GIVES US TWELVE DAYS, MAYBE MORE. MAYBE LESS. YOU PLAN TO OVERTHROW THE EMPEROR IN A FORTNIGHT?
THAT'S ALL I REQUIRE.
IT'S TAKEN TEN YEARS. I'VE SET UP A SPECIAL INFANTRY. WITH NO LOYALTY TO PALPATINE. THEY ANSWER TO ME.
YEAH, WELL, TO US, YOU MEAN.
OF COURSE, GRAND MOFF BARTAM. TO US.
SO. . . ONE DIVISION OF TROOPERS TO OVERTHROW CORUSCANT?
HA! THAT'LL BARELY GET US INSIDE THE PALACE.

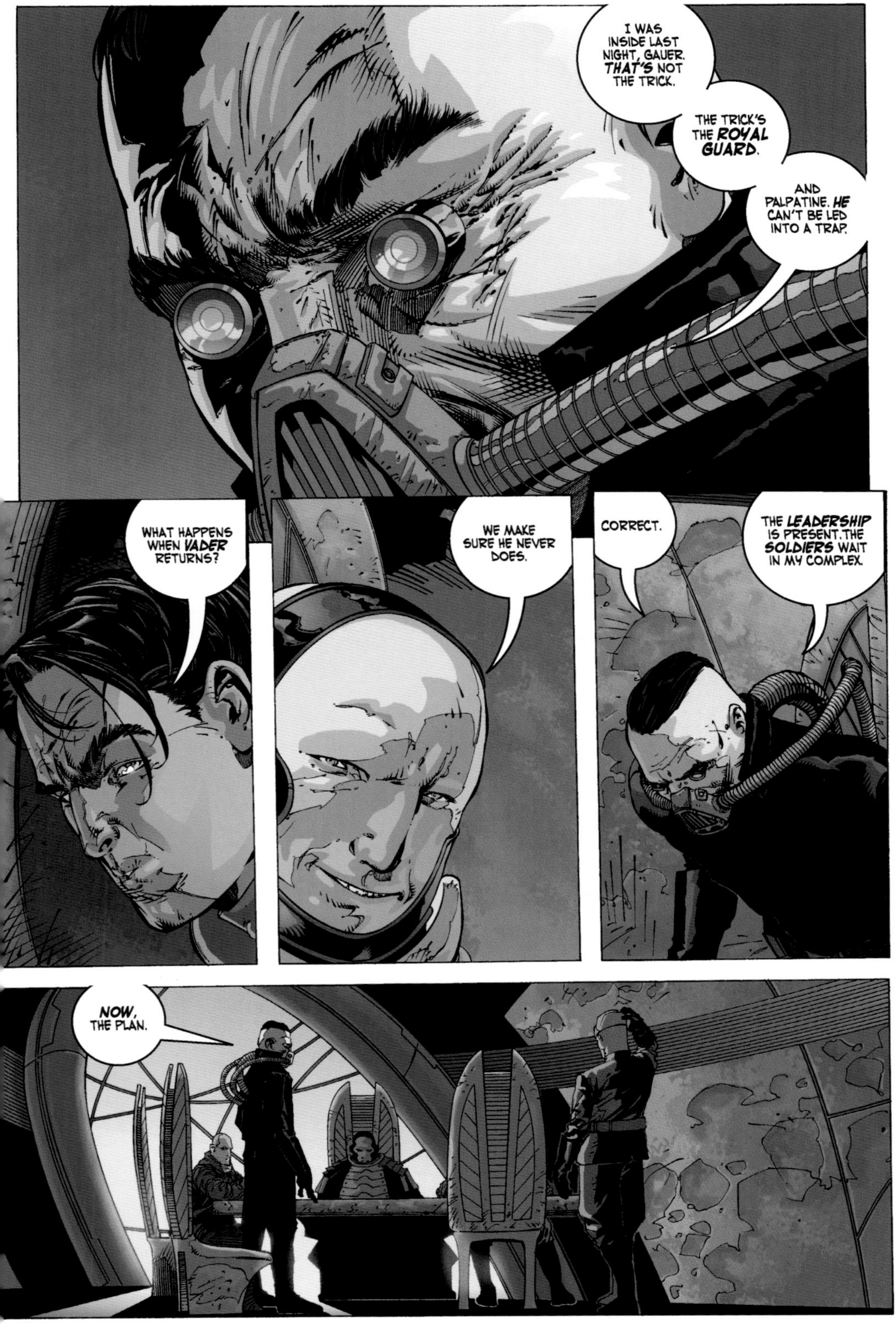

I WAS INSIDE LAST NIGHT, GAUER. THAT'S NOT THE TRICK.
THE TRICK'S THE ROYAL GUARD.
AND PALPATINE. HE CAN'T BE LED INTO A TRAP.
WHAT HAPPENS WHEN VADER RETURNS?
WE MAKE SURE HE NEVER DOES.
CORRECT.
THE LEADERSHIP IS PRESENT. THE SOLDIERS WAIT IN MY COMPLEX.
NOW, THE PLAN.

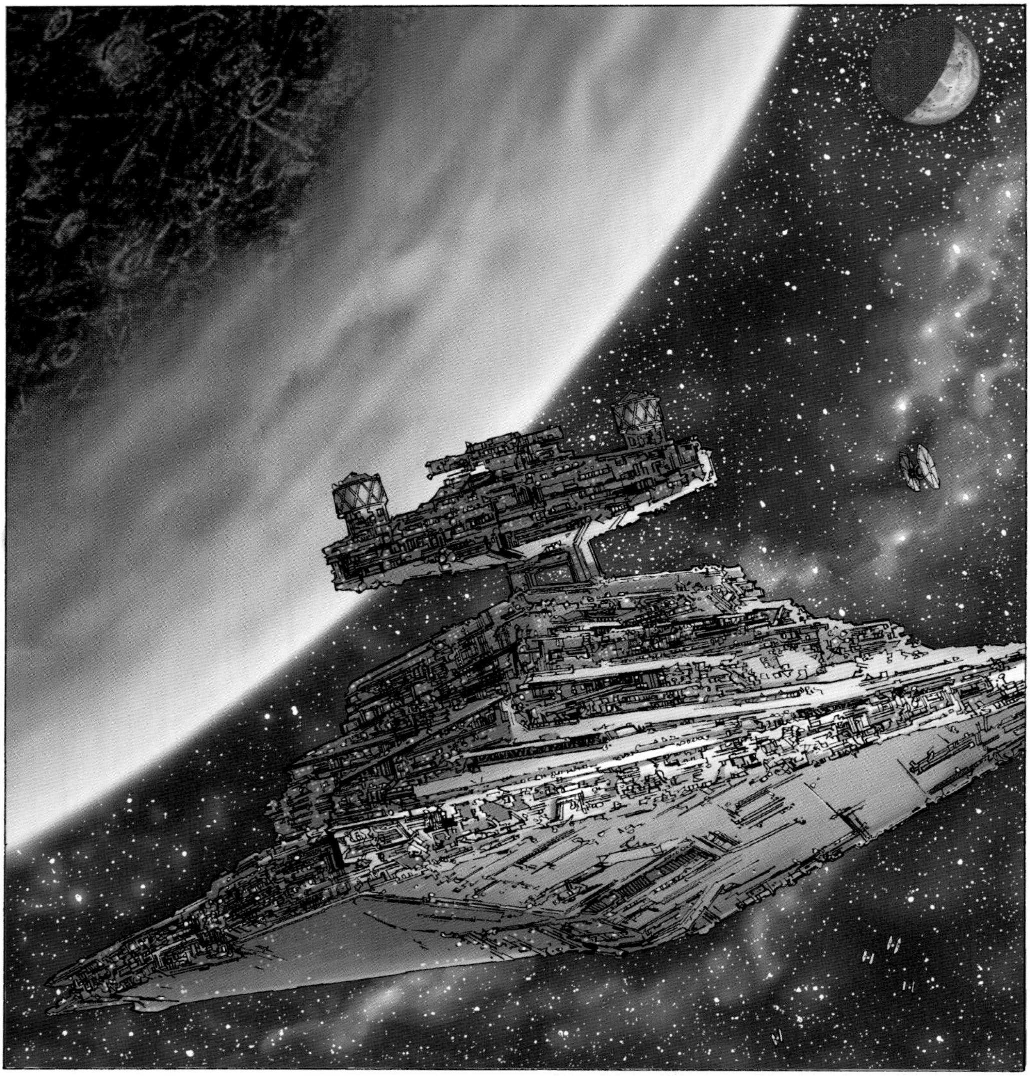

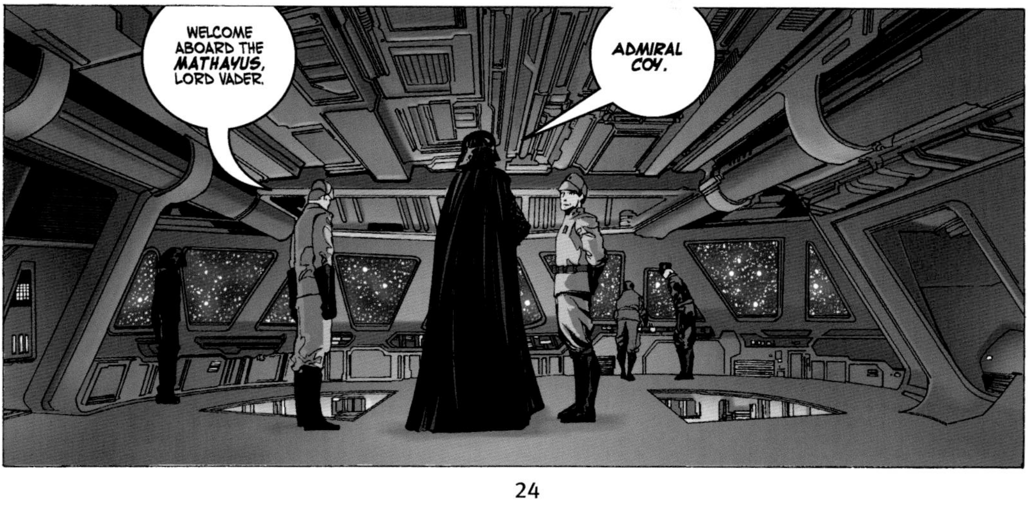
WELCOME ABOARD THE MATHAYUS, LORD VADER.
ADMIRAL COY.

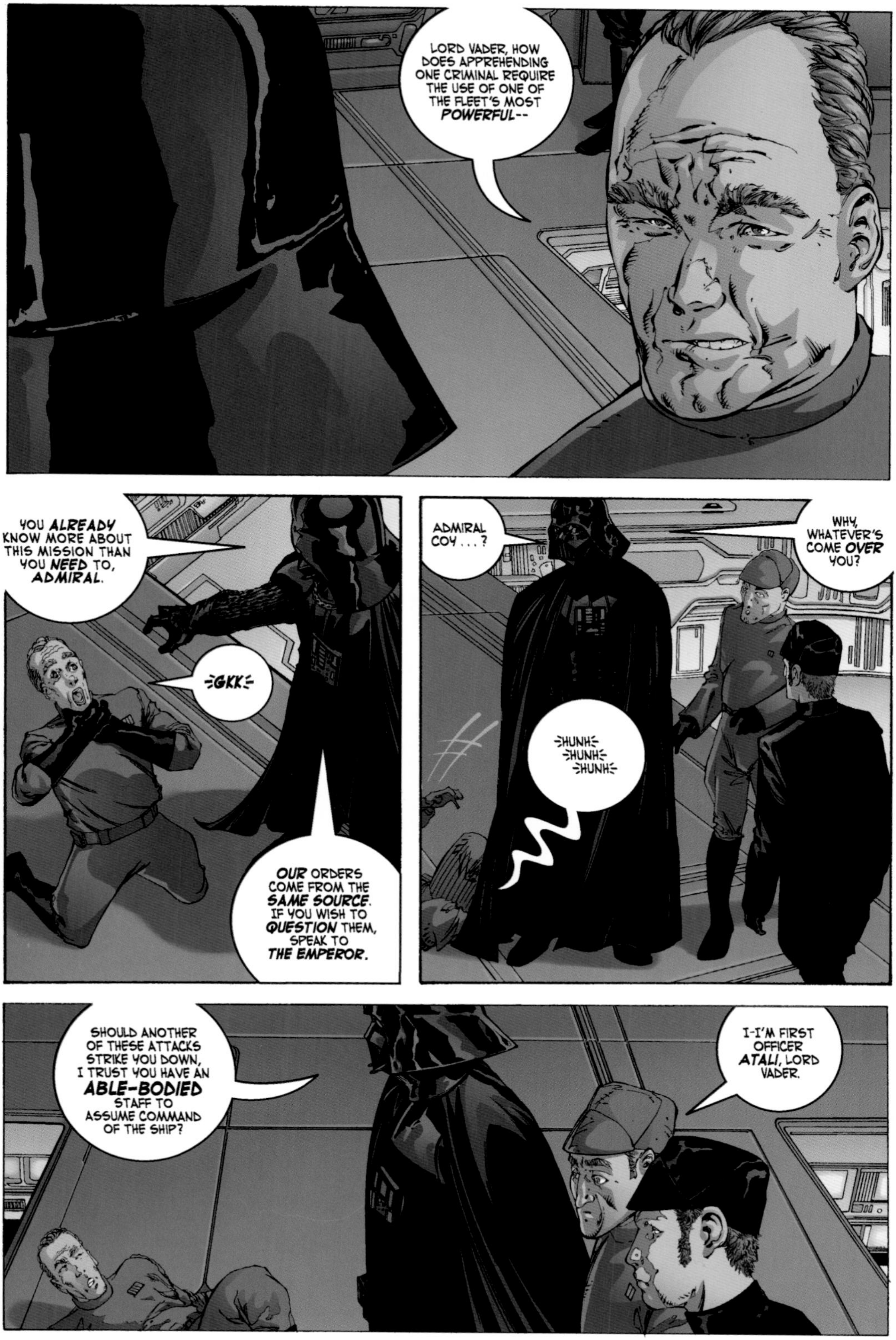
LORD VADER, HOW DOES APPREHENDING ONE CRIMINAL REQUIRE THE USE OF ONE OF THE FLEET'S MOST POWERFUL--
YOU ALREADY KNOW MORE ABOUT THIS MISSION THAN YOU NEED TO, ADMIRAL.
GKK
OUR ORDERS COME FROM THE SAME SOURCE. IF YOU WISH TO QUESTION THEM, SPEAK TO THE EMPEROR.
ADMIRAL COY . . . ?
WHY, WHATEVER'S COME OVER YOU?
HUNH HUNH HUNH
SHOULD ANOTHER OF THESE ATTACKS STRIKE YOU DOWN, I TRUST YOU HAVE AN ABLE-BODIED STAFF TO ASSUME COMMAND OF THE SHIP?
I-I'M FIRST OFFICER ATALI, LORD VADER.

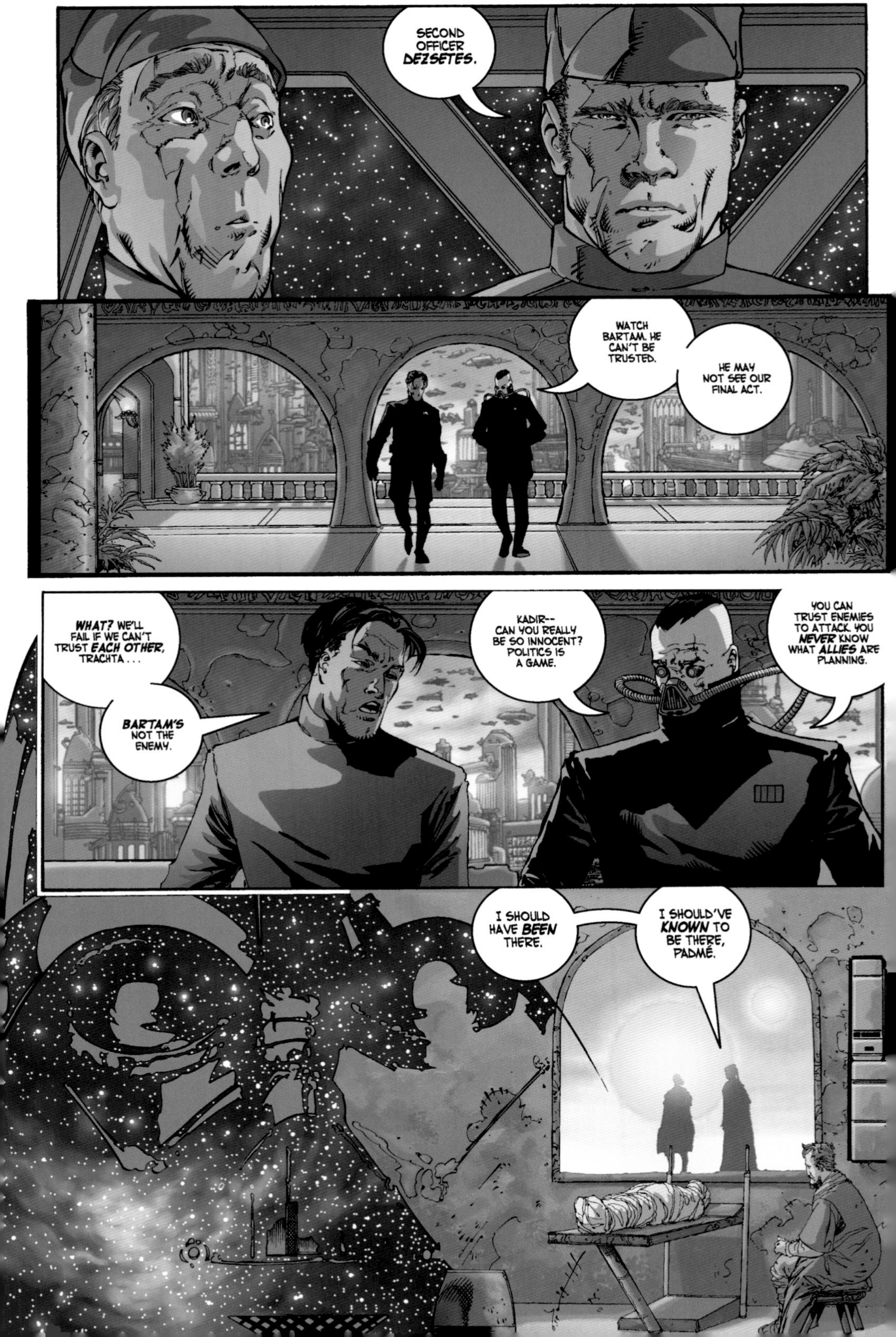
SECOND OFFICER DEZSETES.
WATCH BARTAM. HE CAN'T BE TRUSTED.
HE MAY NOT SEE OUR FINAL ACT.
WHAT? WE'LL FAIL IF WE CAN'T TRUST EACH OTHER, TRACHTA . . .
BARTAM'S NOT THE ENEMY.
KADIR-- CAN YOU REALLY BE SO INNOCENT? POLITICS IS A GAME.
YOU CAN TRUST ENEMIES TO ATTACK. YOU NEVER KNOW WHAT ALLIES ARE PLANNING.
I SHOULD HAVE BEEN THERE.
I SHOULD'VE KNOWN TO BE THERE, PADMÉ.

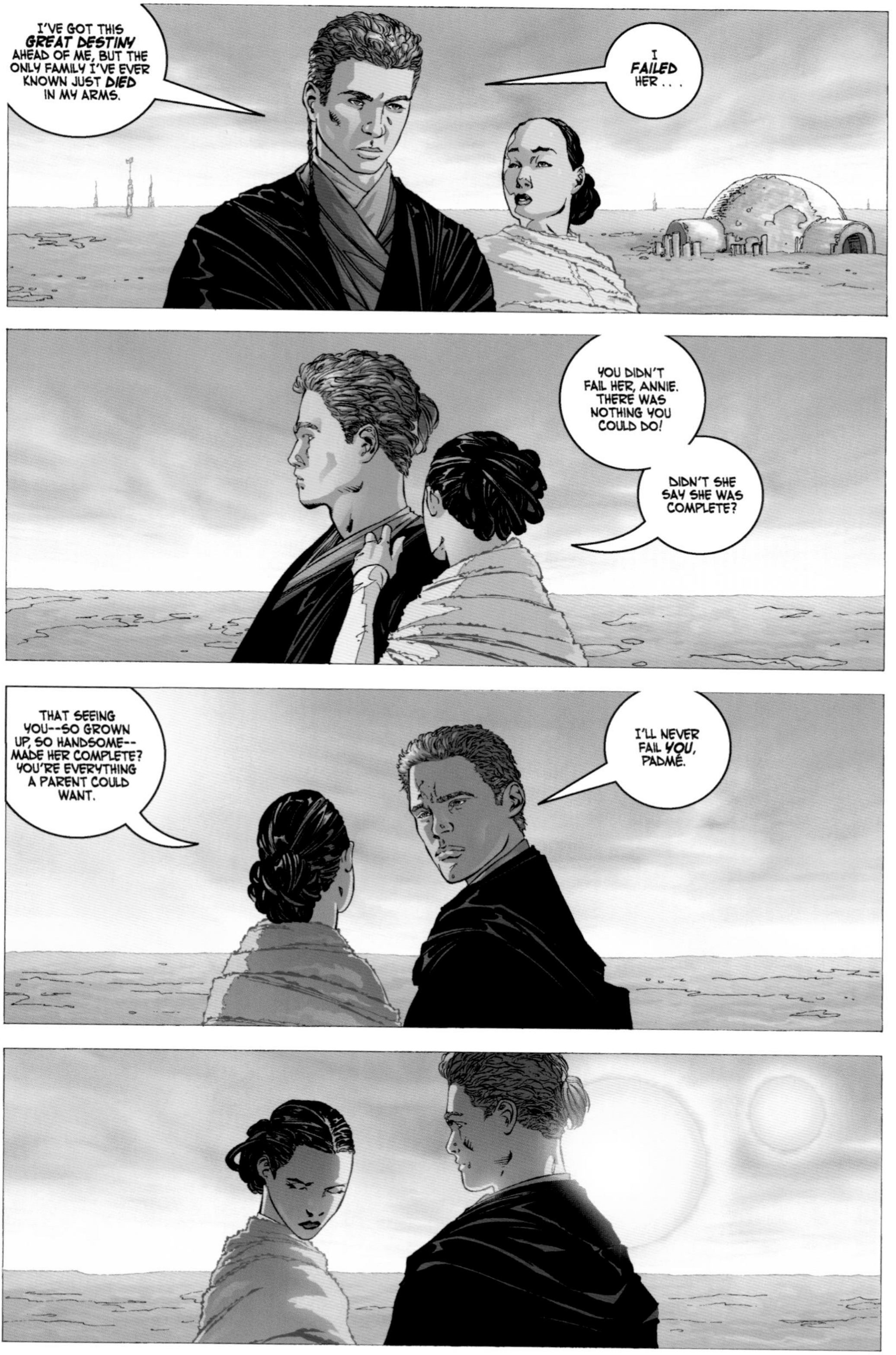
I'VE GOT THIS GREAT DESTINY AHEAD OF ME, BUT THE ONLY FAMILY I'VE EVER KNOWN JUST DIED IN MY ARMS.
I FAILED HER . . .
YOU DIDN'T FAIL HER, ANNIE. THERE WAS NOTHING YOU COULD DO!
DIDN'T SHE SAY SHE WAS COMPLETE?
THAT SEEING YOU--SO GROWN UP, SO HANDSOME--MADE HER COMPLETE? YOU'RE EVERYTHING A PARENT COULD WANT.
I'LL NEVER FAIL YOU, PADMÉ.

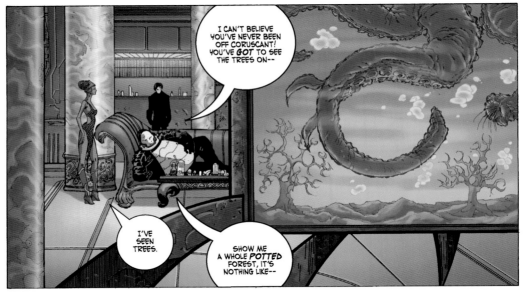

I CAN'T BELIEVE YOU'VE NEVER BEEN OFF CORUSCANT! YOU'VE *GOT* TO SEE THE TREES ON--

I'VE SEEN TREES.

SHOW ME A WHOLE *POTTED* FOREST, IT'S NOTHING LIKE--

EXCUSE ME, DEAR, WHY DON'T YOU COME BACK WHEN JUNIOR HERE TAKES OFF.

I HAVE TO TALK TO YOU ABOUT TRACHTA . . .

I THINK IT'S IMPORTANT HE KNOW WE'RE ALL IN THIS TOGETHER. IT'S *HIS* PLAN--MAYBE IT MAKES SENSE TO SHOW HIM A LITTLE MORE, I DON'T KNOW, *RESPECT.*

DOES HE THINK THAT I DON'T *RESPECT* HIM?

I-- I DON'T KNOW.

HE HASN'T *SAID* THAT?

NO.

DOES HE THINK I'M NOT TAKING THIS *SERIOUSLY* ENOUGH?

MAYBE *THAT'S* ALL IT IS . . .

HM. YOU'RE A SMART KID, KADIR. I GUESS IT WOULDN'T HURT TO TAKE TRACHTA A LITTLE MORE SERIOUSLY.

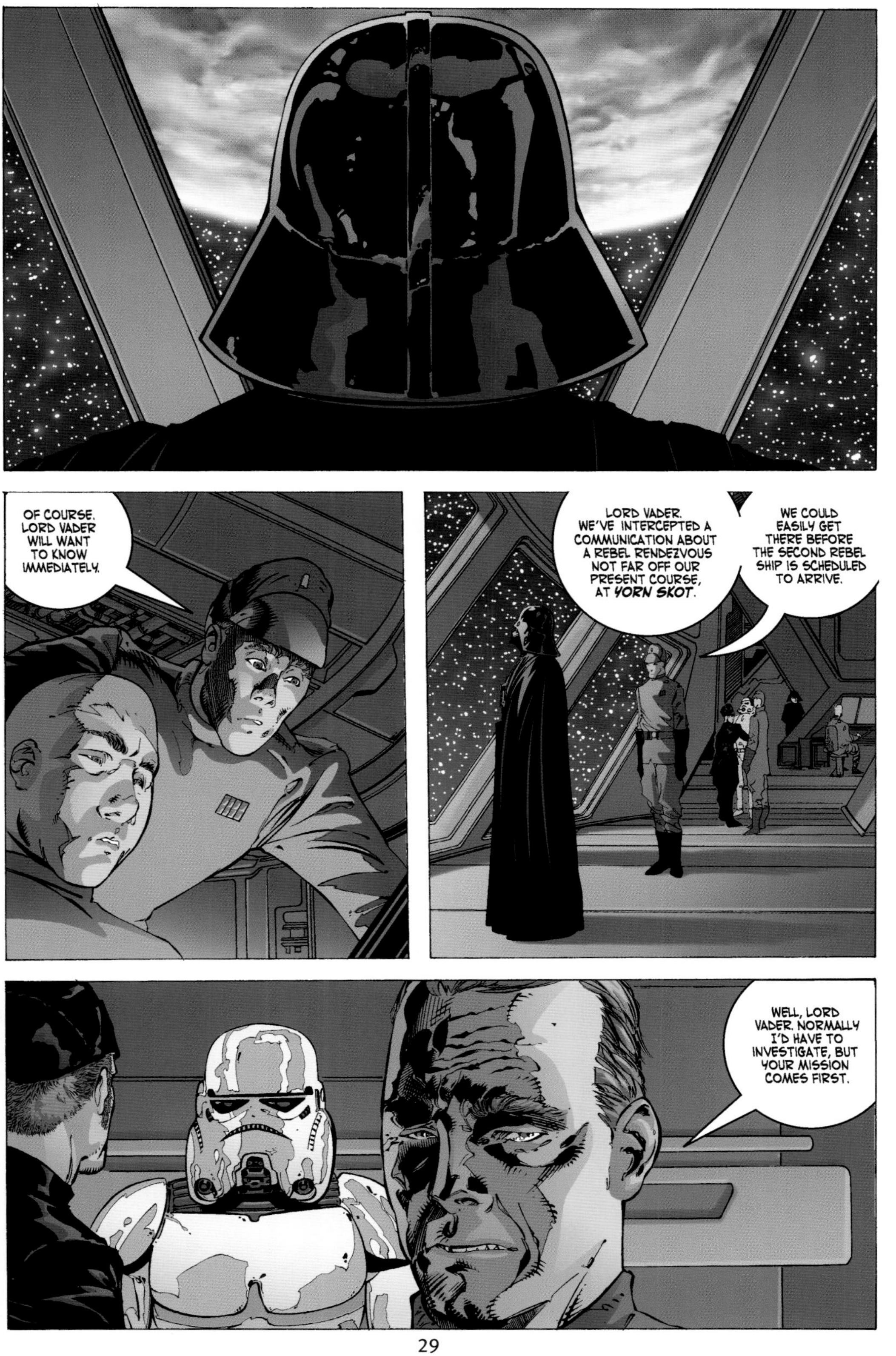
OF COURSE. LORD VADER WILL WANT TO KNOW IMMEDIATELY.
LORD VADER. WE'VE INTERCEPTED A COMMUNICATION ABOUT A REBEL RENDEZVOUS NOT FAR OFF OUR PRESENT COURSE, AT YORN SKOT.
WE COULD EASILY GET THERE BEFORE THE SECOND REBEL SHIP IS SCHEDULED TO ARRIVE.
WELL, LORD VADER. NORMALLY I'D HAVE TO INVESTIGATE, BUT YOUR MISSION COMES FIRST.

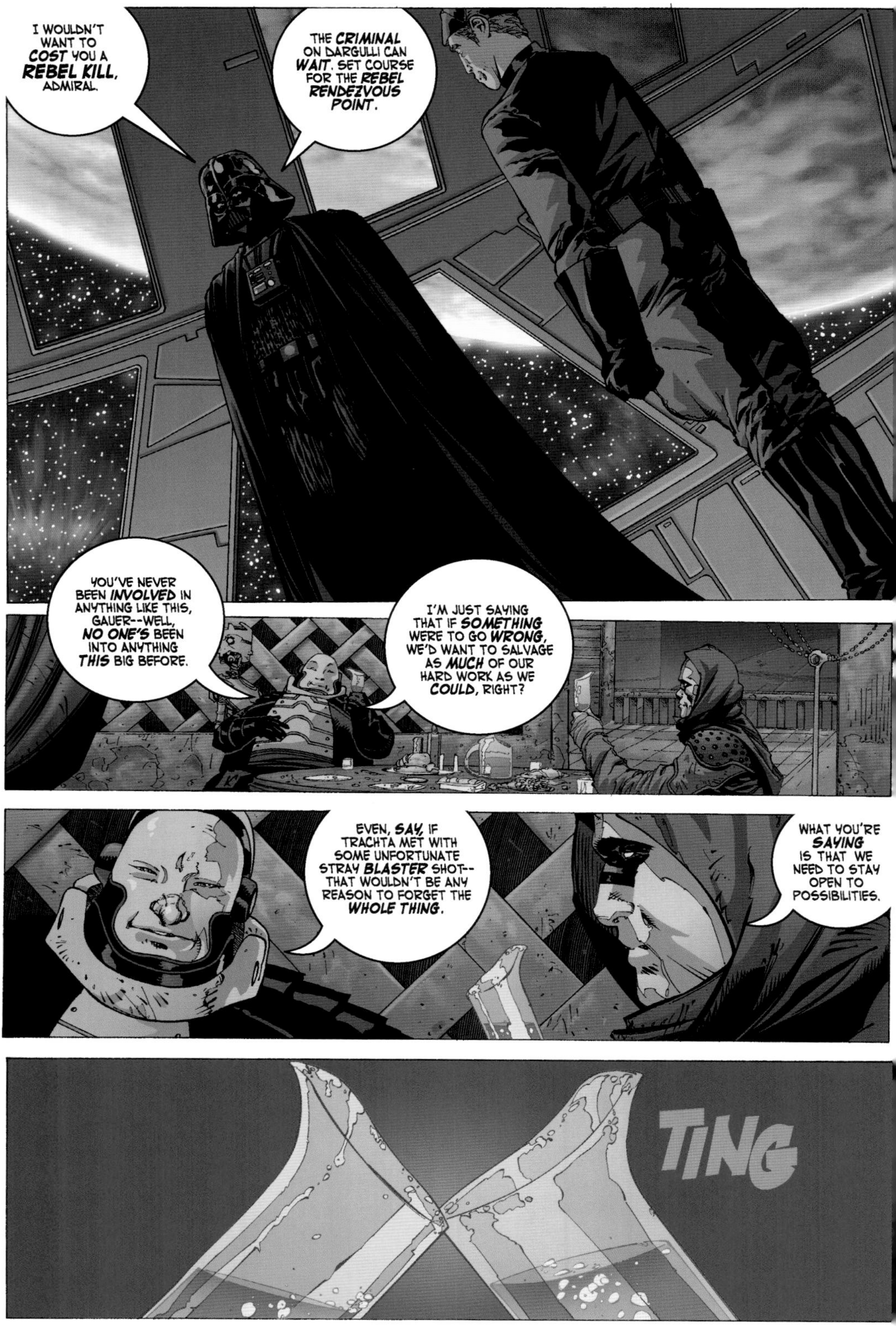
I WOULDN'T WANT TO COST YOU A REBEL KILL, ADMIRAL.
THE CRIMINAL ON DARGULLI CAN WAIT. SET COURSE FOR THE REBEL RENDEZVOUS POINT.
YOU'VE NEVER BEEN INVOLVED IN ANYTHING LIKE THIS, GAUER--WELL, NO ONE'S BEEN INTO ANYTHING THIS BIG BEFORE.
I'M JUST SAYING THAT IF SOMETHING WERE TO GO WRONG, WE'D WANT TO SALVAGE AS MUCH OF OUR HARD WORK AS WE COULD, RIGHT?
EVEN, SAY, IF TRACHTA MET WITH SOME UNFORTUNATE STRAY BLASTER SHOT--THAT WOULDN'T BE ANY REASON TO FORGET THE WHOLE THING.
WHAT YOU'RE SAYING IS THAT WE NEED TO STAY OPEN TO POSSIBILITIES.
TING

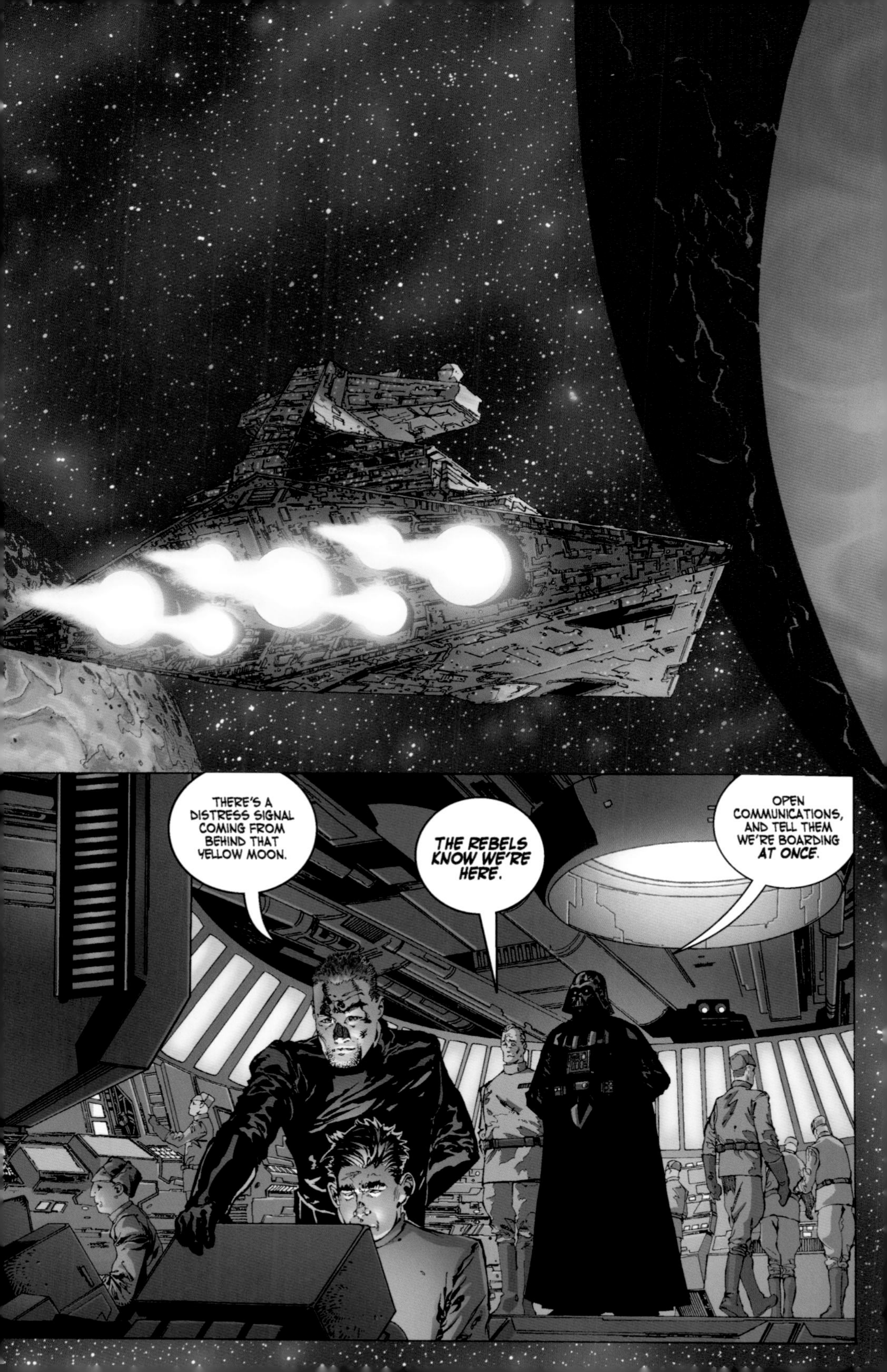
THERE'S A DISTRESS SIGNAL COMING FROM BEHIND THAT YELLOW MOON.
THE REBELS KNOW WE'RE HERE.
OPEN COMMUNICATIONS, AND TELL THEM WE'RE BOARDING AT ONCE.

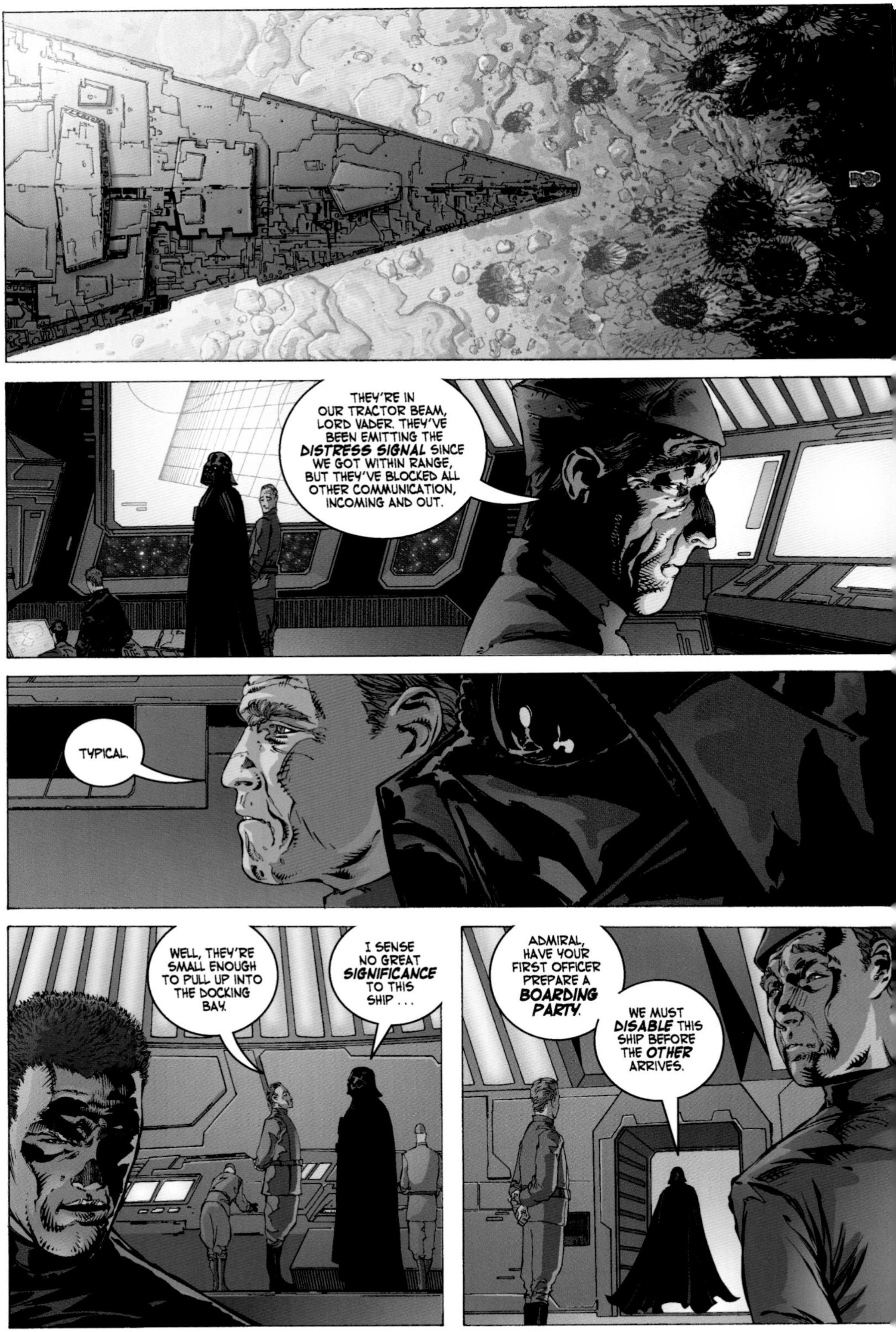
THEY'RE IN OUR TRACTOR BEAM, LORD VADER. THEY'VE BEEN EMITTING THE DISTRESS SIGNAL SINCE WE GOT WITHIN RANGE, BUT THEY'VE BLOCKED ALL OTHER COMMUNICATION, INCOMING AND OUT.
TYPICAL.
WELL, THEY'RE SMALL ENOUGH TO PULL UP INTO THE DOCKING BAY.
I SENSE NO GREAT SIGNIFICANCE TO THIS SHIP . . .
ADMIRAL, HAVE YOUR FIRST OFFICER PREPARE A BOARDING PARTY.
WE MUST DISABLE THIS SHIP BEFORE THE OTHER ARRIVES.

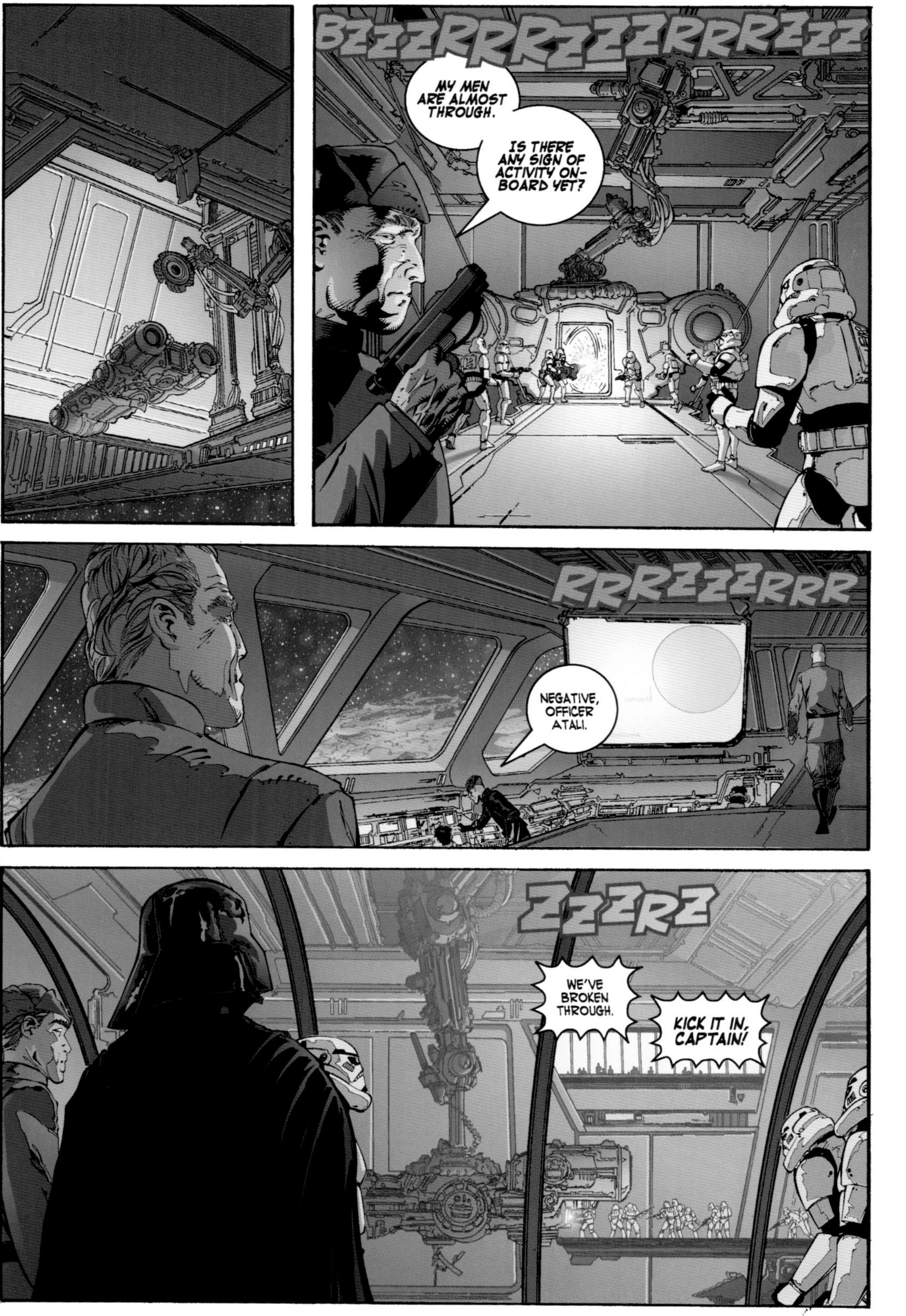
BZZZRRRZZZRRRZZZ
MY MEN ARE ALMOST THROUGH.
IS THERE ANY SIGN OF ACTIVITY ON-BOARD YET?
RRRZZZRRR
NEGATIVE, OFFICER ATALI.
ZZZRZ
WE'VE BROKEN THROUGH.
KICK IT IN, CAPTAIN!

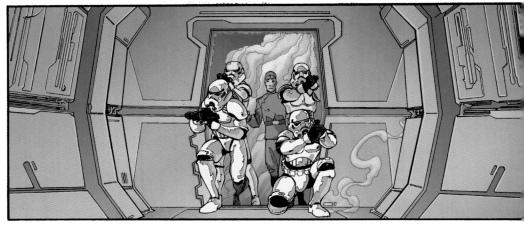

IT'S ABANDONED . . .

. . . THERE'S NO--

CLICK

ADMIRAL COY. HOW DID WE *RECEIVE* THE TRANSMISSION?

THE *DISTRESS SIGNAL?*

NO, ADMIRAL, THE TRANSMISSION WHICH *INFORMED* US OF THIS *RENDEZVOUS.*

HELLO? HELLO?

I SAID THE SHIP APPEARS TO BE ABANDONED!

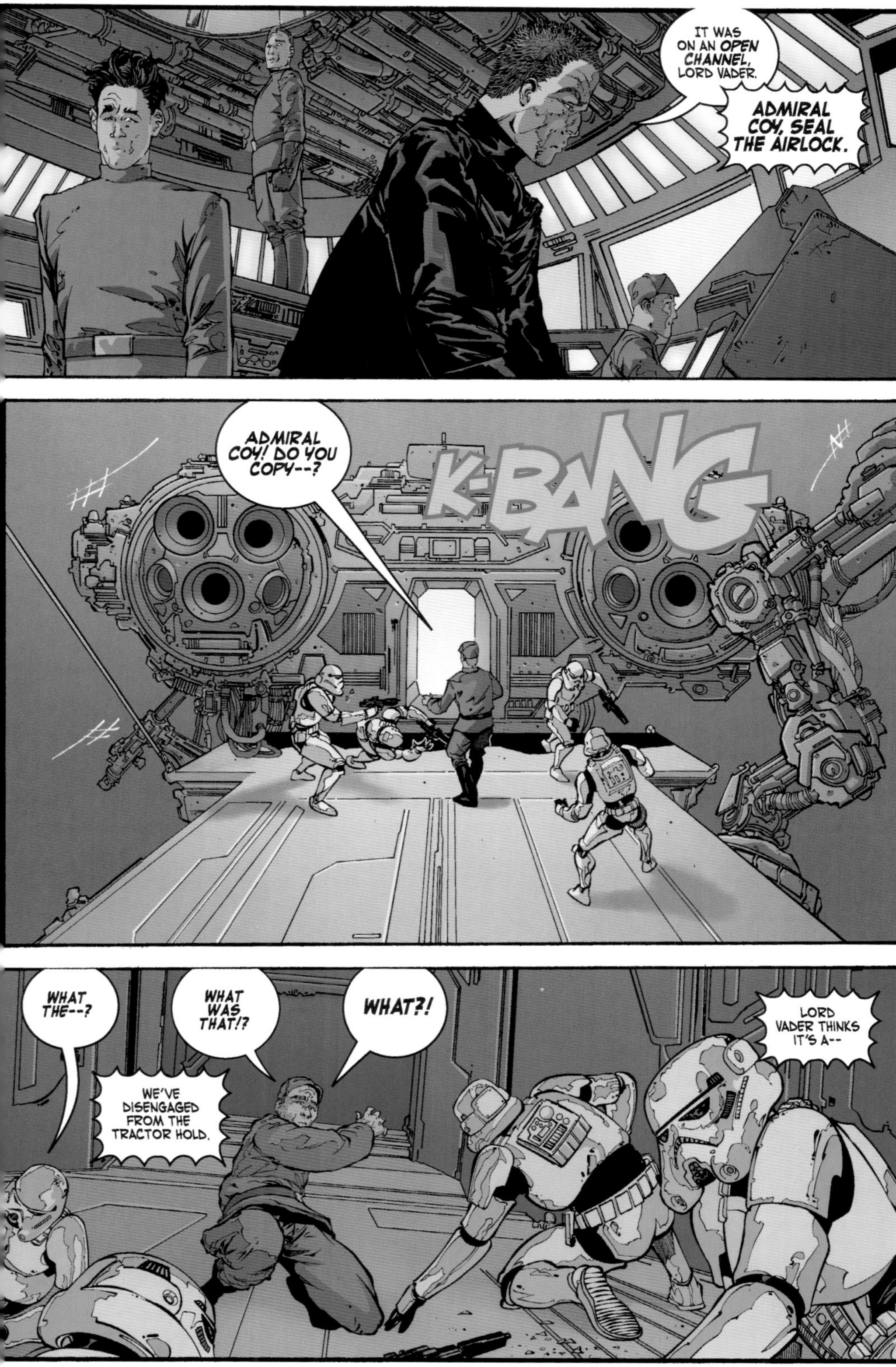

IT WAS ON AN OPEN CHANNEL, LORD VADER.
ADMIRAL COY, SEAL THE AIRLOCK.
ADMIRAL COY! DO YOU COPY--?
K-BANG
WHAT THE--?
WHAT WAS THAT!?
WHAT?!
WE'VE DISENGAGED FROM THE TRACTOR HOLD.
LORD VADER THINKS IT'S A--

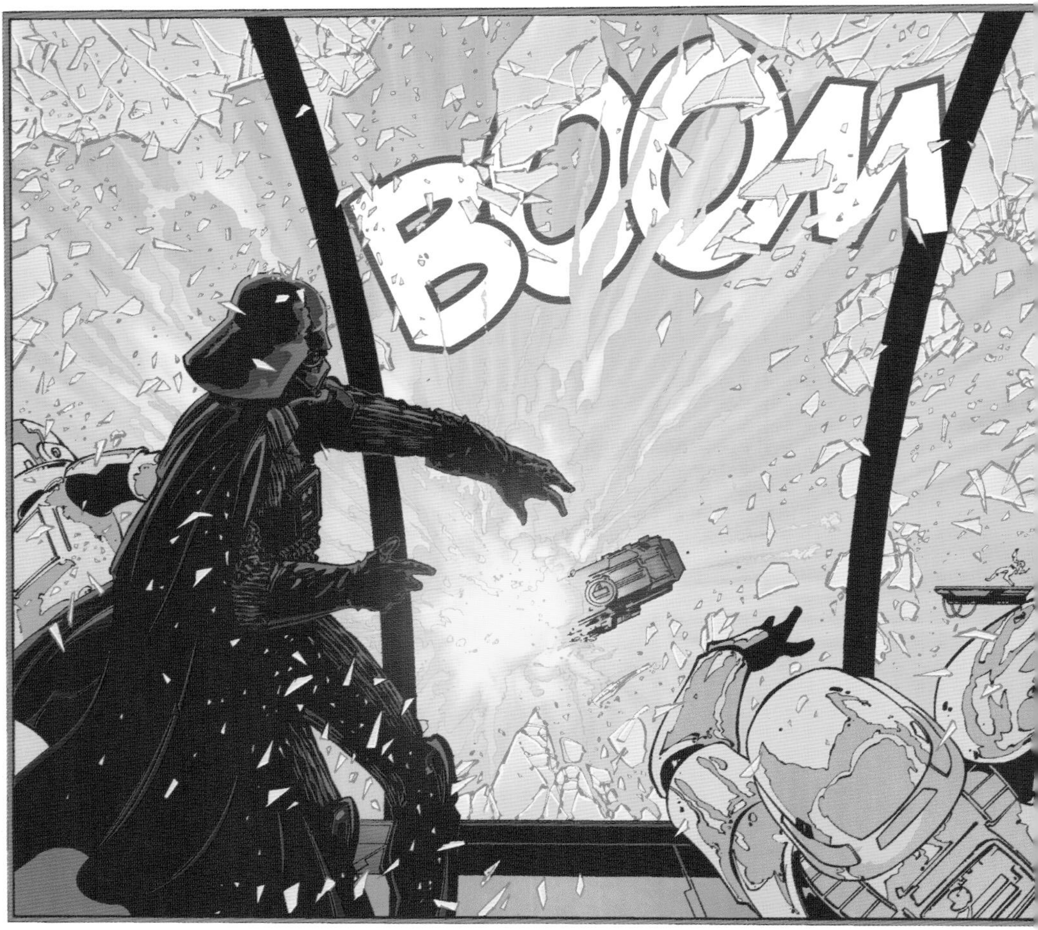
BOOM

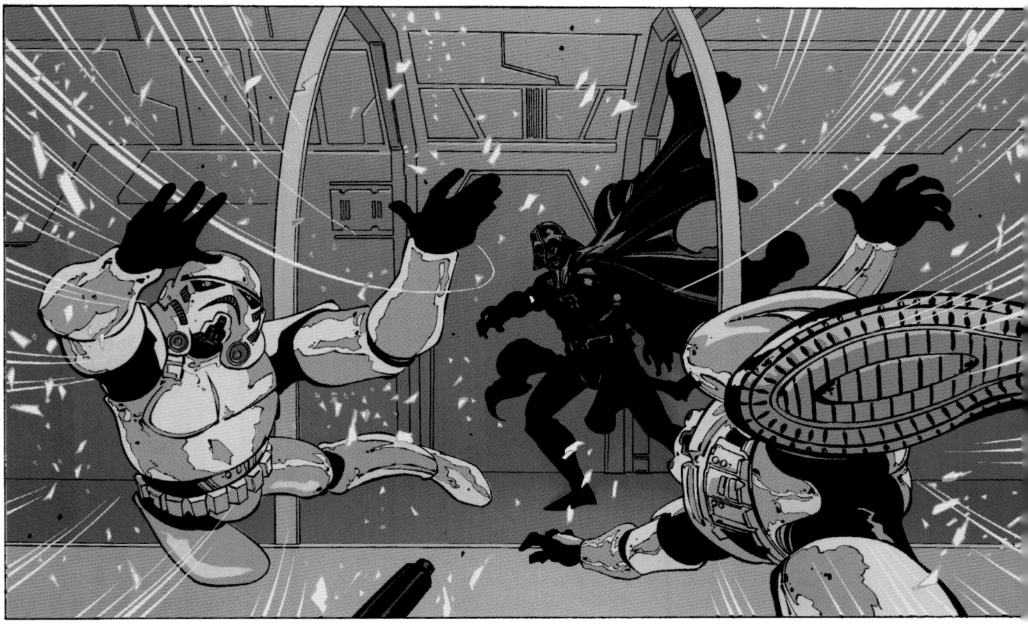

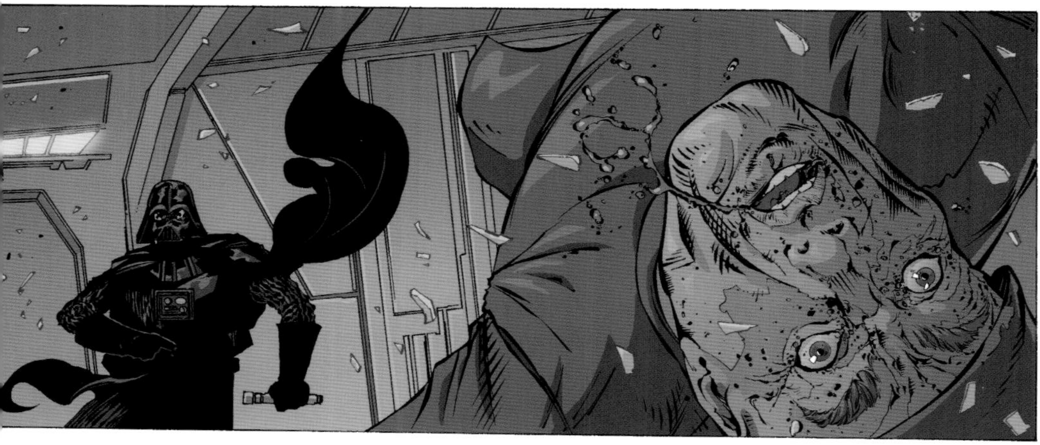

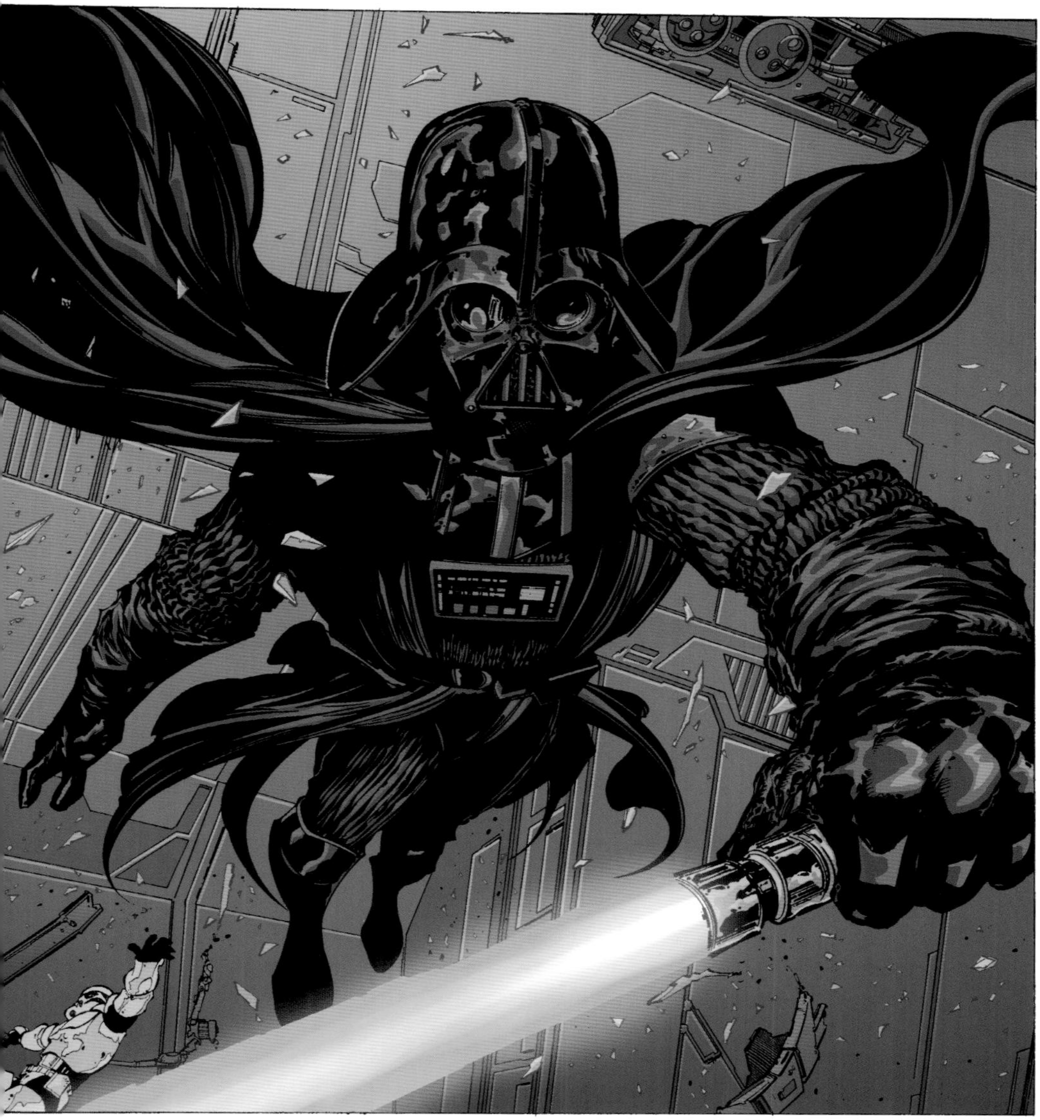

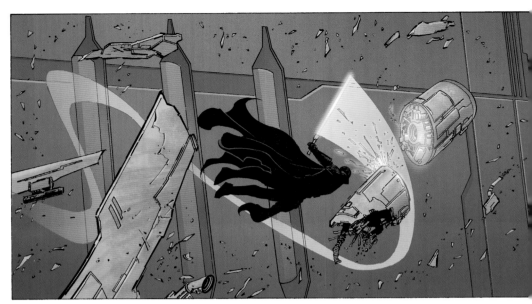

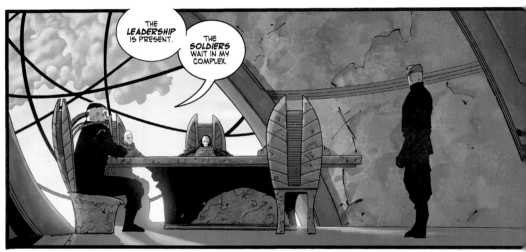

THE **LEADERSHIP** IS PRESENT.

THE **SOLDIERS** WAIT IN MY COMPLEX.

"*NOW*, THE PLAN."

"THE EMPEROR WISHES TO FOLLOW TARKIN, TO VISIT HIS **DEATH STAR.** VADER'S ALREADY GONE."

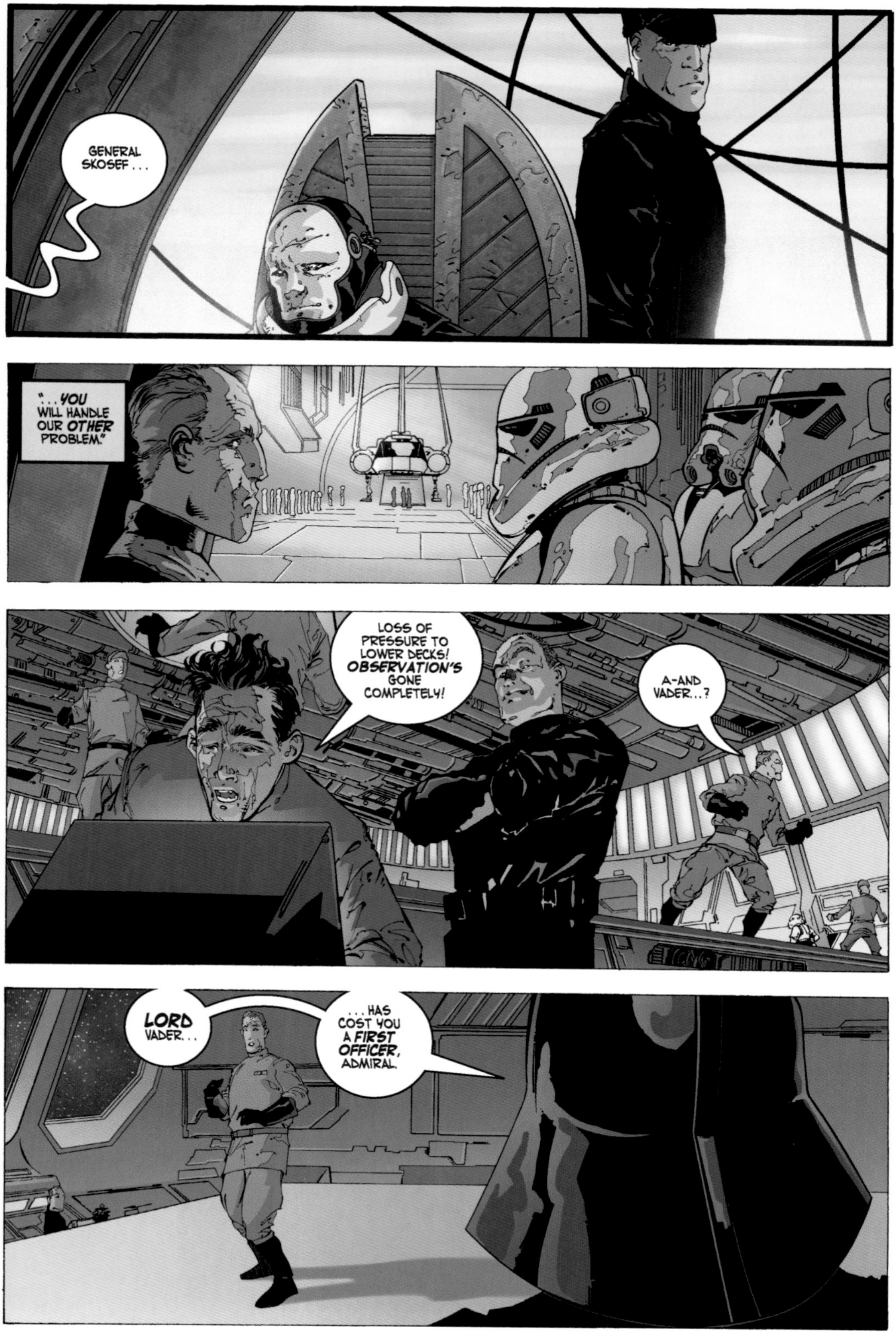
GENERAL SKOSEF . . .
". . . YOU WILL HANDLE OUR OTHER PROBLEM."
LOSS OF PRESSURE TO LOWER DECKS! OBSERVATION'S GONE COMPLETELY!
A-AND VADER...?
LORD VADER. . .
. . . HAS COST YOU A FIRST OFFICER, ADMIRAL.

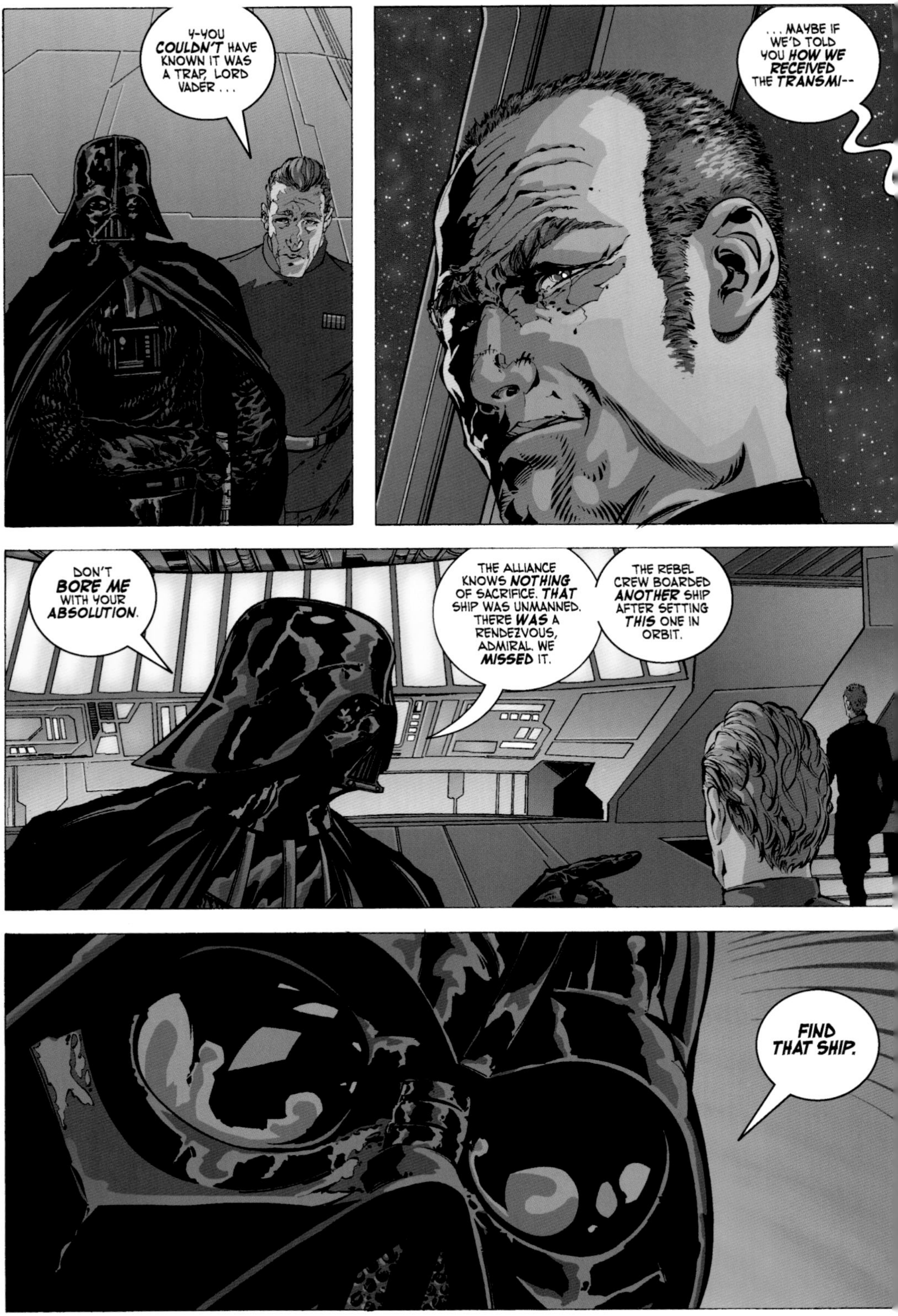
Y-YOU COULDN'T HAVE KNOWN IT WAS A TRAP, LORD VADER . . .
. . . MAYBE IF WE'D TOLD YOU HOW WE RECEIVED THE TRANSMI--
DON'T BORE ME WITH YOUR ABSOLUTION.
THE ALLIANCE KNOWS NOTHING OF SACRIFICE. THAT SHIP WAS UNMANNED. THERE WAS A RENDEZVOUS, ADMIRAL. WE MISSED IT.
THE REBEL CREW BOARDED ANOTHER SHIP AFTER SETTING THIS ONE IN ORBIT.
FIND THAT SHIP.

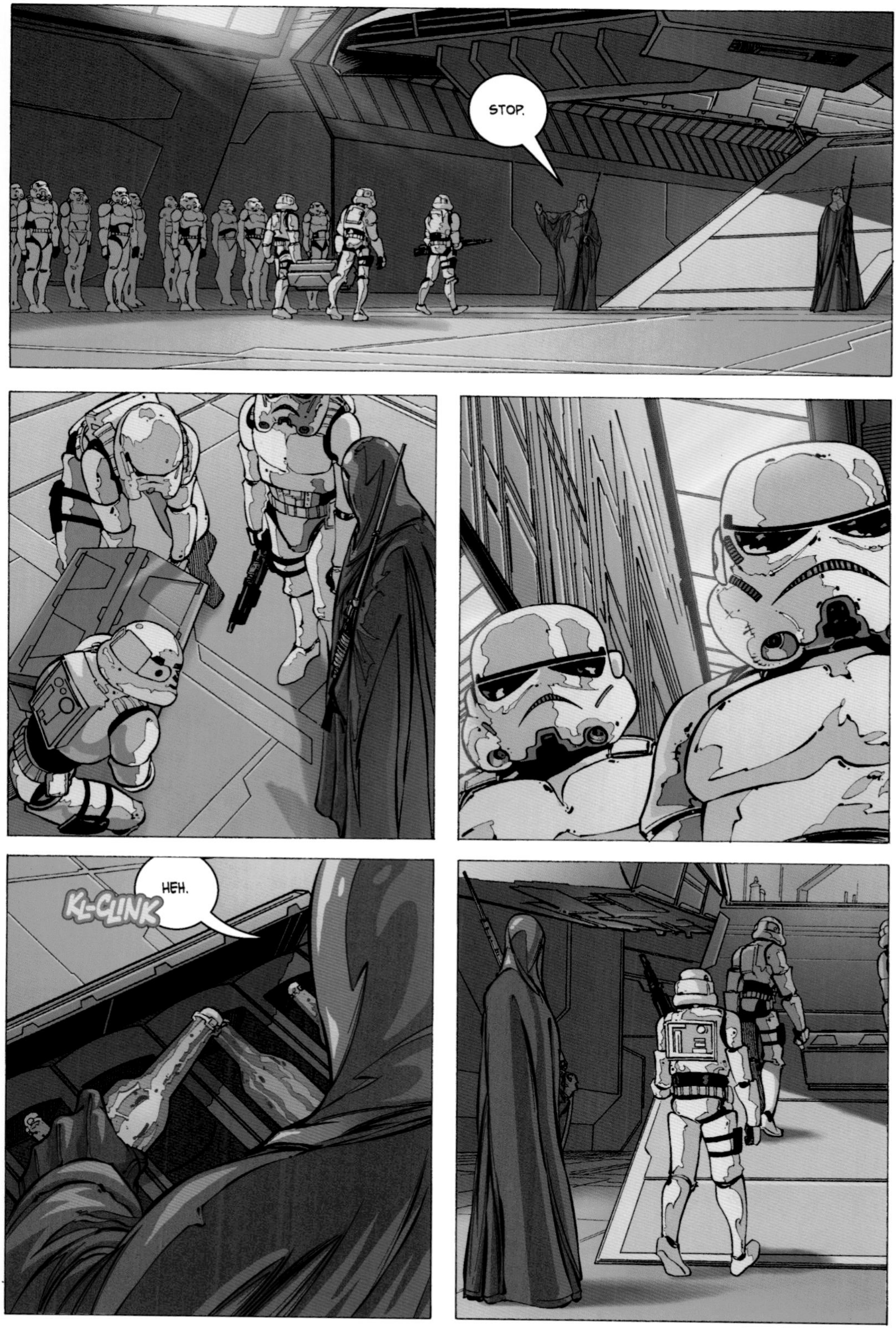
STOP.
KL-CLINK
HEH.

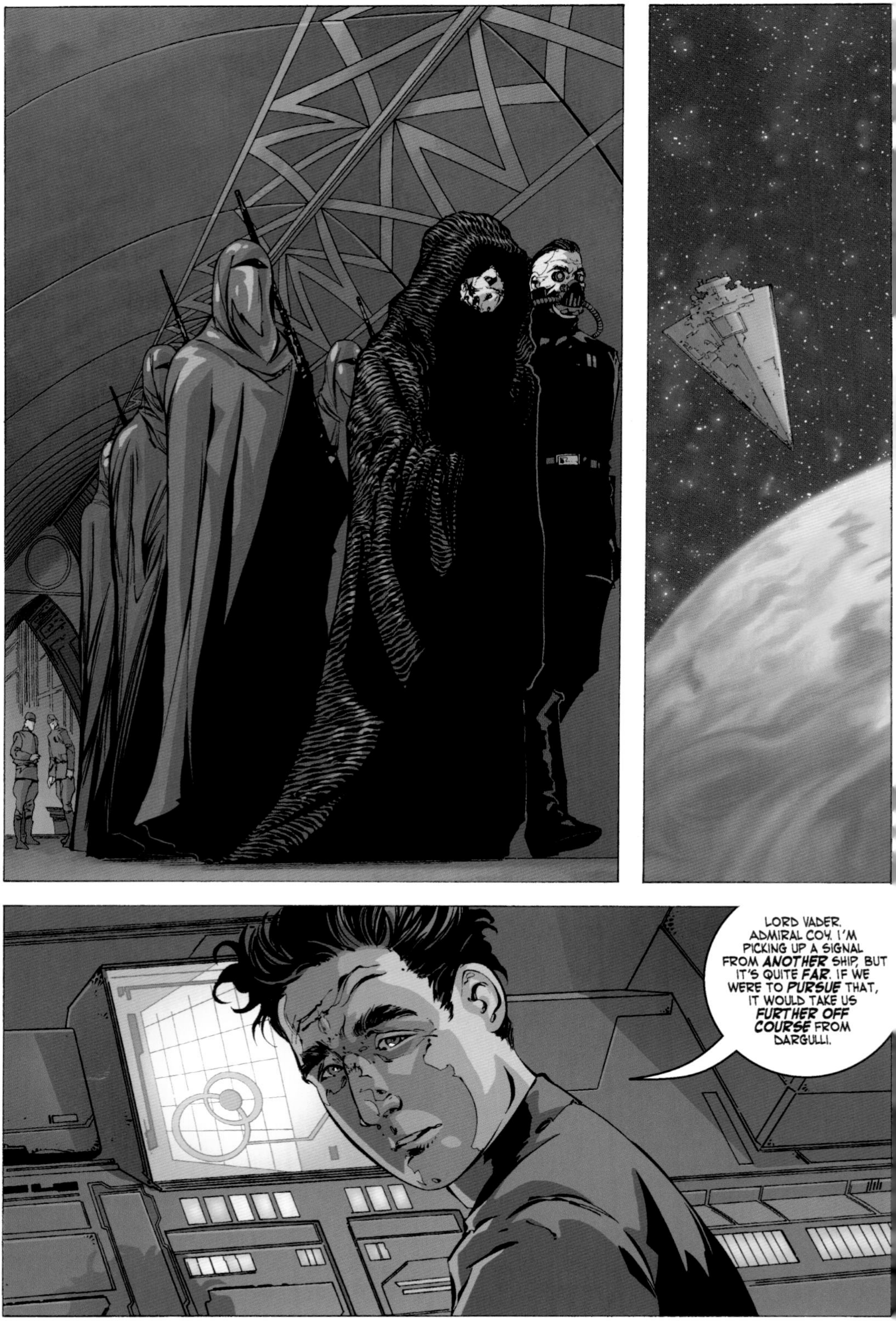

LORD VADER. ADMIRAL COY. I'M PICKING UP A SIGNAL FROM ANOTHER SHIP, BUT IT'S QUITE FAR. IF WE WERE TO PURSUE THAT, IT WOULD TAKE US FURTHER OFF COURSE FROM DARGULLI.

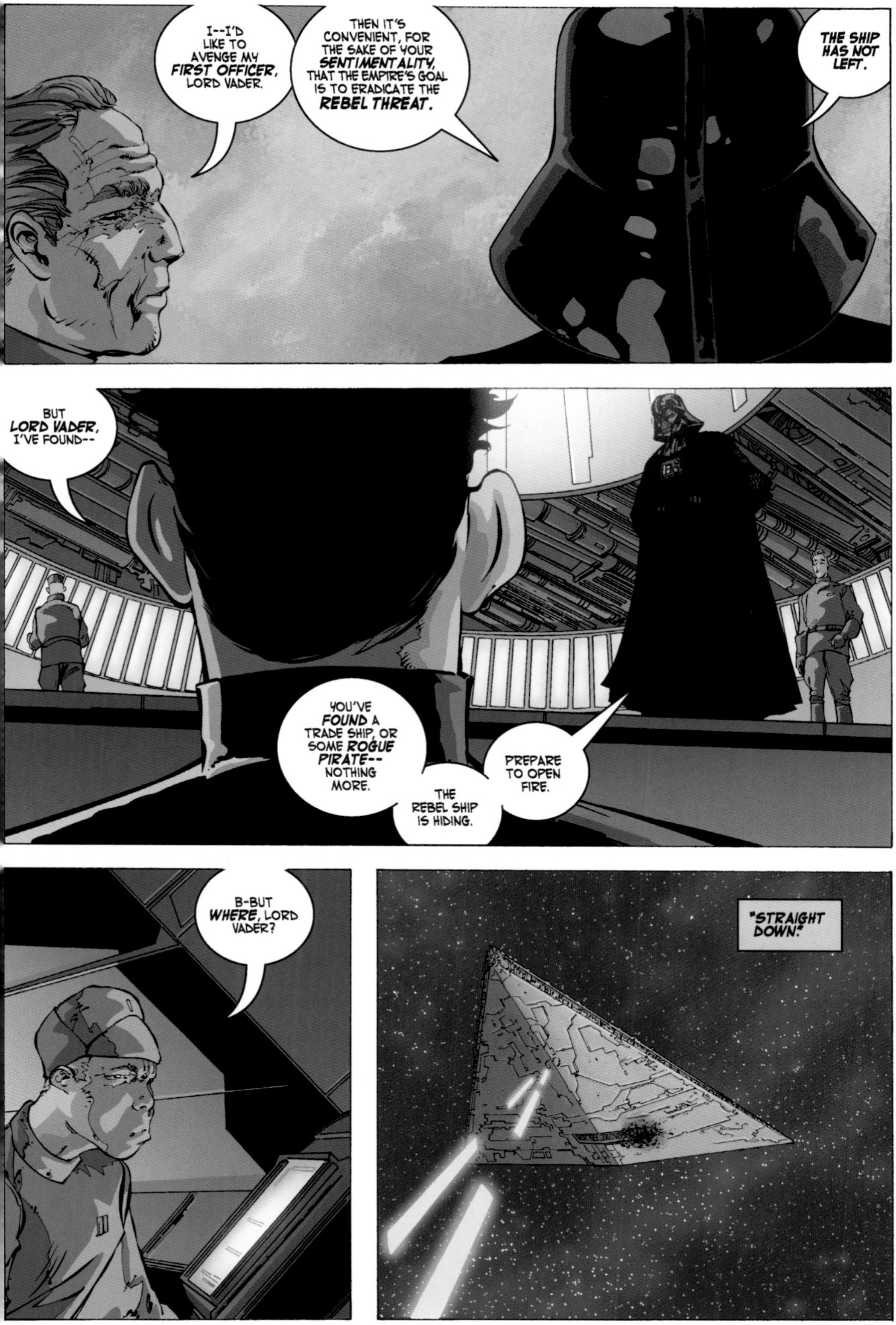

I--I'D LIKE TO AVENGE MY FIRST OFFICER, LORD VADER.
THEN IT'S CONVENIENT, FOR THE SAKE OF YOUR SENTIMENTALITY, THAT THE EMPIRE'S GOAL IS TO ERADICATE THE REBEL THREAT.
THE SHIP HAS NOT LEFT.
BUT LORD VADER, I'VE FOUND--
YOU'VE FOUND A TRADE SHIP, OR SOME ROGUE PIRATE-- NOTHING MORE.
THE REBEL SHIP IS HIDING.
PREPARE TO OPEN FIRE.
B-BUT WHERE, LORD VADER?
"STRAIGHT DOWN."

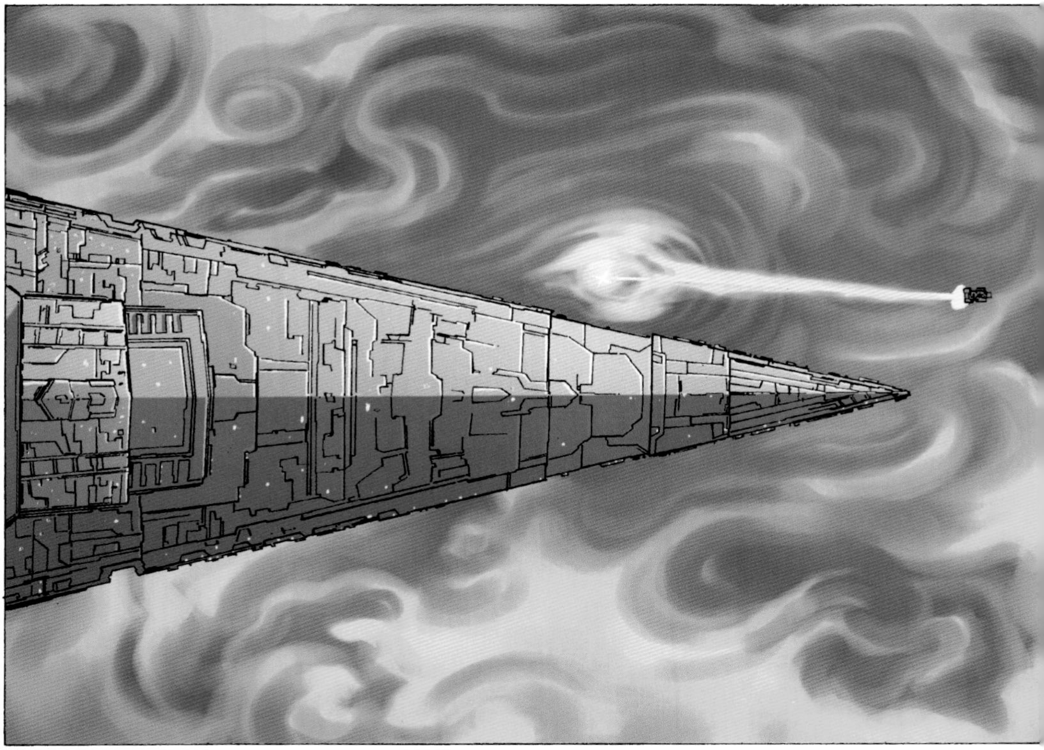

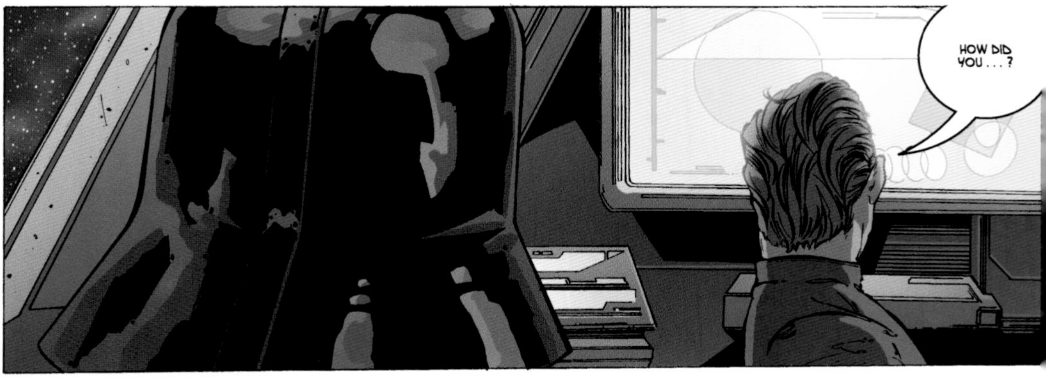
HOW DID YOU . . . ?

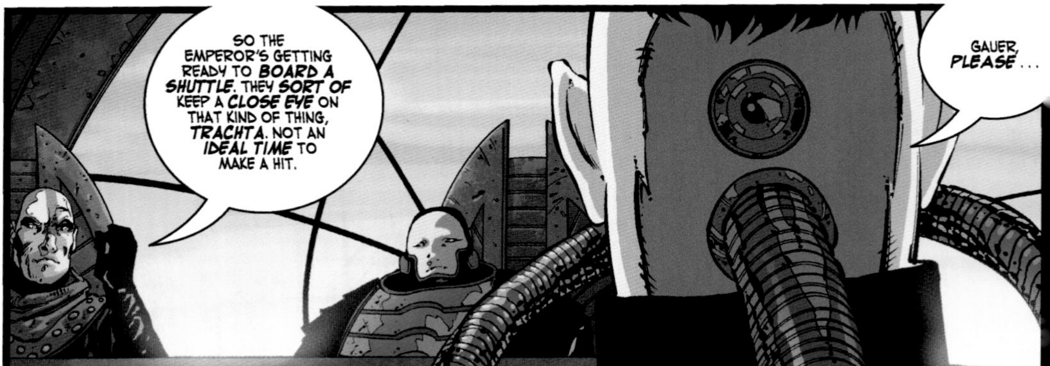
SO THE EMPEROR'S GETTING READY TO **BOARD A SHUTTLE**. THEY **SORT OF** KEEP A **CLOSE EYE** ON THAT KIND OF THING, **TRACHTA**. NOT AN **IDEAL TIME** TO MAKE A HIT.
GAUER, **PLEASE** . . .

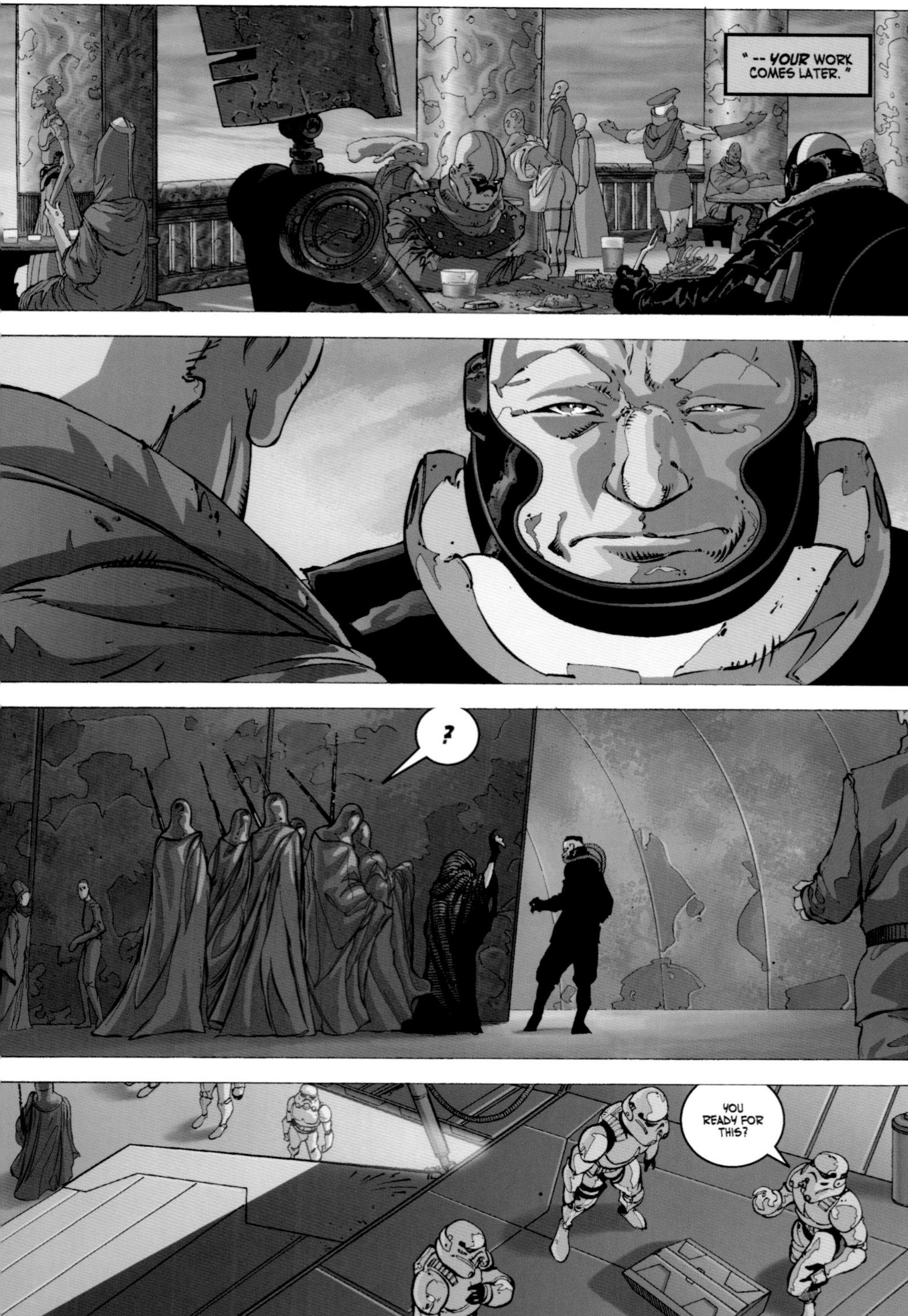
" -- YOUR WORK COMES LATER."
?
YOU READY FOR THIS?

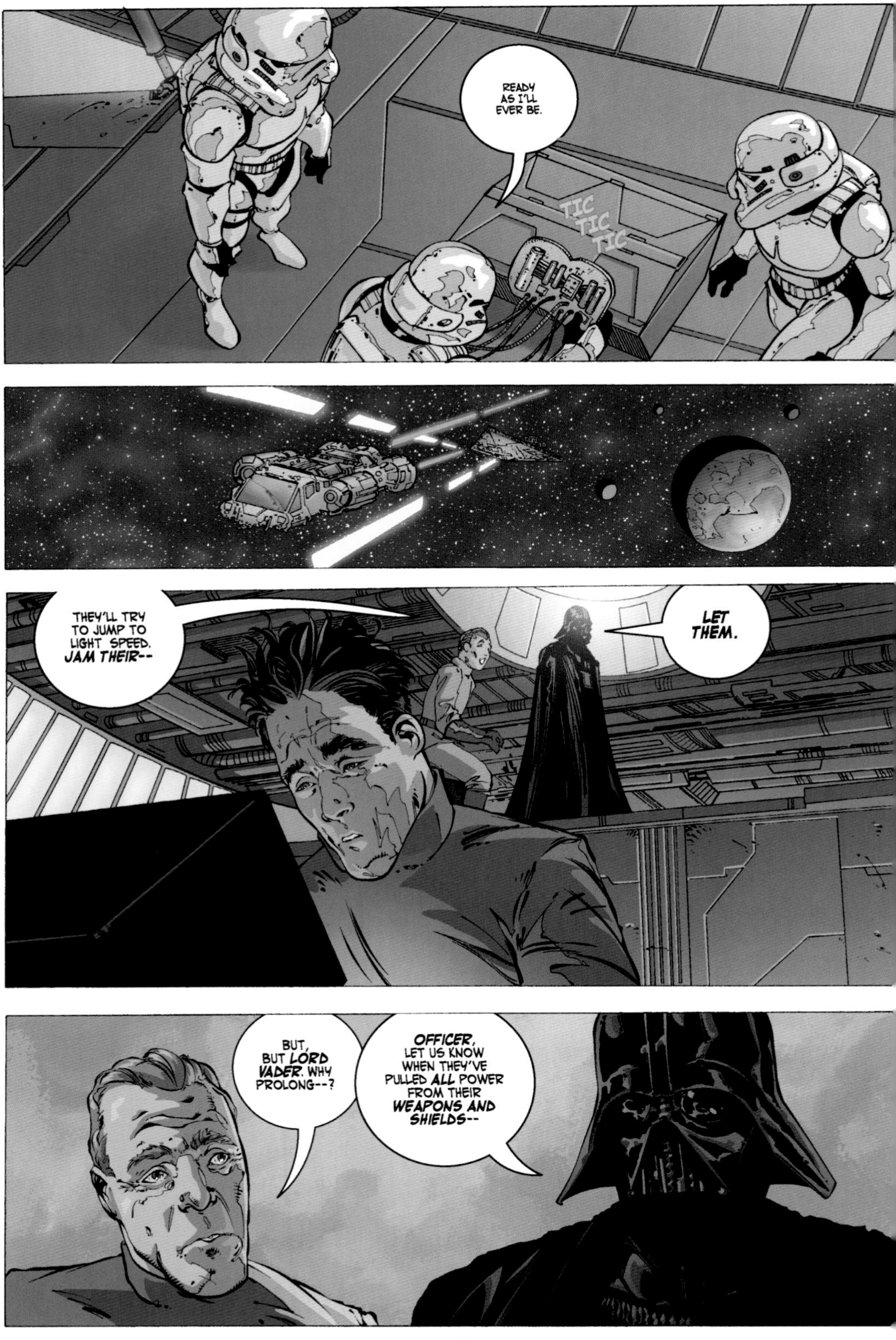
READY AS I'LL EVER BE.
TIC TIC TIC
THEY'LL TRY TO JUMP TO LIGHT SPEED. JAM THEIR--
LET THEM.
BUT, BUT LORD VADER. WHY PROLONG--?
OFFICER, LET US KNOW WHEN THEY'VE PULLED ALL POWER FROM THEIR WEAPONS AND SHIELDS--

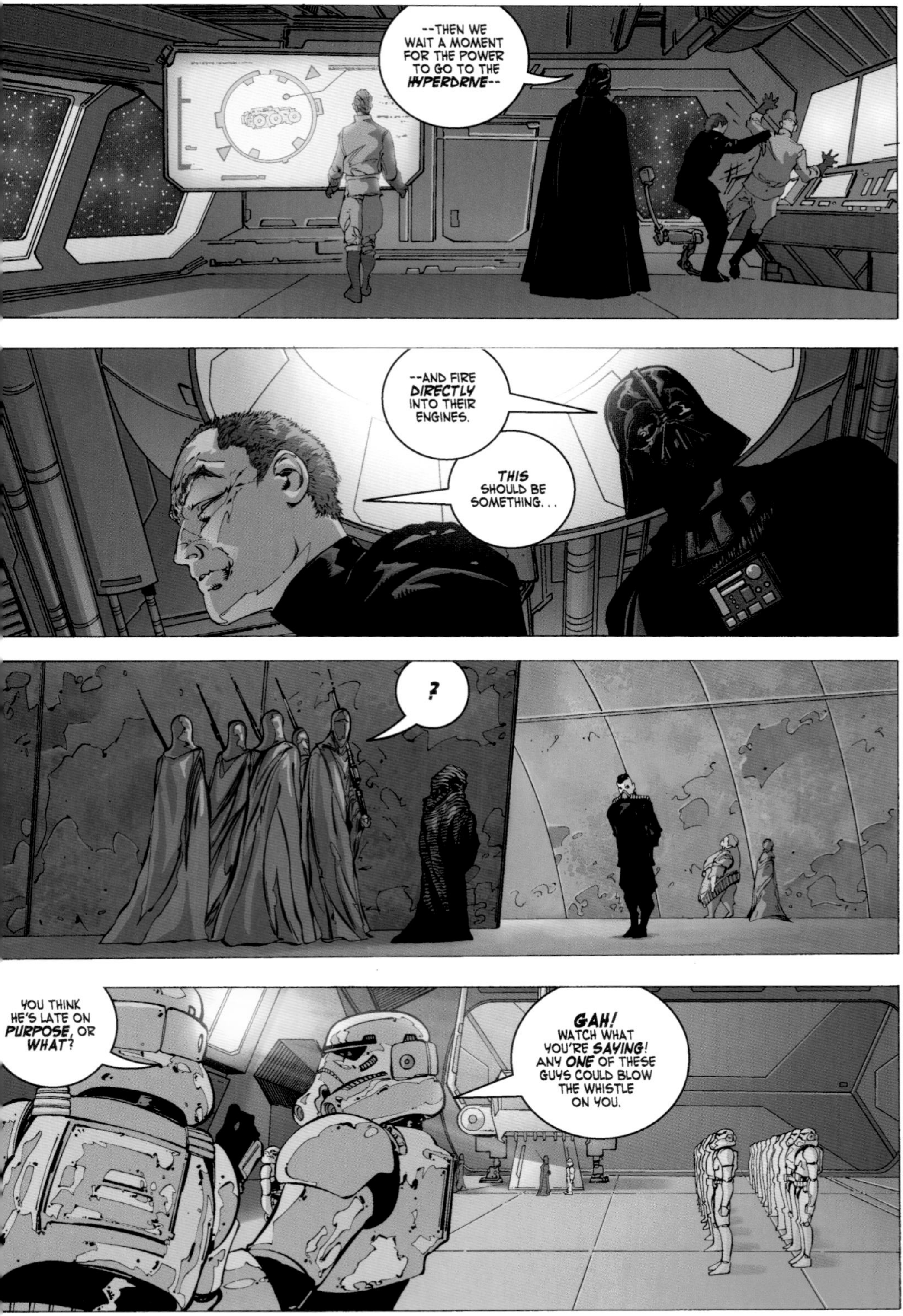
--THEN WE WAIT A MOMENT FOR THE POWER TO GO TO THE HYPERDRIVE--
--AND FIRE DIRECTLY INTO THEIR ENGINES.
THIS SHOULD BE SOMETHING. . .
?
YOU THINK HE'S LATE ON PURPOSE, OR WHAT?
GAH! WATCH WHAT YOU'RE SAYING! ANY ONE OF THESE GUYS COULD BLOW THE WHISTLE ON YOU.

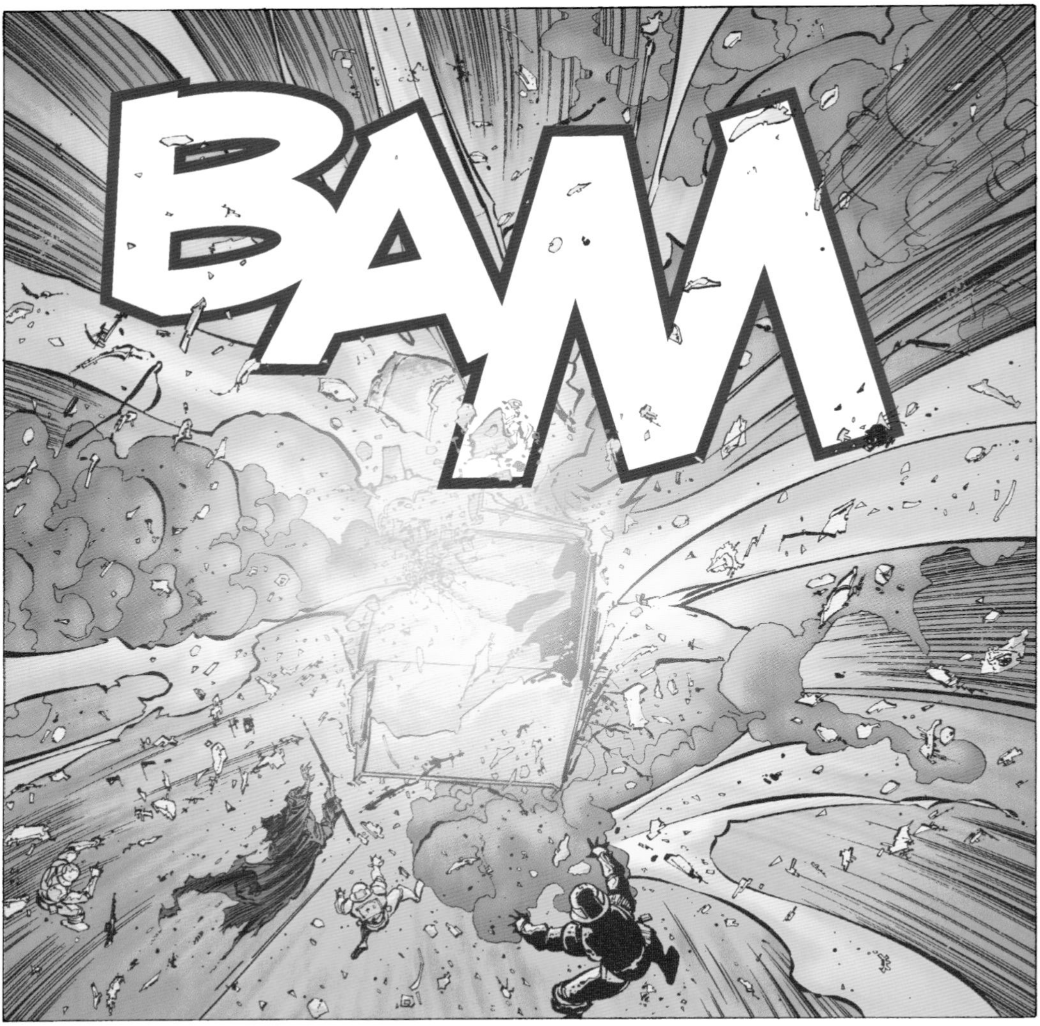
BAM

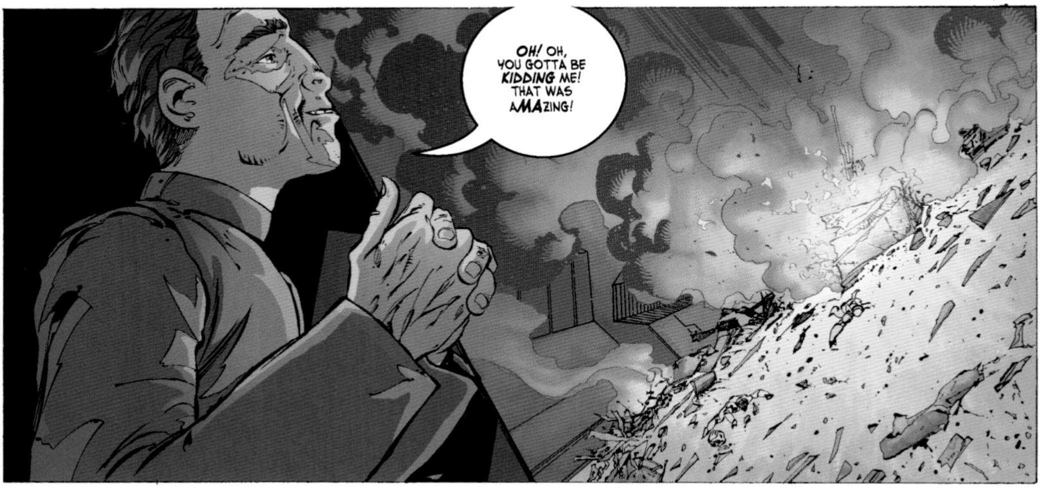
OH! OH, YOU GOTTA BE KIDDING ME! THAT WAS AMAZING!

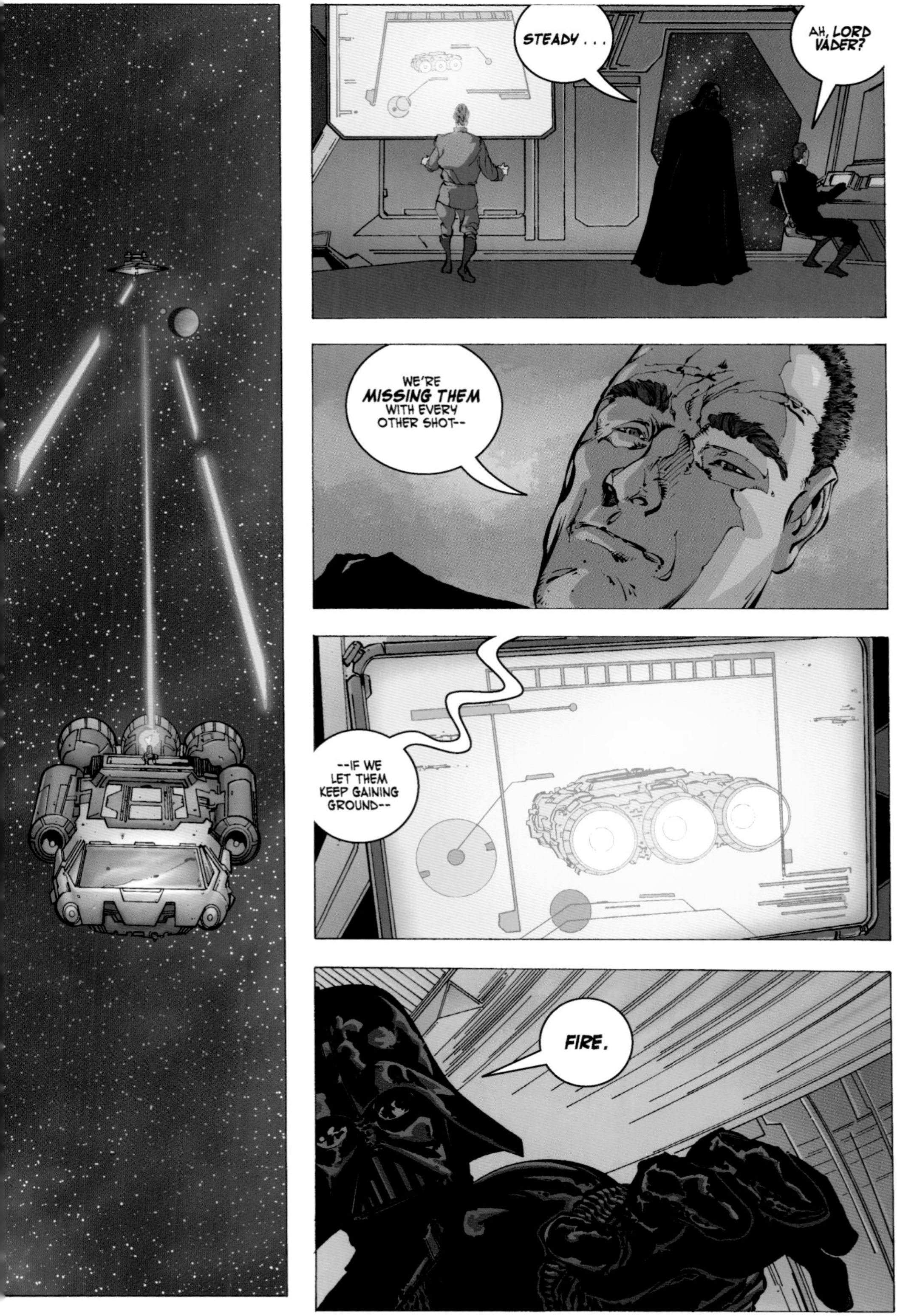

STEADY . . .
AH, LORD VADER?
WE'RE MISSING THEM WITH EVERY OTHER SHOT--
--IF WE LET THEM KEEP GAINING GROUND--
FIRE.

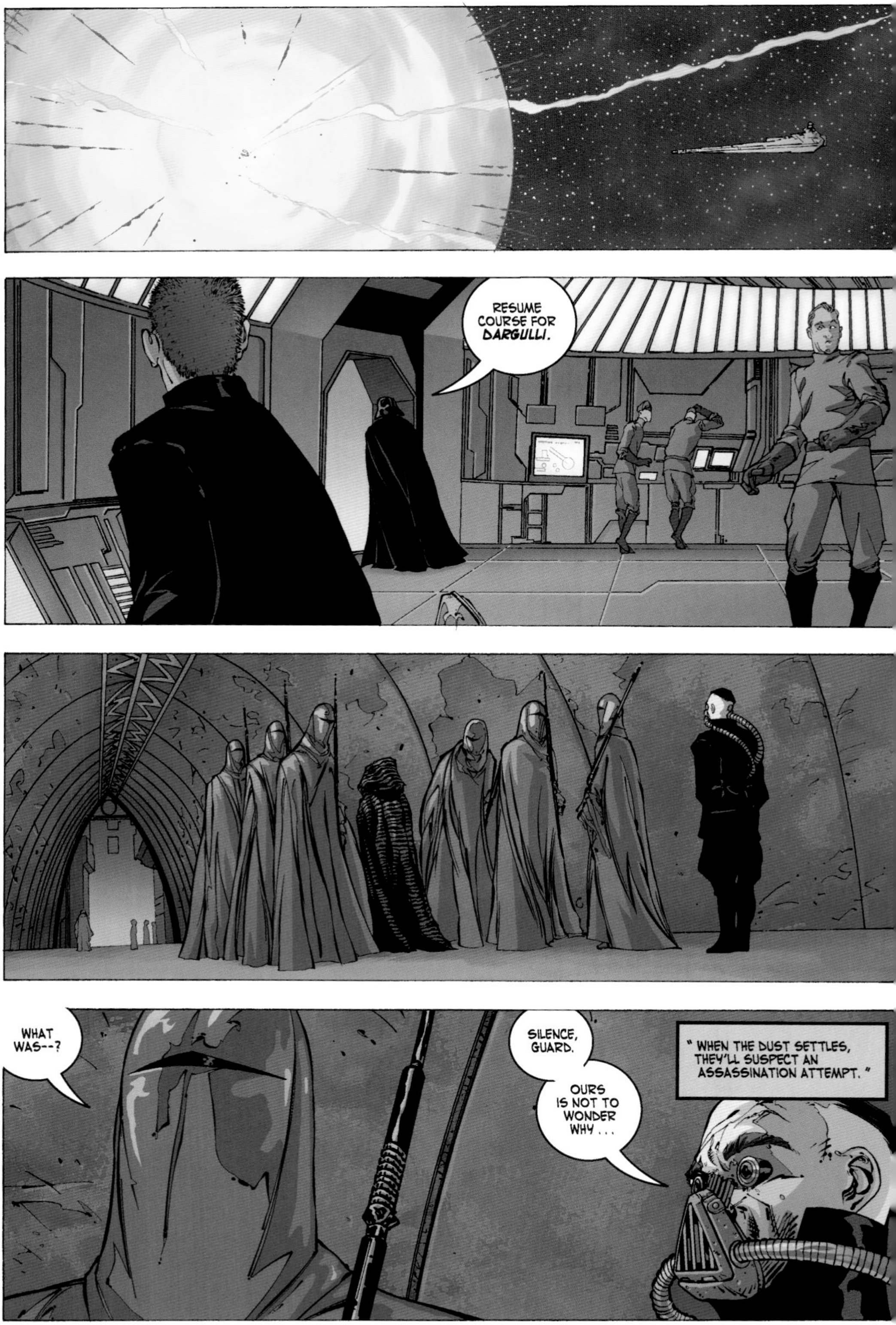
RESUME COURSE FOR DARGULLI.
WHAT WAS--?
SILENCE, GUARD.
OURS IS NOT TO WONDER WHY . . .
" WHEN THE DUST SETTLES, THEY'LL SUSPECT AN ASSASSINATION ATTEMPT. "

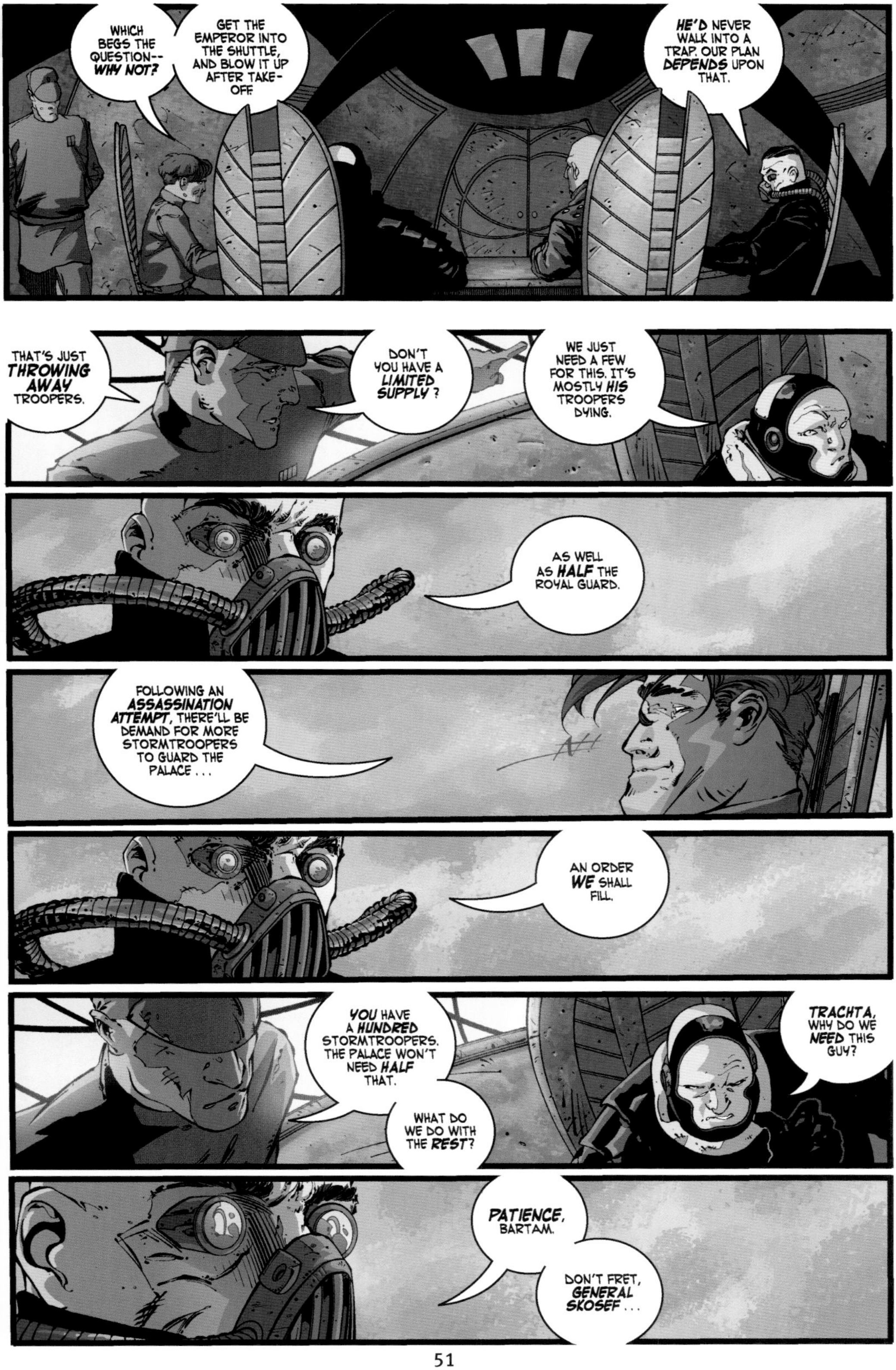

WHICH BEGS THE QUESTION-- WHY NOT?
GET THE EMPEROR INTO THE SHUTTLE, AND BLOW IT UP AFTER TAKE-OFF
HE'D NEVER WALK INTO A TRAP. OUR PLAN DEPENDS UPON THAT.
THAT'S JUST THROWING AWAY TROOPERS.
DON'T YOU HAVE A LIMITED SUPPLY ?
WE JUST NEED A FEW FOR THIS. IT'S MOSTLY HIS TROOPERS DYING.
AS WELL AS HALF THE ROYAL GUARD.
FOLLOWING AN ASSASSINATION ATTEMPT, THERE'LL BE DEMAND FOR MORE STORMTROOPERS TO GUARD THE PALACE . . .
AN ORDER WE SHALL FILL.
YOU HAVE A HUNDRED STORMTROOPERS. THE PALACE WON'T NEED HALF THAT.
WHAT DO WE DO WITH THE REST?
TRACHTA, WHY DO WE NEED THIS GUY?
PATIENCE, BARTAM.
DON'T FRET, GENERAL SKOSEF . . .

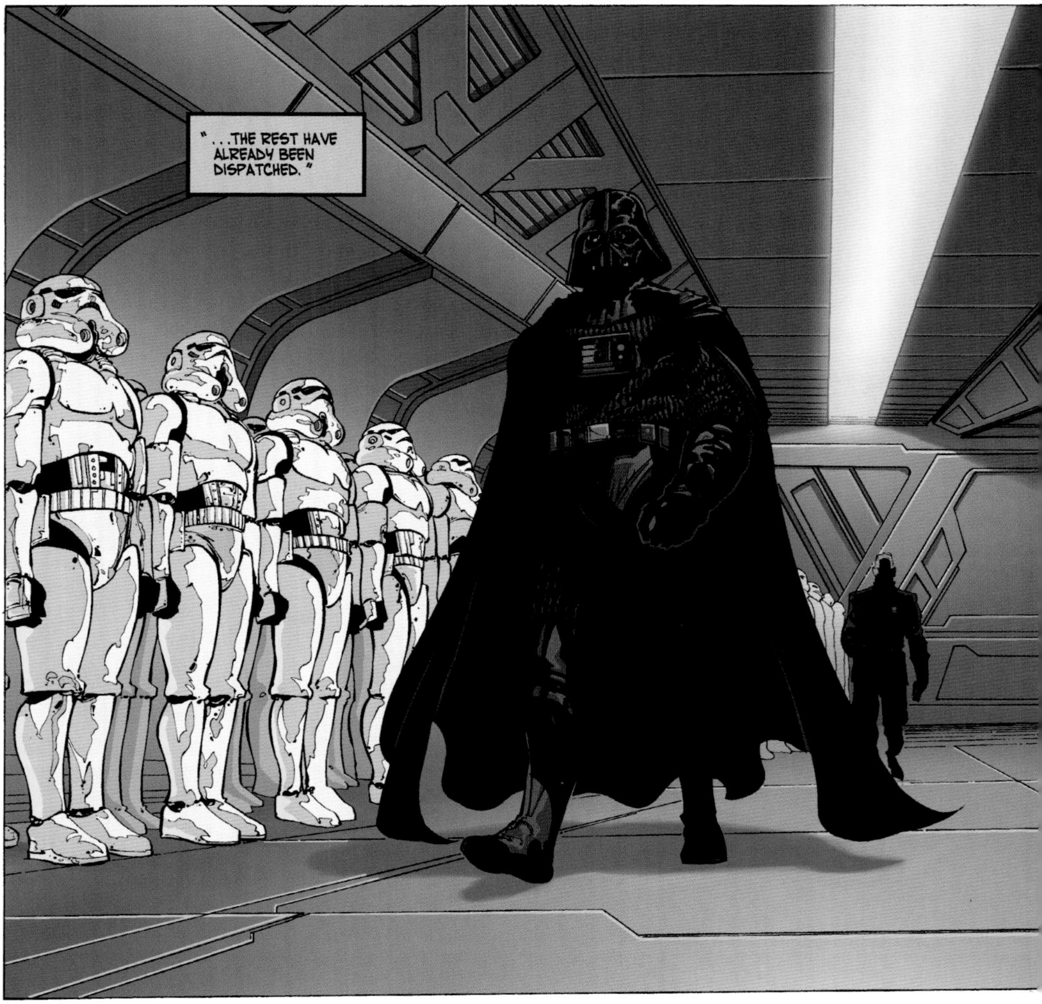
"...THE REST HAVE ALREADY BEEN DISPATCHED."

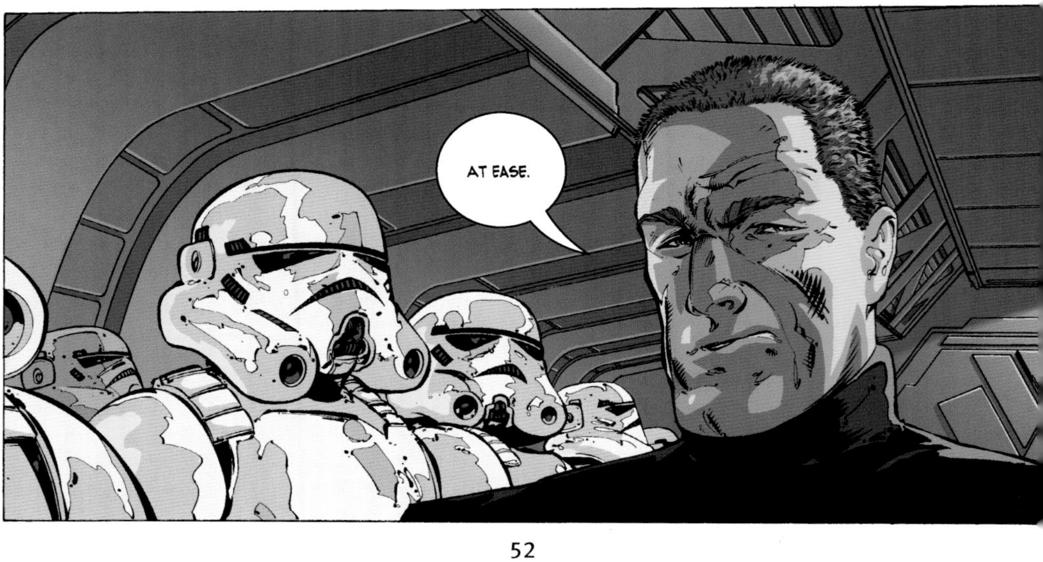
AT EASE.

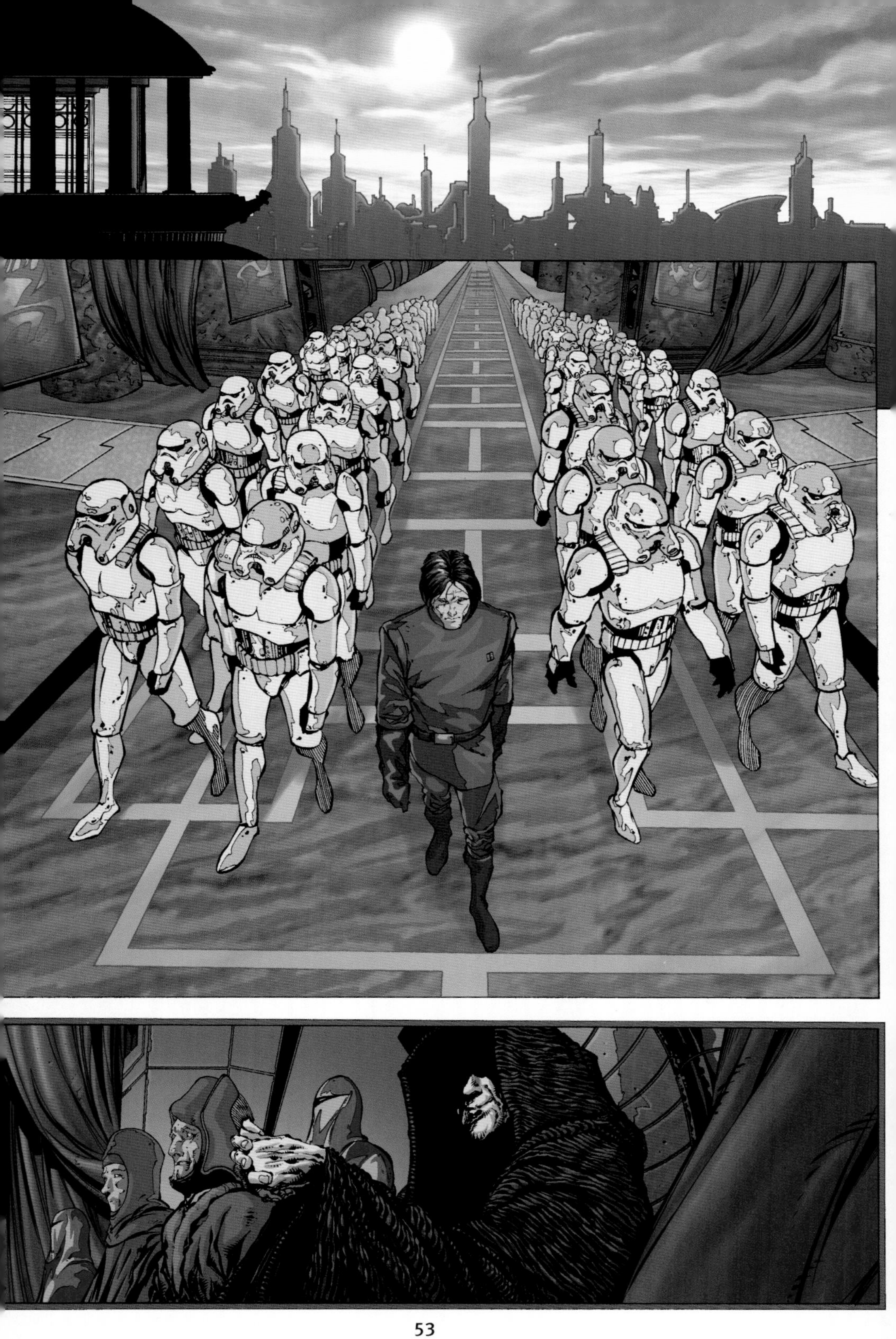

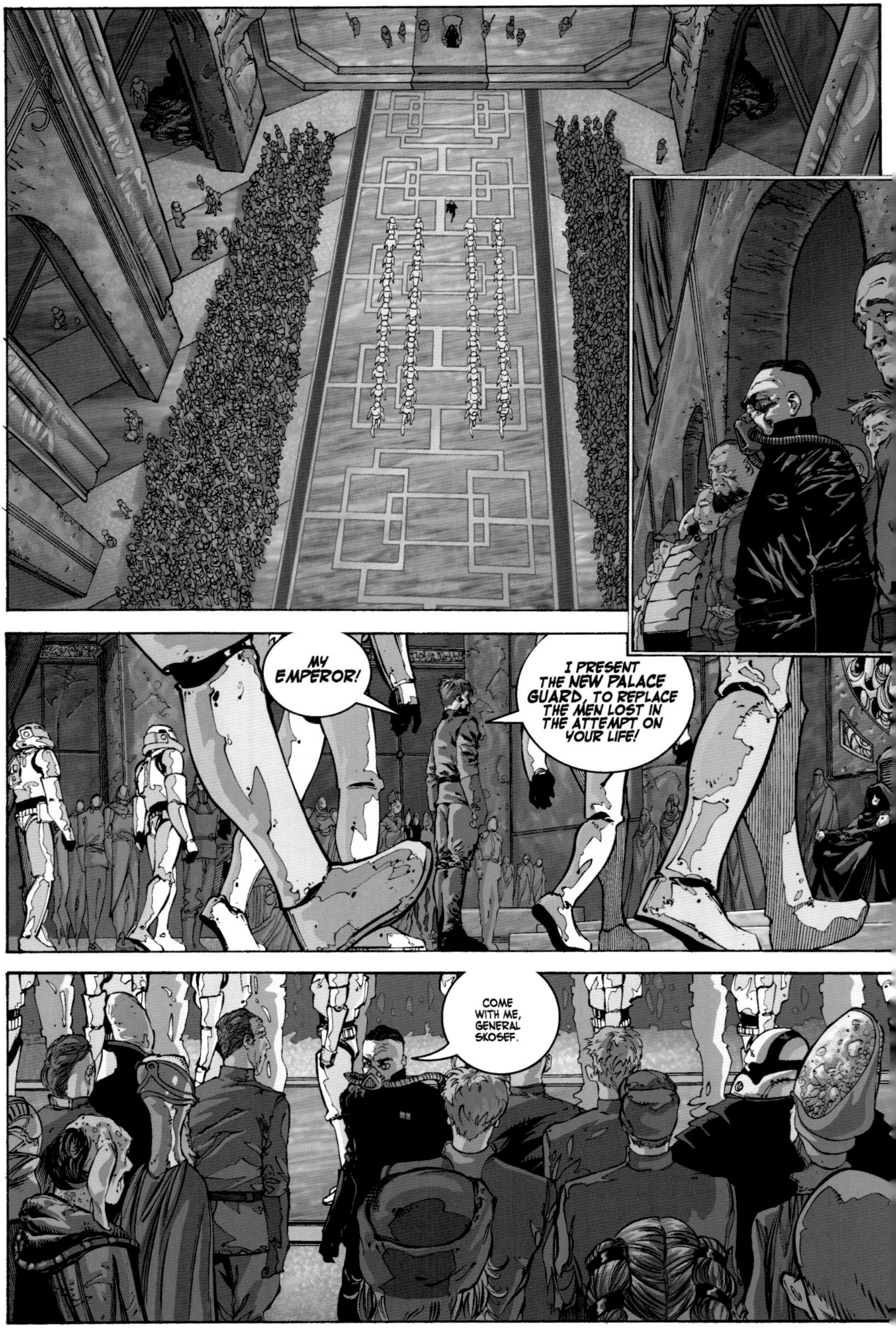
MY EMPEROR!
I PRESENT THE NEW PALACE GUARD, TO REPLACE THE MEN LOST IN THE ATTEMPT ON YOUR LIFE!
COME WITH ME, GENERAL SKOSEF.

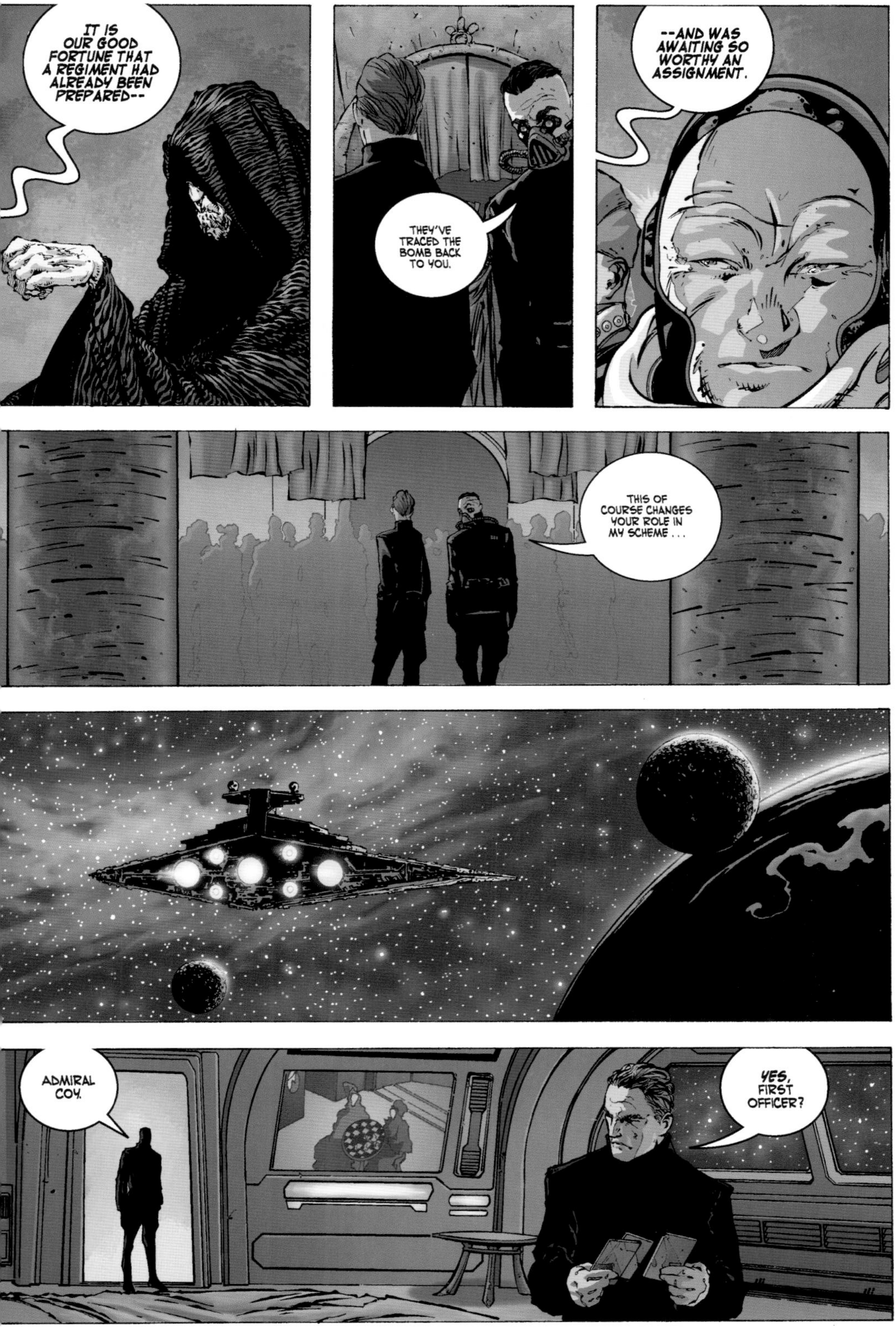
IT IS OUR GOOD FORTUNE THAT A REGIMENT HAD ALREADY BEEN PREPARED--
THEY'VE TRACED THE BOMB BACK TO YOU.
--AND WAS AWAITING SO WORTHY AN ASSIGNMENT.
THIS OF COURSE CHANGES YOUR ROLE IN MY SCHEME . . .
ADMIRAL COY.
YES, FIRST OFFICER?

YOU *LOOKED* LIKE YOU HAD IT IN YOU TO STAND *UP* TO VADER. BUT YOU COULDN'T, COULD YOU? I WAS ALMOST READY TO *RECRUIT* YOU INTO ALL THIS MYSELF.

WH . . . ?

BZ-ZTAK

AAGH!

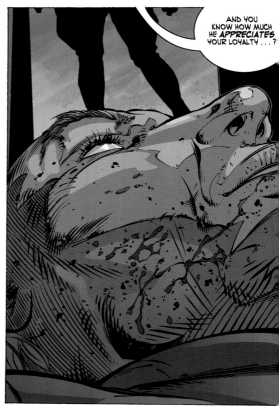

AND YOU KNOW HOW MUCH HE *APPRECIATES* YOUR LOYALTY . . . ?

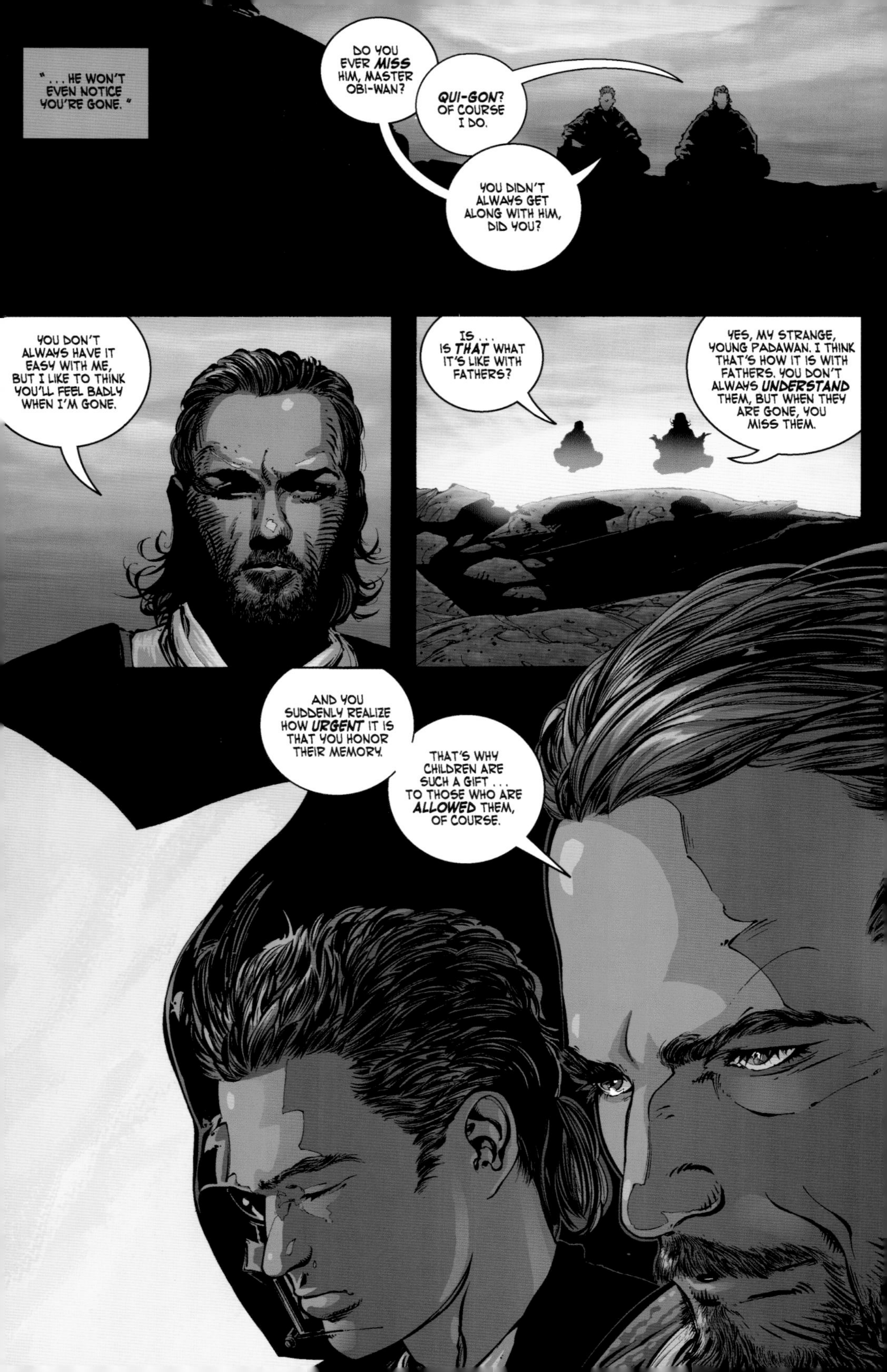
". . . HE WON'T EVEN NOTICE YOU'RE GONE."
DO YOU EVER MISS HIM, MASTER OBI-WAN?
QUI-GON? OF COURSE I DO.
YOU DIDN'T ALWAYS GET ALONG WITH HIM, DID YOU?
YOU DON'T ALWAYS HAVE IT EASY WITH ME, BUT I LIKE TO THINK YOU'LL FEEL BADLY WHEN I'M GONE.
IS . . . IS THAT WHAT IT'S LIKE WITH FATHERS?
YES, MY STRANGE, YOUNG PADAWAN. I THINK THAT'S HOW IT IS WITH FATHERS. YOU DON'T ALWAYS UNDERSTAND THEM, BUT WHEN THEY ARE GONE, YOU MISS THEM.
AND YOU SUDDENLY REALIZE HOW URGENT IT IS THAT YOU HONOR THEIR MEMORY.
THAT'S WHY CHILDREN ARE SUCH A GIFT . . . TO THOSE WHO ARE ALLOWED THEM, OF COURSE.

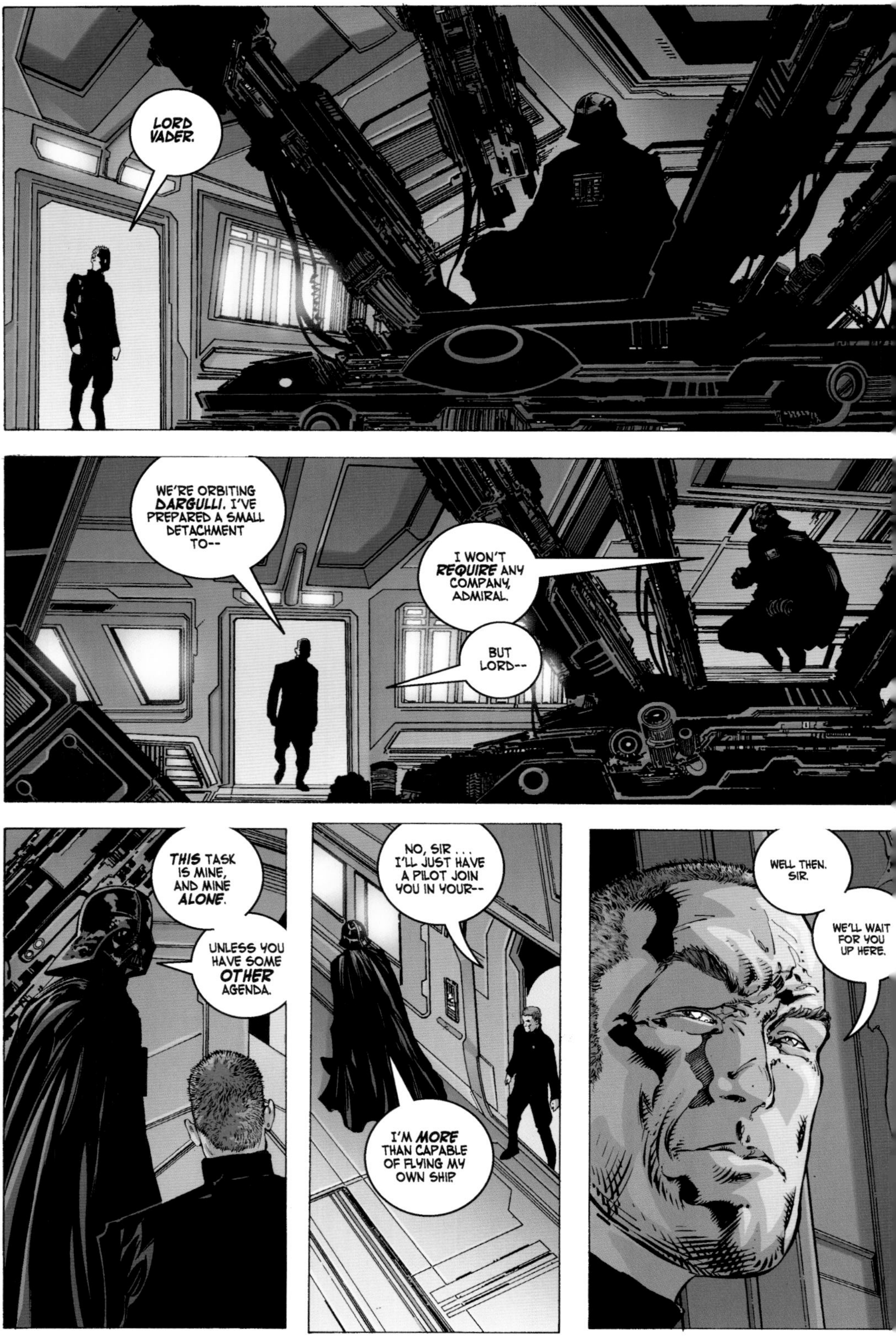

LORD VADER.
WE'RE ORBITING DARGULLI. I'VE PREPARED A SMALL DETACHMENT TO--
I WON'T REQUIRE ANY COMPANY, ADMIRAL.
BUT LORD--
THIS TASK IS MINE, AND MINE ALONE.
UNLESS YOU HAVE SOME OTHER AGENDA.
NO, SIR . . . I'LL JUST HAVE A PILOT JOIN YOU IN YOUR--
I'M MORE THAN CAPABLE OF FLYING MY OWN SHIP.
WELL THEN. SIR.
WE'LL WAIT FOR YOU UP HERE.

" I HEARD YOU'RE LEAVING *CORUSCANT*... "

. . . THAT TRUE?

YEAH. I'M GOING OFFWORLD FOR A WHILE.

" ISN'T THAT DANGEROUS? "

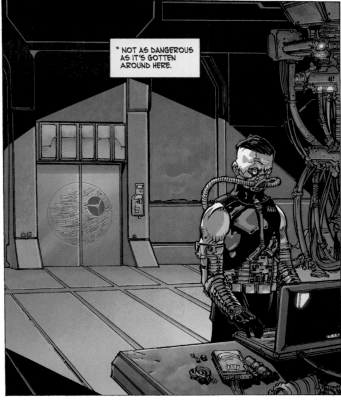

" NOT AS DANGEROUS AS IT'S GOTTEN AROUND HERE.

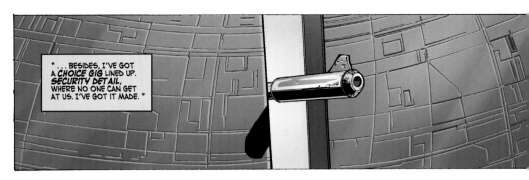

"... BESIDES, I'VE GOT A *CHOICE GIG* LINED UP. *SECURITY DETAIL*, WHERE NO ONE CAN GET AT US. I'VE GOT IT MADE."

YOU SOUND PRETTY SURE OF YOURSELF.

NAH, IT'S JUST, AFTER THAT ATTEMPT ON *PALPATINE*, IT FEELS LIKE THINGS ARE HEATING UP.

TAP

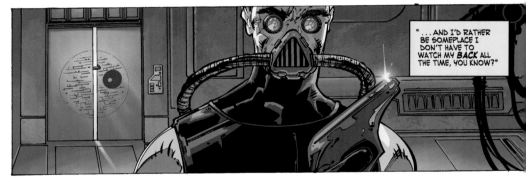

"... AND I'D RATHER BE SOMEPLACE I DON'T HAVE TO WATCH MY *BACK* ALL THE TIME, YOU KNOW?"

BZZT

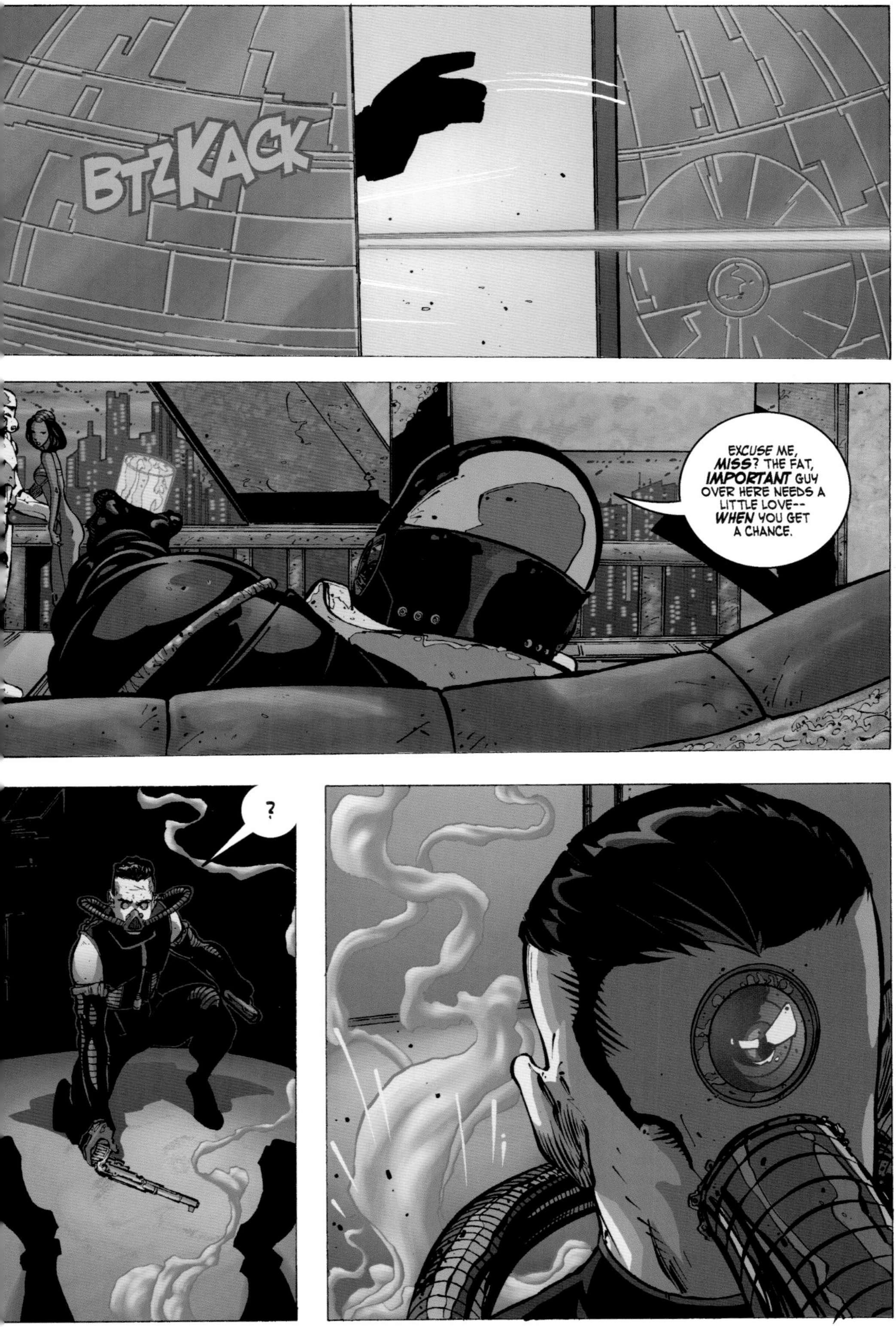
BTZKACK
EXCUSE ME, MISS? THE FAT, IMPORTANT GUY OVER HERE NEEDS A LITTLE LOVE-- WHEN YOU GET A CHANCE.
?

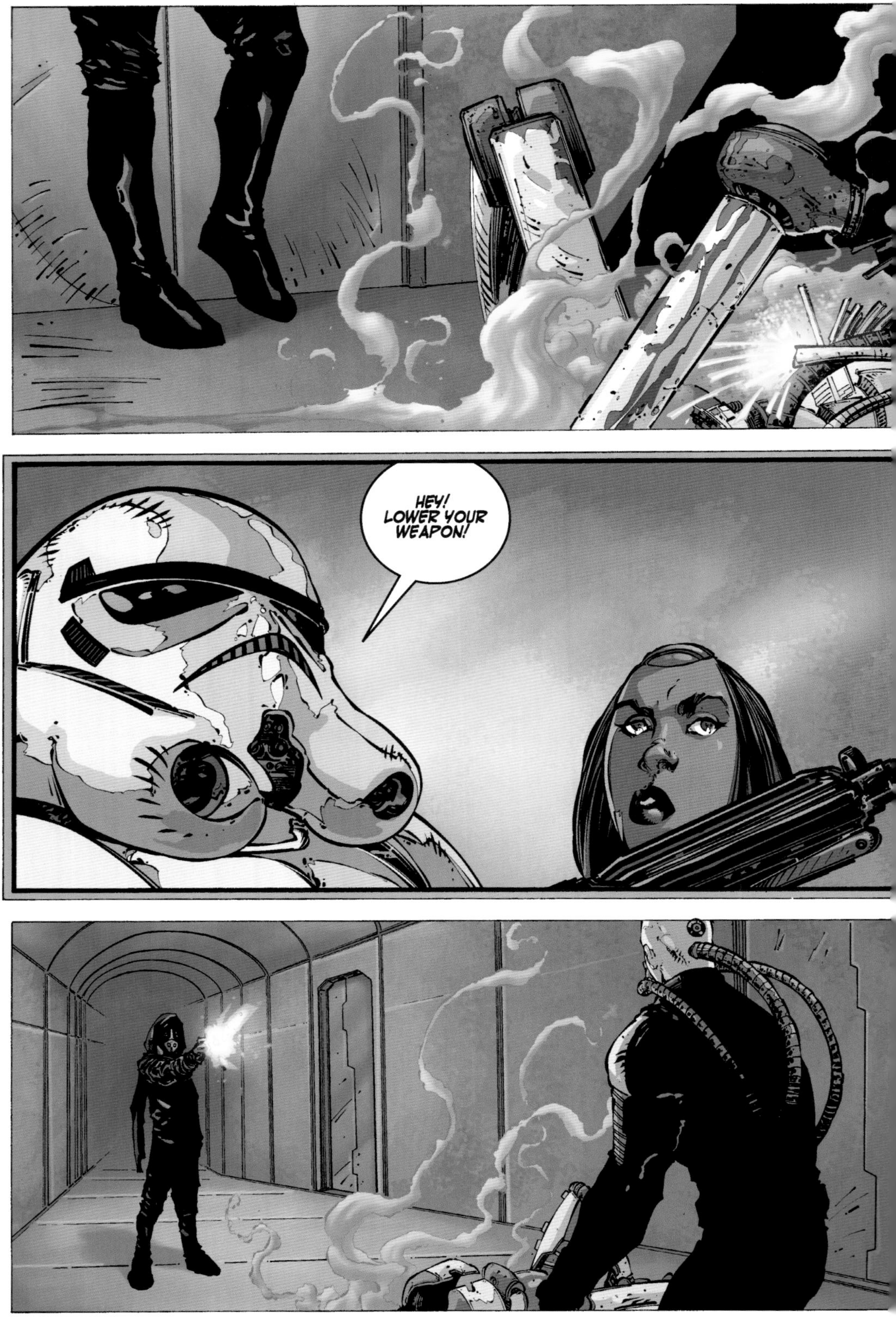
HEY! LOWER YOUR WEAPON!

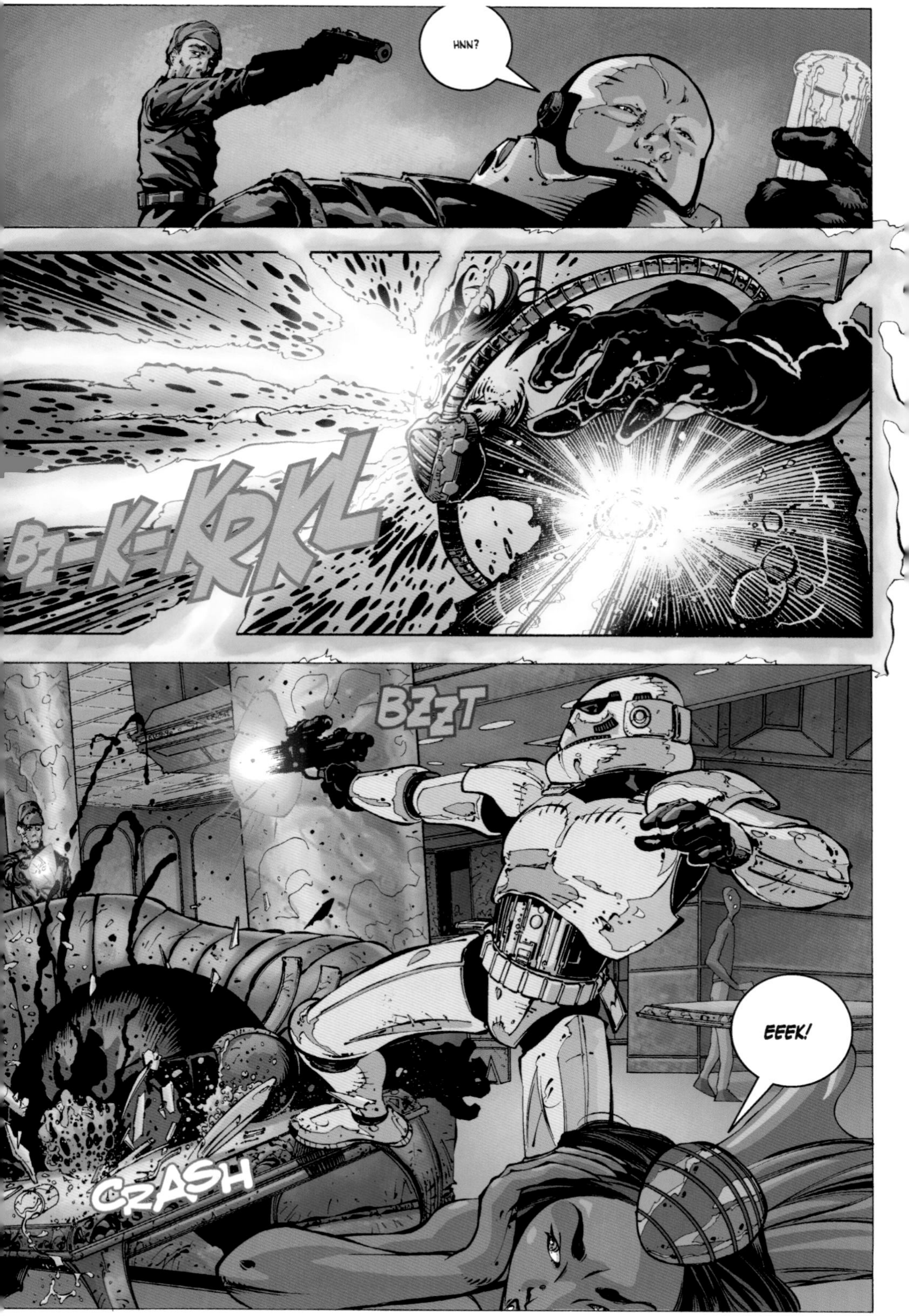
HNN?
BZ-K-KRKL
BZZT
EEEK!
CRASH

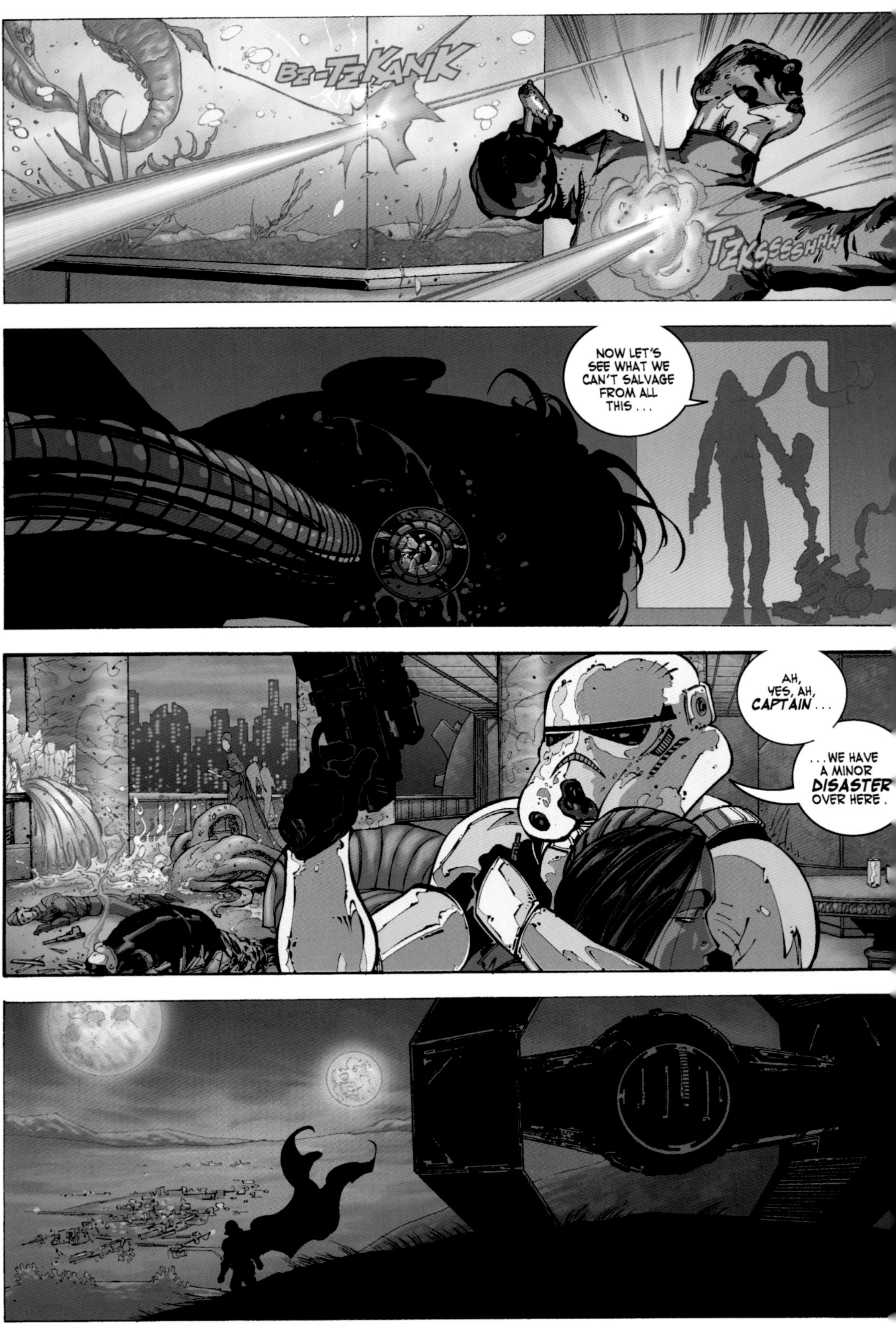
BZ-TZKANK
TZKSSSSHHH
NOW LET'S SEE WHAT WE CAN'T SALVAGE FROM ALL THIS . . .
AH, YES, AH, CAPTAIN . . .
. . . WE HAVE A MINOR DISASTER OVER HERE.

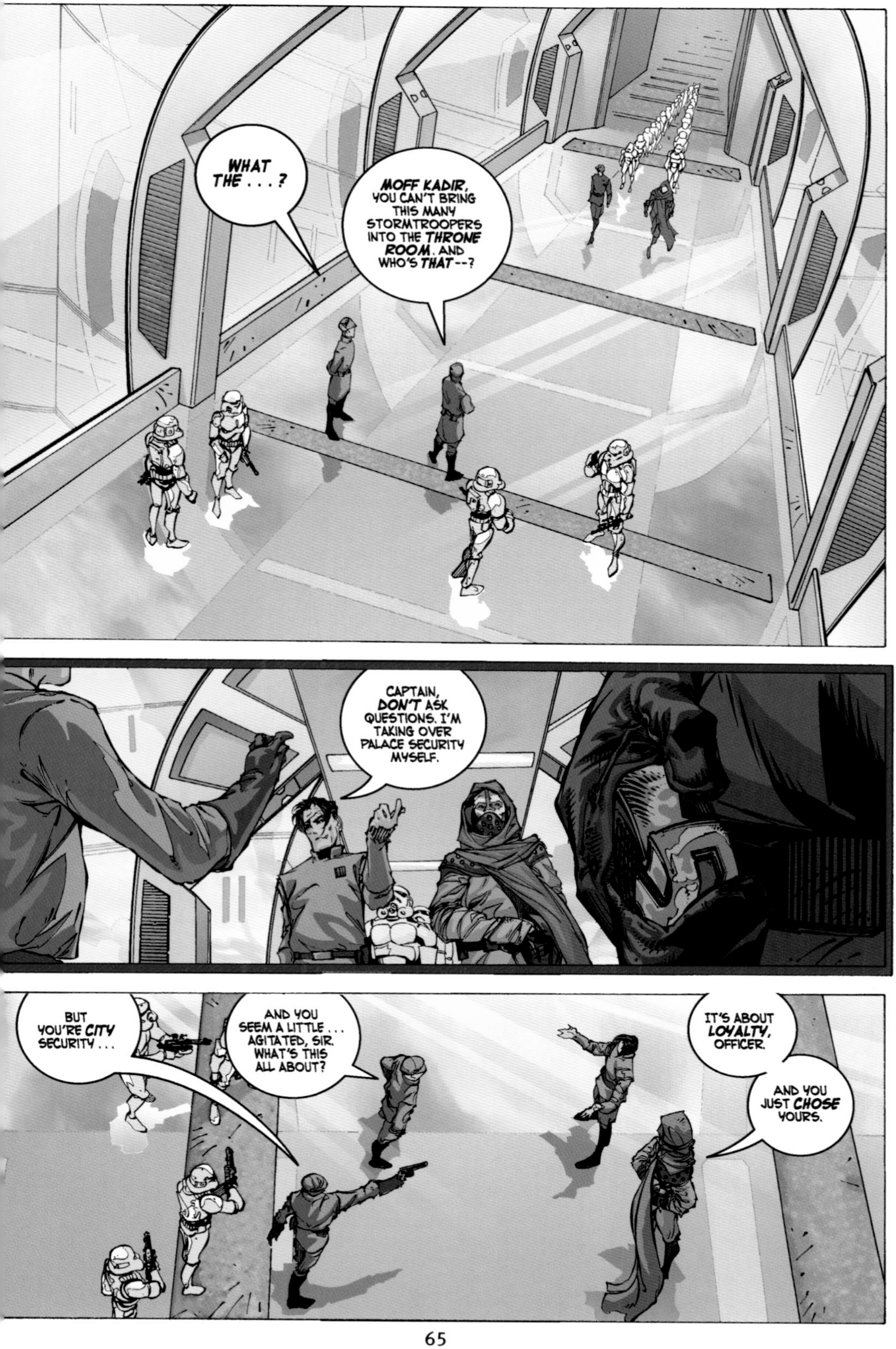
WHAT THE . . . ?
MOFF KADIR, YOU CAN'T BRING THIS MANY STORMTROOPERS INTO THE THRONE ROOM. AND WHO'S THAT--?
CAPTAIN, DON'T ASK QUESTIONS. I'M TAKING OVER PALACE SECURITY MYSELF.
BUT YOU'RE CITY SECURITY . . .
AND YOU SEEM A LITTLE . . . AGITATED, SIR. WHAT'S THIS ALL ABOUT?
IT'S ABOUT LOYALTY, OFFICER.
AND YOU JUST CHOSE YOURS.

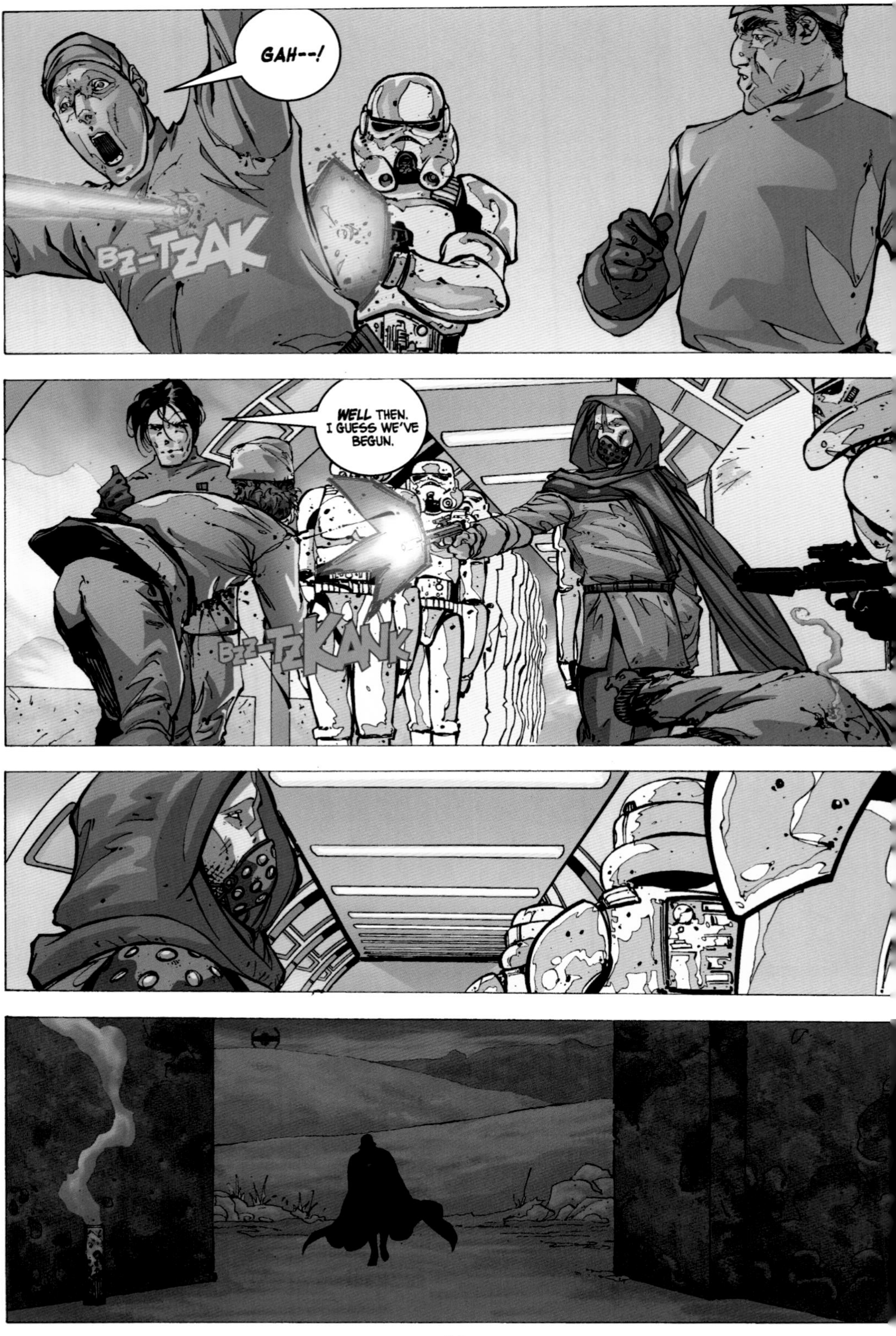
GAH--!
BZ-TZAK
WELL THEN. I GUESS WE'VE BEGUN.
BZZ-TZKANK

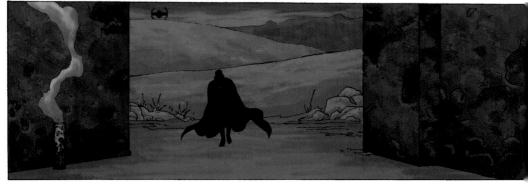

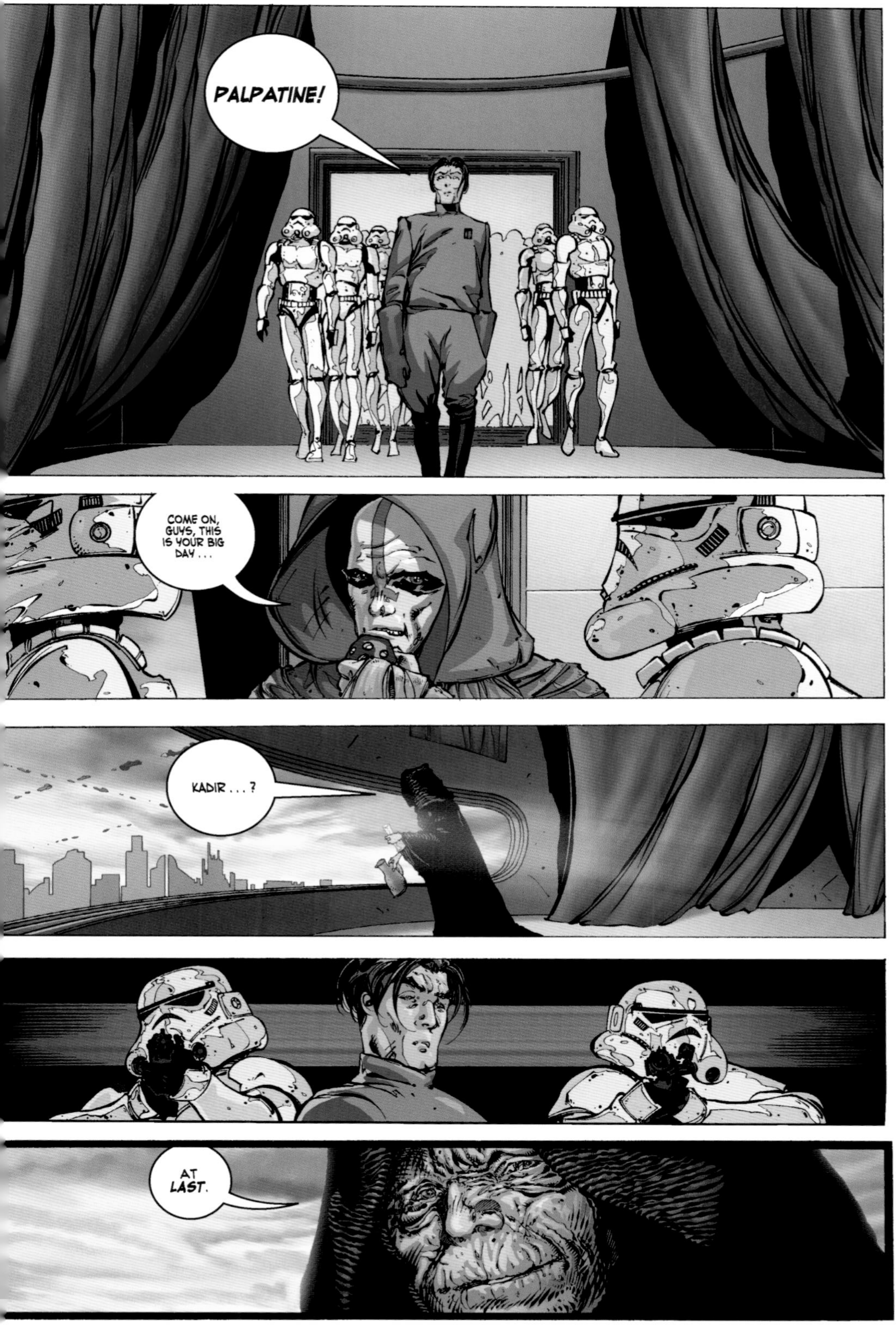
PALPATINE!
COME ON, GUYS, THIS IS YOUR BIG DAY . . .
KADIR . . . ?
AT LAST.

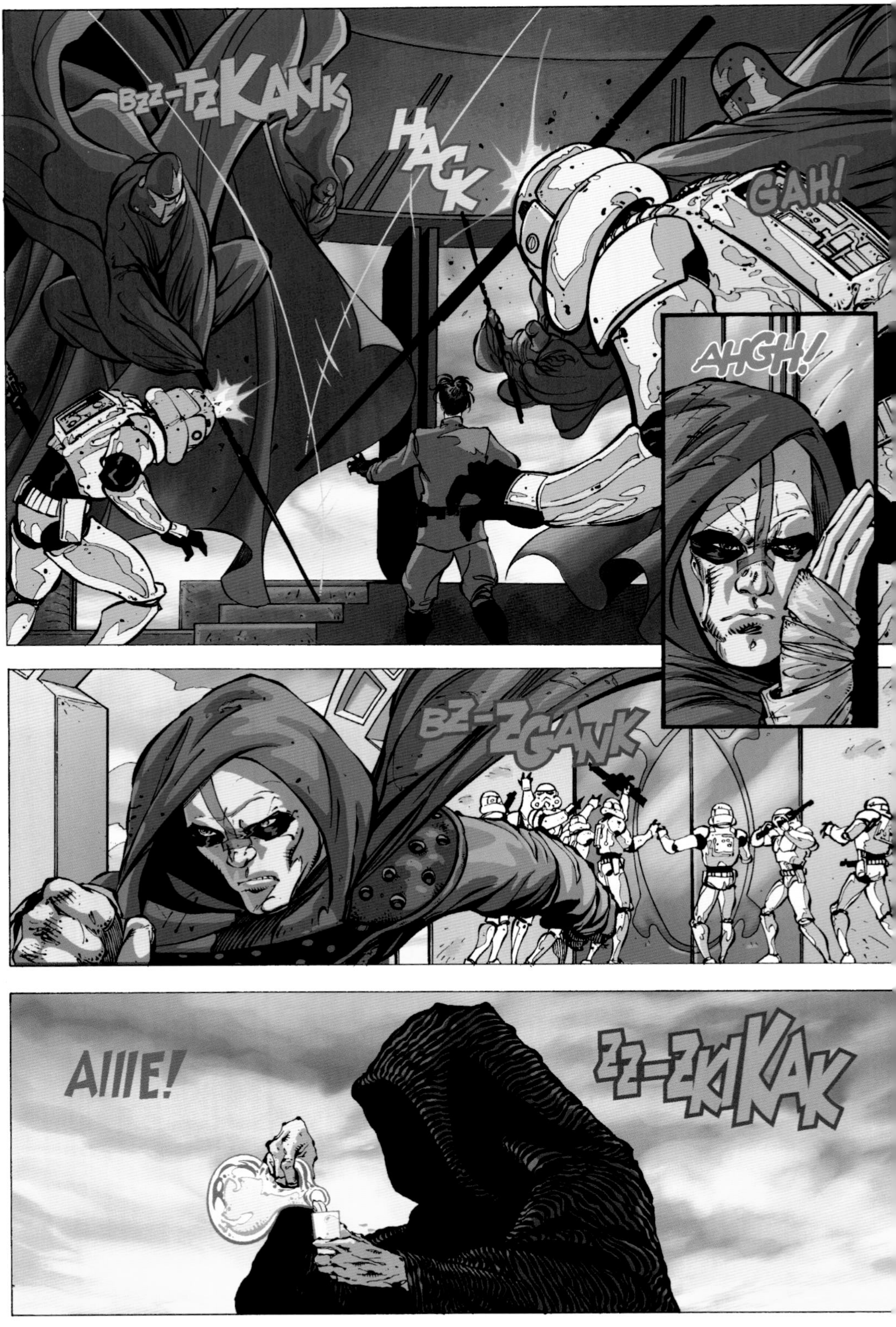
BZZ-TZKANK
HACK
GAH!
AHGH!
BZ-ZGANK
AIIIE!
ZZ-ZKKAK

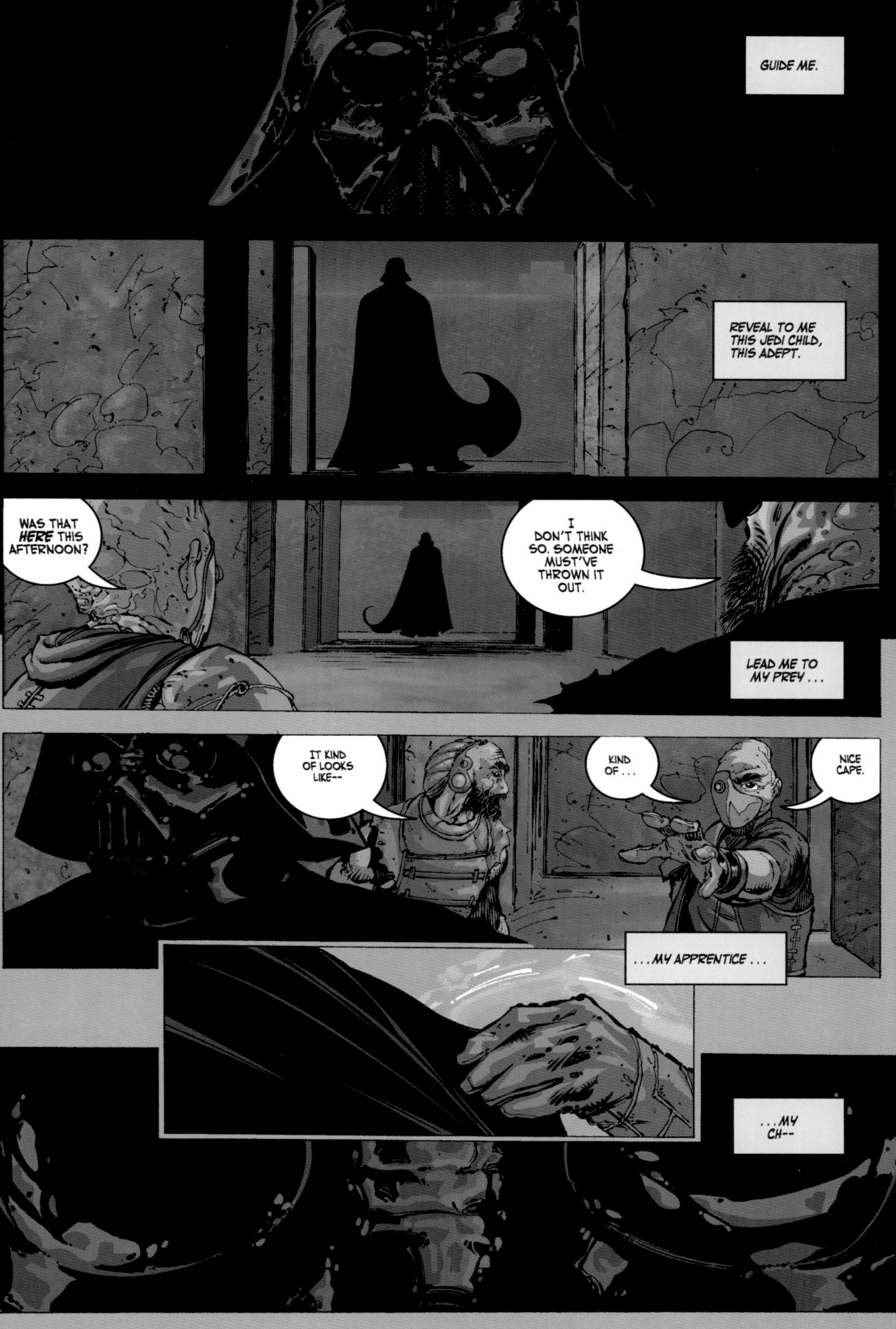
GUIDE ME.
REVEAL TO ME THIS JEDI CHILD, THIS ADEPT.
WAS THAT HERE THIS AFTERNOON?
I DON'T THINK SO. SOMEONE MUST'VE THROWN IT OUT.
LEAD ME TO MY PREY . . .
IT KIND OF LOOKS LIKE--
KIND OF . . .
NICE CAPE.
. . . MY APPRENTICE . . .
. . . MY CH--

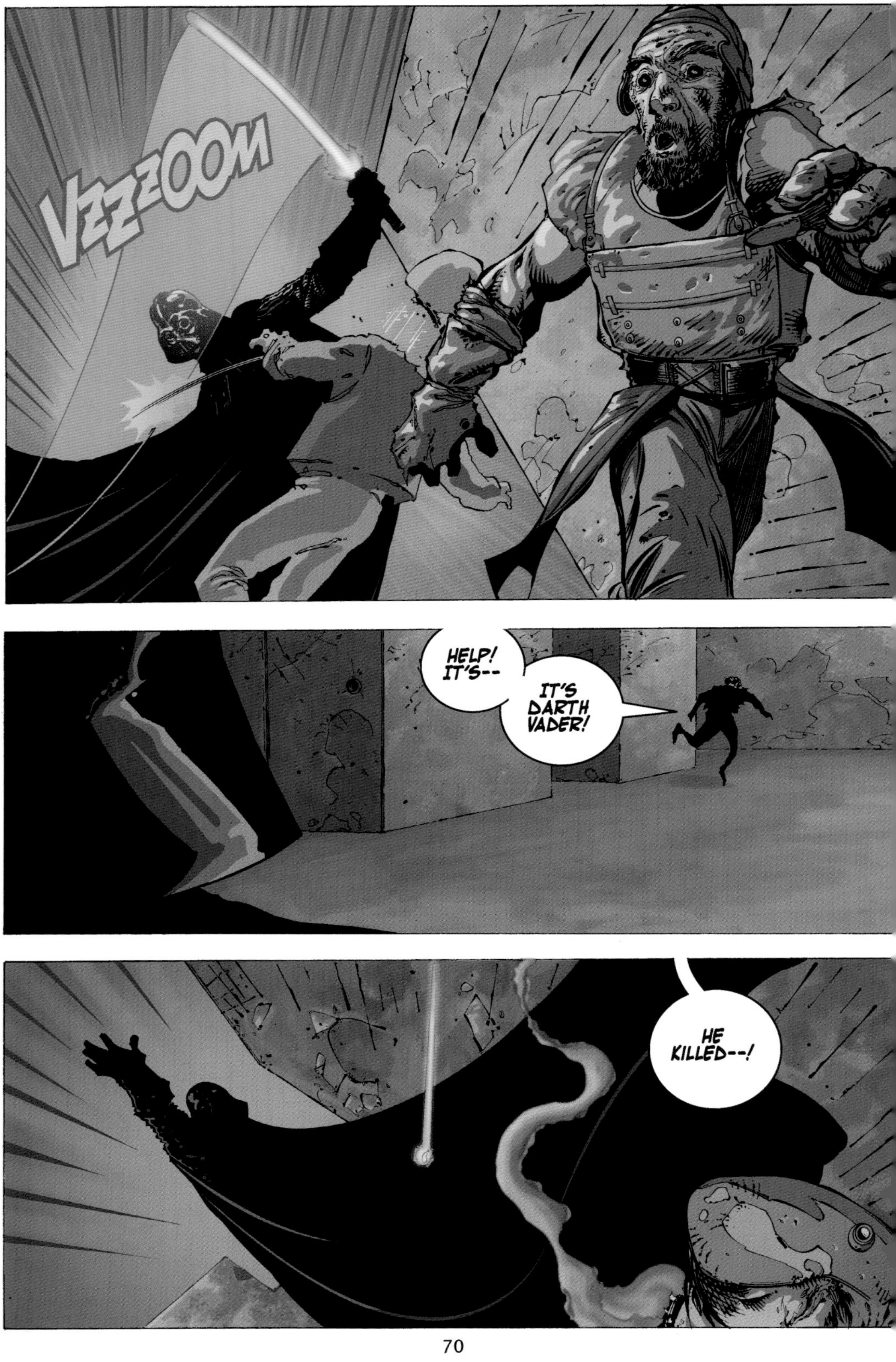
VZZZOOM
HELP! IT'S--
IT'S DARTH VADER!
HE KILLED--!

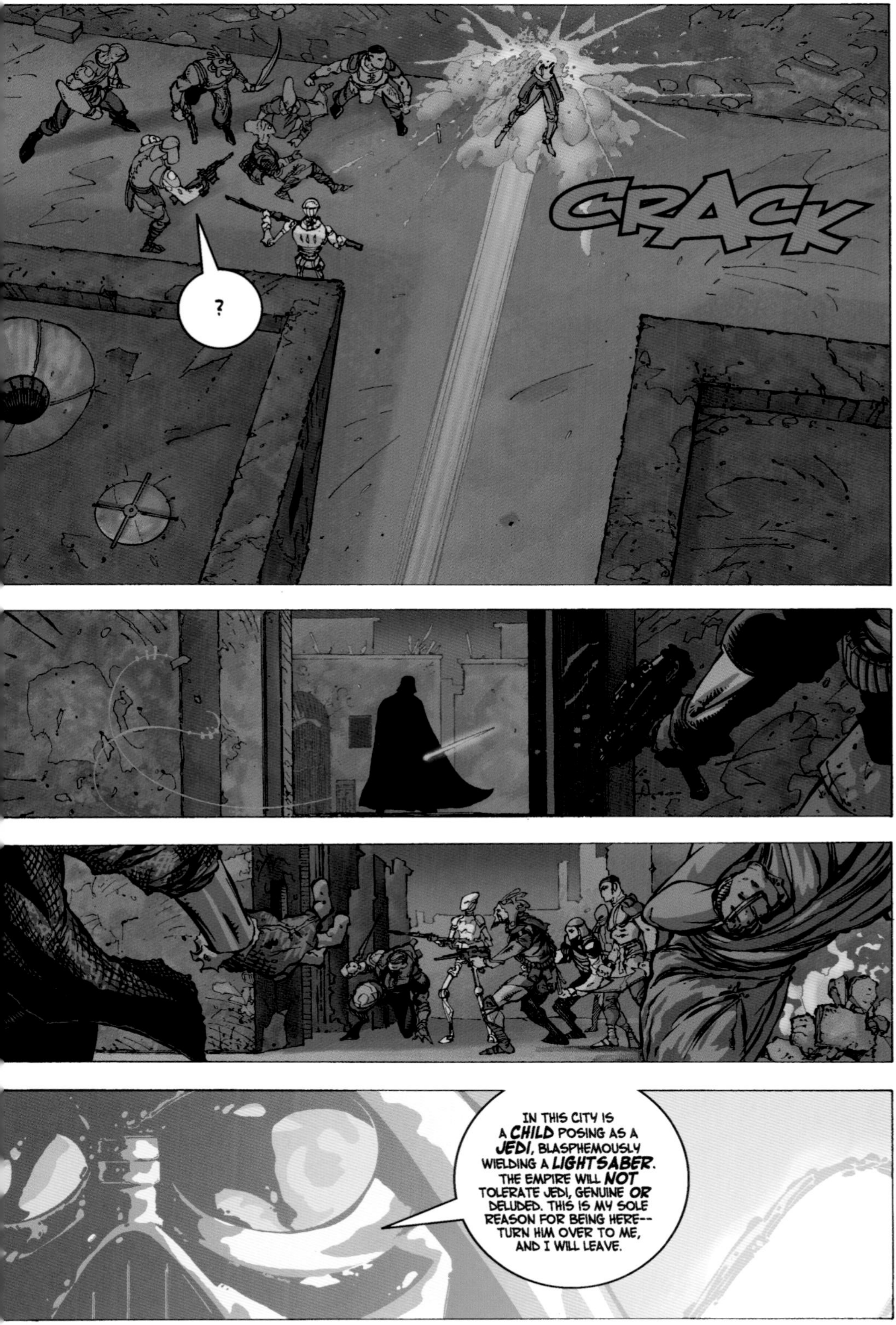
CRACK
?
IN THIS CITY IS A CHILD POSING AS A JEDI, BLASPHEMOUSLY WIELDING A LIGHTSABER. THE EMPIRE WILL NOT TOLERATE JEDI, GENUINE OR DELUDED. THIS IS MY SOLE REASON FOR BEING HERE-- TURN HIM OVER TO ME, AND I WILL LEAVE.

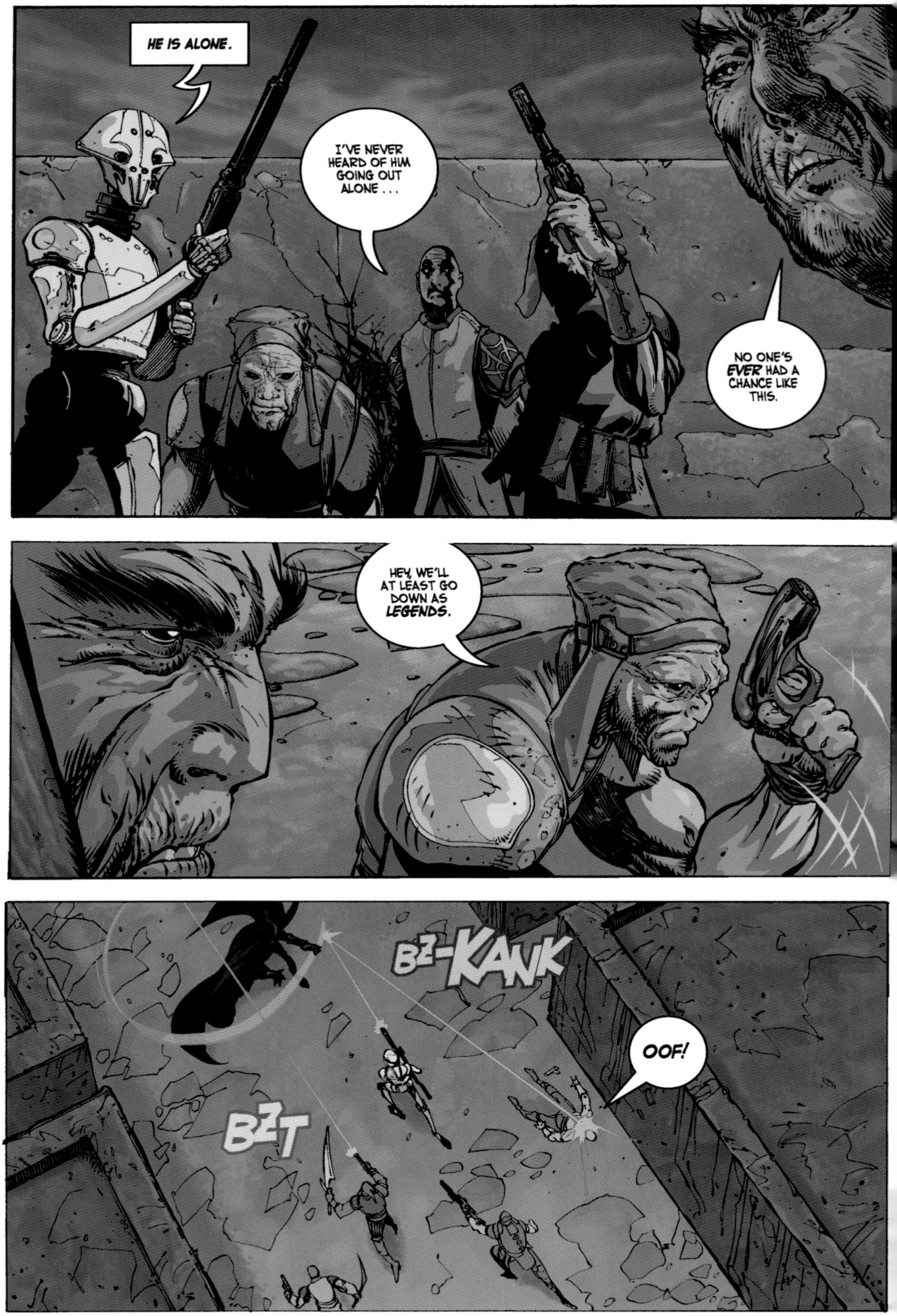
HE IS ALONE.
I'VE NEVER HEARD OF HIM GOING OUT ALONE . . .
NO ONE'S EVER HAD A CHANCE LIKE THIS.
HEY, WE'LL AT LEAST GO DOWN AS LEGENDS.
BZ-KANK
OOF!
BZT

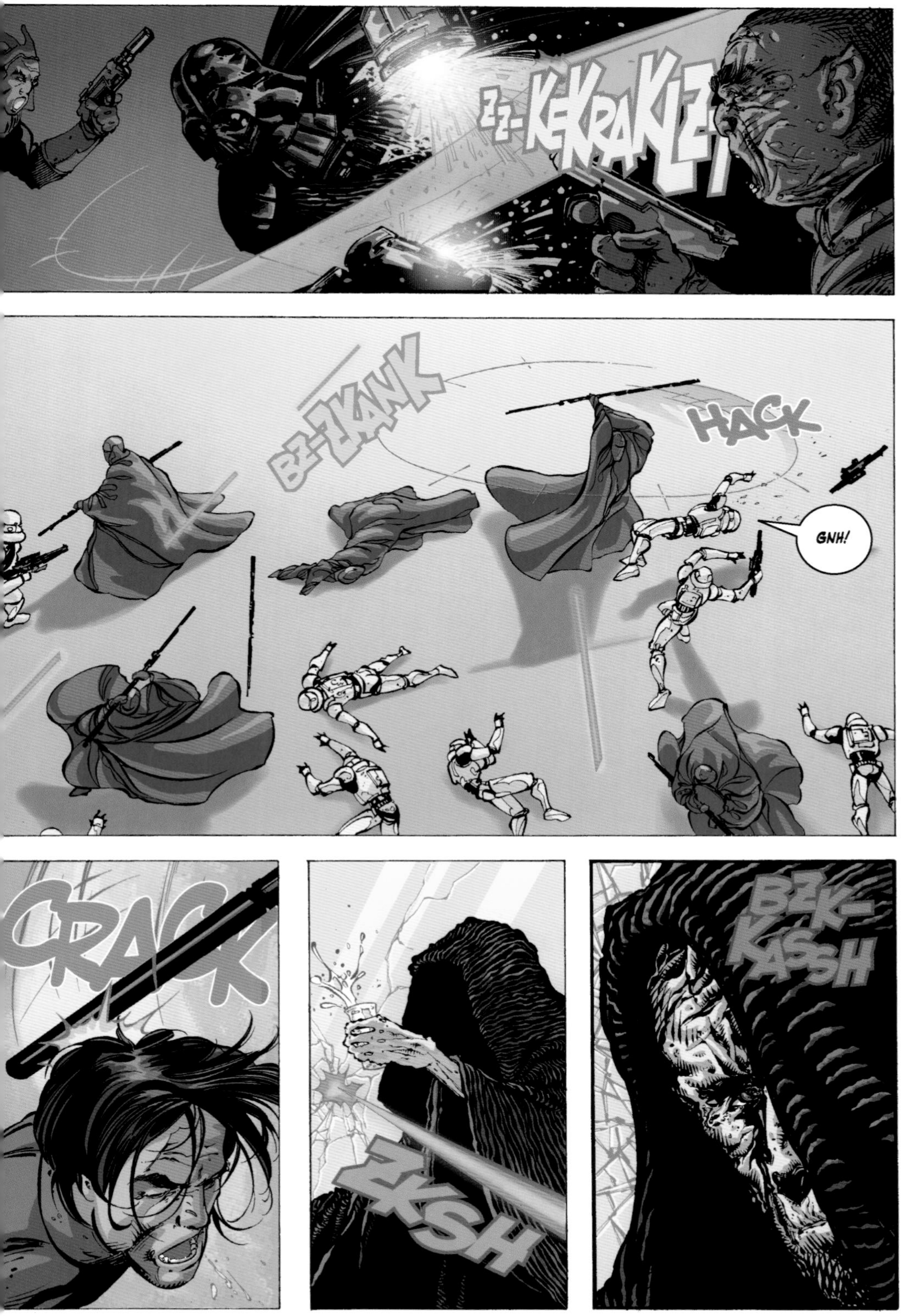
ZZ-KEKRAKLZ-T
BZ-ZWANK
HACK
GNH!
CRACK
ZKSH
BZK-KASSH

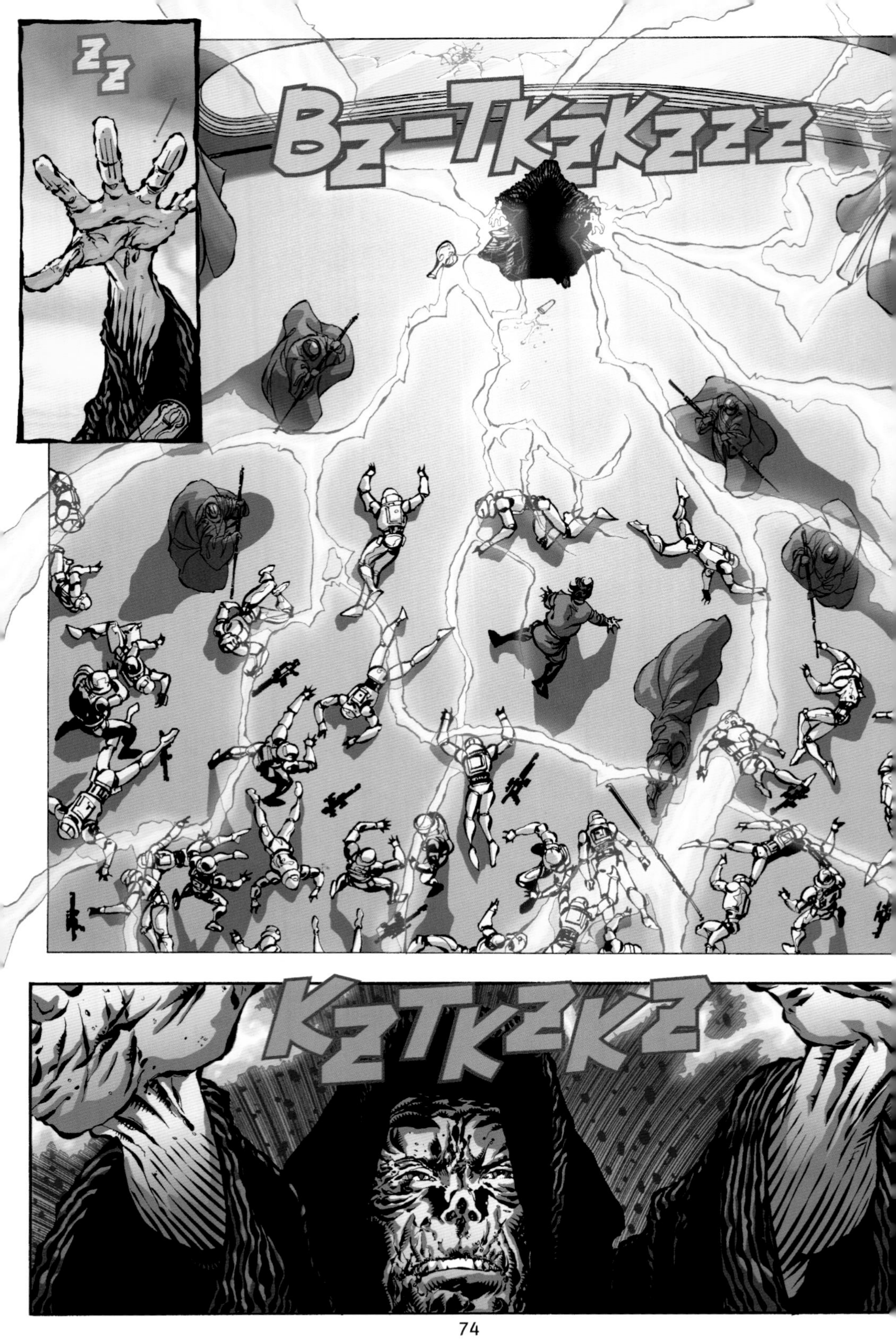

ZZ
BZ-TKZKZZZ
KZTKZKZ

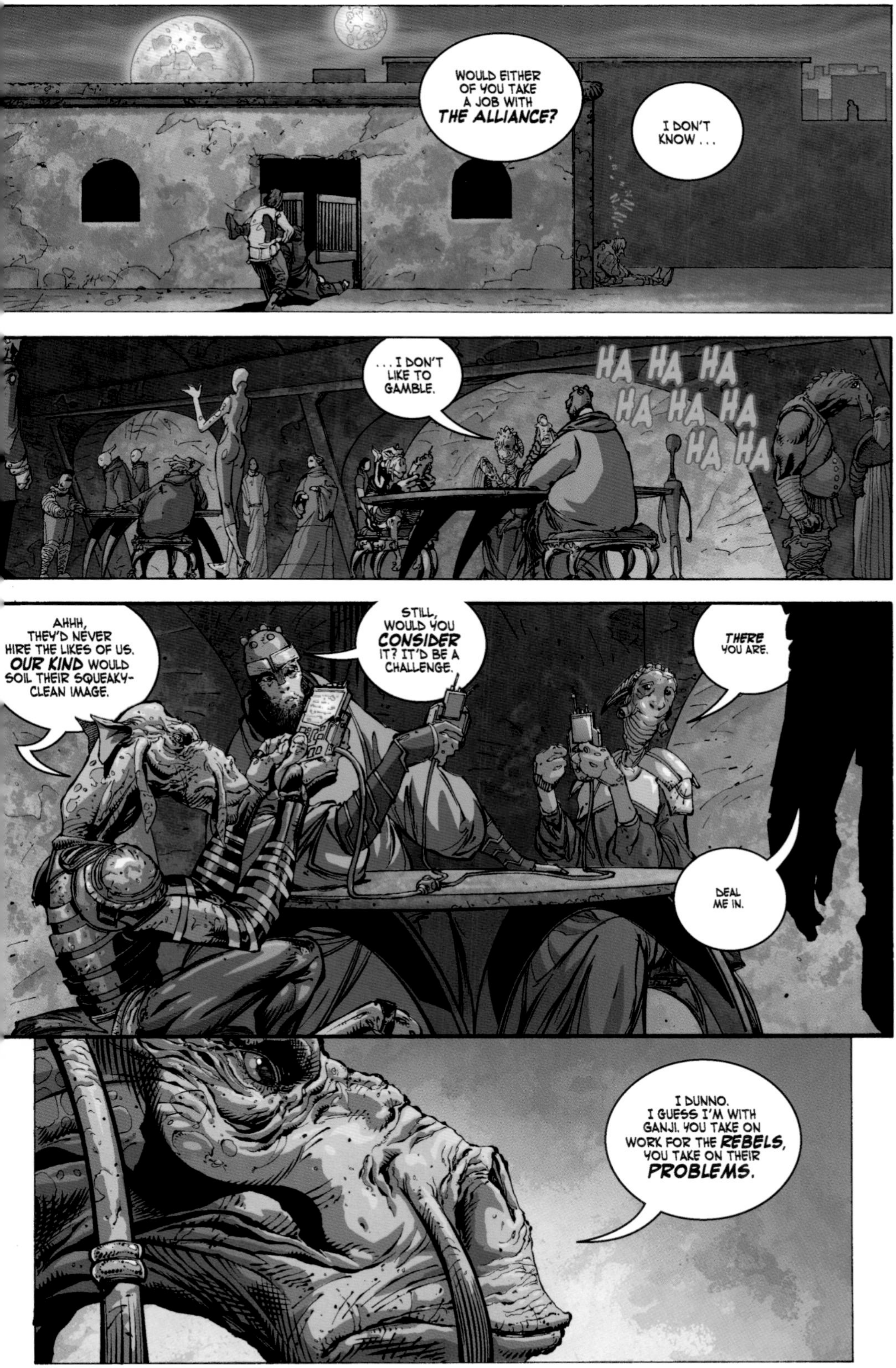
WOULD EITHER OF YOU TAKE A JOB WITH THE ALLIANCE?
I DON'T KNOW . . .
. . . I DON'T LIKE TO GAMBLE.
HA HA HA HA HA HA HA HA
AHHH, THEY'D NEVER HIRE THE LIKES OF US. OUR KIND WOULD SOIL THEIR SQUEAKY-CLEAN IMAGE.
STILL, WOULD YOU CONSIDER IT? IT'D BE A CHALLENGE.
THERE YOU ARE.
DEAL ME IN.
I DUNNO. I GUESS I'M WITH GANJI. YOU TAKE ON WORK FOR THE REBELS, YOU TAKE ON THEIR PROBLEMS.

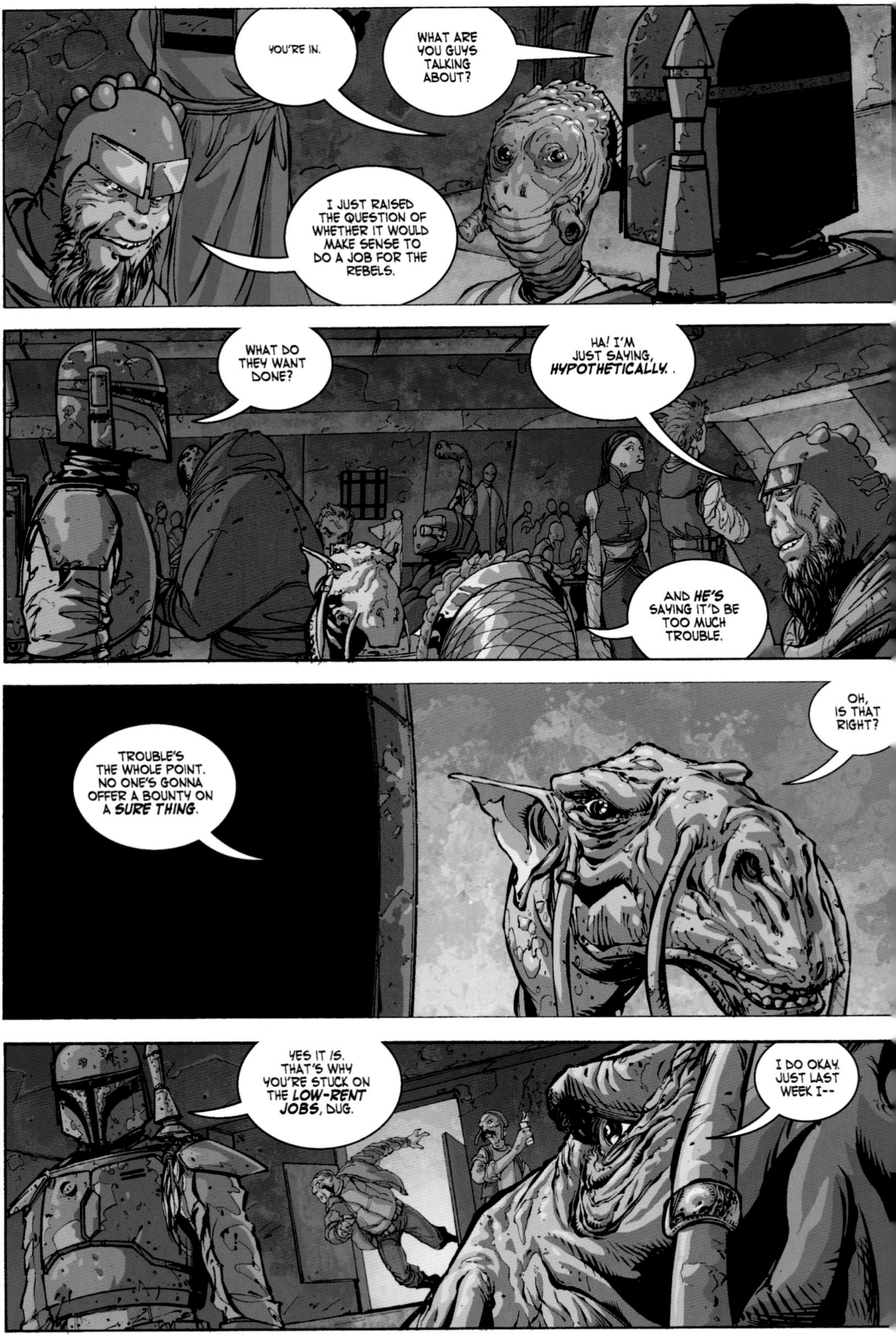

YOU'RE IN.
WHAT ARE YOU GUYS TALKING ABOUT?
I JUST RAISED THE QUESTION OF WHETHER IT WOULD MAKE SENSE TO DO A JOB FOR THE REBELS.
WHAT DO THEY WANT DONE?
HA! I'M JUST SAYING, HYPOTHETICALLY. .
AND HE'S SAYING IT'D BE TOO MUCH TROUBLE.
OH, IS THAT RIGHT?
TROUBLE'S THE WHOLE POINT. NO ONE'S GONNA OFFER A BOUNTY ON A SURE THING.
YES IT IS. THAT'S WHY YOU'RE STUCK ON THE LOW-RENT JOBS, DUG.
I DO OKAY. JUST LAST WEEK I--

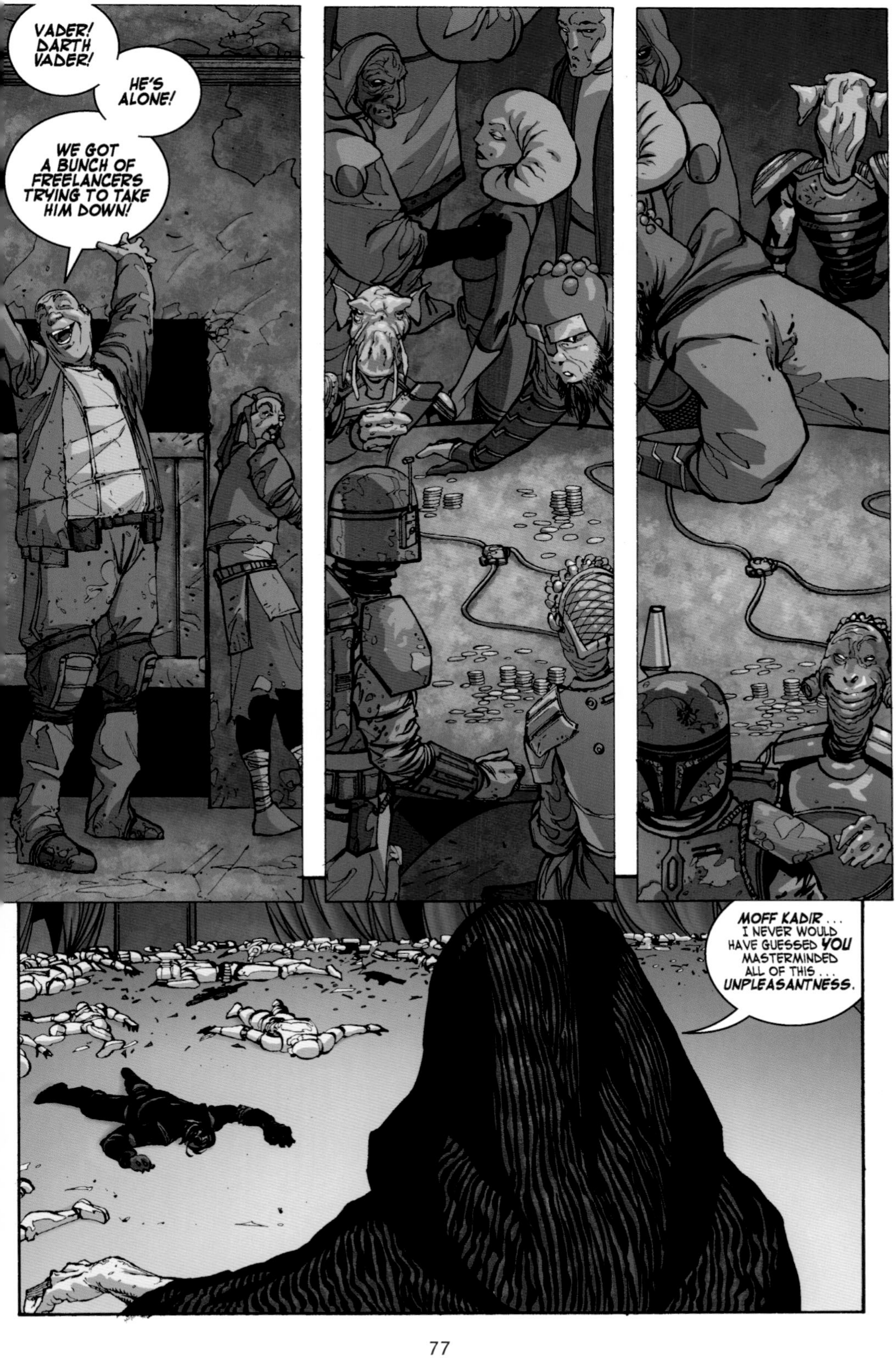
VADER! DARTH VADER!
HE'S ALONE!
WE GOT A BUNCH OF FREELANCERS TRYING TO TAKE HIM DOWN!
MOFF KADIR . . . I NEVER WOULD HAVE GUESSED YOU MASTERMINDED ALL OF THIS . . . UNPLEASANTNESS.

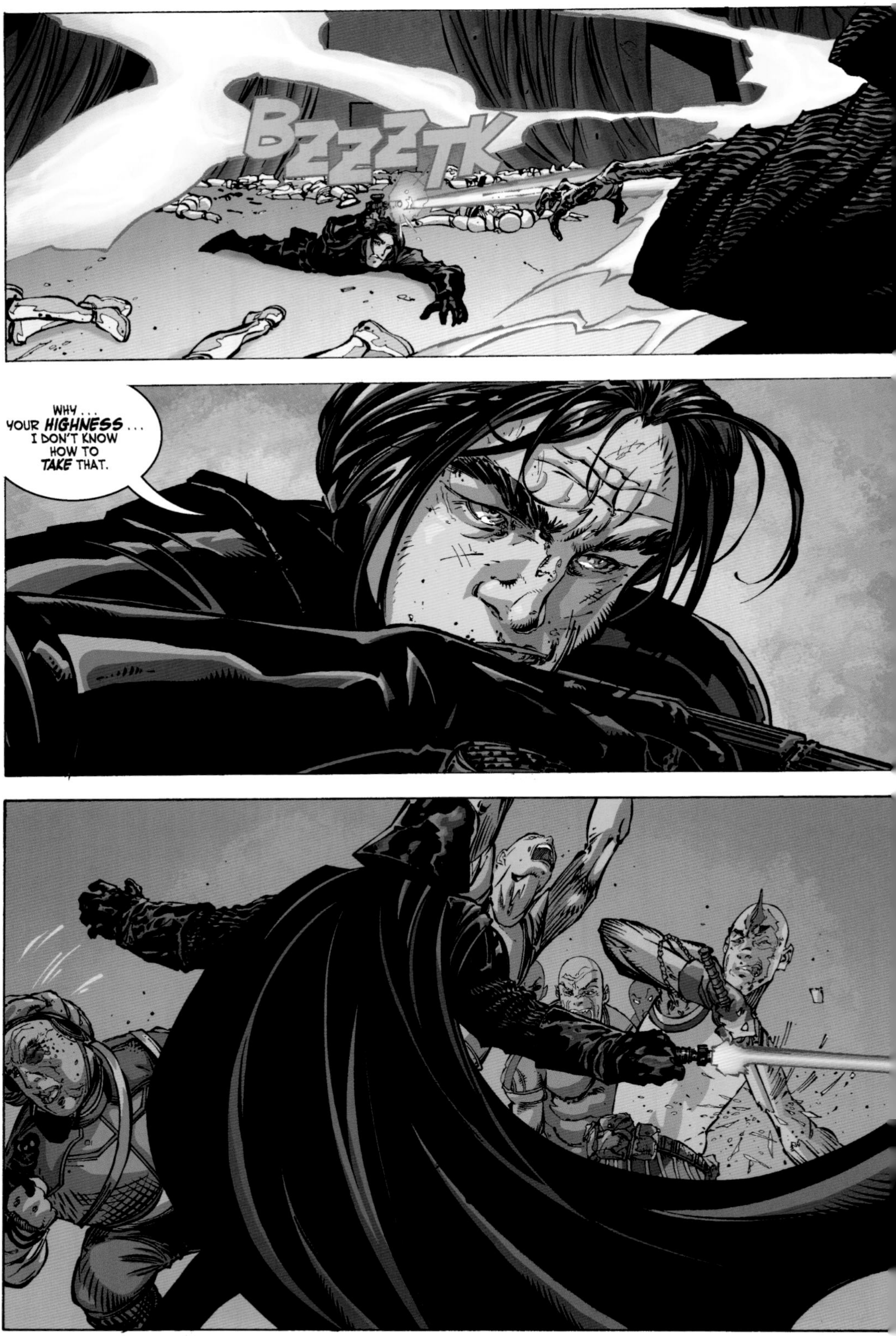
BZZZTK
WHY . . . YOUR HIGHNESS . . . I DON'T KNOW HOW TO TAKE THAT.

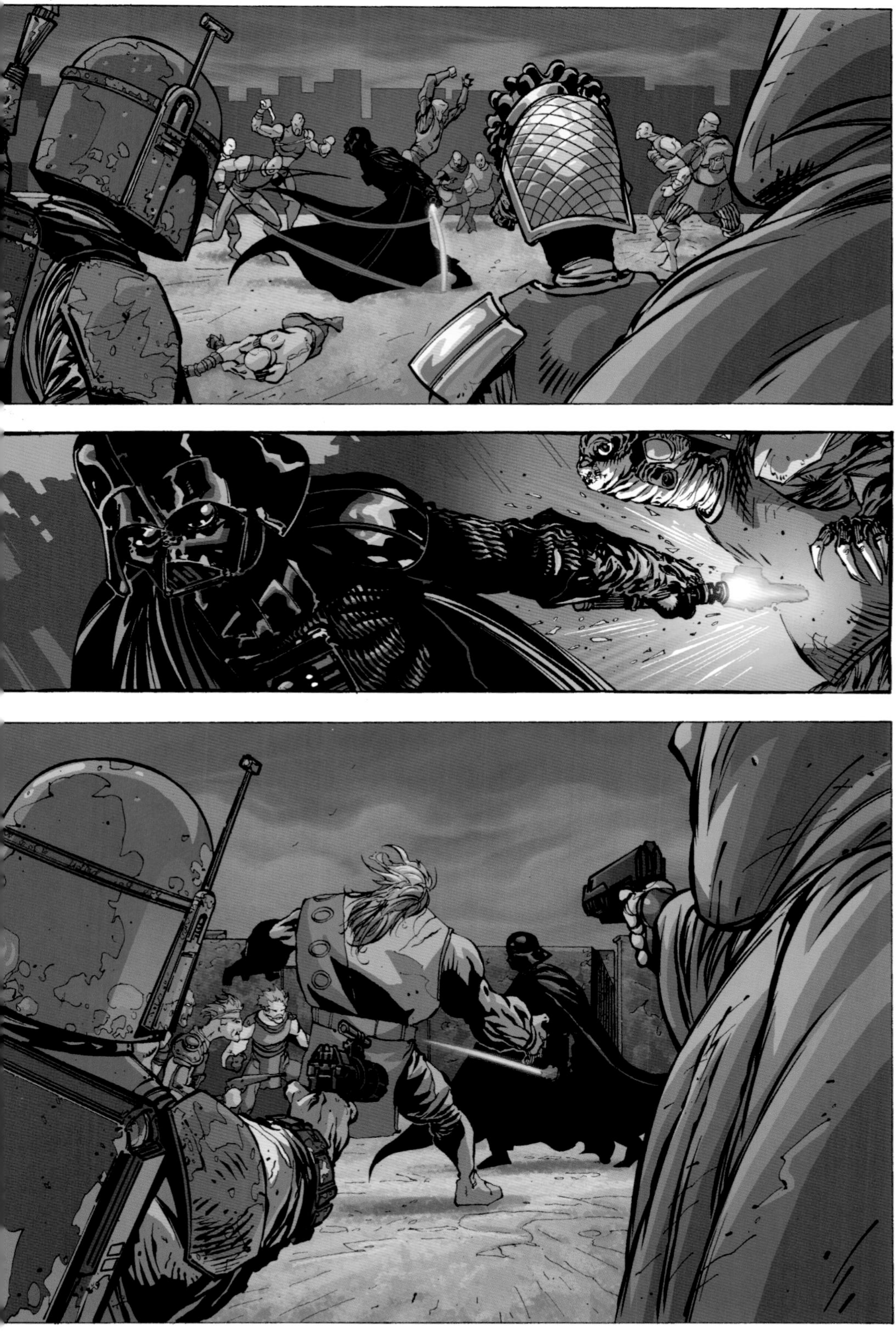

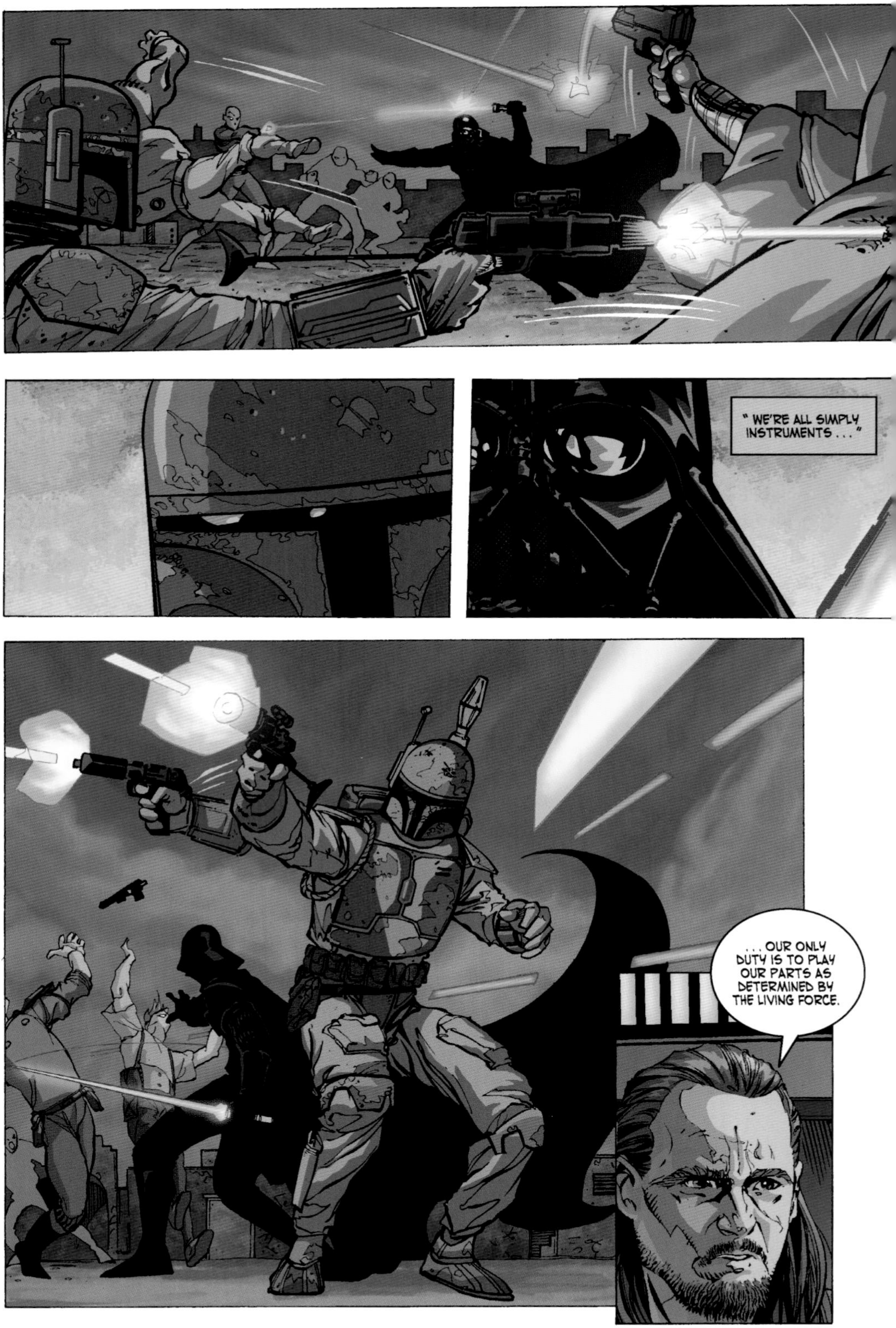
" WE'RE ALL SIMPLY INSTRUMENTS . . . "
. . . OUR ONLY DUTY IS TO PLAY OUR PARTS AS DETERMINED BY THE LIVING FORCE.

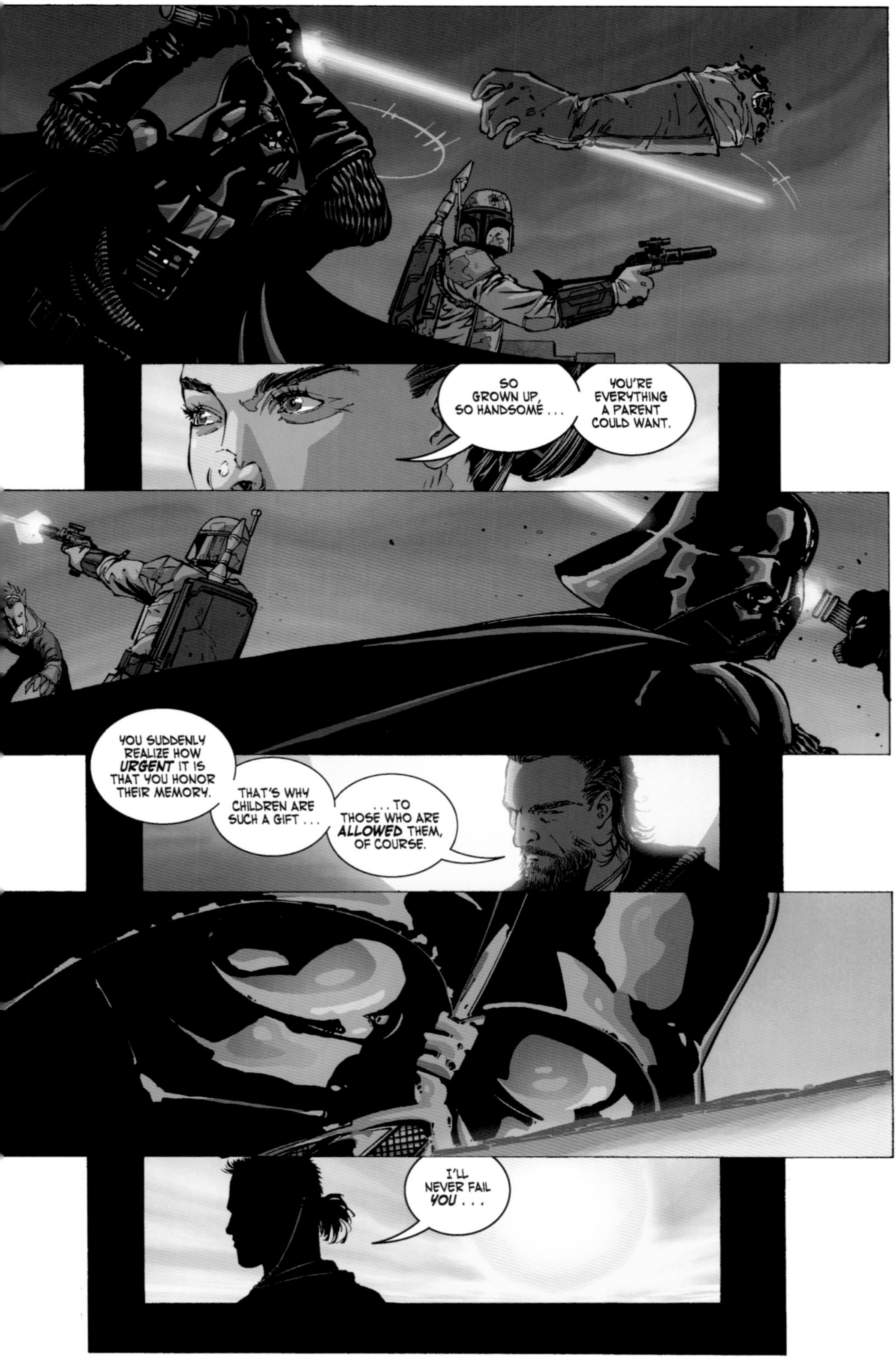
SO GROWN UP, SO HANDSOME . . .
YOU'RE EVERYTHING A PARENT COULD WANT.
YOU SUDDENLY REALIZE HOW **URGENT** IT IS THAT YOU HONOR THEIR MEMORY.
THAT'S WHY CHILDREN ARE SUCH A GIFT . . .
. . . TO THOSE WHO ARE **ALLOWED** THEM, OF COURSE.
I'LL NEVER FAIL **YOU** . . .

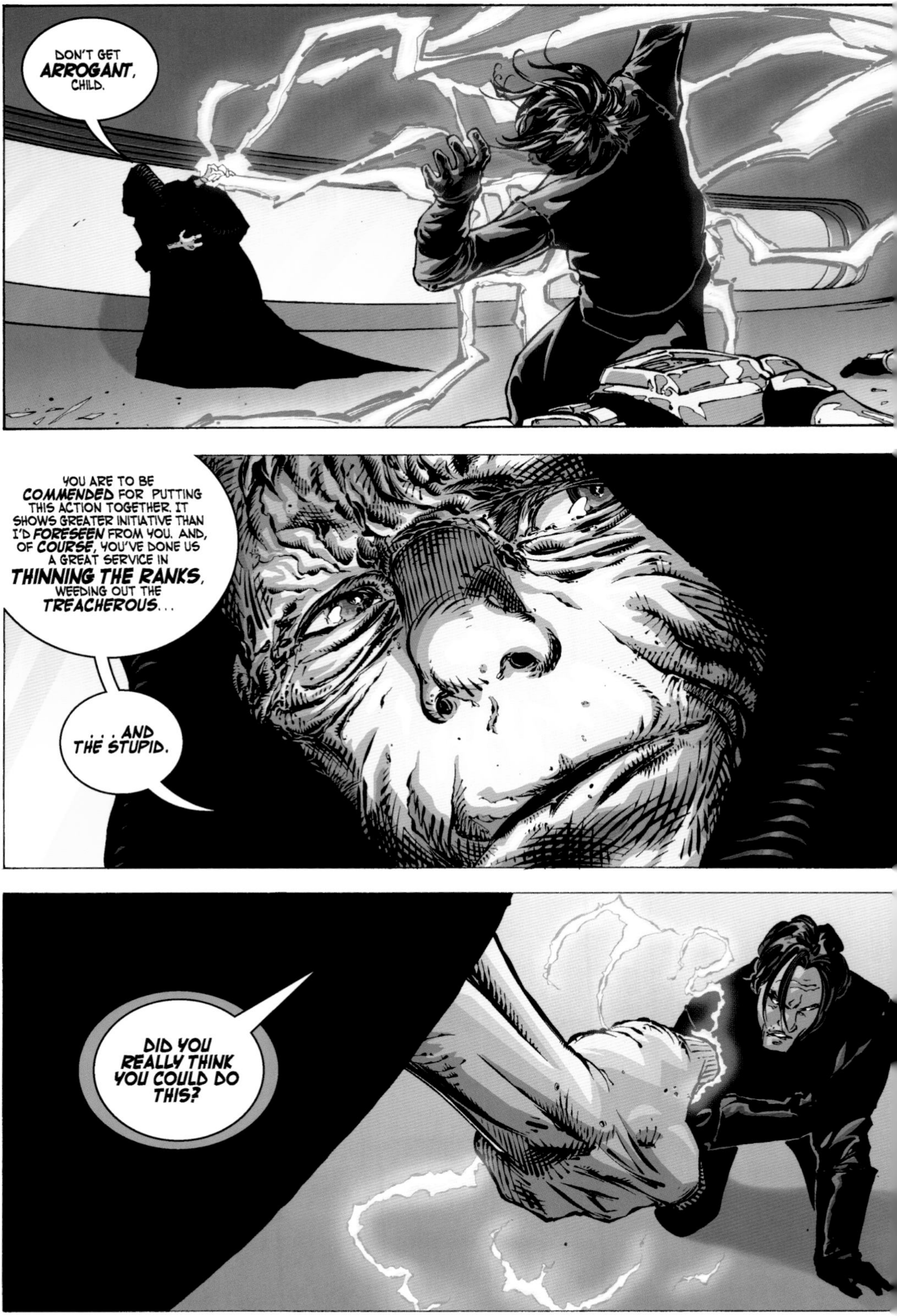
DON'T GET ARROGANT, CHILD.
YOU ARE TO BE COMMENDED FOR PUTTING THIS ACTION TOGETHER. IT SHOWS GREATER INITIATIVE THAN I'D FORESEEN FROM YOU. AND, OF COURSE, YOU'VE DONE US A GREAT SERVICE IN THINNING THE RANKS, WEEDING OUT THE TREACHEROUS...
...AND THE STUPID.
DID YOU REALLY THINK YOU COULD DO THIS?

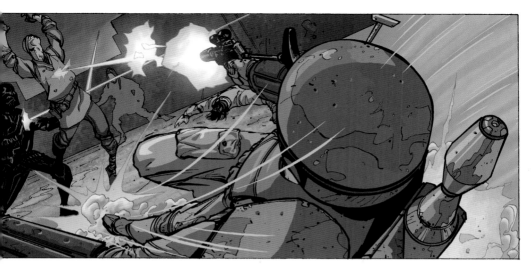

DON'T SLOW DOWN *NOW*, BIG GUY.

LORD VADER!

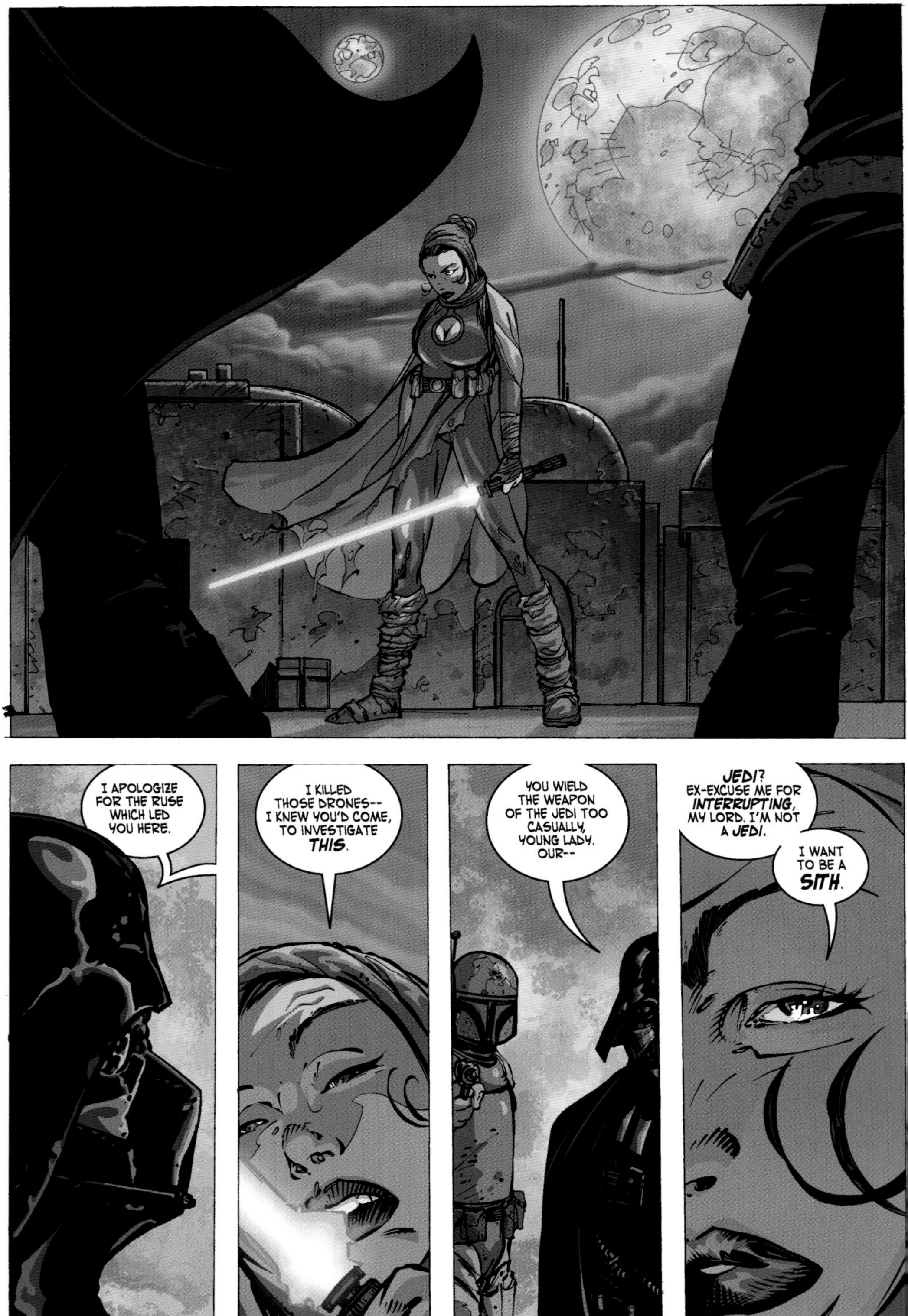
I APOLOGIZE FOR THE RUSE WHICH LED YOU HERE.
I KILLED THOSE DRONES-- I KNEW YOU'D COME, TO INVESTIGATE THIS.
YOU WIELD THE WEAPON OF THE JEDI TOO CASUALLY, YOUNG LADY. OUR--
JEDI? EX-EXCUSE ME FOR INTERRUPTING, MY LORD. I'M NOT A JEDI.
I WANT TO BE A SITH.

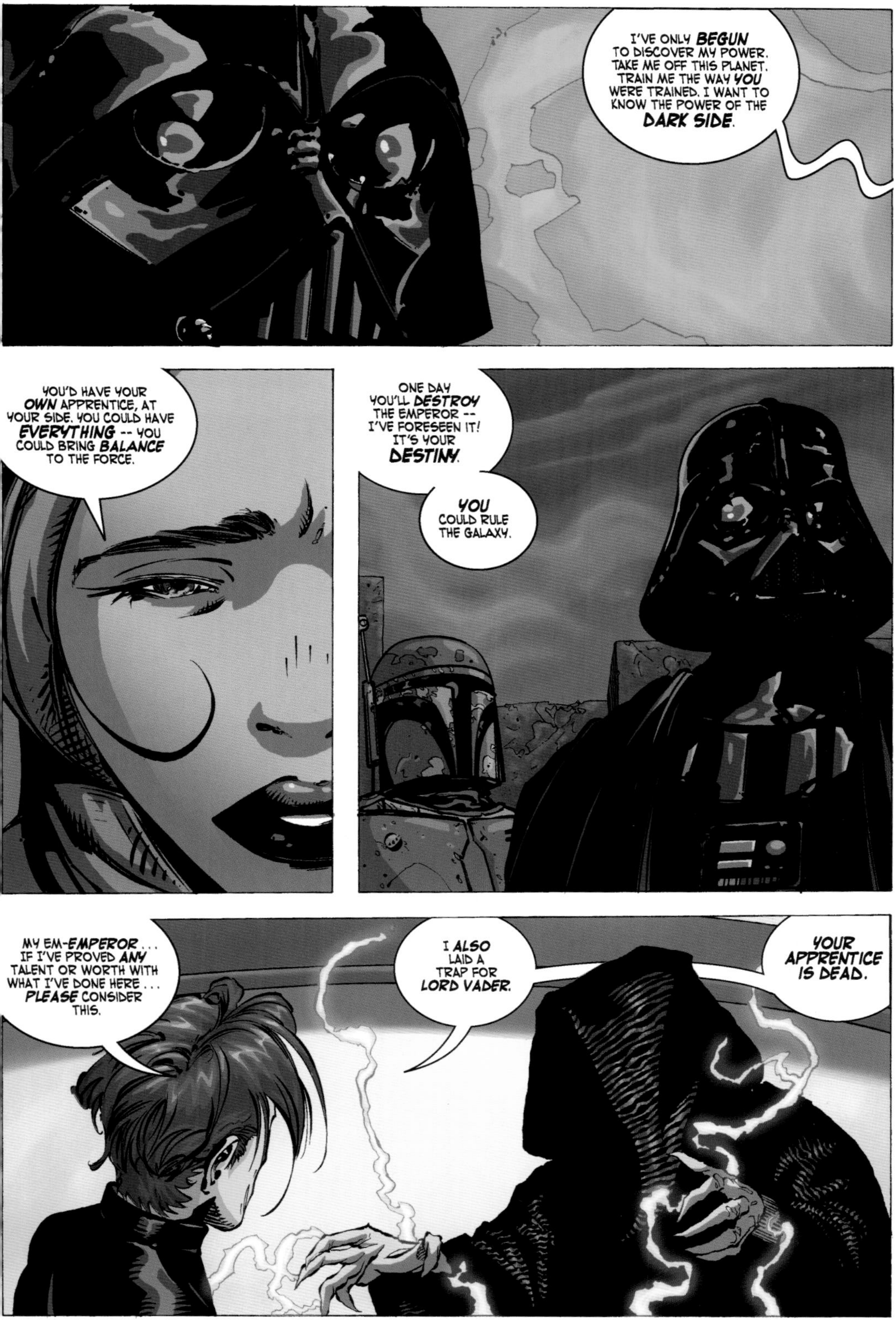
I'VE ONLY BEGUN TO DISCOVER MY POWER. TAKE ME OFF THIS PLANET. TRAIN ME THE WAY YOU WERE TRAINED. I WANT TO KNOW THE POWER OF THE DARK SIDE.
YOU'D HAVE YOUR OWN APPRENTICE, AT YOUR SIDE. YOU COULD HAVE EVERYTHING -- YOU COULD BRING BALANCE TO THE FORCE.
ONE DAY YOU'LL DESTROY THE EMPEROR -- I'VE FORESEEN IT! IT'S YOUR DESTINY.
YOU COULD RULE THE GALAXY.
MY EM-EMPEROR . . . IF I'VE PROVED ANY TALENT OR WORTH WITH WHAT I'VE DONE HERE . . . PLEASE CONSIDER THIS.
I ALSO LAID A TRAP FOR LORD VADER.
YOUR APPRENTICE IS DEAD.

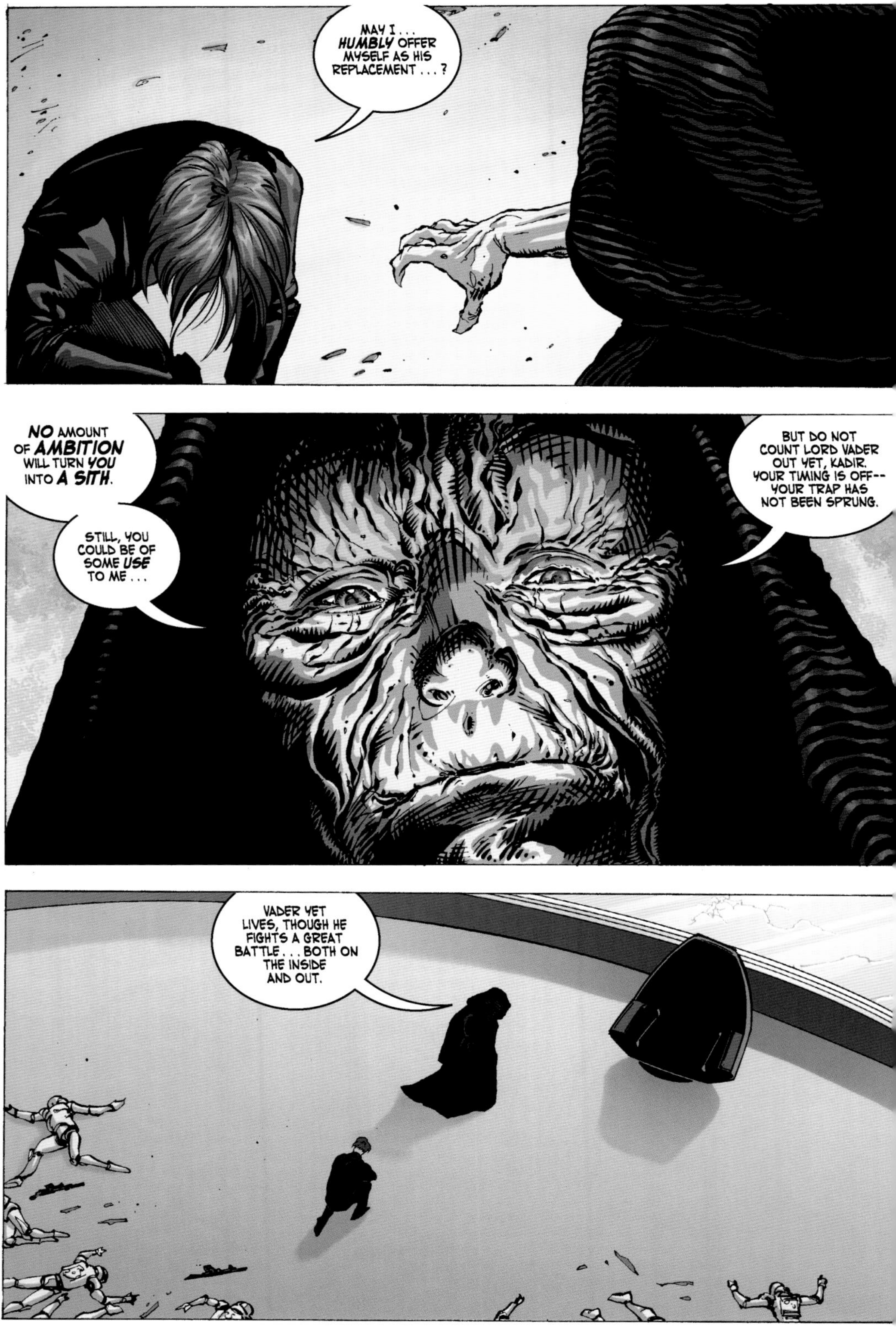
MAY I . . . HUMBLY OFFER MYSELF AS HIS REPLACEMENT . . . ?
NO AMOUNT OF AMBITION WILL TURN YOU INTO A SITH.
STILL, YOU COULD BE OF SOME USE TO ME . . .
BUT DO NOT COUNT LORD VADER OUT YET, KADIR. YOUR TIMING IS OFF-- YOUR TRAP HAS NOT BEEN SPRUNG.
VADER YET LIVES, THOUGH HE FIGHTS A GREAT BATTLE . . . BOTH ON THE INSIDE AND OUT.

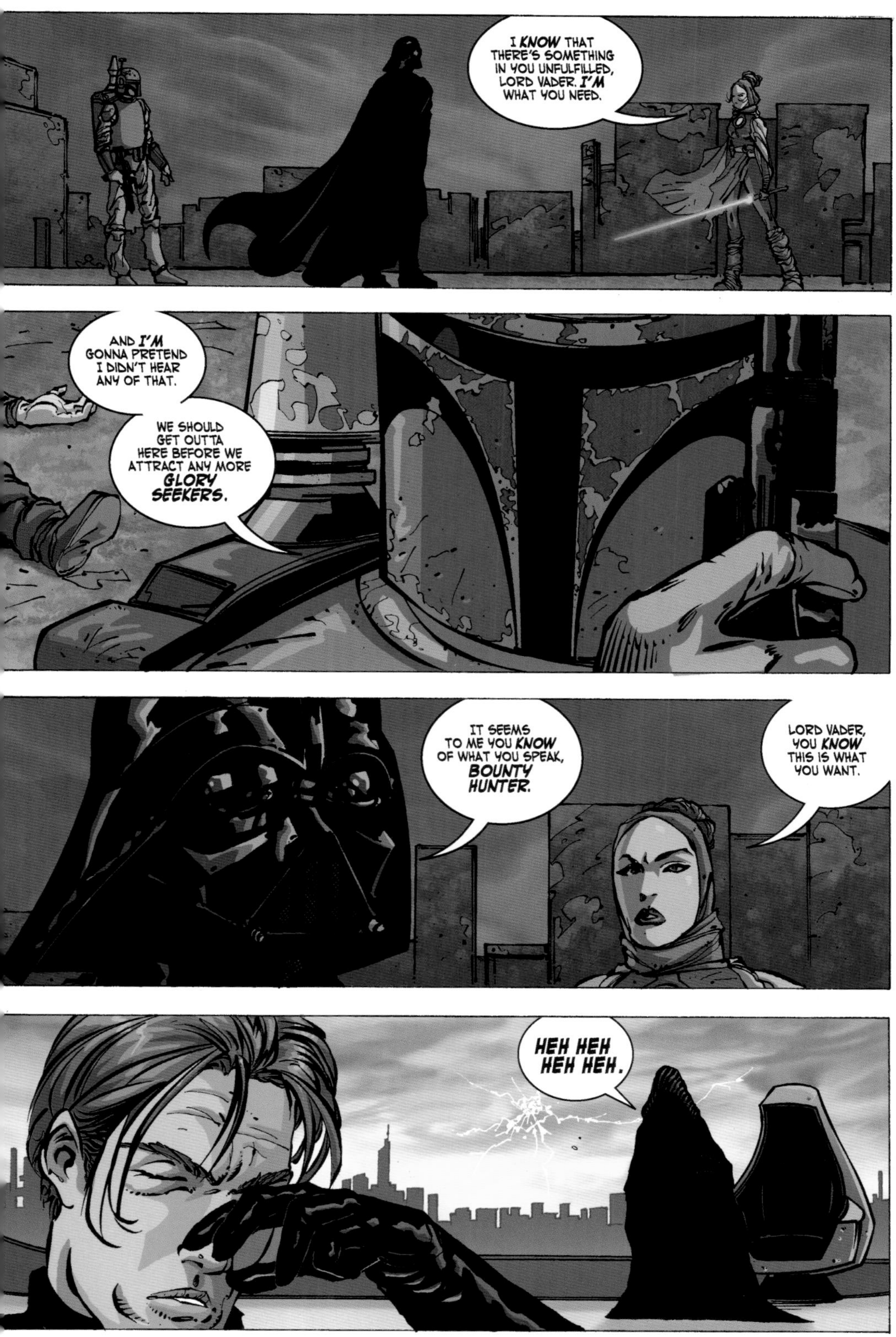
I KNOW THAT THERE'S SOMETHING IN YOU UNFULFILLED, LORD VADER. I'M WHAT YOU NEED.
AND I'M GONNA PRETEND I DIDN'T HEAR ANY OF THAT.
WE SHOULD GET OUTTA HERE BEFORE WE ATTRACT ANY MORE GLORY SEEKERS.
IT SEEMS TO ME YOU KNOW OF WHAT YOU SPEAK, BOUNTY HUNTER.
LORD VADER, YOU KNOW THIS IS WHAT YOU WANT.
HEH HEH HEH HEH.

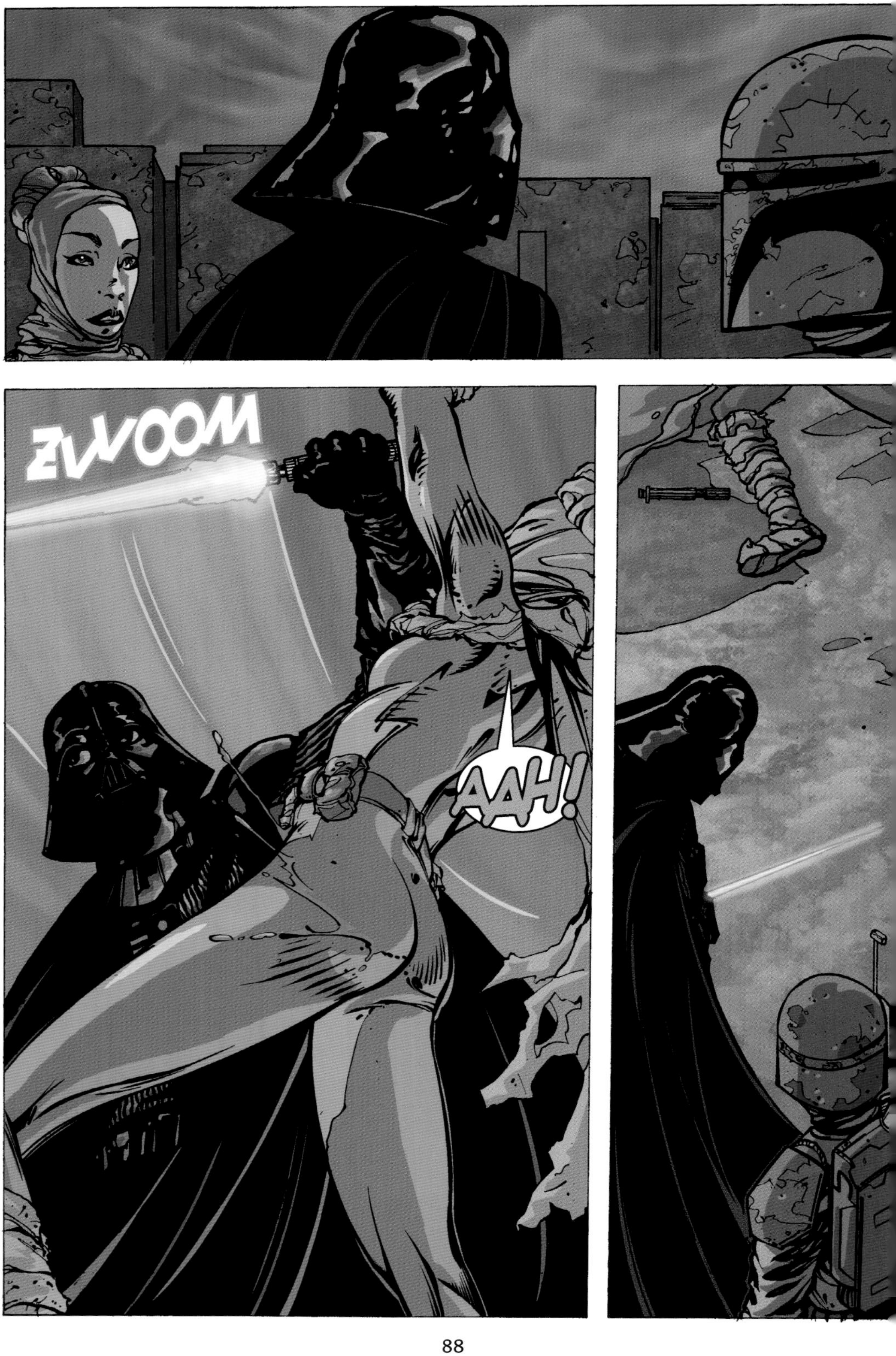
ZVVOOM
AAH!

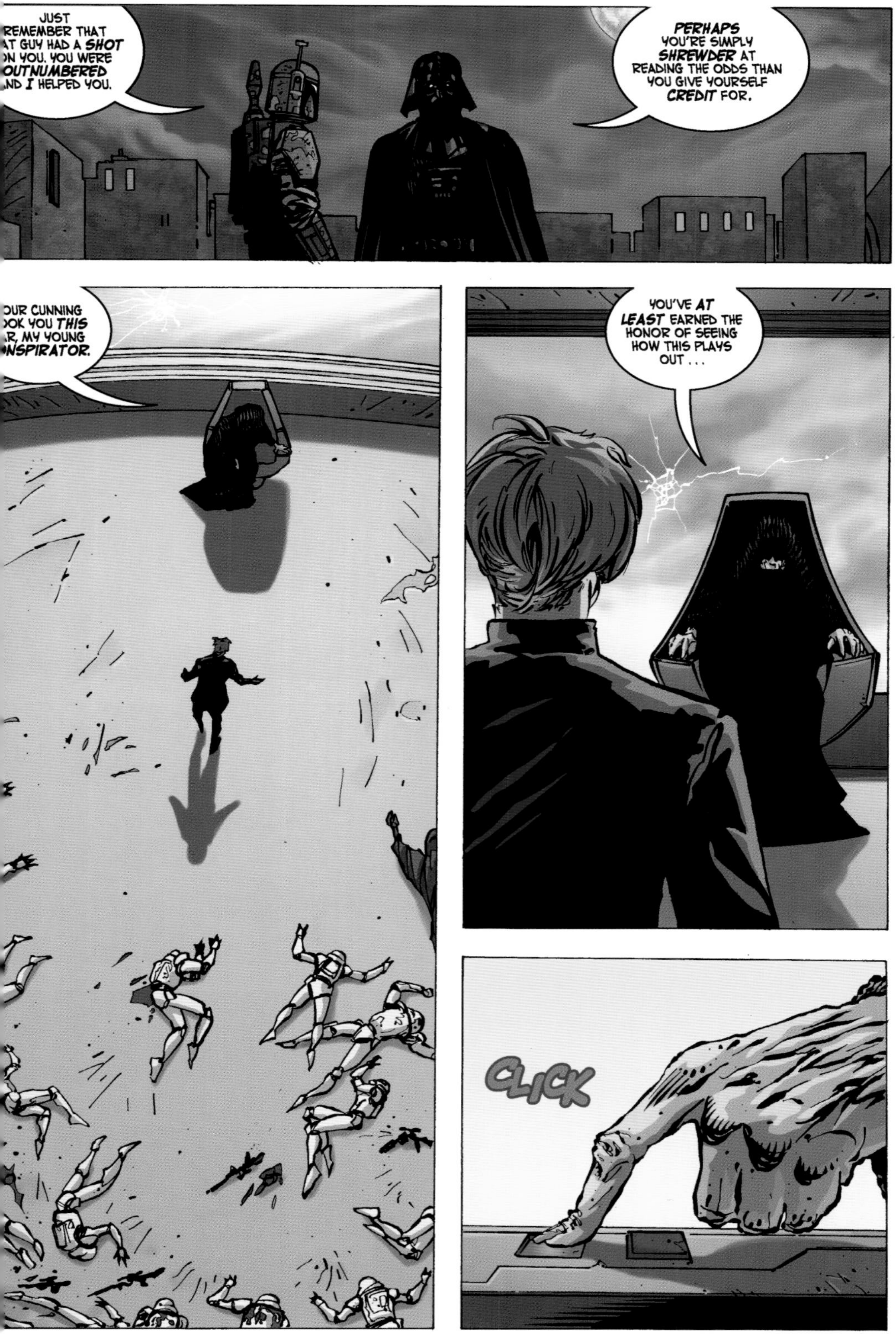
JUST REMEMBER THAT AT GUY HAD A SHOT ON YOU. YOU WERE OUTNUMBERED AND I HELPED YOU.
PERHAPS YOU'RE SIMPLY SHREWDER AT READING THE ODDS THAN YOU GIVE YOURSELF CREDIT FOR.
OUR CUNNING OOK YOU THIS AR, MY YOUNG NSPIRATOR.
YOU'VE AT LEAST EARNED THE HONOR OF SEEING HOW THIS PLAYS OUT . . .
CLICK

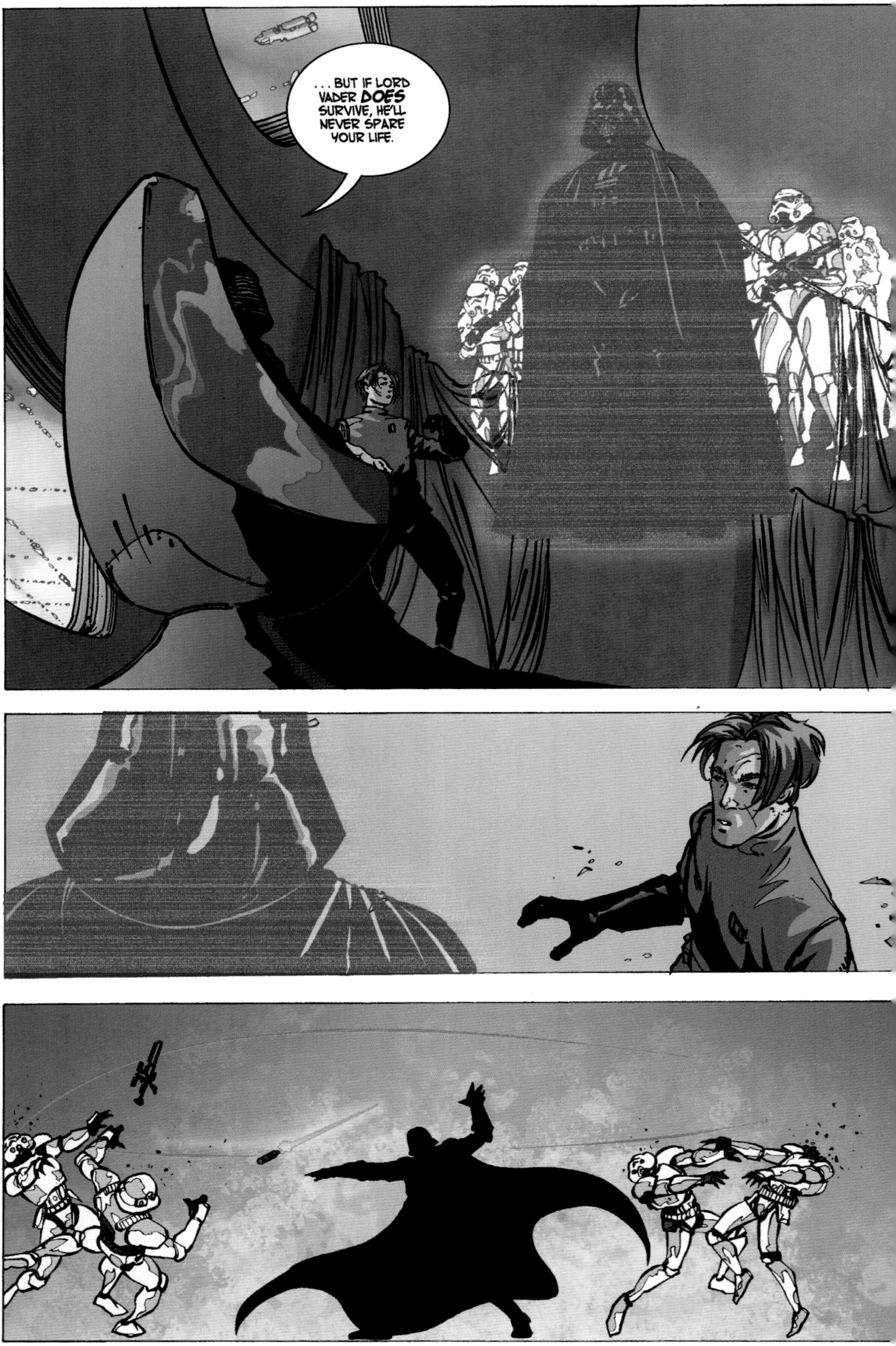
. . . BUT IF LORD VADER DOES SURVIVE, HE'LL NEVER SPARE YOUR LIFE.

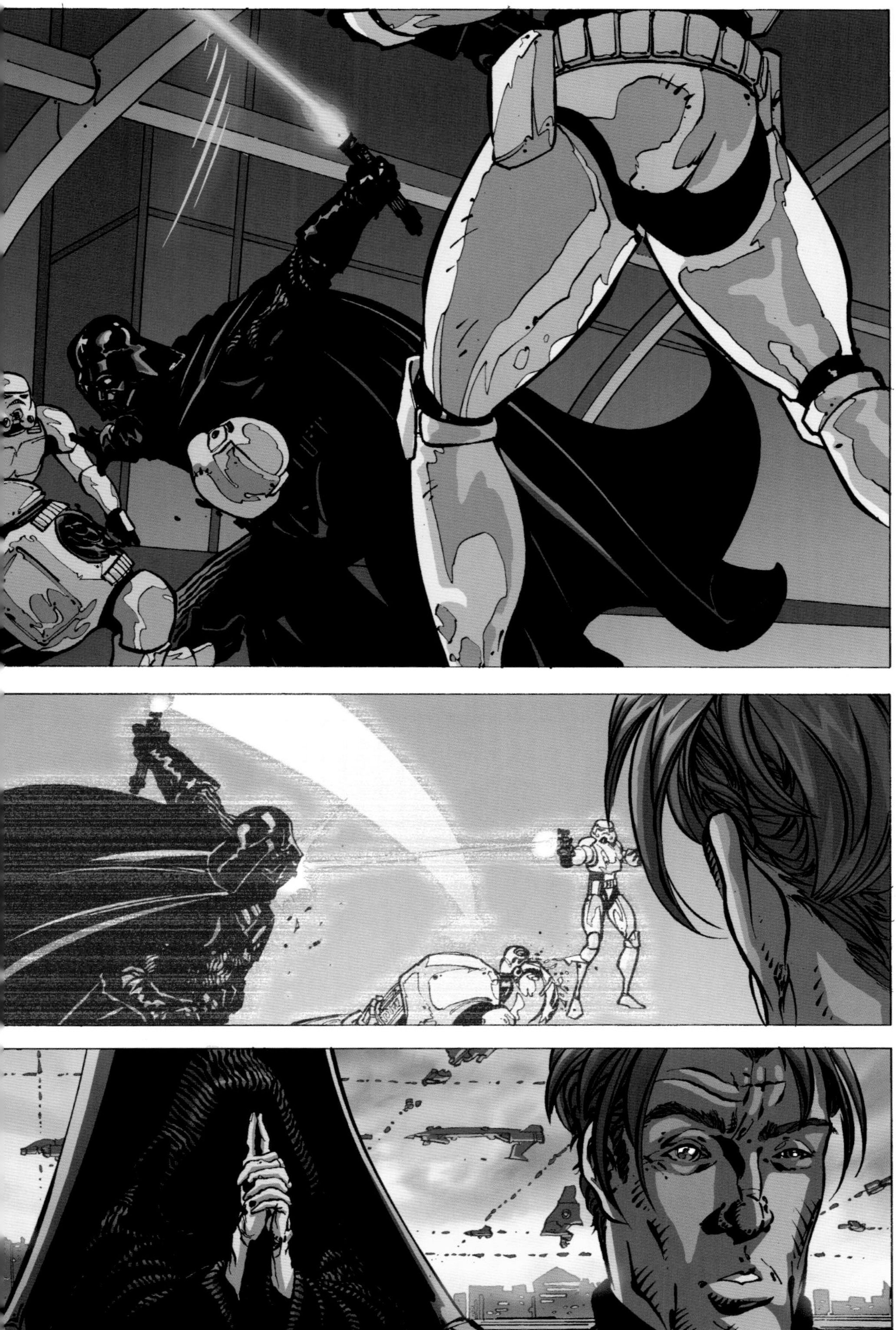

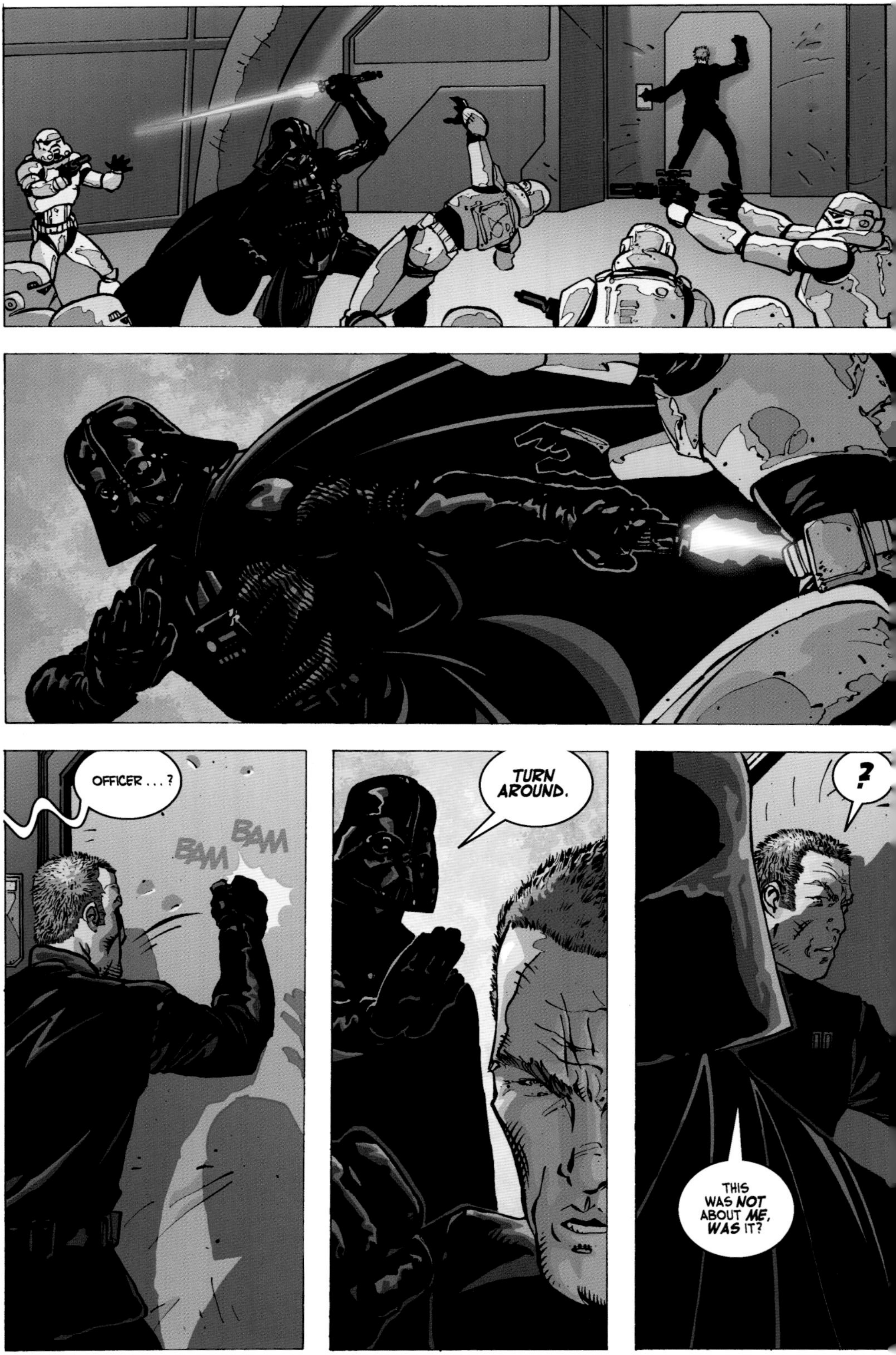
OFFICER . . . ?
BAM BAM
TURN AROUND.
?
THIS WAS NOT ABOUT ME, WAS IT?

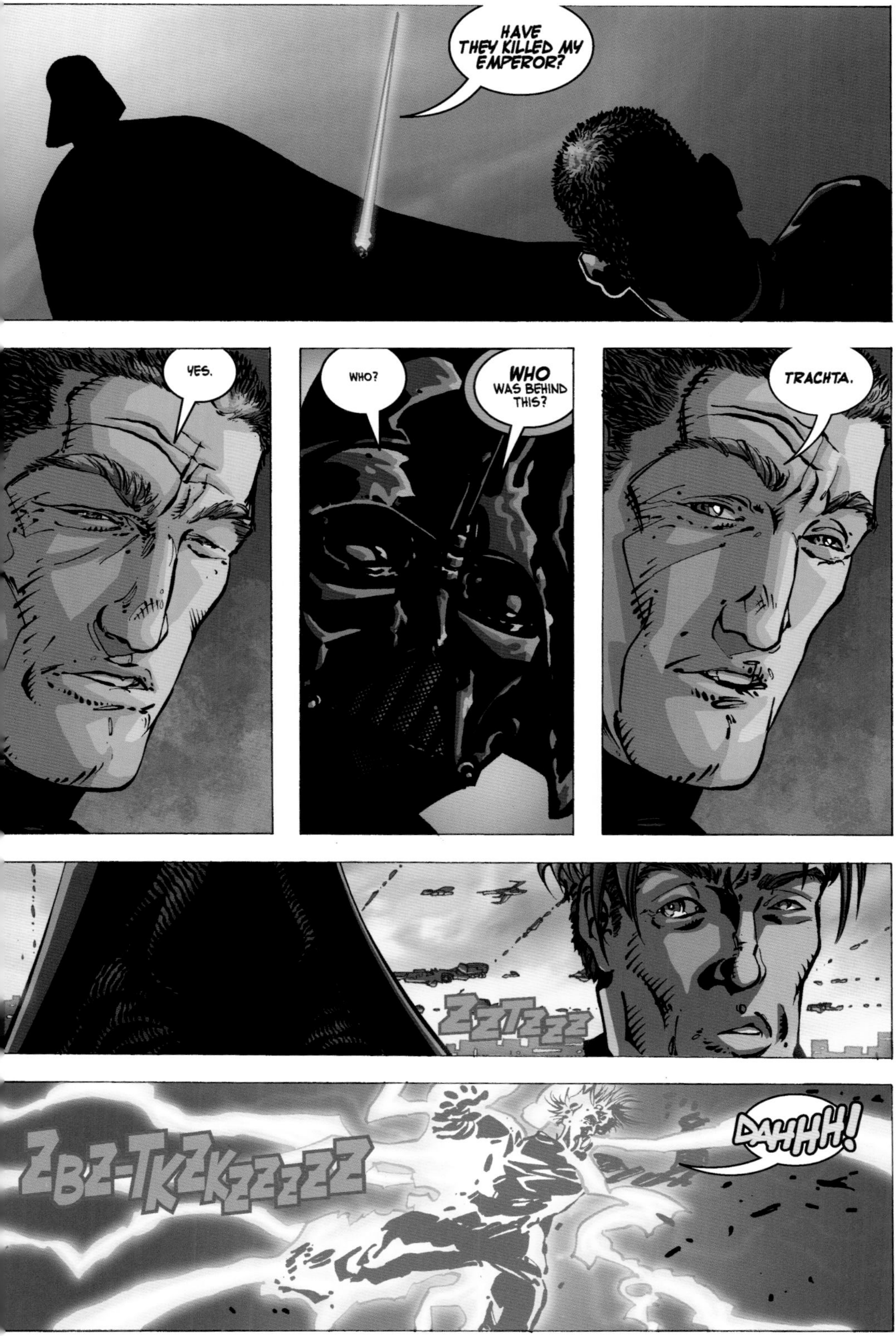
HAVE THEY KILLED MY EMPEROR?
YES.
WHO?
WHO WAS BEHIND THIS?
TRACHTA.
ZZTZZZ
ZBZ-TKZKZZZZZ
DAHHH!

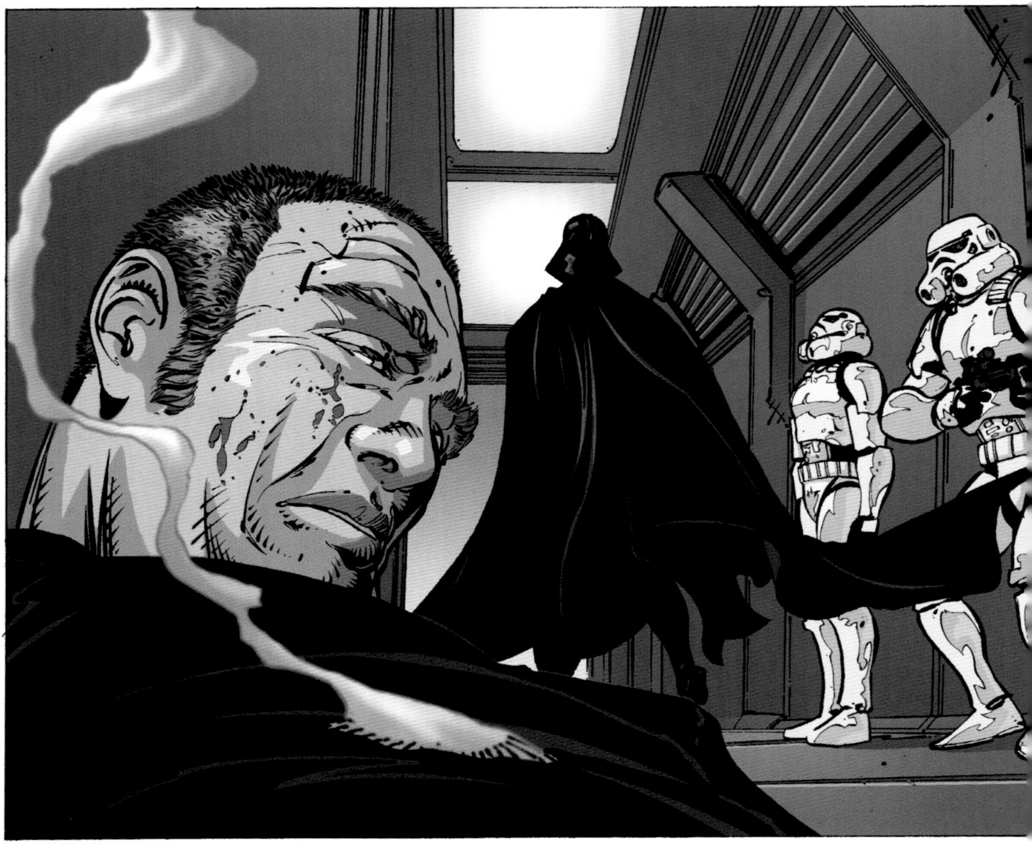
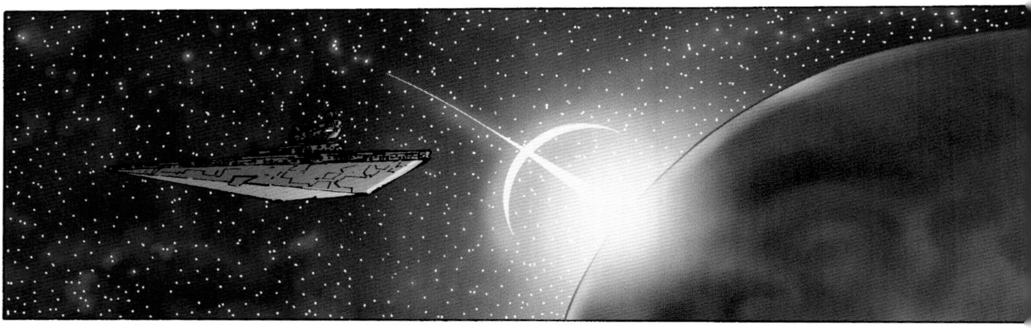
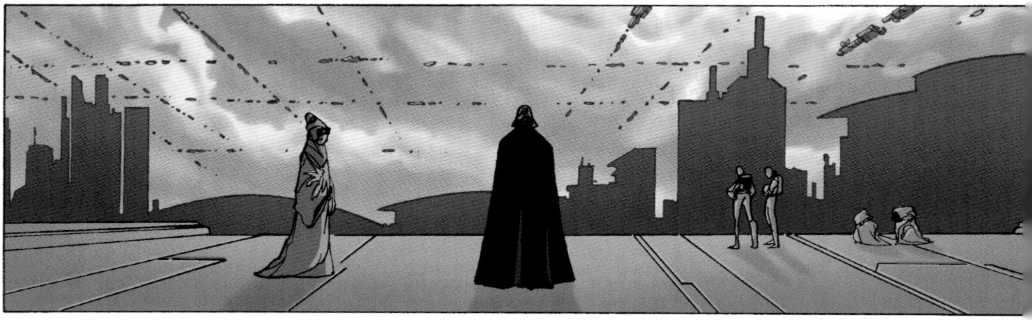

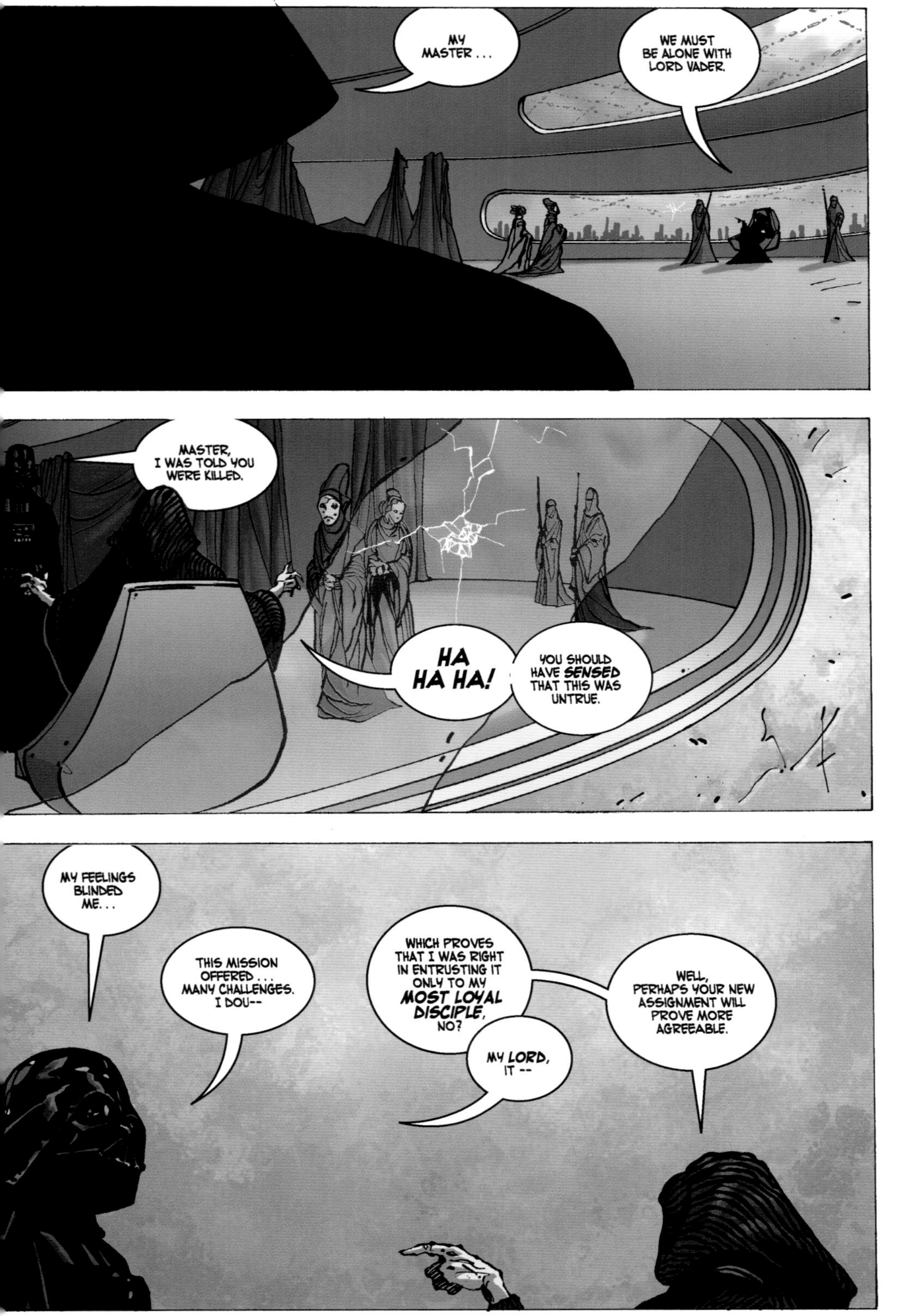
MY MASTER . . .
WE MUST BE ALONE WITH LORD VADER.
MASTER, I WAS TOLD YOU WERE KILLED.
HA HA HA!
YOU SHOULD HAVE SENSED THAT THIS WAS UNTRUE.
MY FEELINGS BLINDED ME. . .
THIS MISSION OFFERED . . . MANY CHALLENGES. I DOU--
WHICH PROVES THAT I WAS RIGHT IN ENTRUSTING IT ONLY TO MY MOST LOYAL DISCIPLE, NO?
MY LORD, IT --
WELL, PERHAPS YOUR NEW ASSIGNMENT WILL PROVE MORE AGREEABLE.

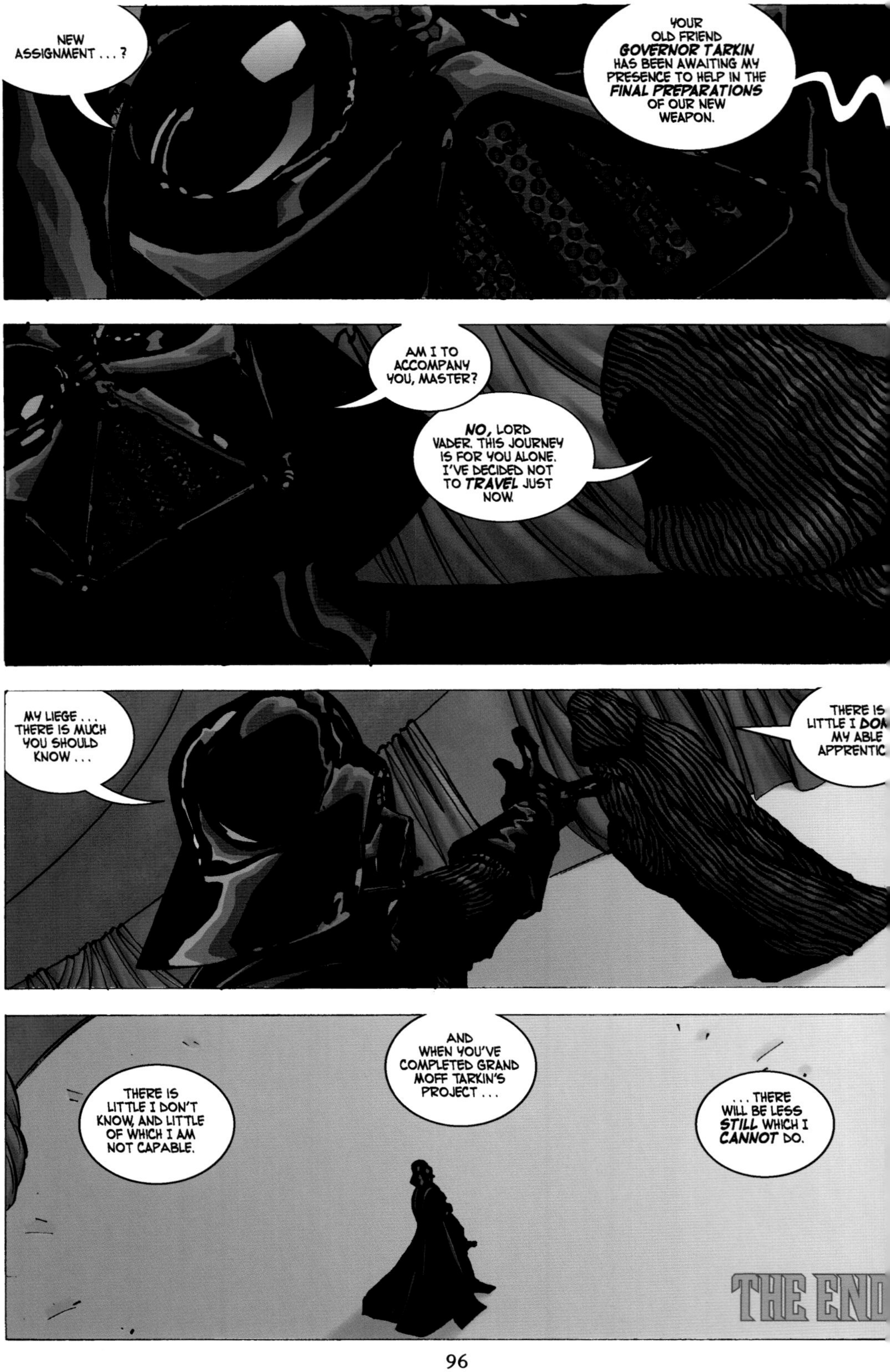
NEW ASSIGNMENT . . . ?
YOUR OLD FRIEND GOVERNOR TARKIN HAS BEEN AWAITING MY PRESENCE TO HELP IN THE FINAL PREPARATIONS OF OUR NEW WEAPON.
AM I TO ACCOMPANY YOU, MASTER?
NO, LORD VADER. THIS JOURNEY IS FOR YOU ALONE. I'VE DECIDED NOT TO TRAVEL JUST NOW.
MY LIEGE . . . THERE IS MUCH YOU SHOULD KNOW . . .
THERE IS LITTLE I DON MY ABLE APPRENTIC
THERE IS LITTLE I DON'T KNOW, AND LITTLE OF WHICH I AM NOT CAPABLE.
AND WHEN YOU'VE COMPLETED GRAND MOFF TARKIN'S PROJECT . . .
. . . THERE WILL BE LESS STILL WHICH I CANNOT DO.
THE END

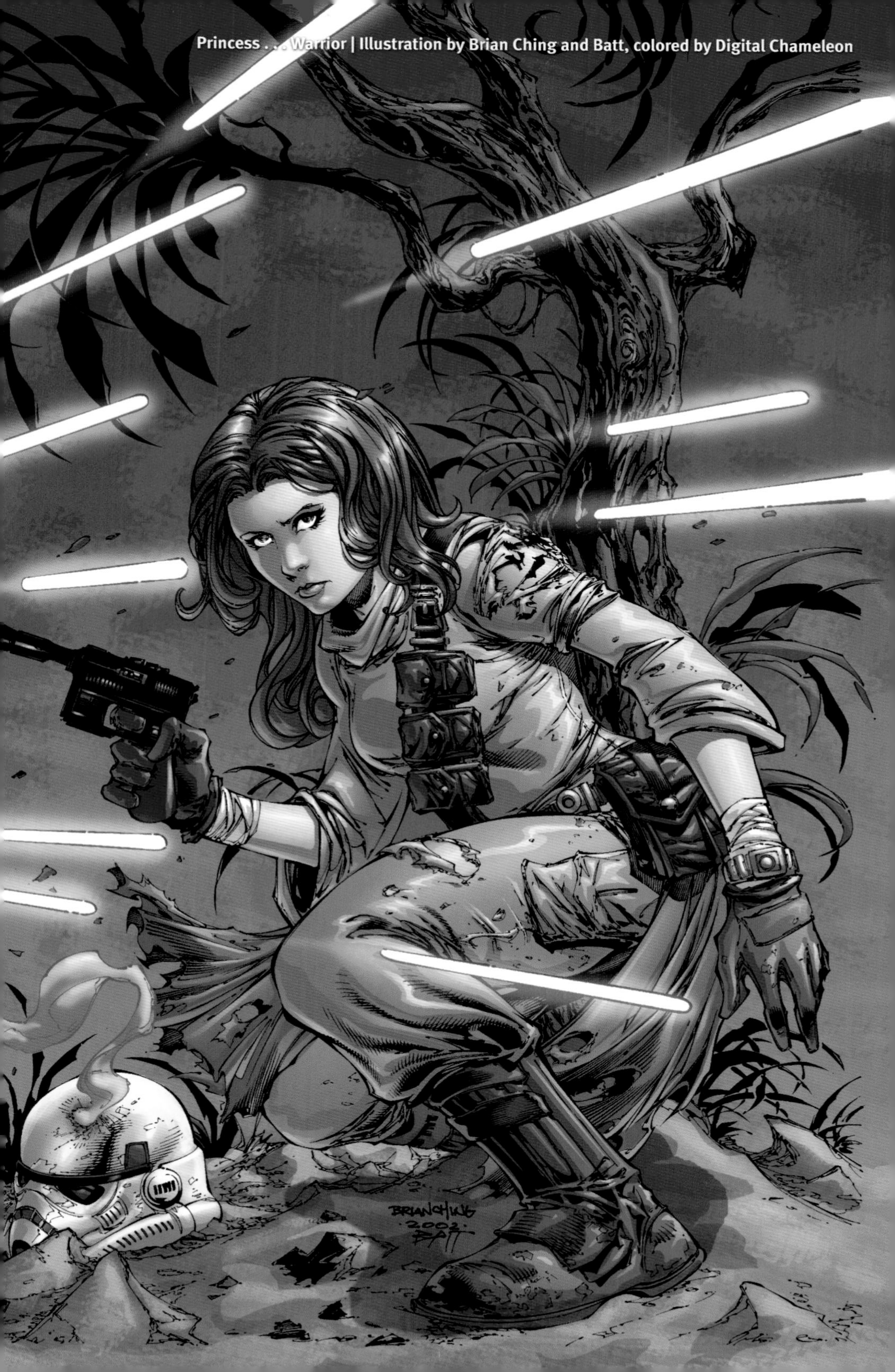

Princess . . . Warrior | Illustration by Brian Ching and Batt, colored by Digital Chameleon

A FEW WEEKS PRIOR TO THE BATTLE OF YAVIN . . .

script by Randy Stradley
      with situations and dialogue from the
      Star Wars radio dramatization by Brian Daley
pencils by Davidé Fabbri
inks by Christian Dalla Vecchia
colors and lettering by Digital Chameleon

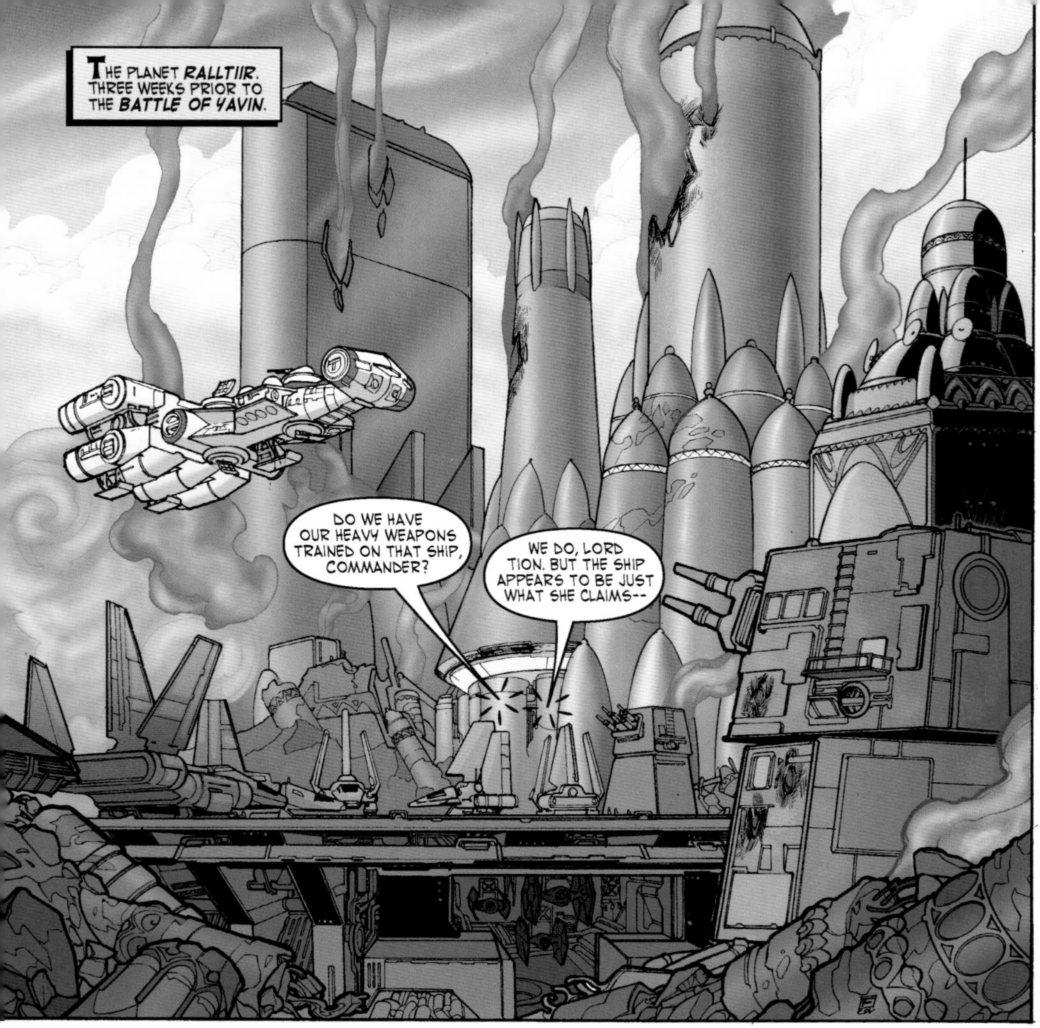
THE PLANET RALLTIIR. THREE WEEKS PRIOR TO THE BATTLE OF YAVIN.
DO WE HAVE OUR HEAVY WEAPONS TRAINED ON THAT SHIP, COMMANDER?
WE DO, LORD TION. BUT THE SHIP APPEARS TO BE JUST WHAT SHE CLAIMS--

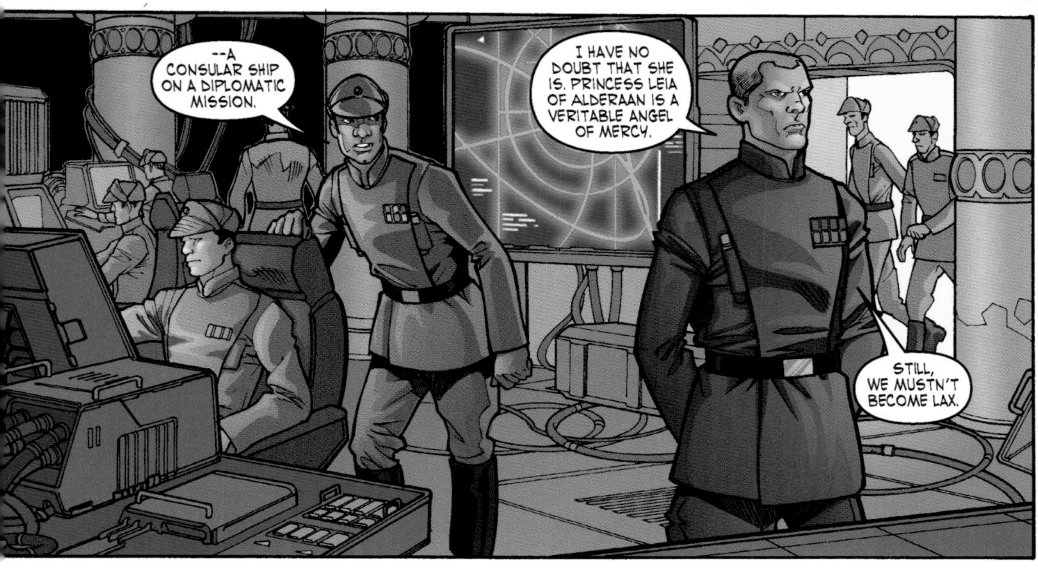
--A CONSULAR SHIP ON A DIPLOMATIC MISSION.
I HAVE NO DOUBT THAT SHE IS. PRINCESS LEIA OF ALDERAAN IS A VERITABLE ANGEL OF MERCY.
STILL, WE MUSTN'T BECOME LAX.

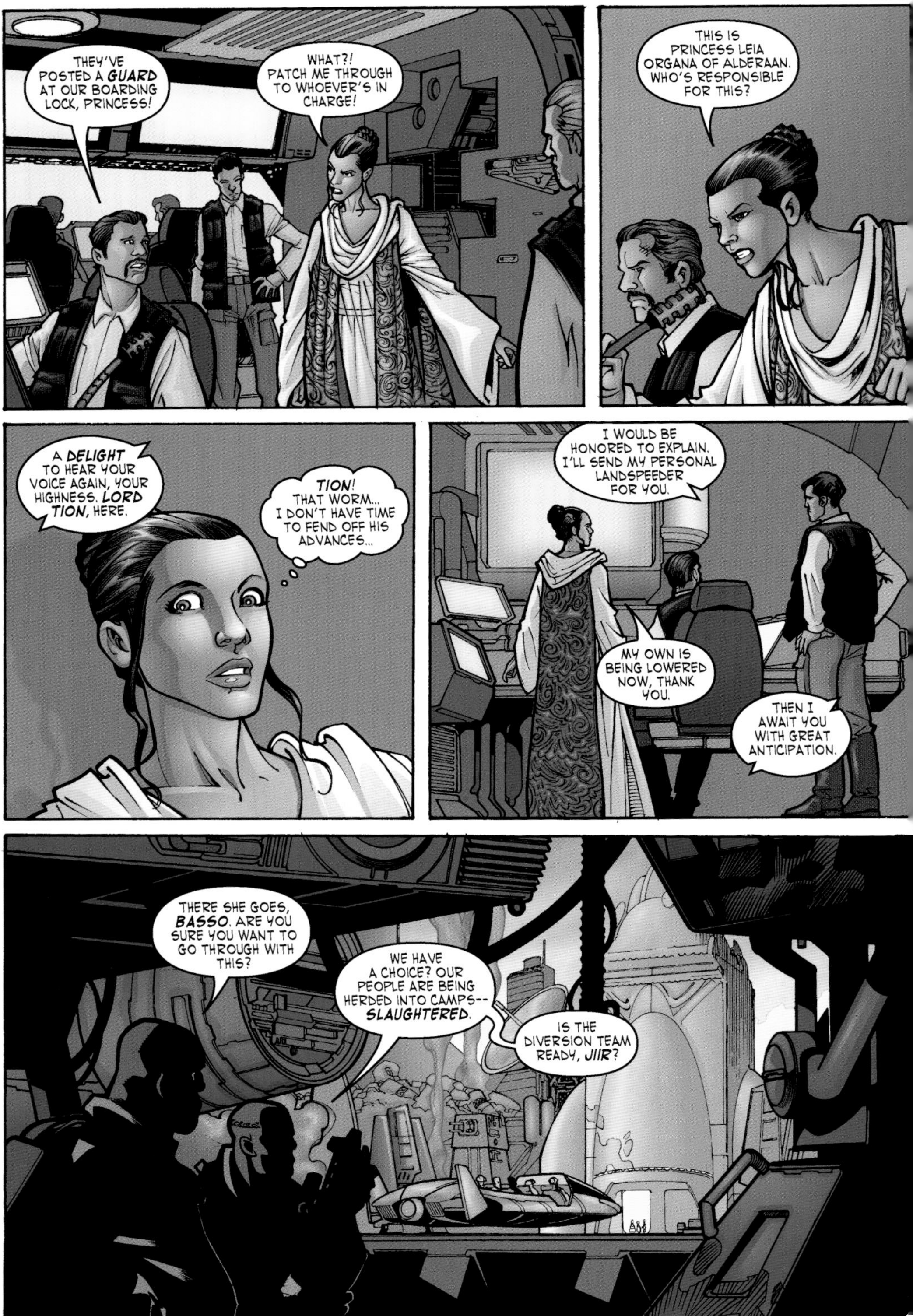
THEY'VE POSTED A GUARD AT OUR BOARDING LOCK, PRINCESS!
WHAT?! PATCH ME THROUGH TO WHOEVER'S IN CHARGE!
THIS IS PRINCESS LEIA ORGANA OF ALDERAAN. WHO'S RESPONSIBLE FOR THIS?
A DELIGHT TO HEAR YOUR VOICE AGAIN, YOUR HIGHNESS. LORD TION, HERE.
TION! THAT WORM... I DON'T HAVE TIME TO FEND OFF HIS ADVANCES...
I WOULD BE HONORED TO EXPLAIN. I'LL SEND MY PERSONAL LANDSPEEDER FOR YOU.
MY OWN IS BEING LOWERED NOW, THANK YOU.
THEN I AWAIT YOU WITH GREAT ANTICIPATION.
THERE SHE GOES, BASSO. ARE YOU SURE YOU WANT TO GO THROUGH WITH THIS?
WE HAVE A CHOICE? OUR PEOPLE ARE BEING HERDED INTO CAMPS-- SLAUGHTERED.
IS THE DIVERSION TEAM READY, JIIR?

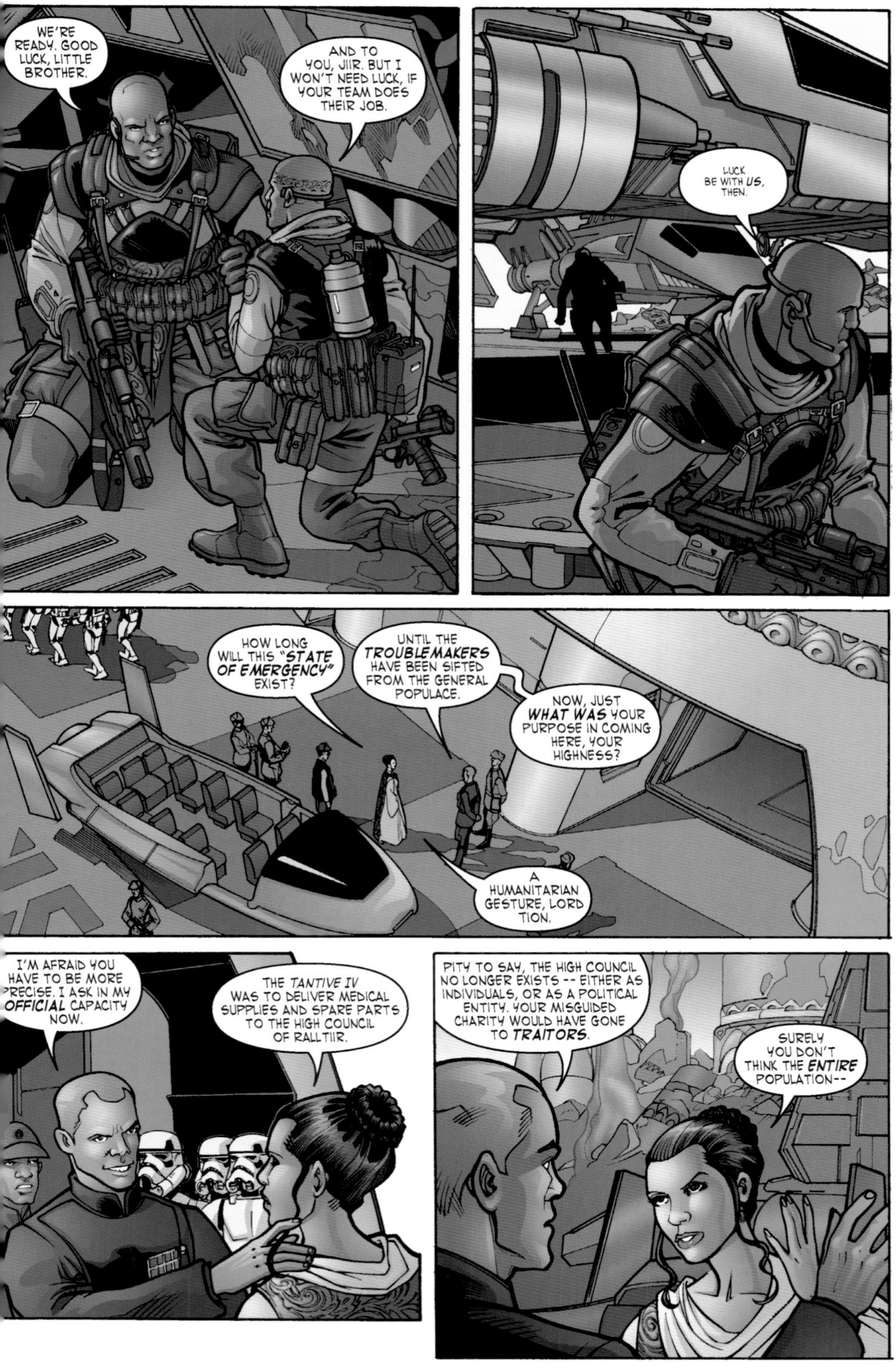

WE'RE READY. GOOD LUCK, LITTLE BROTHER.
AND TO YOU, JIIR. BUT I WON'T NEED LUCK, IF YOUR TEAM DOES THEIR JOB.
LUCK BE WITH *US*, THEN.
HOW LONG WILL THIS "*STATE OF EMERGENCY*" EXIST?
UNTIL THE *TROUBLEMAKERS* HAVE BEEN SIFTED FROM THE GENERAL POPULACE.
NOW, JUST *WHAT WAS* YOUR PURPOSE IN COMING HERE, YOUR HIGHNESS?
A HUMANITARIAN GESTURE, LORD TION.
I'M AFRAID YOU HAVE TO BE MORE PRECISE. I ASK IN MY *OFFICIAL* CAPACITY NOW.
THE *TANTIVE IV* WAS TO DELIVER MEDICAL SUPPLIES AND SPARE PARTS TO THE HIGH COUNCIL OF RALLTIIR.
PITY TO SAY, THE HIGH COUNCIL NO LONGER EXISTS -- EITHER AS INDIVIDUALS, OR AS A POLITICAL ENTITY. YOUR MISGUIDED CHARITY WOULD HAVE GONE TO *TRAITORS*.
SURELY YOU DON'T THINK THE *ENTIRE* POPULATION--

ENOUGH OF THEM WERE SYMPATHETIC TO THE *REBEL ALLIANCE* TO REQUIRE A *PURIFICATION* HERE.

THE EMPIRE WILL EXERT CLOSE GUIDANCE OVER THEM FOR THEIR OWN SAFETY.

"WITH A STARFLEET *BLOCKADE?* WITH IMPRESSMENT GANGS AND *INTERROGATION CENTERS?*"

"I RECOMMEND GREAT CARE IN CHOOSING YOUR WORDS, PRINCESS. I HAVE A HIGH REGARD FOR YOUR FAMILY AND -- IF I MAY SAY SO -- FOR *YOU* YOURSELF. BUT THERE ARE CERTAIN THINGS WHICH EVEN AN *ORGANA* MAY NOT SAY WITH IMPUNITY."

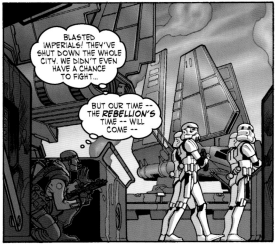

BLASTED *IMPERIALS!* THEY'VE SHUT DOWN THE WHOLE CITY. WE DIDN'T EVEN HAVE A CHANCE TO FIGHT...

BUT OUR TIME -- THE *REBELLION'S* TIME -- WILL COME --

--AND SOONER THAN THEY THINK.

THERE'S THE DIVERSION!

BDOW

BDOW

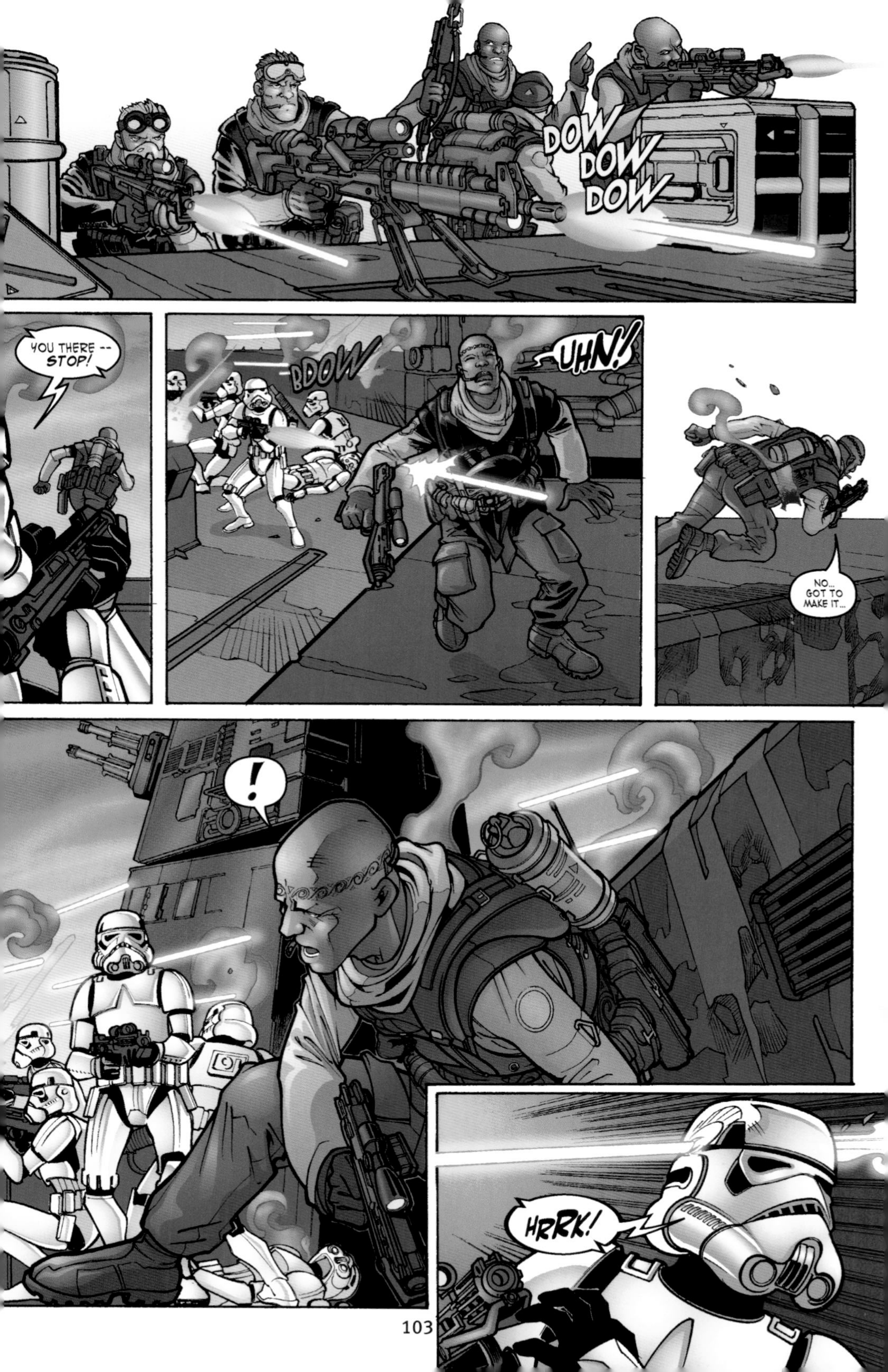
DOW
DOW
DOW
YOU THERE -- STOP!
BDOW
UHN!
NO... GOT TO MAKE IT...
!
HRRK!

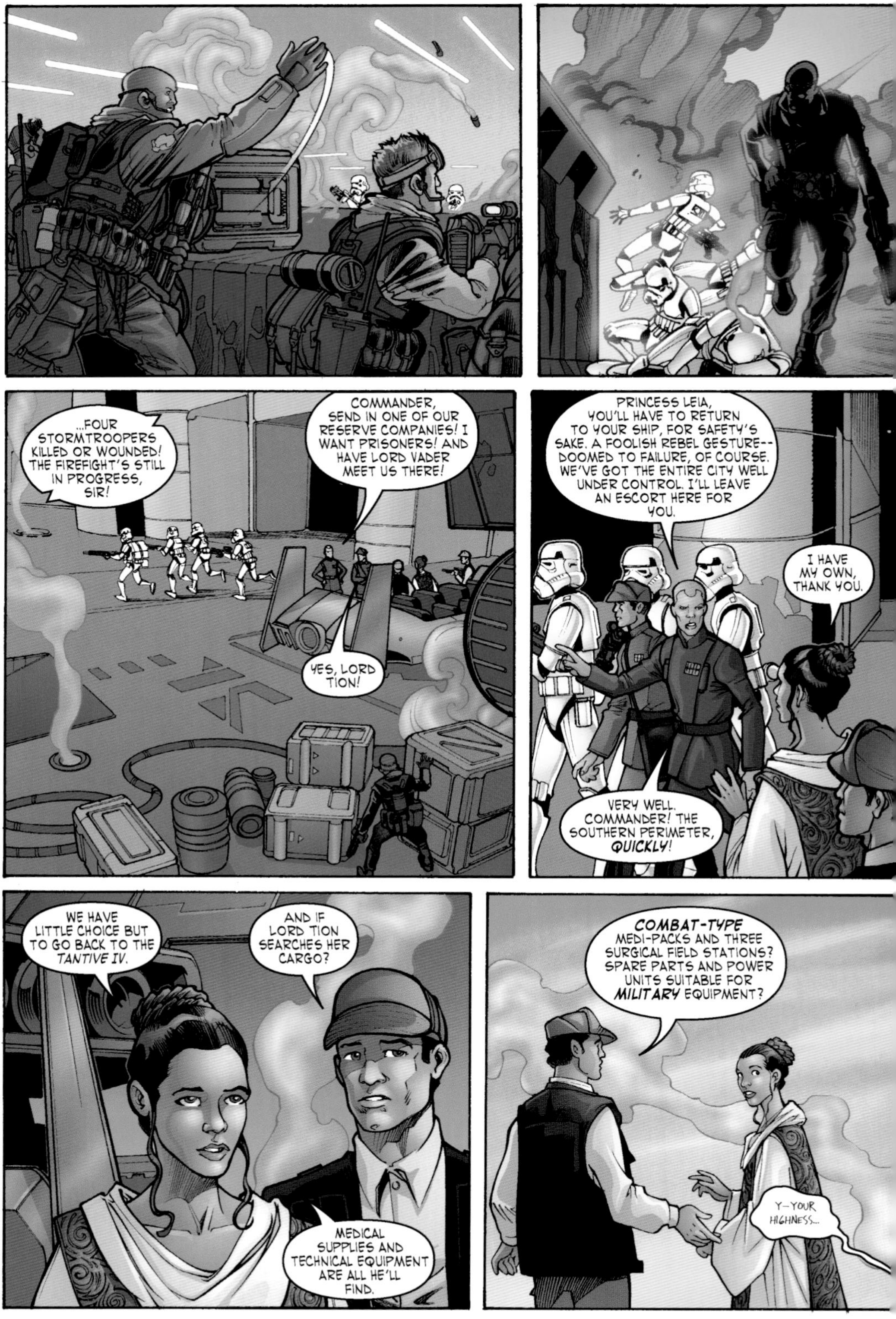
...FOUR STORMTROOPERS KILLED OR WOUNDED! THE FIREFIGHT'S STILL IN PROGRESS, SIR!
COMMANDER, SEND IN ONE OF OUR RESERVE COMPANIES! I WANT PRISONERS! AND HAVE LORD VADER MEET US THERE!
YES, LORD TION!
PRINCESS LEIA, YOU'LL HAVE TO RETURN TO YOUR SHIP, FOR SAFETY'S SAKE. A FOOLISH REBEL GESTURE-- DOOMED TO FAILURE, OF COURSE. WE'VE GOT THE ENTIRE CITY WELL UNDER CONTROL. I'LL LEAVE AN ESCORT HERE FOR YOU.
I HAVE MY OWN, THANK YOU.
VERY WELL. COMMANDER! THE SOUTHERN PERIMETER, QUICKLY!
WE HAVE LITTLE CHOICE BUT TO GO BACK TO THE TANTIVE IV.
AND IF LORD TION SEARCHES HER CARGO?
MEDICAL SUPPLIES AND TECHNICAL EQUIPMENT ARE ALL HE'LL FIND.
COMBAT-TYPE MEDI-PACKS AND THREE SURGICAL FIELD STATIONS? SPARE PARTS AND POWER UNITS SUITABLE FOR MILITARY EQUIPMENT?
Y-YOUR HIGHNESS...

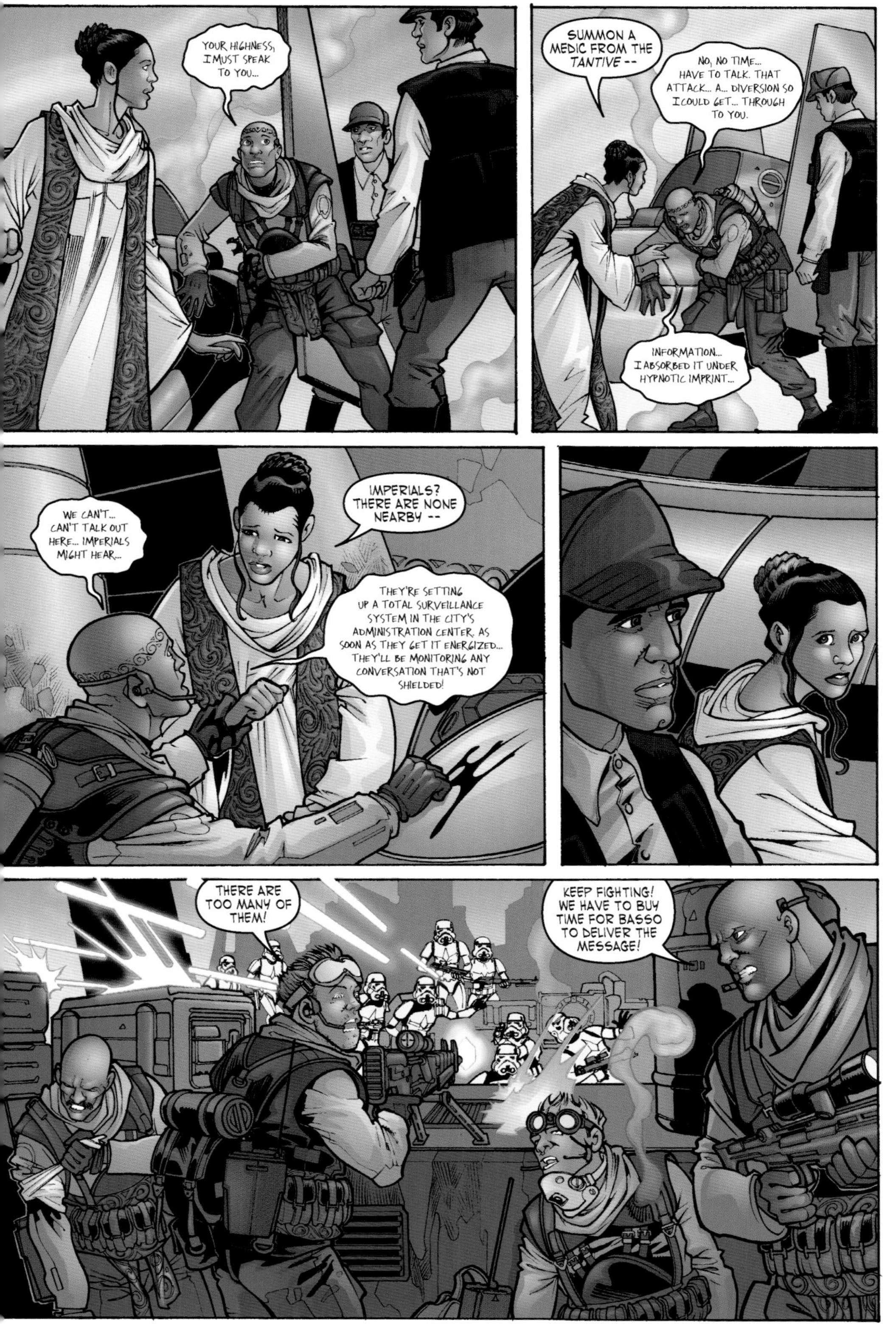
YOUR HIGHNESS, I MUST SPEAK TO YOU...
SUMMON A MEDIC FROM THE *TANTIVE* --
NO, NO TIME... HAVE TO TALK. THAT ATTACK... A... DIVERSION SO I COULD GET... THROUGH TO YOU.
INFORMATION... I ABSORBED IT UNDER HYPNOTIC IMPRINT...
WE CAN'T... CAN'T TALK OUT HERE... IMPERIALS MIGHT HEAR...
IMPERIALS? THERE ARE NONE NEARBY --
THEY'RE SETTING UP A TOTAL SURVEILLANCE SYSTEM IN THE CITY'S ADMINISTRATION CENTER. AS SOON AS THEY GET IT ENERGIZED... THEY'LL BE MONITORING ANY CONVERSATION THAT'S NOT SHIELDED!
THERE ARE TOO MANY OF THEM!
KEEP FIGHTING! WE HAVE TO BUY TIME FOR BASSO TO DELIVER THE MESSAGE!

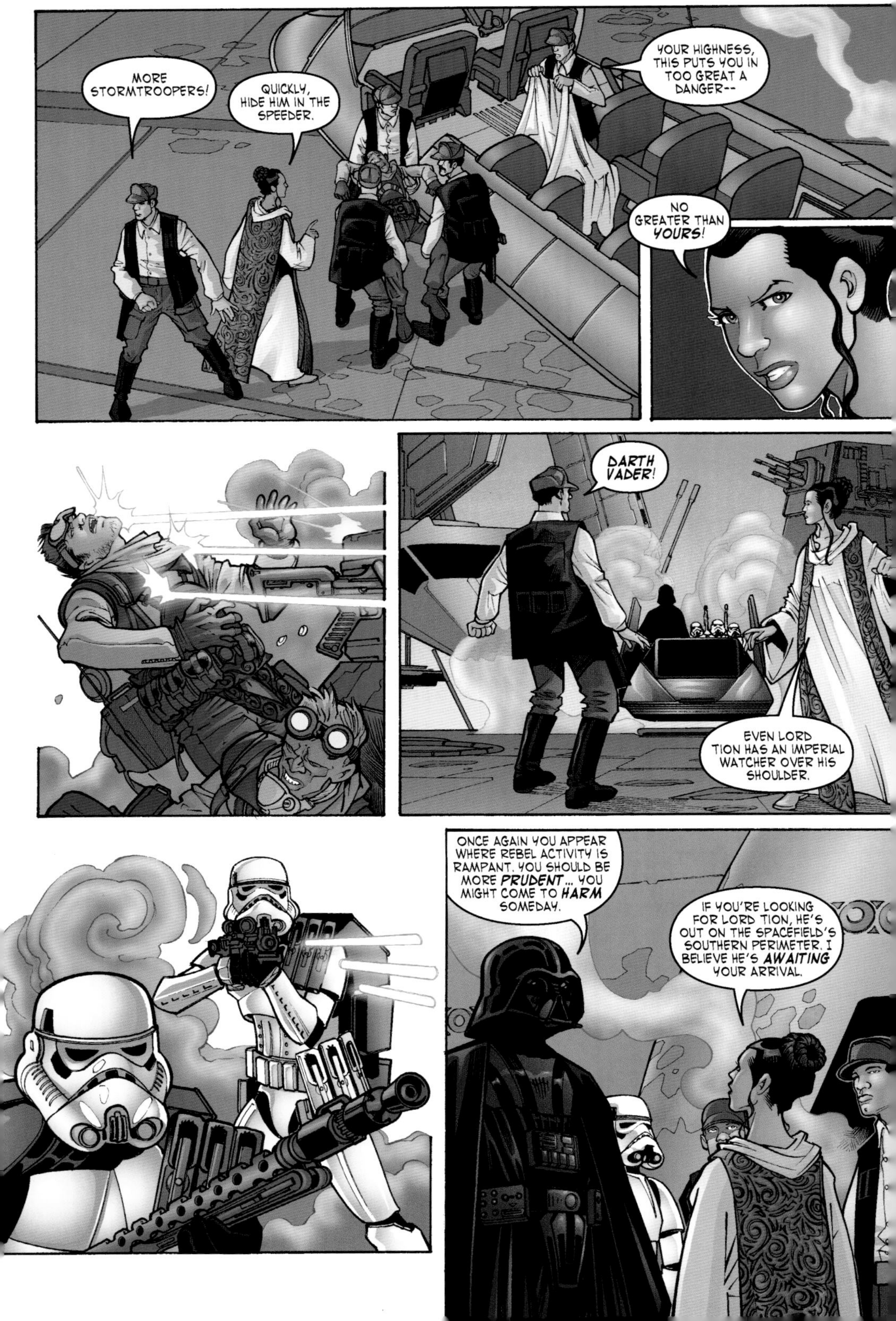
MORE STORMTROOPERS!
QUICKLY, HIDE HIM IN THE SPEEDER.
YOUR HIGHNESS, THIS PUTS YOU IN TOO GREAT A DANGER--
NO GREATER THAN YOURS!
DARTH VADER!
EVEN LORD TION HAS AN IMPERIAL WATCHER OVER HIS SHOULDER.
ONCE AGAIN YOU APPEAR WHERE REBEL ACTIVITY IS RAMPANT. YOU SHOULD BE MORE PRUDENT... YOU MIGHT COME TO HARM SOMEDAY.
IF YOU'RE LOOKING FOR LORD TION, HE'S OUT ON THE SPACEFIELD'S SOUTHERN PERIMETER. I BELIEVE HE'S AWAITING YOUR ARRIVAL.

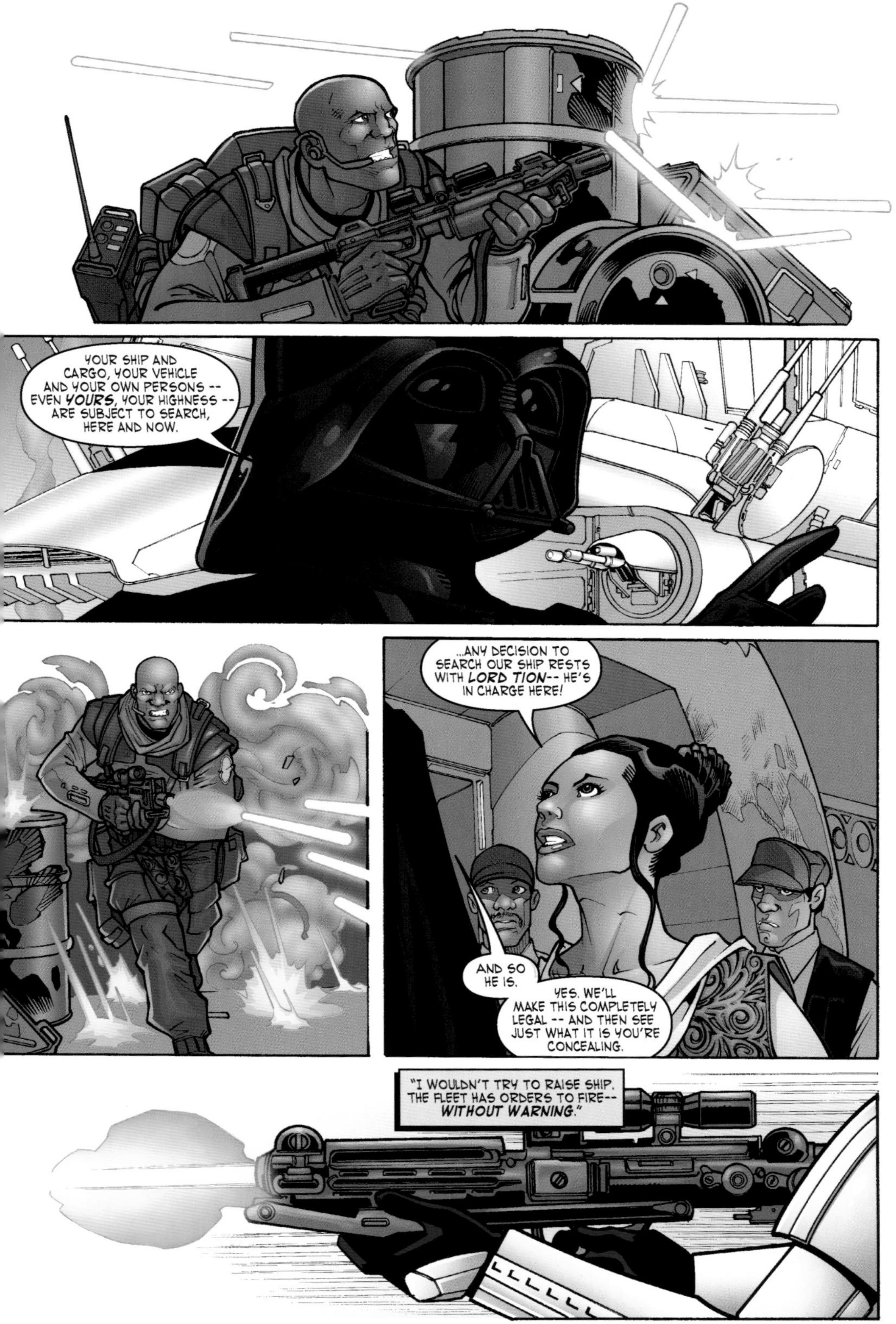
YOUR SHIP AND CARGO, YOUR VEHICLE AND YOUR OWN PERSONS -- EVEN *YOURS*, YOUR HIGHNESS -- ARE SUBJECT TO SEARCH, HERE AND NOW.
...ANY DECISION TO SEARCH OUR SHIP RESTS WITH *LORD TION*-- HE'S IN CHARGE HERE!
AND SO HE IS.
YES. WE'LL MAKE THIS COMPLETELY LEGAL -- AND THEN SEE JUST WHAT IT IS YOU'RE CONCEALING.
"I WOULDN'T TRY TO RAISE SHIP. THE FLEET HAS ORDERS TO FIRE-- *WITHOUT WARNING*."

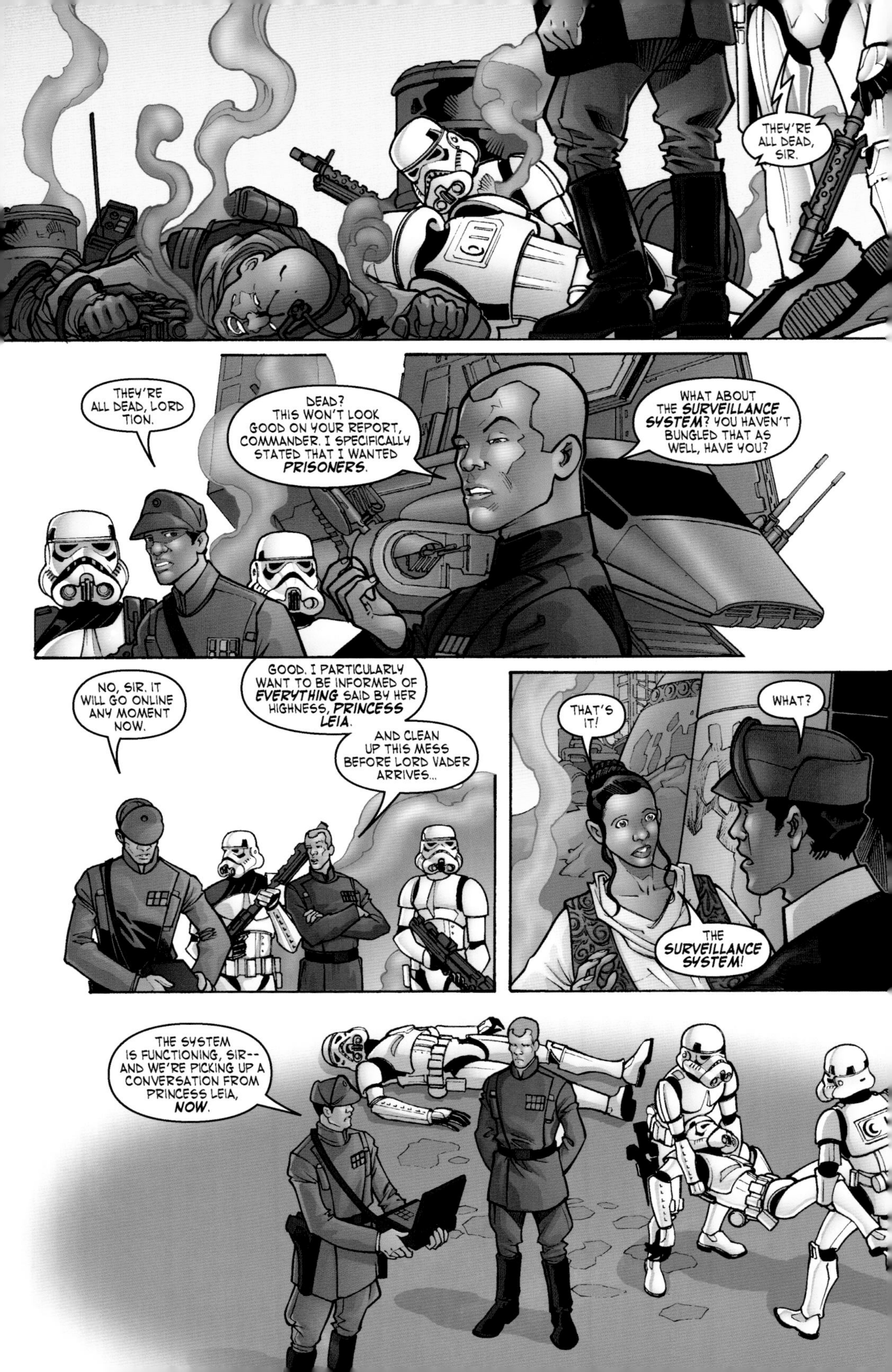
THEY'RE ALL DEAD, SIR.
THEY'RE ALL DEAD, LORD TION.
DEAD? THIS WON'T LOOK GOOD ON YOUR REPORT, COMMANDER. I SPECIFICALLY STATED THAT I WANTED PRISONERS.
WHAT ABOUT THE SURVEILLANCE SYSTEM? YOU HAVEN'T BUNGLED THAT AS WELL, HAVE YOU?
NO, SIR. IT WILL GO ONLINE ANY MOMENT NOW.
GOOD. I PARTICULARLY WANT TO BE INFORMED OF EVERYTHING SAID BY HER HIGHNESS, PRINCESS LEIA.
AND CLEAN UP THIS MESS BEFORE LORD VADER ARRIVES...
THAT'S IT!
WHAT?
THE SURVEILLANCE SYSTEM!
THE SYSTEM IS FUNCTIONING, SIR-- AND WE'RE PICKING UP A CONVERSATION FROM PRINCESS LEIA, NOW.

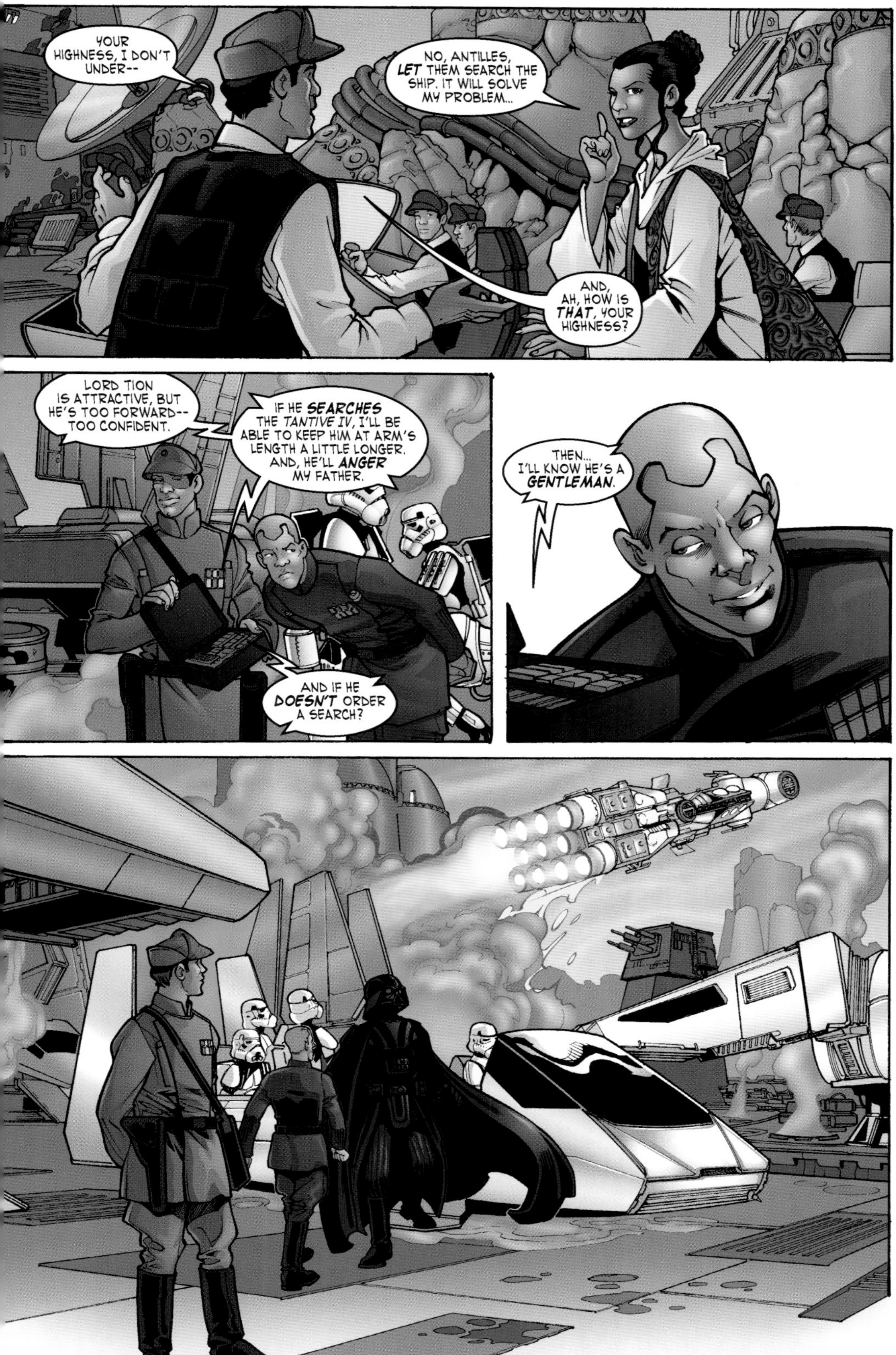
YOUR HIGHNESS, I DON'T UNDER--
NO, ANTILLES, LET THEM SEARCH THE SHIP. IT WILL SOLVE MY PROBLEM...
AND, AH, HOW IS THAT, YOUR HIGHNESS?
LORD TION IS ATTRACTIVE, BUT HE'S TOO FORWARD--TOO CONFIDENT.
IF HE SEARCHES THE TANTIVE IV, I'LL BE ABLE TO KEEP HIM AT ARM'S LENGTH A LITTLE LONGER. AND, HE'LL ANGER MY FATHER.
AND IF HE DOESN'T ORDER A SEARCH?
THEN... I'LL KNOW HE'S A GENTLEMAN.

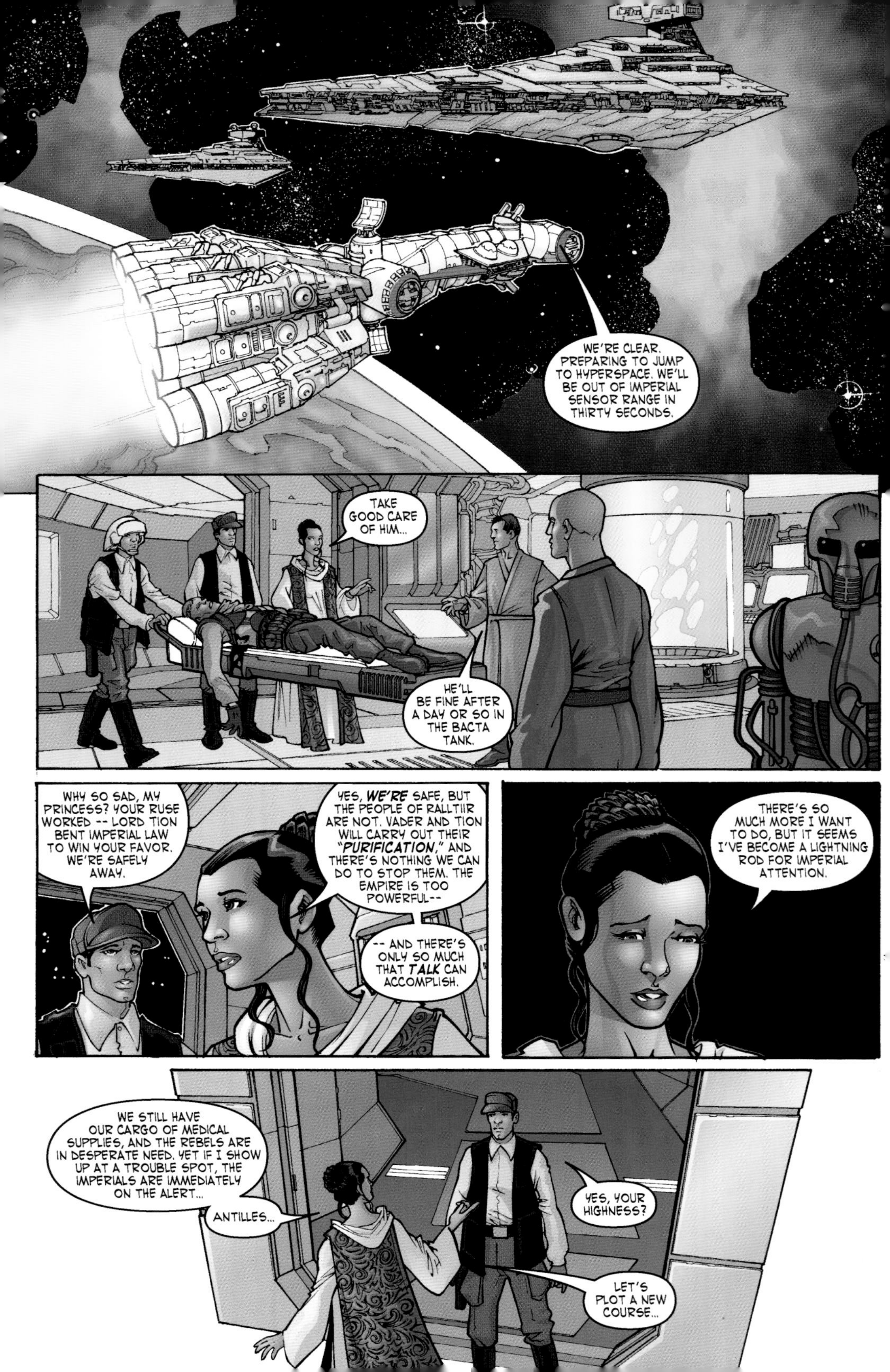
WE'RE CLEAR. PREPARING TO JUMP TO HYPERSPACE. WE'LL BE OUT OF IMPERIAL SENSOR RANGE IN THIRTY SECONDS.
TAKE GOOD CARE OF HIM...
HE'LL BE FINE AFTER A DAY OR SO IN THE BACTA TANK.
WHY SO SAD, MY PRINCESS? YOUR RUSE WORKED -- LORD TION BENT IMPERIAL LAW TO WIN YOUR FAVOR. WE'RE SAFELY AWAY.
YES, WE'RE SAFE, BUT THE PEOPLE OF RALLTIIR ARE NOT. VADER AND TION WILL CARRY OUT THEIR "PURIFICATION," AND THERE'S NOTHING WE CAN DO TO STOP THEM. THE EMPIRE IS TOO POWERFUL--
-- AND THERE'S ONLY SO MUCH THAT TALK CAN ACCOMPLISH.
THERE'S SO MUCH MORE I WANT TO DO, BUT IT SEEMS I'VE BECOME A LIGHTNING ROD FOR IMPERIAL ATTENTION.
WE STILL HAVE OUR CARGO OF MEDICAL SUPPLIES, AND THE REBELS ARE IN DESPERATE NEED. YET IF I SHOW UP AT A TROUBLE SPOT, THE IMPERIALS ARE IMMEDIATELY ON THE ALERT...
ANTILLES...
YES, YOUR HIGHNESS?
LET'S PLOT A NEW COURSE...

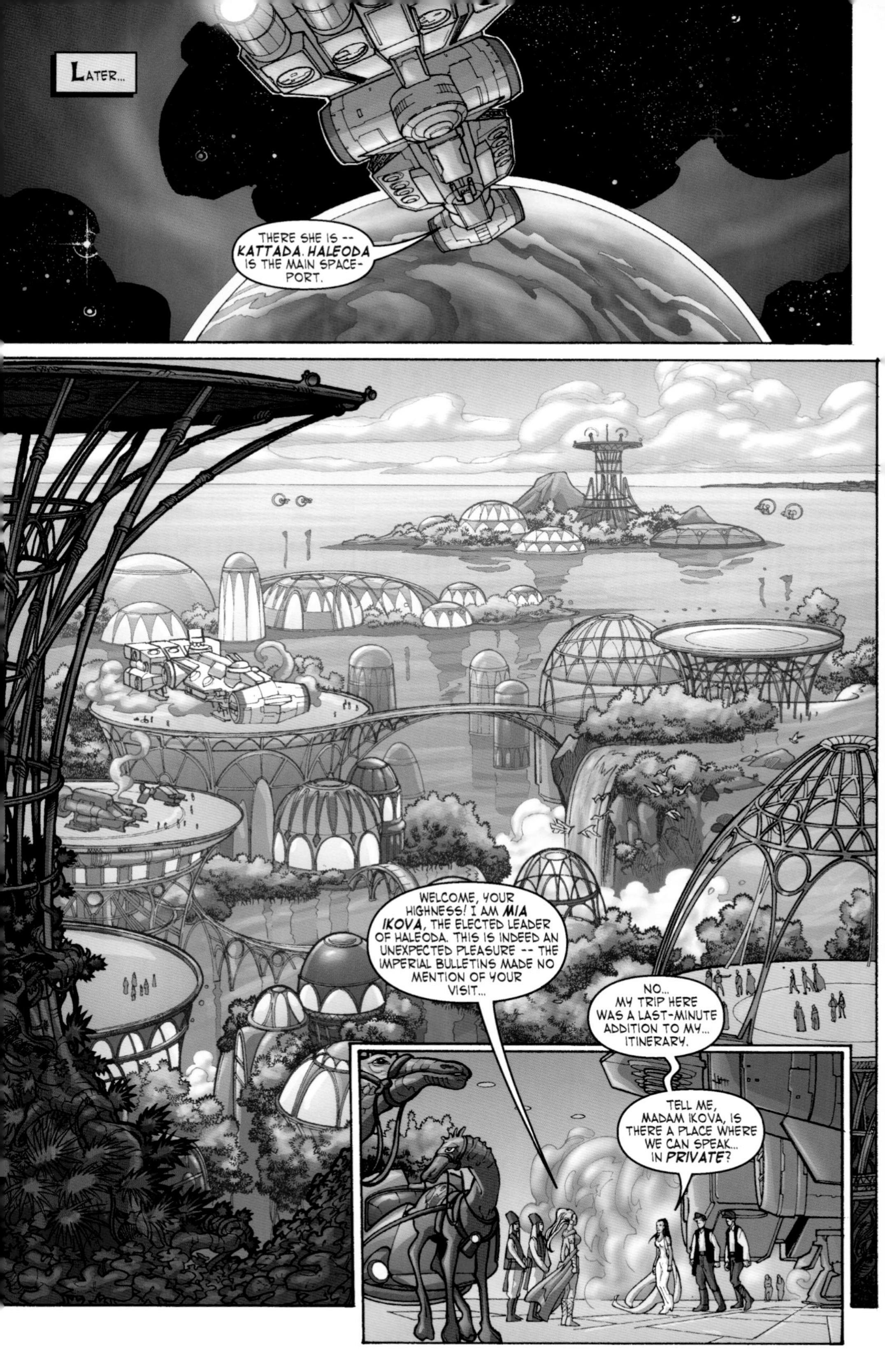
LATER...
THERE SHE IS -- KATTADA. HALEODA IS THE MAIN SPACE-PORT.
WELCOME, YOUR HIGHNESS! I AM MIA IKOVA, THE ELECTED LEADER OF HALEODA. THIS IS INDEED AN UNEXPECTED PLEASURE -- THE IMPERIAL BULLETINS MADE NO MENTION OF YOUR VISIT...
NO... MY TRIP HERE WAS A LAST-MINUTE ADDITION TO MY... ITINERARY.
TELL ME, MADAM IKOVA, IS THERE A PLACE WHERE WE CAN SPEAK... IN PRIVATE?

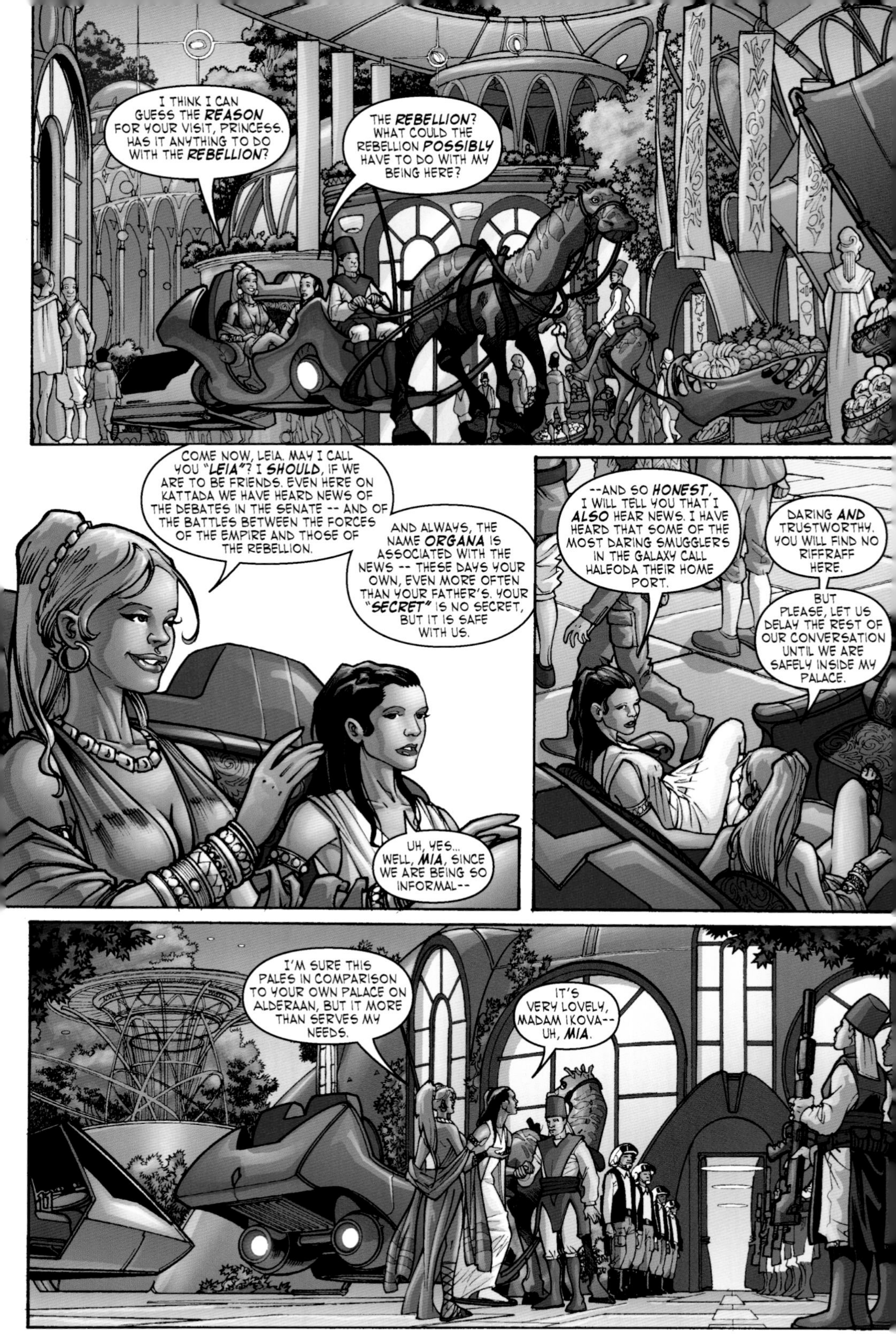
I THINK I CAN GUESS THE REASON FOR YOUR VISIT, PRINCESS. HAS IT ANYTHING TO DO WITH THE REBELLION?
THE REBELLION? WHAT COULD THE REBELLION POSSIBLY HAVE TO DO WITH MY BEING HERE?
COME NOW, LEIA. MAY I CALL YOU "LEIA"? I SHOULD, IF WE ARE TO BE FRIENDS. EVEN HERE ON KATTADA WE HAVE HEARD NEWS OF THE DEBATES IN THE SENATE -- AND OF THE BATTLES BETWEEN THE FORCES OF THE EMPIRE AND THOSE OF THE REBELLION.
AND ALWAYS, THE NAME ORGANA IS ASSOCIATED WITH THE NEWS -- THESE DAYS YOUR OWN, EVEN MORE OFTEN THAN YOUR FATHER'S. YOUR "SECRET" IS NO SECRET, BUT IT IS SAFE WITH US.
UH, YES... WELL, MIA, SINCE WE ARE BEING SO INFORMAL--
--AND SO HONEST, I WILL TELL YOU THAT I ALSO HEAR NEWS. I HAVE HEARD THAT SOME OF THE MOST DARING SMUGGLERS IN THE GALAXY CALL HALEODA THEIR HOME PORT.
DARING AND TRUSTWORTHY. YOU WILL FIND NO RIFFRAFF HERE.
BUT PLEASE, LET US DELAY THE REST OF OUR CONVERSATION UNTIL WE ARE SAFELY INSIDE MY PALACE.
I'M SURE THIS PALES IN COMPARISON TO YOUR OWN PALACE ON ALDERAAN, BUT IT MORE THAN SERVES MY NEEDS.
IT'S VERY LOVELY, MADAM IKOVA-- UH, MIA.

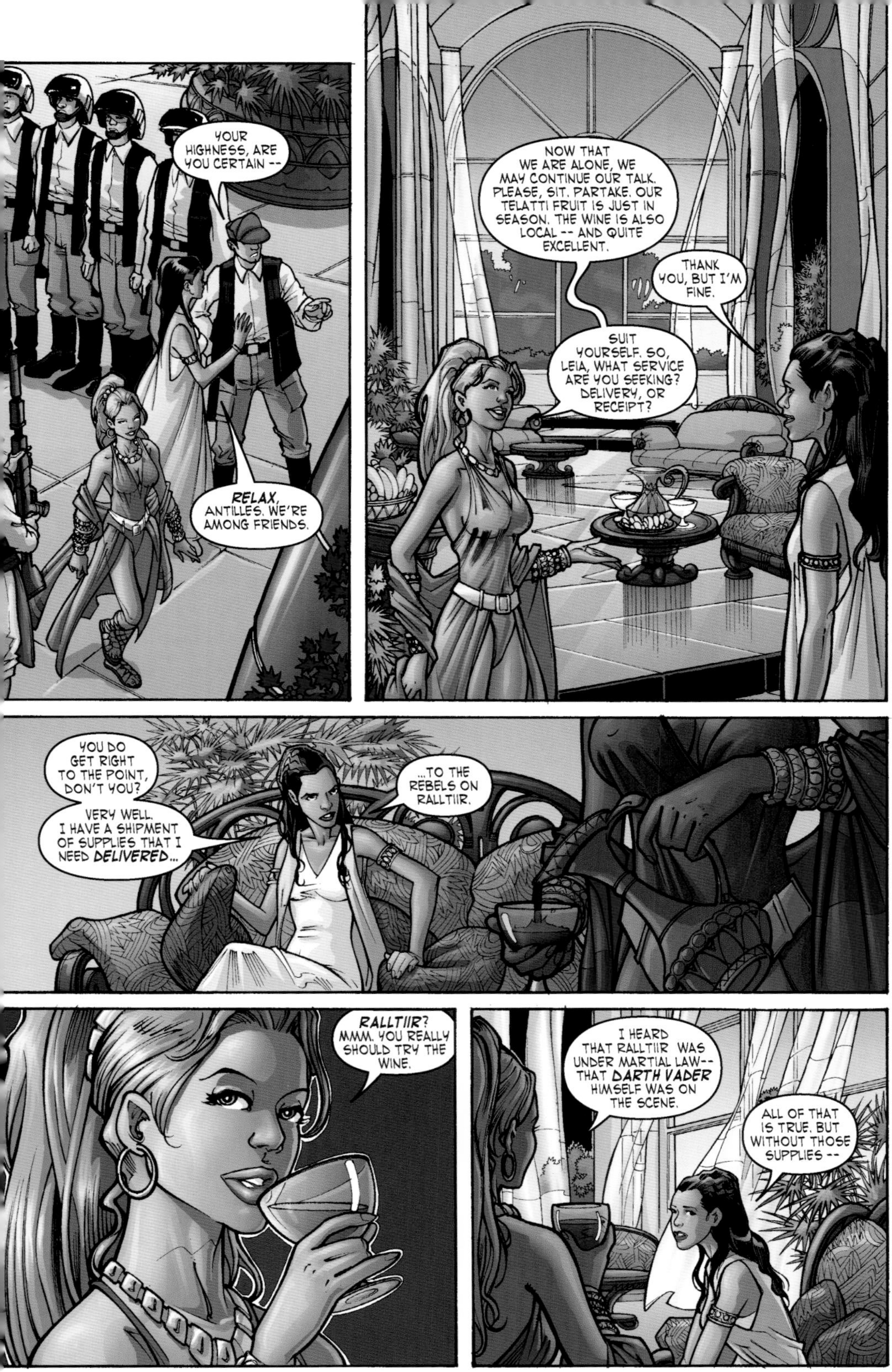
YOUR HIGHNESS, ARE YOU CERTAIN --
RELAX, ANTILLES. WE'RE AMONG FRIENDS.
NOW THAT WE ARE ALONE, WE MAY CONTINUE OUR TALK. PLEASE, SIT. PARTAKE. OUR TELATTI FRUIT IS JUST IN SEASON. THE WINE IS ALSO LOCAL -- AND QUITE EXCELLENT.
THANK YOU, BUT I'M FINE.
SUIT YOURSELF. SO, LEIA, WHAT SERVICE ARE YOU SEEKING? DELIVERY, OR RECEIPT?
YOU DO GET RIGHT TO THE POINT, DON'T YOU?
VERY WELL. I HAVE A SHIPMENT OF SUPPLIES THAT I NEED DELIVERED...
...TO THE REBELS ON RALLTIIR.
RALLTIIR? MMM. YOU REALLY SHOULD TRY THE WINE.
I HEARD THAT RALLTIIR WAS UNDER MARTIAL LAW-- THAT DARTH VADER HIMSELF WAS ON THE SCENE.
ALL OF THAT IS TRUE. BUT WITHOUT THOSE SUPPLIES --

LEIA, PLEASE, SAY NO MORE. CONSIDER YOUR REQUEST *FULFILLED*. KATTADA HAS NO LOVE FOR THE EMPIRE.

BESIDES, MY PILOTS *LOVE* A CHALLENGE.

THANK YOU, MIA. I DON'T KNOW WHAT TO SAY...

PERHAPS I *WILL* TRY SOME OF THE TELATTI...

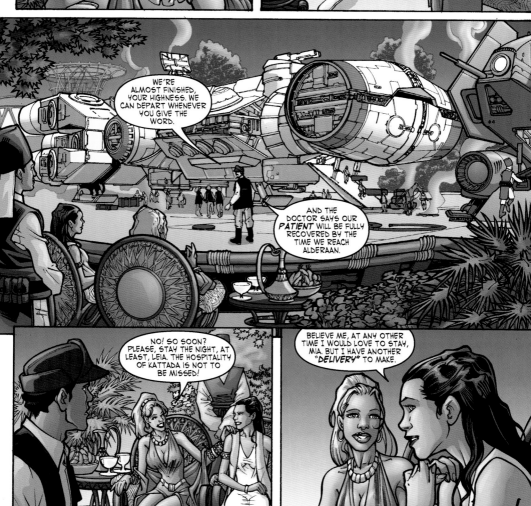

WE'RE ALMOST FINISHED, YOUR HIGHNESS. WE CAN DEPART WHENEVER YOU GIVE THE WORD.

AND THE DOCTOR SAYS OUR *PATIENT* WILL BE FULLY RECOVERED BY THE TIME WE REACH ALDERAAN.

NO! SO SOON? PLEASE, STAY THE NIGHT, AT LEAST, LEIA. THE HOSPITALITY OF KATTADA IS NOT TO BE MISSED!

BELIEVE ME, AT ANY OTHER TIME I WOULD LOVE TO STAY, MIA. BUT I HAVE ANOTHER *"DELIVERY"* TO MAKE.

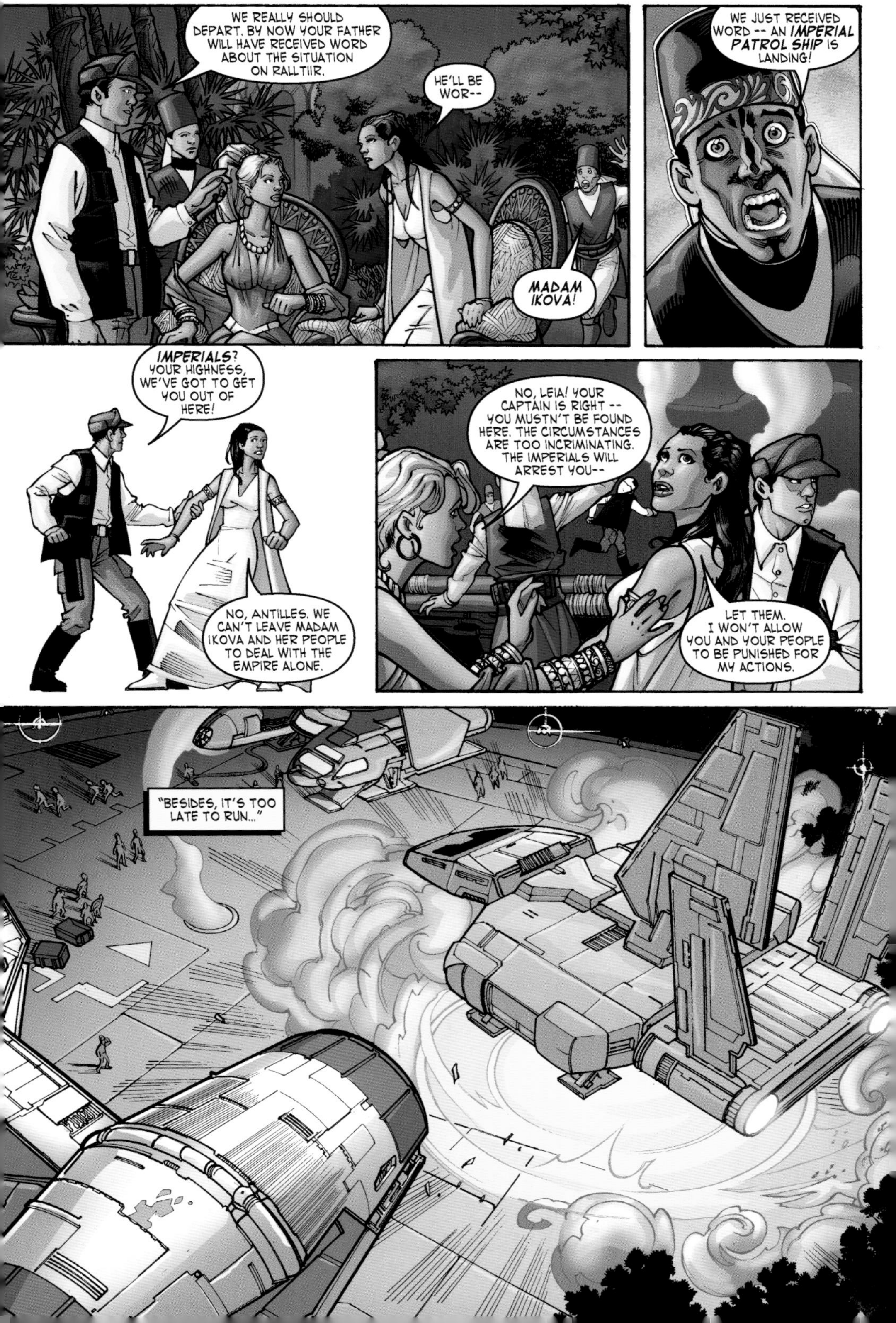
WE REALLY SHOULD DEPART. BY NOW YOUR FATHER WILL HAVE RECEIVED WORD ABOUT THE SITUATION ON RALLTIIR.
HE'LL BE WOR--
MADAM IKOVA!
WE JUST RECEIVED WORD -- AN IMPERIAL PATROL SHIP IS LANDING!
IMPERIALS? YOUR HIGHNESS, WE'VE GOT TO GET YOU OUT OF HERE!
NO, ANTILLES. WE CAN'T LEAVE MADAM IKOVA AND HER PEOPLE TO DEAL WITH THE EMPIRE ALONE.
NO, LEIA! YOUR CAPTAIN IS RIGHT -- YOU MUSTN'T BE FOUND HERE. THE CIRCUMSTANCES ARE TOO INCRIMINATING. THE IMPERIALS WILL ARREST YOU--
LET THEM. I WON'T ALLOW YOU AND YOUR PEOPLE TO BE PUNISHED FOR MY ACTIONS.
"BESIDES, IT'S TOO LATE TO RUN..."

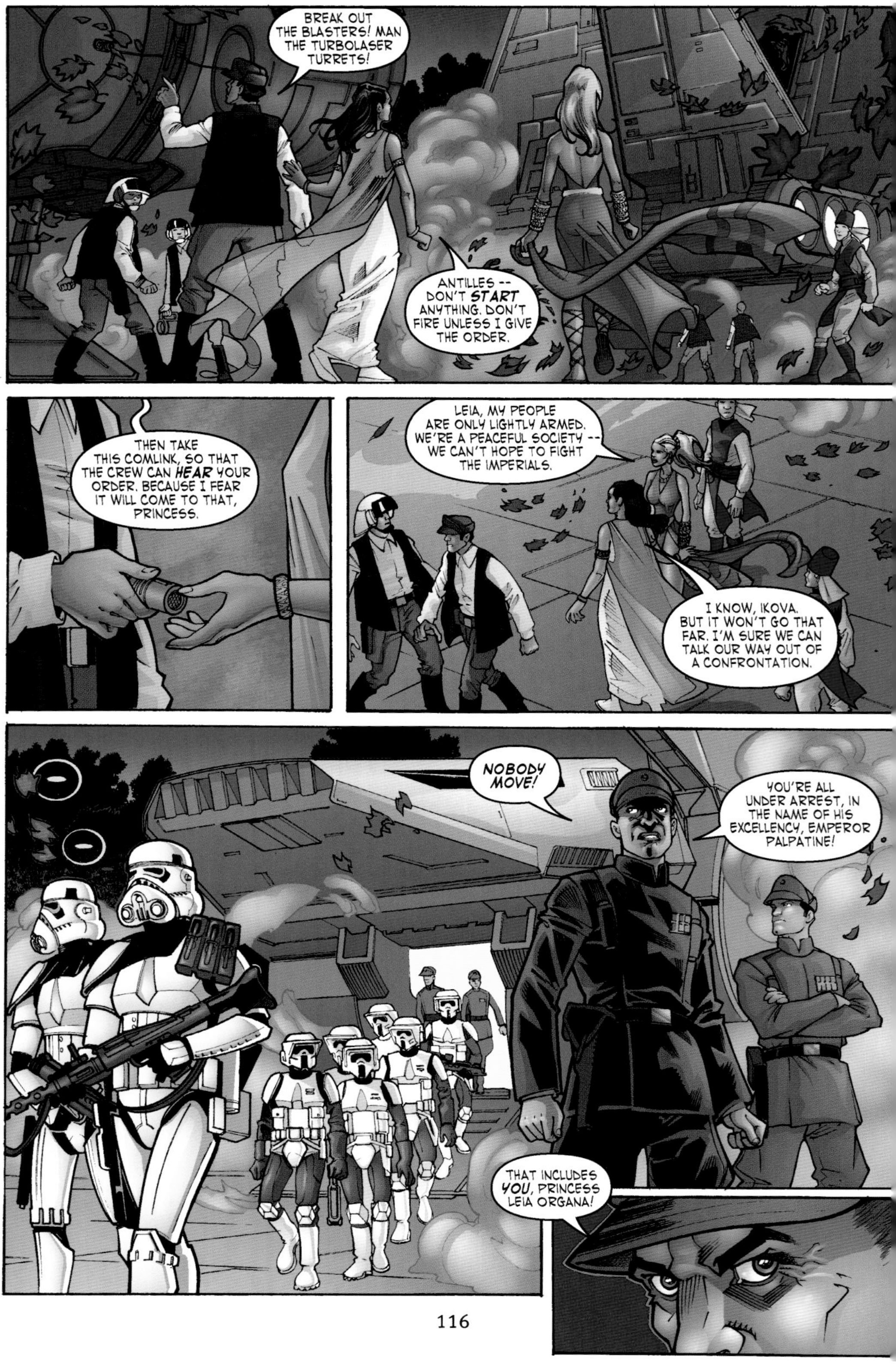
BREAK OUT THE BLASTERS! MAN THE TURBOLASER TURRETS!
ANTILLES -- DON'T START ANYTHING. DON'T FIRE UNLESS I GIVE THE ORDER.
THEN TAKE THIS COMLINK, SO THAT THE CREW CAN HEAR YOUR ORDER. BECAUSE I FEAR IT WILL COME TO THAT, PRINCESS.
LEIA, MY PEOPLE ARE ONLY LIGHTLY ARMED. WE'RE A PEACEFUL SOCIETY -- WE CAN'T HOPE TO FIGHT THE IMPERIALS.
I KNOW, IKOVA. BUT IT WON'T GO THAT FAR. I'M SURE WE CAN TALK OUR WAY OUT OF A CONFRONTATION.
NOBODY MOVE!
YOU'RE ALL UNDER ARREST, IN THE NAME OF HIS EXCELLENCY, EMPEROR PALPATINE!
THAT INCLUDES YOU, PRINCESS LEIA ORGANA!

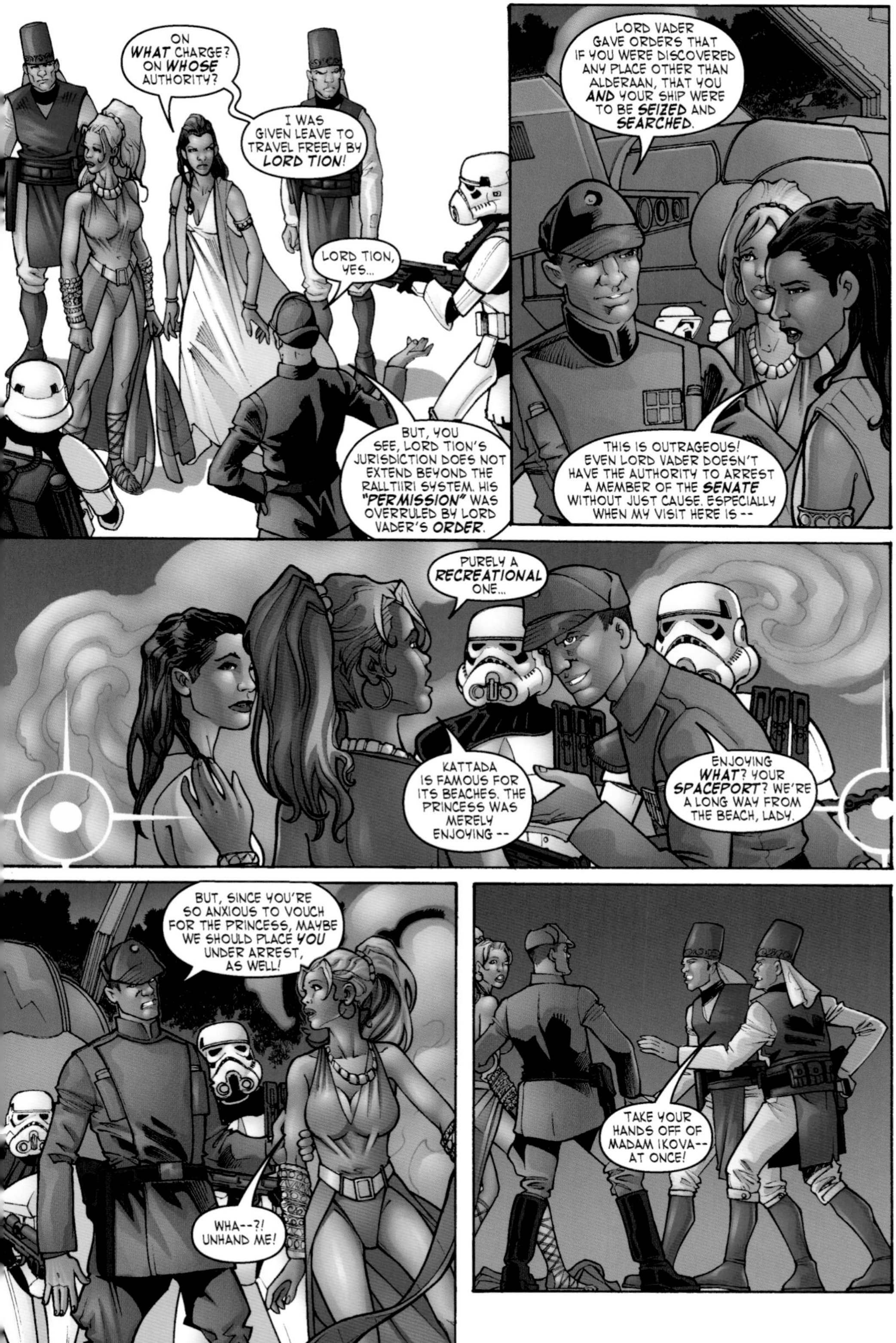
ON WHAT CHARGE? ON WHOSE AUTHORITY?
I WAS GIVEN LEAVE TO TRAVEL FREELY BY LORD TION!
LORD TION, YES...
BUT, YOU SEE, LORD TION'S JURISDICTION DOES NOT EXTEND BEYOND THE RALLTIIRI SYSTEM. HIS "PERMISSION" WAS OVERRULED BY LORD VADER'S ORDER.
LORD VADER GAVE ORDERS THAT IF YOU WERE DISCOVERED ANY PLACE OTHER THAN ALDERAAN, THAT YOU AND YOUR SHIP WERE TO BE SEIZED AND SEARCHED.
THIS IS OUTRAGEOUS! EVEN LORD VADER DOESN'T HAVE THE AUTHORITY TO ARREST A MEMBER OF THE SENATE WITHOUT JUST CAUSE. ESPECIALLY WHEN MY VISIT HERE IS --
PURELY A RECREATIONAL ONE...
KATTADA IS FAMOUS FOR ITS BEACHES. THE PRINCESS WAS MERELY ENJOYING --
ENJOYING WHAT? YOUR SPACEPORT? WE'RE A LONG WAY FROM THE BEACH, LADY.
BUT, SINCE YOU'RE SO ANXIOUS TO VOUCH FOR THE PRINCESS, MAYBE WE SHOULD PLACE YOU UNDER ARREST, AS WELL!
WHA--?! UNHAND ME!
TAKE YOUR HANDS OFF OF MADAM IKOVA-- AT ONCE!

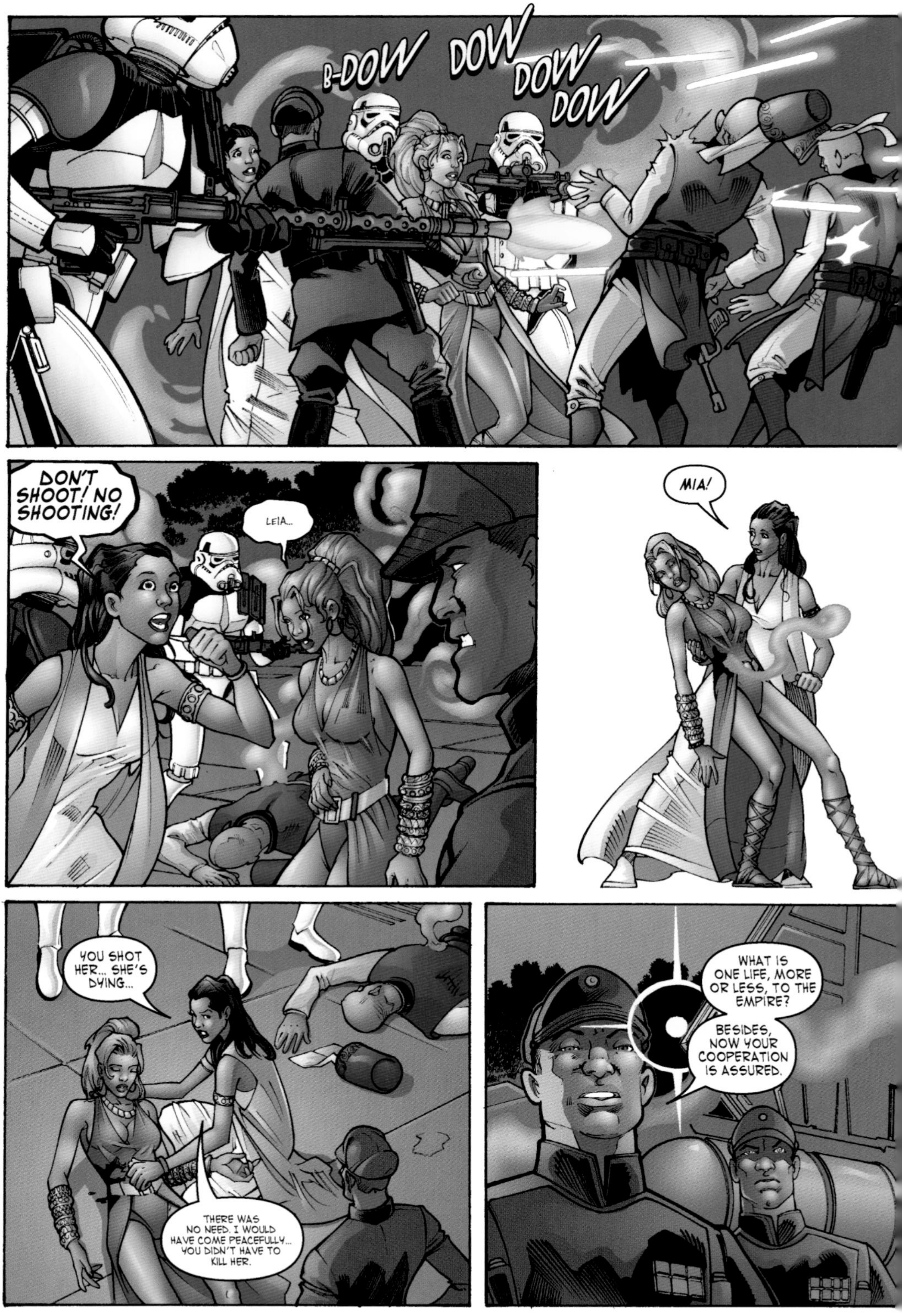
B-DOW DOW DOW DOW
DON'T SHOOT! NO SHOOTING!
LEIA...
MIA!
YOU SHOT HER... SHE'S DYING...
THERE WAS NO NEED. I WOULD HAVE COME PEACEFULLY... YOU DIDN'T HAVE TO KILL HER.
WHAT IS ONE LIFE, MORE OR LESS, TO THE EMPIRE?
BESIDES, NOW YOUR COOPERATION IS ASSURED.

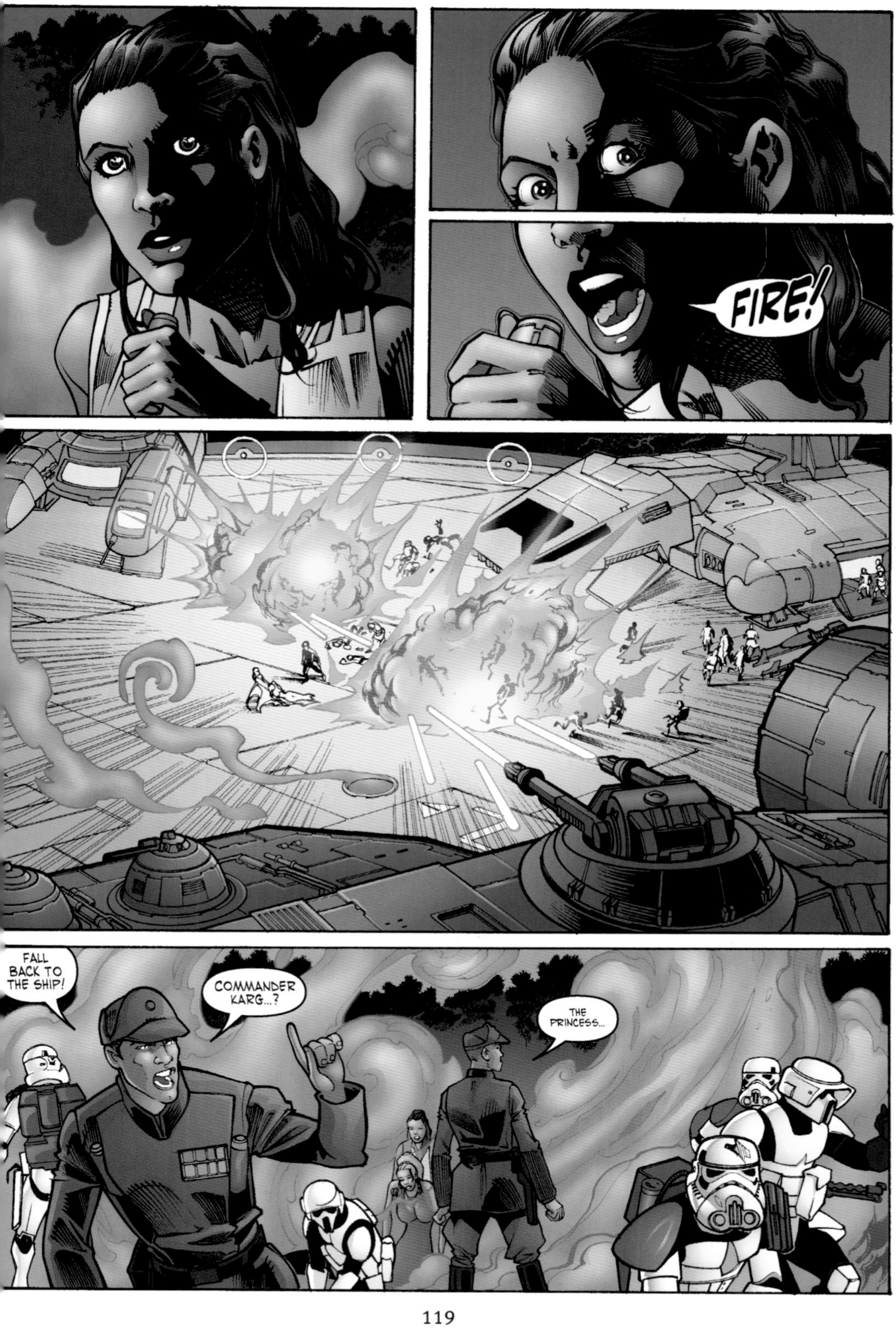

FIRE!
FALL BACK TO THE SHIP!
COMMANDER KARG...?
THE PRINCESS...

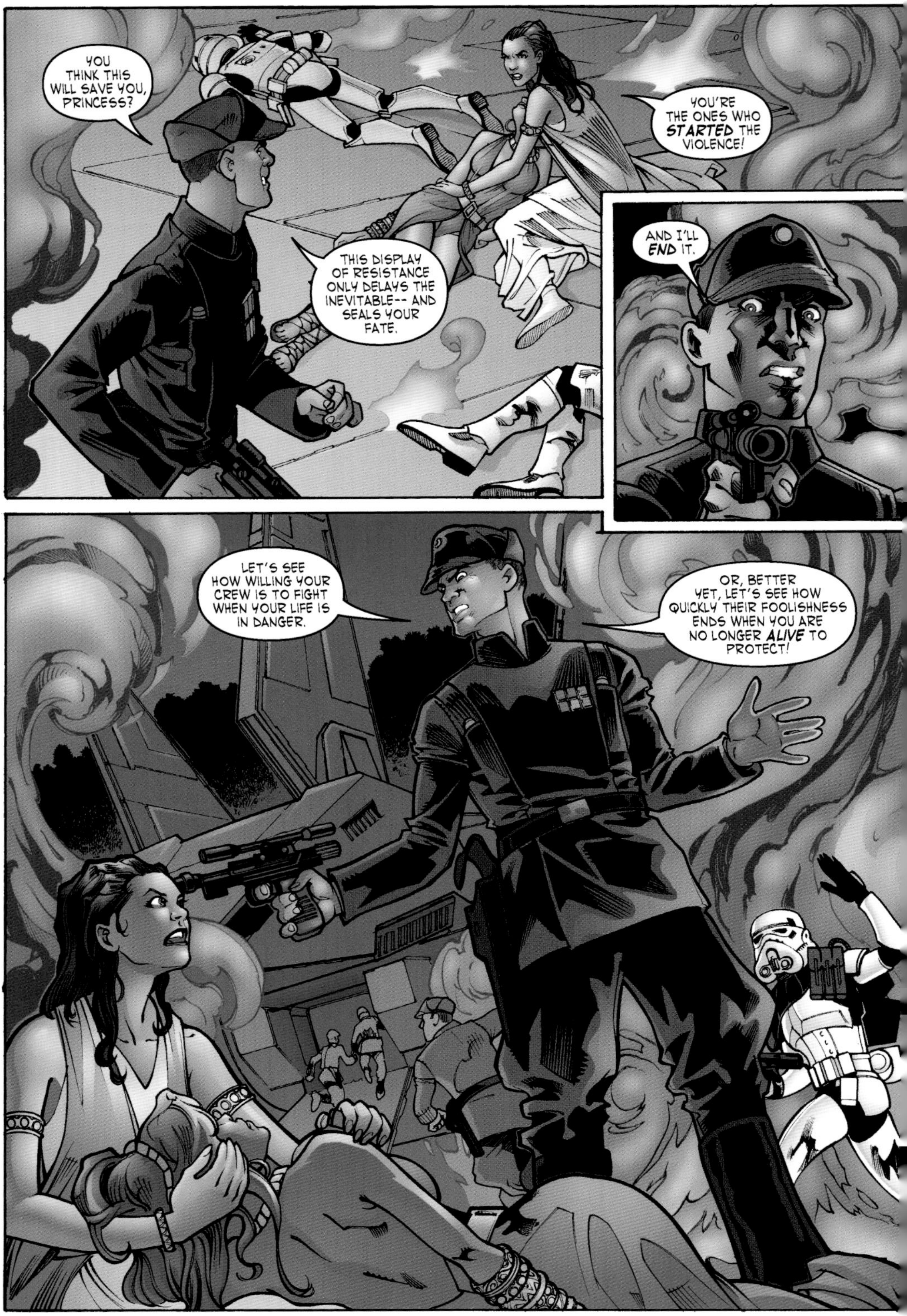
YOU THINK THIS WILL SAVE YOU, PRINCESS?
YOU'RE THE ONES WHO STARTED THE VIOLENCE!
THIS DISPLAY OF RESISTANCE ONLY DELAYS THE INEVITABLE-- AND SEALS YOUR FATE.
AND I'LL END IT.
LET'S SEE HOW WILLING YOUR CREW IS TO FIGHT WHEN YOUR LIFE IS IN DANGER.
OR, BETTER YET, LET'S SEE HOW QUICKLY THEIR FOOLISHNESS ENDS WHEN YOU ARE NO LONGER ALIVE TO PROTECT!

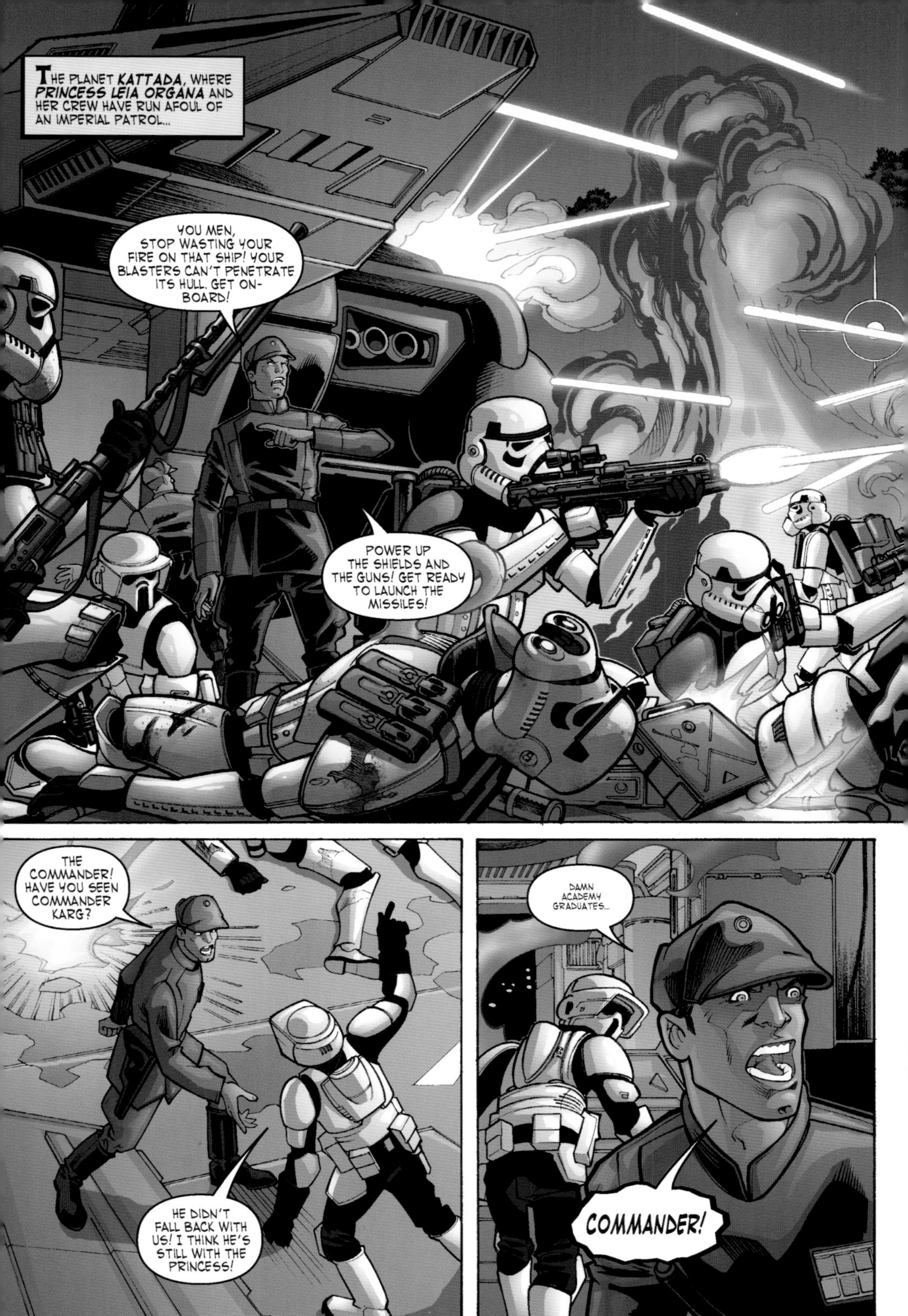
THE PLANET KATTADA, WHERE PRINCESS LEIA ORGANA AND HER CREW HAVE RUN AFOUL OF AN IMPERIAL PATROL...
YOU MEN, STOP WASTING YOUR FIRE ON THAT SHIP! YOUR BLASTERS CAN'T PENETRATE ITS HULL. GET ON-BOARD!
POWER UP THE SHIELDS AND THE GUNS! GET READY TO LAUNCH THE MISSILES!
THE COMMANDER! HAVE YOU SEEN COMMANDER KARG?
HE DIDN'T FALL BACK WITH US! I THINK HE'S STILL WITH THE PRINCESS!
DAMN ACADEMY GRADUATES...
COMMANDER!

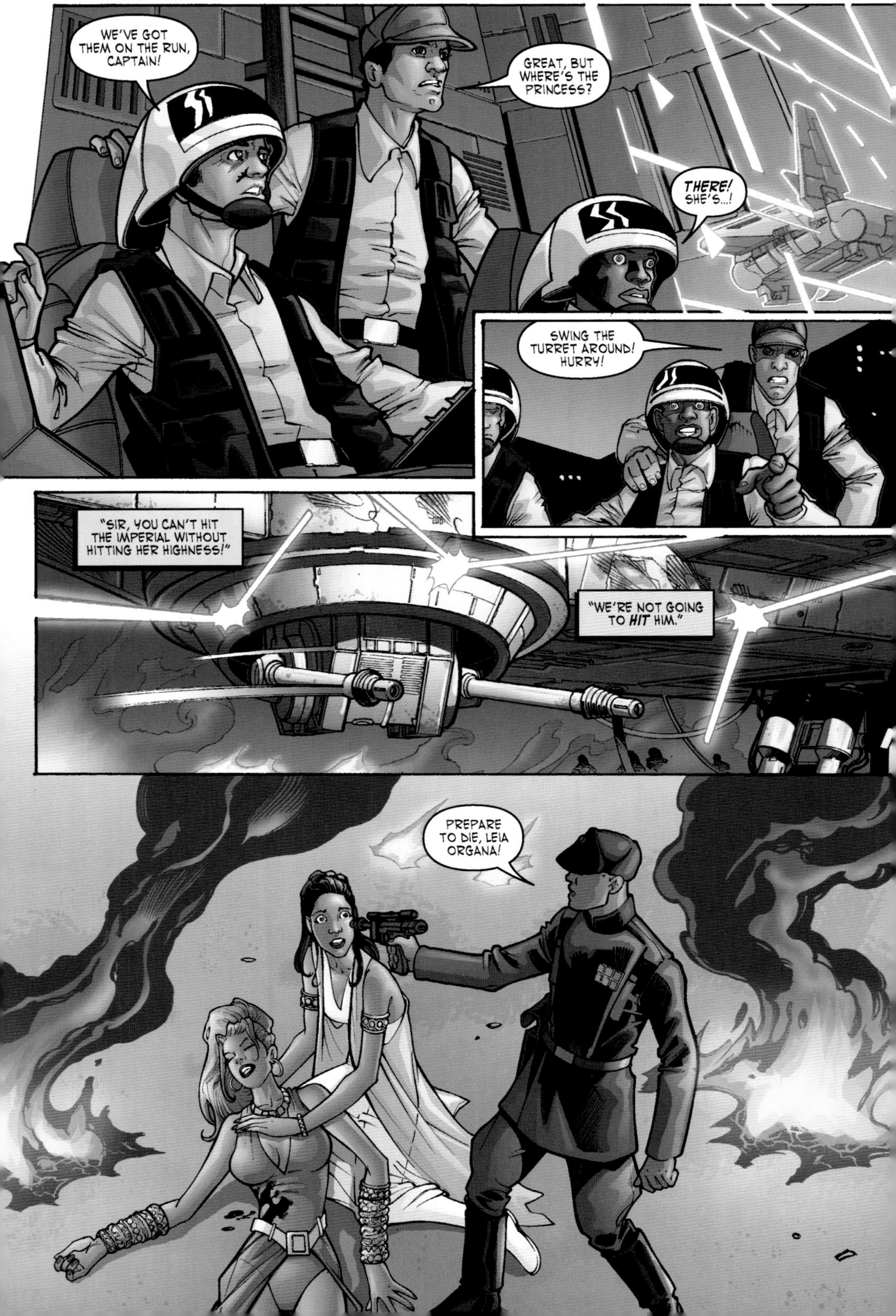
WE'VE GOT THEM ON THE RUN, CAPTAIN!
GREAT, BUT WHERE'S THE PRINCESS?
THERE! SHE'S...!
SWING THE TURRET AROUND! HURRY!
"SIR, YOU CAN'T HIT THE IMPERIAL WITHOUT HITTING HER HIGHNESS!"
"WE'RE NOT GOING TO HIT HIM."
PREPARE TO DIE, LEIA ORGANA!

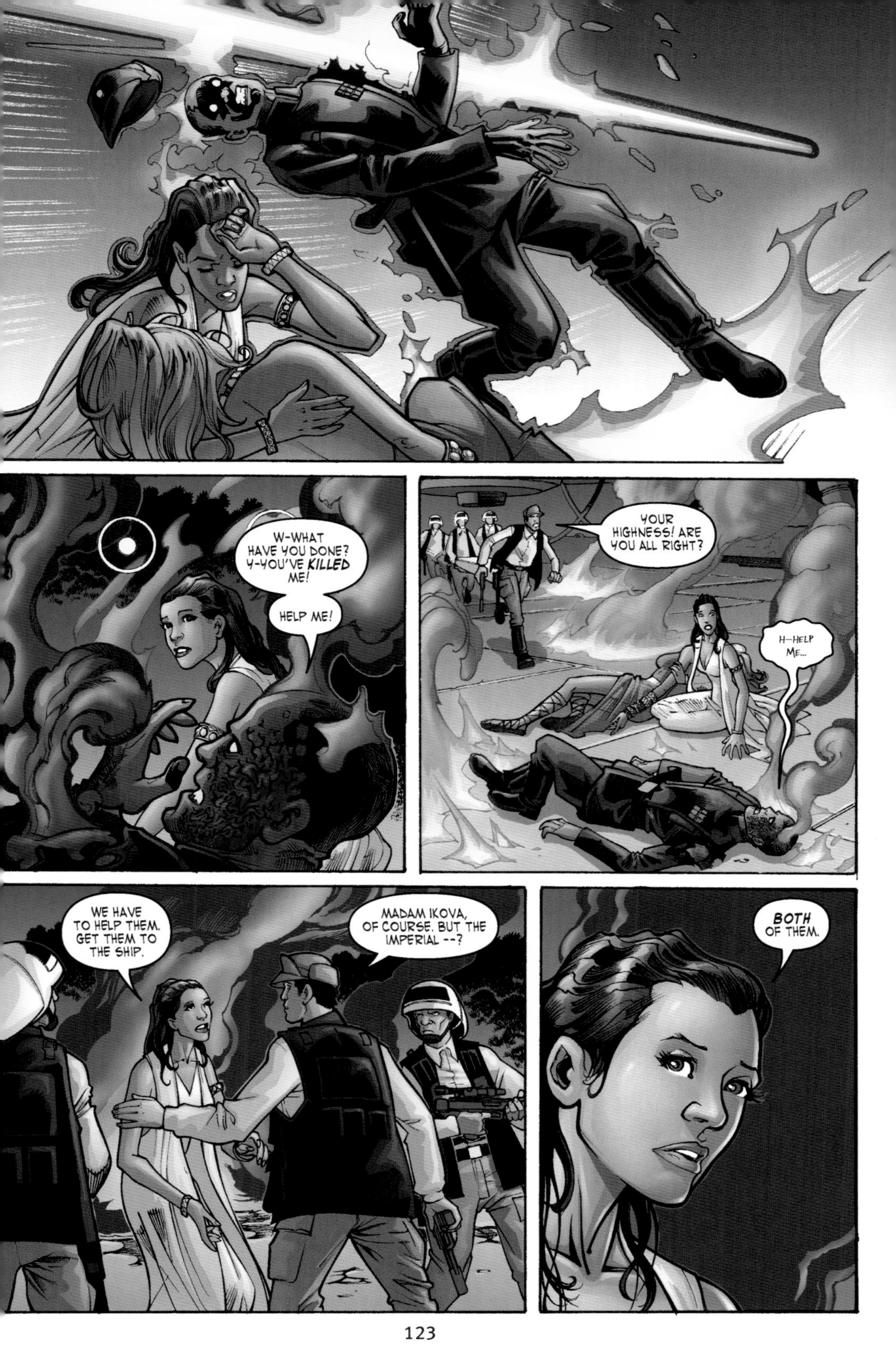
W-WHAT HAVE YOU DONE? Y-YOU'VE *KILLED* ME!
HELP ME!
YOUR HIGHNESS! ARE YOU ALL RIGHT?
H-HELP ME...
WE HAVE TO HELP THEM. GET THEM TO THE SHIP.
MADAM IKOVA, OF COURSE. BUT THE IMPERIAL --?
BOTH OF THEM.

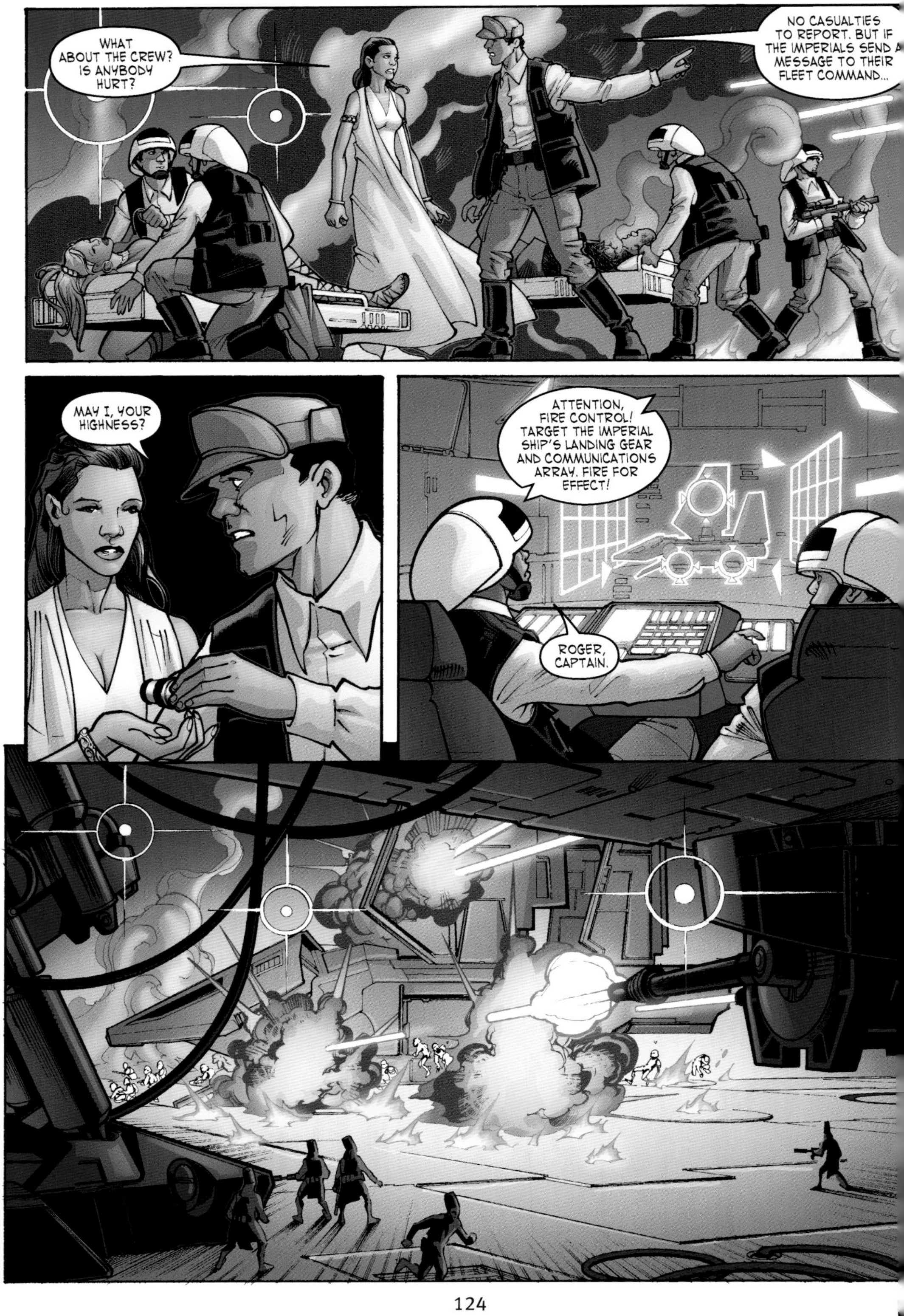
WHAT ABOUT THE CREW? IS ANYBODY HURT?
NO CASUALTIES TO REPORT. BUT IF THE IMPERIALS SEND A MESSAGE TO THEIR FLEET COMMAND...
MAY I, YOUR HIGHNESS?
ATTENTION, FIRE CONTROL! TARGET THE IMPERIAL SHIP'S LANDING GEAR AND COMMUNICATIONS ARRAY. FIRE FOR EFFECT!
ROGER, CAPTAIN.

THAT WILL GIVE THEM SOMETHING TO THINK ABOUT -- BUT WE STILL HAVE A *FIGHT* AHEAD OF US! WE SHOULD FINISH THEM NOW WHILE --

THERE WILL BE *NO MORE* FIGHTING!

BUT, YOUR HIGHNESS...

OUR ONLY CONCERN NOW IS TO SEE TO MADAM IKOVA'S WOUNDS -- AND TO MOVE THE *TANTIVE IV* OUT OF HARM'S WAY!

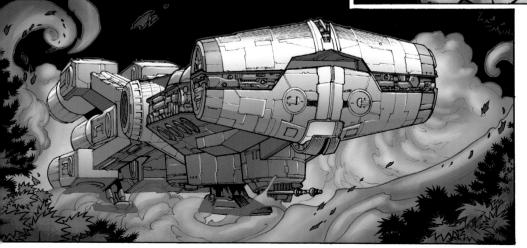

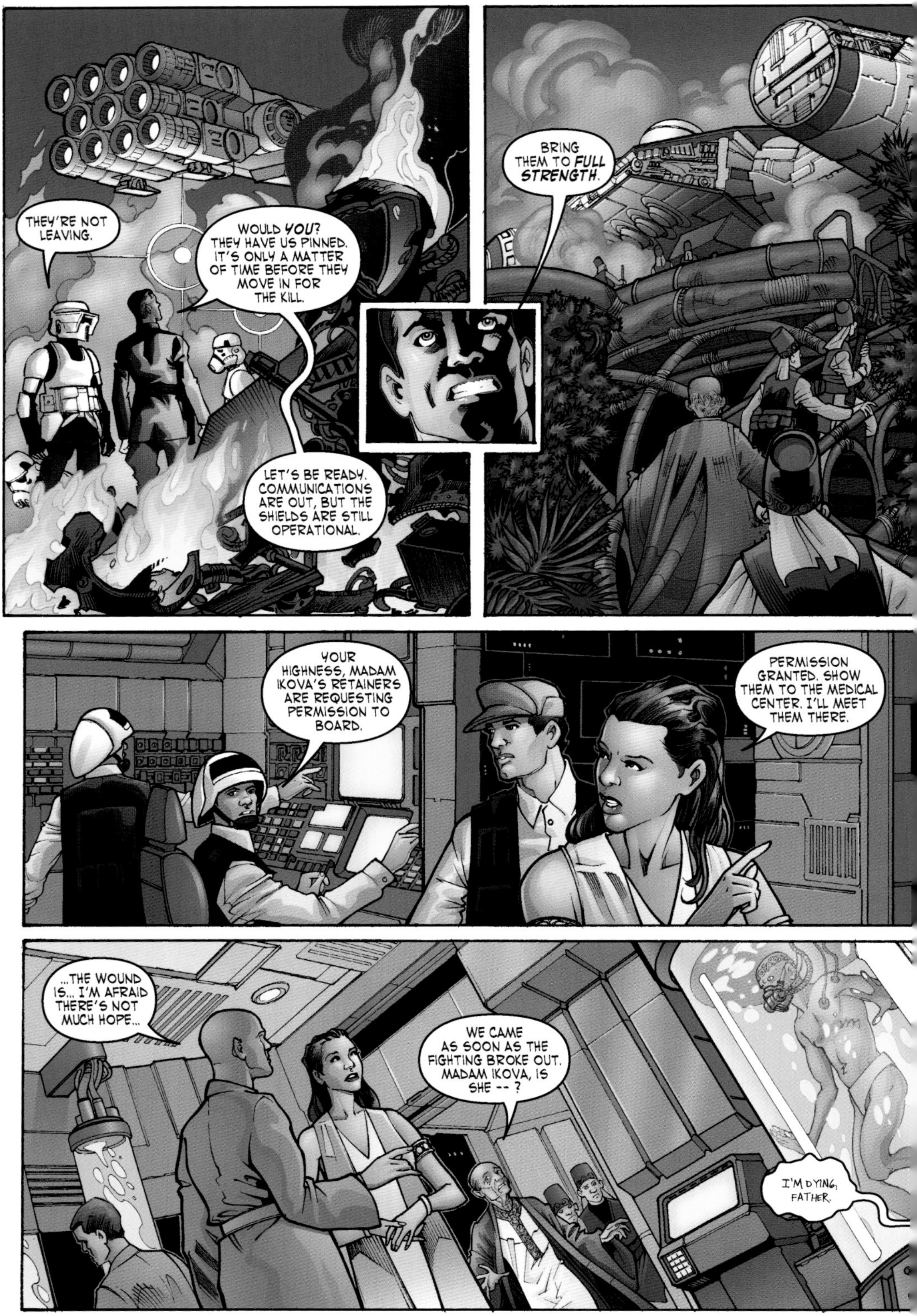
THEY'RE NOT LEAVING.
WOULD YOU? THEY HAVE US PINNED. IT'S ONLY A MATTER OF TIME BEFORE THEY MOVE IN FOR THE KILL.
LET'S BE READY. COMMUNICATIONS ARE OUT, BUT THE SHIELDS ARE STILL OPERATIONAL.
BRING THEM TO FULL STRENGTH.
YOUR HIGHNESS, MADAM IKOVA'S RETAINERS ARE REQUESTING PERMISSION TO BOARD.
PERMISSION GRANTED. SHOW THEM TO THE MEDICAL CENTER. I'LL MEET THEM THERE.
...THE WOUND IS... I'M AFRAID THERE'S NOT MUCH HOPE...
WE CAME AS SOON AS THE FIGHTING BROKE OUT. MADAM IKOVA, IS SHE -- ?
I'M DYING, FATHER.

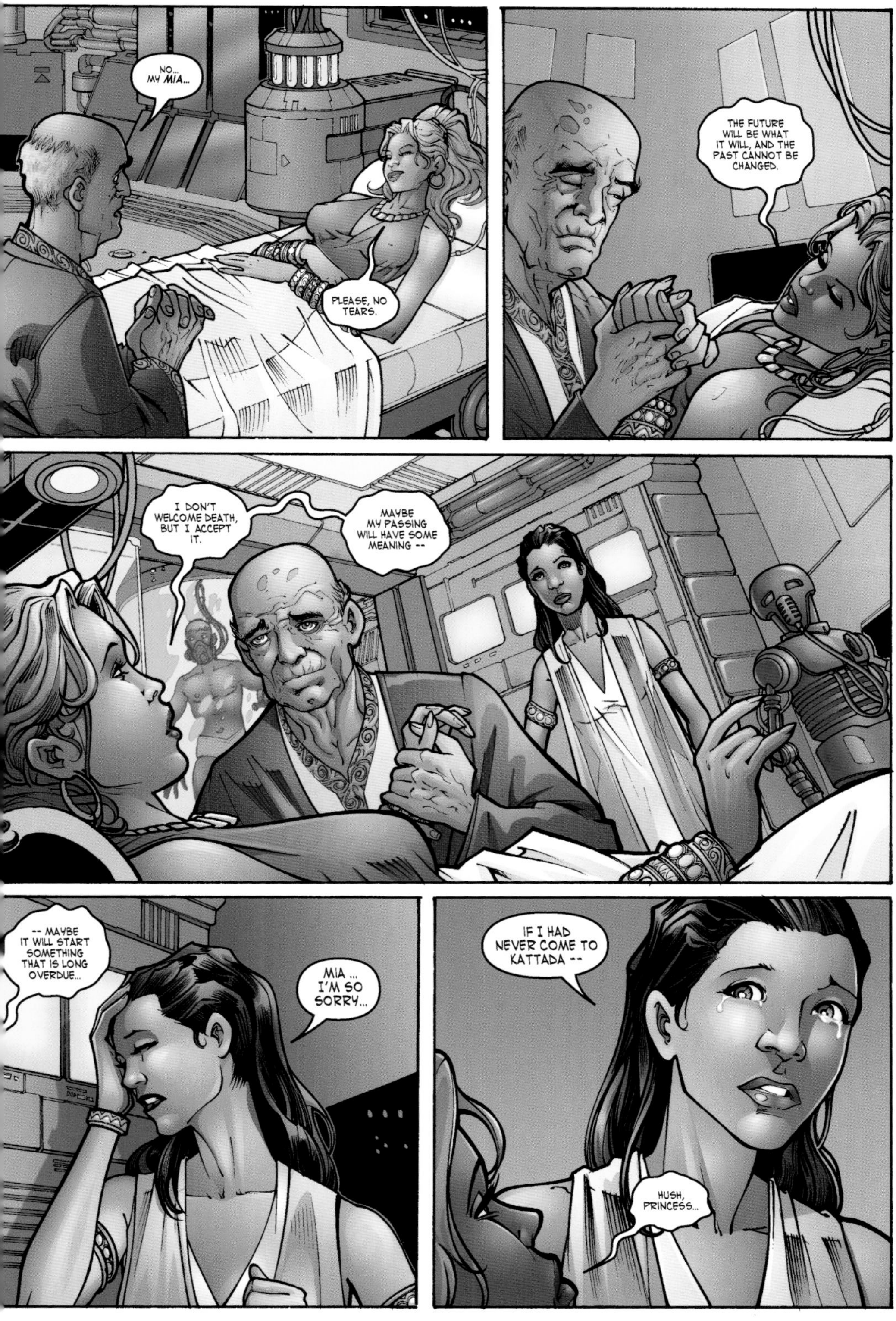
NO... MY MIA...
PLEASE, NO TEARS.
THE FUTURE WILL BE WHAT IT WILL, AND THE PAST CANNOT BE CHANGED.
I DON'T WELCOME DEATH, BUT I ACCEPT IT.
MAYBE MY PASSING WILL HAVE SOME MEANING --
-- MAYBE IT WILL START SOMETHING THAT IS LONG OVERDUE...
MIA ... I'M SO SORRY...
IF I HAD NEVER COME TO KATTADA --
HUSH, PRINCESS...

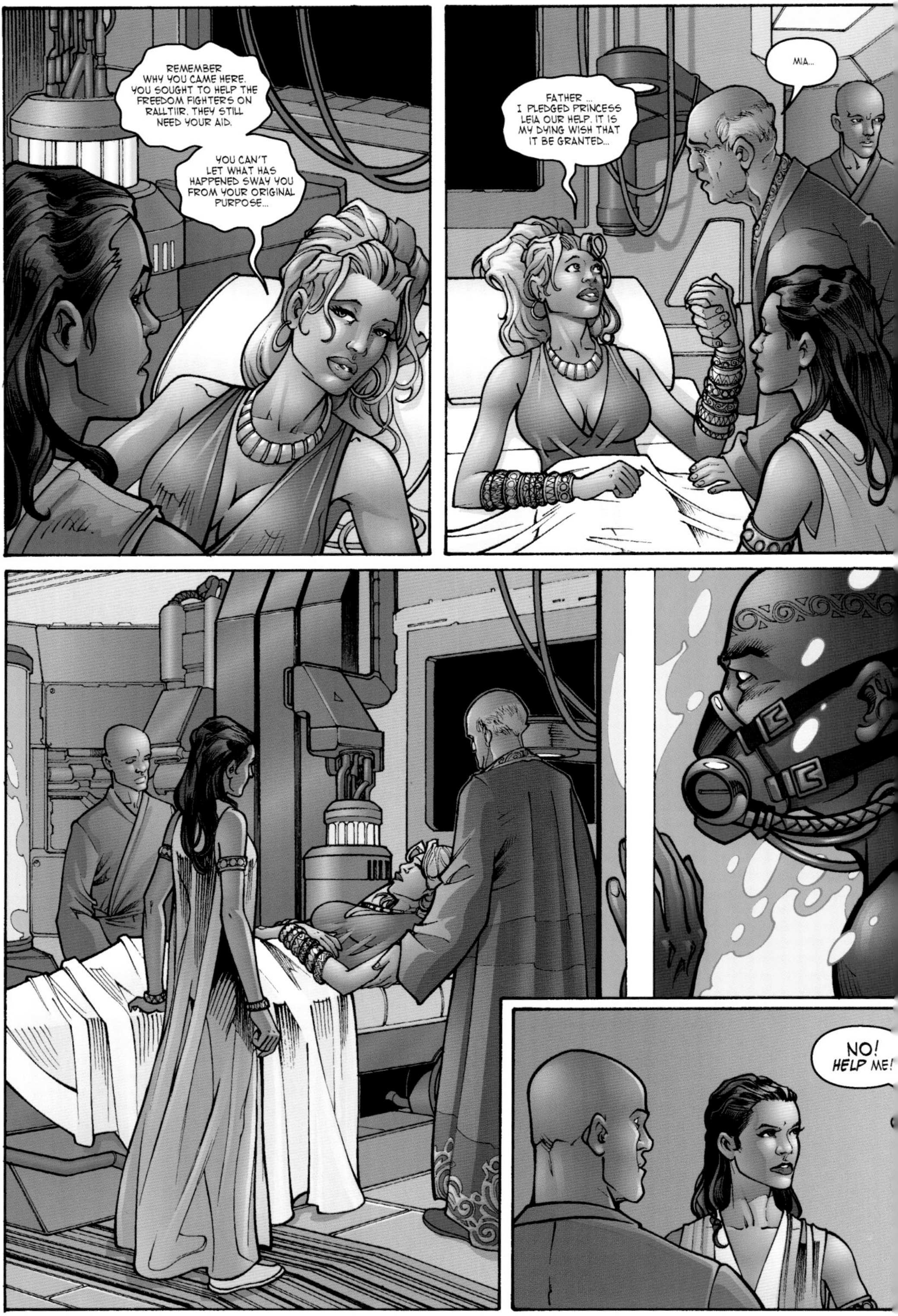

REMEMBER WHY YOU CAME HERE. YOU SOUGHT TO HELP THE FREEDOM FIGHTERS ON RALLTIIR. THEY STILL NEED YOUR AID.
YOU CAN'T LET WHAT HAS HAPPENED SWAY YOU FROM YOUR ORIGINAL PURPOSE...
FATHER ... I PLEDGED PRINCESS LEIA OUR HELP. IT IS MY DYING WISH THAT IT BE GRANTED...
MIA...
NO! HELP ME!

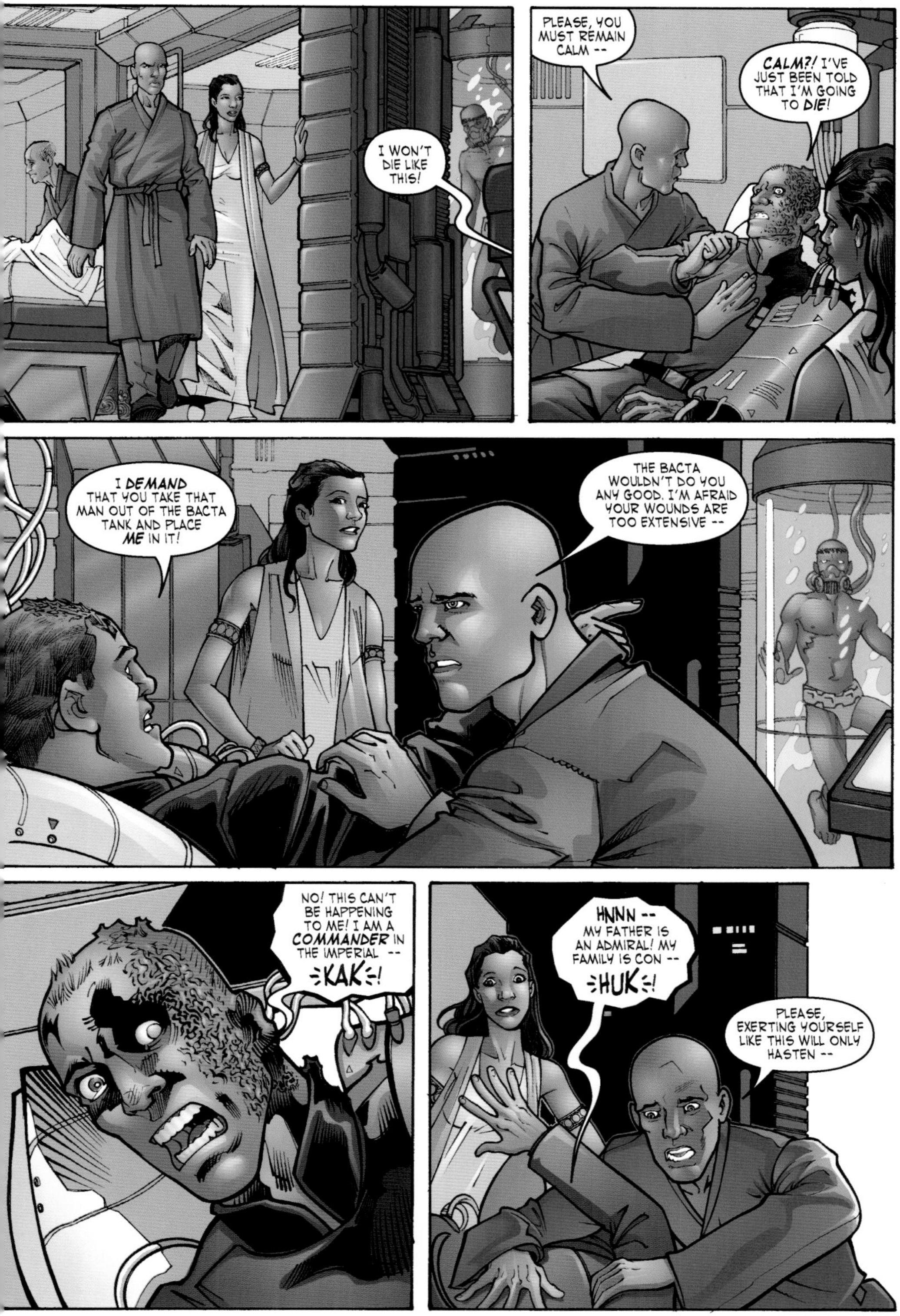
I WON'T DIE LIKE THIS!
PLEASE, YOU MUST REMAIN CALM --
CALM?! I'VE JUST BEEN TOLD THAT I'M GOING TO DIE!
I DEMAND THAT YOU TAKE THAT MAN OUT OF THE BACTA TANK AND PLACE ME IN IT!
THE BACTA WOULDN'T DO YOU ANY GOOD. I'M AFRAID YOUR WOUNDS ARE TOO EXTENSIVE --
NO! THIS CAN'T BE HAPPENING TO ME! I AM A COMMANDER IN THE IMPERIAL --
KAK!
HNNN -- MY FATHER IS AN ADMIRAL! MY FAMILY IS CON --
HUK!
PLEASE, EXERTING YOURSELF LIKE THIS WILL ONLY HASTEN --

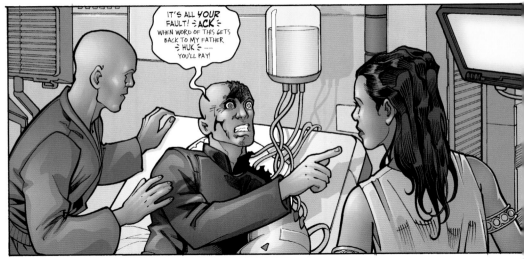

IT'S ALL *YOUR* FAULT! ÷ACK÷ WHEN WORD OF THIS GETS BACK TO MY FATHER ÷HUK÷ -- YOU'LL PAY!

...YOU'LL PAY...

I'M SORRY YOU HAD TO WITNESS THAT, YOUR HIGHNESS.

BUT HE WAS RIGHT -- WHEN WORD OF THIS GETS OUT, YOU WILL BE NAMED AN ENEMY OF THE EMPIRE. THEN EVEN YOUR ROYAL STATUS WON'T BE ABLE TO SHIELD YOU.

THEIR COMMUNICATIONS ARE CUT, BUT THEIR SHIELDS ARE OPERATIVE. THE ONLY WAY TO GET AT THEM IS WITH A *GROUND ASSAULT*.

THE IMPERIALS KNOW THAT ALL THEY HAVE TO DO IS WAIT. EVENTUALLY, ANOTHER PATROL WILL BE DISPATCHED TO LOCATE THEM --

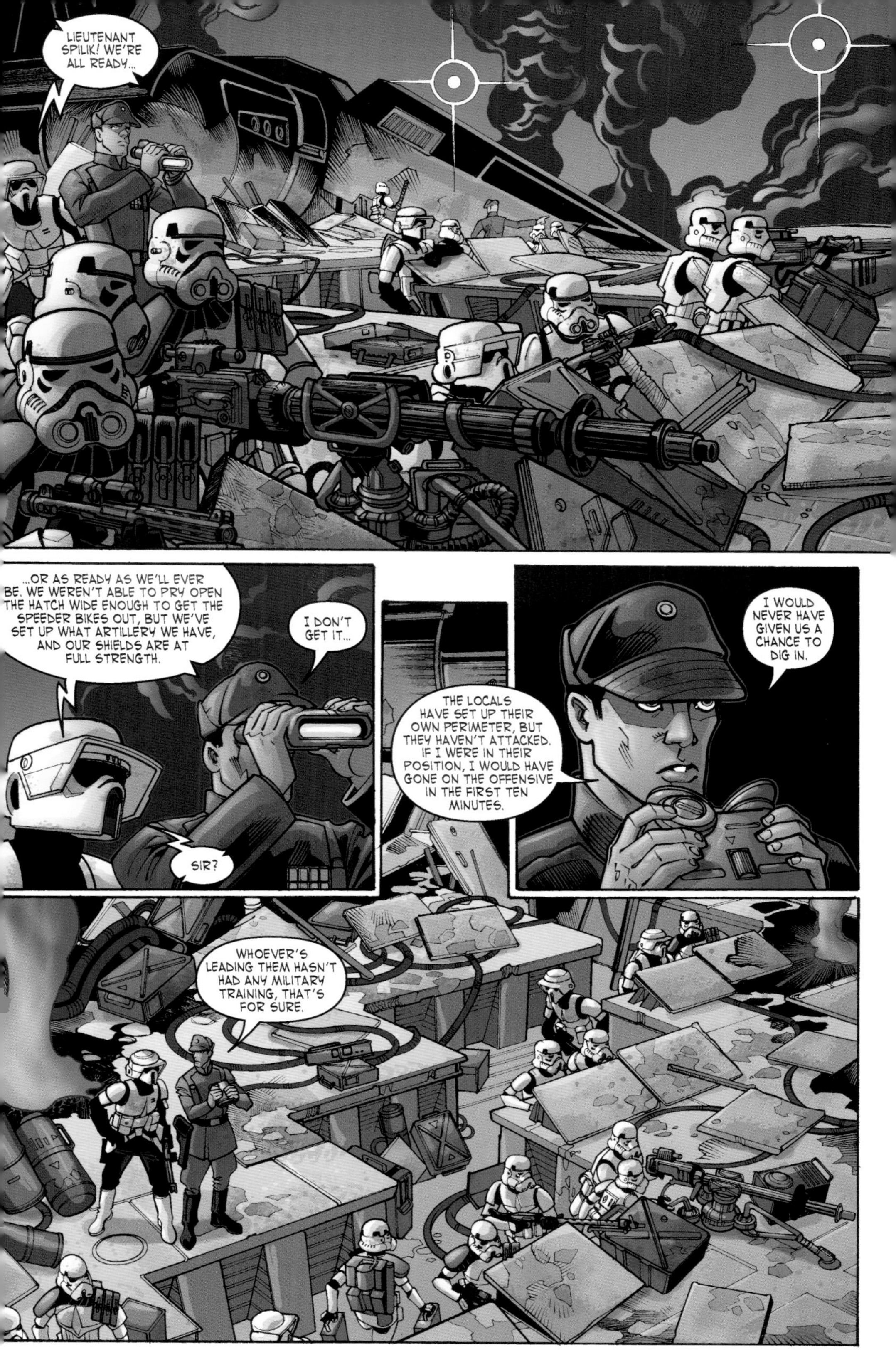
LIEUTENANT SPILIK! WE'RE ALL READY...
...OR AS READY AS WE'LL EVER BE. WE WEREN'T ABLE TO PRY OPEN THE HATCH WIDE ENOUGH TO GET THE SPEEDER BIKES OUT, BUT WE'VE SET UP WHAT ARTILLERY WE HAVE, AND OUR SHIELDS ARE AT FULL STRENGTH.
I DON'T GET IT...
SIR?
THE LOCALS HAVE SET UP THEIR OWN PERIMETER, BUT THEY HAVEN'T ATTACKED. IF I WERE IN THEIR POSITION, I WOULD HAVE GONE ON THE OFFENSIVE IN THE FIRST TEN MINUTES.
I WOULD NEVER HAVE GIVEN US A CHANCE TO DIG IN.
WHOEVER'S LEADING THEM HASN'T HAD ANY MILITARY TRAINING, THAT'S FOR SURE.

ARE YOU SURE YOU WANT ADVICE FROM *ME*? I'M NO OFFICER...

MAYBE NOT, *BASSO*, BUT YOU'RE THE ONLY ONE WITH THE EXPERIENCE I NEED. CAPTAIN ANTILLES KNOWS SHIP-TO-SHIP COMBAT -- HE'S RUN HIS SHARE OF BLOCKADES. BUT HE'S NEVER HAD TO DEPLOY *GROUND TROOPS*.

YOU'RE THE CLOSEST THING TO A *VETERAN* THAT WE HAVE. PLEASE, I DON'T KNOW WHAT TO DO NEXT...

BUT YOU KNOW THAT YOU HAVE TO DO *SOMETHING*, RIGHT?

YOU *KNOW* THAT PEOPLE WILL *DIE*.

I DON'T LIKE TO THINK ABOUT --

IN THE HEAT OF THE MOMENT, WITH MIA'S LIFE AT STAKE, IT WAS DIFFERENT. THIS ... *PLANNING* ... SEEMS SO COLDBLOODED...

I'D LIKE TO AVOID BLOODSHED, IF IT'S POSSIBLE.

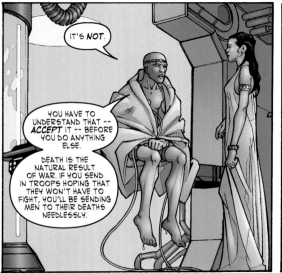

IT'S *NOT*.

YOU HAVE TO UNDERSTAND THAT -- *ACCEPT* IT -- BEFORE YOU DO ANYTHING ELSE.

DEATH IS THE NATURAL RESULT OF WAR. IF YOU SEND IN TROOPS HOPING THAT THEY WON'T HAVE TO FIGHT, YOU'LL BE SENDING MEN TO THEIR DEATHS NEEDLESSLY.

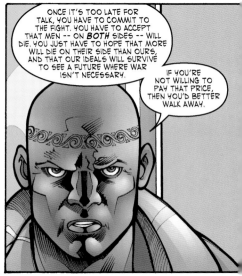

ONCE IT'S TOO LATE FOR TALK, YOU HAVE TO COMMIT TO THE FIGHT. YOU HAVE TO ACCEPT THAT MEN -- ON *BOTH* SIDES -- WILL DIE. YOU JUST HAVE TO HOPE THAT MORE WILL DIE ON THEIR SIDE THAN OURS, AND THAT OUR IDEALS WILL SURVIVE TO SEE A FUTURE WHERE WAR ISN'T NECESSARY.

IF YOU'RE NOT WILLING TO PAY THAT PRICE, THEN YOU'D BETTER WALK AWAY.

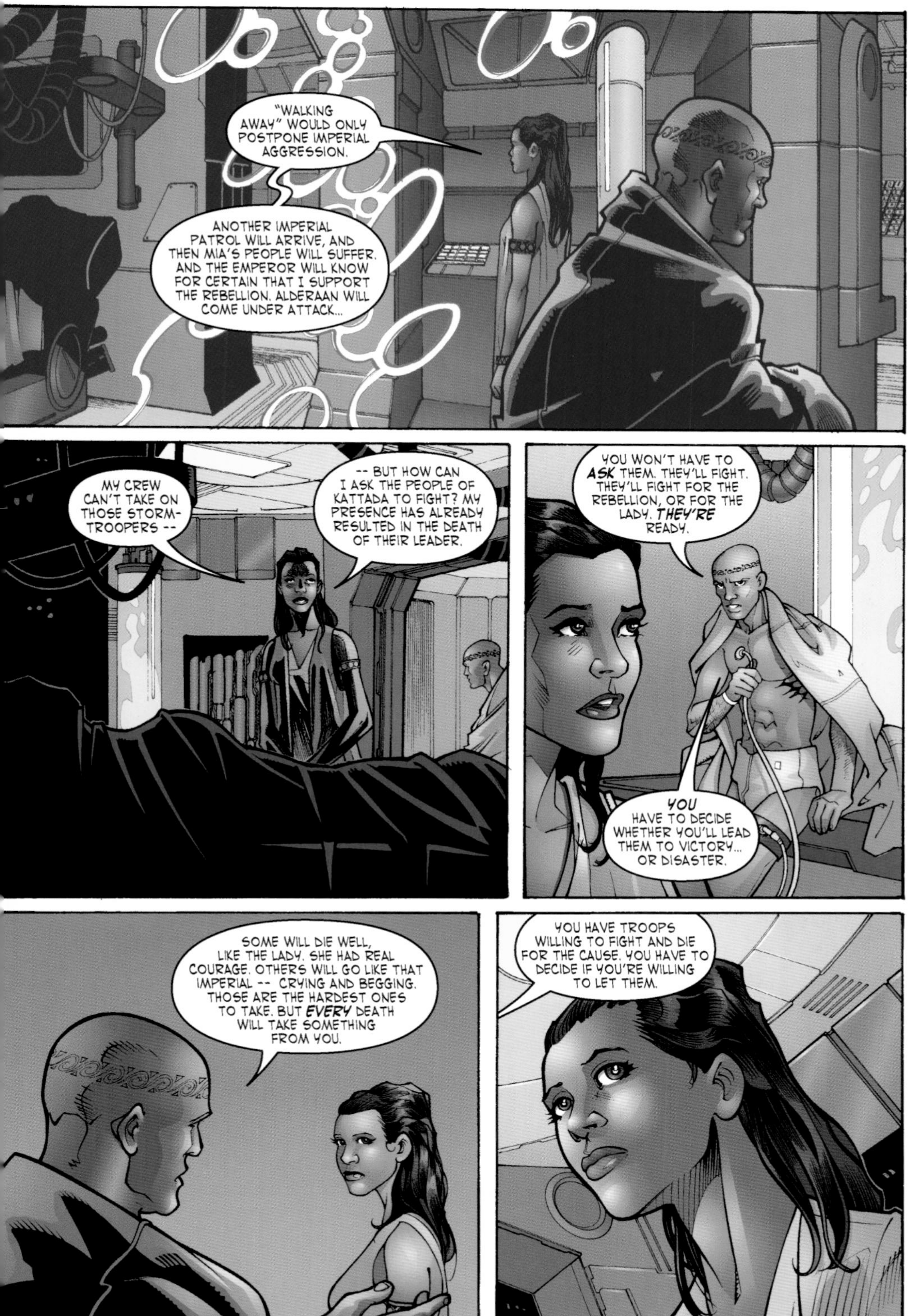
"WALKING AWAY" WOULD ONLY POSTPONE IMPERIAL AGGRESSION.
ANOTHER IMPERIAL PATROL WILL ARRIVE, AND THEN MIA'S PEOPLE WILL SUFFER. AND THE EMPEROR WILL KNOW FOR CERTAIN THAT I SUPPORT THE REBELLION. ALDERAAN WILL COME UNDER ATTACK...
MY CREW CAN'T TAKE ON THOSE STORM-TROOPERS --
-- BUT HOW CAN I ASK THE PEOPLE OF KATTADA TO FIGHT? MY PRESENCE HAS ALREADY RESULTED IN THE DEATH OF THEIR LEADER.
YOU WON'T HAVE TO ASK THEM. THEY'LL FIGHT. THEY'LL FIGHT FOR THE REBELLION, OR FOR THE LADY. THEY'RE READY.
YOU HAVE TO DECIDE WHETHER YOU'LL LEAD THEM TO VICTORY... OR DISASTER.
SOME WILL DIE WELL, LIKE THE LADY. SHE HAD REAL COURAGE. OTHERS WILL GO LIKE THAT IMPERIAL -- CRYING AND BEGGING. THOSE ARE THE HARDEST ONES TO TAKE. BUT EVERY DEATH WILL TAKE SOMETHING FROM YOU.
YOU HAVE TROOPS WILLING TO FIGHT AND DIE FOR THE CAUSE. YOU HAVE TO DECIDE IF YOU'RE WILLING TO LET THEM.

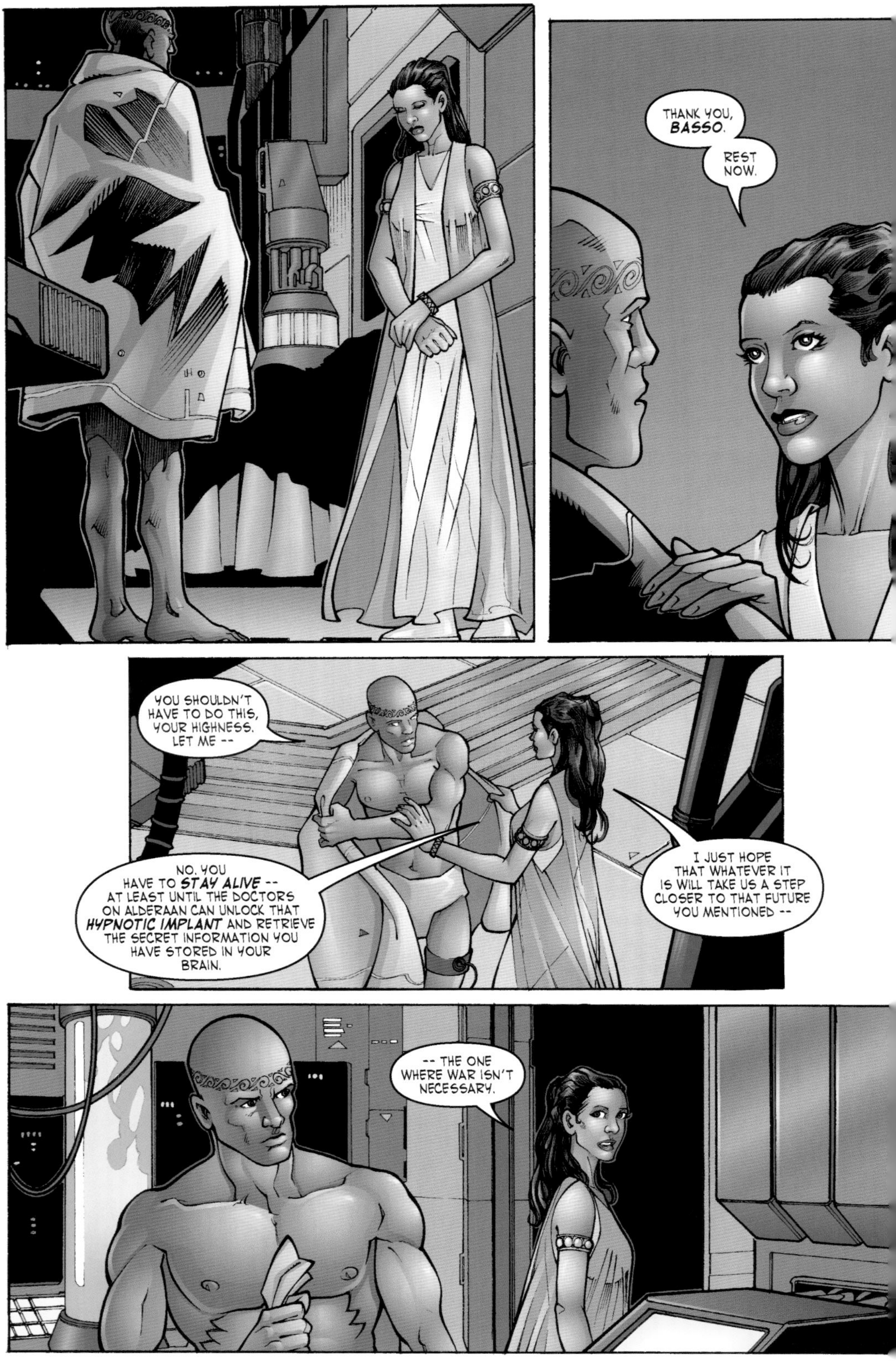
THANK YOU, BASSO.
REST NOW.
YOU SHOULDN'T HAVE TO DO THIS, YOUR HIGHNESS. LET ME --
NO. YOU HAVE TO STAY ALIVE -- AT LEAST UNTIL THE DOCTORS ON ALDERAAN CAN UNLOCK THAT HYPNOTIC IMPLANT AND RETRIEVE THE SECRET INFORMATION YOU HAVE STORED IN YOUR BRAIN.
I JUST HOPE THAT WHATEVER IT IS WILL TAKE US A STEP CLOSER TO THAT FUTURE YOU MENTIONED --
-- THE ONE WHERE WAR ISN'T NECESSARY.

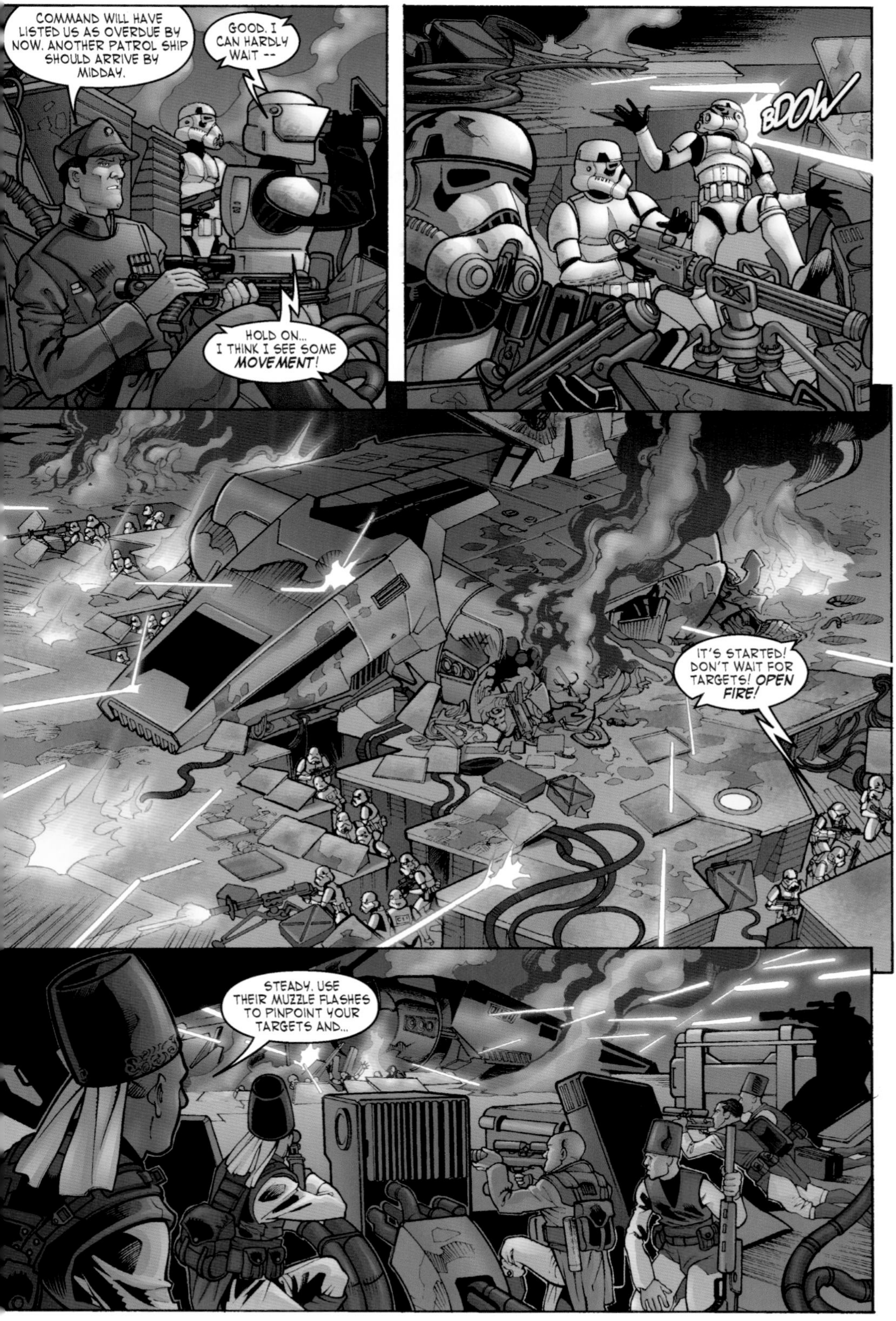
COMMAND WILL HAVE LISTED US AS OVERDUE BY NOW. ANOTHER PATROL SHIP SHOULD ARRIVE BY MIDDAY.
GOOD. I CAN HARDLY WAIT --
HOLD ON... I THINK I SEE SOME *MOVEMENT*!
BDOW
IT'S STARTED! DON'T WAIT FOR TARGETS! *OPEN FIRE!*
STEADY. USE THEIR MUZZLE FLASHES TO PINPOINT YOUR TARGETS AND...

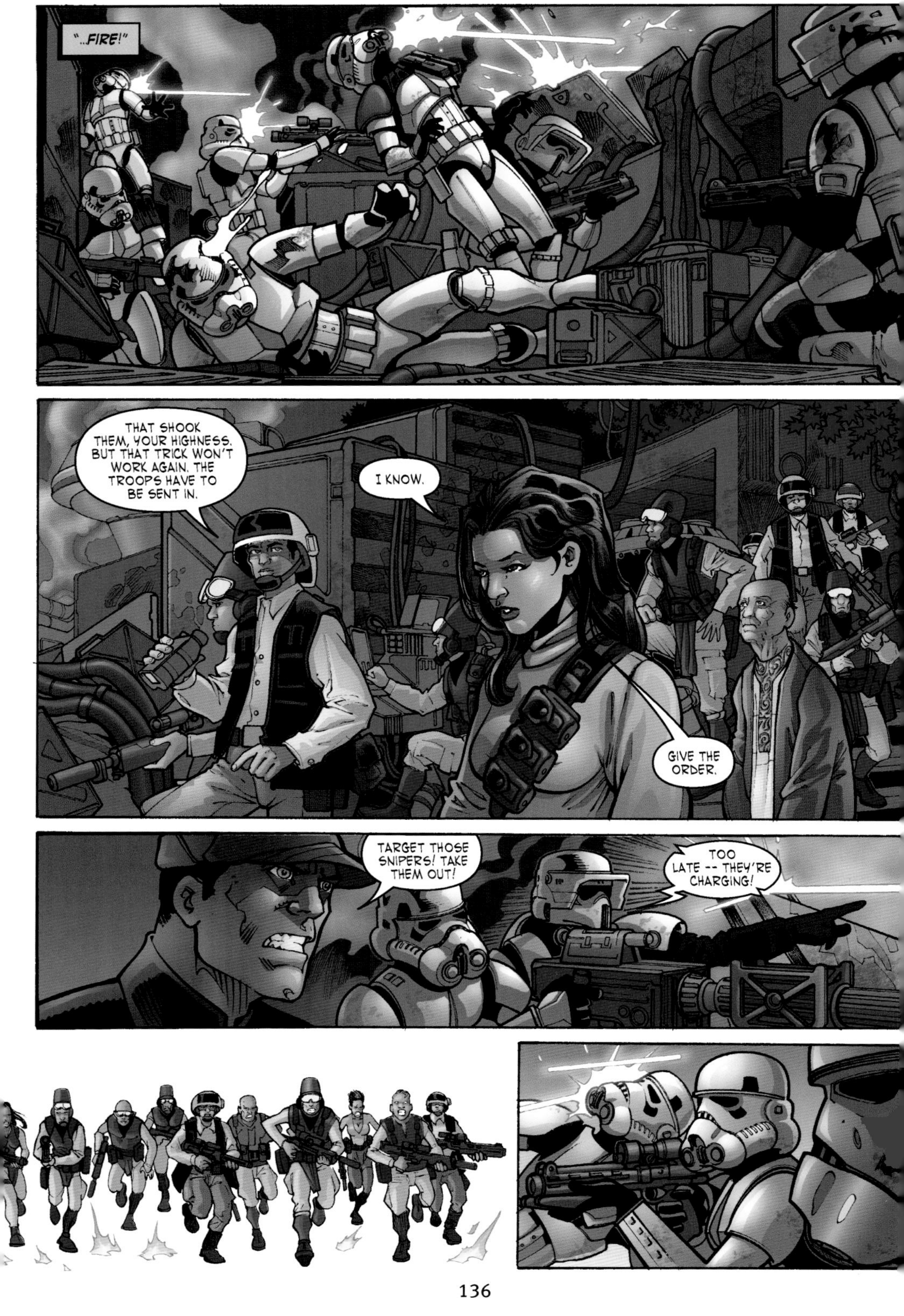
"...FIRE!"
THAT SHOOK THEM, YOUR HIGHNESS. BUT THAT TRICK WON'T WORK AGAIN. THE TROOPS HAVE TO BE SENT IN.
I KNOW.
GIVE THE ORDER.
TARGET THOSE SNIPERS! TAKE THEM OUT!
TOO LATE -- THEY'RE CHARGING!

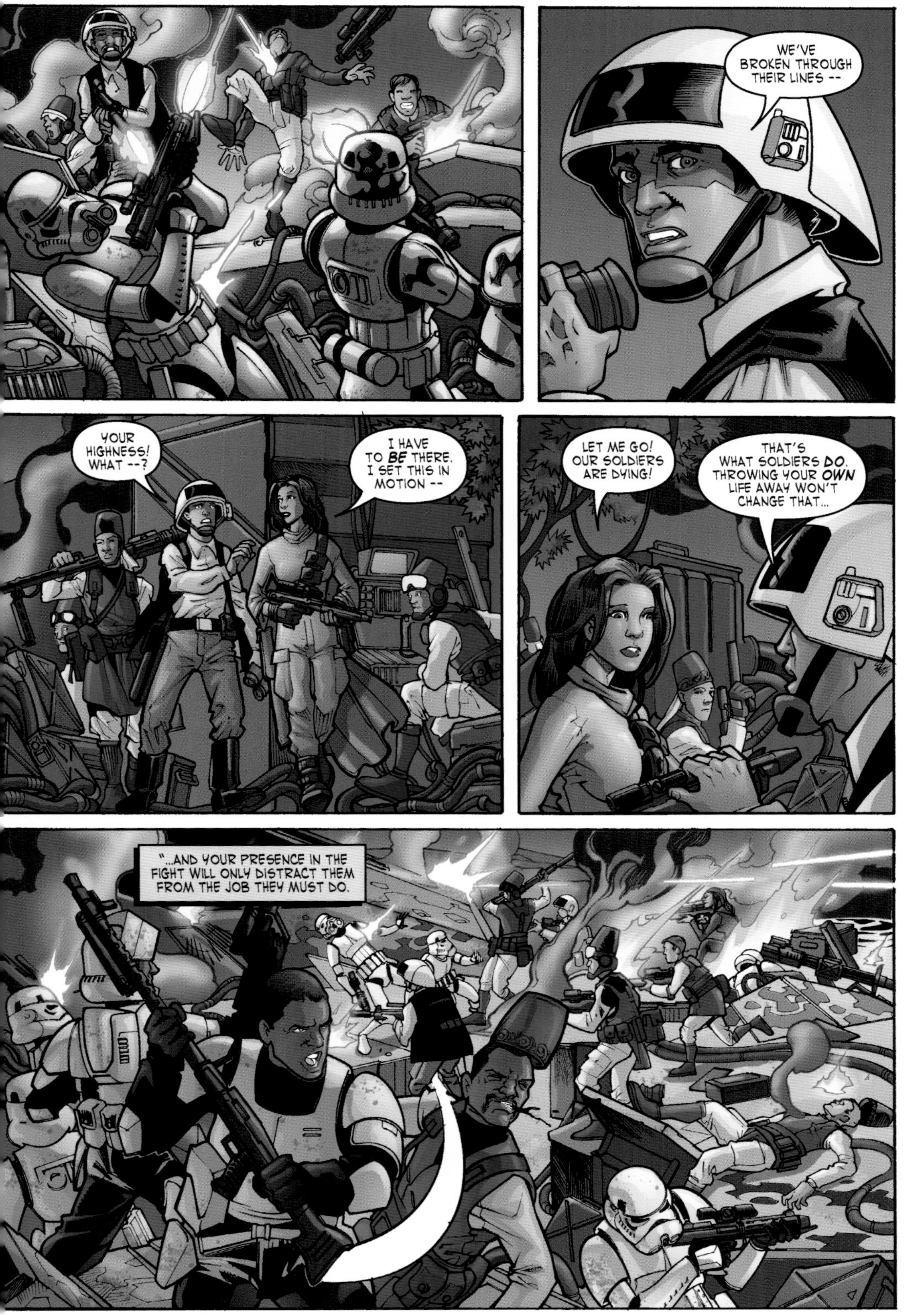
WE'VE BROKEN THROUGH THEIR LINES --
YOUR HIGHNESS! WHAT --?
I HAVE TO BE THERE. I SET THIS IN MOTION --
LET ME GO! OUR SOLDIERS ARE DYING!
THAT'S WHAT SOLDIERS DO. THROWING YOUR OWN LIFE AWAY WON'T CHANGE THAT...
"...AND YOUR PRESENCE IN THE FIGHT WILL ONLY DISTRACT THEM FROM THE JOB THEY MUST DO.

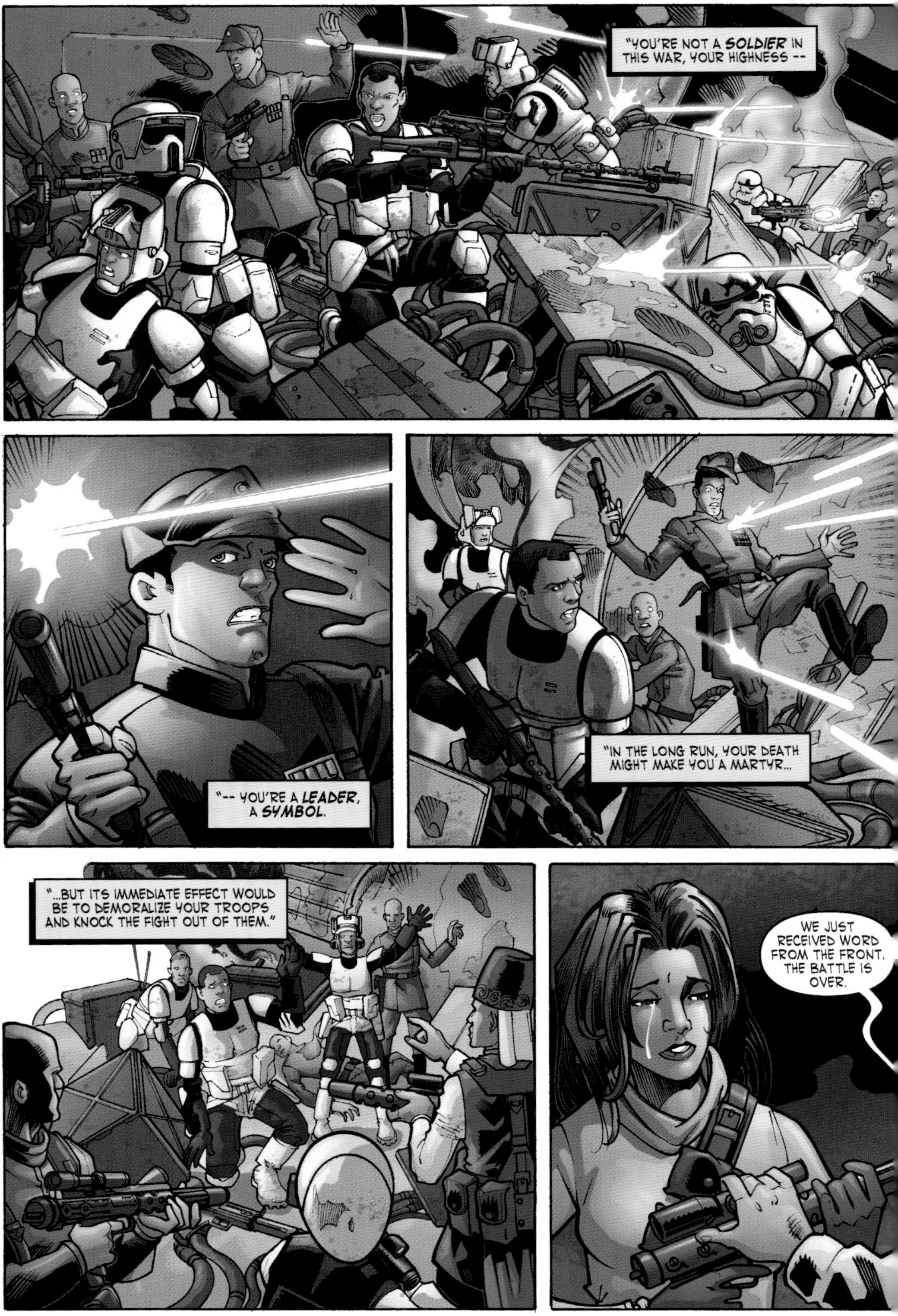
"YOU'RE NOT A SOLDIER IN THIS WAR, YOUR HIGHNESS --
"-- YOU'RE A LEADER, A SYMBOL.
"IN THE LONG RUN, YOUR DEATH MIGHT MAKE YOU A MARTYR...
"...BUT ITS IMMEDIATE EFFECT WOULD BE TO DEMORALIZE YOUR TROOPS AND KNOCK THE FIGHT OUT OF THEM."
WE JUST RECEIVED WORD FROM THE FRONT. THE BATTLE IS OVER.

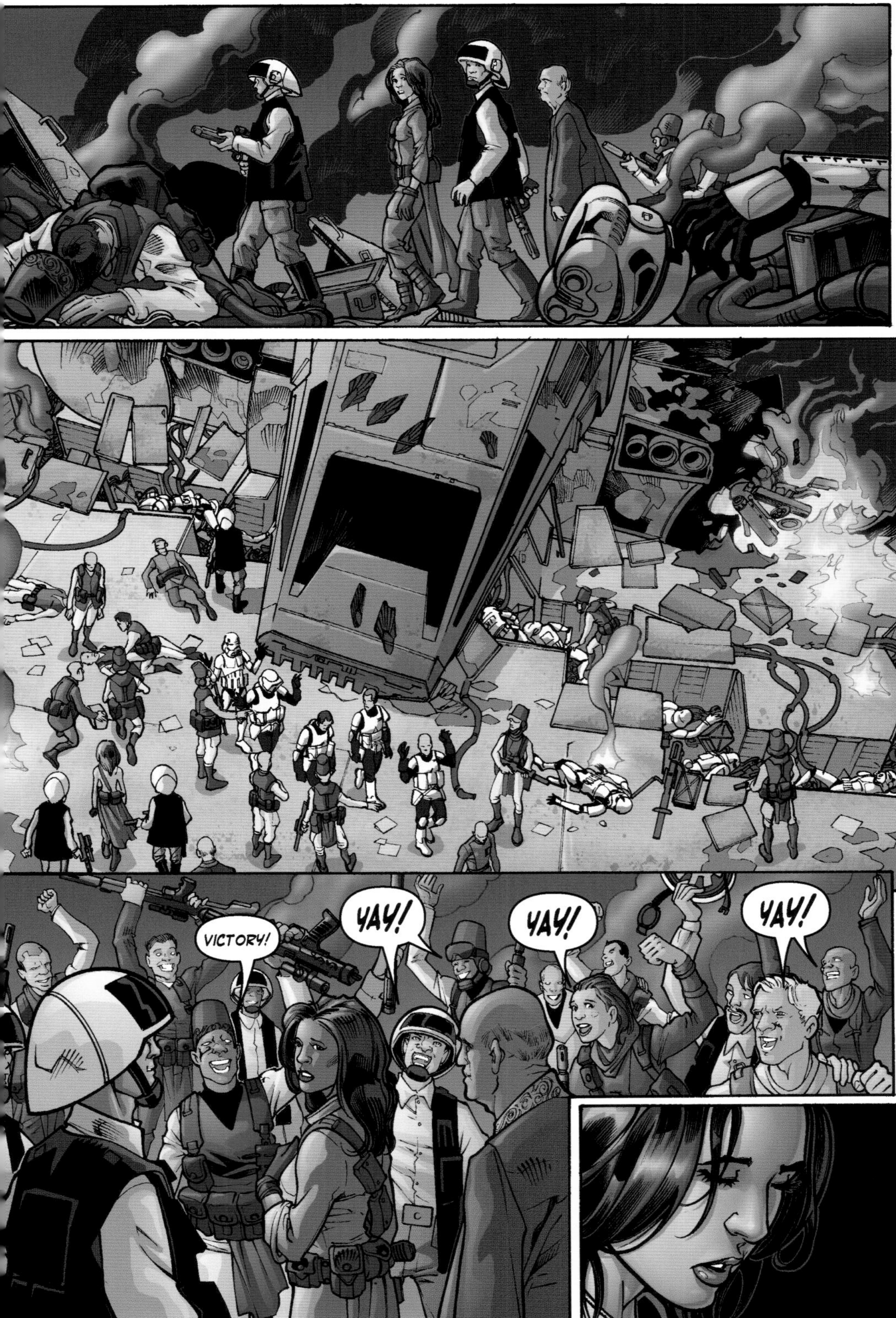
VICTORY!
YAY!
YAY!
YAY!

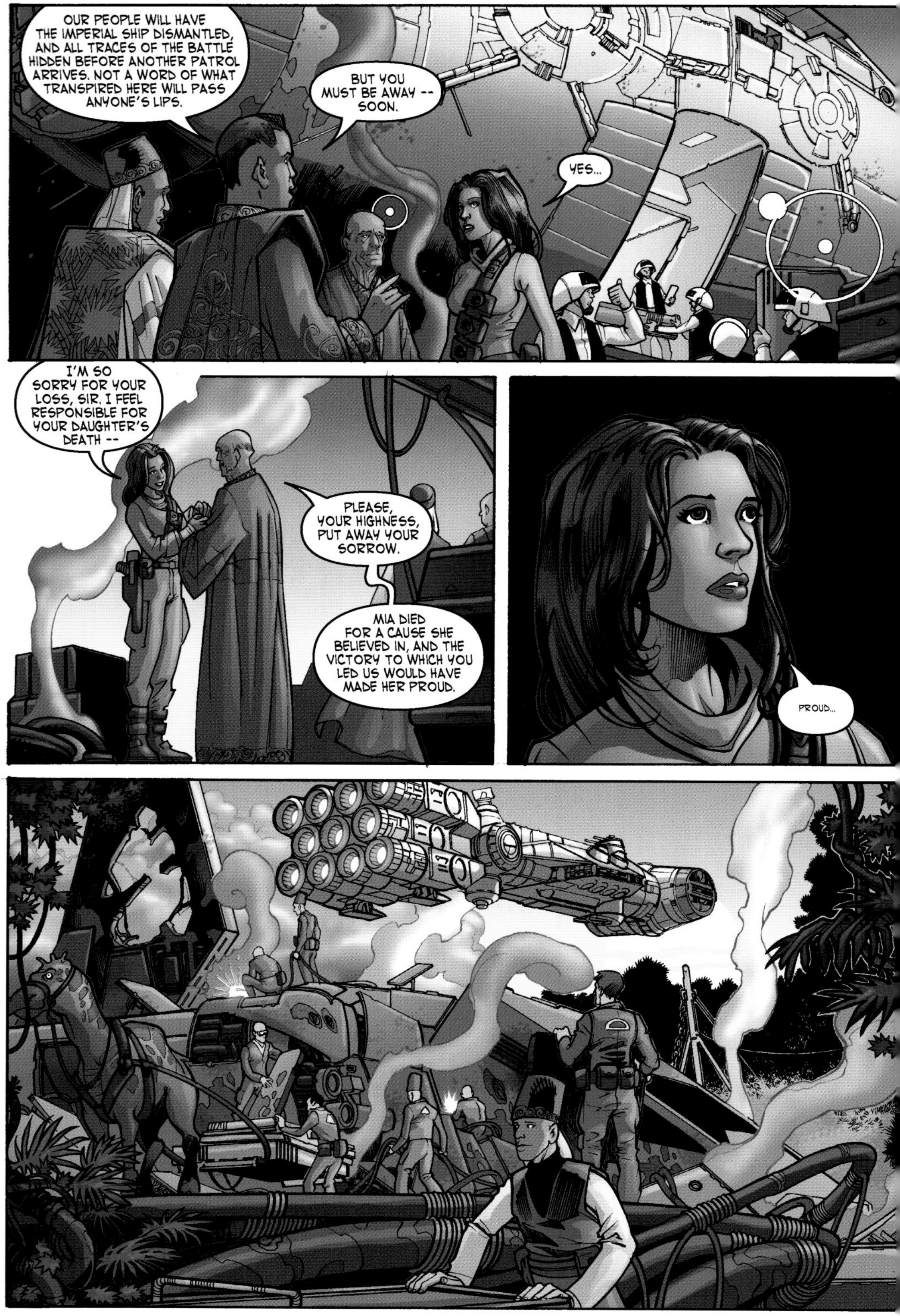
OUR PEOPLE WILL HAVE THE IMPERIAL SHIP DISMANTLED, AND ALL TRACES OF THE BATTLE HIDDEN BEFORE ANOTHER PATROL ARRIVES. NOT A WORD OF WHAT TRANSPIRED HERE WILL PASS ANYONE'S LIPS.
BUT YOU MUST BE AWAY -- SOON.
YES...
I'M SO SORRY FOR YOUR LOSS, SIR. I FEEL RESPONSIBLE FOR YOUR DAUGHTER'S DEATH --
PLEASE, YOUR HIGHNESS, PUT AWAY YOUR SORROW.
MIA DIED FOR A CAUSE SHE BELIEVED IN, AND THE VICTORY TO WHICH YOU LED US WOULD HAVE MADE HER PROUD.
PROUD...

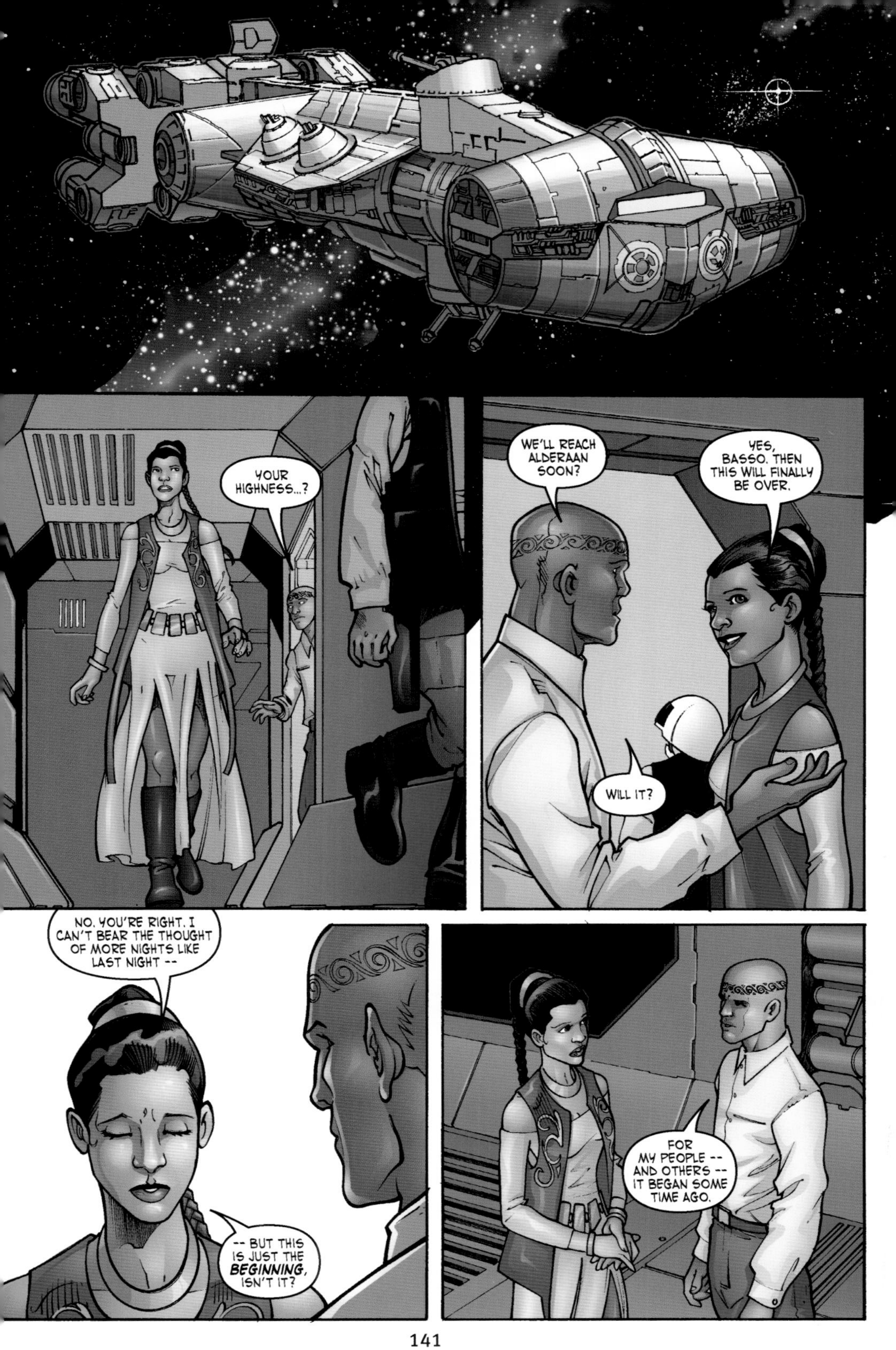
YOUR HIGHNESS...?
WE'LL REACH ALDERAAN SOON?
YES, BASSO. THEN THIS WILL FINALLY BE OVER.
WILL IT?
NO. YOU'RE RIGHT. I CAN'T BEAR THE THOUGHT OF MORE NIGHTS LIKE LAST NIGHT --
-- BUT THIS IS JUST THE *BEGINNING*, ISN'T IT?
FOR MY PEOPLE -- AND OTHERS -- IT BEGAN SOME TIME AGO.

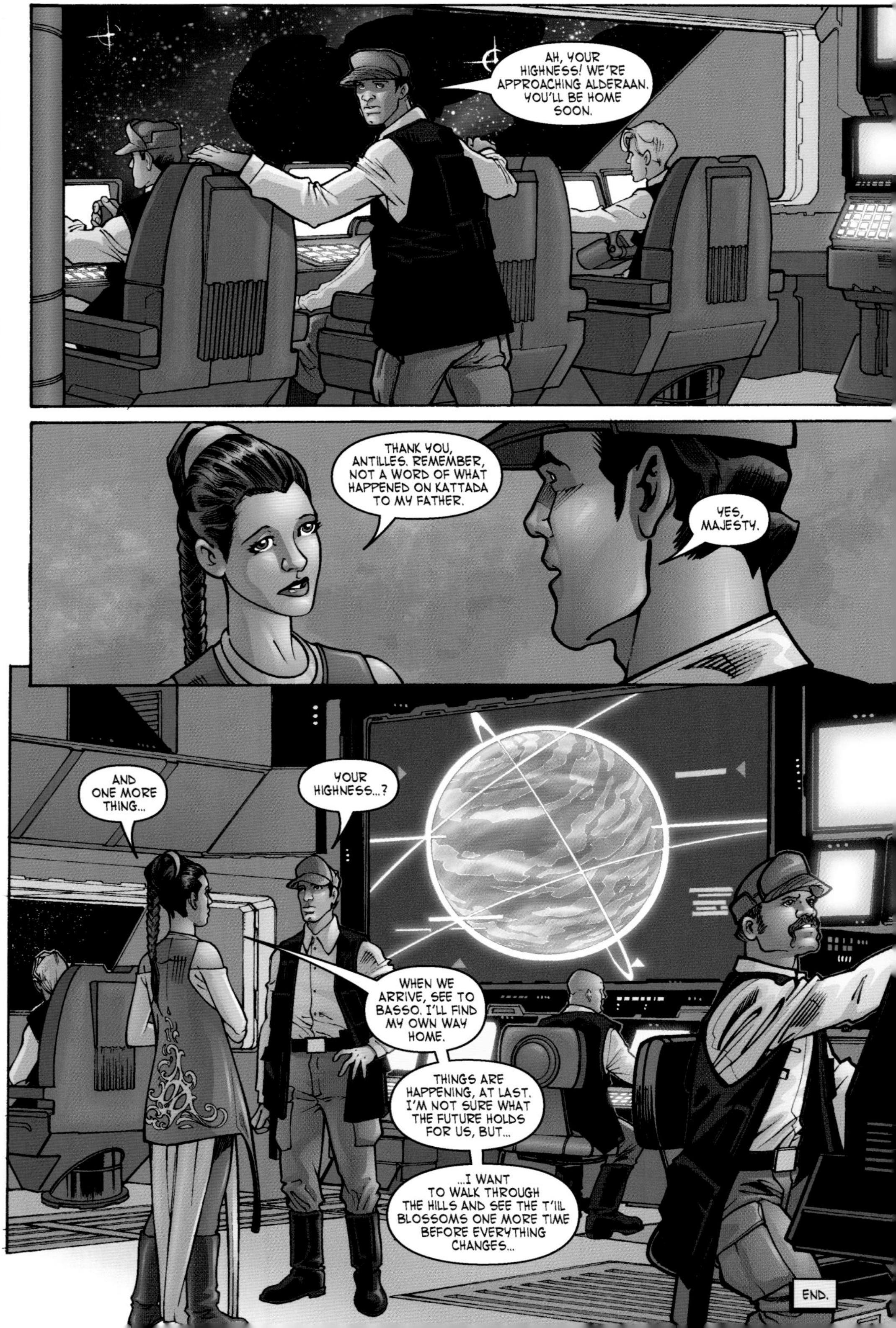
AH, YOUR HIGHNESS! WE'RE APPROACHING ALDERAAN. YOU'LL BE HOME SOON.
THANK YOU, ANTILLES. REMEMBER, NOT A WORD OF WHAT HAPPENED ON KATTADA TO MY FATHER.
YES, MAJESTY.
AND ONE MORE THING...
YOUR HIGHNESS...?
WHEN WE ARRIVE, SEE TO BASSO. I'LL FIND MY OWN WAY HOME.
THINGS ARE HAPPENING, AT LAST. I'M NOT SURE WHAT THE FUTURE HOLDS FOR US, BUT...
...I WANT TO WALK THROUGH THE HILLS AND SEE THE T'IIL BLOSSOMS ONE MORE TIME BEFORE EVERYTHING CHANGES...
END.

The Short, Happy Life of Roons Sewell | Illustration by Kilian Plunkett

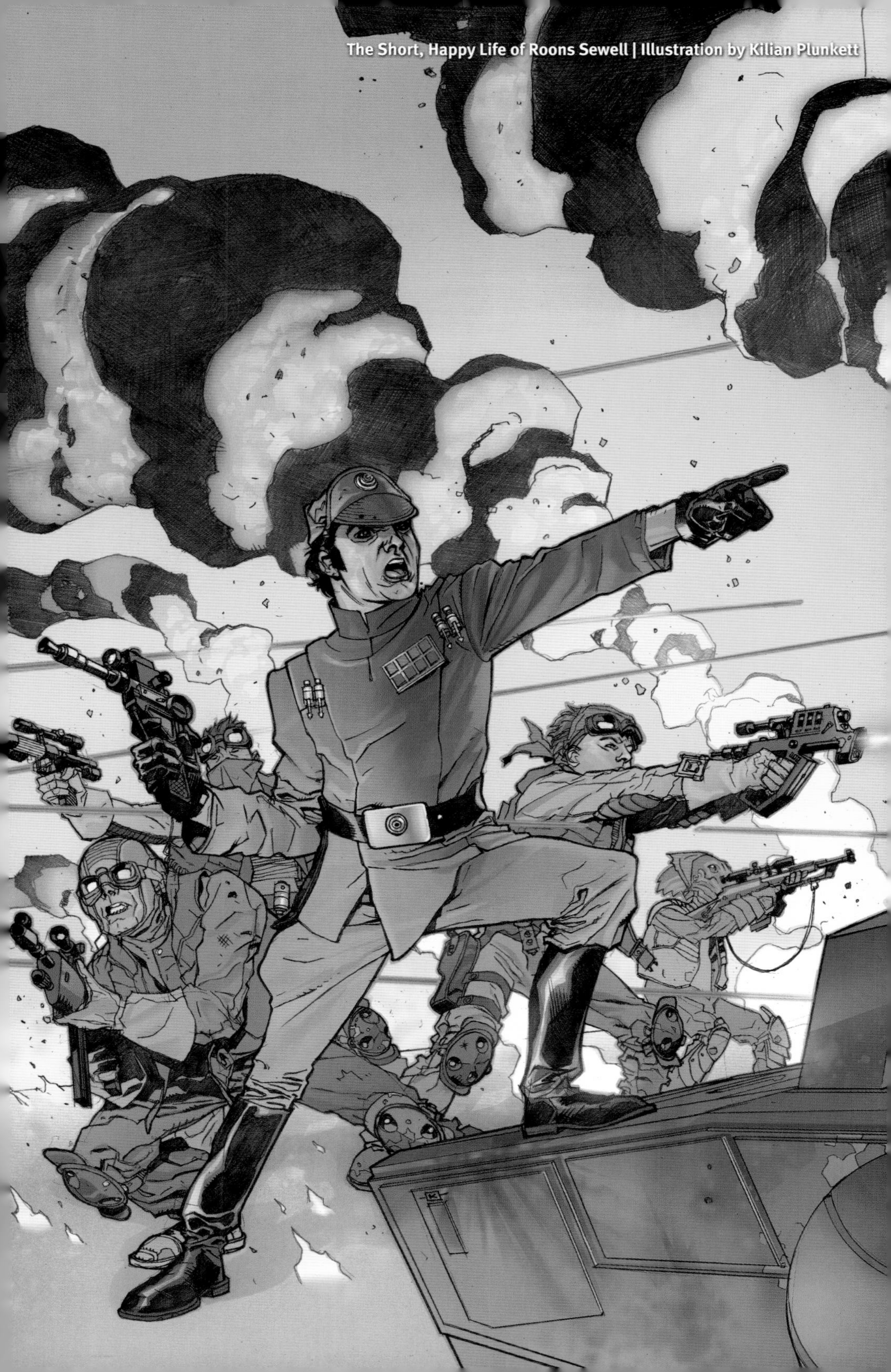

JUST PRIOR TO THE BATTLE OF YAVIN . . .

script by Paul Chadwick
art by Tomás Giorello
colors by Joe Wayne
lettering by Sno Cone Studios

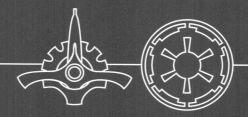

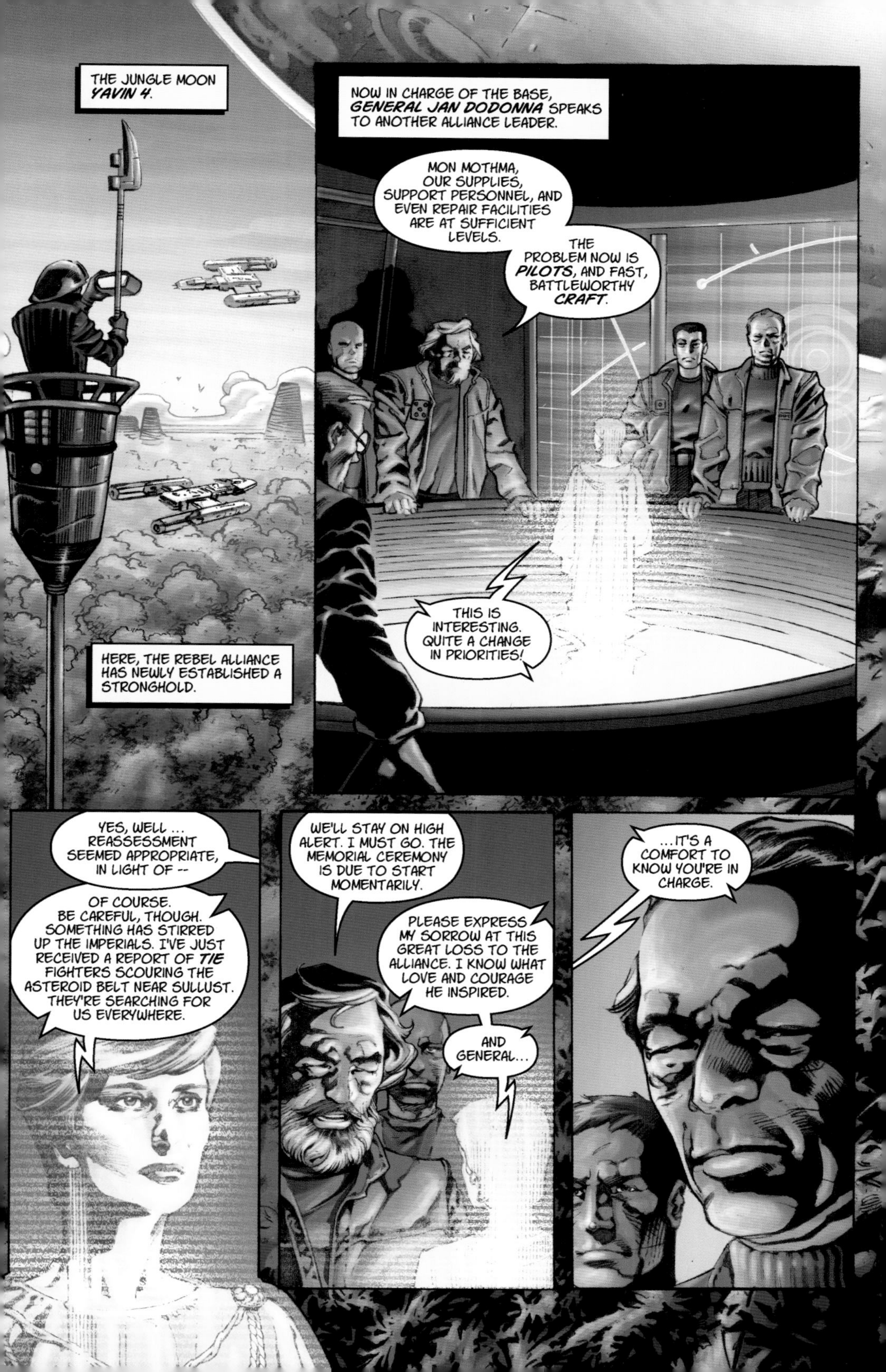
THE JUNGLE MOON YAVIN 4.
HERE, THE REBEL ALLIANCE HAS NEWLY ESTABLISHED A STRONGHOLD.
NOW IN CHARGE OF THE BASE, GENERAL JAN DODONNA SPEAKS TO ANOTHER ALLIANCE LEADER.
MON MOTHMA, OUR SUPPLIES, SUPPORT PERSONNEL, AND EVEN REPAIR FACILITIES ARE AT SUFFICIENT LEVELS.
THE PROBLEM NOW IS PILOTS, AND FAST, BATTLEWORTHY CRAFT.
THIS IS INTERESTING. QUITE A CHANGE IN PRIORITIES!
YES, WELL ... REASSESSMENT SEEMED APPROPRIATE, IN LIGHT OF --
OF COURSE. BE CAREFUL, THOUGH. SOMETHING HAS STIRRED UP THE IMPERIALS. I'VE JUST RECEIVED A REPORT OF TIE FIGHTERS SCOURING THE ASTEROID BELT NEAR SULLUST. THEY'RE SEARCHING FOR US EVERYWHERE.
WE'LL STAY ON HIGH ALERT. I MUST GO. THE MEMORIAL CEREMONY IS DUE TO START MOMENTARILY.
PLEASE EXPRESS MY SORROW AT THIS GREAT LOSS TO THE ALLIANCE. I KNOW WHAT LOVE AND COURAGE HE INSPIRED.
AND GENERAL...
...IT'S A COMFORT TO KNOW YOU'RE IN CHARGE.

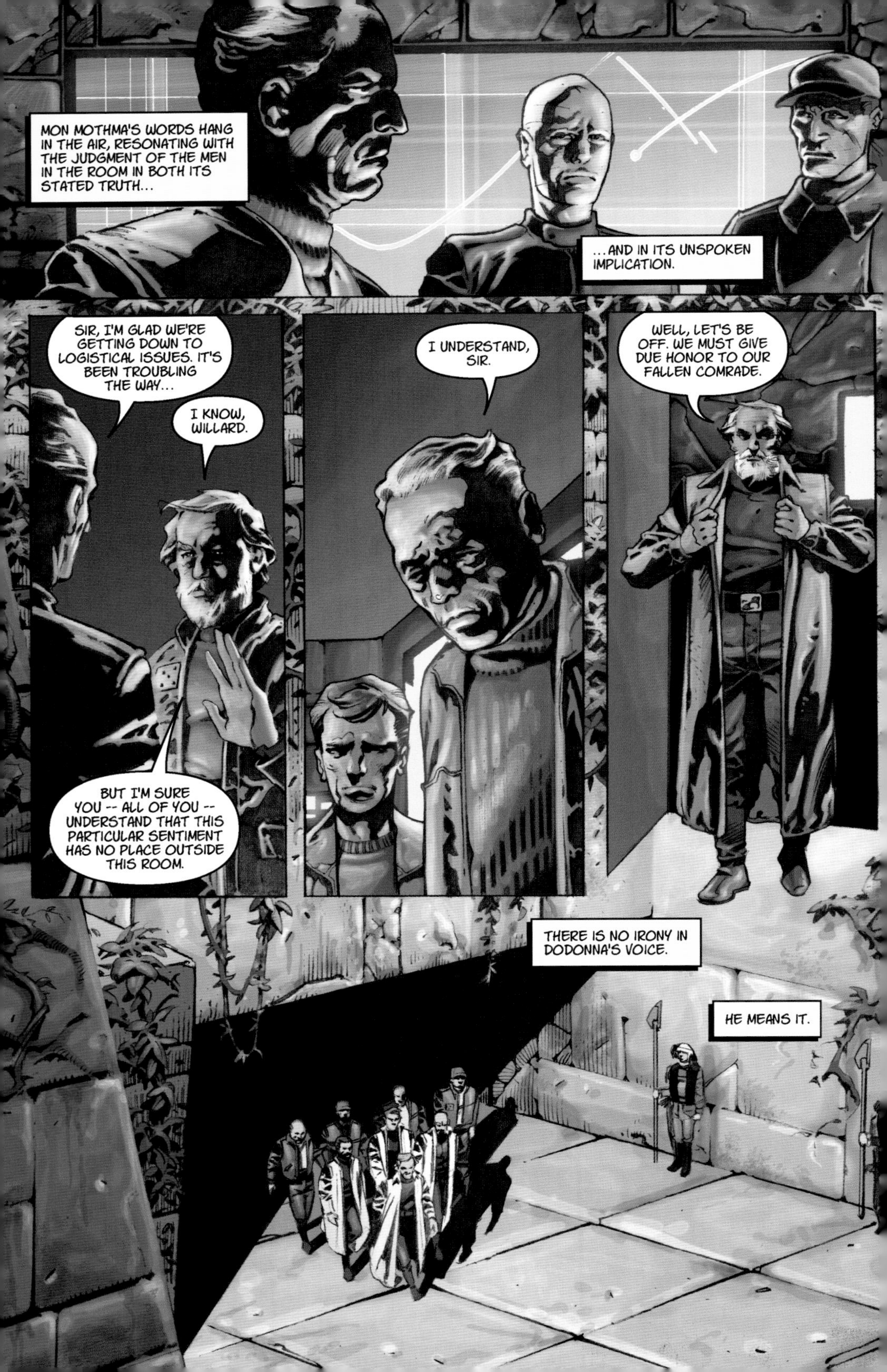
MON MOTHMA'S WORDS HANG IN THE AIR, RESONATING WITH THE JUDGMENT OF THE MEN IN THE ROOM IN BOTH ITS STATED TRUTH...
...AND IN ITS UNSPOKEN IMPLICATION.
SIR, I'M GLAD WE'RE GETTING DOWN TO LOGISTICAL ISSUES. IT'S BEEN TROUBLING THE WAY...
I KNOW, WILLARD.
BUT I'M SURE YOU -- ALL OF YOU -- UNDERSTAND THAT THIS PARTICULAR SENTIMENT HAS NO PLACE OUTSIDE THIS ROOM.
I UNDERSTAND, SIR.
WELL, LET'S BE OFF. WE MUST GIVE DUE HONOR TO OUR FALLEN COMRADE.
THERE IS NO IRONY IN DODONNA'S VOICE.
HE MEANS IT.

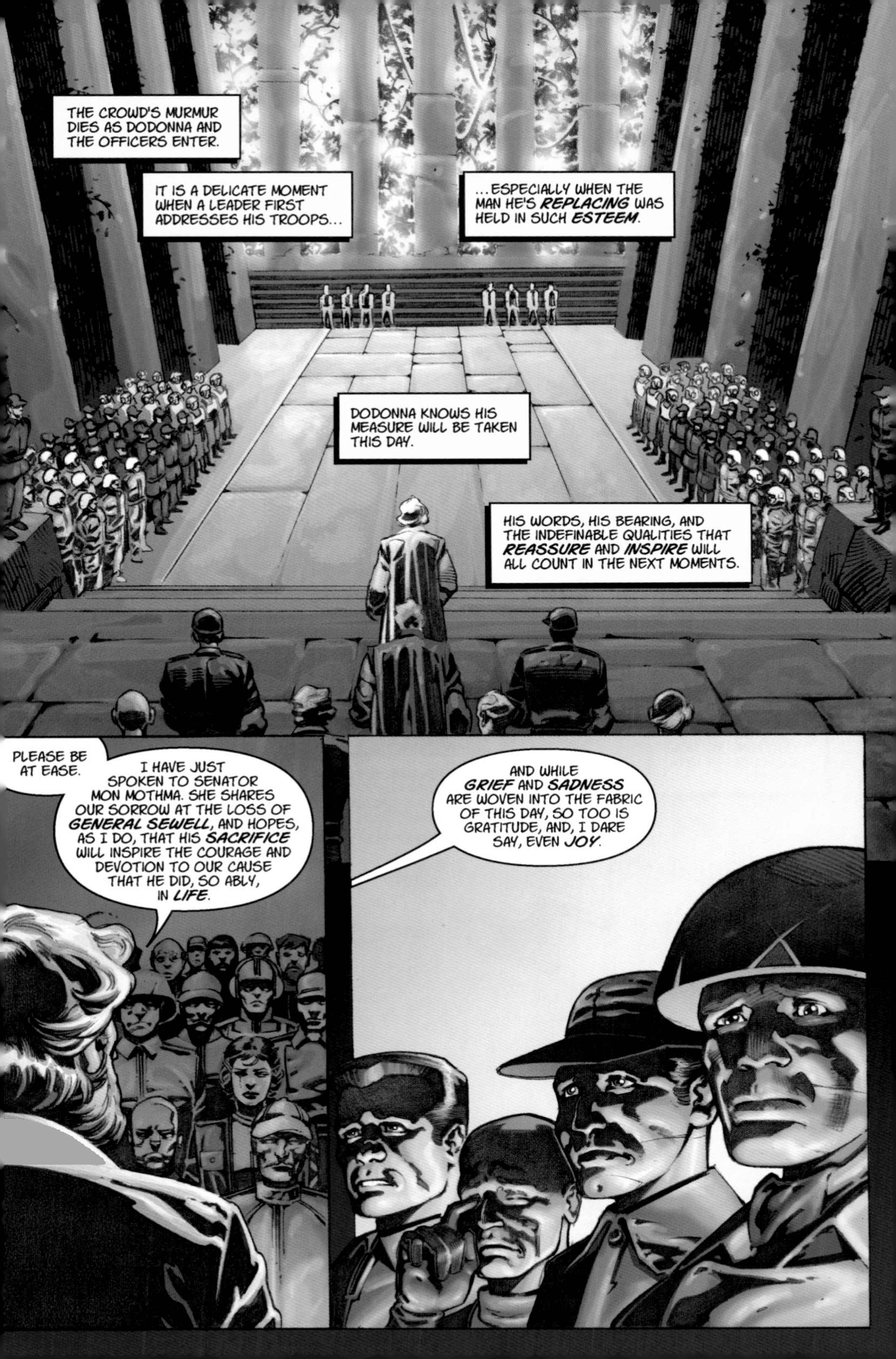

THE CROWD'S MURMUR DIES AS DODONNA AND THE OFFICERS ENTER.
IT IS A DELICATE MOMENT WHEN A LEADER FIRST ADDRESSES HIS TROOPS...
...ESPECIALLY WHEN THE MAN HE'S REPLACING WAS HELD IN SUCH ESTEEM.
DODONNA KNOWS HIS MEASURE WILL BE TAKEN THIS DAY.
HIS WORDS, HIS BEARING, AND THE INDEFINABLE QUALITIES THAT REASSURE AND INSPIRE WILL ALL COUNT IN THE NEXT MOMENTS.
PLEASE BE AT EASE.
I HAVE JUST SPOKEN TO SENATOR MON MOTHMA. SHE SHARES OUR SORROW AT THE LOSS OF GENERAL SEWELL, AND HOPES, AS I DO, THAT HIS SACRIFICE WILL INSPIRE THE COURAGE AND DEVOTION TO OUR CAUSE THAT HE DID, SO ABLY, IN LIFE.
AND WHILE GRIEF AND SADNESS ARE WOVEN INTO THE FABRIC OF THIS DAY, SO TOO IS GRATITUDE, AND, I DARE SAY, EVEN JOY.

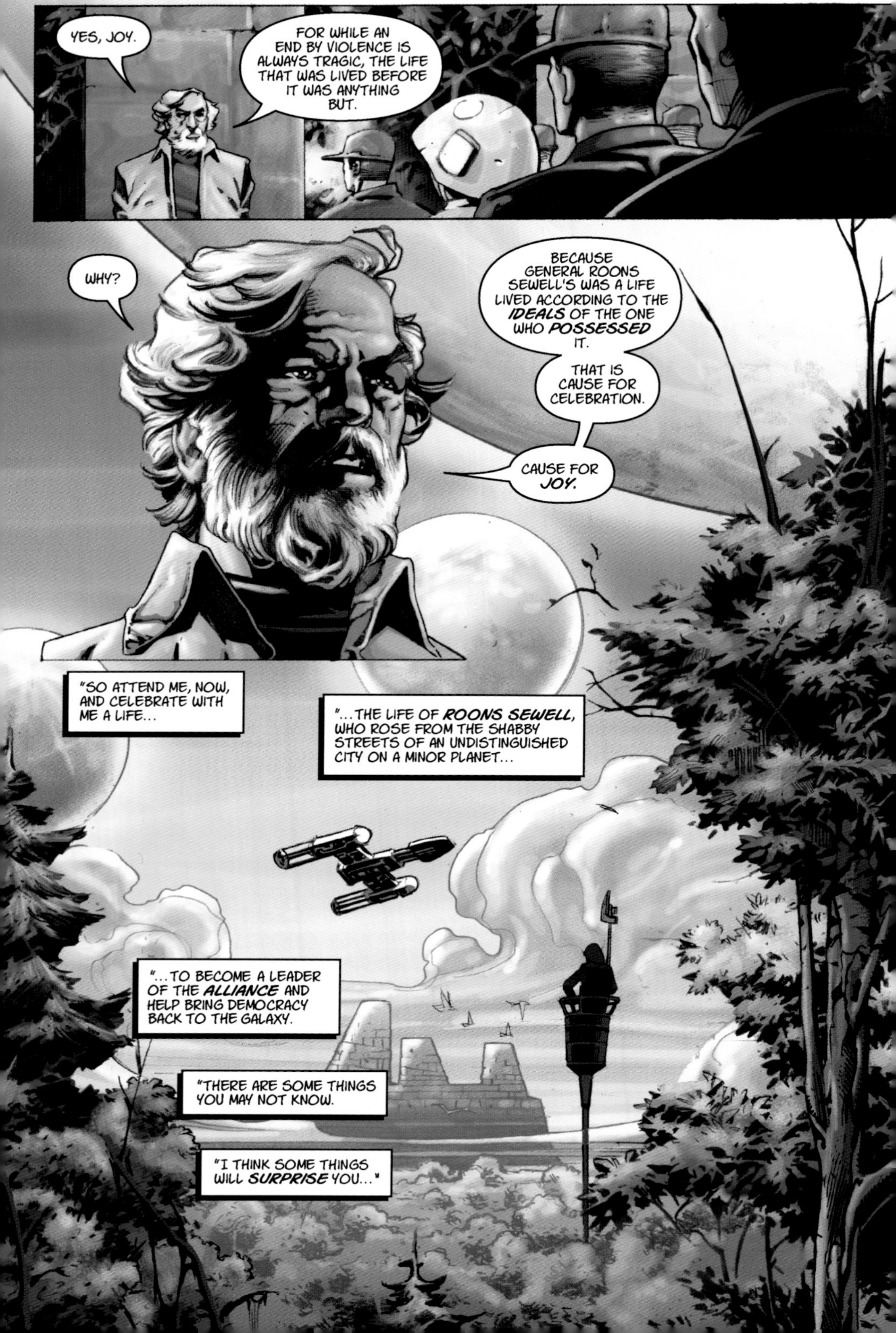
YES, JOY.
FOR WHILE AN END BY VIOLENCE IS ALWAYS TRAGIC, THE LIFE THAT WAS LIVED BEFORE IT WAS ANYTHING BUT.
WHY?
BECAUSE GENERAL ROONS SEWELL'S WAS A LIFE LIVED ACCORDING TO THE IDEALS OF THE ONE WHO POSSESSED IT.
THAT IS CAUSE FOR CELEBRATION.
CAUSE FOR JOY.
"SO ATTEND ME, NOW, AND CELEBRATE WITH ME A LIFE...
"...THE LIFE OF ROONS SEWELL, WHO ROSE FROM THE SHABBY STREETS OF AN UNDISTINGUISHED CITY ON A MINOR PLANET...
"...TO BECOME A LEADER OF THE ALLIANCE AND HELP BRING DEMOCRACY BACK TO THE GALAXY.
"THERE ARE SOME THINGS YOU MAY NOT KNOW.
"I THINK SOME THINGS WILL SURPRISE YOU..."

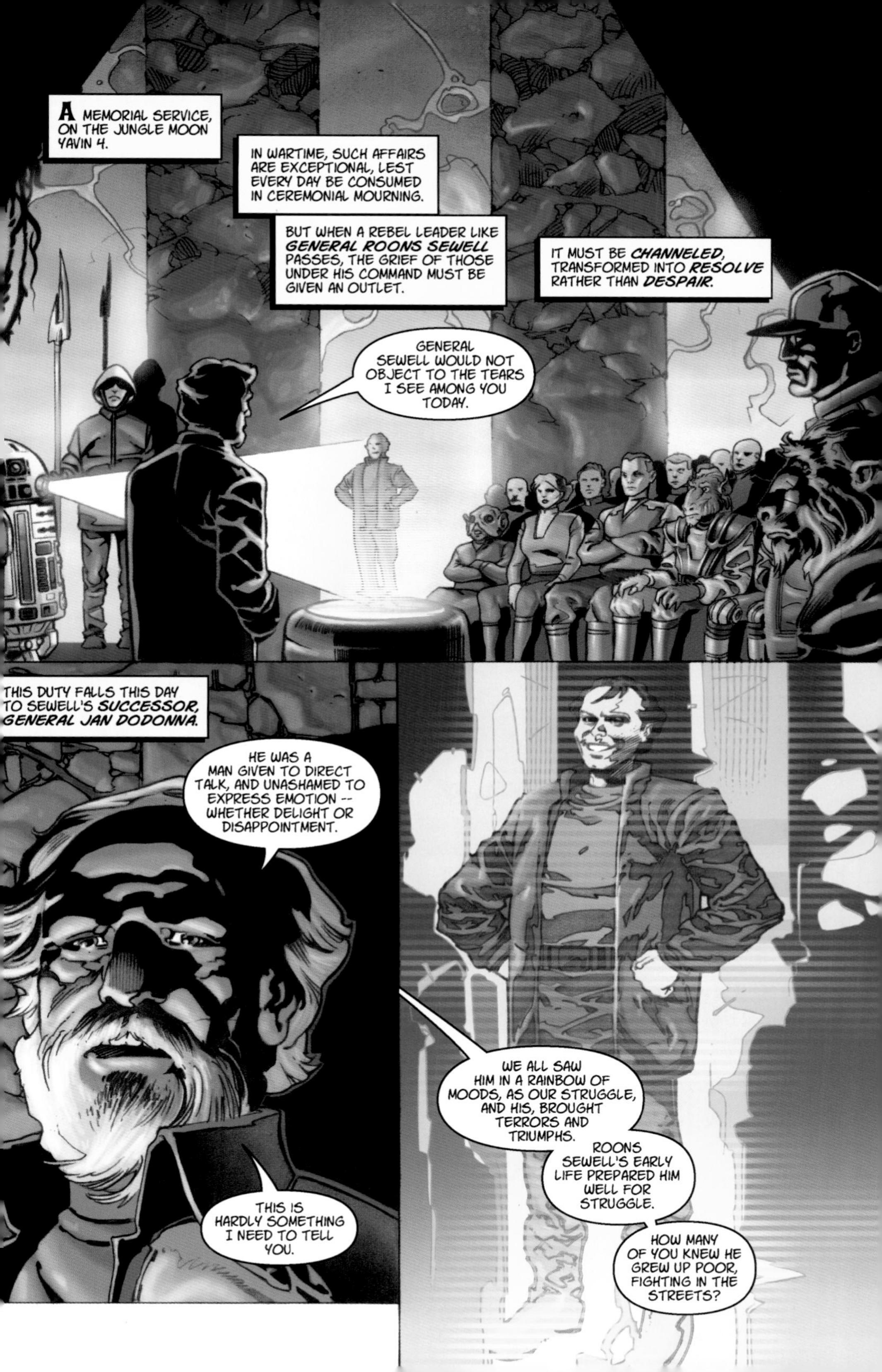
A MEMORIAL SERVICE, ON THE JUNGLE MOON YAVIN 4.
IN WARTIME, SUCH AFFAIRS ARE EXCEPTIONAL, LEST EVERY DAY BE CONSUMED IN CEREMONIAL MOURNING.
BUT WHEN A REBEL LEADER LIKE GENERAL ROONS SEWELL PASSES, THE GRIEF OF THOSE UNDER HIS COMMAND MUST BE GIVEN AN OUTLET.
IT MUST BE CHANNELED, TRANSFORMED INTO RESOLVE RATHER THAN DESPAIR.
GENERAL SEWELL WOULD NOT OBJECT TO THE TEARS I SEE AMONG YOU TODAY.
THIS DUTY FALLS THIS DAY TO SEWELL'S SUCCESSOR, GENERAL JAN DODONNA.
HE WAS A MAN GIVEN TO DIRECT TALK, AND UNASHAMED TO EXPRESS EMOTION -- WHETHER DELIGHT OR DISAPPOINTMENT.
THIS IS HARDLY SOMETHING I NEED TO TELL YOU.
WE ALL SAW HIM IN A RAINBOW OF MOODS, AS OUR STRUGGLE, AND HIS, BROUGHT TERRORS AND TRIUMPHS.
ROONS SEWELL'S EARLY LIFE PREPARED HIM WELL FOR STRUGGLE.
HOW MANY OF YOU KNEW HE GREW UP POOR, FIGHTING IN THE STREETS?

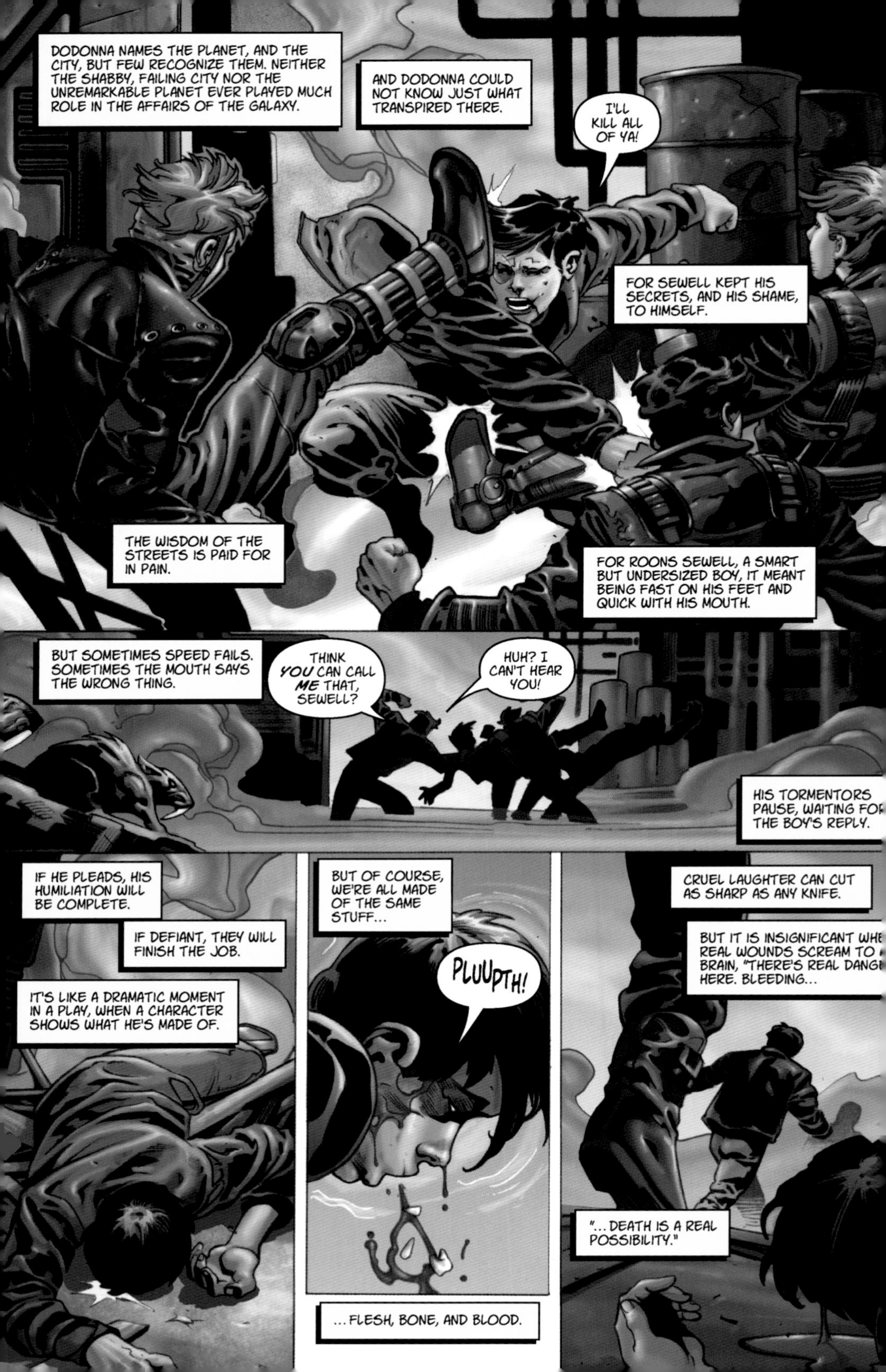
DODONNA NAMES THE PLANET, AND THE CITY, BUT FEW RECOGNIZE THEM. NEITHER THE SHABBY, FAILING CITY NOR THE UNREMARKABLE PLANET EVER PLAYED MUCH ROLE IN THE AFFAIRS OF THE GALAXY.
AND DODONNA COULD NOT KNOW JUST WHAT TRANSPIRED THERE.
I'LL KILL ALL OF YA!
FOR SEWELL KEPT HIS SECRETS, AND HIS SHAME, TO HIMSELF.
THE WISDOM OF THE STREETS IS PAID FOR IN PAIN.
FOR ROONS SEWELL, A SMART BUT UNDERSIZED BOY, IT MEANT BEING FAST ON HIS FEET AND QUICK WITH HIS MOUTH.
BUT SOMETIMES SPEED FAILS. SOMETIMES THE MOUTH SAYS THE WRONG THING.
THINK *YOU* CAN CALL *ME* THAT, SEWELL?
HUH? I CAN'T HEAR YOU!
HIS TORMENTORS PAUSE, WAITING FOR THE BOY'S REPLY.
IF HE PLEADS, HIS HUMILIATION WILL BE COMPLETE.
IF DEFIANT, THEY WILL FINISH THE JOB.
IT'S LIKE A DRAMATIC MOMENT IN A PLAY, WHEN A CHARACTER SHOWS WHAT HE'S MADE OF.
BUT OF COURSE, WE'RE ALL MADE OF THE SAME STUFF...
PLUUPTH!
...FLESH, BONE, AND BLOOD.
CRUEL LAUGHTER CAN CUT AS SHARP AS ANY KNIFE.
BUT IT IS INSIGNIFICANT WHE REAL WOUNDS SCREAM TO BRAIN, "THERE'S REAL DANG HERE. BLEEDING...
"...DEATH IS A REAL POSSIBILITY."

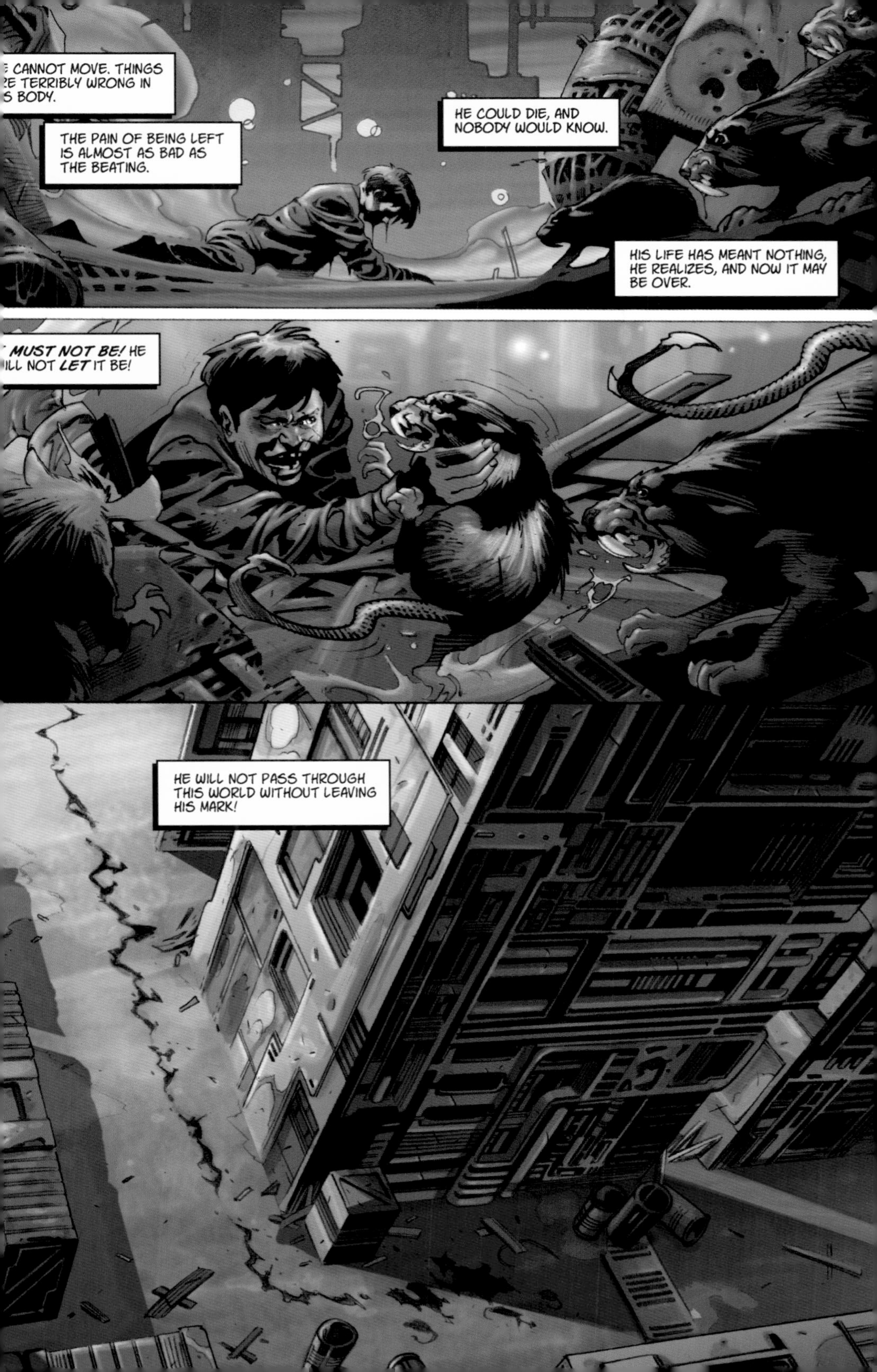
E CANNOT MOVE. THINGS
RE TERRIBLY WRONG IN
S BODY.
THE PAIN OF BEING LEFT
IS ALMOST AS BAD AS
THE BEATING.
HE COULD DIE, AND
NOBODY WOULD KNOW.
HIS LIFE HAS MEANT NOTHING,
HE REALIZES, AND NOW IT MAY
BE OVER.
MUST NOT BE! HE
ILL NOT LET IT BE!
HE WILL NOT PASS THROUGH
THIS WORLD WITHOUT LEAVING
HIS MARK!

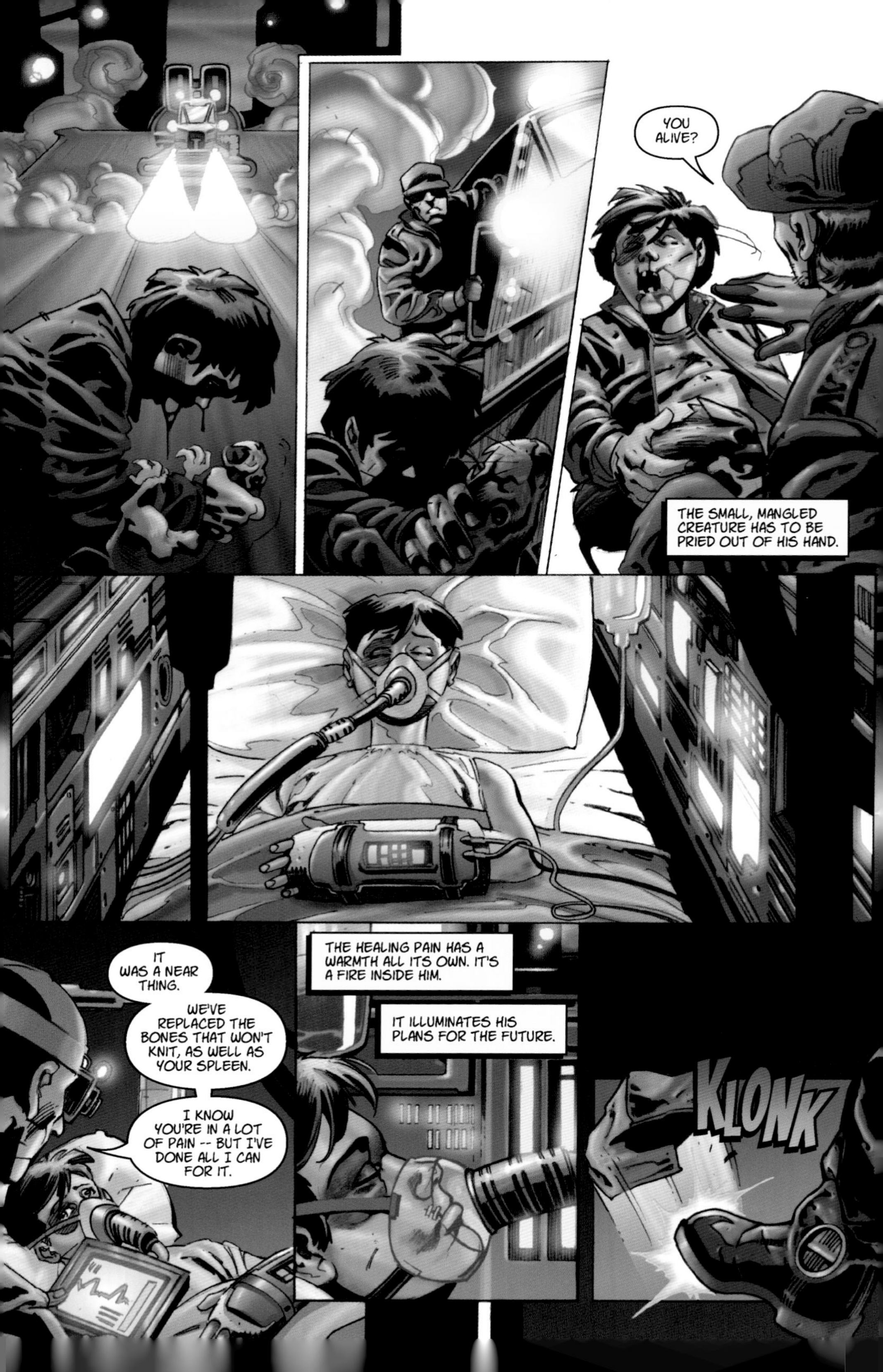
YOU ALIVE?
THE SMALL, MANGLED CREATURE HAS TO BE PRIED OUT OF HIS HAND.
IT WAS A NEAR THING.
WE'VE REPLACED THE BONES THAT WON'T KNIT, AS WELL AS YOUR SPLEEN.
I KNOW YOU'RE IN A LOT OF PAIN -- BUT I'VE DONE ALL I CAN FOR IT.
THE HEALING PAIN HAS A WARMTH ALL ITS OWN. IT'S A FIRE INSIDE HIM.
IT ILLUMINATES HIS PLANS FOR THE FUTURE.
KLONK

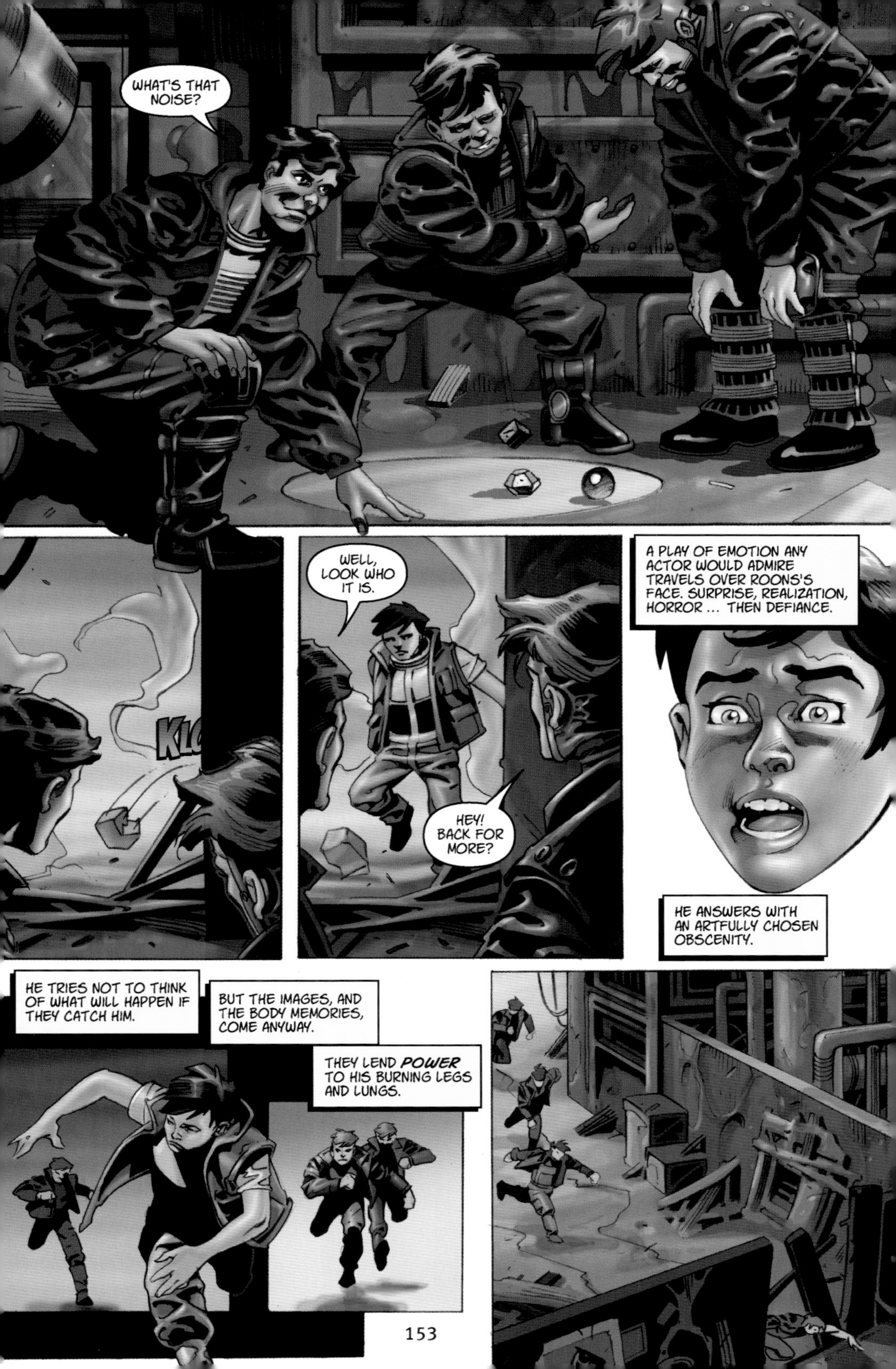
WHAT'S THAT NOISE?
WELL, LOOK WHO IT IS.
HEY! BACK FOR MORE?
A PLAY OF EMOTION ANY ACTOR WOULD ADMIRE TRAVELS OVER ROONS'S FACE. SURPRISE, REALIZATION, HORROR ... THEN DEFIANCE.
HE ANSWERS WITH AN ARTFULLY CHOSEN OBSCENITY.
HE TRIES NOT TO THINK OF WHAT WILL HAPPEN IF THEY CATCH HIM.
BUT THE IMAGES, AND THE BODY MEMORIES, COME ANYWAY.
THEY LEND *POWER* TO HIS BURNING LEGS AND LUNGS.

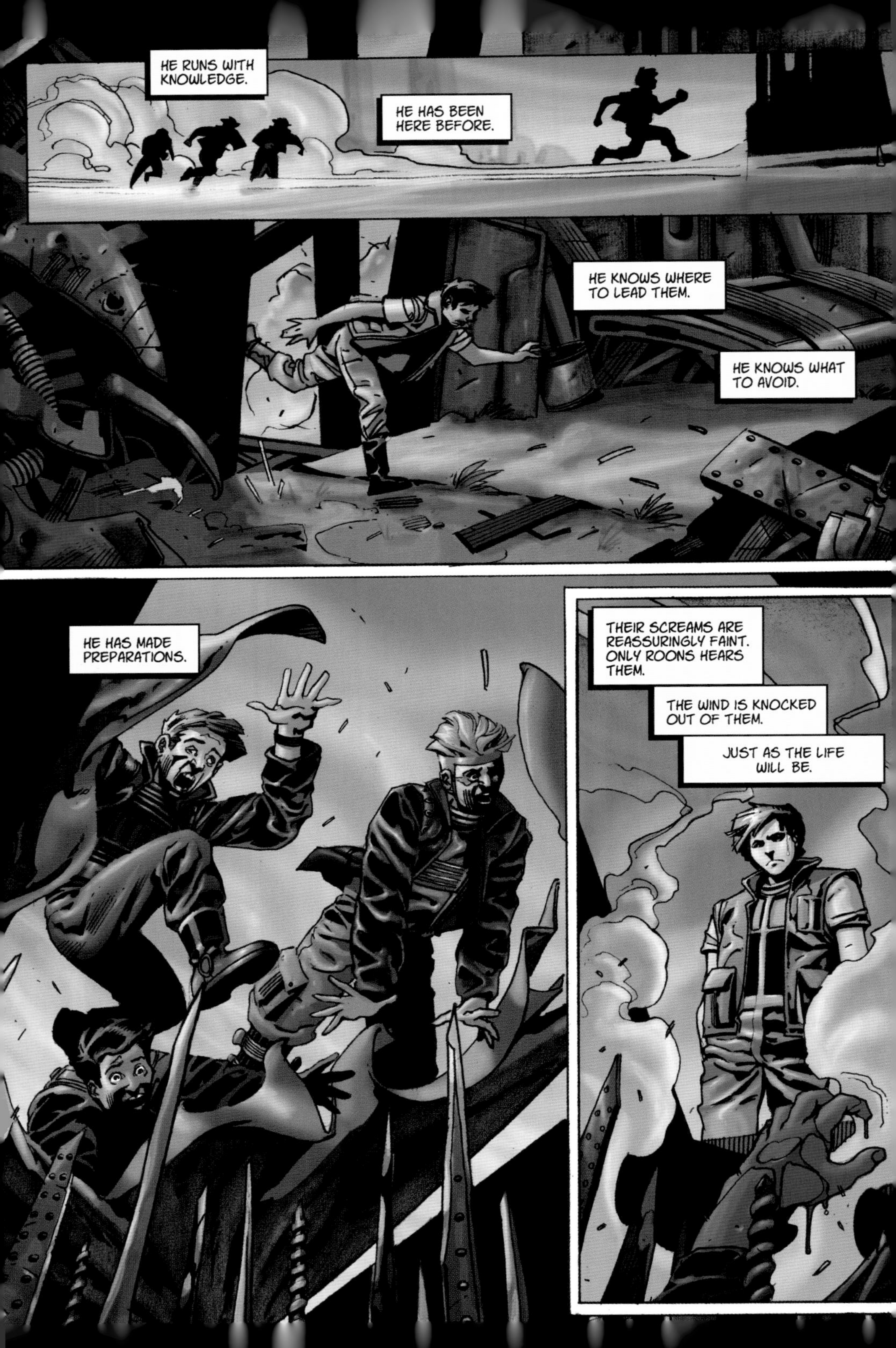
HE RUNS WITH KNOWLEDGE.
HE HAS BEEN HERE BEFORE.
HE KNOWS WHERE TO LEAD THEM.
HE KNOWS WHAT TO AVOID.
HE HAS MADE PREPARATIONS.
THEIR SCREAMS ARE REASSURINGLY FAINT. ONLY ROONS HEARS THEM.
THE WIND IS KNOCKED OUT OF THEM.
JUST AS THE LIFE WILL BE.

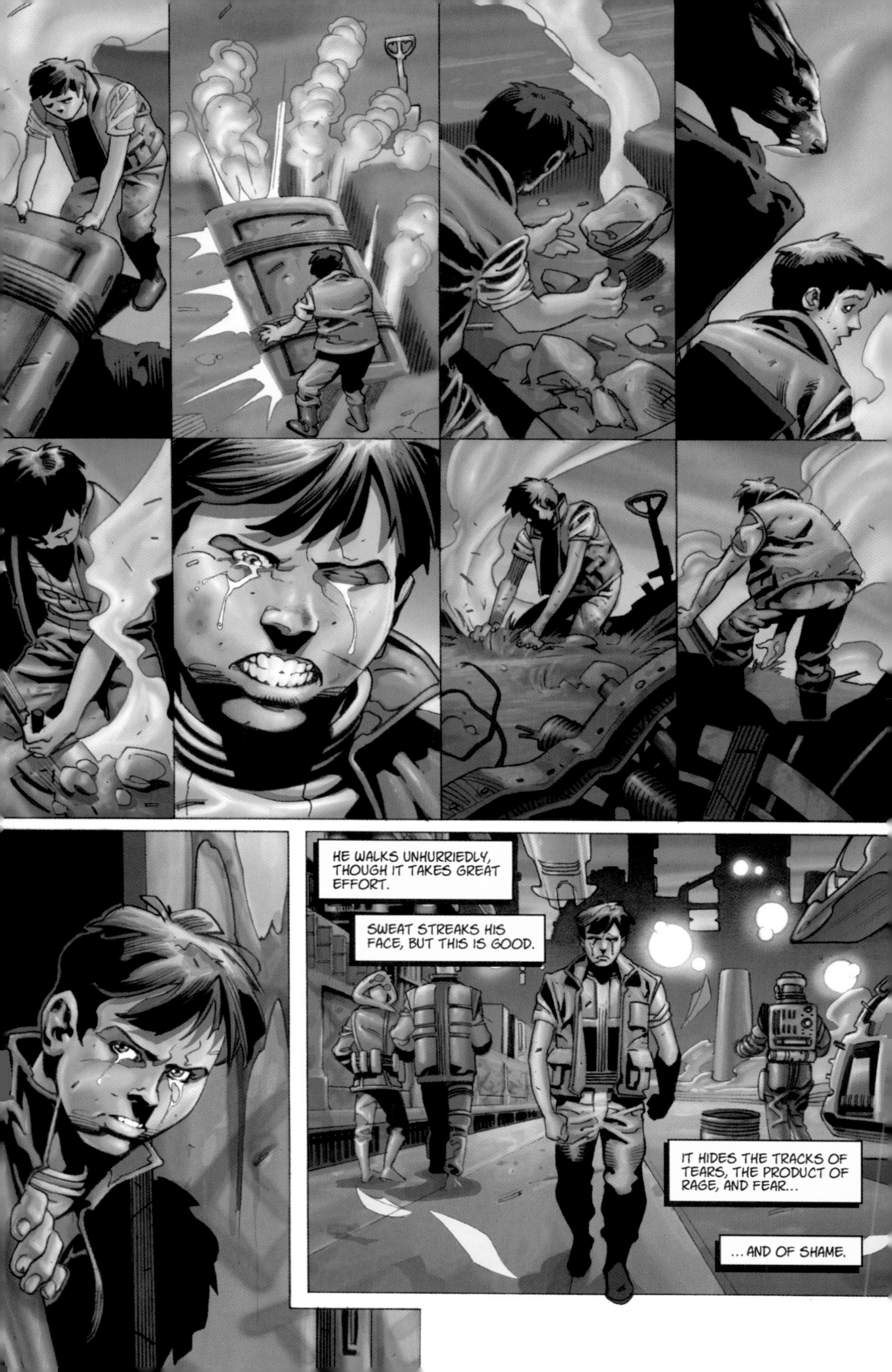
HE WALKS UNHURRIEDLY, THOUGH IT TAKES GREAT EFFORT.
SWEAT STREAKS HIS FACE, BUT THIS IS GOOD.
IT HIDES THE TRACKS OF TEARS, THE PRODUCT OF RAGE, AND FEAR...
...AND OF SHAME.

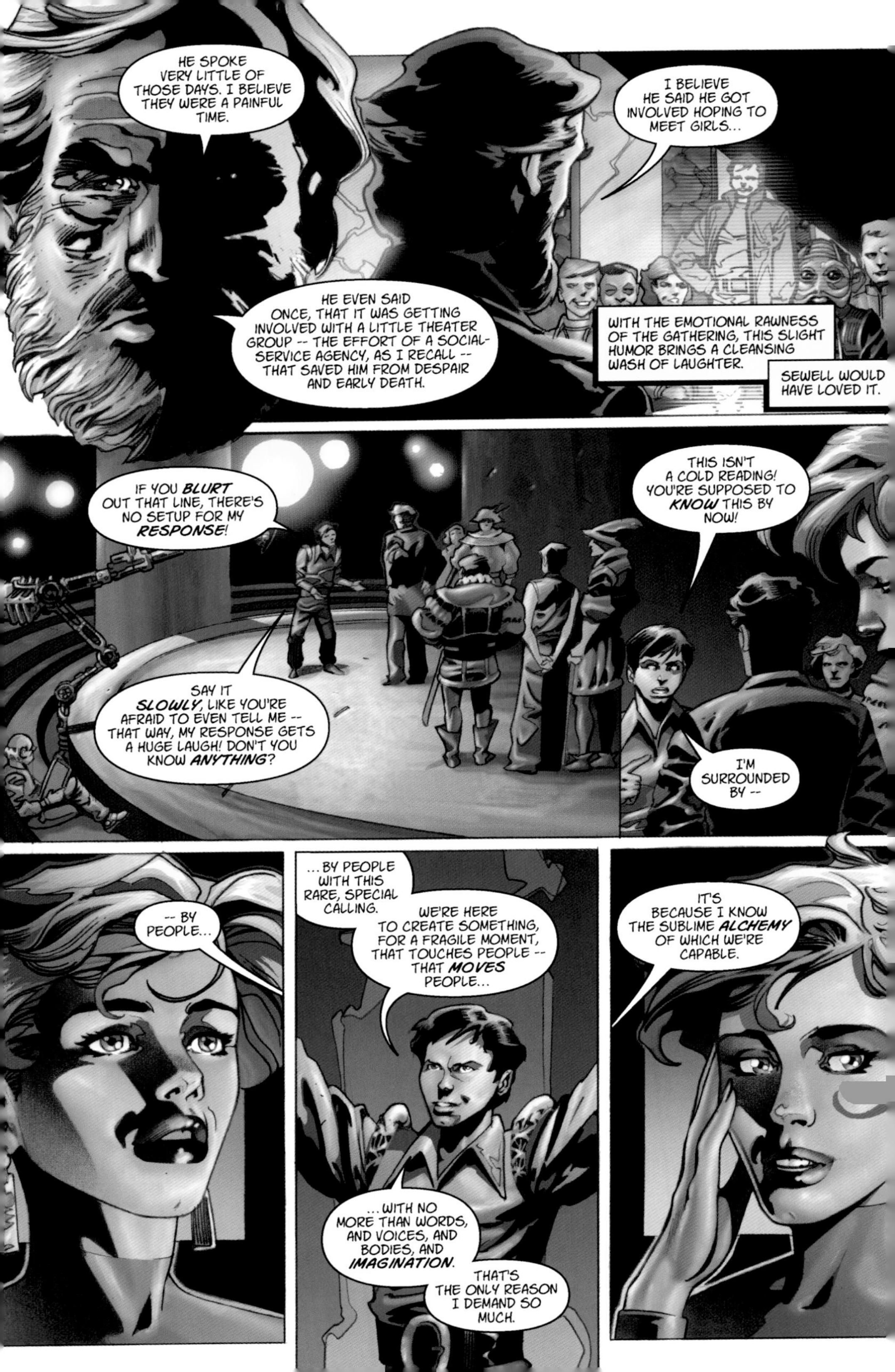

HE SPOKE VERY LITTLE OF THOSE DAYS. I BELIEVE THEY WERE A PAINFUL TIME.
I BELIEVE HE SAID HE GOT INVOLVED HOPING TO MEET GIRLS...
HE EVEN SAID ONCE, THAT IT WAS GETTING INVOLVED WITH A LITTLE THEATER GROUP -- THE EFFORT OF A SOCIAL-SERVICE AGENCY, AS I RECALL -- THAT SAVED HIM FROM DESPAIR AND EARLY DEATH.
WITH THE EMOTIONAL RAWNESS OF THE GATHERING, THIS SLIGHT HUMOR BRINGS A CLEANSING WASH OF LAUGHTER.
SEWELL WOULD HAVE LOVED IT.
IF YOU BLURT OUT THAT LINE, THERE'S NO SETUP FOR MY RESPONSE!
SAY IT SLOWLY, LIKE YOU'RE AFRAID TO EVEN TELL ME -- THAT WAY, MY RESPONSE GETS A HUGE LAUGH! DON'T YOU KNOW ANYTHING?
THIS ISN'T A COLD READING! YOU'RE SUPPOSED TO KNOW THIS BY NOW!
I'M SURROUNDED BY --
-- BY PEOPLE...
...BY PEOPLE WITH THIS RARE, SPECIAL CALLING.
WE'RE HERE TO CREATE SOMETHING, FOR A FRAGILE MOMENT, THAT TOUCHES PEOPLE -- THAT MOVES PEOPLE...
...WITH NO MORE THAN WORDS, AND VOICES, AND BODIES, AND IMAGINATION.
THAT'S THE ONLY REASON I DEMAND SO MUCH.
IT'S BECAUSE I KNOW THE SUBLIME ALCHEMY OF WHICH WE'RE CAPABLE.

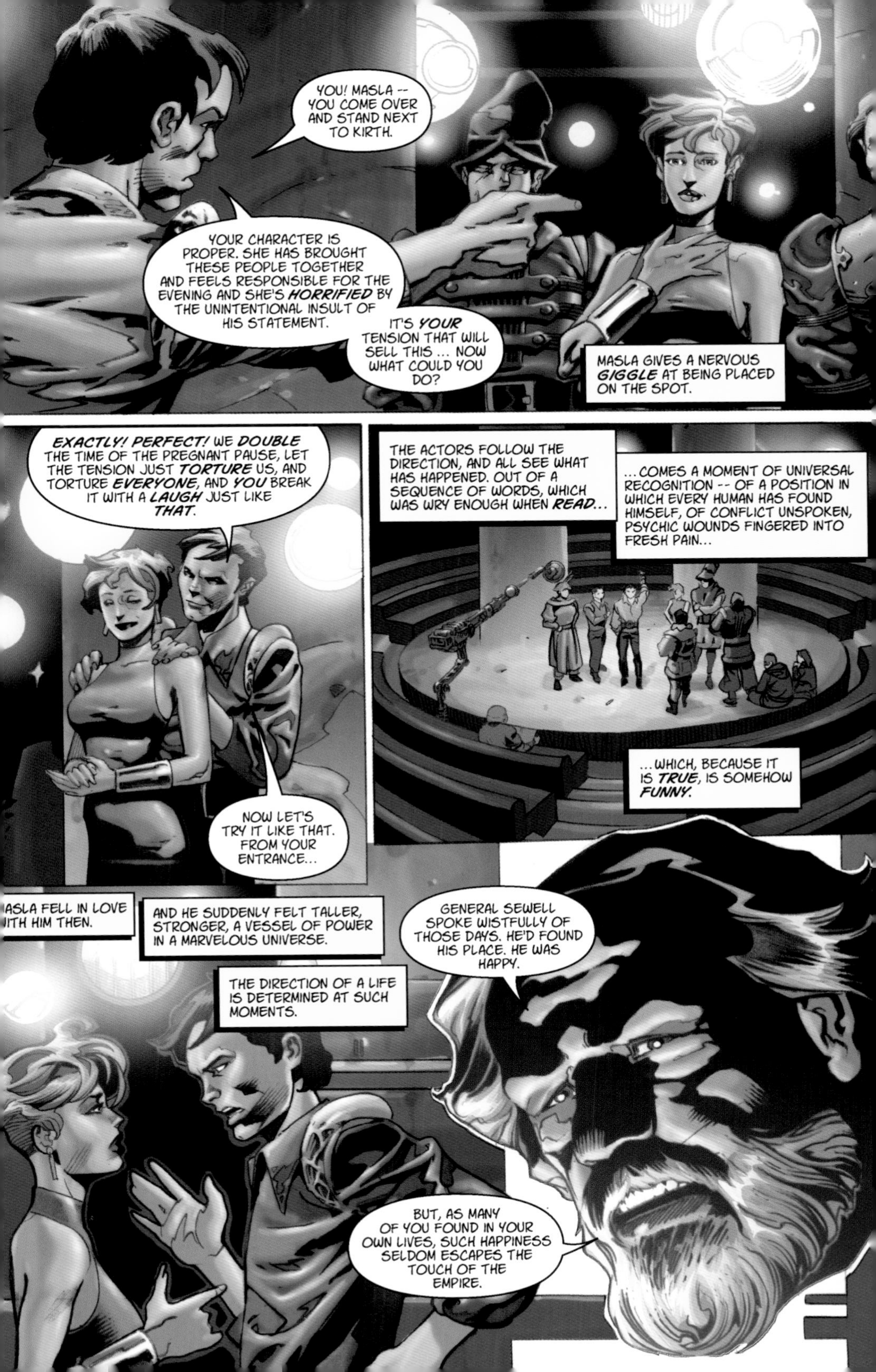
YOU! MASLA -- YOU COME OVER AND STAND NEXT TO KIRTH.
YOUR CHARACTER IS PROPER. SHE HAS BROUGHT THESE PEOPLE TOGETHER AND FEELS RESPONSIBLE FOR THE EVENING AND SHE'S HORRIFIED BY THE UNINTENTIONAL INSULT OF HIS STATEMENT.
IT'S YOUR TENSION THAT WILL SELL THIS ... NOW WHAT COULD YOU DO?
MASLA GIVES A NERVOUS GIGGLE AT BEING PLACED ON THE SPOT.
EXACTLY! PERFECT! WE DOUBLE THE TIME OF THE PREGNANT PAUSE, LET THE TENSION JUST TORTURE US, AND TORTURE EVERYONE, AND YOU BREAK IT WITH A LAUGH JUST LIKE THAT.
NOW LET'S TRY IT LIKE THAT. FROM YOUR ENTRANCE...
THE ACTORS FOLLOW THE DIRECTION, AND ALL SEE WHAT HAS HAPPENED. OUT OF A SEQUENCE OF WORDS, WHICH WAS WRY ENOUGH WHEN READ...
...COMES A MOMENT OF UNIVERSAL RECOGNITION -- OF A POSITION IN WHICH EVERY HUMAN HAS FOUND HIMSELF, OF CONFLICT UNSPOKEN, PSYCHIC WOUNDS FINGERED INTO FRESH PAIN...
...WHICH, BECAUSE IT IS TRUE, IS SOMEHOW FUNNY.
ASLA FELL IN LOVE ITH HIM THEN.
AND HE SUDDENLY FELT TALLER, STRONGER, A VESSEL OF POWER IN A MARVELOUS UNIVERSE.
GENERAL SEWELL SPOKE WISTFULLY OF THOSE DAYS. HE'D FOUND HIS PLACE. HE WAS HAPPY.
THE DIRECTION OF A LIFE IS DETERMINED AT SUCH MOMENTS.
BUT, AS MANY OF YOU FOUND IN YOUR OWN LIVES, SUCH HAPPINESS SELDOM ESCAPES THE TOUCH OF THE EMPIRE.

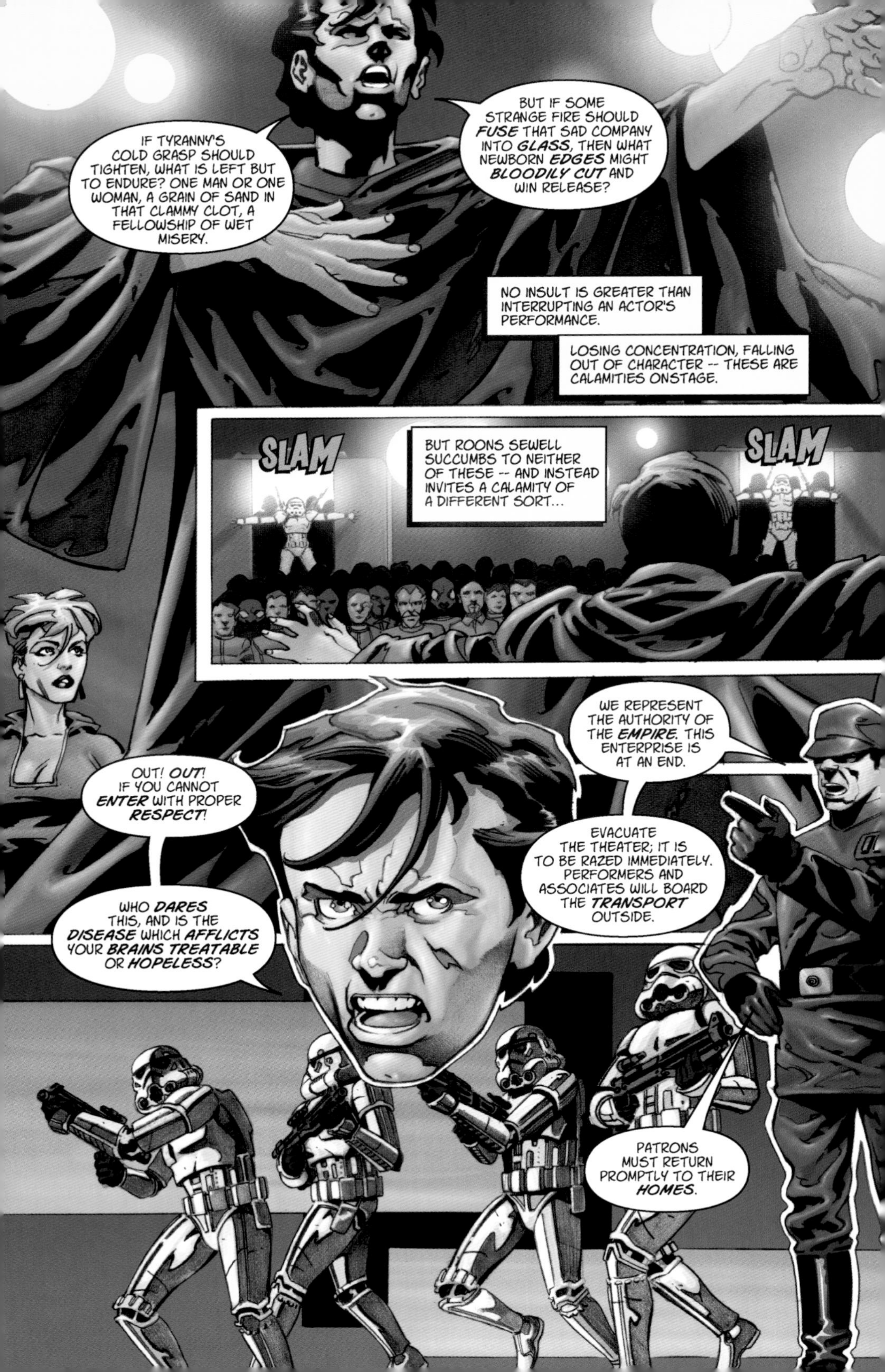

IF TYRANNY'S COLD GRASP SHOULD TIGHTEN, WHAT IS LEFT BUT TO ENDURE? ONE MAN OR ONE WOMAN, A GRAIN OF SAND IN THAT CLAMMY CLOT, A FELLOWSHIP OF WET MISERY.
BUT IF SOME STRANGE FIRE SHOULD FUSE THAT SAD COMPANY INTO GLASS, THEN WHAT NEWBORN EDGES MIGHT BLOODILY CUT AND WIN RELEASE?
NO INSULT IS GREATER THAN INTERRUPTING AN ACTOR'S PERFORMANCE.
LOSING CONCENTRATION, FALLING OUT OF CHARACTER -- THESE ARE CALAMITIES ONSTAGE.
SLAM
BUT ROONS SEWELL SUCCUMBS TO NEITHER OF THESE -- AND INSTEAD INVITES A CALAMITY OF A DIFFERENT SORT...
SLAM
OUT! OUT! IF YOU CANNOT ENTER WITH PROPER RESPECT!
WHO DARES THIS, AND IS THE DISEASE WHICH AFFLICTS YOUR BRAINS TREATABLE OR HOPELESS?
WE REPRESENT THE AUTHORITY OF THE EMPIRE. THIS ENTERPRISE IS AT AN END.
EVACUATE THE THEATER; IT IS TO BE RAZED IMMEDIATELY. PERFORMERS AND ASSOCIATES WILL BOARD THE TRANSPORT OUTSIDE.
PATRONS MUST RETURN PROMPTLY TO THEIR HOMES.

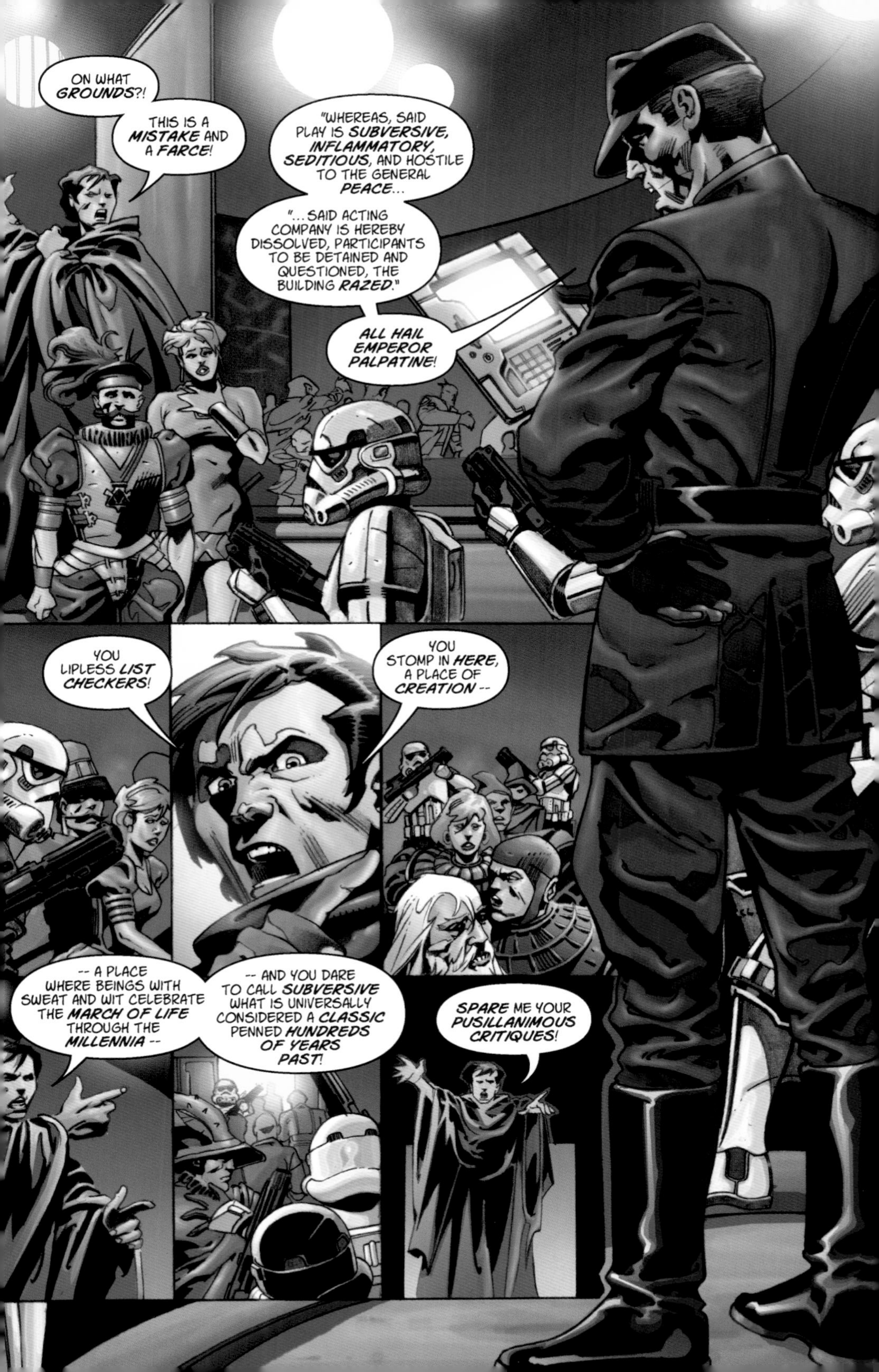
ON WHAT GROUNDS?!
THIS IS A MISTAKE AND A FARCE!
"WHEREAS, SAID PLAY IS SUBVERSIVE, INFLAMMATORY, SEDITIOUS, AND HOSTILE TO THE GENERAL PEACE...
"...SAID ACTING COMPANY IS HEREBY DISSOLVED, PARTICIPANTS TO BE DETAINED AND QUESTIONED, THE BUILDING RAZED."
ALL HAIL EMPEROR PALPATINE!
YOU LIPLESS LIST CHECKERS!
YOU STOMP IN HERE, A PLACE OF CREATION --
-- A PLACE WHERE BEINGS WITH SWEAT AND WIT CELEBRATE THE MARCH OF LIFE THROUGH THE MILLENNIA --
-- AND YOU DARE TO CALL SUBVERSIVE WHAT IS UNIVERSALLY CONSIDERED A CLASSIC PENNED HUNDREDS OF YEARS PAST!
SPARE ME YOUR PUSILLANIMOUS CRITIQUES!

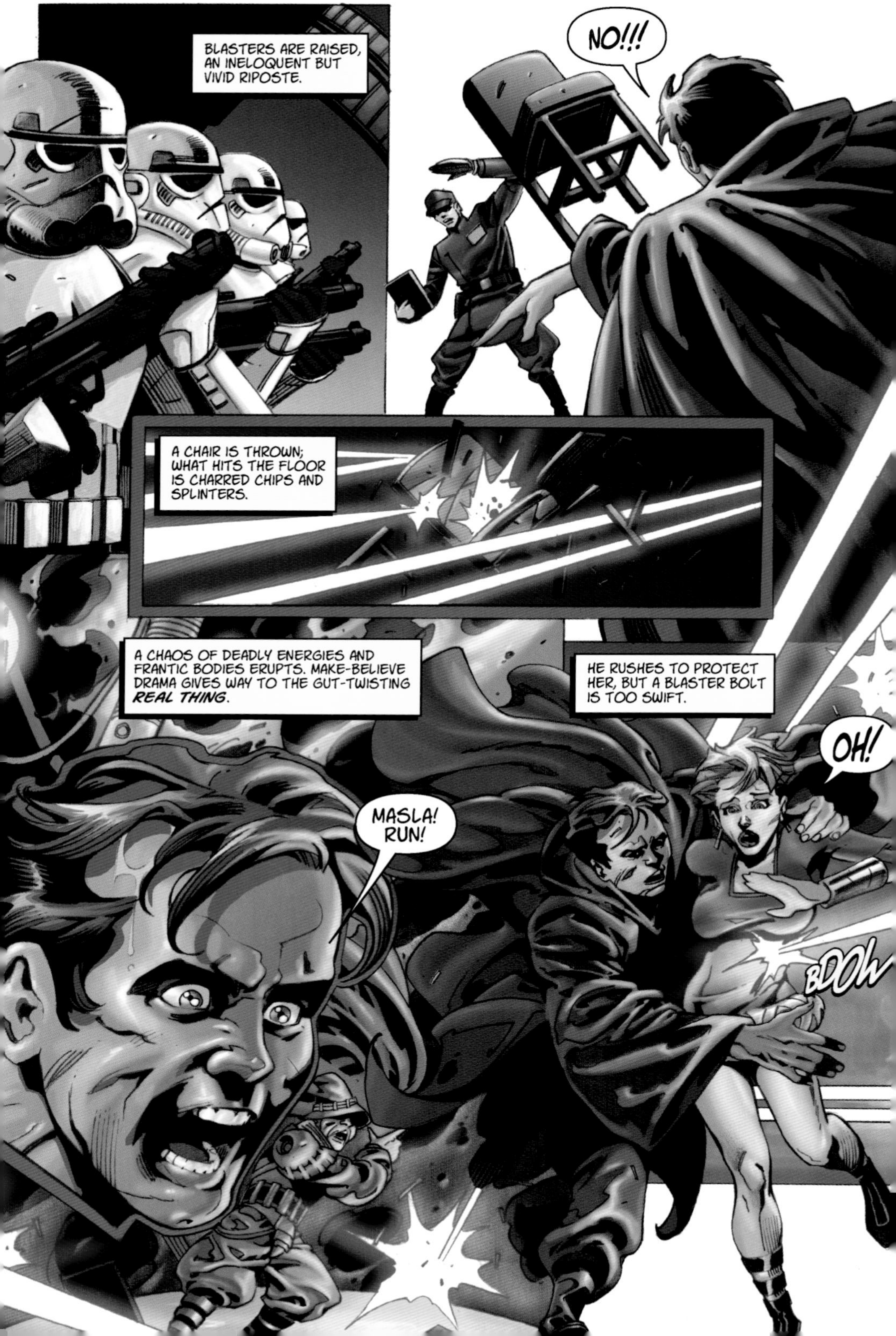
BLASTERS ARE RAISED, AN INELOQUENT BUT VIVID RIPOSTE.
NO!!!
A CHAIR IS THROWN; WHAT HITS THE FLOOR IS CHARRED CHIPS AND SPLINTERS.
A CHAOS OF DEADLY ENERGIES AND FRANTIC BODIES ERUPTS. MAKE-BELIEVE DRAMA GIVES WAY TO THE GUT-TWISTING *REAL THING*.
HE RUSHES TO PROTECT HER, BUT A BLASTER BOLT IS TOO SWIFT.
OH!
MASLA! RUN!
BDOW

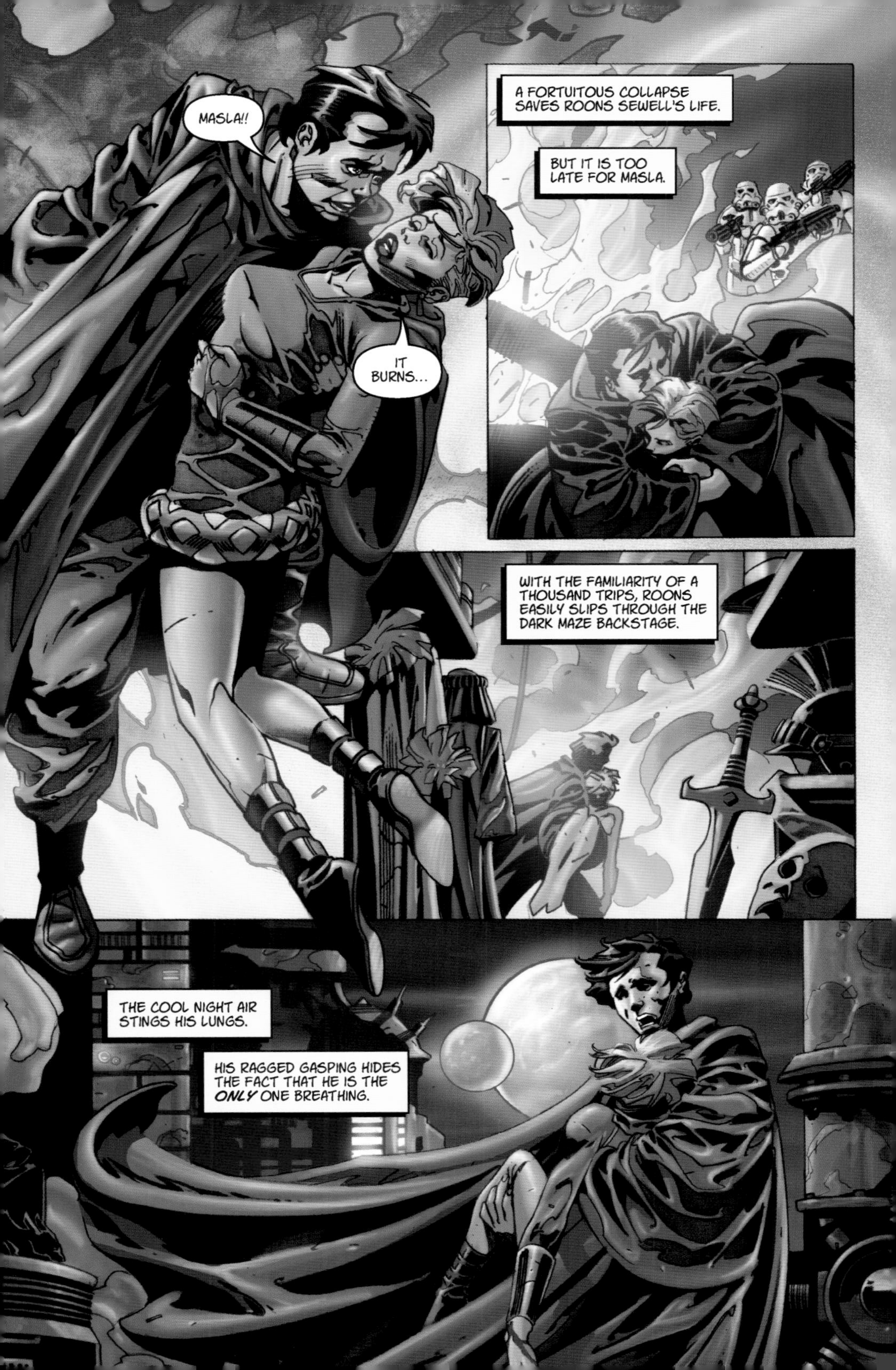
MASLA!!
IT BURNS...
A FORTUITOUS COLLAPSE SAVES ROONS SEWELL'S LIFE.
BUT IT IS TOO LATE FOR MASLA.
WITH THE FAMILIARITY OF A THOUSAND TRIPS, ROONS EASILY SLIPS THROUGH THE DARK MAZE BACKSTAGE.
THE COOL NIGHT AIR STINGS HIS LUNGS.
HIS RAGGED GASPING HIDES THE FACT THAT HE IS THE *ONLY* ONE BREATHING.

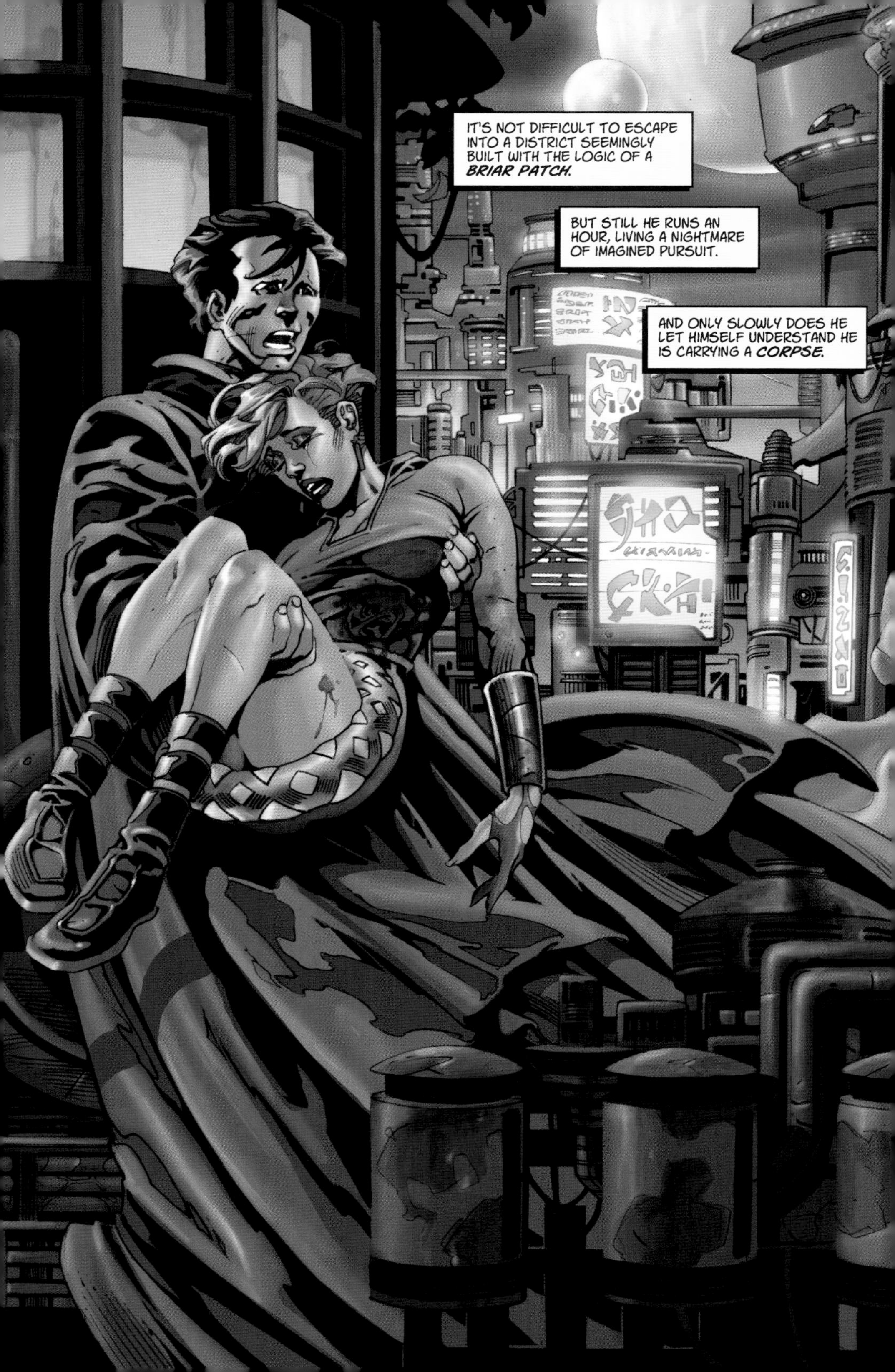
IT'S NOT DIFFICULT TO ESCAPE INTO A DISTRICT SEEMINGLY BUILT WITH THE LOGIC OF A *BRIAR PATCH*.
BUT STILL HE RUNS AN HOUR, LIVING A NIGHTMARE OF IMAGINED PURSUIT.
AND ONLY SLOWLY DOES HE LET HIMSELF UNDERSTAND HE IS CARRYING A *CORPSE*.

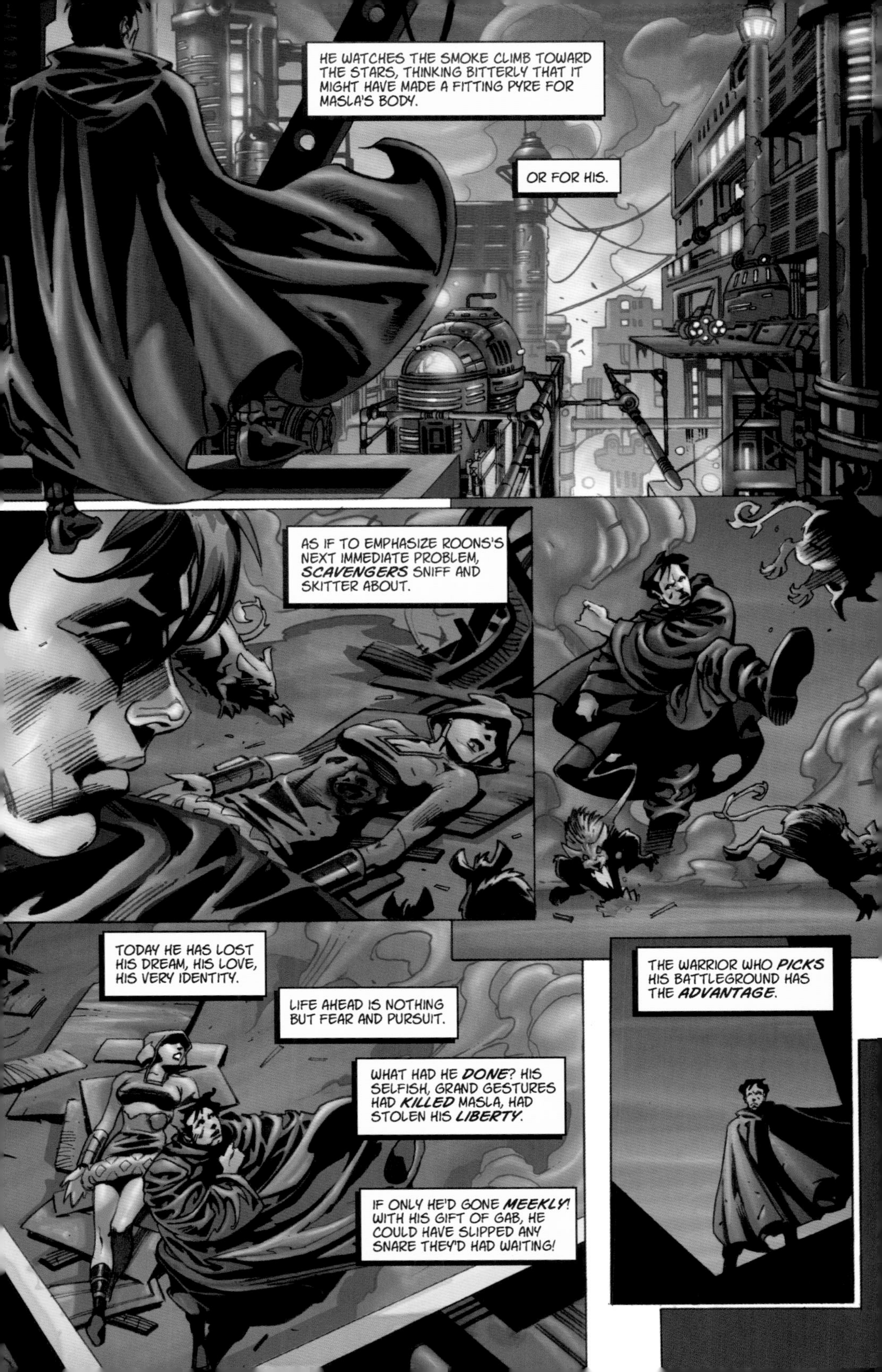
HE WATCHES THE SMOKE CLIMB TOWARD THE STARS, THINKING BITTERLY THAT IT MIGHT HAVE MADE A FITTING PYRE FOR MASLA'S BODY.
OR FOR HIS.
AS IF TO EMPHASIZE ROONS'S NEXT IMMEDIATE PROBLEM, SCAVENGERS SNIFF AND SKITTER ABOUT.
TODAY HE HAS LOST HIS DREAM, HIS LOVE, HIS VERY IDENTITY.
LIFE AHEAD IS NOTHING BUT FEAR AND PURSUIT.
WHAT HAD HE DONE? HIS SELFISH, GRAND GESTURES HAD KILLED MASLA, HAD STOLEN HIS LIBERTY.
IF ONLY HE'D GONE MEEKLY! WITH HIS GIFT OF GAB, HE COULD HAVE SLIPPED ANY SNARE THEY'D HAD WAITING!
THE WARRIOR WHO PICKS HIS BATTLEGROUND HAS THE ADVANTAGE.

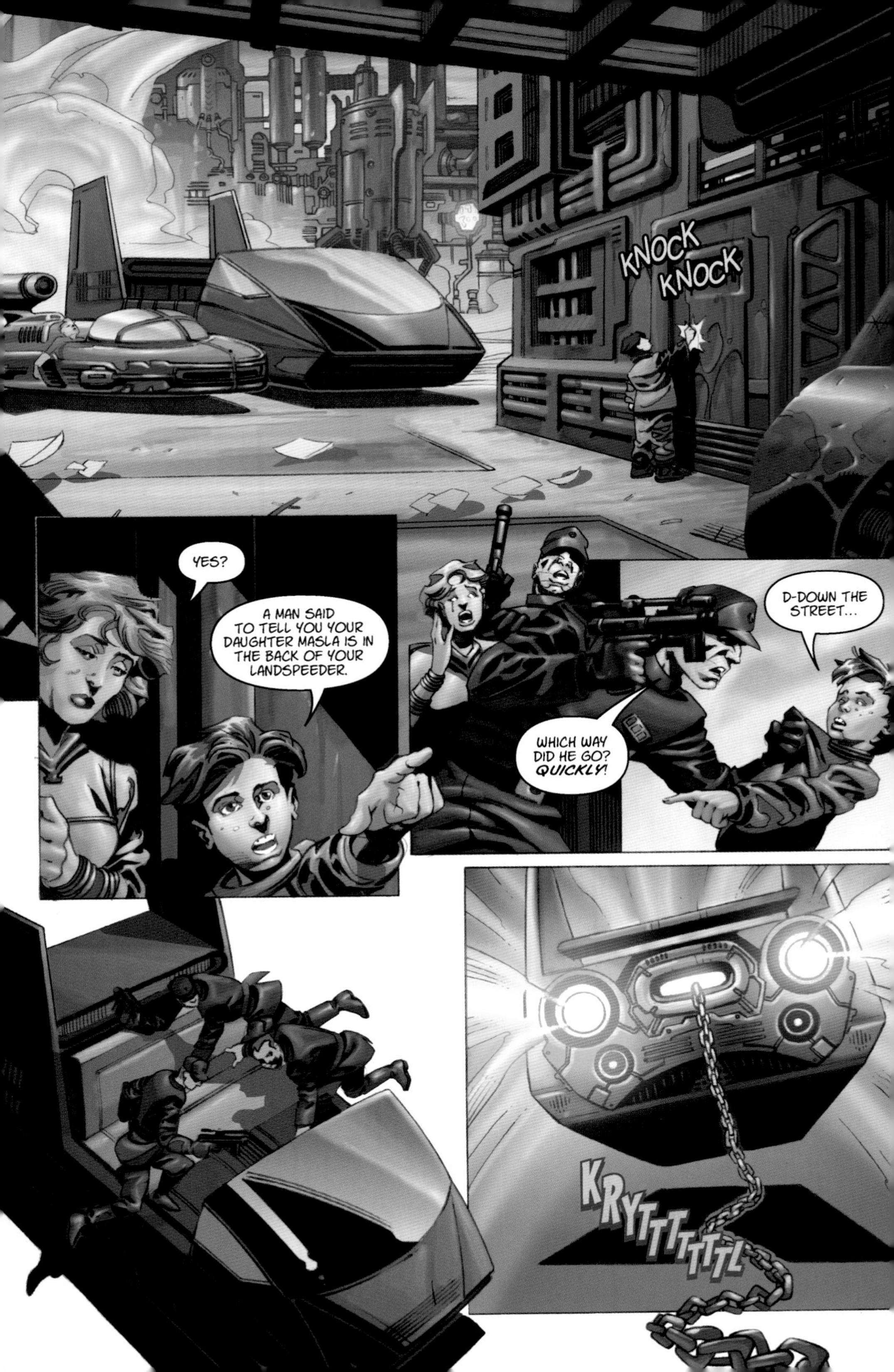
KNOCK
KNOCK
YES?
A MAN SAID TO TELL YOU YOUR DAUGHTER MASLA IS IN THE BACK OF YOUR LANDSPEEDER.
WHICH WAY DID HE GO? *QUICKLY*!
D-DOWN THE STREET...
KRYTTTTTTTL

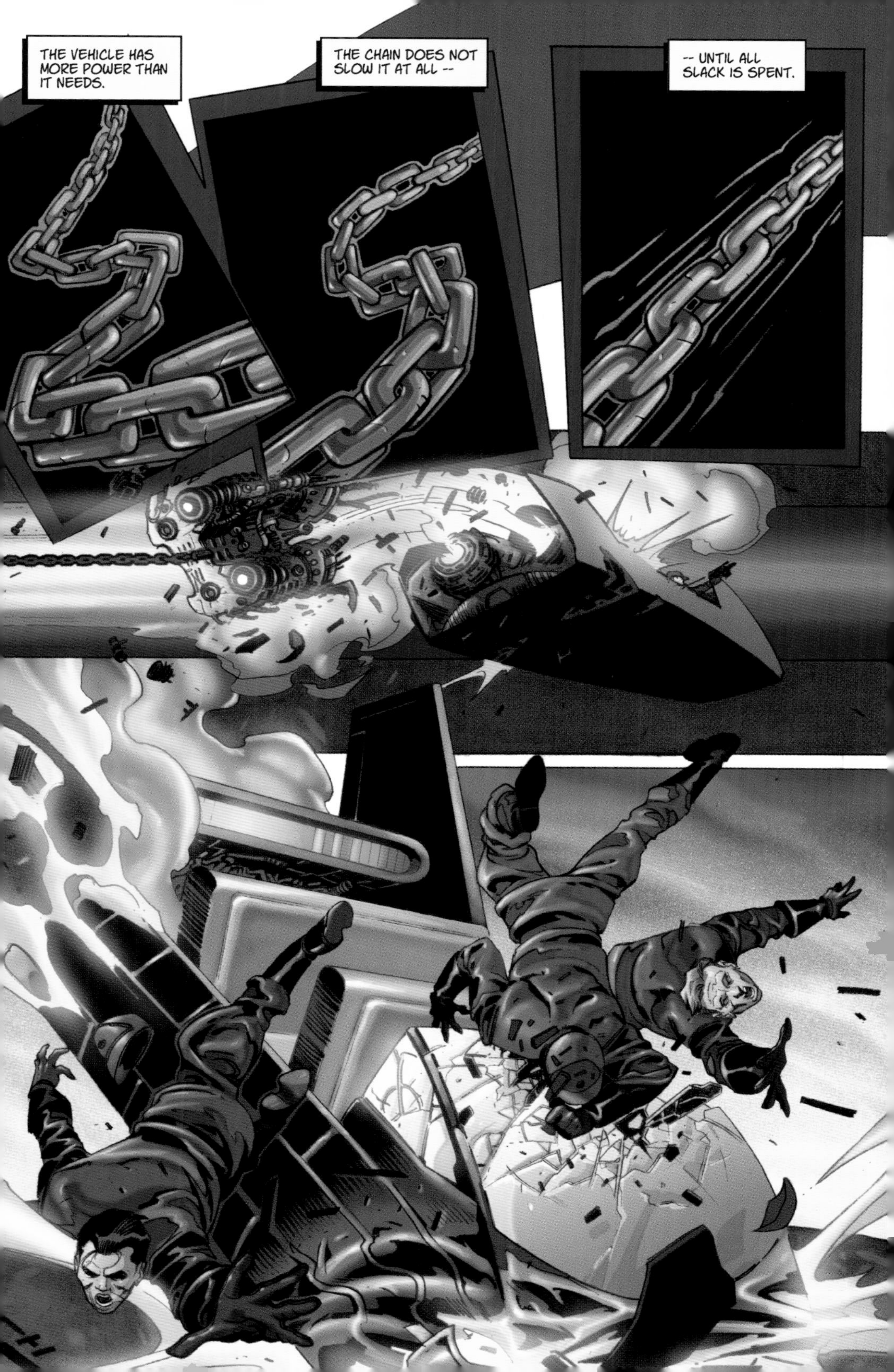
THE VEHICLE HAS MORE POWER THAN IT NEEDS.
THE CHAIN DOES NOT SLOW IT AT ALL --
-- UNTIL ALL SLACK IS SPENT.

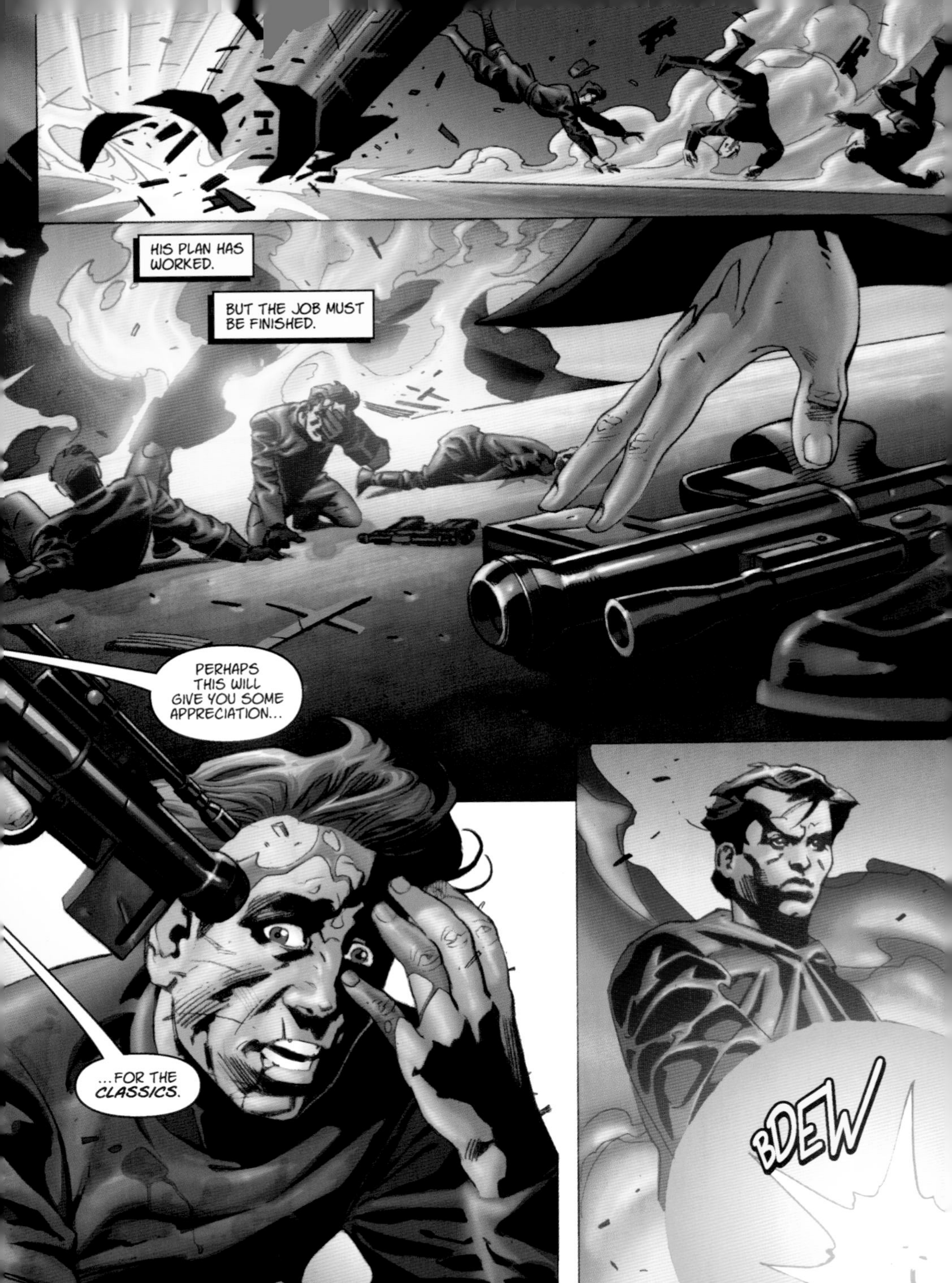
HIS PLAN HAS WORKED.
BUT THE JOB MUST BE FINISHED.
PERHAPS THIS WILL GIVE YOU SOME APPRECIATION...
...FOR THE *CLASSICS*.
BDEW

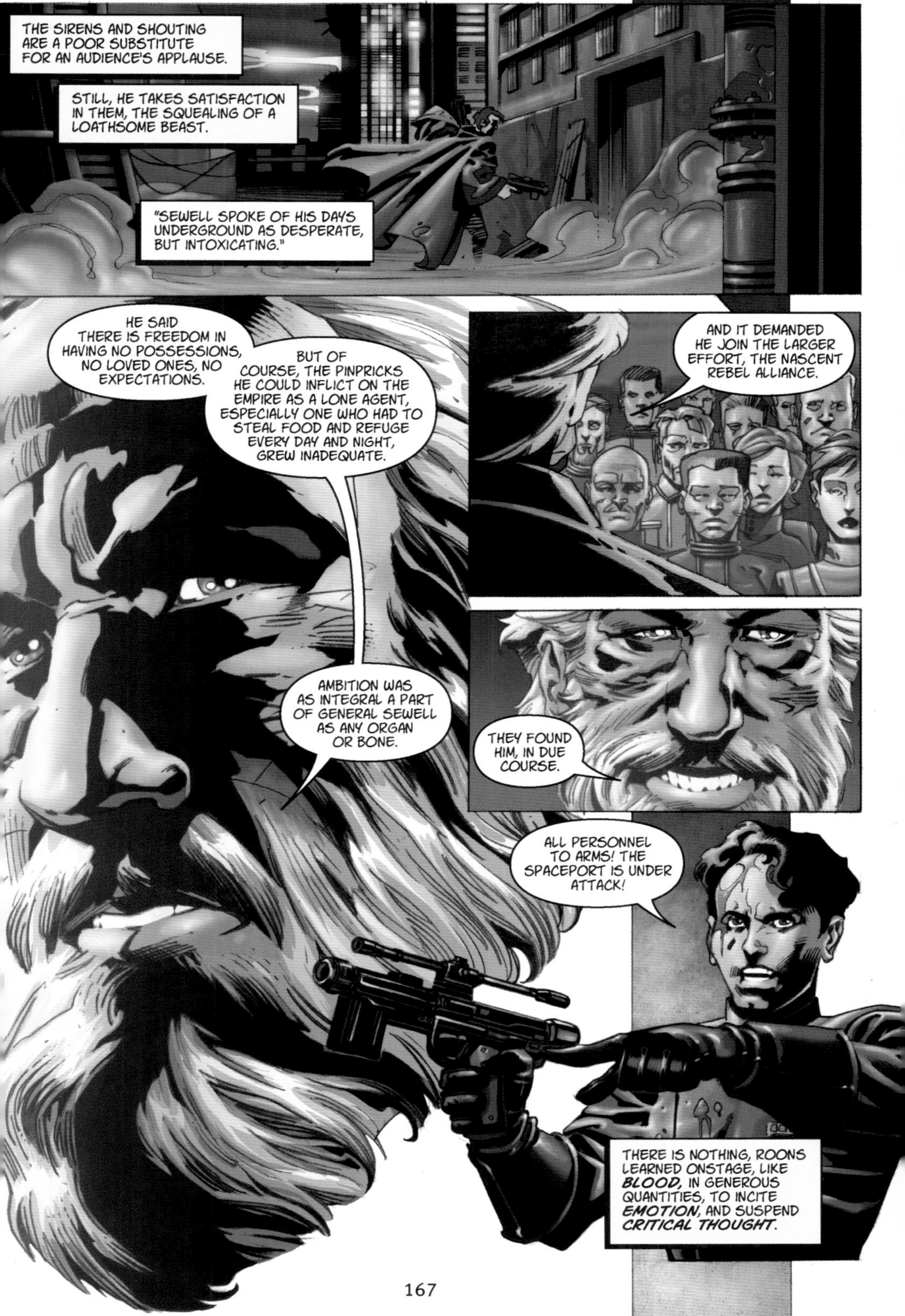
THE SIRENS AND SHOUTING ARE A POOR SUBSTITUTE FOR AN AUDIENCE'S APPLAUSE.
STILL, HE TAKES SATISFACTION IN THEM, THE SQUEALING OF A LOATHSOME BEAST.
"SEWELL SPOKE OF HIS DAYS UNDERGROUND AS DESPERATE, BUT INTOXICATING."
HE SAID THERE IS FREEDOM IN HAVING NO POSSESSIONS, NO LOVED ONES, NO EXPECTATIONS.
BUT OF COURSE, THE PINPRICKS HE COULD INFLICT ON THE EMPIRE AS A LONE AGENT, ESPECIALLY ONE WHO HAD TO STEAL FOOD AND REFUGE EVERY DAY AND NIGHT, GREW INADEQUATE.
AMBITION WAS AS INTEGRAL A PART OF GENERAL SEWELL AS ANY ORGAN OR BONE.
AND IT DEMANDED HE JOIN THE LARGER EFFORT, THE NASCENT REBEL ALLIANCE.
THEY FOUND HIM, IN DUE COURSE.
ALL PERSONNEL TO ARMS! THE SPACEPORT IS UNDER ATTACK!
THERE IS NOTHING, ROONS LEARNED ONSTAGE, LIKE ***BLOOD,*** IN GENEROUS QUANTITIES, TO INCITE ***EMOTION,*** AND SUSPEND ***CRITICAL THOUGHT***.

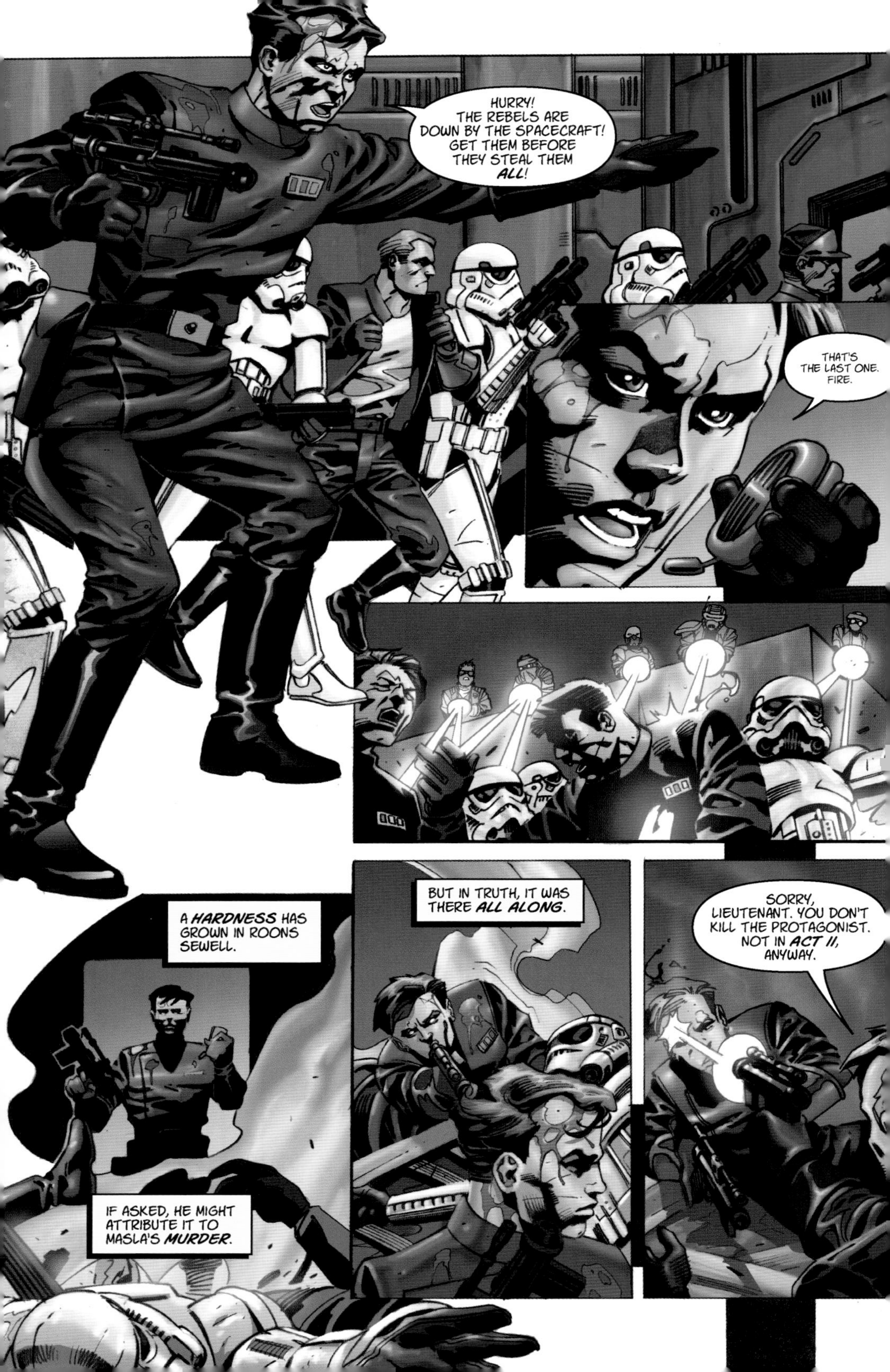
HURRY! THE REBELS ARE DOWN BY THE SPACECRAFT! GET THEM BEFORE THEY STEAL THEM ALL!
THAT'S THE LAST ONE. FIRE.
A HARDNESS HAS GROWN IN ROONS SEWELL.
IF ASKED, HE MIGHT ATTRIBUTE IT TO MASLA'S MURDER.
BUT IN TRUTH, IT WAS THERE ALL ALONG.
SORRY, LIEUTENANT. YOU DON'T KILL THE PROTAGONIST. NOT IN ACT II, ANYWAY.

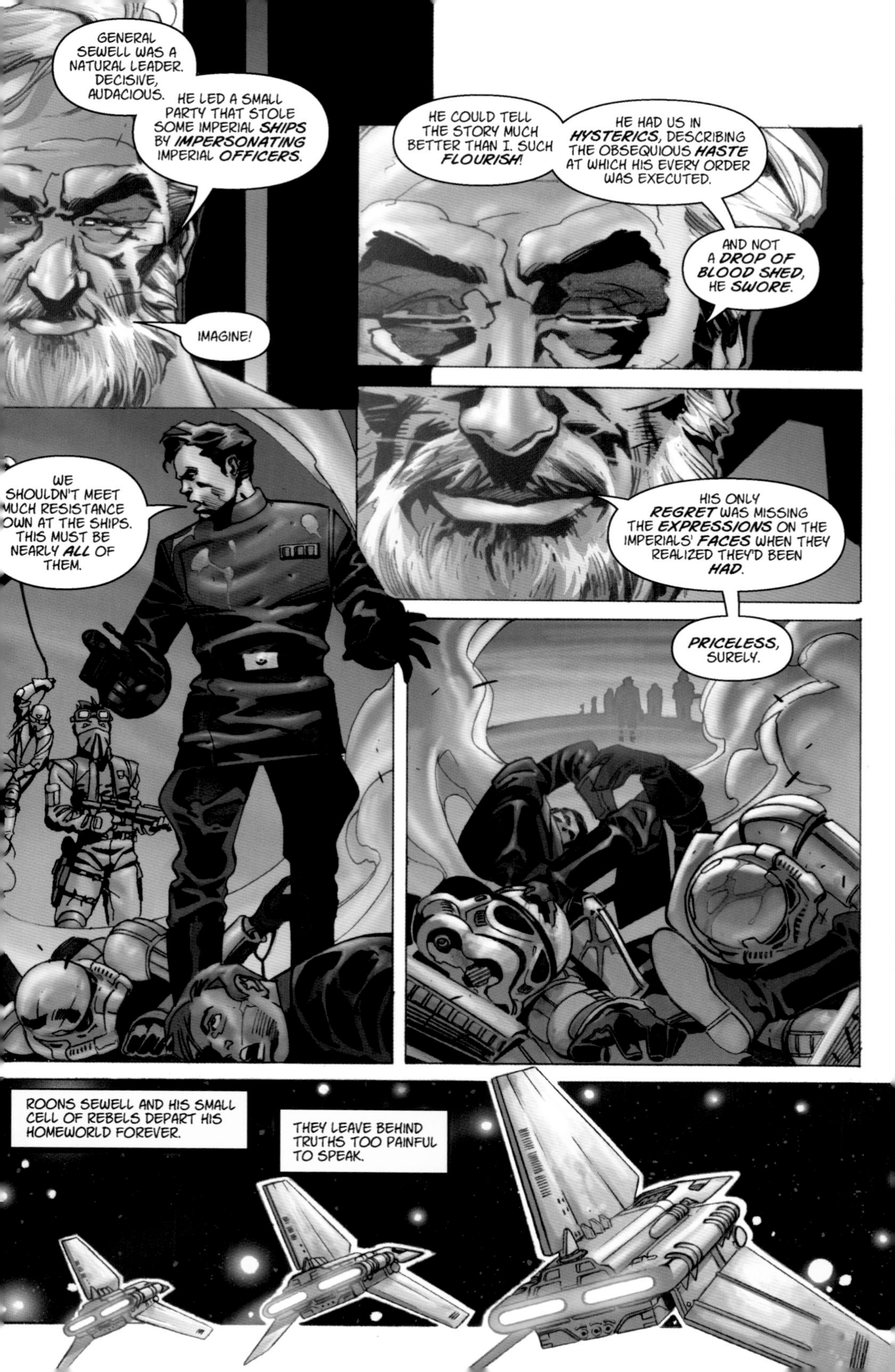
GENERAL SEWELL WAS A NATURAL LEADER. DECISIVE, AUDACIOUS.
HE LED A SMALL PARTY THAT STOLE SOME IMPERIAL SHIPS BY IMPERSONATING IMPERIAL OFFICERS.
IMAGINE!
HE COULD TELL THE STORY MUCH BETTER THAN I. SUCH FLOURISH!
HE HAD US IN HYSTERICS, DESCRIBING THE OBSEQUIOUS HASTE AT WHICH HIS EVERY ORDER WAS EXECUTED.
AND NOT A DROP OF BLOOD SHED, HE SWORE.
WE SHOULDN'T MEET MUCH RESISTANCE OWN AT THE SHIPS. THIS MUST BE NEARLY ALL OF THEM.
HIS ONLY REGRET WAS MISSING THE EXPRESSIONS ON THE IMPERIALS' FACES WHEN THEY REALIZED THEY'D BEEN HAD.
PRICELESS, SURELY.
ROONS SEWELL AND HIS SMALL CELL OF REBELS DEPART HIS HOMEWORLD FOREVER.
THEY LEAVE BEHIND TRUTHS TOO PAINFUL TO SPEAK.

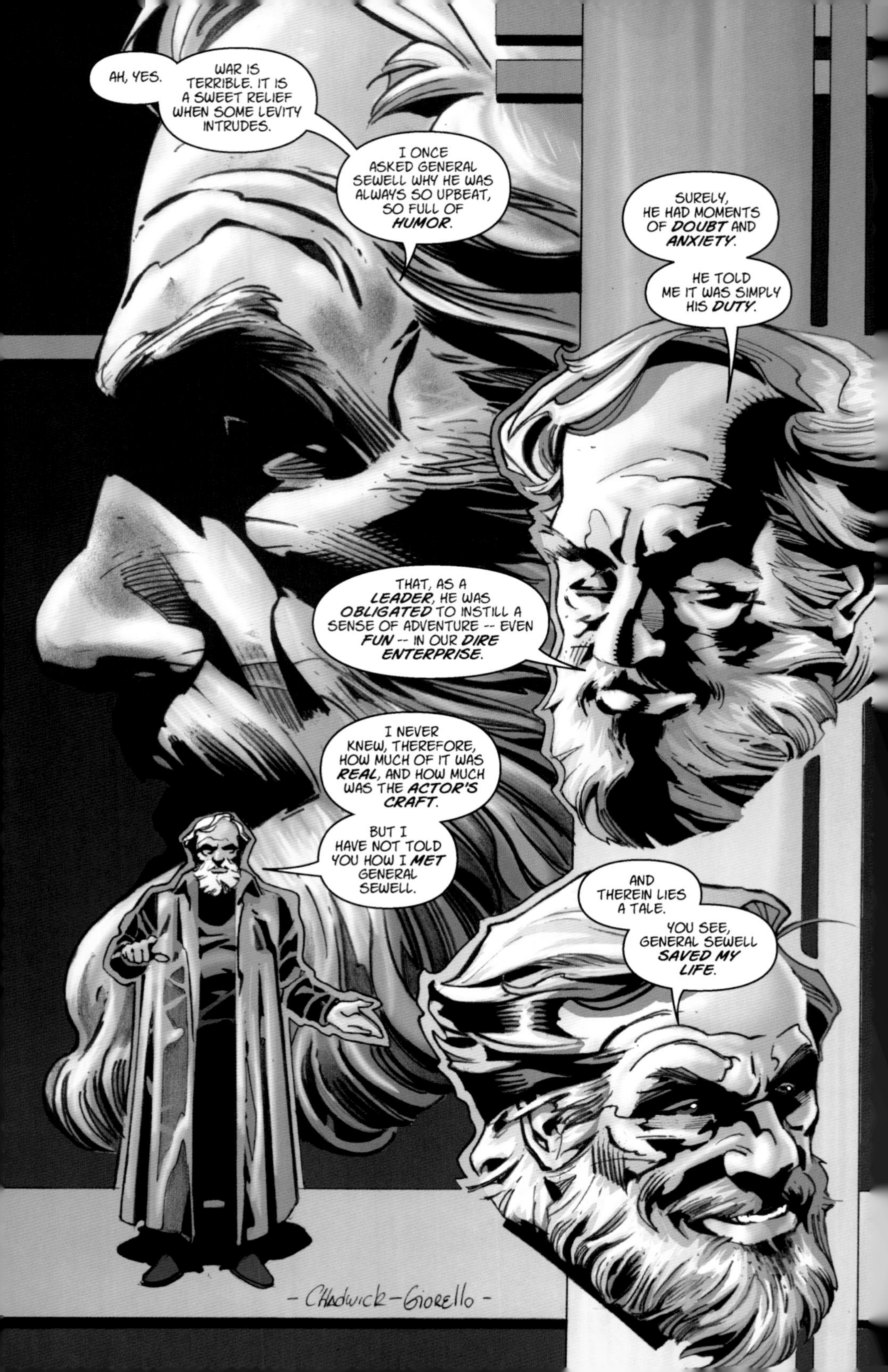
AH, YES.
WAR IS TERRIBLE. IT IS A SWEET RELIEF WHEN SOME LEVITY INTRUDES.
I ONCE ASKED GENERAL SEWELL WHY HE WAS ALWAYS SO UPBEAT, SO FULL OF HUMOR.
SURELY, HE HAD MOMENTS OF DOUBT AND ANXIETY.
HE TOLD ME IT WAS SIMPLY HIS DUTY.
THAT, AS A LEADER, HE WAS OBLIGATED TO INSTILL A SENSE OF ADVENTURE -- EVEN FUN -- IN OUR DIRE ENTERPRISE.
I NEVER KNEW, THEREFORE, HOW MUCH OF IT WAS REAL, AND HOW MUCH WAS THE ACTOR'S CRAFT.
BUT I HAVE NOT TOLD YOU HOW I MET GENERAL SEWELL.
AND THEREIN LIES A TALE.
YOU SEE, GENERAL SEWELL SAVED MY LIFE.
- CHADWICK - GIORELLO -

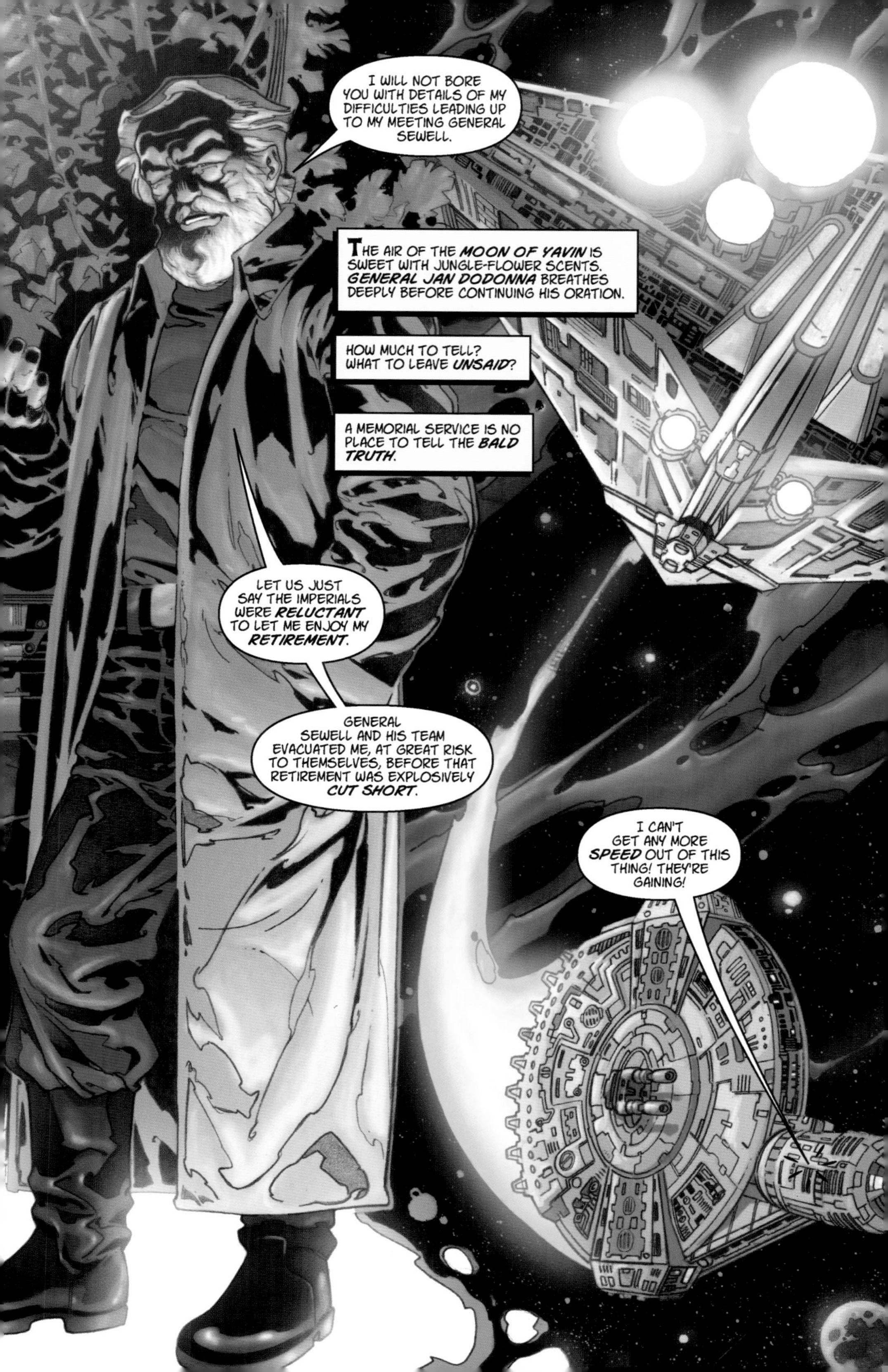
I WILL NOT BORE YOU WITH DETAILS OF MY DIFFICULTIES LEADING UP TO MY MEETING GENERAL SEWELL.
THE AIR OF THE MOON OF YAVIN IS SWEET WITH JUNGLE-FLOWER SCENTS. GENERAL JAN DODONNA BREATHES DEEPLY BEFORE CONTINUING HIS ORATION.
HOW MUCH TO TELL? WHAT TO LEAVE UNSAID?
A MEMORIAL SERVICE IS NO PLACE TO TELL THE BALD TRUTH.
LET US JUST SAY THE IMPERIALS WERE RELUCTANT TO LET ME ENJOY MY RETIREMENT.
GENERAL SEWELL AND HIS TEAM EVACUATED ME, AT GREAT RISK TO THEMSELVES, BEFORE THAT RETIREMENT WAS EXPLOSIVELY CUT SHORT.
I CAN'T GET ANY MORE SPEED OUT OF THIS THING! THEY'RE GAINING!

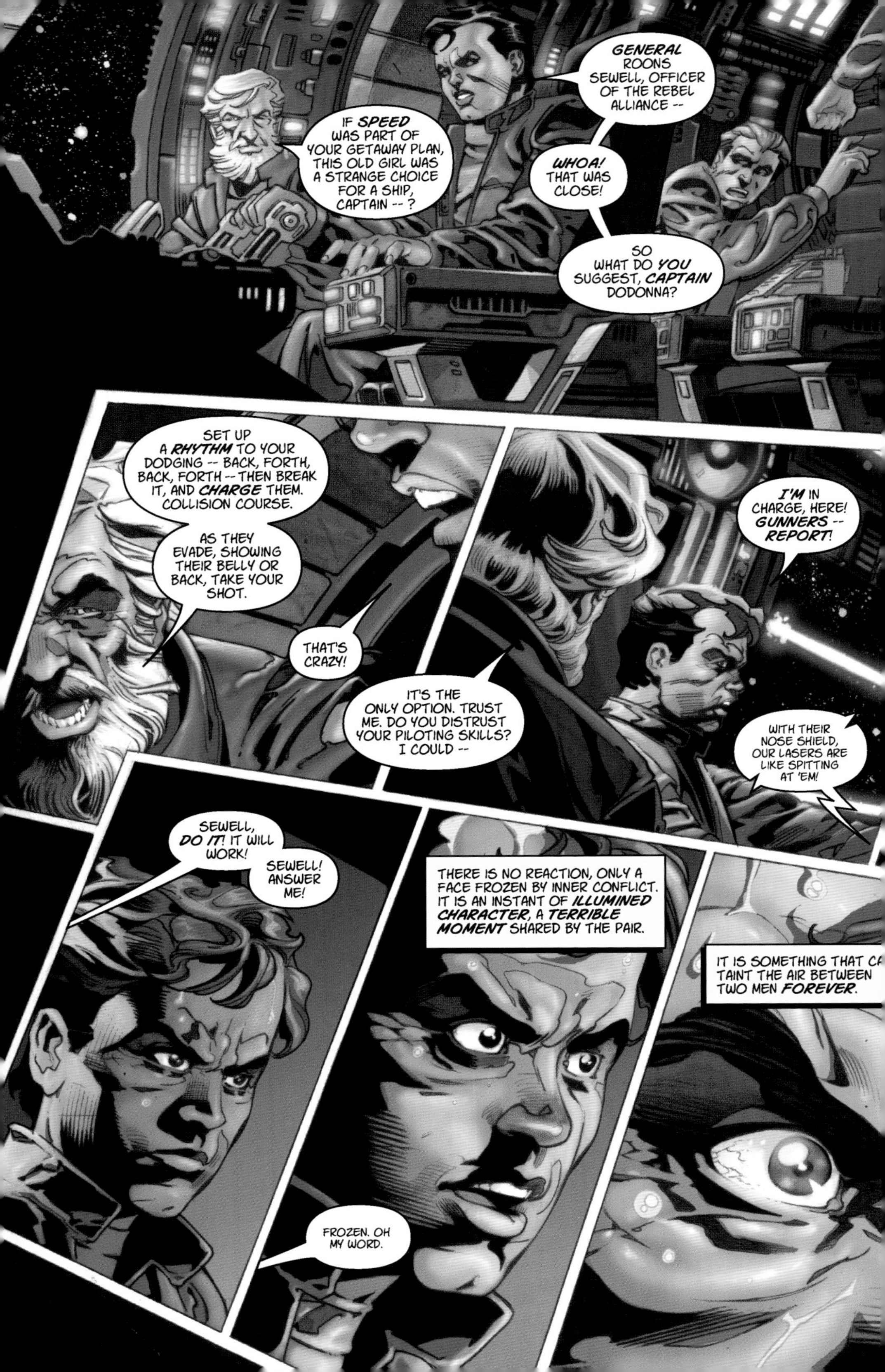
GENERAL ROONS SEWELL, OFFICER OF THE REBEL ALLIANCE --
IF SPEED WAS PART OF YOUR GETAWAY PLAN, THIS OLD GIRL WAS A STRANGE CHOICE FOR A SHIP, CAPTAIN -- ?
WHOA! THAT WAS CLOSE!
SO WHAT DO YOU SUGGEST, CAPTAIN DODONNA?
SET UP A RHYTHM TO YOUR DODGING -- BACK, FORTH, BACK, FORTH -- THEN BREAK IT, AND CHARGE THEM. COLLISION COURSE.
AS THEY EVADE, SHOWING THEIR BELLY OR BACK, TAKE YOUR SHOT.
THAT'S CRAZY!
IT'S THE ONLY OPTION. TRUST ME. DO YOU DISTRUST YOUR PILOTING SKILLS? I COULD --
I'M IN CHARGE, HERE! GUNNERS -- REPORT!
WITH THEIR NOSE SHIELD, OUR LASERS ARE LIKE SPITTING AT 'EM!
SEWELL, DO IT! IT WILL WORK!
SEWELL! ANSWER ME!
FROZEN. OH MY WORD.
THERE IS NO REACTION, ONLY A FACE FROZEN BY INNER CONFLICT. IT IS AN INSTANT OF ILLUMINED CHARACTER, A TERRIBLE MOMENT SHARED BY THE PAIR.
IT IS SOMETHING THAT CA
TAINT THE AIR BETWEEN TWO MEN FOREVER.

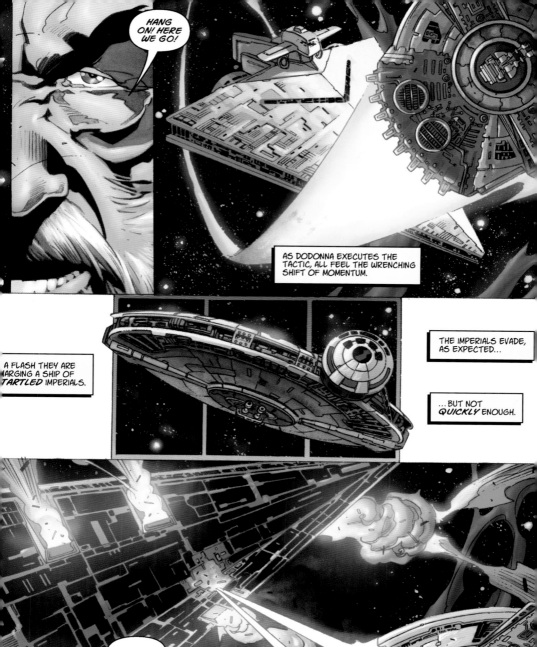

HANG ON! HERE WE GO!

AS DODONNA EXECUTES THE TACTIC, ALL FEEL THE WRENCHING SHIFT OF MOMENTUM.

A FLASH THEY ARE ARGING A SHIP OF TARTLED IMPERIALS.

THE IMPERIALS EVADE, AS EXPECTED...

...BUT NOT QUICKLY ENOUGH.

NOW!!

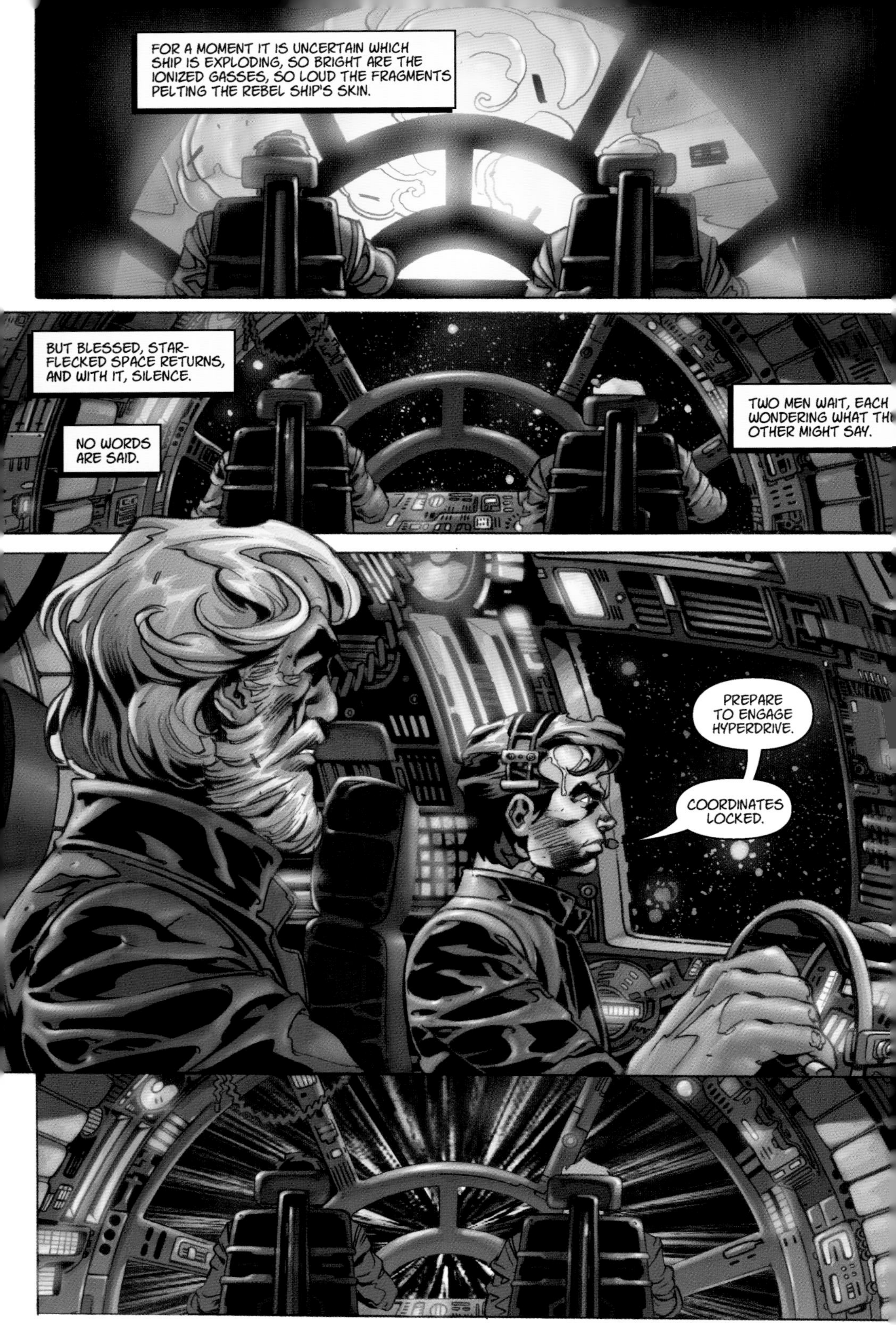
FOR A MOMENT IT IS UNCERTAIN WHICH SHIP IS EXPLODING, SO BRIGHT ARE THE IONIZED GASSES, SO LOUD THE FRAGMENTS PELTING THE REBEL SHIP'S SKIN.
BUT BLESSED, STAR-FLECKED SPACE RETURNS, AND WITH IT, SILENCE.
NO WORDS ARE SAID.
TWO MEN WAIT, EACH WONDERING WHAT TH
OTHER MIGHT SAY.
PREPARE TO ENGAGE HYPERDRIVE.
COORDINATES LOCKED.

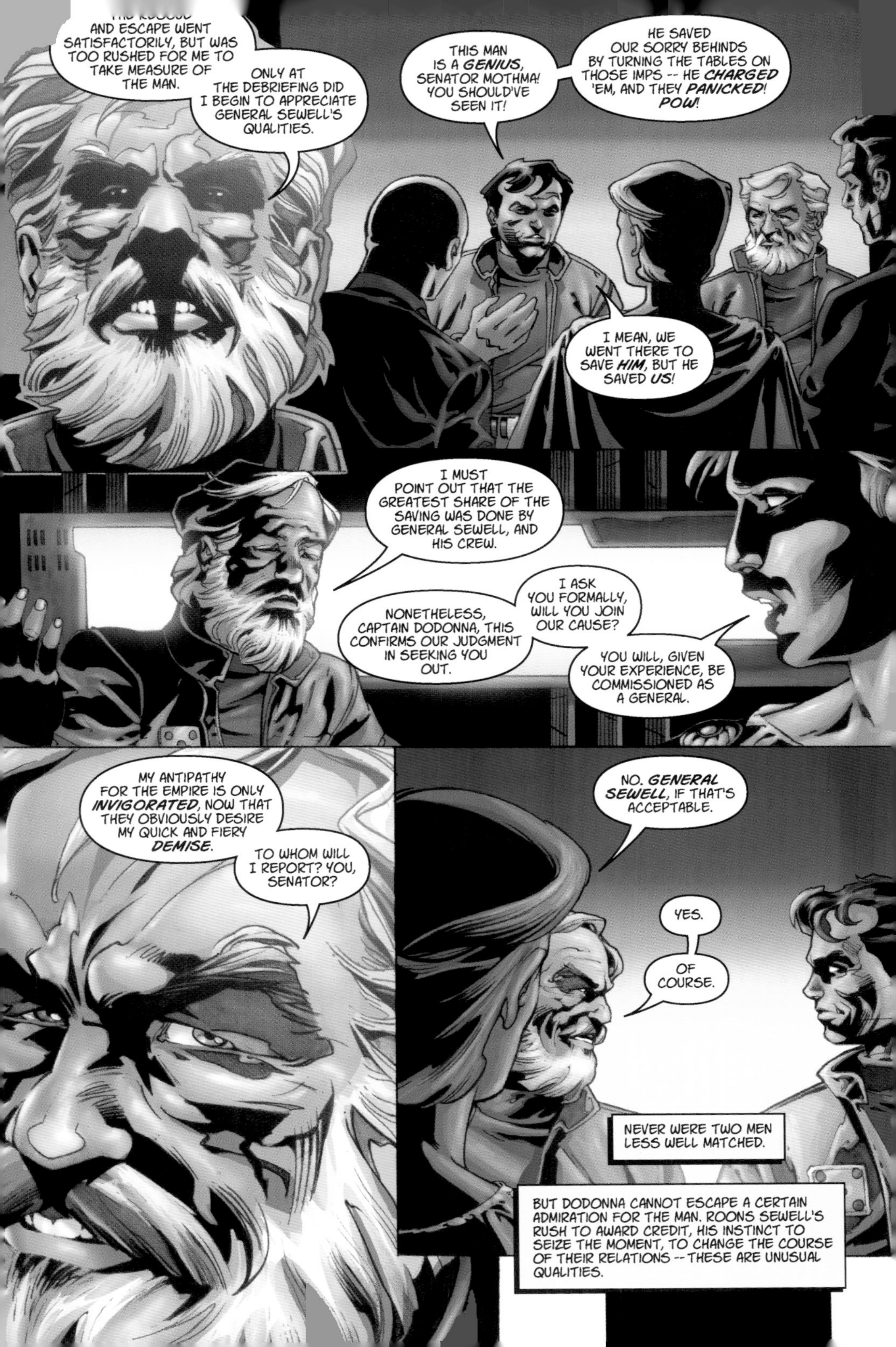
AND ESCAPE WENT SATISFACTORILY, BUT WAS TOO RUSHED FOR ME TO TAKE MEASURE OF THE MAN.
ONLY AT THE DEBRIEFING DID I BEGIN TO APPRECIATE GENERAL SEWELL'S QUALITIES.
THIS MAN IS A GENIUS, SENATOR MOTHMA! YOU SHOULD'VE SEEN IT!
HE SAVED OUR SORRY BEHINDS BY TURNING THE TABLES ON THOSE IMPS -- HE CHARGED 'EM, AND THEY PANICKED! POW!
I MEAN, WE WENT THERE TO SAVE HIM, BUT HE SAVED US!
I MUST POINT OUT THAT THE GREATEST SHARE OF THE SAVING WAS DONE BY GENERAL SEWELL, AND HIS CREW.
NONETHELESS, CAPTAIN DODONNA, THIS CONFIRMS OUR JUDGMENT IN SEEKING YOU OUT.
I ASK YOU FORMALLY, WILL YOU JOIN OUR CAUSE?
YOU WILL, GIVEN YOUR EXPERIENCE, BE COMMISSIONED AS A GENERAL.
MY ANTIPATHY FOR THE EMPIRE IS ONLY INVIGORATED, NOW THAT THEY OBVIOUSLY DESIRE MY QUICK AND FIERY DEMISE.
TO WHOM WILL I REPORT? YOU, SENATOR?
NO. GENERAL SEWELL, IF THAT'S ACCEPTABLE.
YES.
OF COURSE.
NEVER WERE TWO MEN LESS WELL MATCHED.
BUT DODONNA CANNOT ESCAPE A CERTAIN ADMIRATION FOR THE MAN. ROONS SEWELL'S RUSH TO AWARD CREDIT, HIS INSTINCT TO SEIZE THE MOMENT, TO CHANGE THE COURSE OF THEIR RELATIONS -- THESE ARE UNUSUAL QUALITIES.

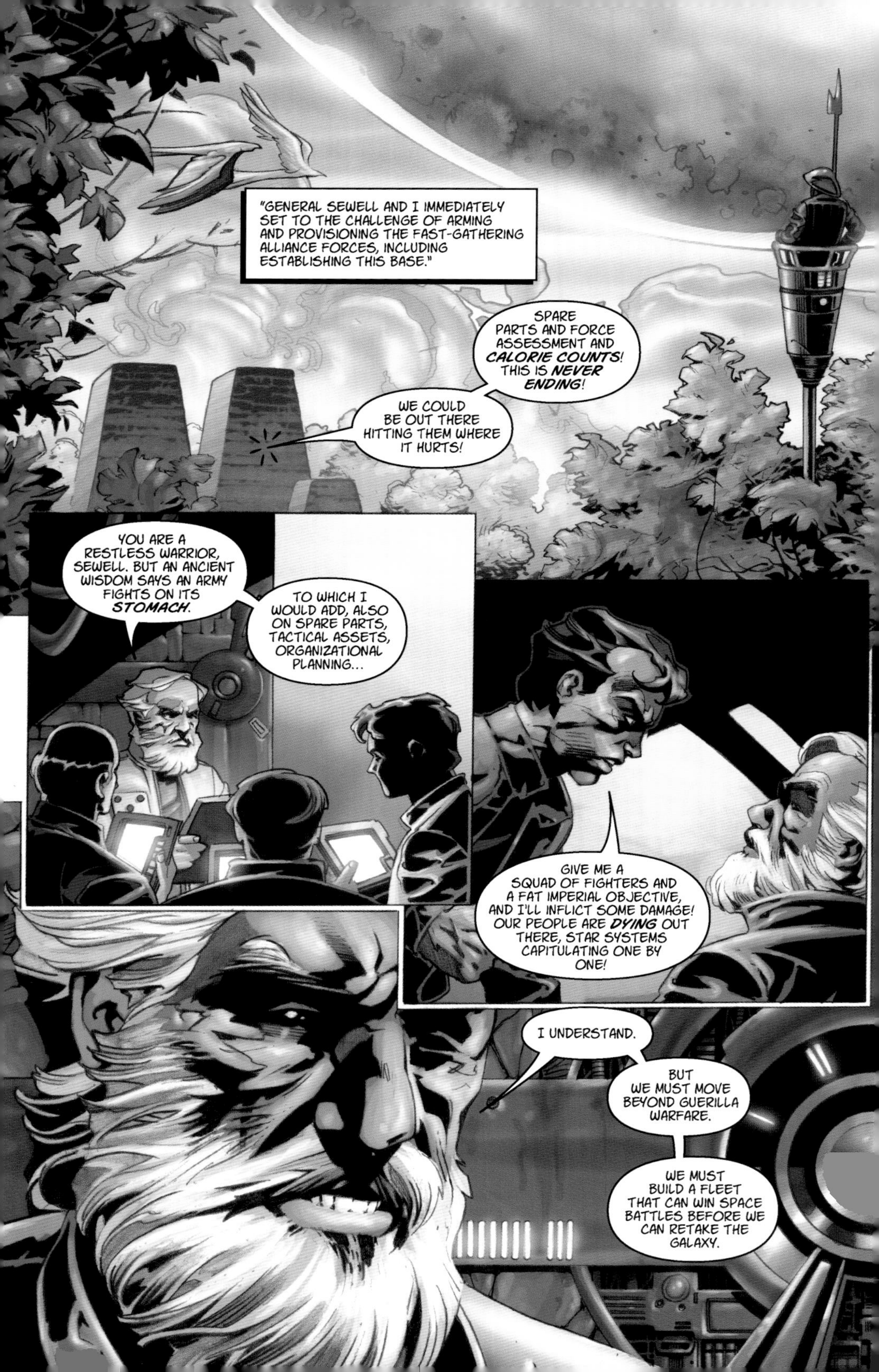
"GENERAL SEWELL AND I IMMEDIATELY SET TO THE CHALLENGE OF ARMING AND PROVISIONING THE FAST-GATHERING ALLIANCE FORCES, INCLUDING ESTABLISHING THIS BASE."
SPARE PARTS AND FORCE ASSESSMENT AND CALORIE COUNTS! THIS IS NEVER ENDING!
WE COULD BE OUT THERE HITTING THEM WHERE IT HURTS!
YOU ARE A RESTLESS WARRIOR, SEWELL. BUT AN ANCIENT WISDOM SAYS AN ARMY FIGHTS ON ITS STOMACH.
TO WHICH I WOULD ADD, ALSO ON SPARE PARTS, TACTICAL ASSETS, ORGANIZATIONAL PLANNING...
GIVE ME A SQUAD OF FIGHTERS AND A FAT IMPERIAL OBJECTIVE, AND I'LL INFLICT SOME DAMAGE! OUR PEOPLE ARE DYING OUT THERE, STAR SYSTEMS CAPITULATING ONE BY ONE!
I UNDERSTAND.
BUT WE MUST MOVE BEYOND GUERILLA WARFARE.
WE MUST BUILD A FLEET THAT CAN WIN SPACE BATTLES BEFORE WE CAN RETAKE THE GALAXY.

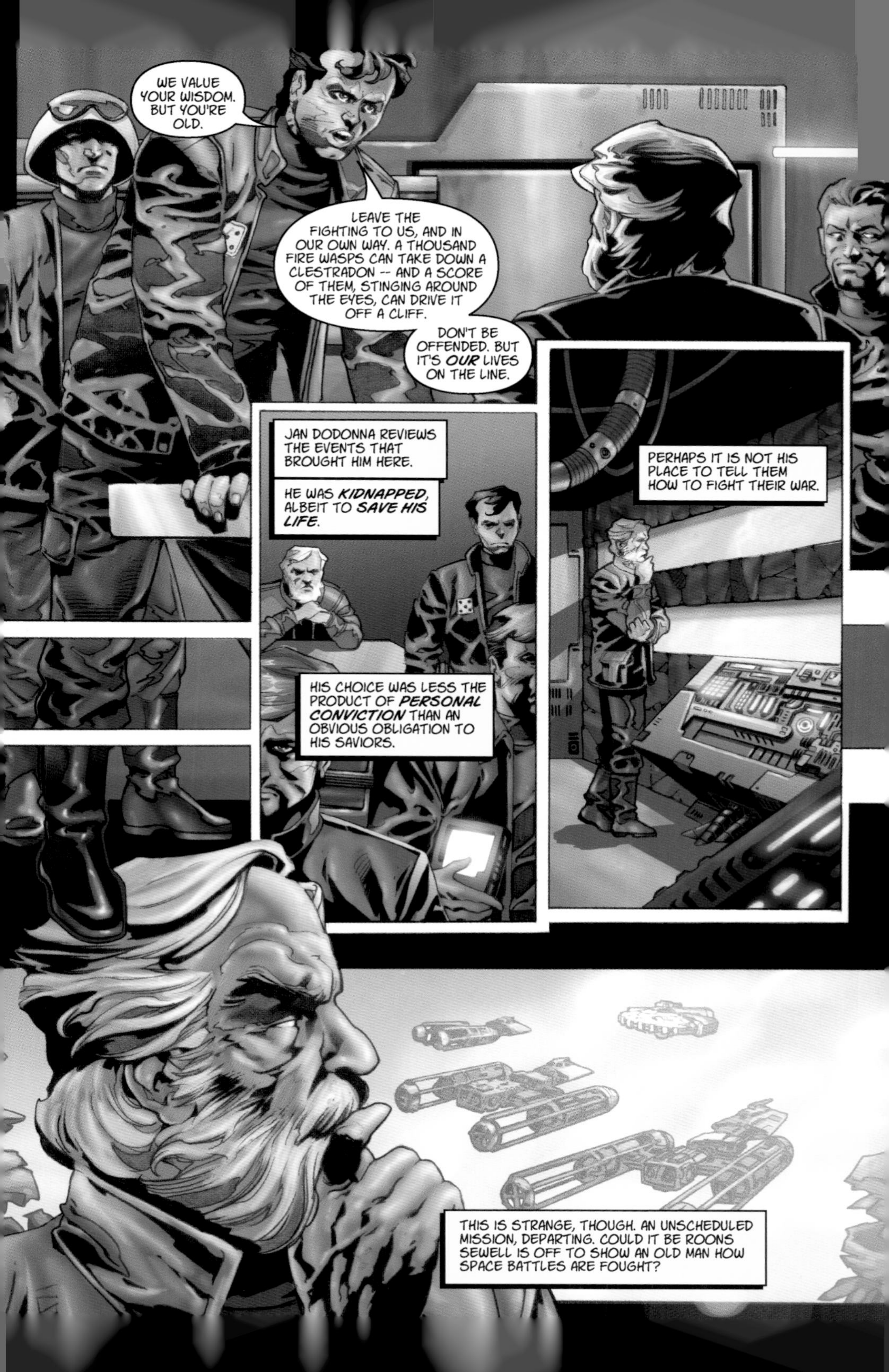
WE VALUE YOUR WISDOM. BUT YOU'RE OLD.
LEAVE THE FIGHTING TO US, AND IN OUR OWN WAY. A THOUSAND FIRE WASPS CAN TAKE DOWN A CLESTRADON -- AND A SCORE OF THEM, STINGING AROUND THE EYES, CAN DRIVE IT OFF A CLIFF.
DON'T BE OFFENDED. BUT IT'S OUR LIVES ON THE LINE.
JAN DODONNA REVIEWS THE EVENTS THAT BROUGHT HIM HERE.
HE WAS KIDNAPPED, ALBEIT TO SAVE HIS LIFE.
HIS CHOICE WAS LESS THE PRODUCT OF PERSONAL CONVICTION THAN AN OBVIOUS OBLIGATION TO HIS SAVIORS.
PERHAPS IT IS NOT HIS PLACE TO TELL THEM HOW TO FIGHT THEIR WAR.
THIS IS STRANGE, THOUGH. AN UNSCHEDULED MISSION, DEPARTING. COULD IT BE ROONS SEWELL IS OFF TO SHOW AN OLD MAN HOW SPACE BATTLES ARE FOUGHT?

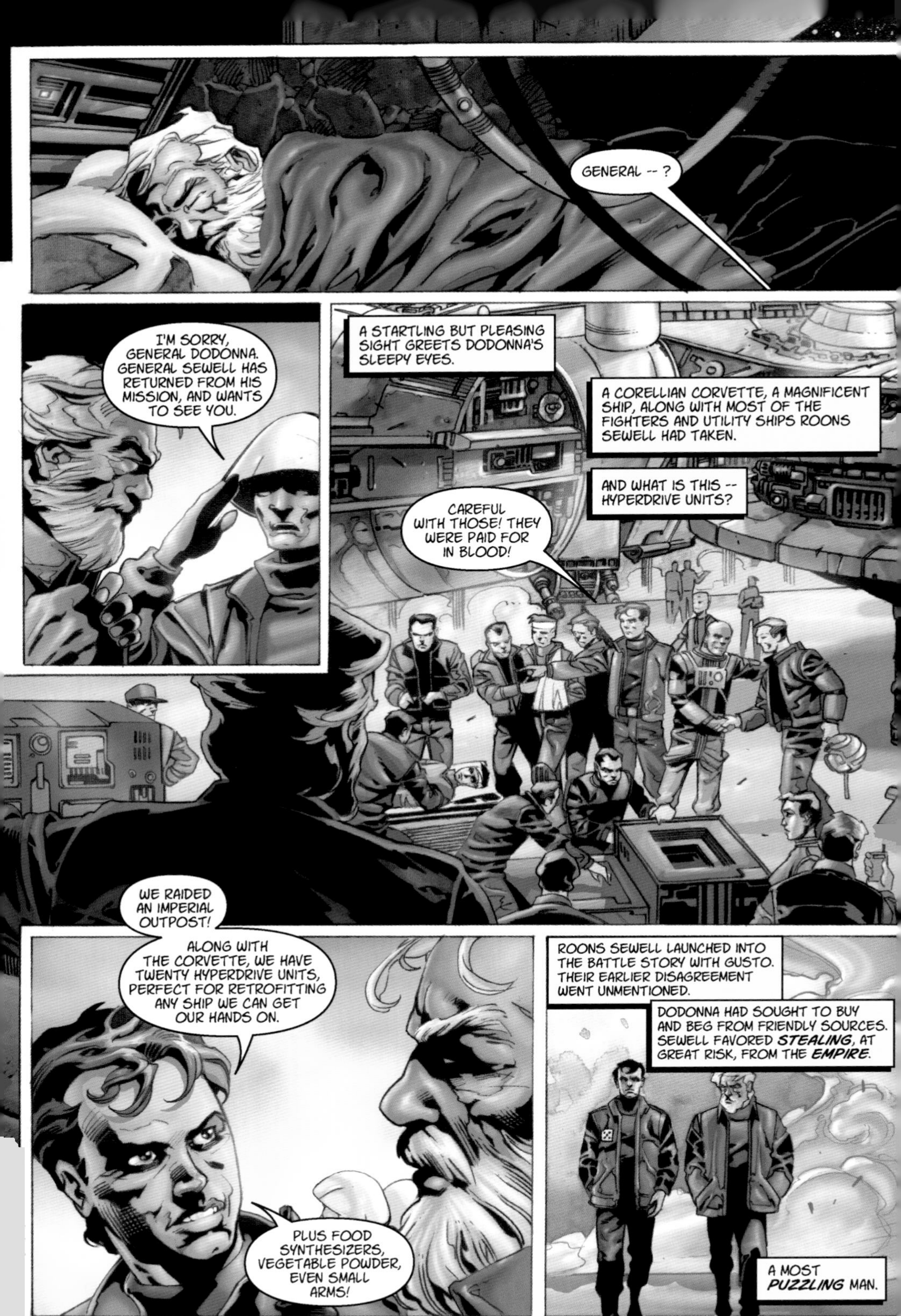
GENERAL -- ?
I'M SORRY, GENERAL DODONNA. GENERAL SEWELL HAS RETURNED FROM HIS MISSION, AND WANTS TO SEE YOU.
A STARTLING BUT PLEASING SIGHT GREETS DODONNA'S SLEEPY EYES.
A CORELLIAN CORVETTE, A MAGNIFICENT SHIP, ALONG WITH MOST OF THE FIGHTERS AND UTILITY SHIPS ROONS SEWELL HAD TAKEN.
AND WHAT IS THIS -- HYPERDRIVE UNITS?
CAREFUL WITH THOSE! THEY WERE PAID FOR IN BLOOD!
WE RAIDED AN IMPERIAL OUTPOST!
ALONG WITH THE CORVETTE, WE HAVE TWENTY HYPERDRIVE UNITS, PERFECT FOR RETROFITTING ANY SHIP WE CAN GET OUR HANDS ON.
PLUS FOOD SYNTHESIZERS, VEGETABLE POWDER, EVEN SMALL ARMS!
ROONS SEWELL LAUNCHED INTO THE BATTLE STORY WITH GUSTO. THEIR EARLIER DISAGREEMENT WENT UNMENTIONED.
DODONNA HAD SOUGHT TO BUY AND BEG FROM FRIENDLY SOURCES. SEWELL FAVORED STEALING, AT GREAT RISK, FROM THE EMPIRE.
A MOST PUZZLING MAN.

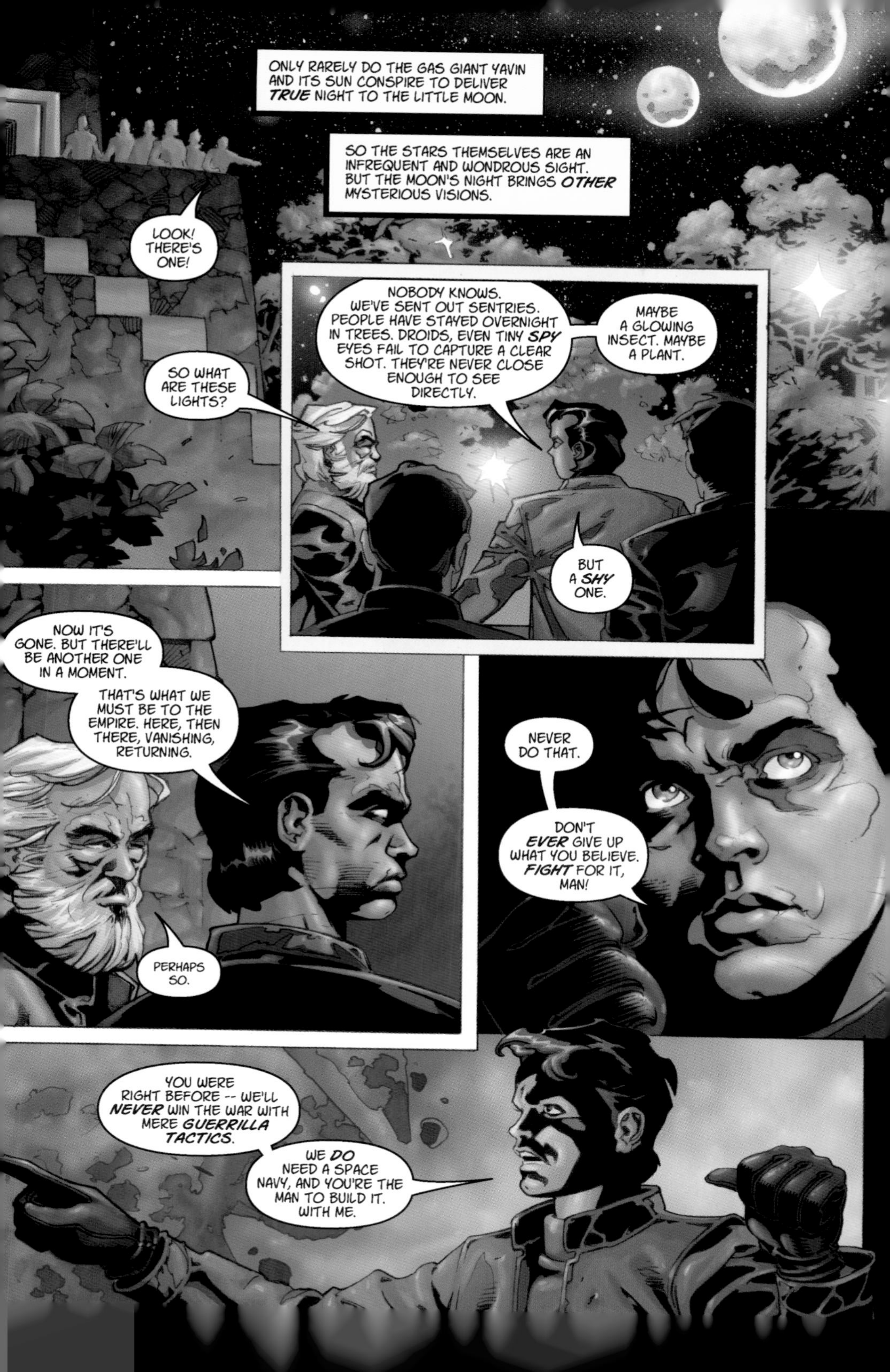
ONLY RARELY DO THE GAS GIANT YAVIN AND ITS SUN CONSPIRE TO DELIVER TRUE NIGHT TO THE LITTLE MOON.
SO THE STARS THEMSELVES ARE AN INFREQUENT AND WONDROUS SIGHT. BUT THE MOON'S NIGHT BRINGS OTHER MYSTERIOUS VISIONS.
LOOK! THERE'S ONE!
SO WHAT ARE THESE LIGHTS?
NOBODY KNOWS. WE'VE SENT OUT SENTRIES. PEOPLE HAVE STAYED OVERNIGHT IN TREES. DROIDS, EVEN TINY SPY EYES FAIL TO CAPTURE A CLEAR SHOT. THEY'RE NEVER CLOSE ENOUGH TO SEE DIRECTLY.
MAYBE A GLOWING INSECT. MAYBE A PLANT.
BUT A SHY ONE.
NOW IT'S GONE. BUT THERE'LL BE ANOTHER ONE IN A MOMENT.
THAT'S WHAT WE MUST BE TO THE EMPIRE. HERE, THEN THERE, VANISHING, RETURNING.
PERHAPS SO.
NEVER DO THAT.
DON'T EVER GIVE UP WHAT YOU BELIEVE. FIGHT FOR IT, MAN!
YOU WERE RIGHT BEFORE -- WE'LL NEVER WIN THE WAR WITH MERE GUERRILLA TACTICS.
WE DO NEED A SPACE NAVY, AND YOU'RE THE MAN TO BUILD IT. WITH ME.

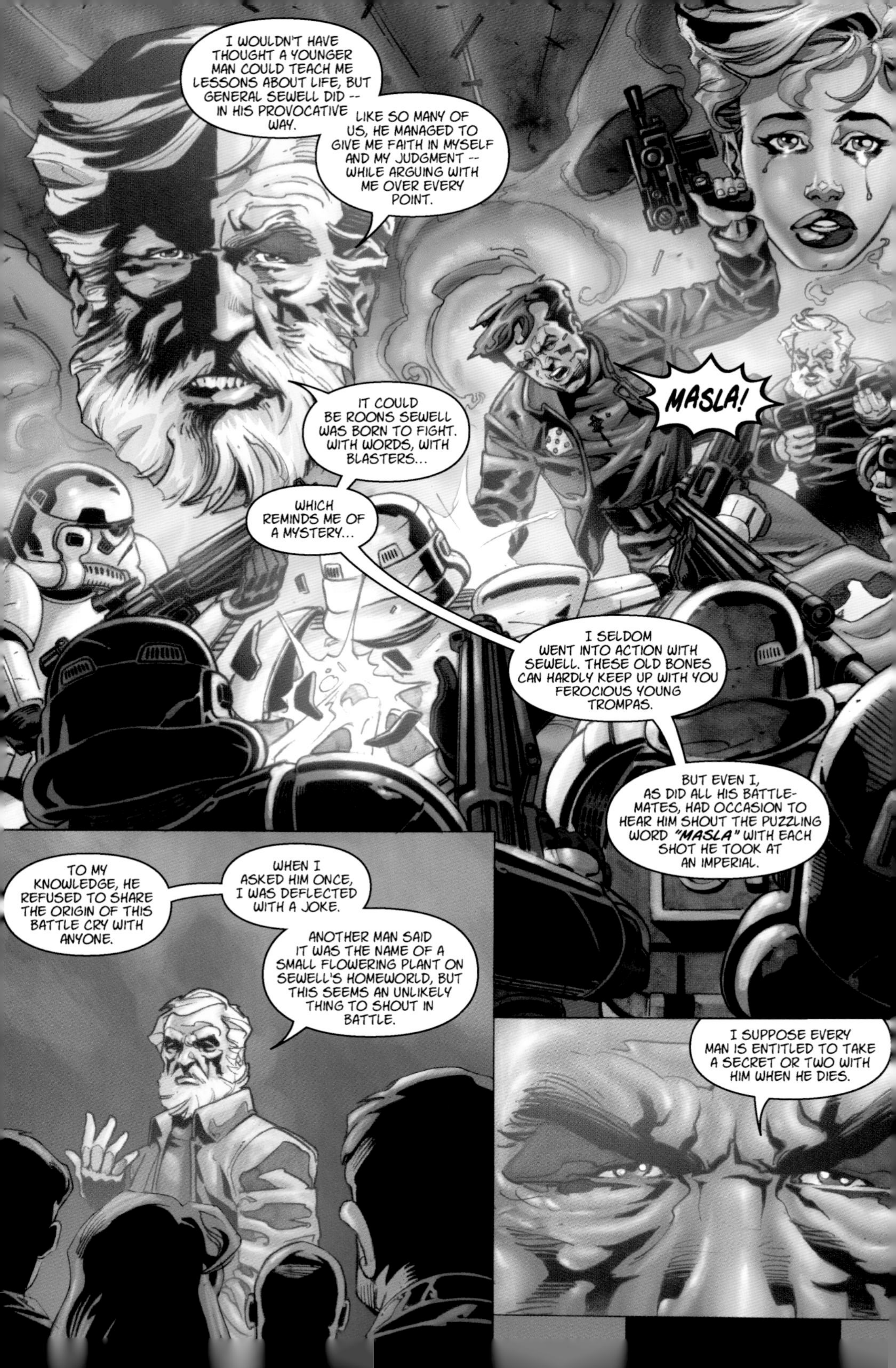
I WOULDN'T HAVE THOUGHT A YOUNGER MAN COULD TEACH ME LESSONS ABOUT LIFE, BUT GENERAL SEWELL DID -- IN HIS PROVOCATIVE WAY.
LIKE SO MANY OF US, HE MANAGED TO GIVE ME FAITH IN MYSELF AND MY JUDGMENT -- WHILE ARGUING WITH ME OVER EVERY POINT.
IT COULD BE ROONS SEWELL WAS BORN TO FIGHT. WITH WORDS, WITH BLASTERS...
WHICH REMINDS ME OF A MYSTERY...
MASLA!
I SELDOM WENT INTO ACTION WITH SEWELL. THESE OLD BONES CAN HARDLY KEEP UP WITH YOU FEROCIOUS YOUNG TROMPAS.
BUT EVEN I, AS DID ALL HIS BATTLE-MATES, HAD OCCASION TO HEAR HIM SHOUT THE PUZZLING WORD "MASLA" WITH EACH SHOT HE TOOK AT AN IMPERIAL.
TO MY KNOWLEDGE, HE REFUSED TO SHARE THE ORIGIN OF THIS BATTLE CRY WITH ANYONE.
WHEN I ASKED HIM ONCE, I WAS DEFLECTED WITH A JOKE.
ANOTHER MAN SAID IT WAS THE NAME OF A SMALL FLOWERING PLANT ON SEWELL'S HOMEWORLD, BUT THIS SEEMS AN UNLIKELY THING TO SHOUT IN BATTLE.
I SUPPOSE EVERY MAN IS ENTITLED TO TAKE A SECRET OR TWO WITH HIM WHEN HE DIES.

SEWELL HAD HIS QUIRKS.
YAVIN IV IS A JUNGLE WORLD, AND SO WE SHARE OUR LIVING SPACE WITH A GOOD NUMBER OF VERMIN, AS YOU WELL KNOW.

SEWELL TOLERATED THE INSECTS, THE FLYERS, THE SLITHERERS. BUT ONE FURRED CRAWLER -- I SEE SMILES, TELLING ME YOU KNOW THIS STORY -- HE COULD NEVER ABIDE...

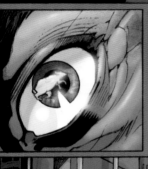

I'LL GET YOU!!

SK-K-OW

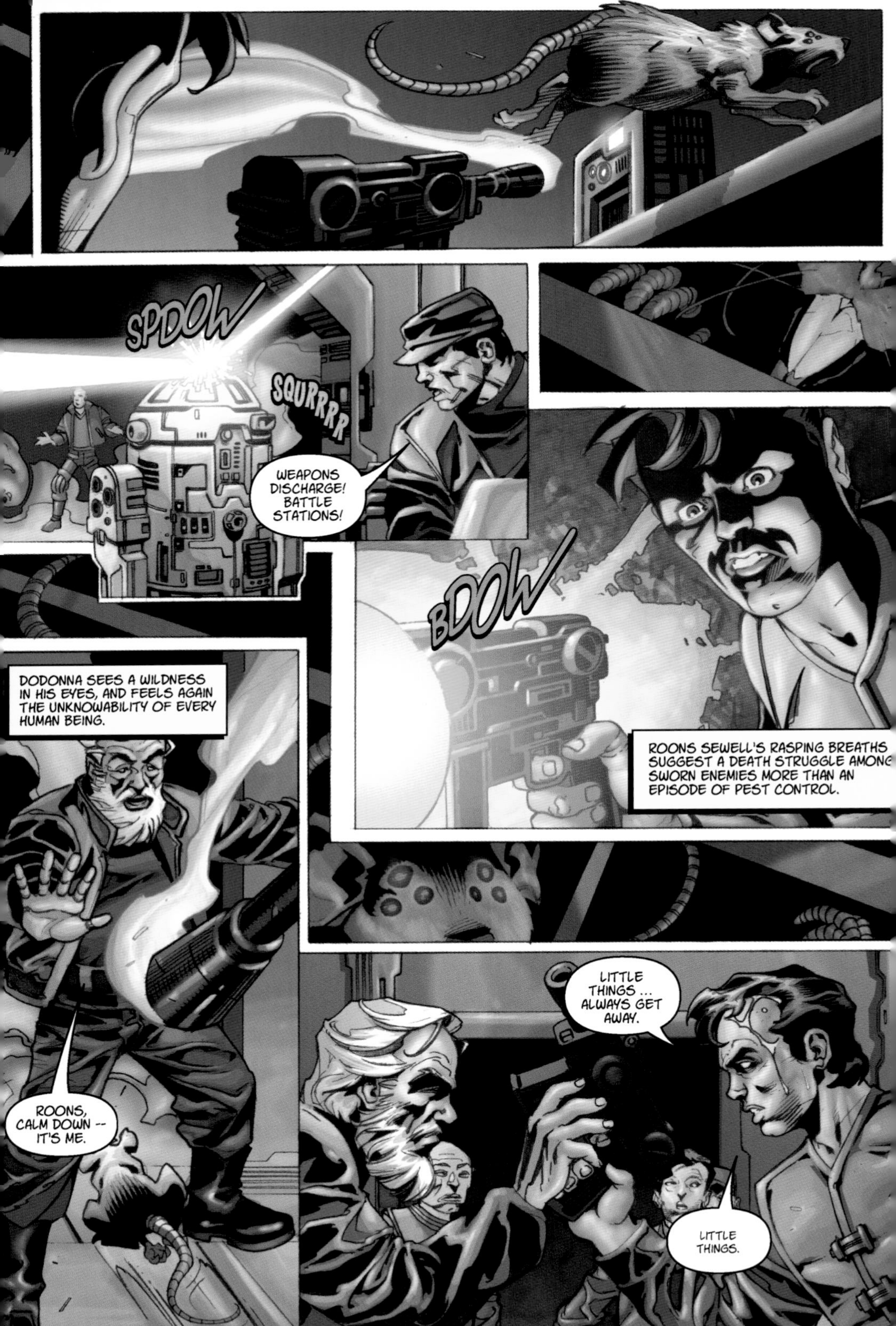
SPDOW
SQURRRR
WEAPONS DISCHARGE! BATTLE STATIONS!
BDOW
DODONNA SEES A WILDNESS IN HIS EYES, AND FEELS AGAIN THE UNKNOWABILITY OF EVERY HUMAN BEING.
ROONS SEWELL'S RASPING BREATHS SUGGEST A DEATH STRUGGLE AMONG SWORN ENEMIES MORE THAN AN EPISODE OF PEST CONTROL.
ROONS, CALM DOWN -- IT'S ME.
LITTLE THINGS ... ALWAYS GET AWAY.
LITTLE THINGS.

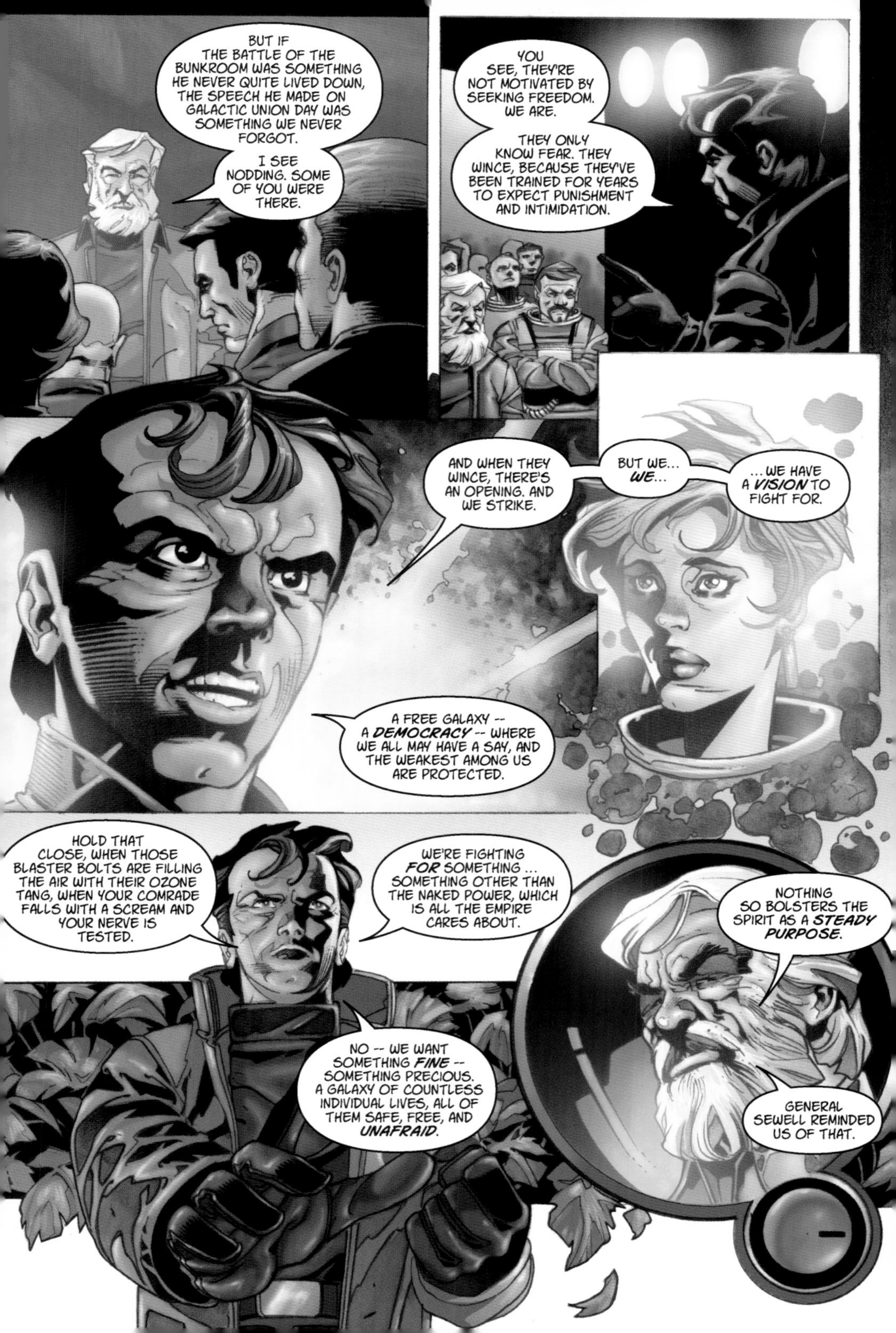
BUT IF THE BATTLE OF THE BUNKROOM WAS SOMETHING HE NEVER QUITE LIVED DOWN, THE SPEECH HE MADE ON GALACTIC UNION DAY WAS SOMETHING WE NEVER FORGOT.
I SEE NODDING. SOME OF YOU WERE THERE.
YOU SEE, THEY'RE NOT MOTIVATED BY SEEKING FREEDOM. WE ARE.
THEY ONLY KNOW FEAR. THEY WINCE, BECAUSE THEY'VE BEEN TRAINED FOR YEARS TO EXPECT PUNISHMENT AND INTIMIDATION.
AND WHEN THEY WINCE, THERE'S AN OPENING. AND WE STRIKE.
BUT WE... WE...
...WE HAVE A VISION TO FIGHT FOR.
A FREE GALAXY -- A DEMOCRACY -- WHERE WE ALL MAY HAVE A SAY, AND THE WEAKEST AMONG US ARE PROTECTED.
HOLD THAT CLOSE, WHEN THOSE BLASTER BOLTS ARE FILLING THE AIR WITH THEIR OZONE TANG, WHEN YOUR COMRADE FALLS WITH A SCREAM AND YOUR NERVE IS TESTED.
WE'RE FIGHTING FOR SOMETHING ... SOMETHING OTHER THAN THE NAKED POWER, WHICH IS ALL THE EMPIRE CARES ABOUT.
NO -- WE WANT SOMETHING FINE -- SOMETHING PRECIOUS. A GALAXY OF COUNTLESS INDIVIDUAL LIVES, ALL OF THEM SAFE, FREE, AND UNAFRAID.
NOTHING SO BOLSTERS THE SPIRIT AS A STEADY PURPOSE.
GENERAL SEWELL REMINDED US OF THAT.

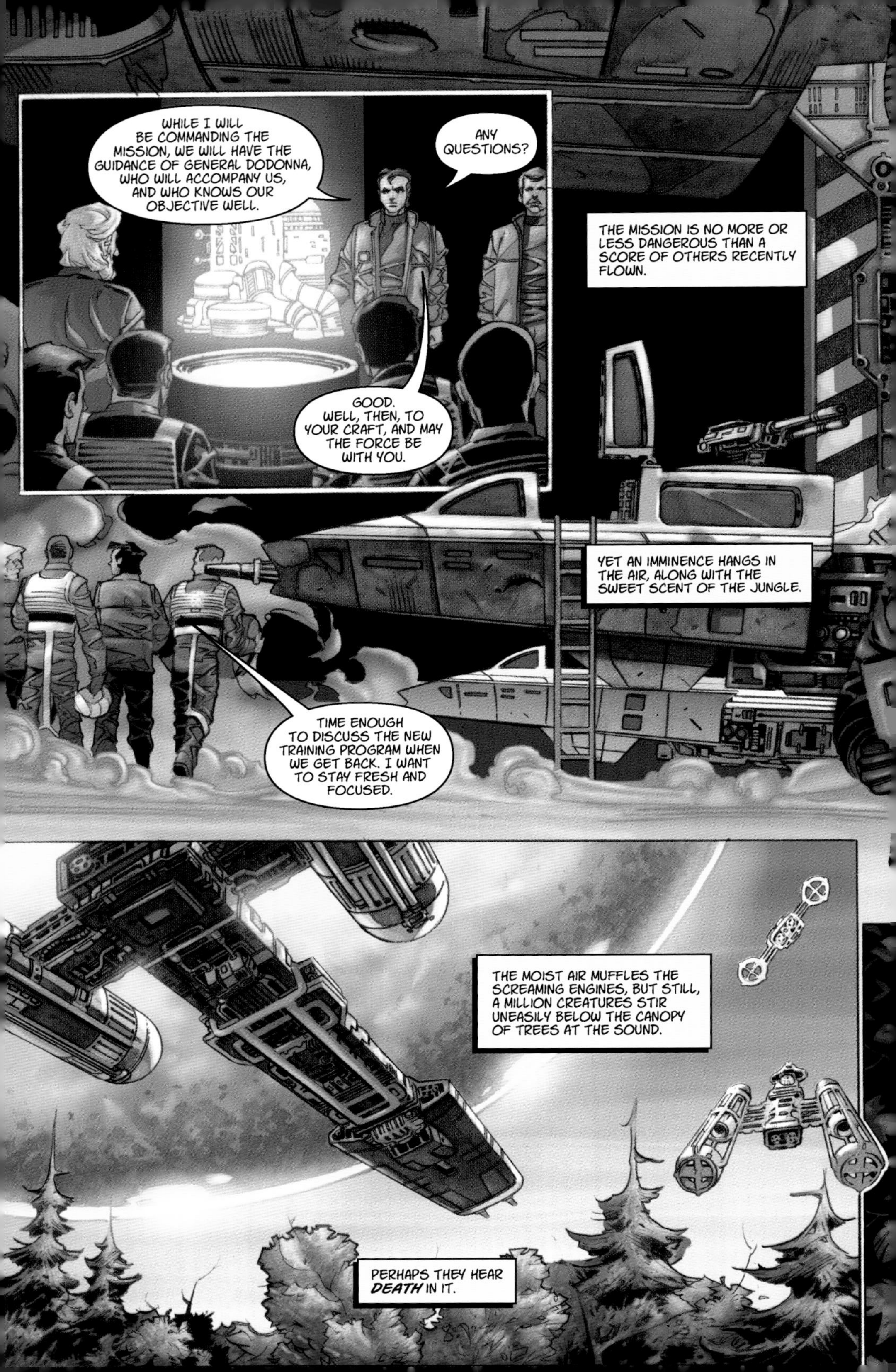
WHILE I WILL BE COMMANDING THE MISSION, WE WILL HAVE THE GUIDANCE OF GENERAL DODONNA, WHO WILL ACCOMPANY US, AND WHO KNOWS OUR OBJECTIVE WELL.
ANY QUESTIONS?
GOOD. WELL, THEN, TO YOUR CRAFT, AND MAY THE FORCE BE WITH YOU.
THE MISSION IS NO MORE OR LESS DANGEROUS THAN A SCORE OF OTHERS RECENTLY FLOWN.
YET AN IMMINENCE HANGS IN THE AIR, ALONG WITH THE SWEET SCENT OF THE JUNGLE.
TIME ENOUGH TO DISCUSS THE NEW TRAINING PROGRAM WHEN WE GET BACK. I WANT TO STAY FRESH AND FOCUSED.
THE MOIST AIR MUFFLES THE SCREAMING ENGINES, BUT STILL, A MILLION CREATURES STIR UNEASILY BELOW THE CANOPY OF TREES AT THE SOUND.
PERHAPS THEY HEAR ***DEATH*** IN IT.

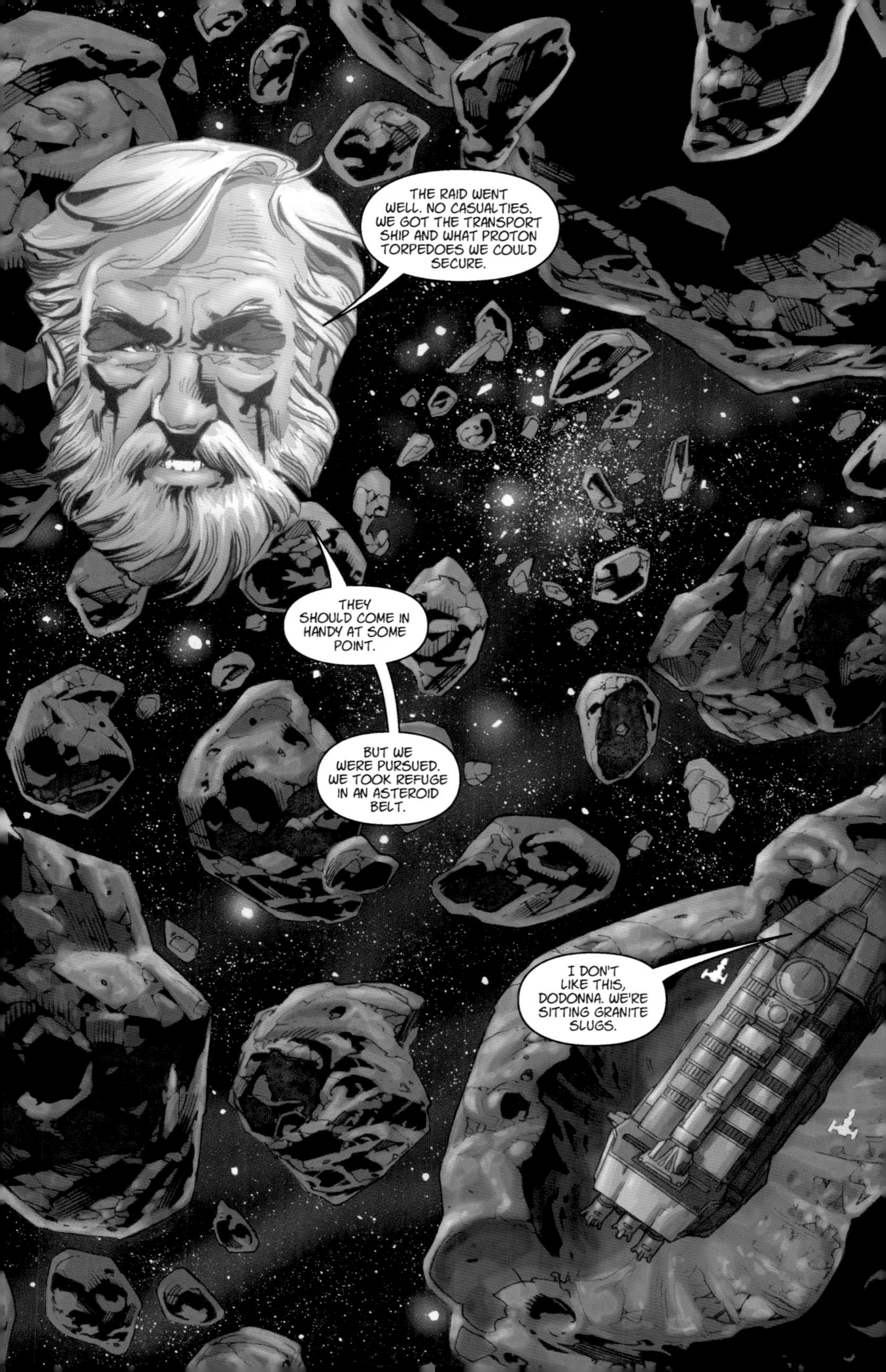
THE RAID WENT WELL. NO CASUALTIES. WE GOT THE TRANSPORT SHIP AND WHAT PROTON TORPEDOES WE COULD SECURE.
THEY SHOULD COME IN HANDY AT SOME POINT.
BUT WE WERE PURSUED. WE TOOK REFUGE IN AN ASTEROID BELT.
I DON'T LIKE THIS, DODONNA. WE'RE SITTING GRANITE SLUGS.

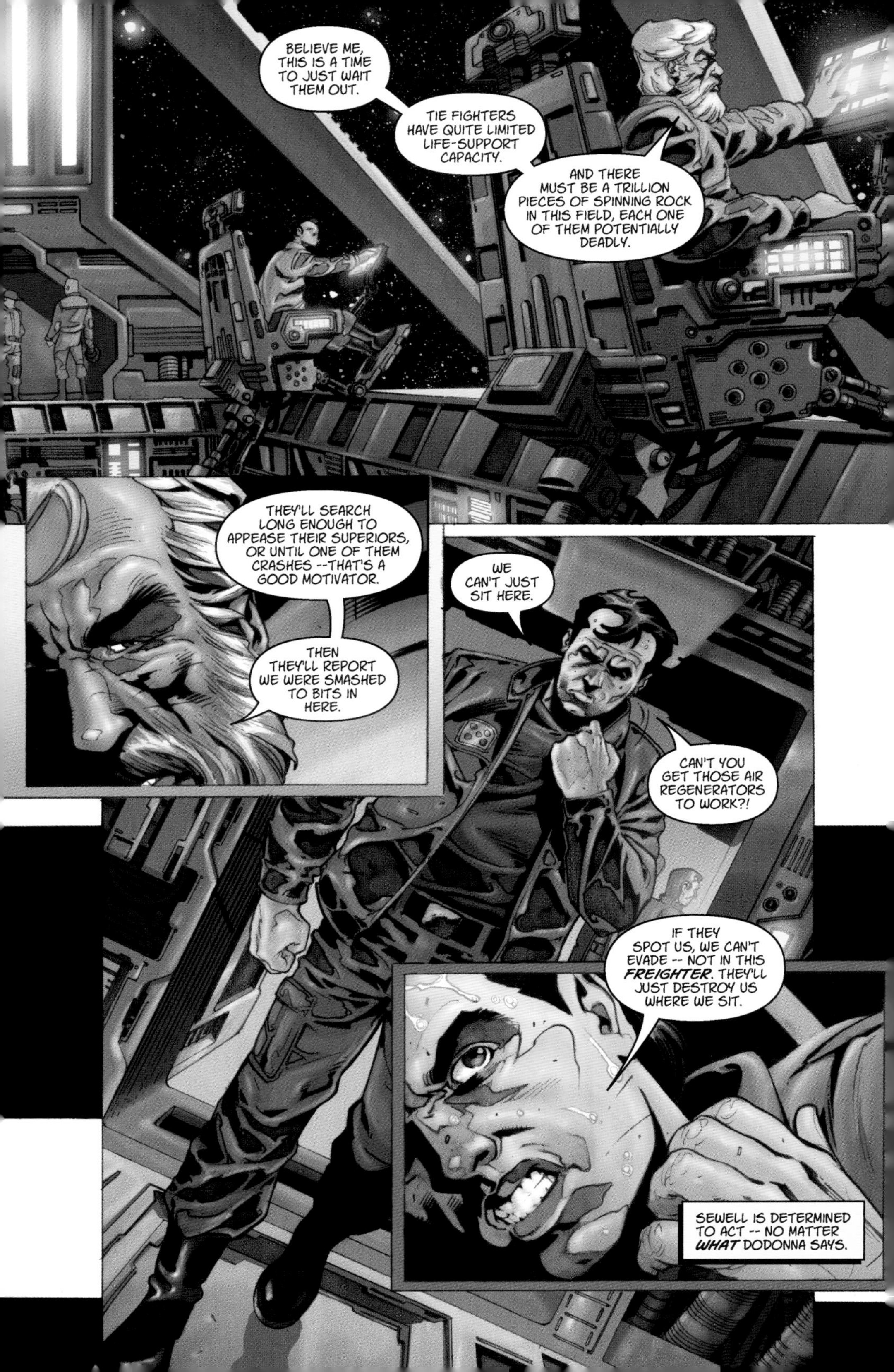
BELIEVE ME, THIS IS A TIME TO JUST WAIT THEM OUT.
TIE FIGHTERS HAVE QUITE LIMITED LIFE-SUPPORT CAPACITY.
AND THERE MUST BE A TRILLION PIECES OF SPINNING ROCK IN THIS FIELD, EACH ONE OF THEM POTENTIALLY DEADLY.
THEY'LL SEARCH LONG ENOUGH TO APPEASE THEIR SUPERIORS, OR UNTIL ONE OF THEM CRASHES --THAT'S A GOOD MOTIVATOR.
THEN THEY'LL REPORT WE WERE SMASHED TO BITS IN HERE.
WE CAN'T JUST SIT HERE.
CAN'T YOU GET THOSE AIR REGENERATORS TO WORK?!
IF THEY SPOT US, WE CAN'T EVADE -- NOT IN THIS ***FREIGHTER***. THEY'LL JUST DESTROY US WHERE WE SIT.
SEWELL IS DETERMINED TO ACT -- NO MATTER ***WHAT*** DODONNA SAYS.

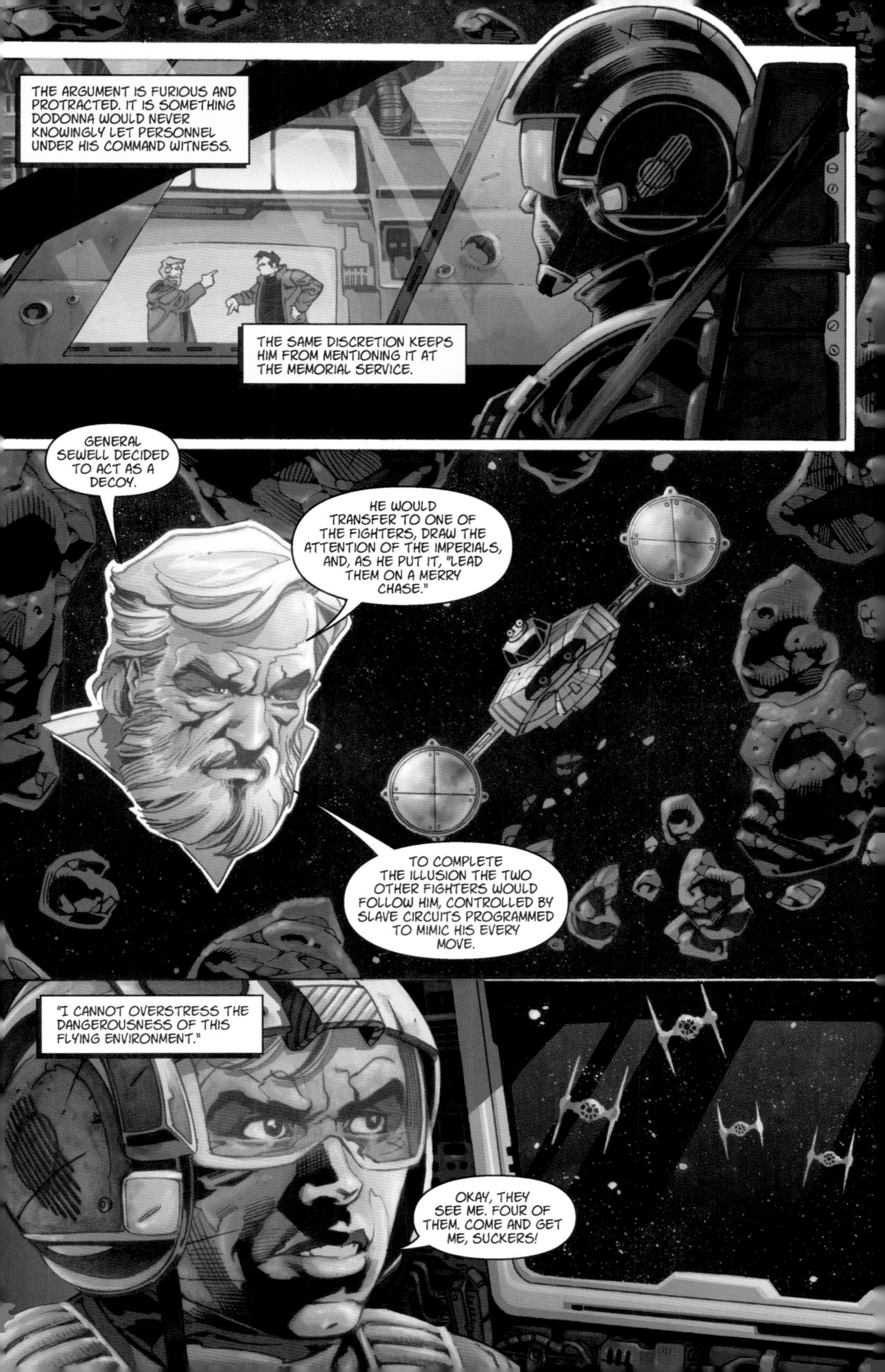

THE ARGUMENT IS FURIOUS AND PROTRACTED. IT IS SOMETHING DODONNA WOULD NEVER KNOWINGLY LET PERSONNEL UNDER HIS COMMAND WITNESS.
THE SAME DISCRETION KEEPS HIM FROM MENTIONING IT AT THE MEMORIAL SERVICE.
GENERAL SEWELL DECIDED TO ACT AS A DECOY.
HE WOULD TRANSFER TO ONE OF THE FIGHTERS, DRAW THE ATTENTION OF THE IMPERIALS, AND, AS HE PUT IT, "LEAD THEM ON A MERRY CHASE."
TO COMPLETE THE ILLUSION THE TWO OTHER FIGHTERS WOULD FOLLOW HIM, CONTROLLED BY SLAVE CIRCUITS PROGRAMMED TO MIMIC HIS EVERY MOVE.
"I CANNOT OVERSTRESS THE DANGEROUSNESS OF THIS FLYING ENVIRONMENT."
OKAY, THEY SEE ME. FOUR OF THEM. COME AND GET ME, SUCKERS!

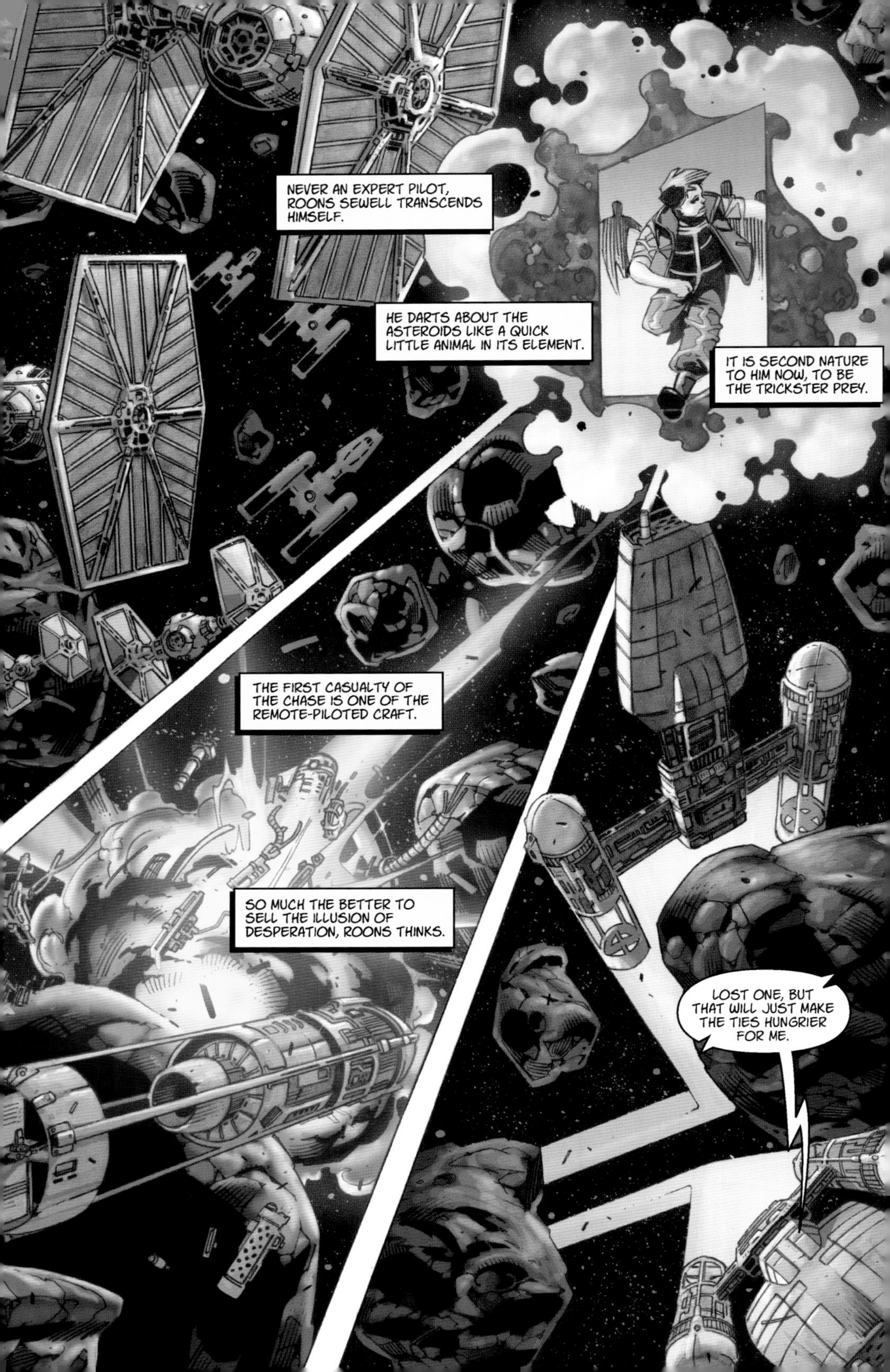

NEVER AN EXPERT PILOT, ROONS SEWELL TRANSCENDS HIMSELF.
HE DARTS ABOUT THE ASTEROIDS LIKE A QUICK LITTLE ANIMAL IN ITS ELEMENT.
IT IS SECOND NATURE TO HIM NOW, TO BE THE TRICKSTER PREY.
THE FIRST CASUALTY OF THE CHASE IS ONE OF THE REMOTE-PILOTED CRAFT.
SO MUCH THE BETTER TO SELL THE ILLUSION OF DESPERATION, ROONS THINKS.
LOST ONE, BUT THAT WILL JUST MAKE THE TIES HUNGRIER FOR ME.

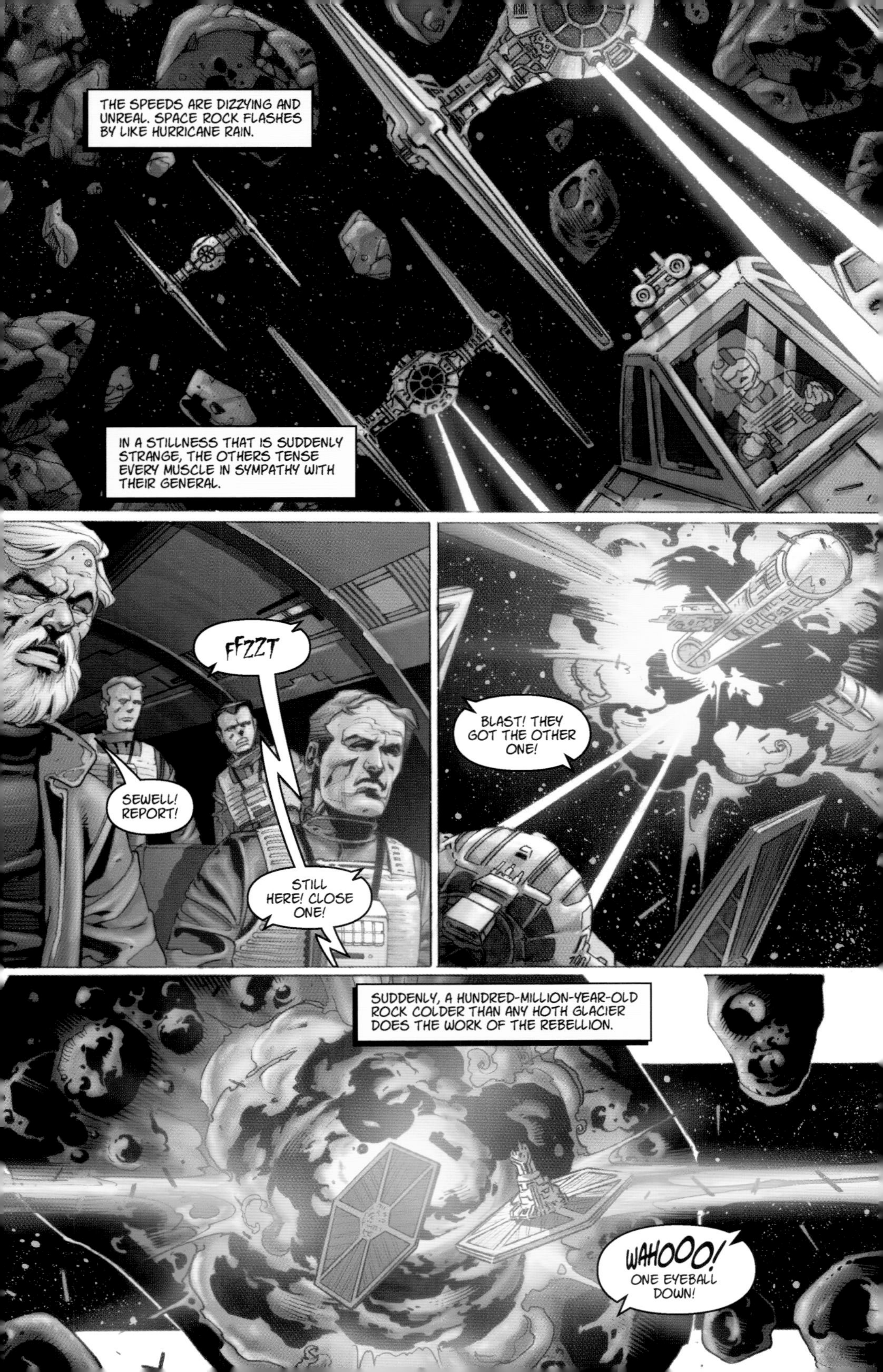
THE SPEEDS ARE DIZZYING AND UNREAL. SPACE ROCK FLASHES BY LIKE HURRICANE RAIN.
IN A STILLNESS THAT IS SUDDENLY STRANGE, THE OTHERS TENSE EVERY MUSCLE IN SYMPATHY WITH THEIR GENERAL.
SEWELL! REPORT!
FFZZT
STILL HERE! CLOSE ONE!
BLAST! THEY GOT THE OTHER ONE!
SUDDENLY, A HUNDRED-MILLION-YEAR-OLD ROCK COLDER THAN ANY HOTH GLACIER DOES THE WORK OF THE REBELLION.
WAHOOO! ONE EYEBALL DOWN!

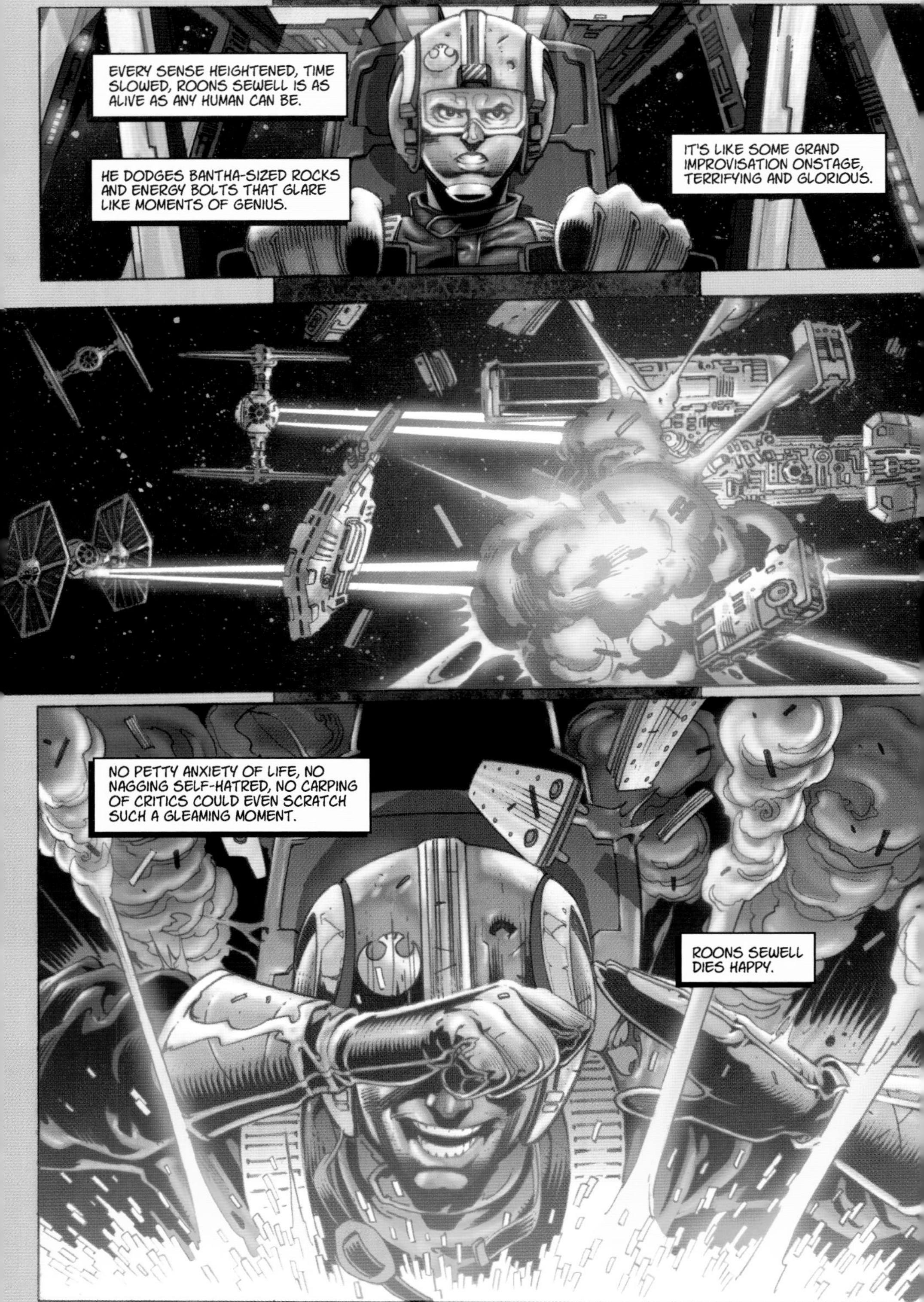
EVERY SENSE HEIGHTENED, TIME SLOWED, ROONS SEWELL IS AS ALIVE AS ANY HUMAN CAN BE.
HE DODGES BANTHA-SIZED ROCKS AND ENERGY BOLTS THAT GLARE LIKE MOMENTS OF GENIUS.
IT'S LIKE SOME GRAND IMPROVISATION ONSTAGE, TERRIFYING AND GLORIOUS.
NO PETTY ANXIETY OF LIFE, NO NAGGING SELF-HATRED, NO CARPING OF CRITICS COULD EVEN SCRATCH SUCH A GLEAMING MOMENT.
ROONS SEWELL DIES HAPPY.

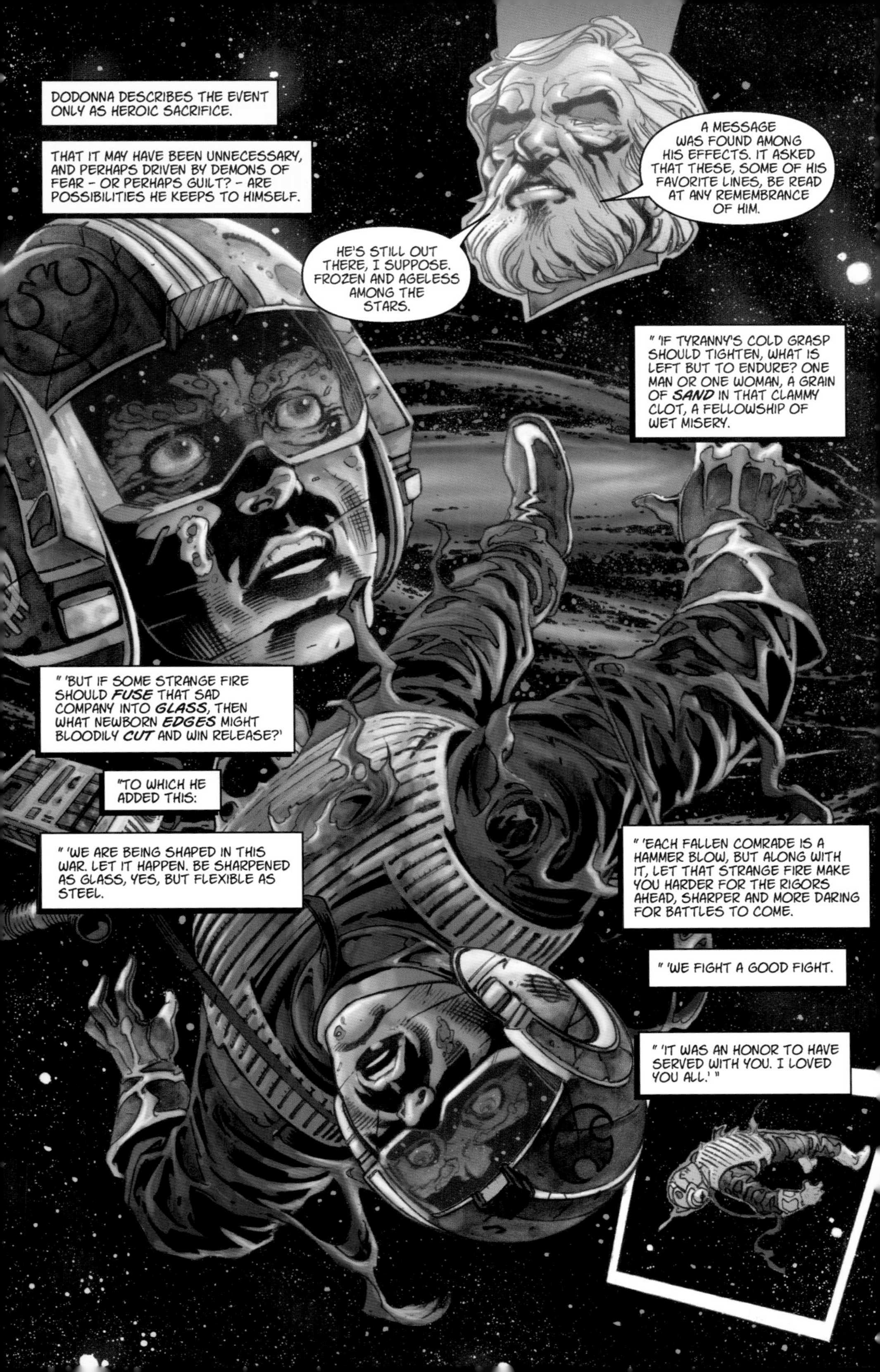
DODONNA DESCRIBES THE EVENT ONLY AS HEROIC SACRIFICE.
THAT IT MAY HAVE BEEN UNNECESSARY, AND PERHAPS DRIVEN BY DEMONS OF FEAR – OR PERHAPS GUILT? – ARE POSSIBILITIES HE KEEPS TO HIMSELF.
HE'S STILL OUT THERE, I SUPPOSE. FROZEN AND AGELESS AMONG THE STARS.
A MESSAGE WAS FOUND AMONG HIS EFFECTS. IT ASKED THAT THESE, SOME OF HIS FAVORITE LINES, BE READ AT ANY REMEMBRANCE OF HIM.
" 'IF TYRANNY'S COLD GRASP SHOULD TIGHTEN, WHAT IS LEFT BUT TO ENDURE? ONE MAN OR ONE WOMAN, A GRAIN OF SAND IN THAT CLAMMY CLOT, A FELLOWSHIP OF WET MISERY.
" 'BUT IF SOME STRANGE FIRE SHOULD FUSE THAT SAD COMPANY INTO GLASS, THEN WHAT NEWBORN EDGES MIGHT BLOODILY CUT AND WIN RELEASE?'
"TO WHICH HE ADDED THIS:
" 'WE ARE BEING SHAPED IN THIS WAR. LET IT HAPPEN. BE SHARPENED AS GLASS, YES, BUT FLEXIBLE AS STEEL.
" 'EACH FALLEN COMRADE IS A HAMMER BLOW, BUT ALONG WITH IT, LET THAT STRANGE FIRE MAKE YOU HARDER FOR THE RIGORS AHEAD, SHARPER AND MORE DARING FOR BATTLES TO COME.
" 'WE FIGHT A GOOD FIGHT.
" 'IT WAS AN HONOR TO HAVE SERVED WITH YOU. I LOVED YOU ALL.' "

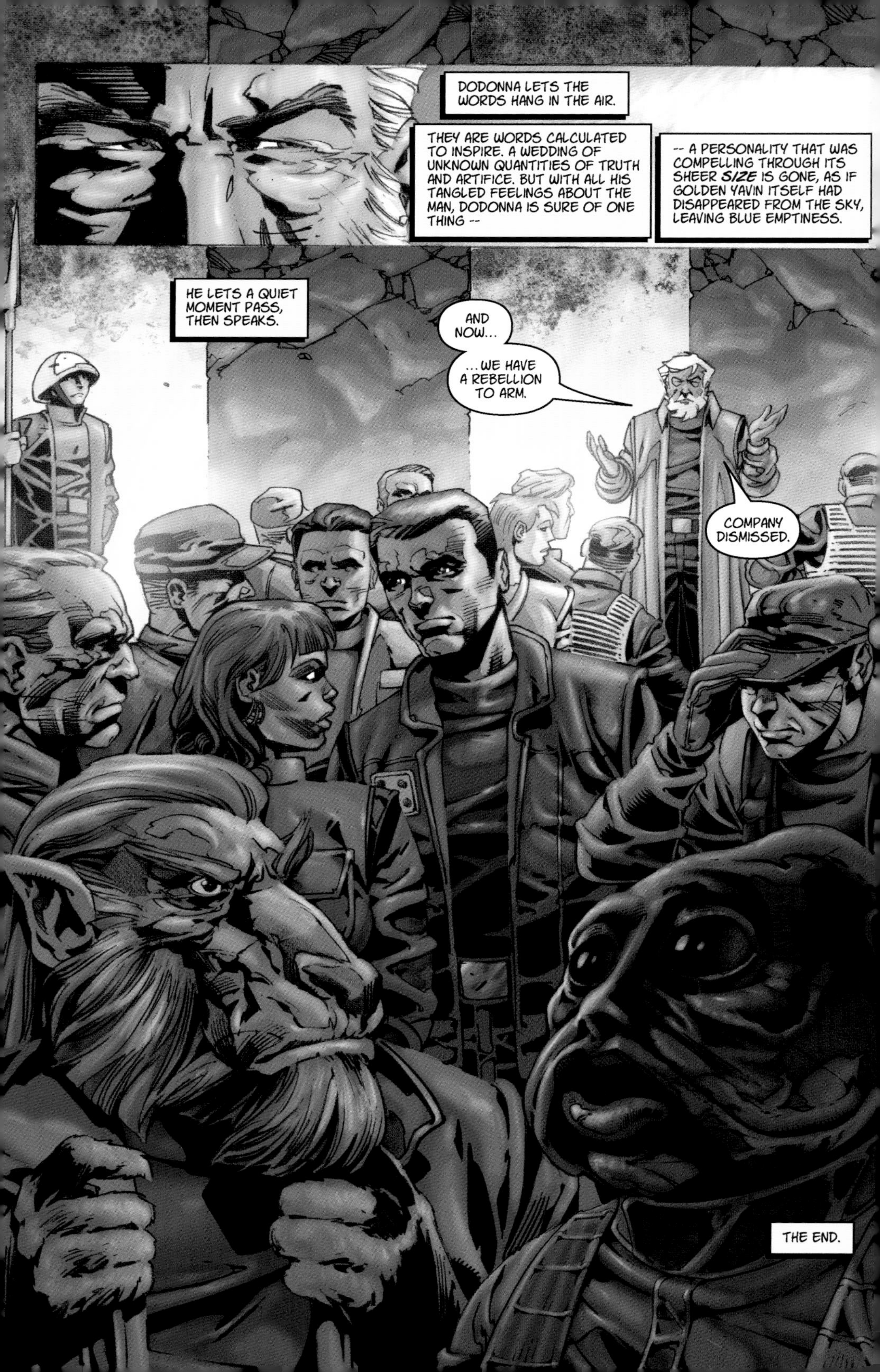
DODONNA LETS THE WORDS HANG IN THE AIR.
THEY ARE WORDS CALCULATED TO INSPIRE. A WEDDING OF UNKNOWN QUANTITIES OF TRUTH AND ARTIFICE. BUT WITH ALL HIS TANGLED FEELINGS ABOUT THE MAN, DODONNA IS SURE OF ONE THING --
-- A PERSONALITY THAT WAS COMPELLING THROUGH ITS SHEER *SIZE* IS GONE, AS IF GOLDEN YAVIN ITSELF HAD DISAPPEARED FROM THE SKY, LEAVING BLUE EMPTINESS.
HE LETS A QUIET MOMENT PASS, THEN SPEAKS.
AND NOW...
...WE HAVE A REBELLION TO ARM.
COMPANY DISMISSED.
THE END.

What Sin Loyalty? | Illustration by David Michael Beck, colored by Brad Anderson

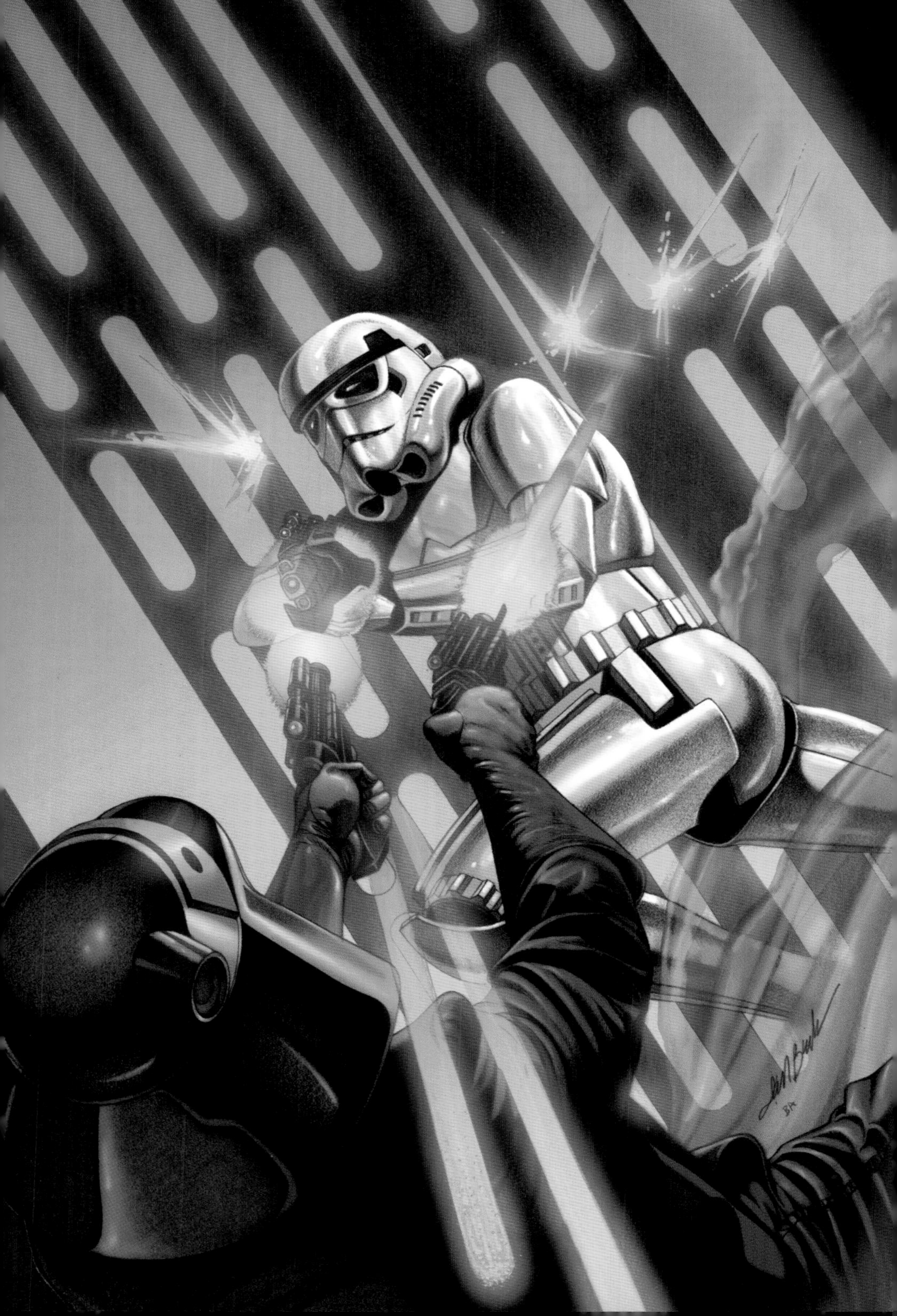

CONCURRENT WITH THE BATTLE OF YAVIN . . .

script by Jeremy Barlow
art by Patrick Blaine
colors by Studio F
lettering by Sno Cone Studios

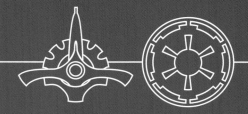

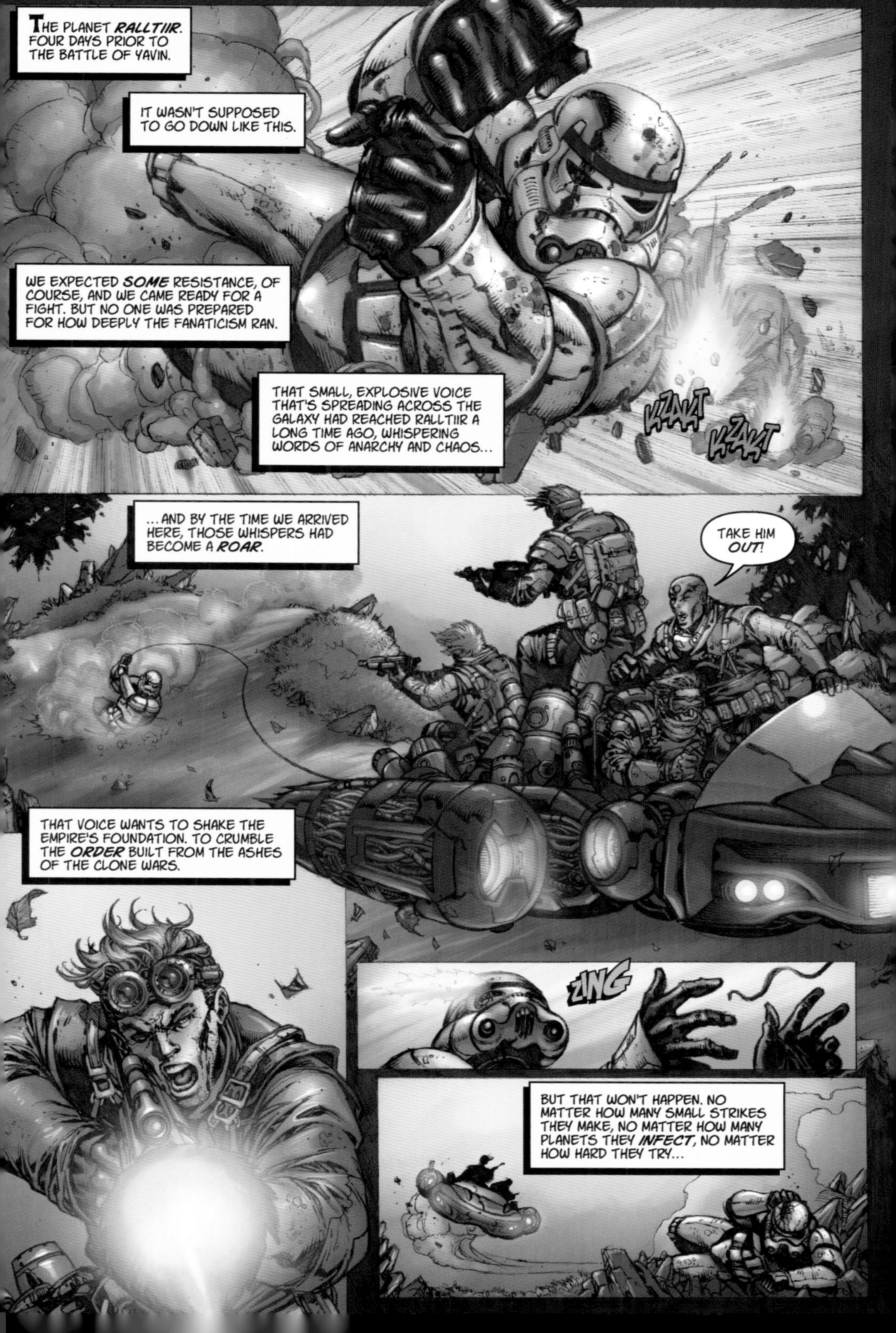
THE PLANET RALLTIIR. FOUR DAYS PRIOR TO THE BATTLE OF YAVIN.
IT WASN'T SUPPOSED TO GO DOWN LIKE THIS.
WE EXPECTED SOME RESISTANCE, OF COURSE, AND WE CAME READY FOR A FIGHT. BUT NO ONE WAS PREPARED FOR HOW DEEPLY THE FANATICISM RAN.
THAT SMALL, EXPLOSIVE VOICE THAT'S SPREADING ACROSS THE GALAXY HAD REACHED RALLTIIR A LONG TIME AGO, WHISPERING WORDS OF ANARCHY AND CHAOS...
KZAKT
KZAKT
...AND BY THE TIME WE ARRIVED HERE, THOSE WHISPERS HAD BECOME A ROAR.
TAKE HIM OUT!
THAT VOICE WANTS TO SHAKE THE EMPIRE'S FOUNDATION. TO CRUMBLE THE ORDER BUILT FROM THE ASHES OF THE CLONE WARS.
ZING
BUT THAT WON'T HAPPEN. NO MATTER HOW MANY SMALL STRIKES THEY MAKE, NO MATTER HOW MANY PLANETS THEY INFECT, NO MATTER HOW HARD THEY TRY...

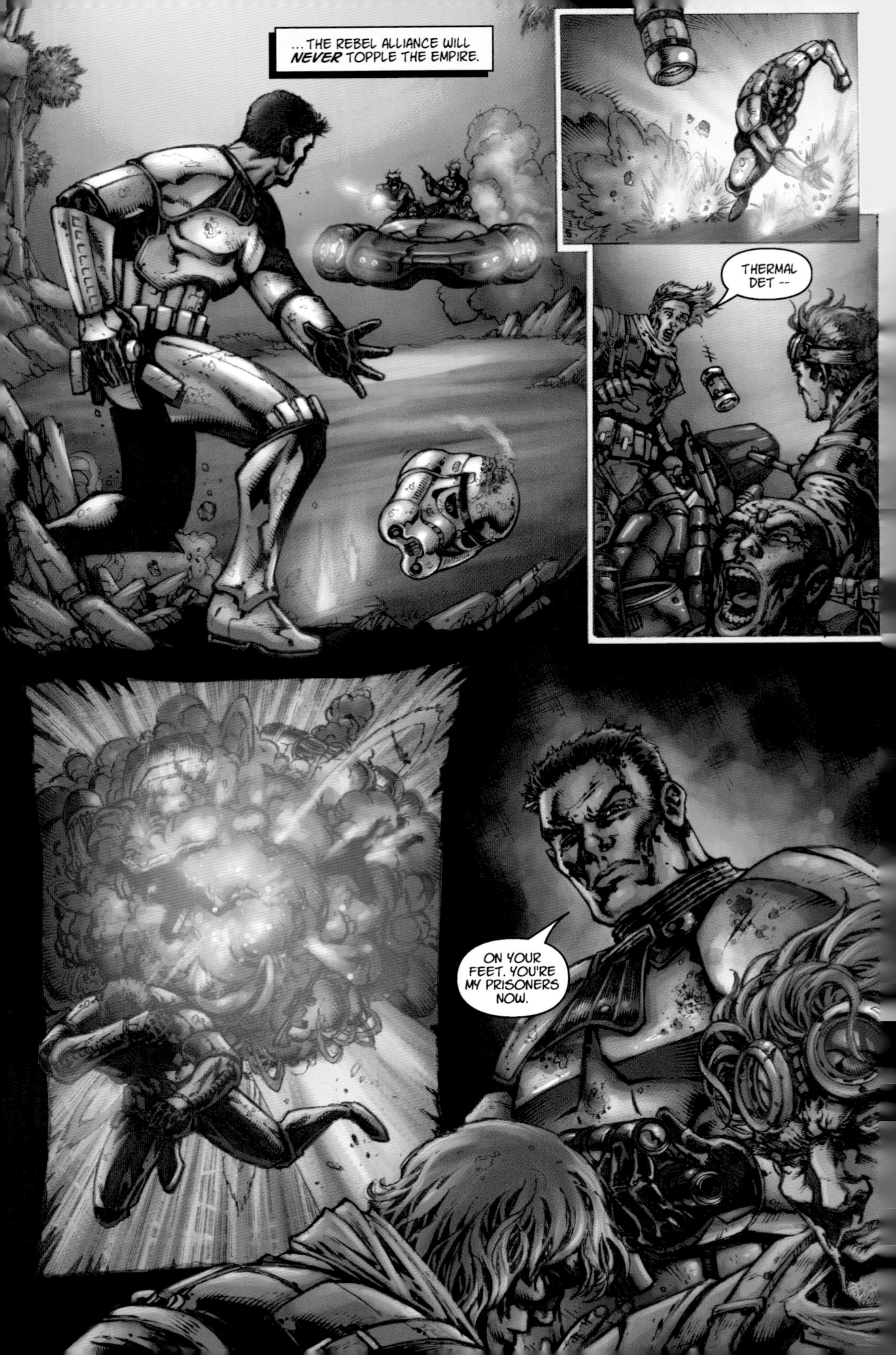
...THE REBEL ALLIANCE WILL NEVER TOPPLE THE EMPIRE.
THERMAL DET --
ON YOUR FEET. YOU'RE MY PRISONERS NOW.

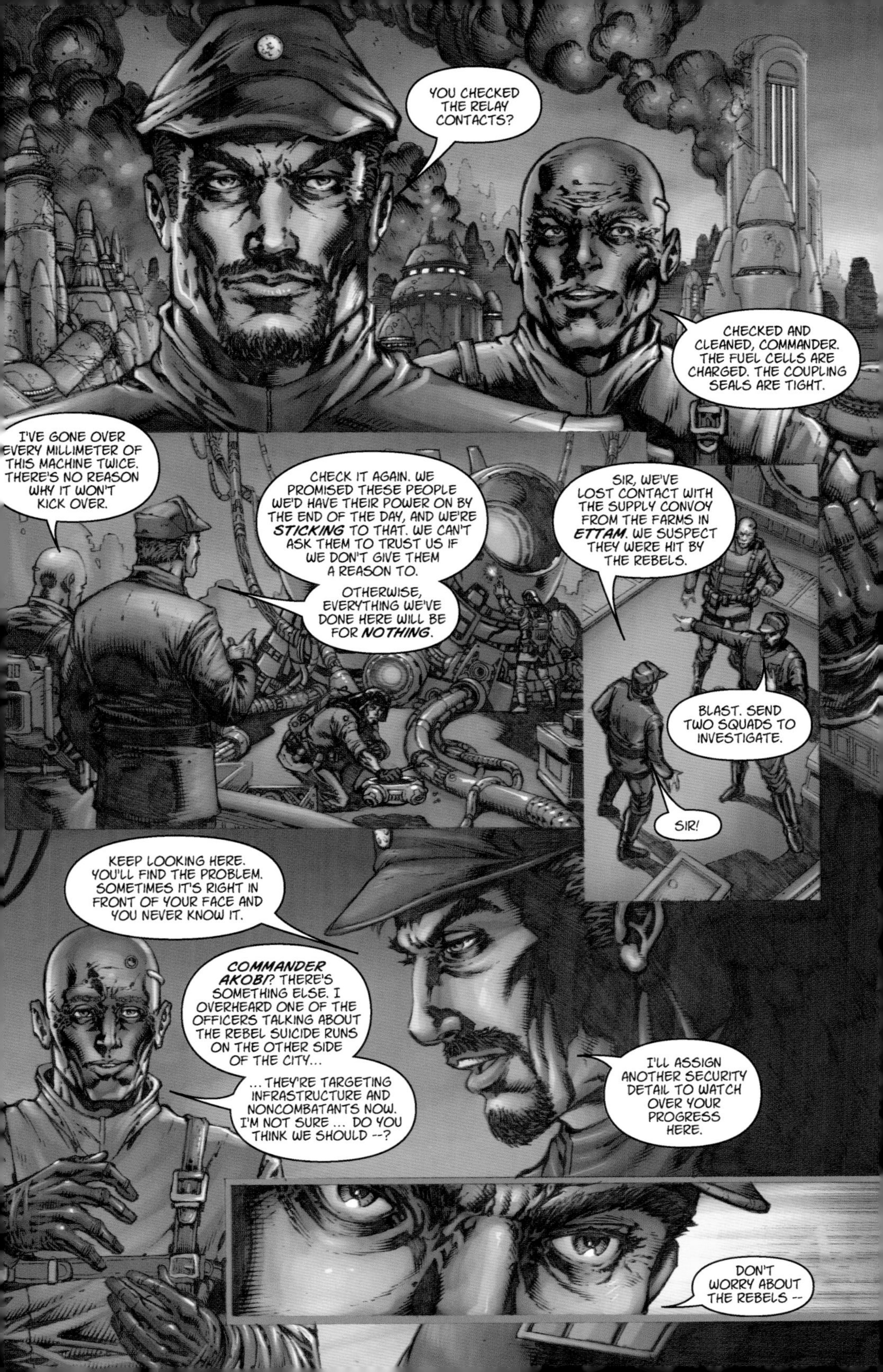
YOU CHECKED THE RELAY CONTACTS?
CHECKED AND CLEANED, COMMANDER. THE FUEL CELLS ARE CHARGED. THE COUPLING SEALS ARE TIGHT.
I'VE GONE OVER EVERY MILLIMETER OF THIS MACHINE TWICE. THERE'S NO REASON WHY IT WON'T KICK OVER.
CHECK IT AGAIN. WE PROMISED THESE PEOPLE WE'D HAVE THEIR POWER ON BY THE END OF THE DAY, AND WE'RE *STICKING* TO THAT. WE CAN'T ASK THEM TO TRUST US IF WE DON'T GIVE THEM A REASON TO.
OTHERWISE, EVERYTHING WE'VE DONE HERE WILL BE FOR *NOTHING*.
SIR, WE'VE LOST CONTACT WITH THE SUPPLY CONVOY FROM THE FARMS IN *ETTAM*. WE SUSPECT THEY WERE HIT BY THE REBELS.
BLAST. SEND TWO SQUADS TO INVESTIGATE.
SIR!
KEEP LOOKING HERE. YOU'LL FIND THE PROBLEM. SOMETIMES IT'S RIGHT IN FRONT OF YOUR FACE AND YOU NEVER KNOW IT.
COMMANDER AKOBI? THERE'S SOMETHING ELSE. I OVERHEARD ONE OF THE OFFICERS TALKING ABOUT THE REBEL SUICIDE RUNS ON THE OTHER SIDE OF THE CITY...
... THEY'RE TARGETING INFRASTRUCTURE AND NONCOMBATANTS NOW. I'M NOT SURE ... DO YOU THINK WE SHOULD --?
I'LL ASSIGN ANOTHER SECURITY DETAIL TO WATCH OVER YOUR PROGRESS HERE.
DON'T WORRY ABOUT THE REBELS --

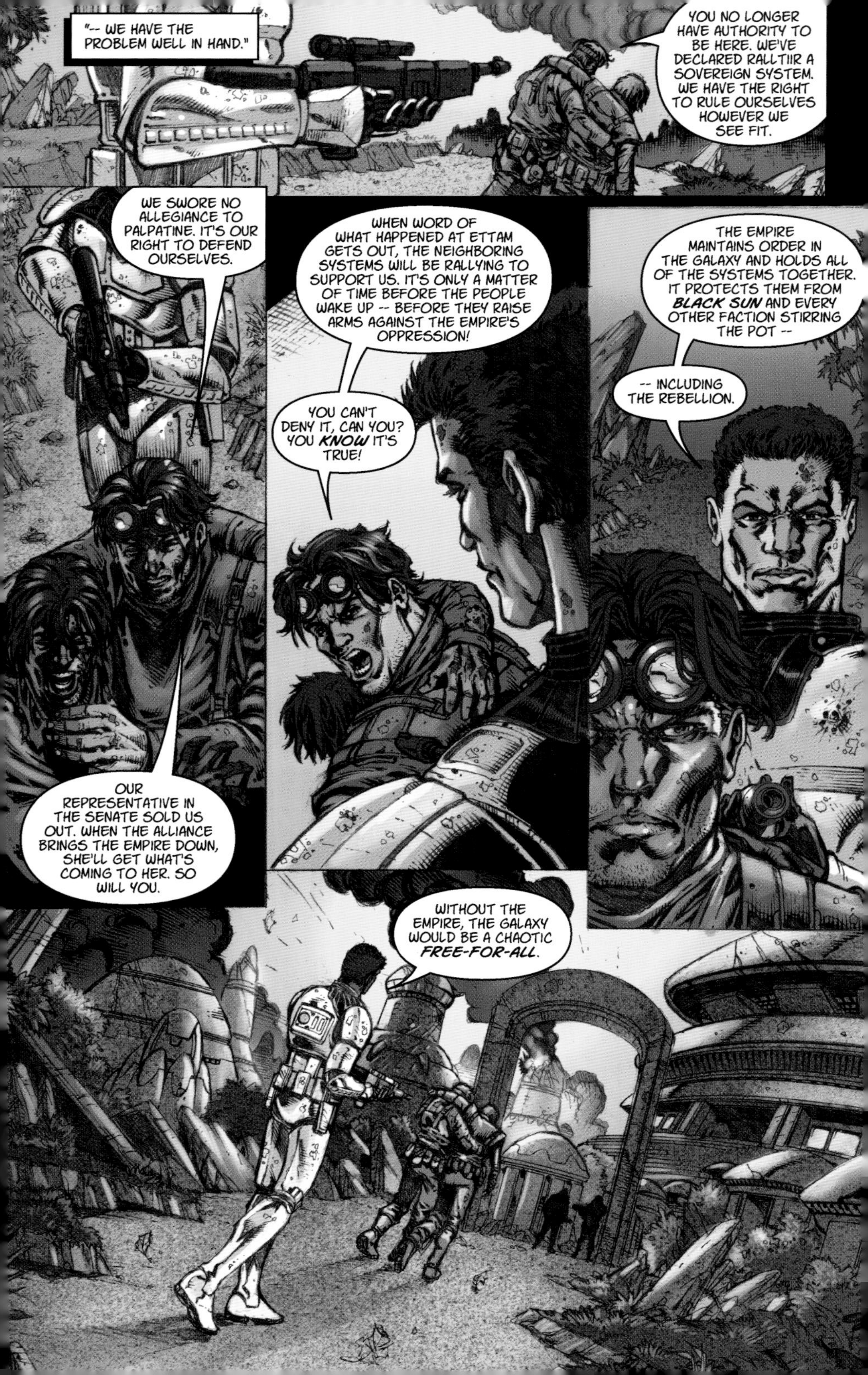
"-- WE HAVE THE PROBLEM WELL IN HAND."
YOU NO LONGER HAVE AUTHORITY TO BE HERE. WE'VE DECLARED RALLTIIR A SOVEREIGN SYSTEM. WE HAVE THE RIGHT TO RULE OURSELVES HOWEVER WE SEE FIT.
WE SWORE NO ALLEGIANCE TO PALPATINE. IT'S OUR RIGHT TO DEFEND OURSELVES.
OUR REPRESENTATIVE IN THE SENATE SOLD US OUT. WHEN THE ALLIANCE BRINGS THE EMPIRE DOWN, SHE'LL GET WHAT'S COMING TO HER. SO WILL YOU.
WHEN WORD OF WHAT HAPPENED AT ETTAM GETS OUT, THE NEIGHBORING SYSTEMS WILL BE RALLYING TO SUPPORT US. IT'S ONLY A MATTER OF TIME BEFORE THE PEOPLE WAKE UP -- BEFORE THEY RAISE ARMS AGAINST THE EMPIRE'S OPPRESSION!
YOU CAN'T DENY IT, CAN YOU? YOU *KNOW* IT'S TRUE!
THE EMPIRE MAINTAINS ORDER IN THE GALAXY AND HOLDS ALL OF THE SYSTEMS TOGETHER. IT PROTECTS THEM FROM *BLACK SUN* AND EVERY OTHER FACTION STIRRING THE POT --
-- INCLUDING THE REBELLION.
WITHOUT THE EMPIRE, THE GALAXY WOULD BE A CHAOTIC *FREE-FOR-ALL*.

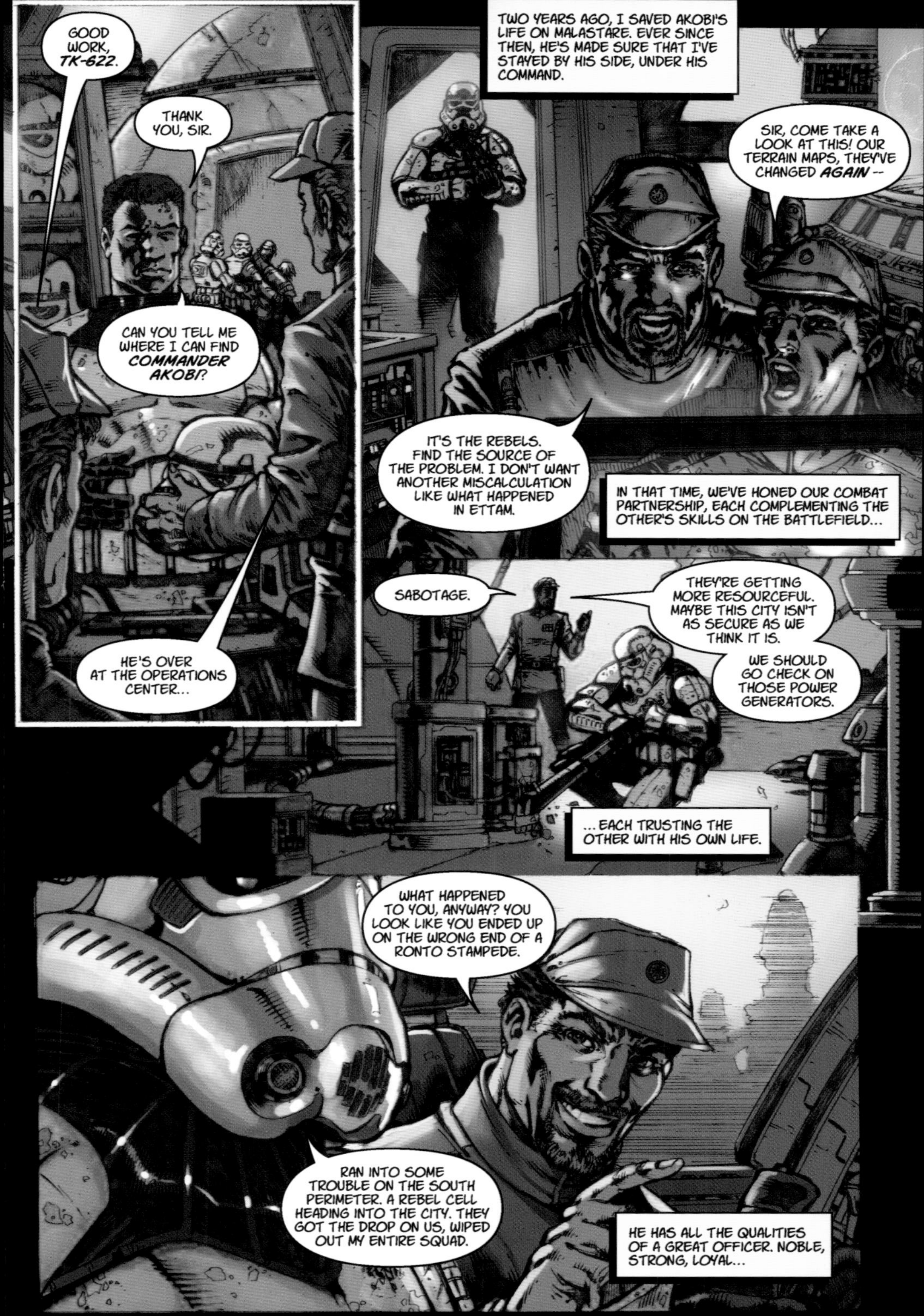
GOOD WORK, TK-622.
THANK YOU, SIR.
CAN YOU TELL ME WHERE I CAN FIND COMMANDER AKOBI?
HE'S OVER AT THE OPERATIONS CENTER...
TWO YEARS AGO, I SAVED AKOBI'S LIFE ON MALASTARE. EVER SINCE THEN, HE'S MADE SURE THAT I'VE STAYED BY HIS SIDE, UNDER HIS COMMAND.
SIR, COME TAKE A LOOK AT THIS! OUR TERRAIN MAPS, THEY'VE CHANGED AGAIN --
IT'S THE REBELS. FIND THE SOURCE OF THE PROBLEM. I DON'T WANT ANOTHER MISCALCULATION LIKE WHAT HAPPENED IN ETTAM.
IN THAT TIME, WE'VE HONED OUR COMBAT PARTNERSHIP, EACH COMPLEMENTING THE OTHER'S SKILLS ON THE BATTLEFIELD...
SABOTAGE.
THEY'RE GETTING MORE RESOURCEFUL. MAYBE THIS CITY ISN'T AS SECURE AS WE THINK IT IS.
WE SHOULD GO CHECK ON THOSE POWER GENERATORS.
... EACH TRUSTING THE OTHER WITH HIS OWN LIFE.
WHAT HAPPENED TO YOU, ANYWAY? YOU LOOK LIKE YOU ENDED UP ON THE WRONG END OF A RONTO STAMPEDE.
RAN INTO SOME TROUBLE ON THE SOUTH PERIMETER. A REBEL CELL HEADING INTO THE CITY. THEY GOT THE DROP ON US, WIPED OUT MY ENTIRE SQUAD.
HE HAS ALL THE QUALITIES OF A GREAT OFFICER. NOBLE, STRONG, LOYAL...

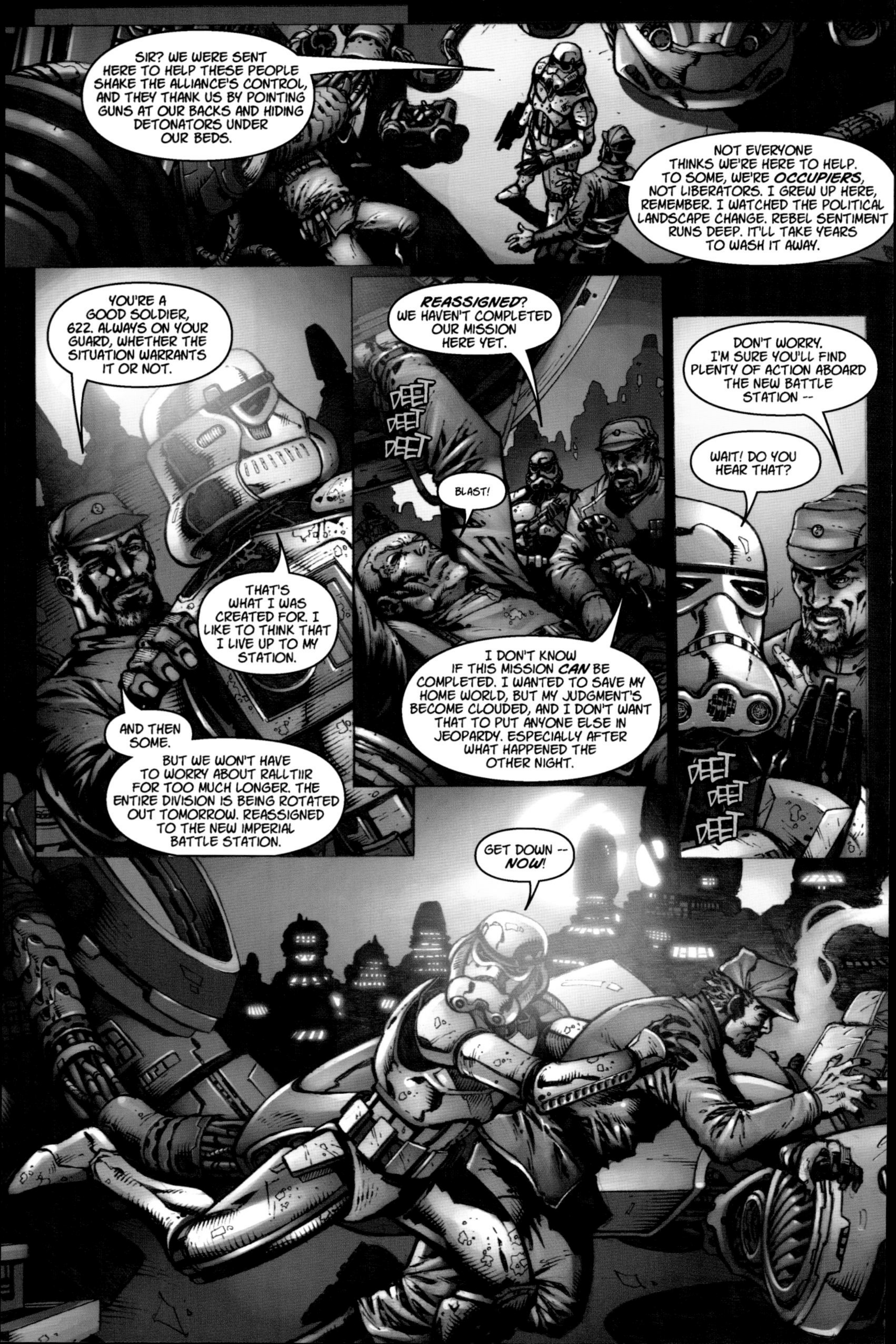
SIR? WE WERE SENT HERE TO HELP THESE PEOPLE SHAKE THE ALLIANCE'S CONTROL, AND THEY THANK US BY POINTING GUNS AT OUR BACKS AND HIDING DETONATORS UNDER OUR BEDS.
NOT EVERYONE THINKS WE'RE HERE TO HELP. TO SOME, WE'RE *OCCUPIERS*, NOT LIBERATORS. I GREW UP HERE, REMEMBER. I WATCHED THE POLITICAL LANDSCAPE CHANGE. REBEL SENTIMENT RUNS DEEP. IT'LL TAKE YEARS TO WASH IT AWAY.
YOU'RE A GOOD SOLDIER, 622. ALWAYS ON YOUR GUARD, WHETHER THE SITUATION WARRANTS IT OR NOT.
THAT'S WHAT I WAS CREATED FOR. I LIKE TO THINK THAT I LIVE UP TO MY STATION.
AND THEN SOME.
BUT WE WON'T HAVE TO WORRY ABOUT RALLTIIR FOR TOO MUCH LONGER. THE ENTIRE DIVISION IS BEING ROTATED OUT TOMORROW. REASSIGNED TO THE NEW IMPERIAL BATTLE STATION.
REASSIGNED? WE HAVEN'T COMPLETED OUR MISSION HERE YET.
DEET DEET DEET
BLAST!
I DON'T KNOW IF THIS MISSION ***CAN*** BE COMPLETED. I WANTED TO SAVE MY HOME WORLD, BUT MY JUDGMENT'S BECOME CLOUDED, AND I DON'T WANT THAT TO PUT ANYONE ELSE IN JEOPARDY. ESPECIALLY AFTER WHAT HAPPENED THE OTHER NIGHT.
DON'T WORRY. I'M SURE YOU'LL FIND PLENTY OF ACTION ABOARD THE NEW BATTLE STATION --
WAIT! DO YOU HEAR THAT?
DEET DEET DEET
GET DOWN -- ***NOW***!

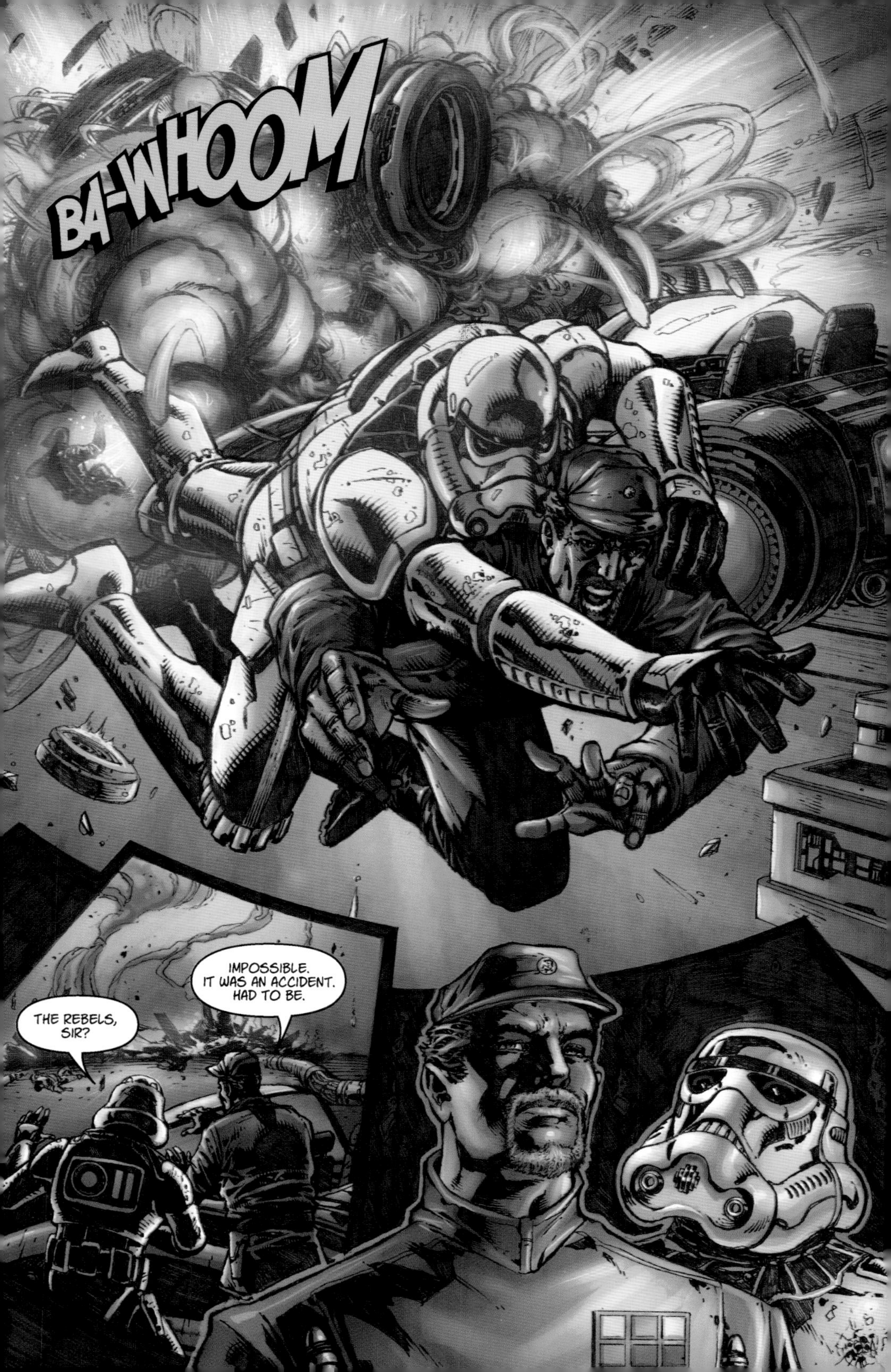
BA-WHOOM
THE REBELS, SIR?
IMPOSSIBLE. IT WAS AN ACCIDENT. HAD TO BE.

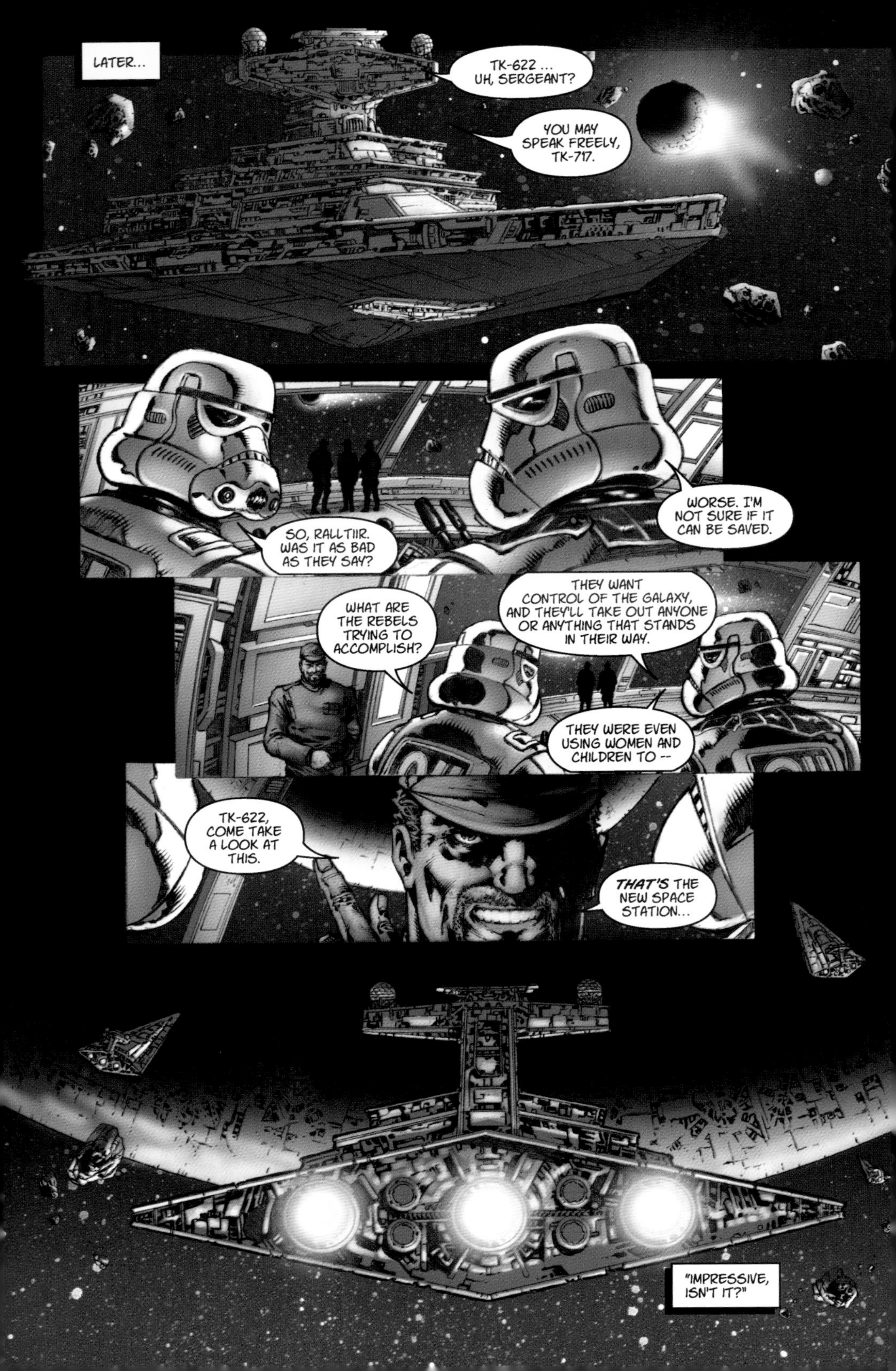
LATER...
TK-622 ... UH, SERGEANT?
YOU MAY SPEAK FREELY, TK-717.
SO, RALLTIIR. WAS IT AS BAD AS THEY SAY?
WORSE. I'M NOT SURE IF IT CAN BE SAVED.
WHAT ARE THE REBELS TRYING TO ACCOMPLISH?
THEY WANT CONTROL OF THE GALAXY, AND THEY'LL TAKE OUT ANYONE OR ANYTHING THAT STANDS IN THEIR WAY.
THEY WERE EVEN USING WOMEN AND CHILDREN TO --
TK-622, COME TAKE A LOOK AT THIS.
THAT'S THE NEW SPACE STATION...
"IMPRESSIVE, ISN'T IT?"

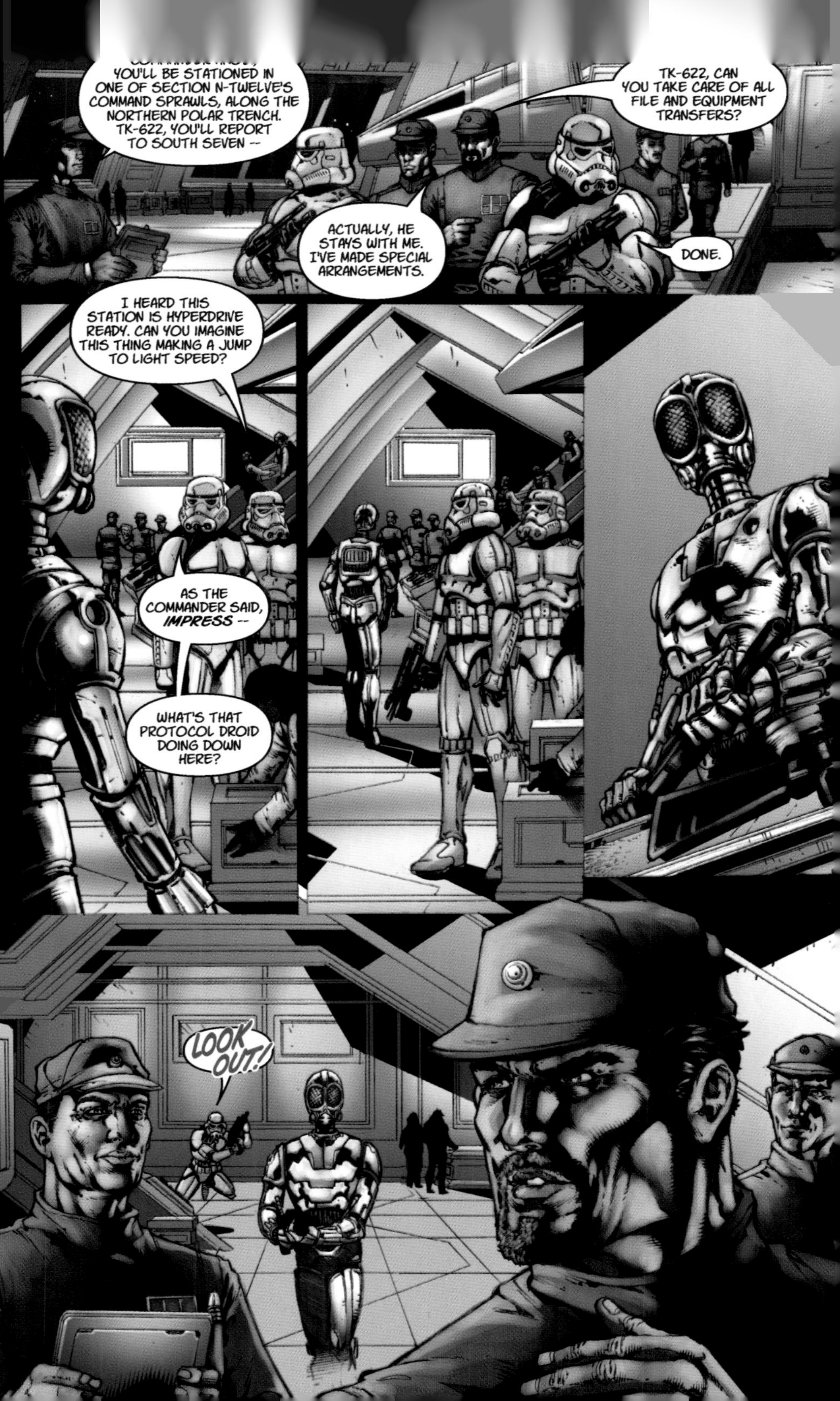

YOU'LL BE STATIONED IN ONE OF SECTION N-TWELVE'S COMMAND SPRAWLS, ALONG THE NORTHERN POLAR TRENCH. TK-622, YOU'LL REPORT TO SOUTH SEVEN --
ACTUALLY, HE STAYS WITH ME. I'VE MADE SPECIAL ARRANGEMENTS.
TK-622, CAN YOU TAKE CARE OF ALL FILE AND EQUIPMENT TRANSFERS?
DONE.
I HEARD THIS STATION IS HYPERDRIVE READY. CAN YOU IMAGINE THIS THING MAKING A JUMP TO LIGHT SPEED?
AS THE COMMANDER SAID, *IMPRESS* --
WHAT'S THAT PROTOCOL DROID DOING DOWN HERE?
LOOK OUT!

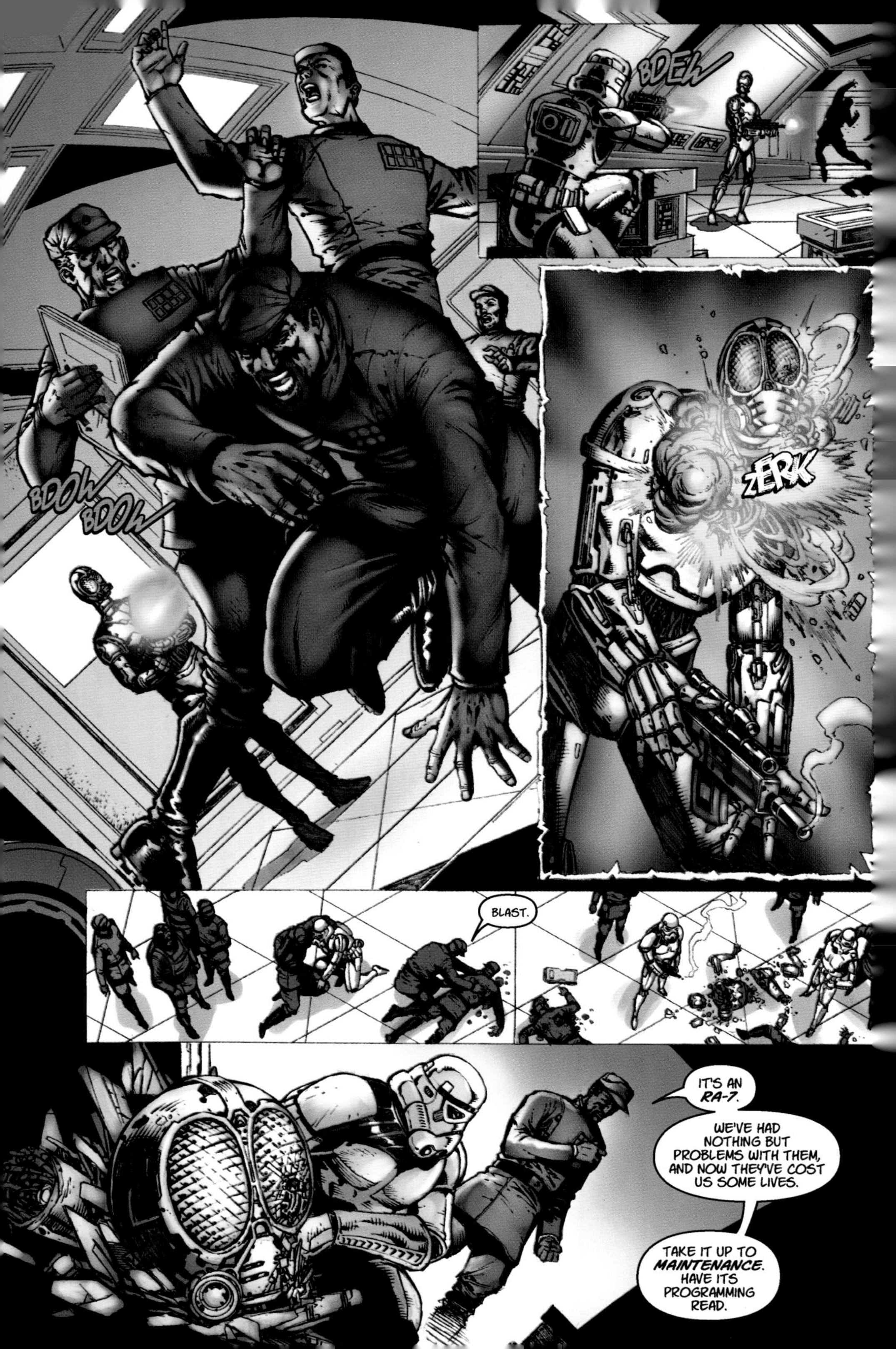
BDEW
BDOW
BDOW
ZERK
BLAST.
IT'S AN *RA-7*.
WE'VE HAD NOTHING BUT PROBLEMS WITH THEM, AND NOW THEY'VE COST US SOME LIVES.
TAKE IT UP TO *MAINTENANCE*. HAVE ITS PROGRAMMING READ.

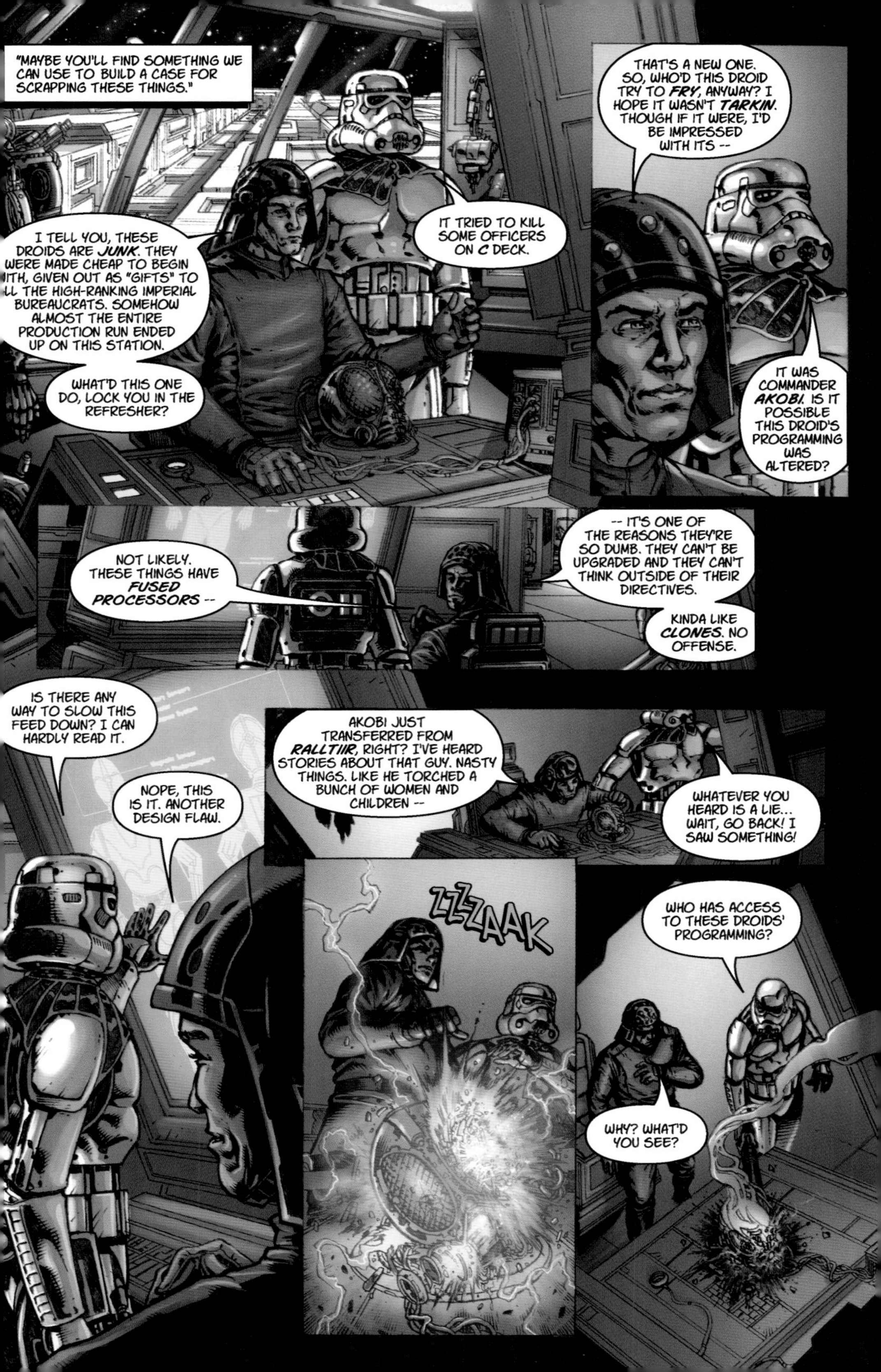

"MAYBE YOU'LL FIND SOMETHING WE CAN USE TO BUILD A CASE FOR SCRAPPING THESE THINGS."
IT TRIED TO KILL SOME OFFICERS ON C DECK.
I TELL YOU, THESE DROIDS ARE JUNK. THEY WERE MADE CHEAP TO BEGIN WITH, GIVEN OUT AS "GIFTS" TO ALL THE HIGH-RANKING IMPERIAL BUREAUCRATS. SOMEHOW ALMOST THE ENTIRE PRODUCTION RUN ENDED UP ON THIS STATION.
WHAT'D THIS ONE DO, LOCK YOU IN THE REFRESHER?
THAT'S A NEW ONE. SO, WHO'D THIS DROID TRY TO FRY, ANYWAY? I HOPE IT WASN'T TARKIN. THOUGH IF IT WERE, I'D BE IMPRESSED WITH ITS --
IT WAS COMMANDER AKOBI. IS IT POSSIBLE THIS DROID'S PROGRAMMING WAS ALTERED?
NOT LIKELY. THESE THINGS HAVE FUSED PROCESSORS --
-- IT'S ONE OF THE REASONS THEY'RE SO DUMB. THEY CAN'T BE UPGRADED AND THEY CAN'T THINK OUTSIDE OF THEIR DIRECTIVES.
KINDA LIKE CLONES. NO OFFENSE.
IS THERE ANY WAY TO SLOW THIS FEED DOWN? I CAN HARDLY READ IT.
NOPE, THIS IS IT. ANOTHER DESIGN FLAW.
AKOBI JUST TRANSFERRED FROM RALLTIIR, RIGHT? I'VE HEARD STORIES ABOUT THAT GUY. NASTY THINGS. LIKE HE TORCHED A BUNCH OF WOMEN AND CHILDREN --
WHATEVER YOU HEARD IS A LIE... WAIT, GO BACK! I SAW SOMETHING!
ZZZZAAK
WHO HAS ACCESS TO THESE DROIDS' PROGRAMMING?
WHY? WHAT'D YOU SEE?

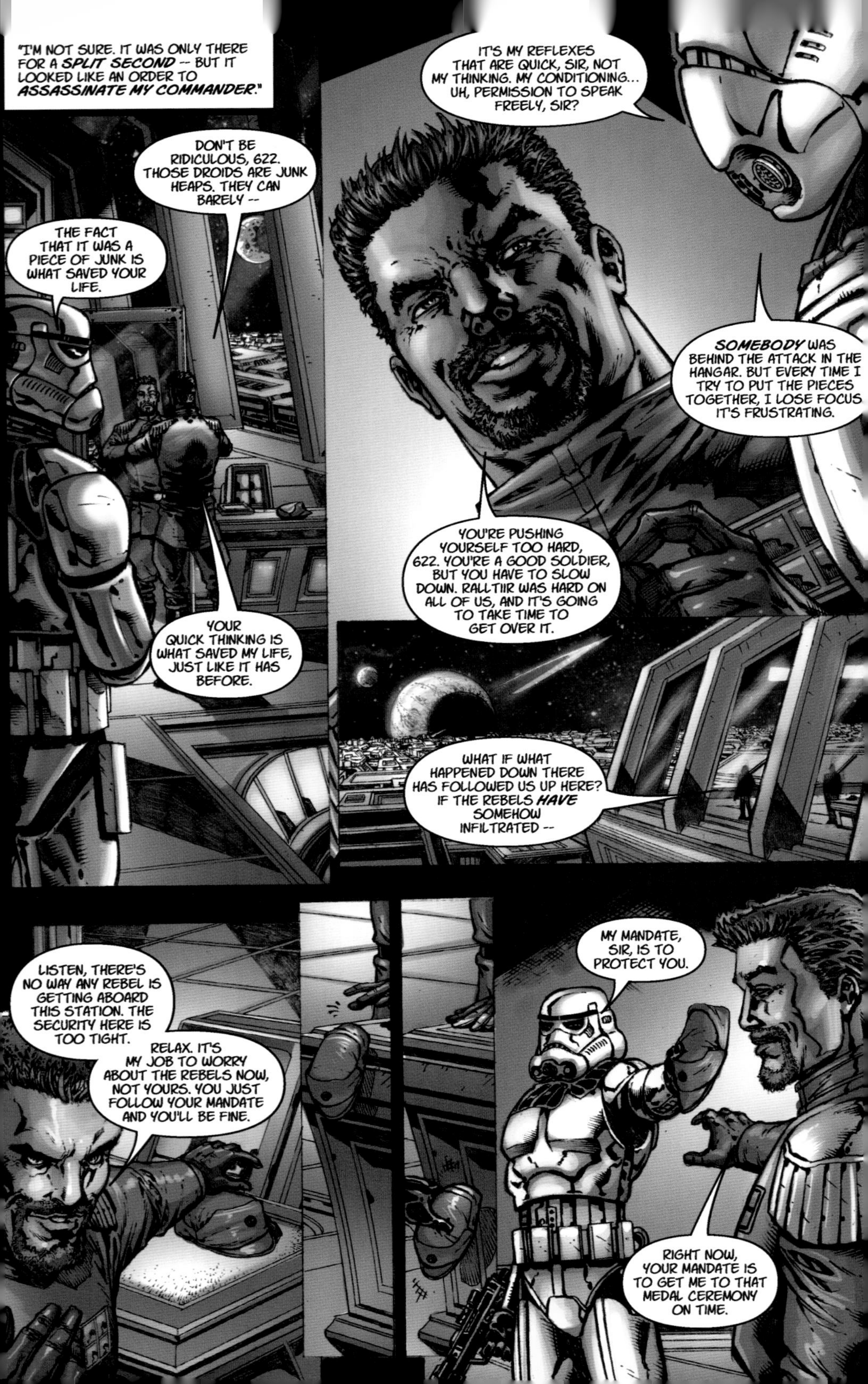
"I'M NOT SURE. IT WAS ONLY THERE FOR A SPLIT SECOND -- BUT IT LOOKED LIKE AN ORDER TO ASSASSINATE MY COMMANDER."
DON'T BE RIDICULOUS, 622. THOSE DROIDS ARE JUNK HEAPS. THEY CAN BARELY --
THE FACT THAT IT WAS A PIECE OF JUNK IS WHAT SAVED YOUR LIFE.
YOUR QUICK THINKING IS WHAT SAVED MY LIFE, JUST LIKE IT HAS BEFORE.
IT'S MY REFLEXES THAT ARE QUICK, SIR, NOT MY THINKING. MY CONDITIONING... UH, PERMISSION TO SPEAK FREELY, SIR?
SOMEBODY WAS BEHIND THE ATTACK IN THE HANGAR. BUT EVERY TIME I TRY TO PUT THE PIECES TOGETHER, I LOSE FOCUS. IT'S FRUSTRATING.
YOU'RE PUSHING YOURSELF TOO HARD, 622. YOU'RE A GOOD SOLDIER, BUT YOU HAVE TO SLOW DOWN. RALLTIIR WAS HARD ON ALL OF US, AND IT'S GOING TO TAKE TIME TO GET OVER IT.
WHAT IF WHAT HAPPENED DOWN THERE HAS FOLLOWED US UP HERE? IF THE REBELS HAVE SOMEHOW INFILTRATED --
LISTEN, THERE'S NO WAY ANY REBEL IS GETTING ABOARD THIS STATION. THE SECURITY HERE IS TOO TIGHT.
RELAX. IT'S MY JOB TO WORRY ABOUT THE REBELS NOW, NOT YOURS. YOU JUST FOLLOW YOUR MANDATE AND YOU'LL BE FINE.
MY MANDATE, SIR, IS TO PROTECT YOU.
RIGHT NOW, YOUR MANDATE IS TO GET ME TO THAT MEDAL CEREMONY ON TIME.

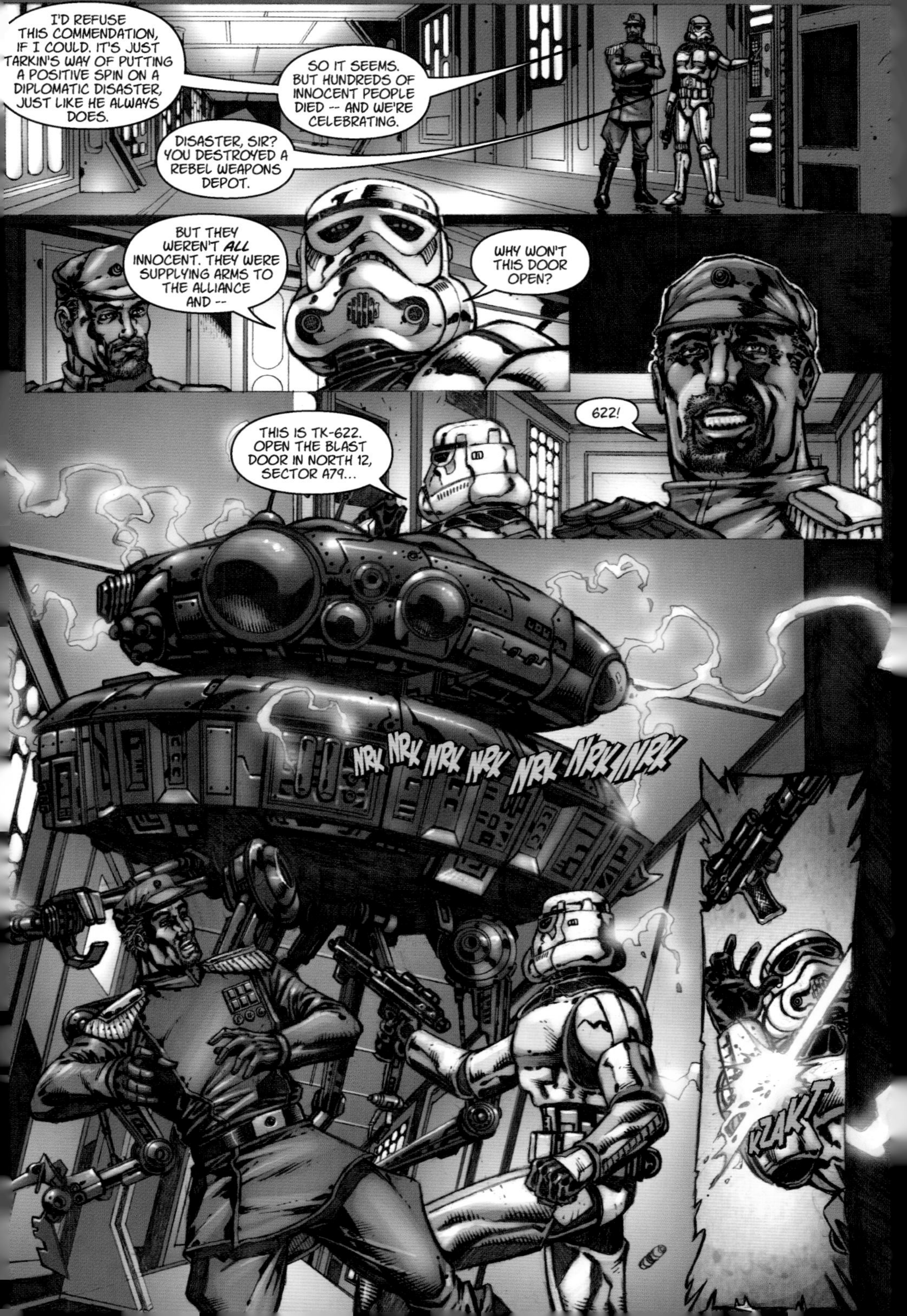
I'D REFUSE THIS COMMENDATION, IF I COULD. IT'S JUST TARKIN'S WAY OF PUTTING A POSITIVE SPIN ON A DIPLOMATIC DISASTER, JUST LIKE HE ALWAYS DOES.
DISASTER, SIR? YOU DESTROYED A REBEL WEAPONS DEPOT.
SO IT SEEMS. BUT HUNDREDS OF INNOCENT PEOPLE DIED -- AND WE'RE CELEBRATING.
BUT THEY WEREN'T ALL INNOCENT. THEY WERE SUPPLYING ARMS TO THE ALLIANCE AND --
WHY WON'T THIS DOOR OPEN?
THIS IS TK-622. OPEN THE BLAST DOOR IN NORTH 12, SECTOR A79...
622!
NRK NRK NRK NRK NRK NRK NRK
KZAKT

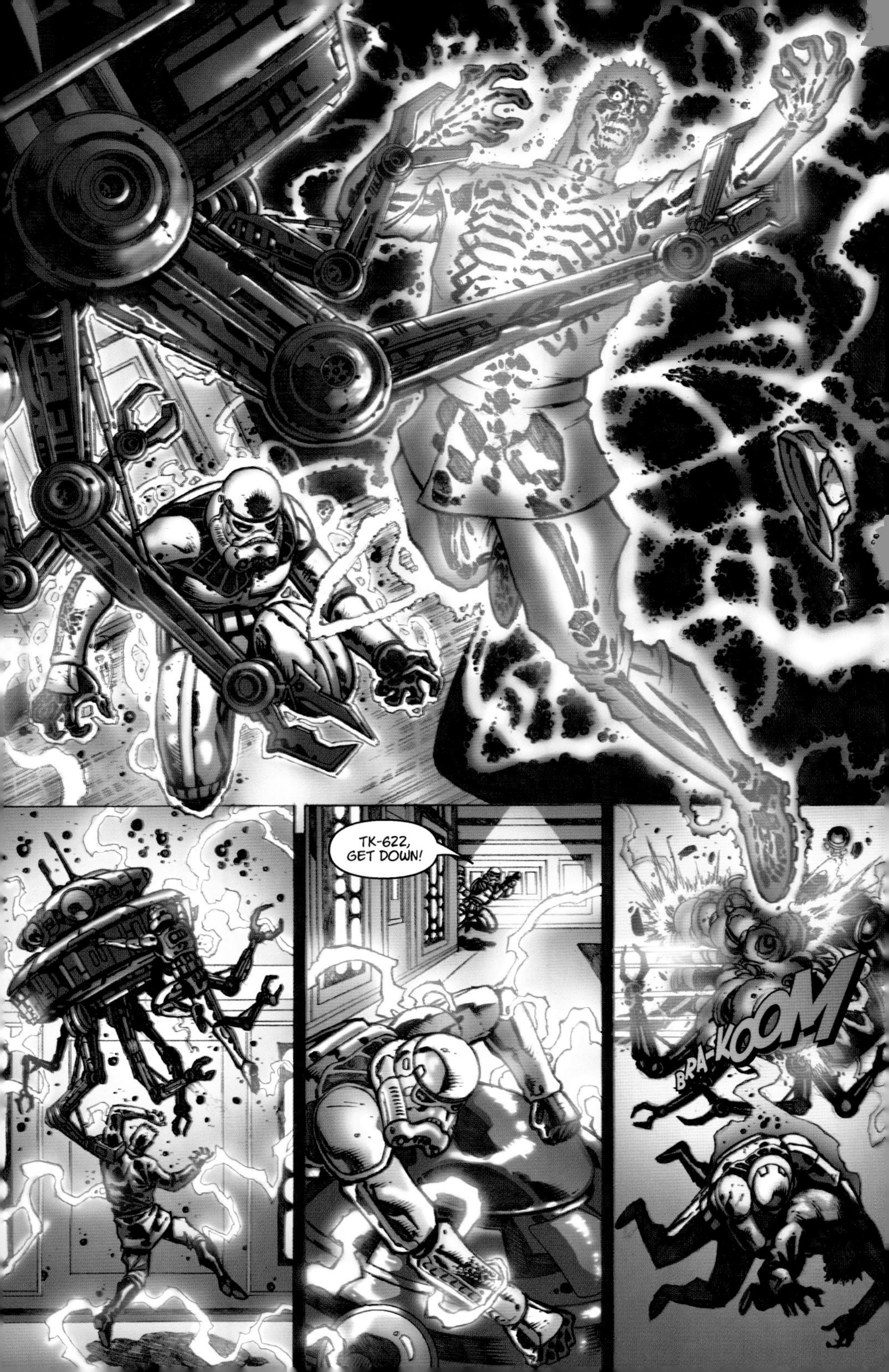
TK-622, GET DOWN!
BRA-KOOM

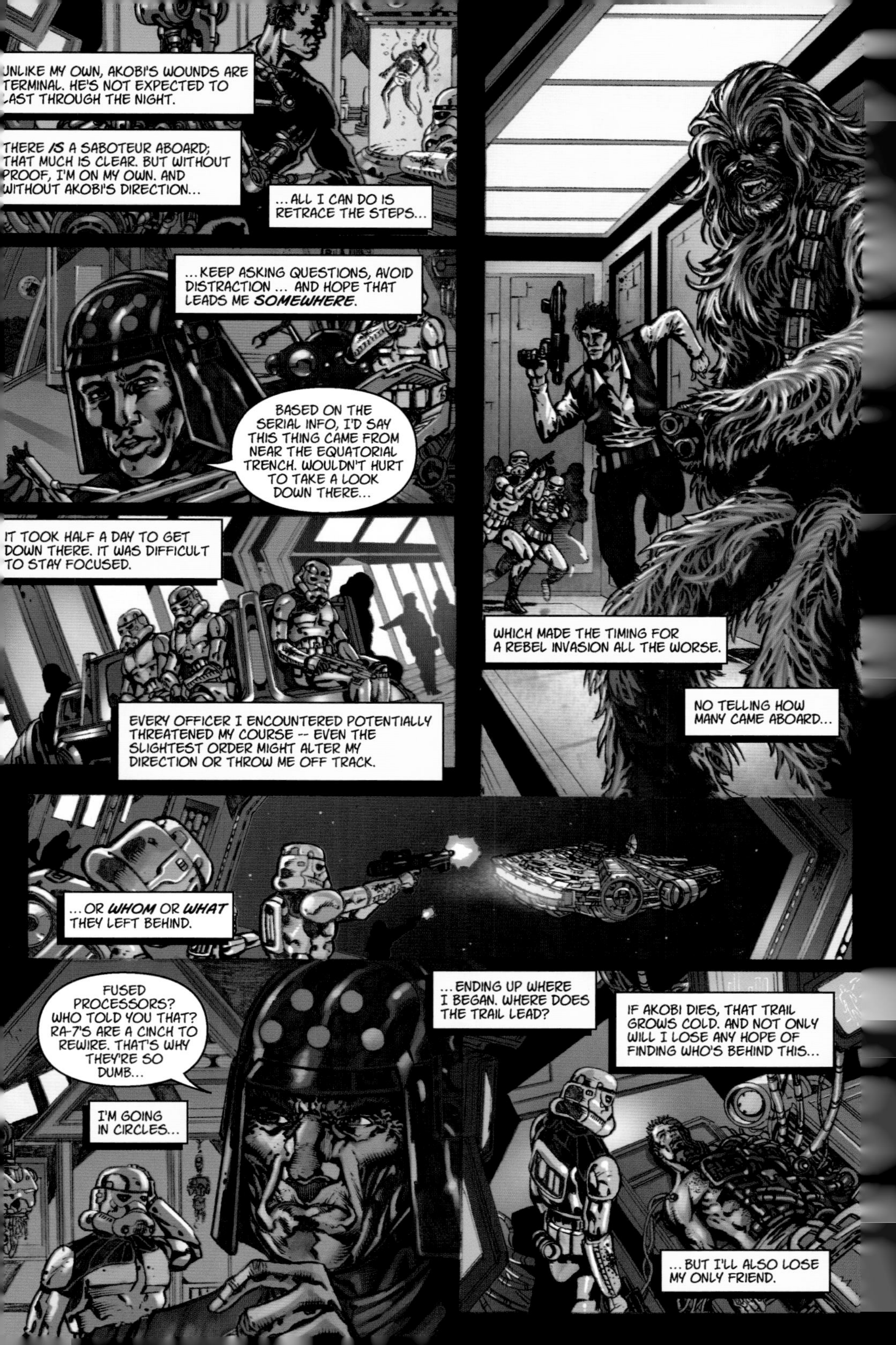
UNLIKE MY OWN, AKOBI'S WOUNDS ARE TERMINAL. HE'S NOT EXPECTED TO LAST THROUGH THE NIGHT.
THERE *IS* A SABOTEUR ABOARD; THAT MUCH IS CLEAR. BUT WITHOUT PROOF, I'M ON MY OWN. AND WITHOUT AKOBI'S DIRECTION...
...ALL I CAN DO IS RETRACE THE STEPS...
...KEEP ASKING QUESTIONS, AVOID DISTRACTION ... AND HOPE THAT LEADS ME *SOMEWHERE*.
BASED ON THE SERIAL INFO, I'D SAY THIS THING CAME FROM NEAR THE EQUATORIAL TRENCH. WOULDN'T HURT TO TAKE A LOOK DOWN THERE...
IT TOOK HALF A DAY TO GET DOWN THERE. IT WAS DIFFICULT TO STAY FOCUSED.
EVERY OFFICER I ENCOUNTERED POTENTIALLY THREATENED MY COURSE -- EVEN THE SLIGHTEST ORDER MIGHT ALTER MY DIRECTION OR THROW ME OFF TRACK.
WHICH MADE THE TIMING FOR A REBEL INVASION ALL THE WORSE.
NO TELLING HOW MANY CAME ABOARD...
...OR *WHOM* OR *WHAT* THEY LEFT BEHIND.
FUSED PROCESSORS? WHO TOLD YOU THAT? RA-7'S ARE A CINCH TO REWIRE. THAT'S WHY THEY'RE SO DUMB...
I'M GOING IN CIRCLES...
...ENDING UP WHERE I BEGAN. WHERE DOES THE TRAIL LEAD?
IF AKOBI DIES, THAT TRAIL GROWS COLD. AND NOT ONLY WILL I LOSE ANY HOPE OF FINDING WHO'S BEHIND THIS...
...BUT I'LL ALSO LOSE MY ONLY FRIEND.

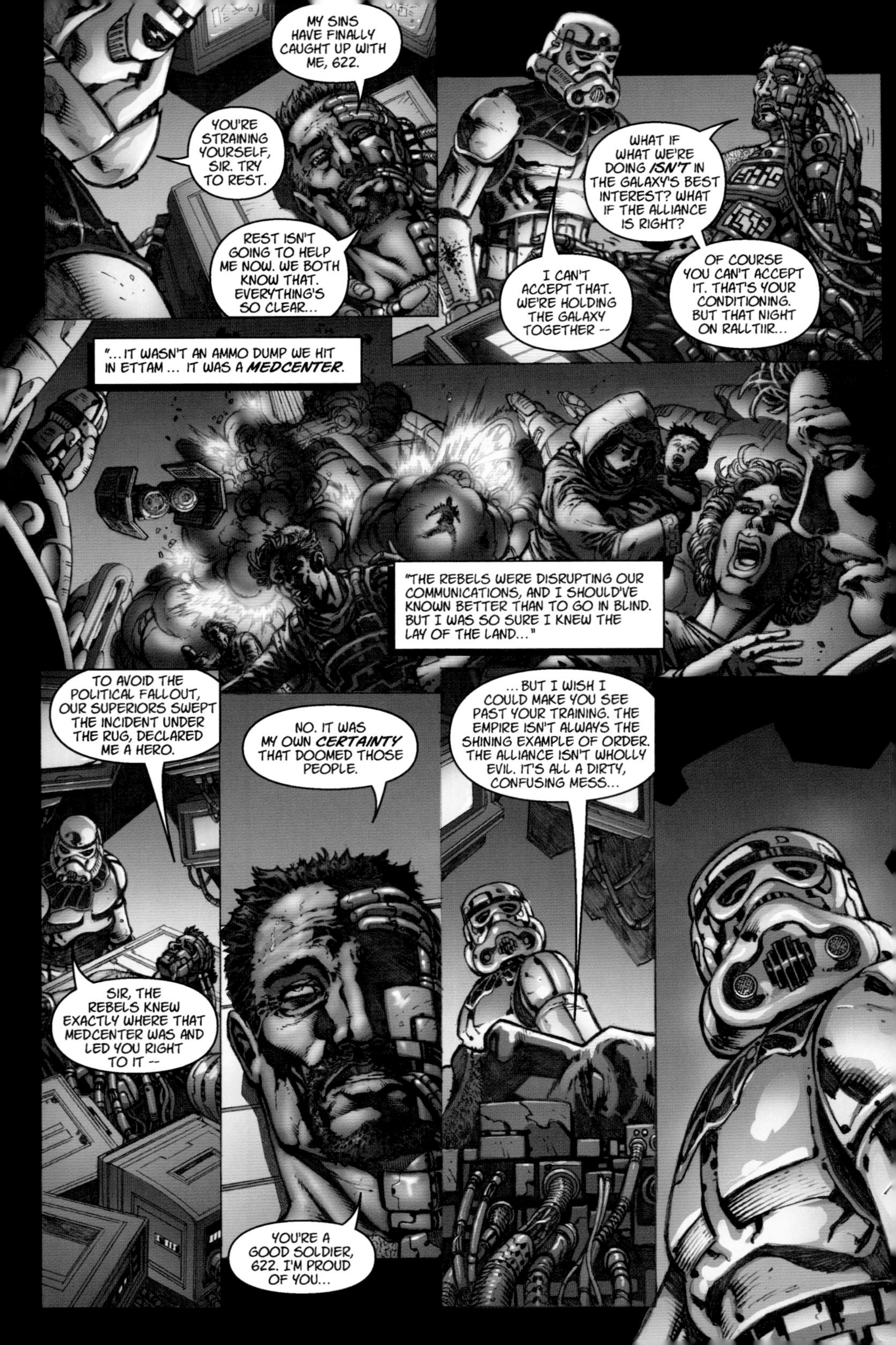
MY SINS HAVE FINALLY CAUGHT UP WITH ME, 622.
YOU'RE STRAINING YOURSELF, SIR. TRY TO REST.
REST ISN'T GOING TO HELP ME NOW. WE BOTH KNOW THAT. EVERYTHING'S SO CLEAR...
WHAT IF WHAT WE'RE DOING *ISN'T* IN THE GALAXY'S BEST INTEREST? WHAT IF THE ALLIANCE IS RIGHT?
I CAN'T ACCEPT THAT. WE'RE HOLDING THE GALAXY TOGETHER --
OF COURSE YOU CAN'T ACCEPT IT. THAT'S YOUR CONDITIONING. BUT THAT NIGHT ON RALLTIIR...
"...IT WASN'T AN AMMO DUMP WE HIT IN ETTAM ... IT WAS A *MEDCENTER*.
"THE REBELS WERE DISRUPTING OUR COMMUNICATIONS, AND I SHOULD'VE KNOWN BETTER THAN TO GO IN BLIND. BUT I WAS SO SURE I KNEW THE LAY OF THE LAND..."
TO AVOID THE POLITICAL FALLOUT, OUR SUPERIORS SWEPT THE INCIDENT UNDER THE RUG, DECLARED ME A HERO.
SIR, THE REBELS KNEW EXACTLY WHERE THAT MEDCENTER WAS AND LED YOU RIGHT TO IT --
NO. IT WAS MY OWN *CERTAINTY* THAT DOOMED THOSE PEOPLE.
YOU'RE A GOOD SOLDIER, 622. I'M PROUD OF YOU...
...BUT I WISH I COULD MAKE YOU SEE PAST YOUR TRAINING. THE EMPIRE ISN'T ALWAYS THE SHINING EXAMPLE OF ORDER. THE ALLIANCE ISN'T WHOLLY EVIL. IT'S ALL A DIRTY, CONFUSING MESS...

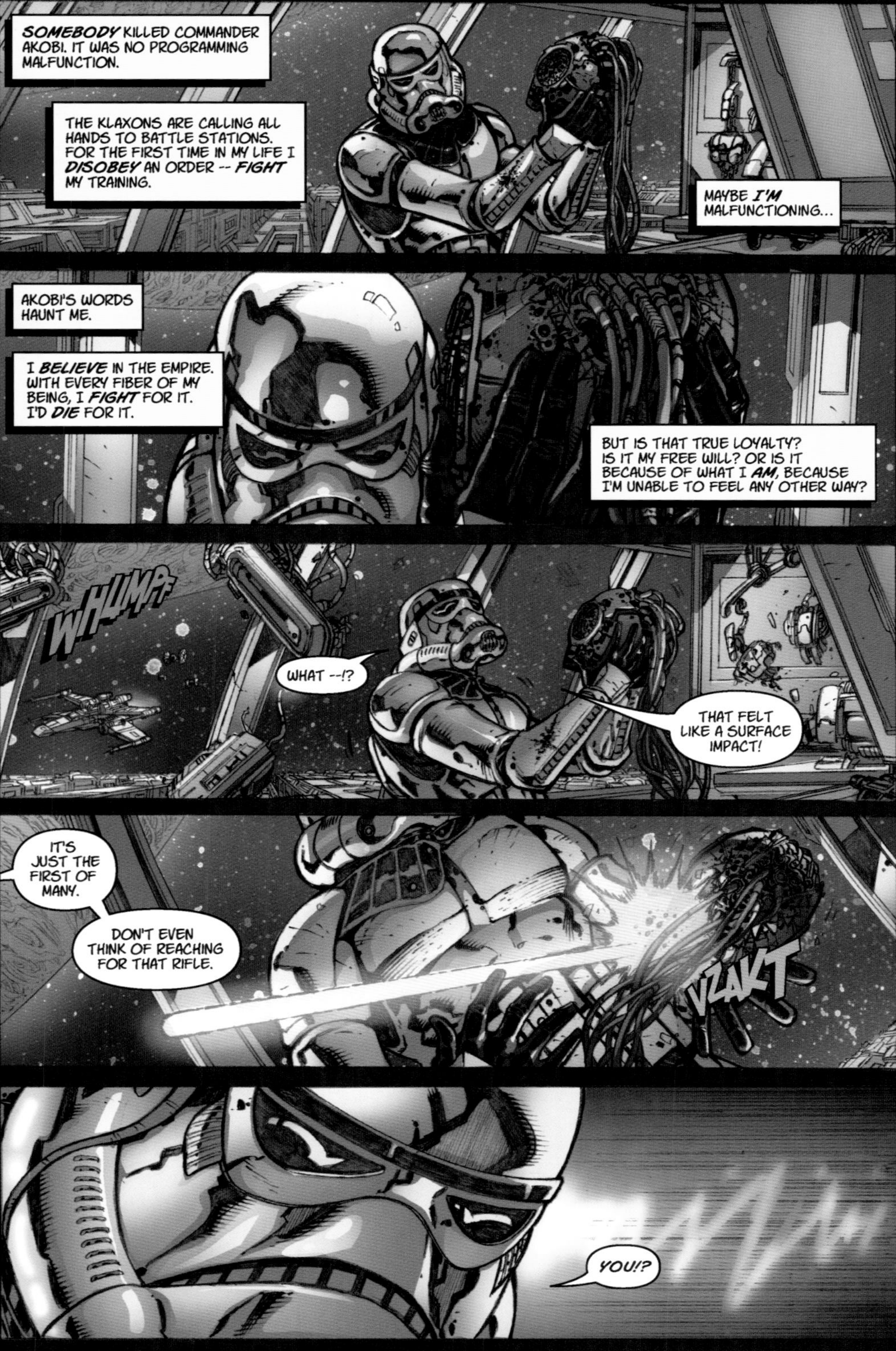
SOMEBODY KILLED COMMANDER AKOBI. IT WAS NO PROGRAMMING MALFUNCTION.
THE KLAXONS ARE CALLING ALL HANDS TO BATTLE STATIONS. FOR THE FIRST TIME IN MY LIFE I DISOBEY AN ORDER -- FIGHT MY TRAINING.
MAYBE I'M MALFUNCTIONING...
AKOBI'S WORDS HAUNT ME.
I BELIEVE IN THE EMPIRE. WITH EVERY FIBER OF MY BEING, I FIGHT FOR IT. I'D DIE FOR IT.
BUT IS THAT TRUE LOYALTY? IS IT MY FREE WILL? OR IS IT BECAUSE OF WHAT I AM, BECAUSE I'M UNABLE TO FEEL ANY OTHER WAY?
WHUMPF
WHAT --!?
THAT FELT LIKE A SURFACE IMPACT!
IT'S JUST THE FIRST OF MANY.
DON'T EVEN THINK OF REACHING FOR THAT RIFLE.
VZAKT
YOU!?

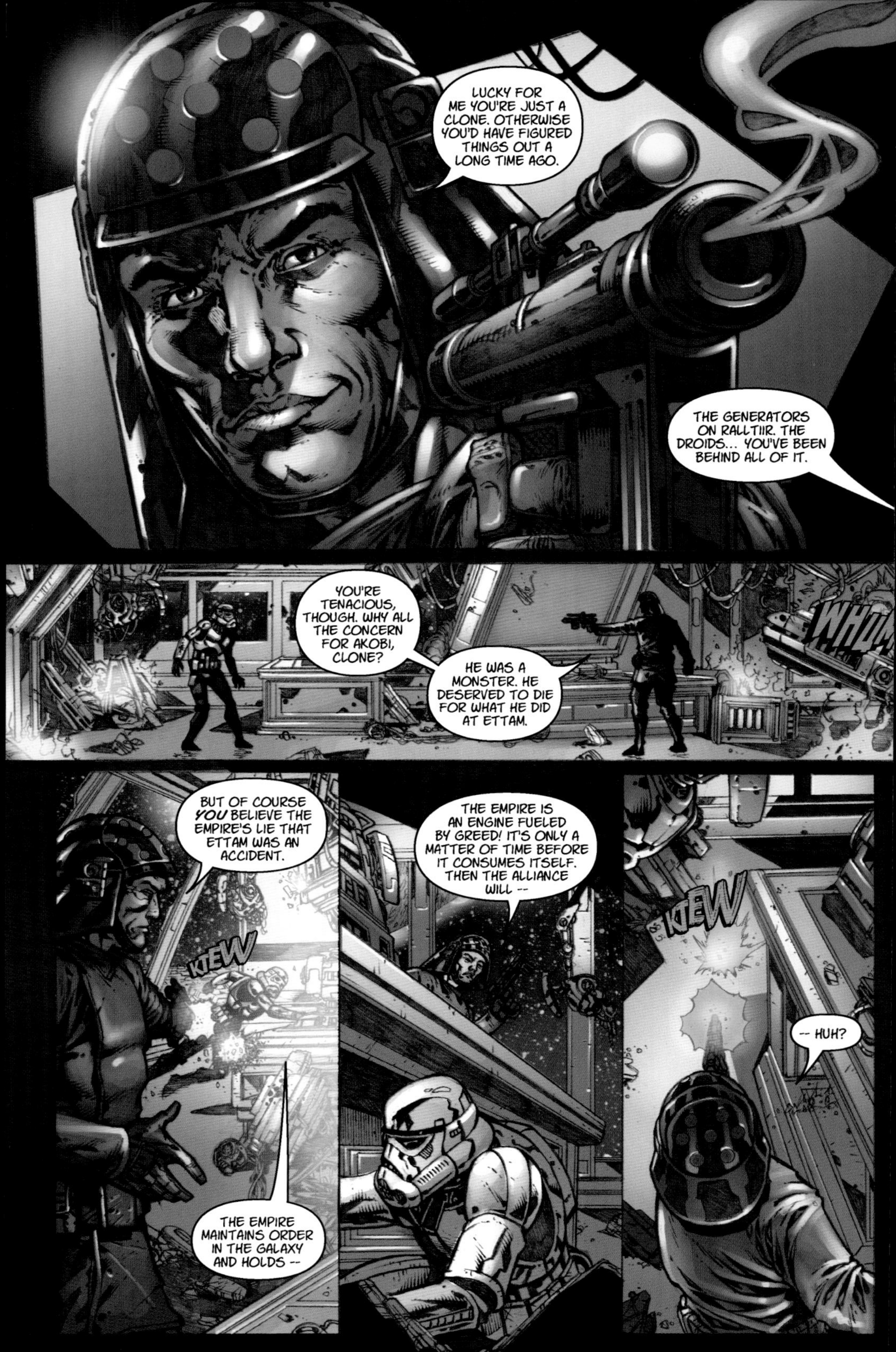
LUCKY FOR ME YOU'RE JUST A CLONE. OTHERWISE YOU'D HAVE FIGURED THINGS OUT A LONG TIME AGO.
THE GENERATORS ON RALLTIIR. THE DROIDS... YOU'VE BEEN BEHIND ALL OF IT.
YOU'RE TENACIOUS, THOUGH. WHY ALL THE CONCERN FOR AKOBI, CLONE?
HE WAS A MONSTER. HE DESERVED TO DIE FOR WHAT HE DID AT ETTAM.
WHUM
BUT OF COURSE *YOU* BELIEVE THE EMPIRE'S LIE THAT ETTAM WAS AN ACCIDENT.
KTEW
THE EMPIRE MAINTAINS ORDER IN THE GALAXY AND HOLDS --
THE EMPIRE IS AN ENGINE FUELED BY GREED! IT'S ONLY A MATTER OF TIME BEFORE IT CONSUMES ITSELF. THEN THE ALLIANCE WILL --
KTEW
-- HUH?

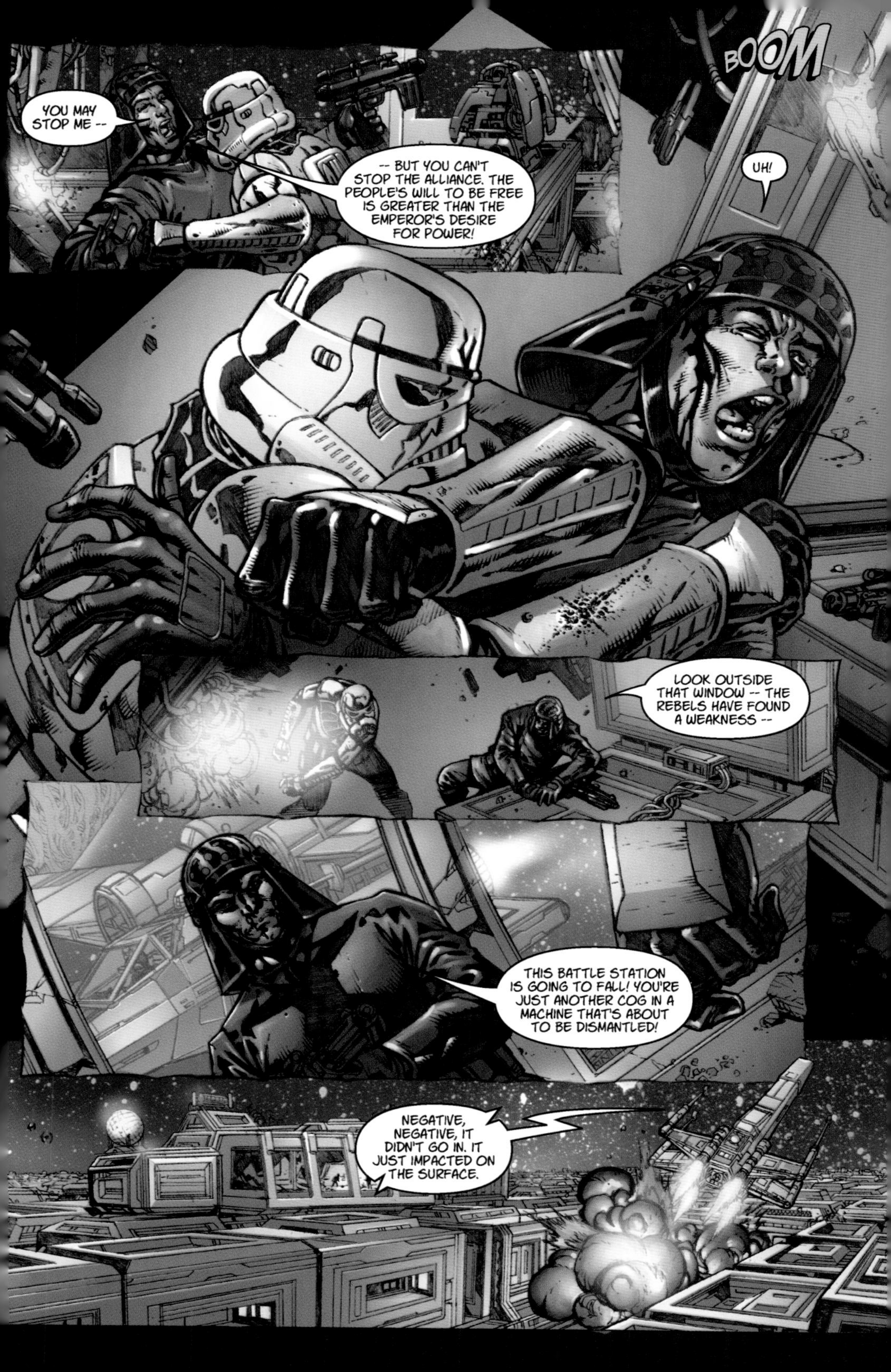
YOU MAY STOP ME --
-- BUT YOU CAN'T STOP THE ALLIANCE. THE PEOPLE'S WILL TO BE FREE IS GREATER THAN THE EMPEROR'S DESIRE FOR POWER!
BOOM
UH!
LOOK OUTSIDE THAT WINDOW -- THE REBELS HAVE FOUND A WEAKNESS --
THIS BATTLE STATION IS GOING TO FALL! YOU'RE JUST ANOTHER COG IN A MACHINE THAT'S ABOUT TO BE DISMANTLED!
NEGATIVE, NEGATIVE, IT DIDN'T GO IN. IT JUST IMPACTED ON THE SURFACE.

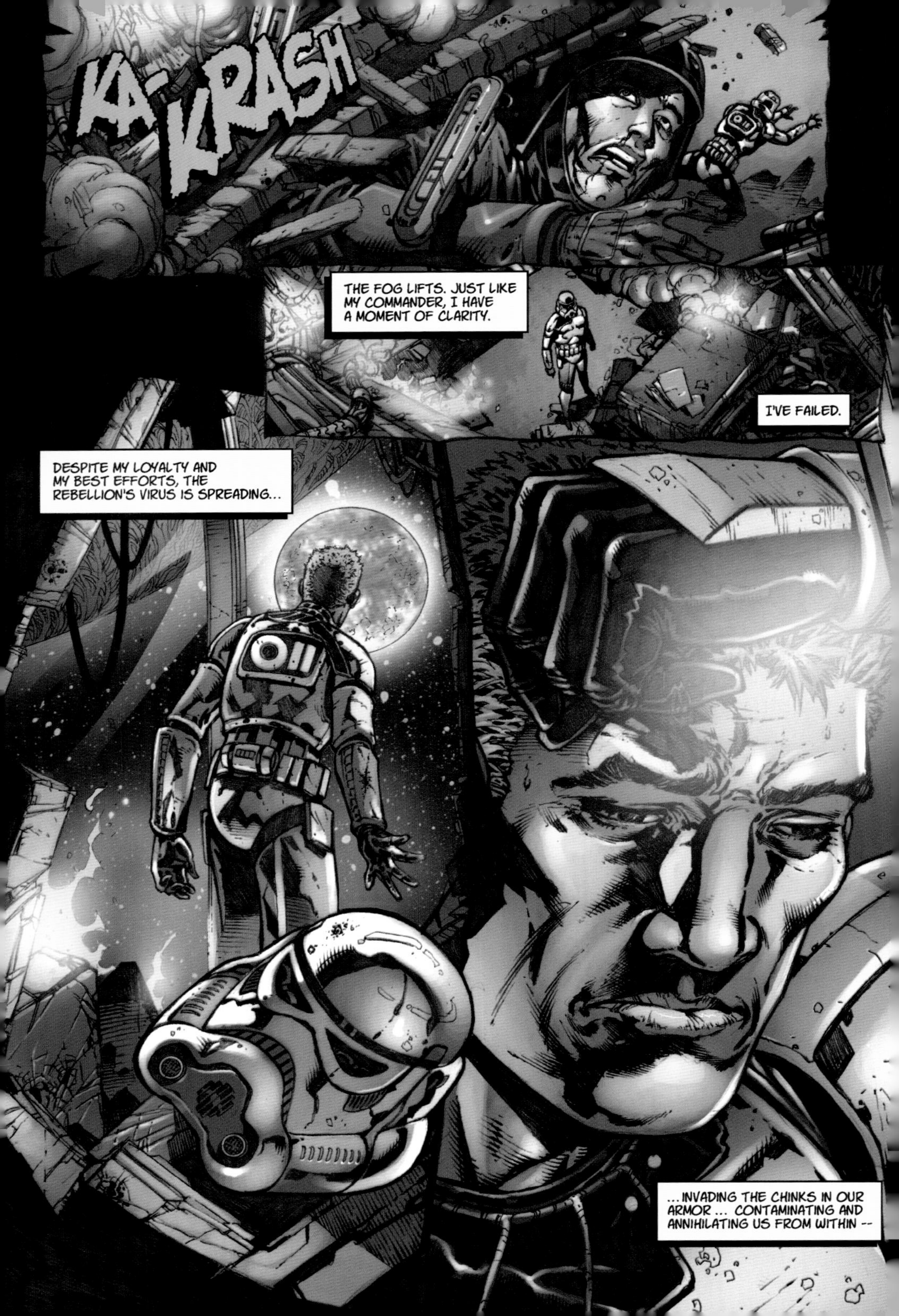
KA-KRASH
THE FOG LIFTS. JUST LIKE MY COMMANDER, I HAVE A MOMENT OF CLARITY.
I'VE FAILED.
DESPITE MY LOYALTY AND MY BEST EFFORTS, THE REBELLION'S VIRUS IS SPREADING...
...INVADING THE CHINKS IN OUR ARMOR ... CONTAMINATING AND ANNIHILATING US FROM WITHIN --

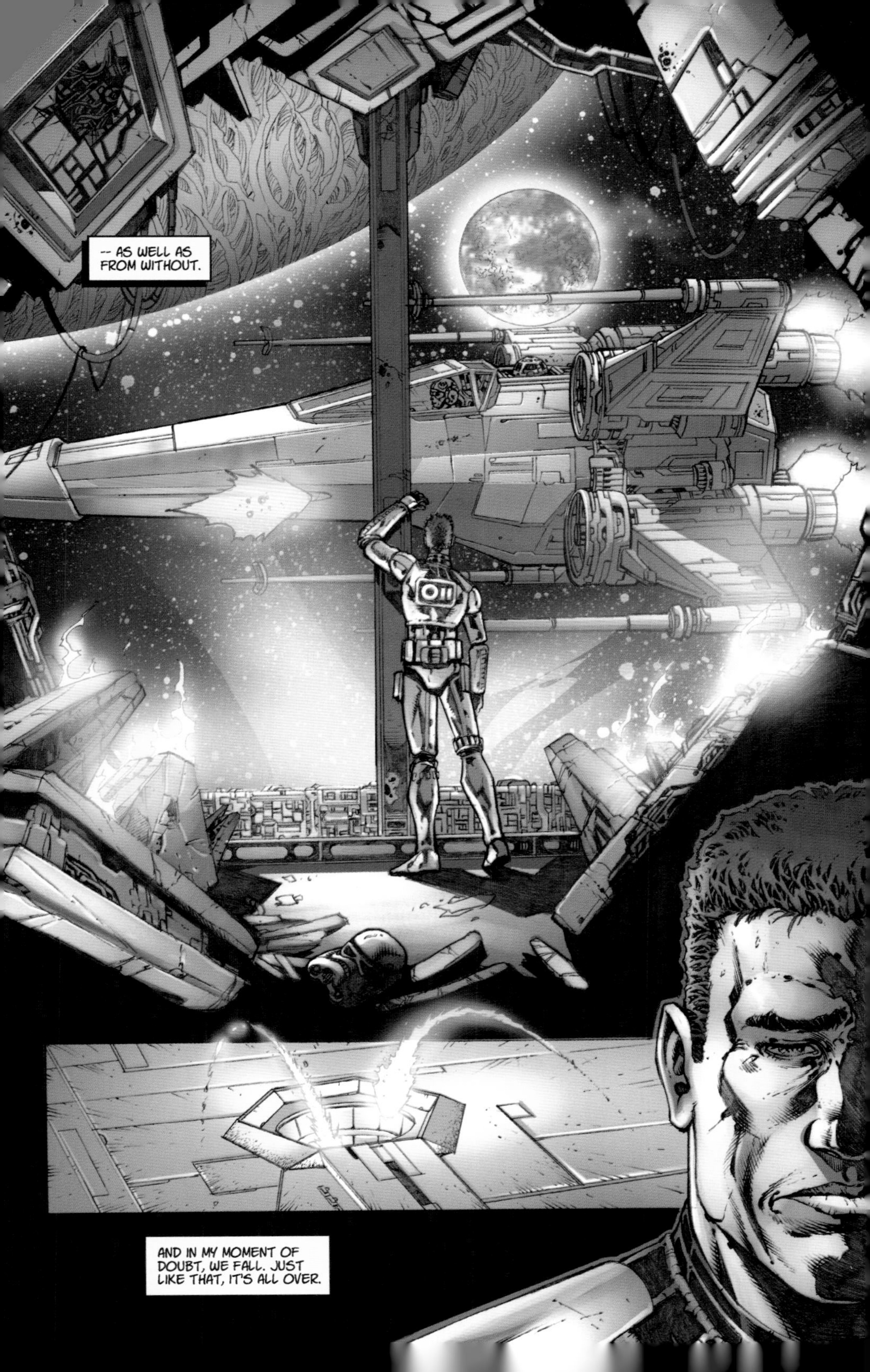
-- AS WELL AS FROM WITHOUT.
O11
AND IN MY MOMENT OF DOUBT, WE FALL. JUST LIKE THAT, IT'S ALL OVER.

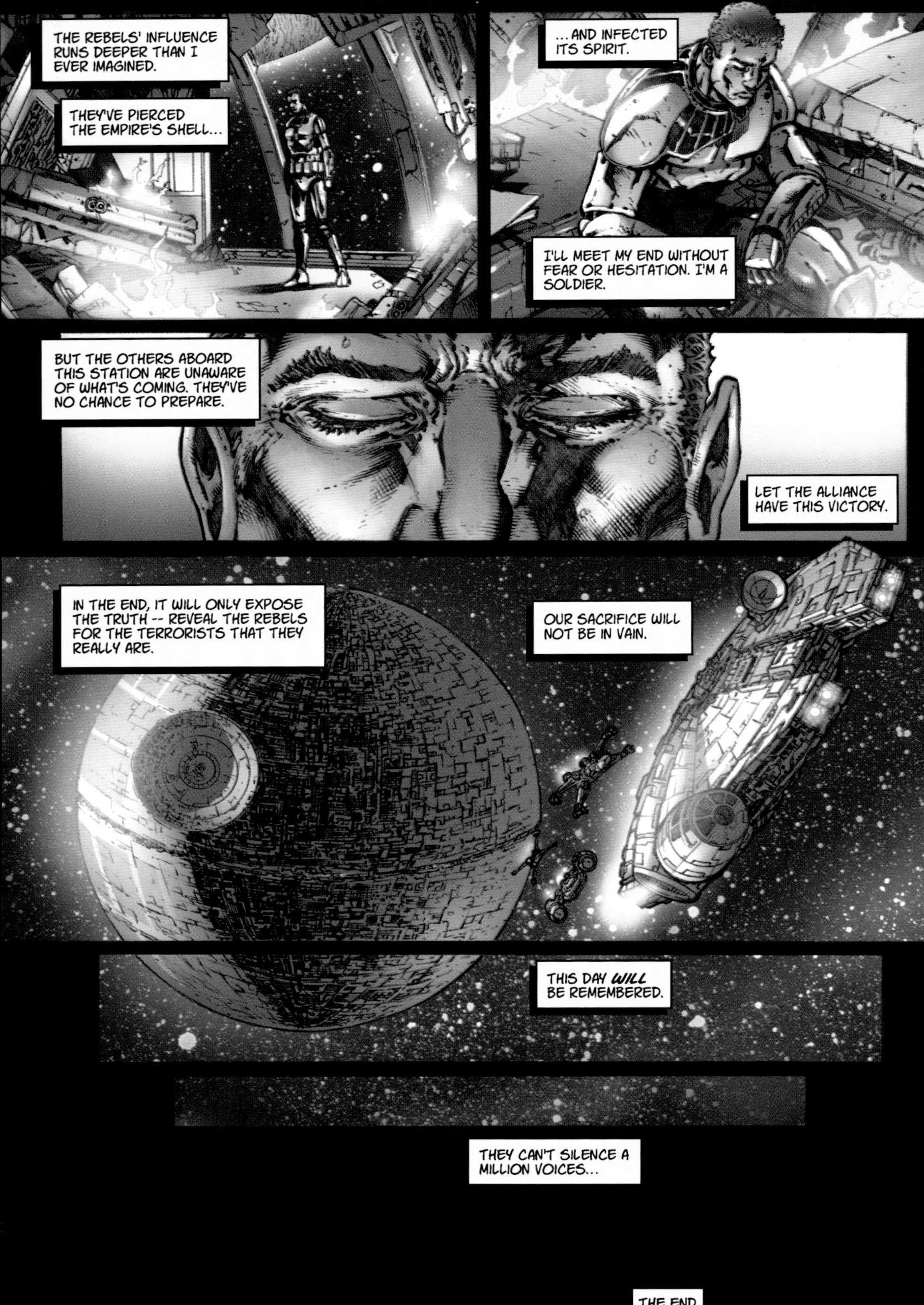
THE REBELS' INFLUENCE RUNS DEEPER THAN I EVER IMAGINED.
THEY'VE PIERCED THE EMPIRE'S SHELL...
...AND INFECTED ITS SPIRIT.
I'LL MEET MY END WITHOUT FEAR OR HESITATION. I'M A SOLDIER.
BUT THE OTHERS ABOARD THIS STATION ARE UNAWARE OF WHAT'S COMING. THEY'VE NO CHANCE TO PREPARE.
LET THE ALLIANCE HAVE THIS VICTORY.
IN THE END, IT WILL ONLY EXPOSE THE TRUTH -- REVEAL THE REBELS FOR THE TERRORISTS THAT THEY REALLY ARE.
OUR SACRIFICE WILL NOT BE IN VAIN.
THIS DAY *WILL* BE REMEMBERED.
THEY CAN'T SILENCE A MILLION VOICES...
THE END

The Savage Heart | Illustration by Francisco Ruiz Velasco

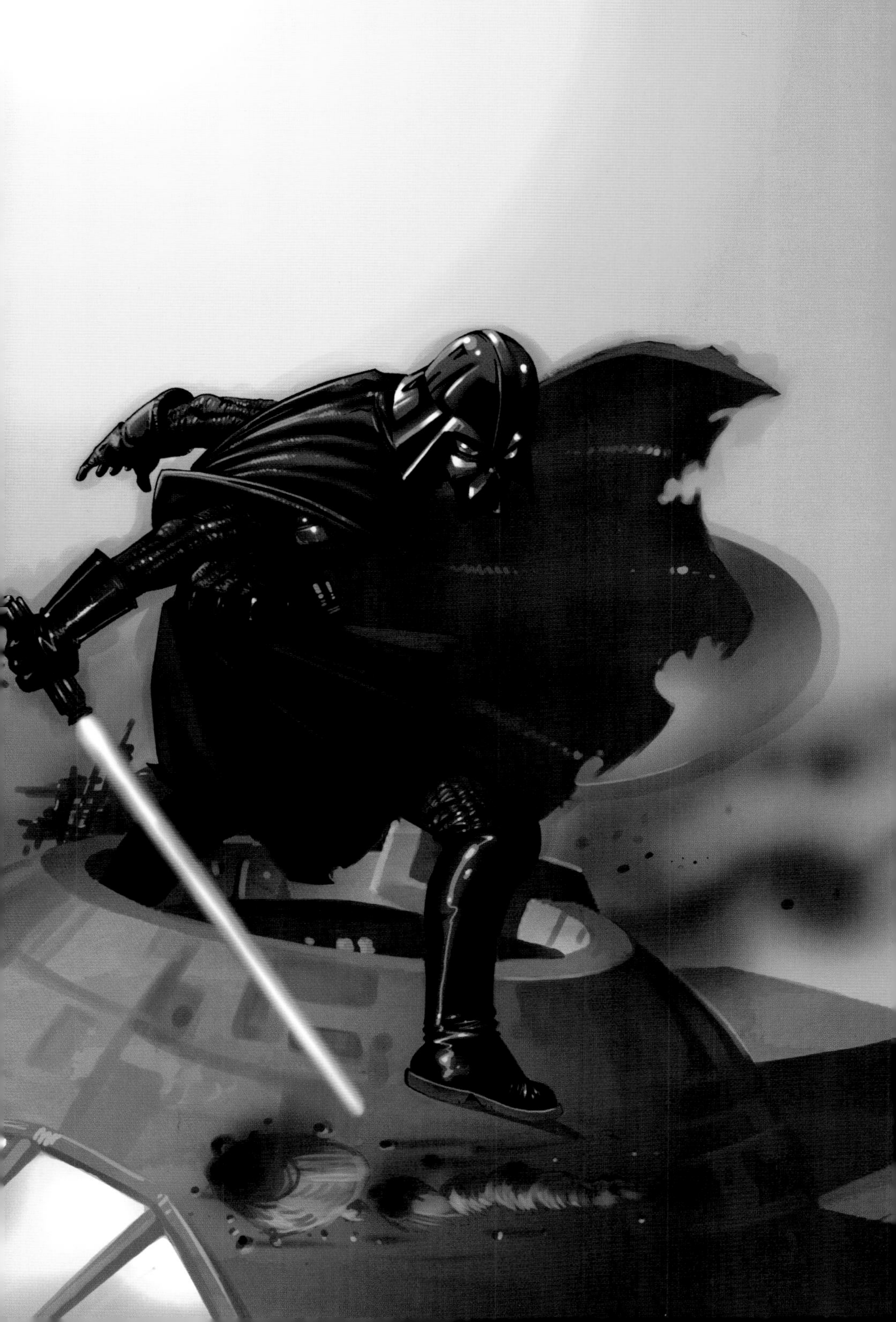

IMMEDIATELY FOLLOWING THE BATTLE OF YAVIN . . .

script by Paul Alden
art and colors by Raúl Treviño
lettering by Michael David Thomas

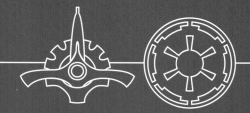

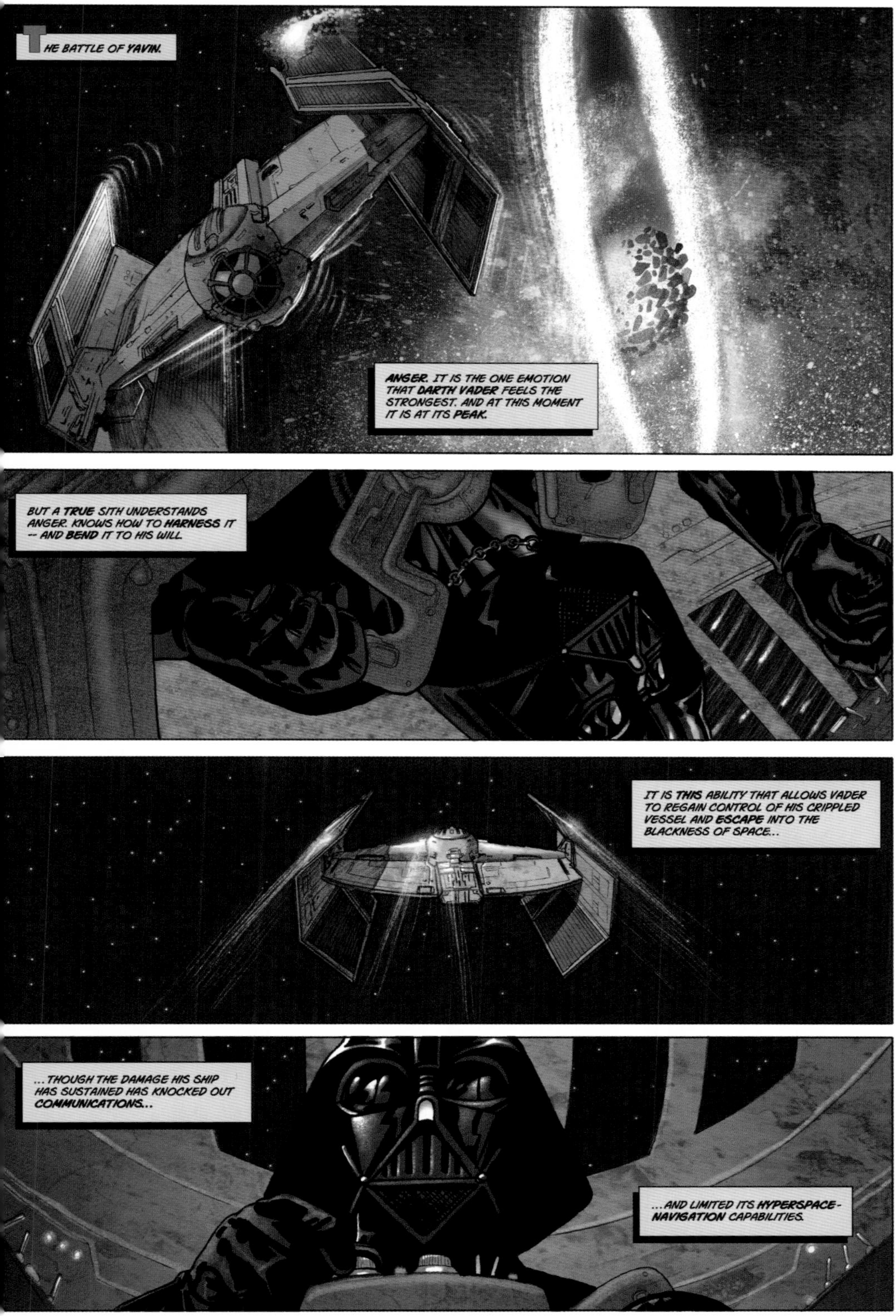
THE BATTLE OF YAVIN.
ANGER. IT IS THE ONE EMOTION THAT DARTH VADER FEELS THE STRONGEST. AND AT THIS MOMENT IT IS AT ITS PEAK.
BUT A TRUE SITH UNDERSTANDS ANGER. KNOWS HOW TO HARNESS IT -- AND BEND IT TO HIS WILL.
IT IS THIS ABILITY THAT ALLOWS VADER TO REGAIN CONTROL OF HIS CRIPPLED VESSEL AND ESCAPE INTO THE BLACKNESS OF SPACE...
...THOUGH THE DAMAGE HIS SHIP HAS SUSTAINED HAS KNOCKED OUT COMMUNICATIONS...
...AND LIMITED ITS HYPERSPACE-NAVIGATION CAPABILITIES.

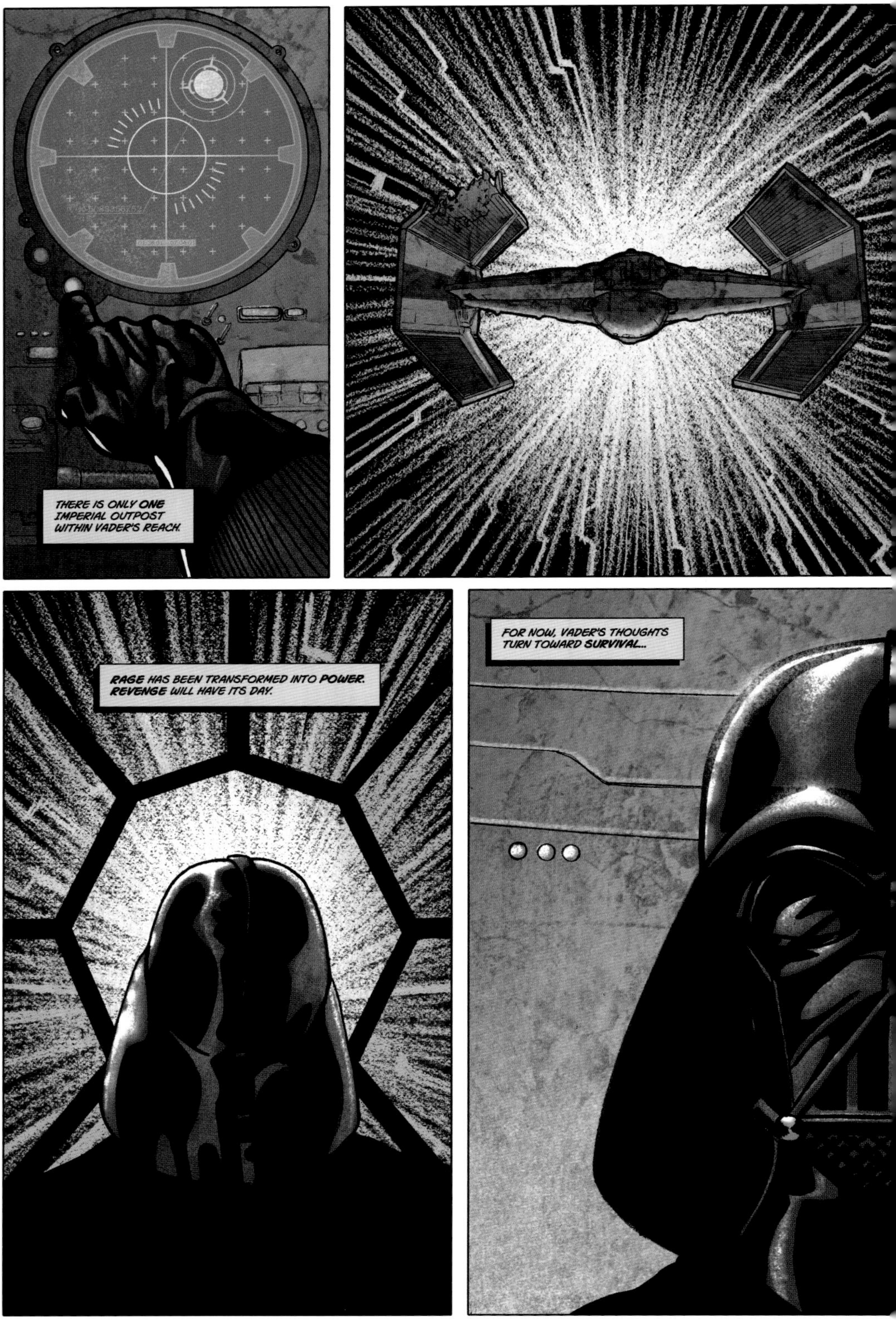
THERE IS ONLY ONE IMPERIAL OUTPOST WITHIN VADER'S REACH.
RAGE HAS BEEN TRANSFORMED INTO POWER. REVENGE WILL HAVE ITS DAY.
FOR NOW, VADER'S THOUGHTS TURN TOWARD SURVIVAL...

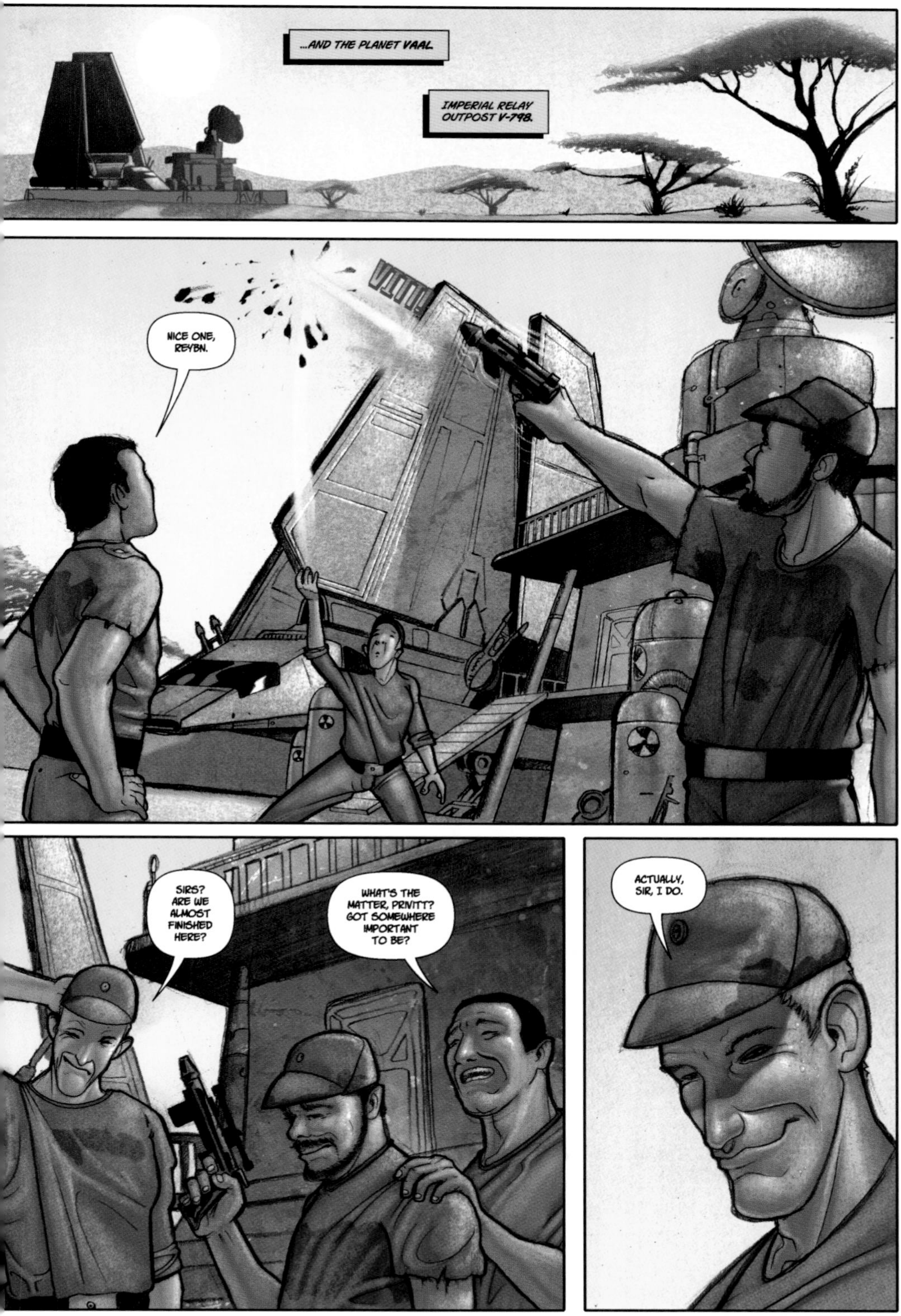
...AND THE PLANET VAAL.
IMPERIAL RELAY OUTPOST V-798.
NICE ONE, REYBN.
SIRS? ARE WE ALMOST FINISHED HERE?
WHAT'S THE MATTER, PRIVITT? GOT SOMEWHERE IMPORTANT TO BE?
ACTUALLY, SIR, I DO.

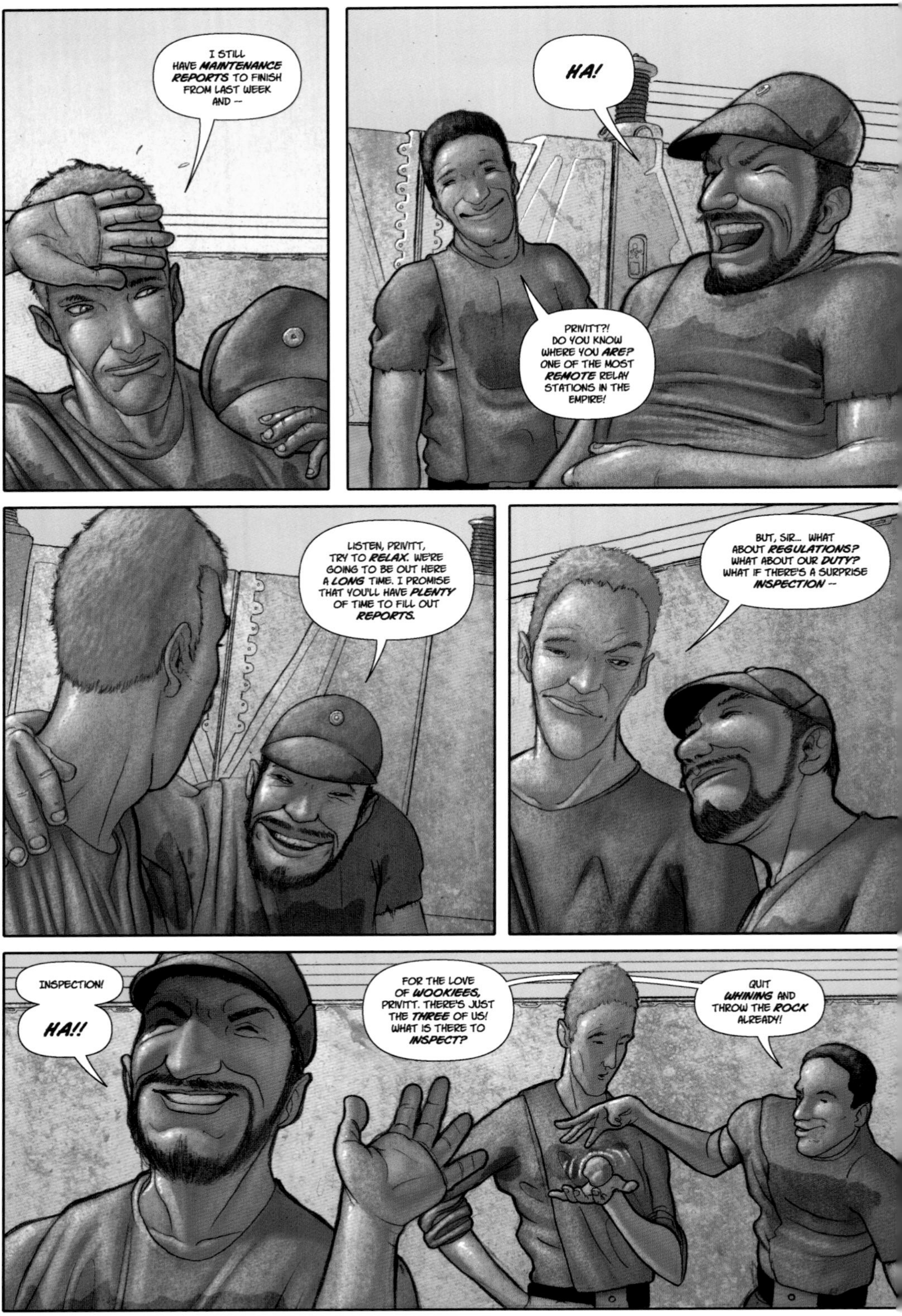
I STILL HAVE MAINTENANCE REPORTS TO FINISH FROM LAST WEEK AND --
HA!
PRIVITT?! DO YOU KNOW WHERE YOU ARE? ONE OF THE MOST REMOTE RELAY STATIONS IN THE EMPIRE!
LISTEN, PRIVITT, TRY TO RELAX. WE'RE GOING TO BE OUT HERE A LONG TIME. I PROMISE THAT YOU'LL HAVE PLENTY OF TIME TO FILL OUT REPORTS.
BUT, SIR... WHAT ABOUT REGULATIONS? WHAT ABOUT OUR DUTY? WHAT IF THERE'S A SURPRISE INSPECTION --
INSPECTION!
HA!!
FOR THE LOVE OF WOOKIEES, PRIVITT. THERE'S JUST THE THREE OF US! WHAT IS THERE TO INSPECT?
QUIT WHINING AND THROW THE ROCK ALREADY!

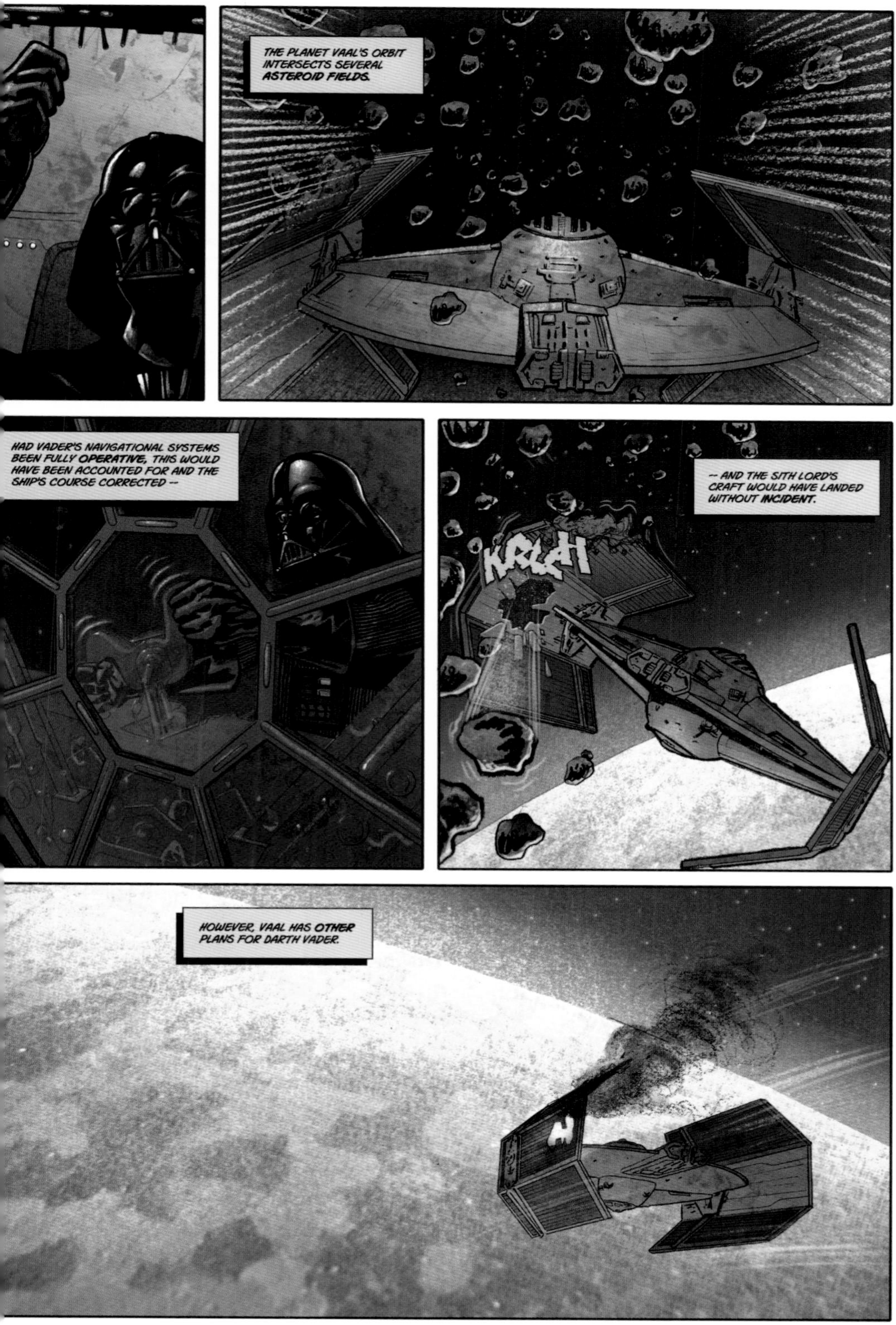
THE PLANET VAAL'S ORBIT INTERSECTS SEVERAL ASTEROID FIELDS.
HAD VADER'S NAVIGATIONAL SYSTEMS BEEN FULLY OPERATIVE, THIS WOULD HAVE BEEN ACCOUNTED FOR AND THE SHIP'S COURSE CORRECTED --
-- AND THE SITH LORD'S CRAFT WOULD HAVE LANDED WITHOUT INCIDENT.
KRASH
HOWEVER, VAAL HAS OTHER PLANS FOR DARTH VADER.

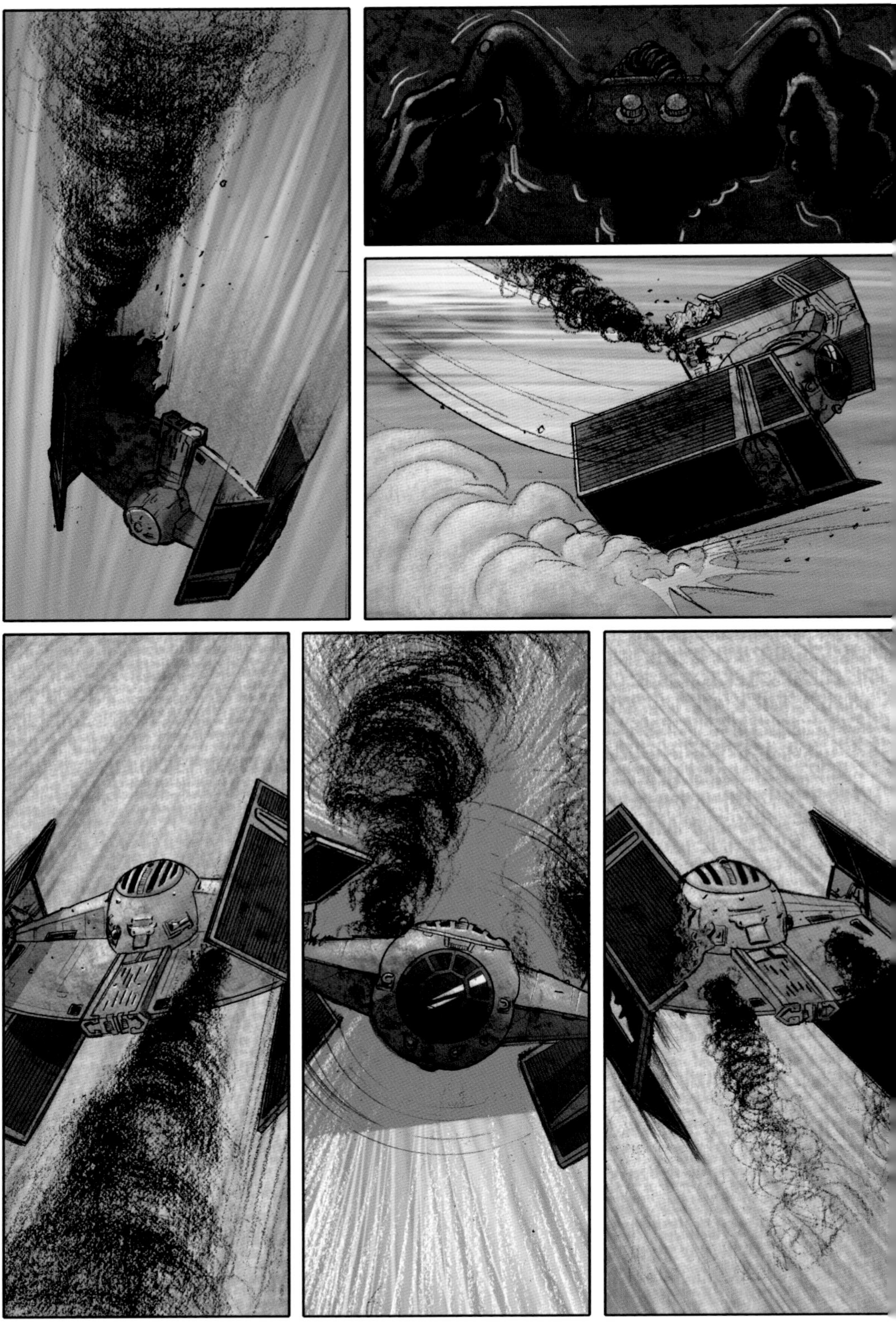

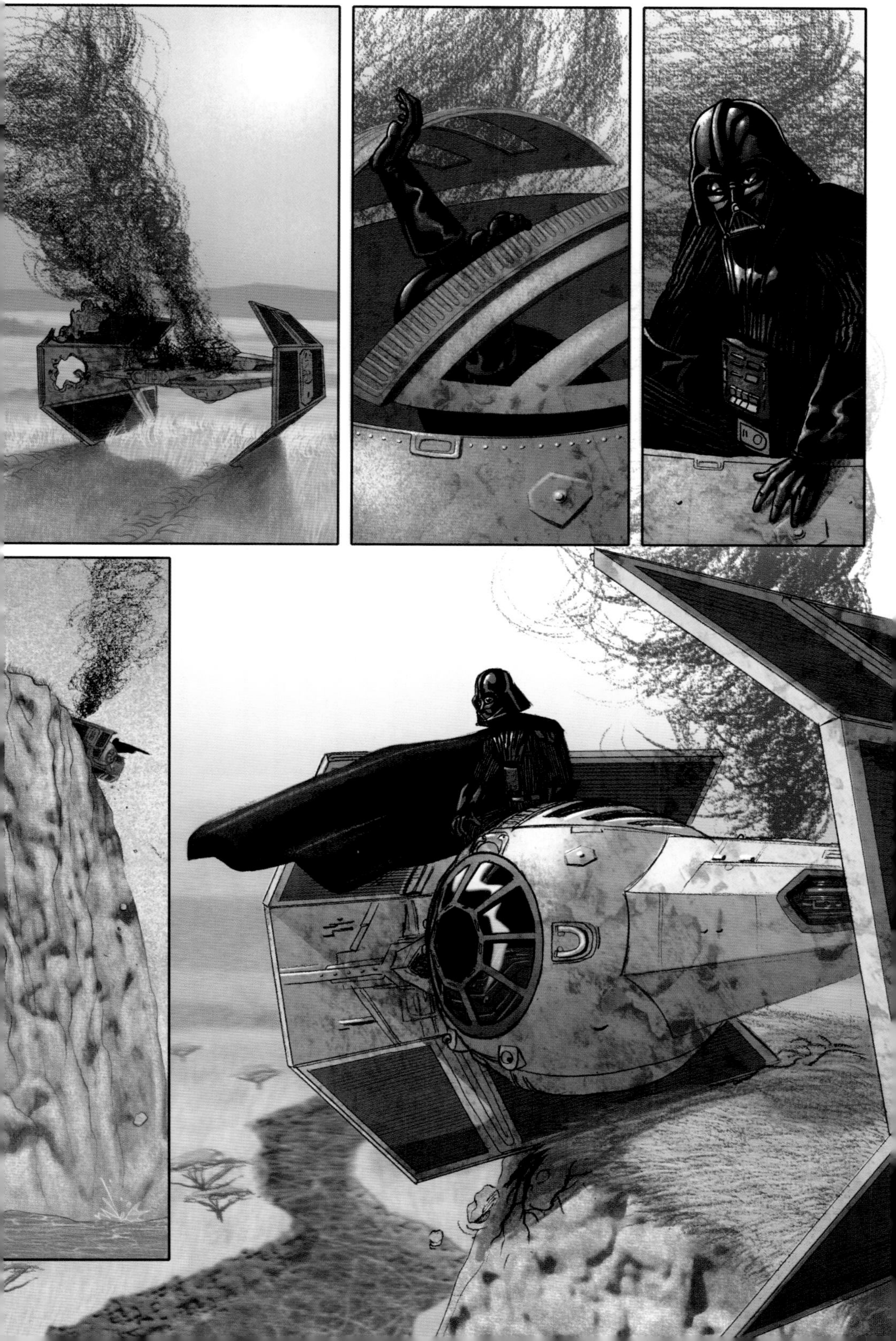

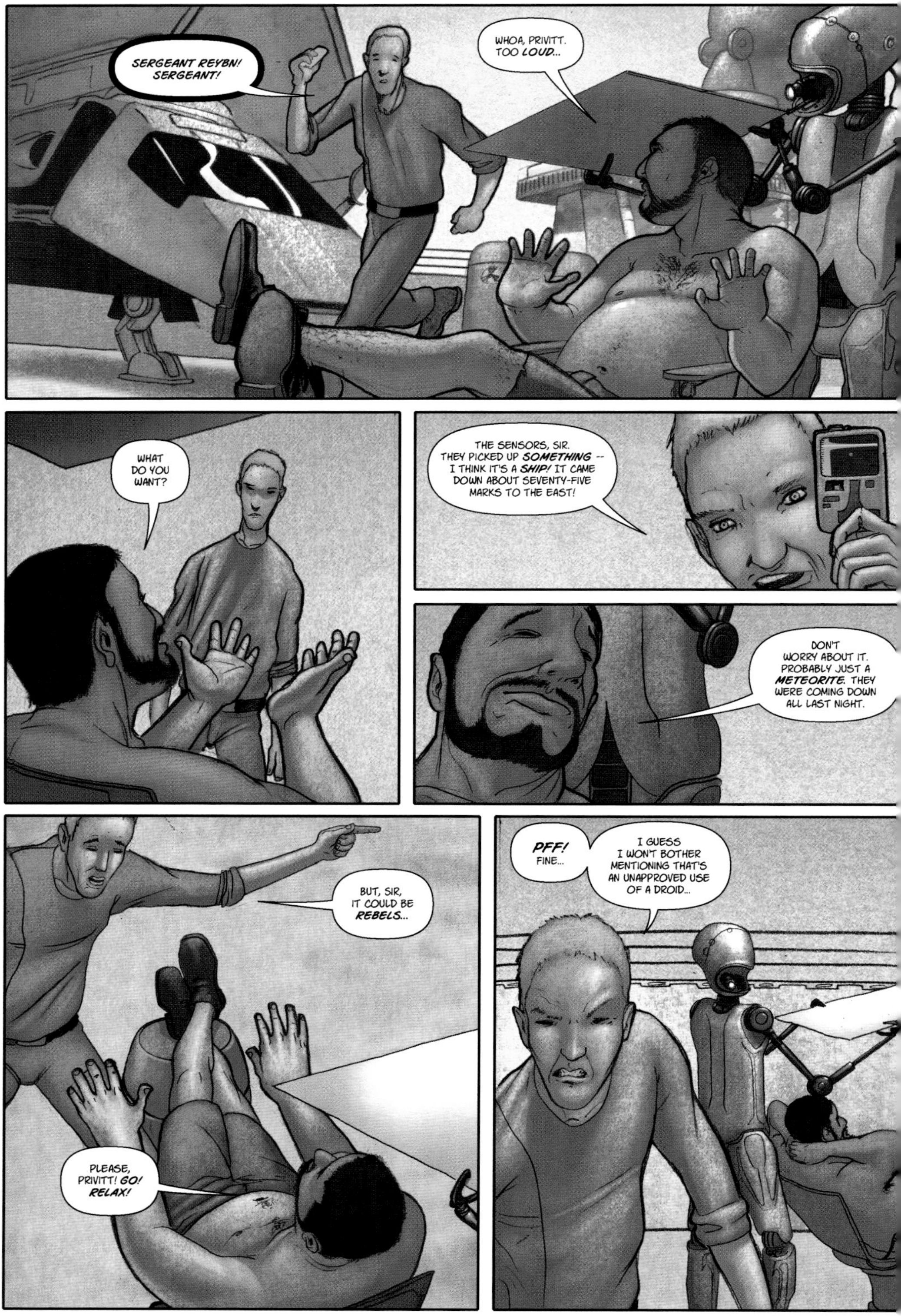
SERGEANT REYBN! SERGEANT!
WHOA, PRIVITT. TOO LOUD...
WHAT DO YOU WANT?
THE SENSORS, SIR. THEY PICKED UP SOMETHING -- I THINK IT'S A SHIP! IT CAME DOWN ABOUT SEVENTY-FIVE MARKS TO THE EAST!
DON'T WORRY ABOUT IT. PROBABLY JUST A METEORITE. THEY WERE COMING DOWN ALL LAST NIGHT.
BUT, SIR, IT COULD BE REBELS...
PLEASE, PRIVITT! GO! RELAX!
PFF! FINE...
I GUESS I WON'T BOTHER MENTIONING THAT'S AN UNAPPROVED USE OF A DROID...

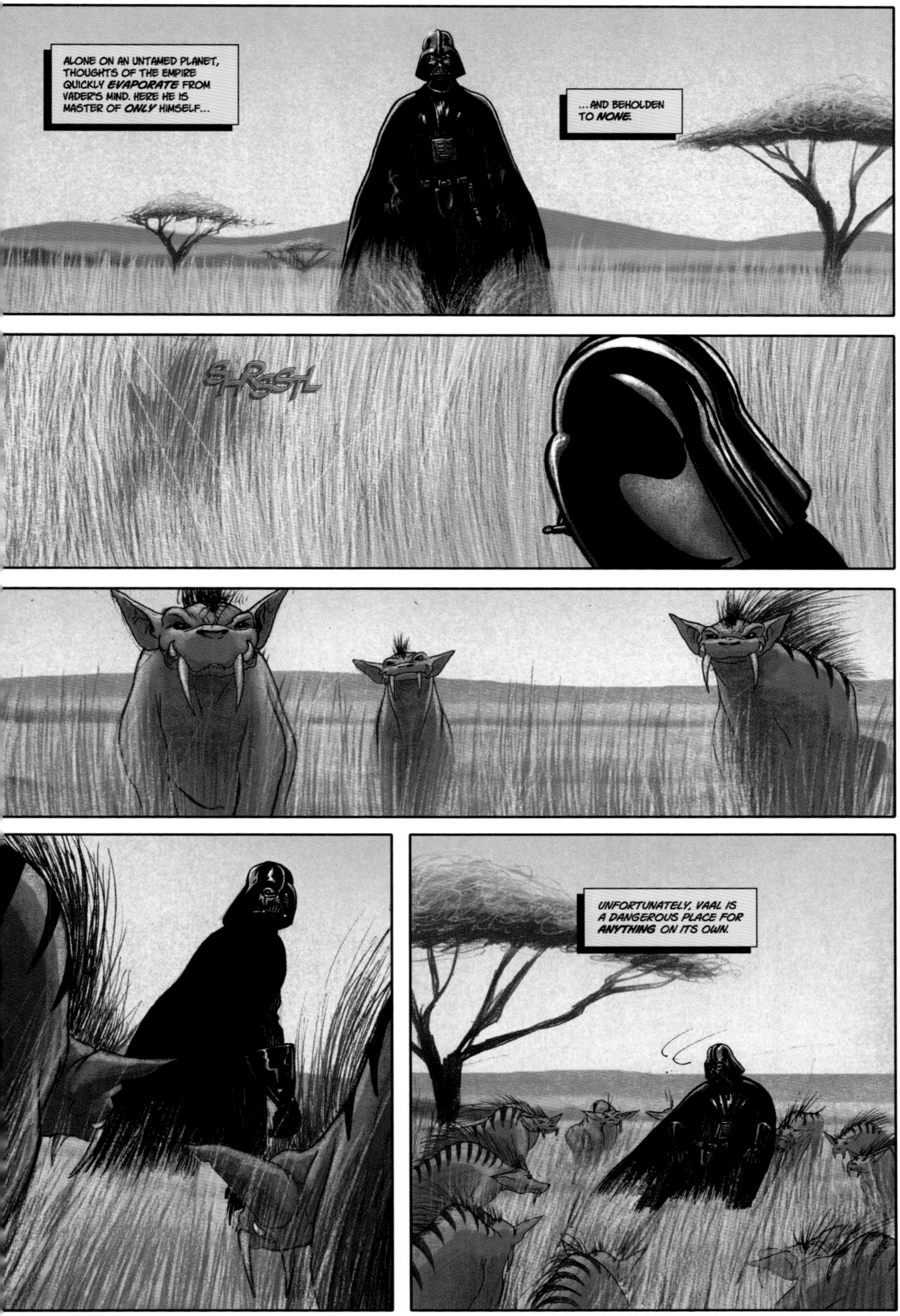
ALONE ON AN UNTAMED PLANET, THOUGHTS OF THE EMPIRE QUICKLY EVAPORATE FROM VADER'S MIND. HERE HE IS MASTER OF ONLY HIMSELF...
...AND BEHOLDEN TO NONE.
UNFORTUNATELY, VAAL IS A DANGEROUS PLACE FOR ANYTHING ON ITS OWN.

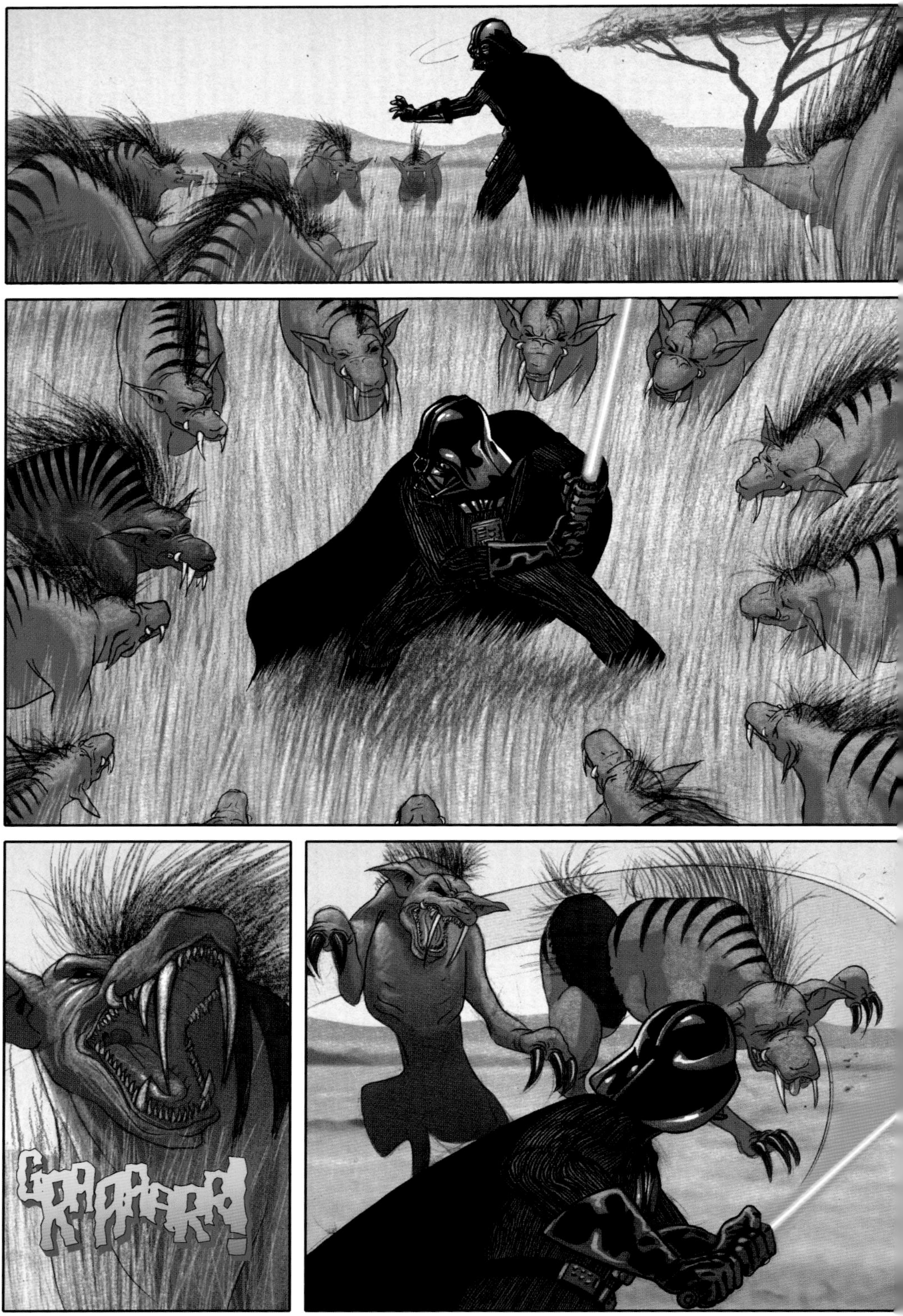
GRAAARRR!

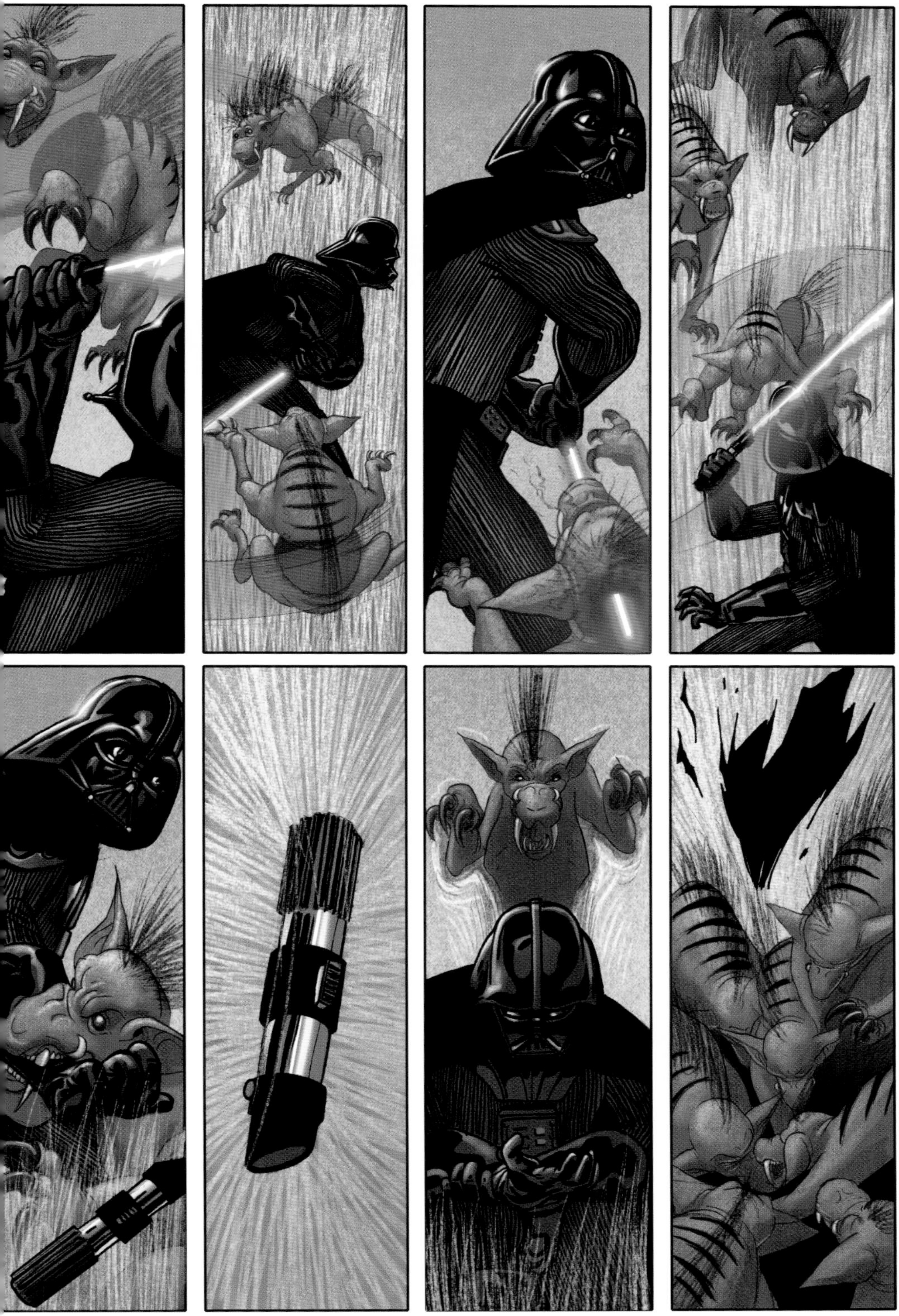

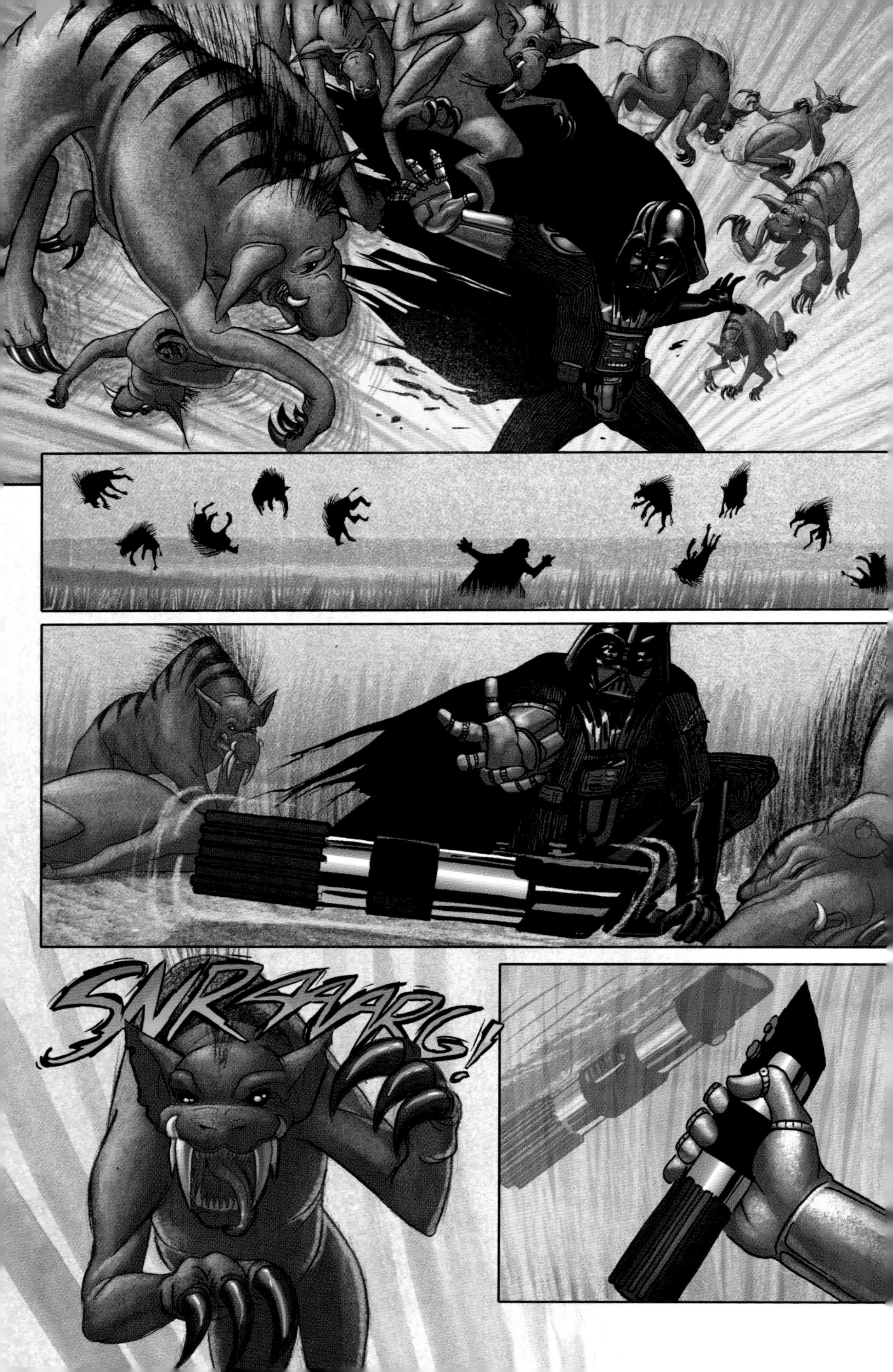
SNRAAARG!

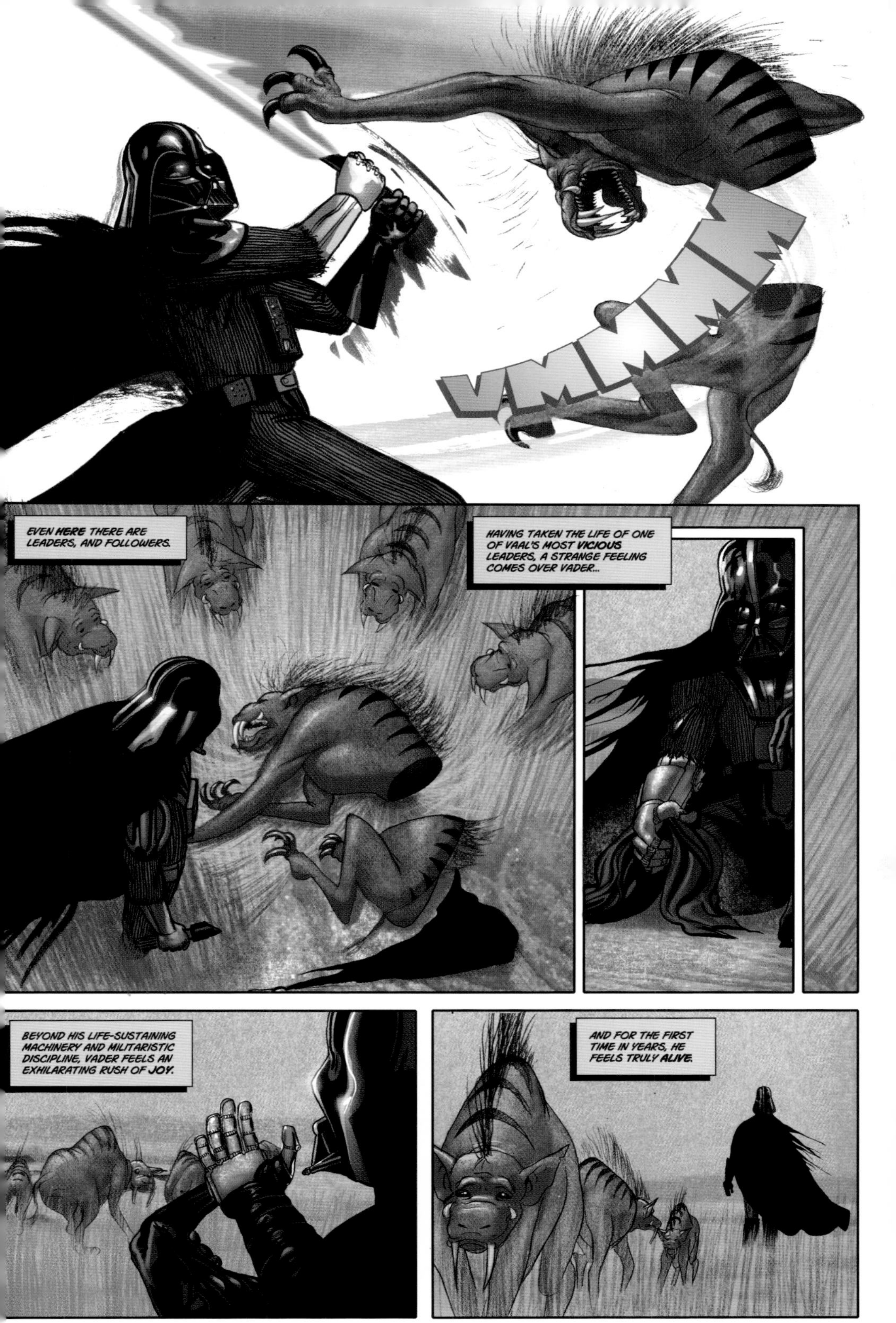
VMMMMM
EVEN HERE THERE ARE LEADERS, AND FOLLOWERS.
HAVING TAKEN THE LIFE OF ONE OF VAAL'S MOST VICIOUS LEADERS, A STRANGE FEELING COMES OVER VADER...
BEYOND HIS LIFE-SUSTAINING MACHINERY AND MILITARISTIC DISCIPLINE, VADER FEELS AN EXHILARATING RUSH OF JOY.
AND FOR THE FIRST TIME IN YEARS, HE FEELS TRULY ALIVE.

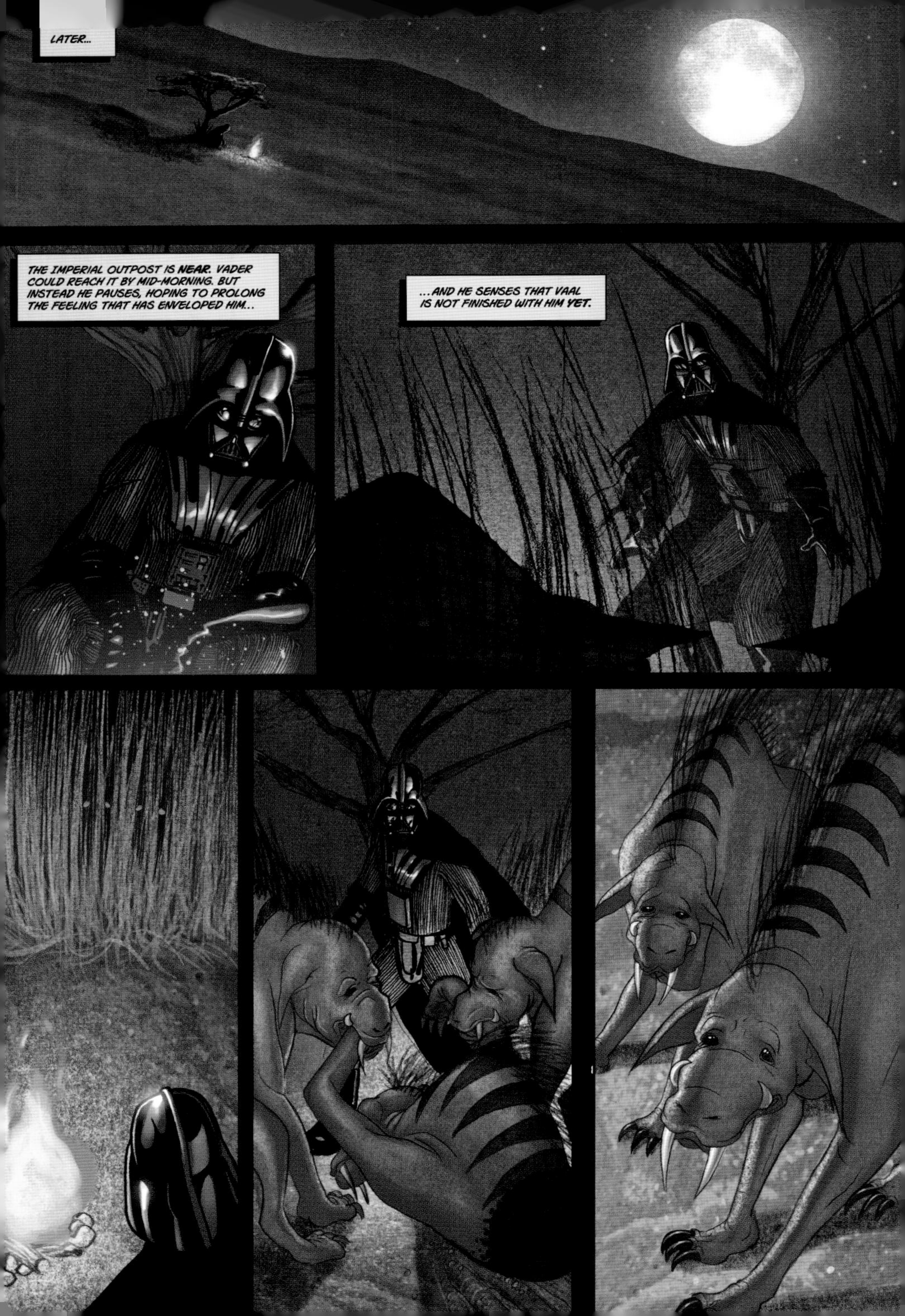
LATER...
THE IMPERIAL OUTPOST IS NEAR. VADER COULD REACH IT BY MID-MORNING. BUT INSTEAD HE PAUSES, HOPING TO PROLONG THE FEELING THAT HAS ENVELOPED HIM...
...AND HE SENSES THAT VAAL IS NOT FINISHED WITH HIM YET.

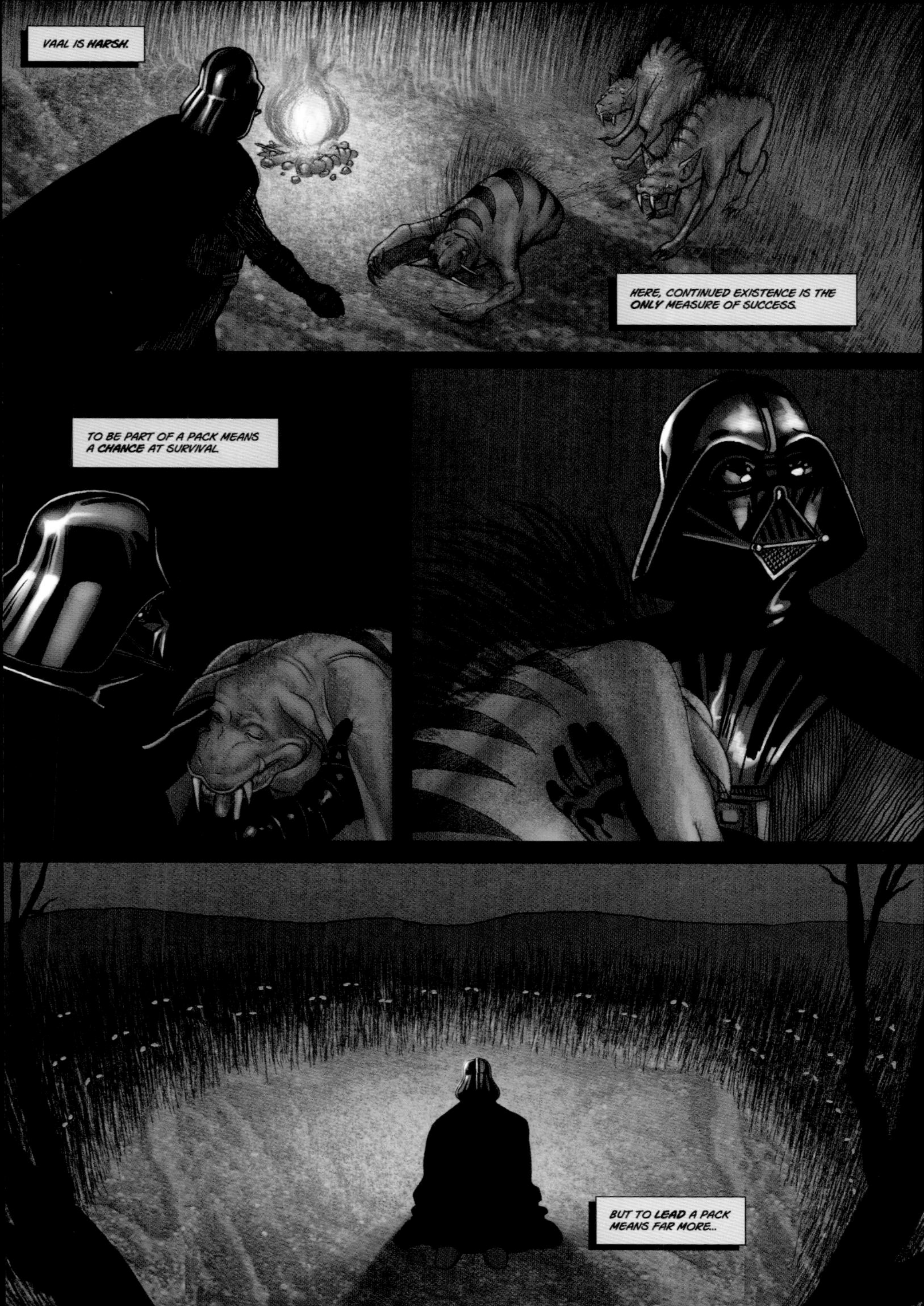
VAAL IS HARSH.
HERE, CONTINUED EXISTENCE IS THE ONLY MEASURE OF SUCCESS.
TO BE PART OF A PACK MEANS A CHANCE AT SURVIVAL.
BUT TO LEAD A PACK MEANS FAR MORE...

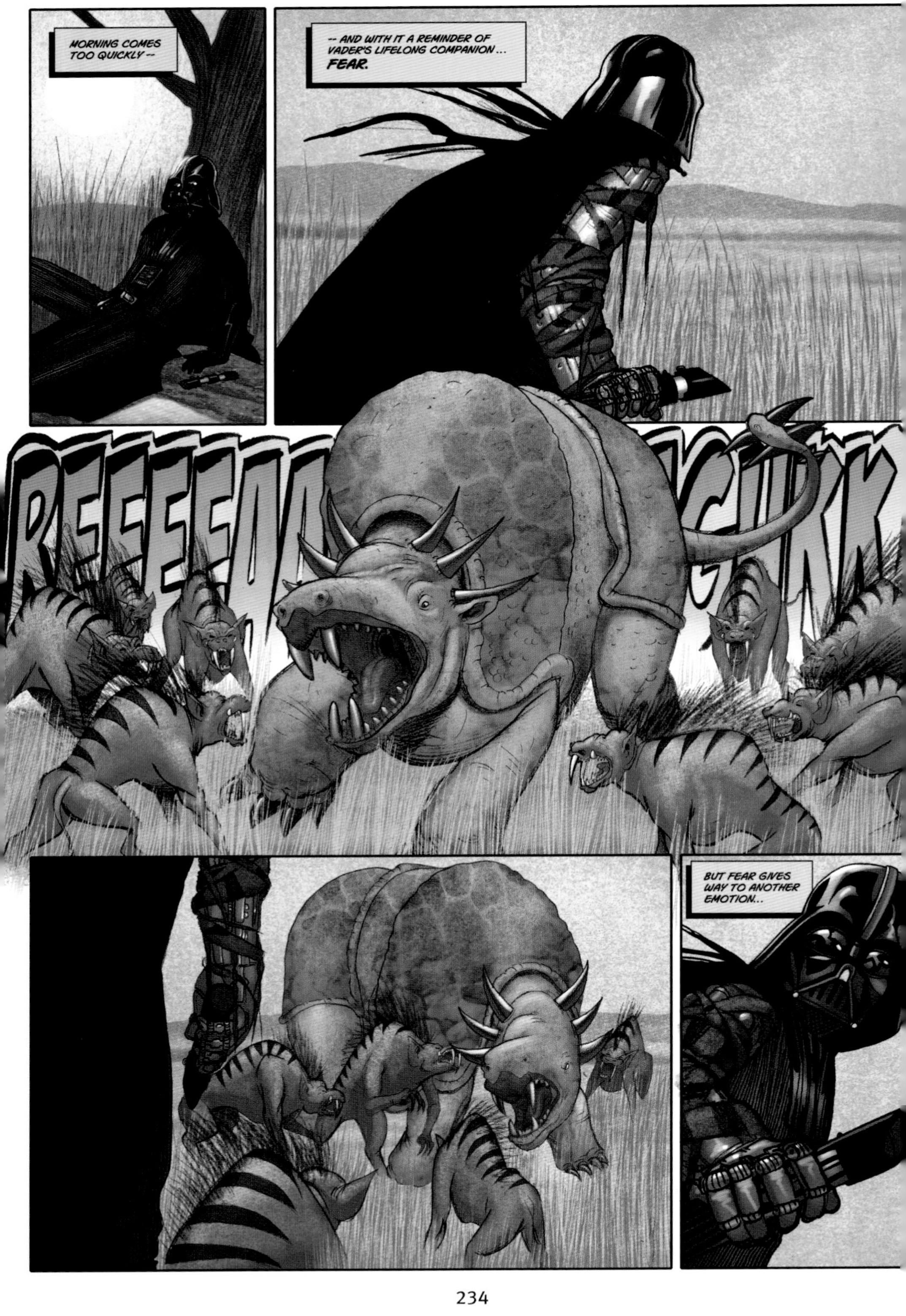
MORNING COMES TOO QUICKLY --
-- AND WITH IT A REMINDER OF VADER'S LIFELONG COMPANION... FEAR.
BUT FEAR GIVES WAY TO ANOTHER EMOTION...

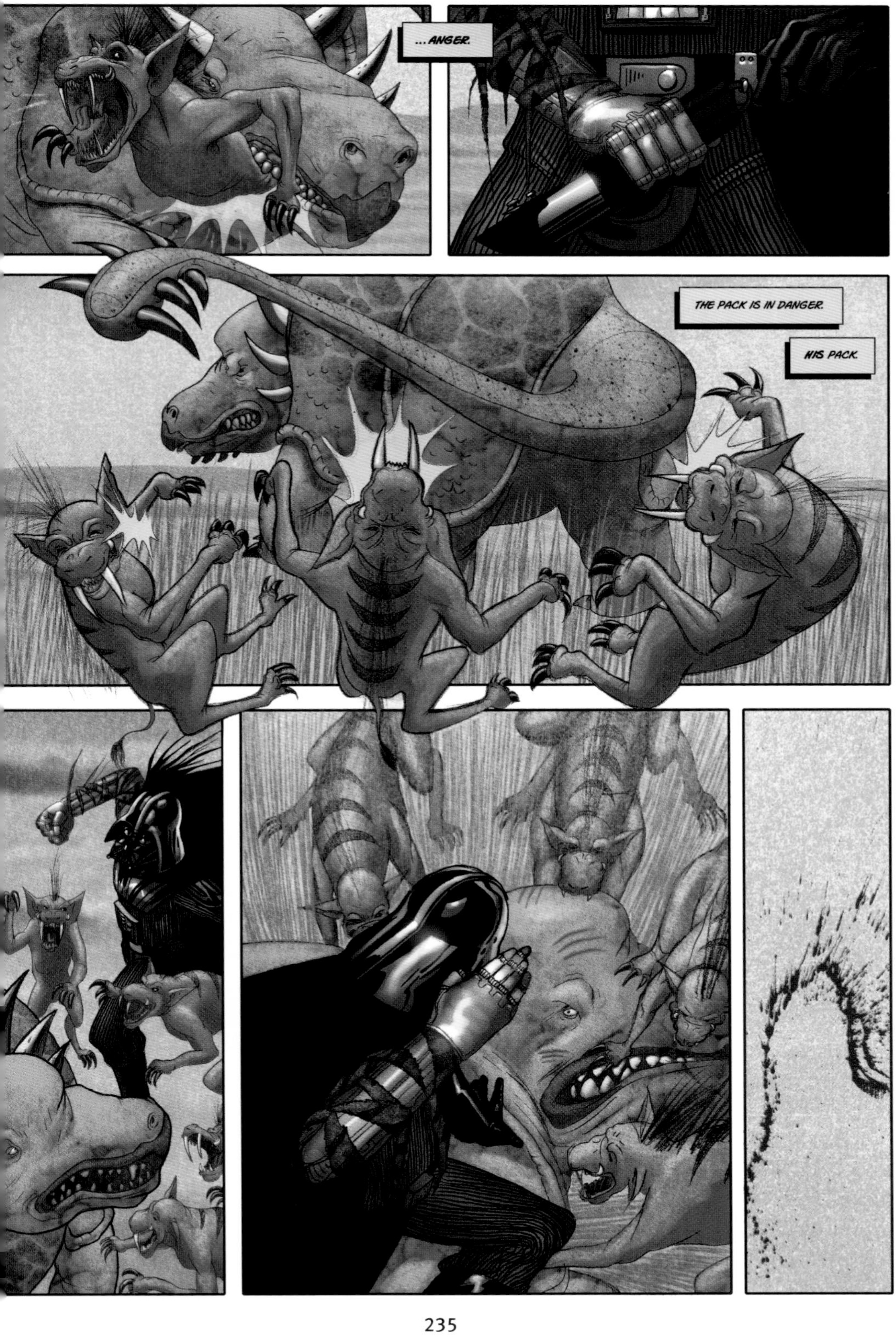
...ANGER.
THE PACK IS IN DANGER.
HIS PACK.

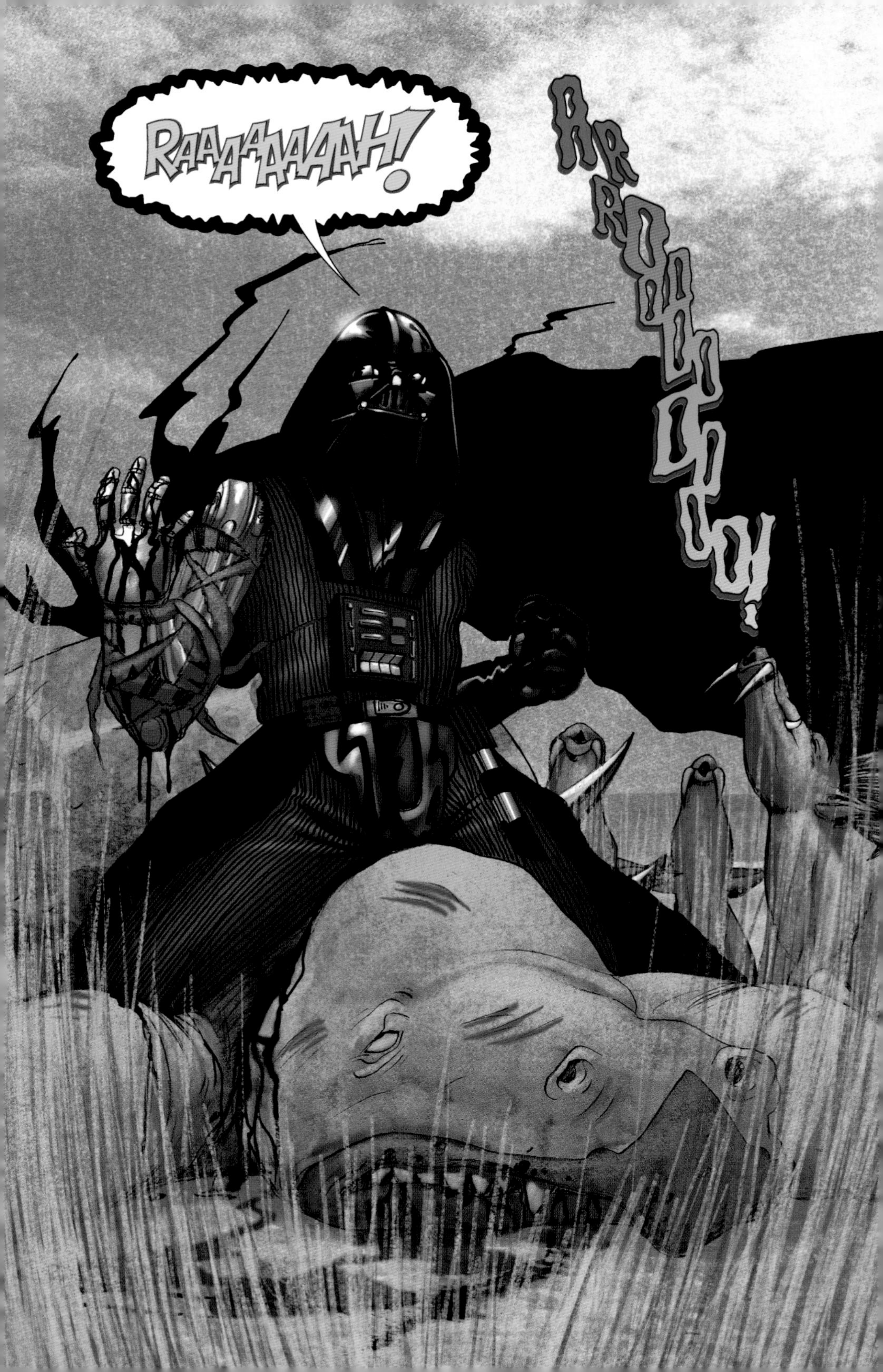
RAAAAAAAAH!
ARROOOOOOO!

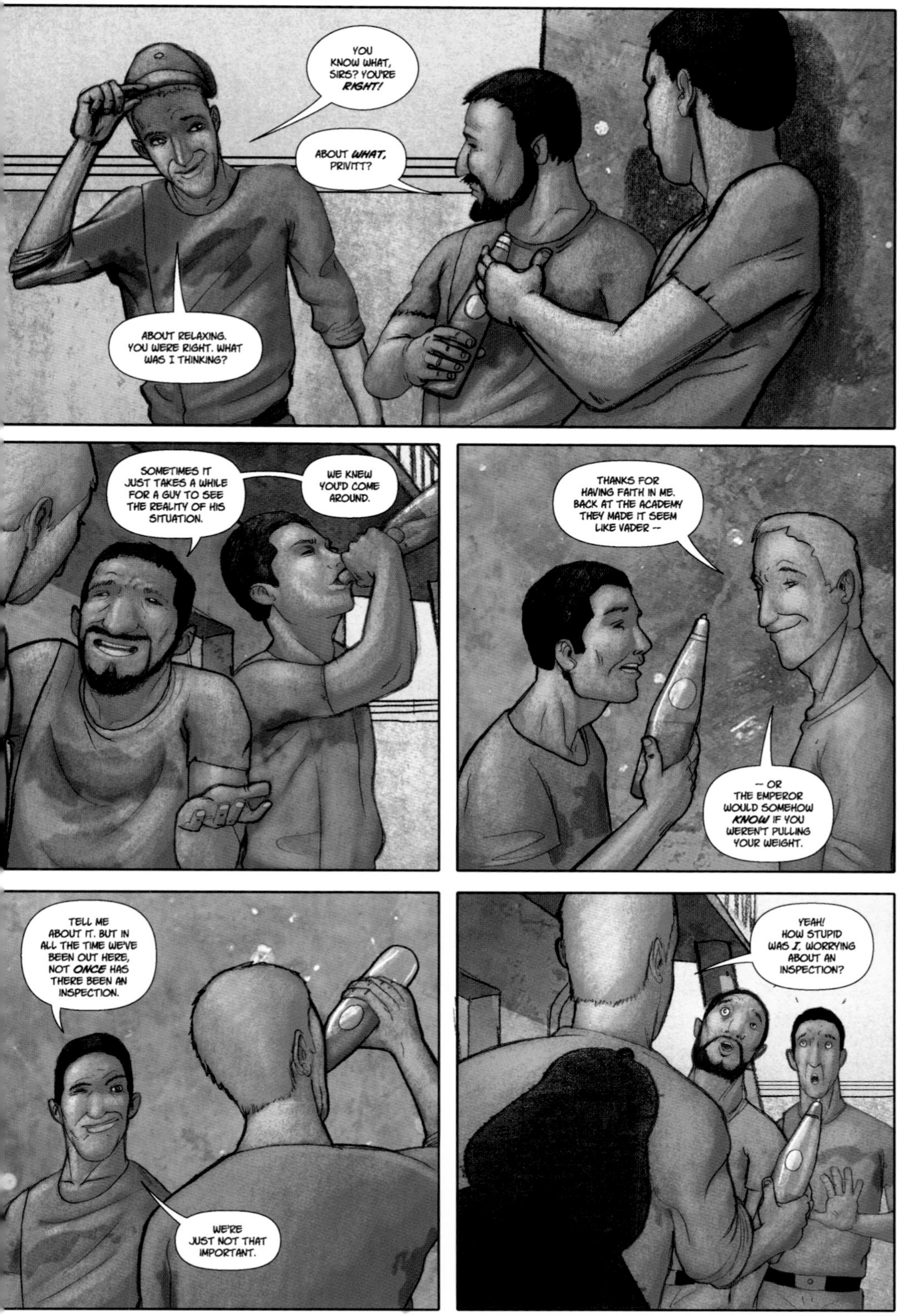
YOU KNOW WHAT, SIRS? YOU'RE *RIGHT!*
ABOUT *WHAT,* PRIVITT?
ABOUT RELAXING. YOU WERE RIGHT. WHAT WAS I THINKING?
SOMETIMES IT JUST TAKES A WHILE FOR A GUY TO SEE THE REALITY OF HIS SITUATION.
WE KNEW YOU'D COME AROUND.
THANKS FOR HAVING FAITH IN ME. BACK AT THE ACADEMY THEY MADE IT SEEM LIKE VADER --
-- OR THE EMPEROR WOULD SOMEHOW *KNOW* IF YOU WEREN'T PULLING YOUR WEIGHT.
TELL ME ABOUT IT. BUT IN ALL THE TIME WE'VE BEEN OUT HERE, NOT *ONCE* HAS THERE BEEN AN INSPECTION.
WE'RE JUST NOT THAT IMPORTANT.
YEAH! HOW STUPID WAS *I,* WORRYING ABOUT AN INSPECTION?

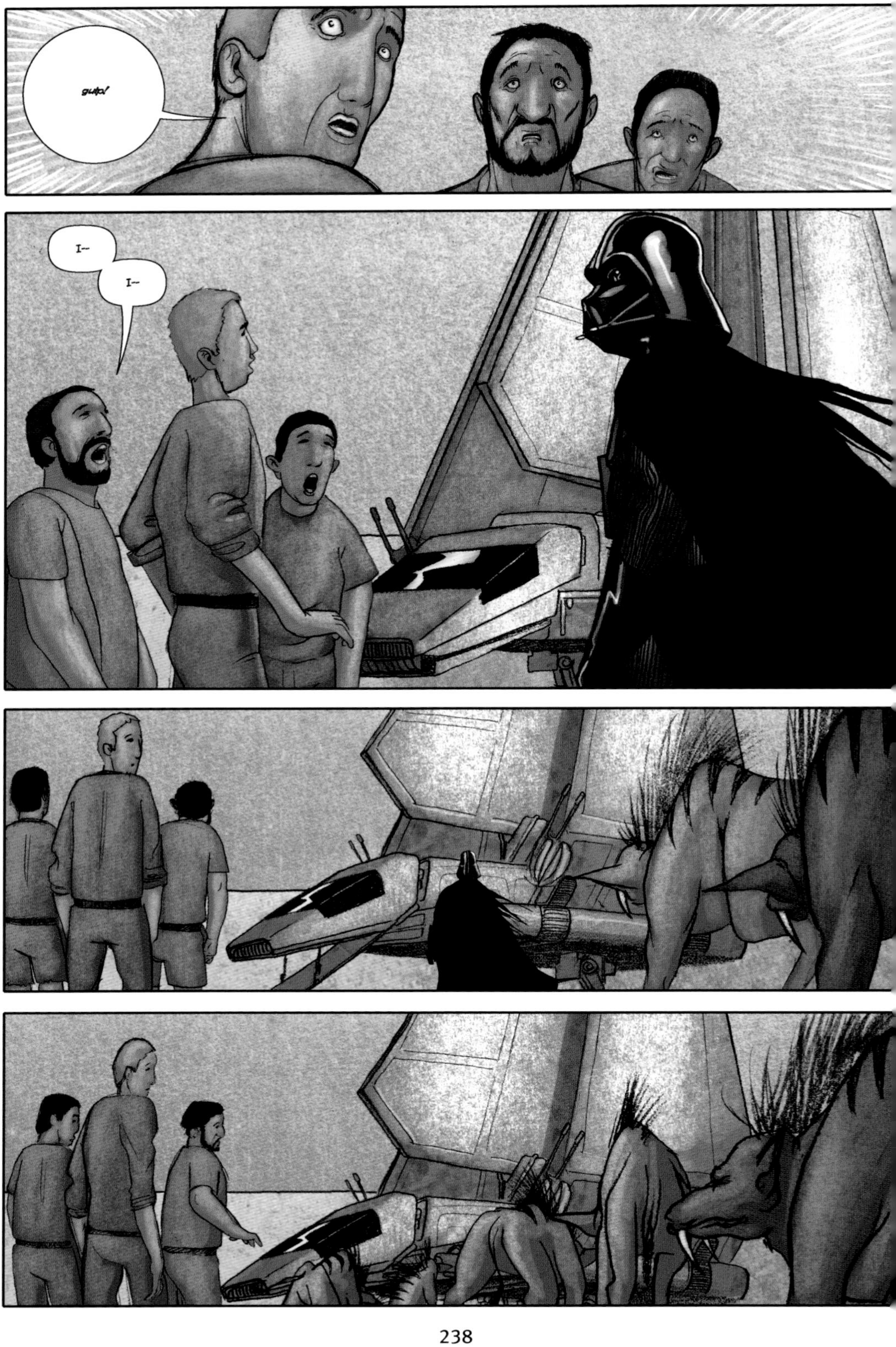
gulp!
I--
I--

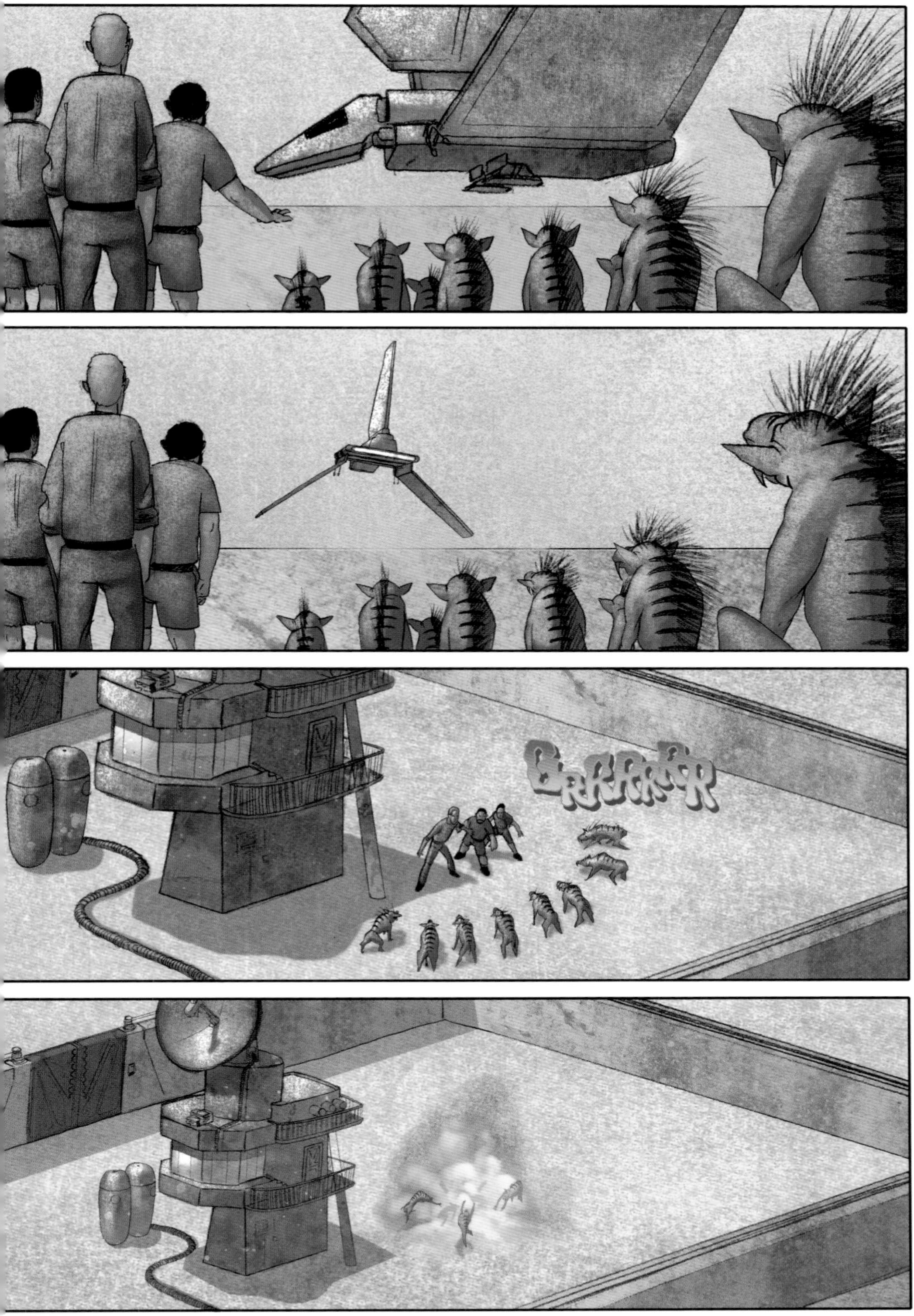
GRRAARR

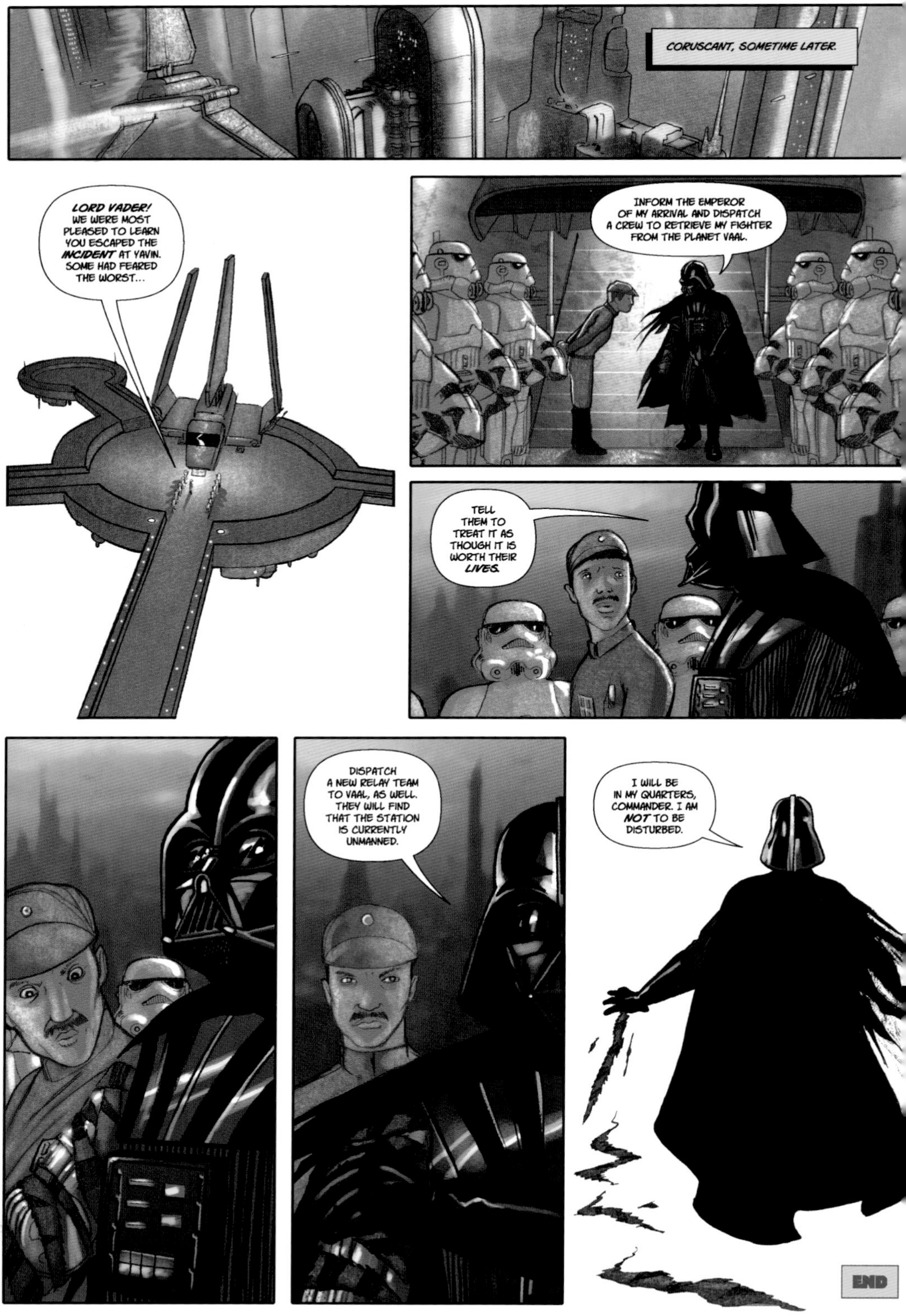
CORUSCANT, SOMETIME LATER.
LORD VADER! WE WERE MOST PLEASED TO LEARN YOU ESCAPED THE INCIDENT AT YAVIN. SOME HAD FEARED THE WORST...
INFORM THE EMPEROR OF MY ARRIVAL AND DISPATCH A CREW TO RETRIEVE MY FIGHTER FROM THE PLANET VAAL.
TELL THEM TO TREAT IT AS THOUGH IT IS WORTH THEIR LIVES.
DISPATCH A NEW RELAY TEAM TO VAAL, AS WELL. THEY WILL FIND THAT THE STATION IS CURRENTLY UNMANNED.
I WILL BE IN MY QUARTERS, COMMANDER. I AM NOT TO BE DISTURBED.
END

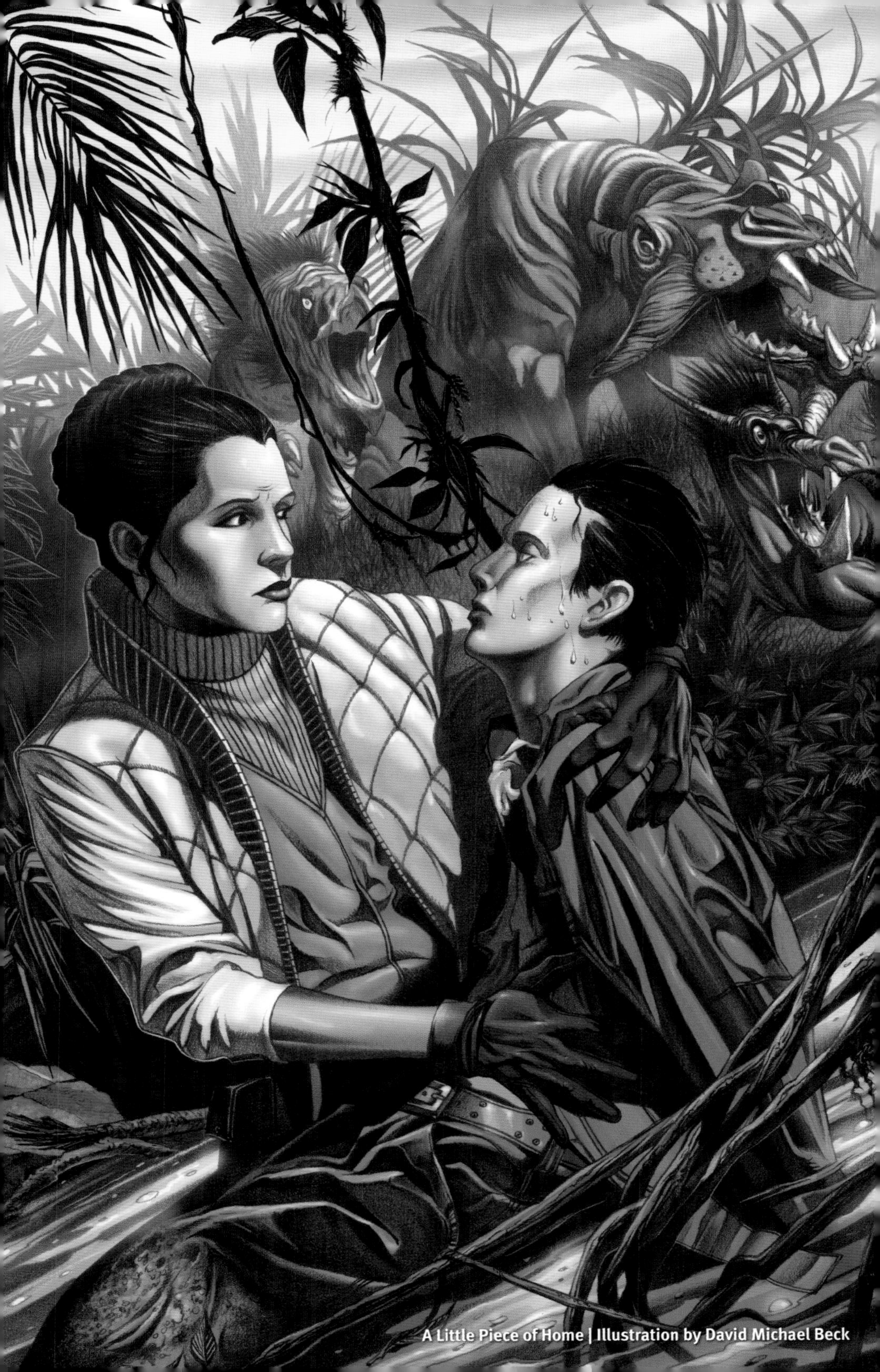

A Little Piece of Home | Illustration by David Michael Beck

APPROXIMATELY SIX MONTHS AFTER THE BATTLE
OF YAVIN . . .

script by Ron Marz
pencils by Tomás Giorello
colors by Brad Anderson and Michael Atiyeh
lettering by Sno Cone Studios

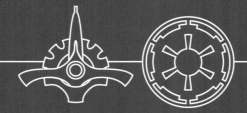

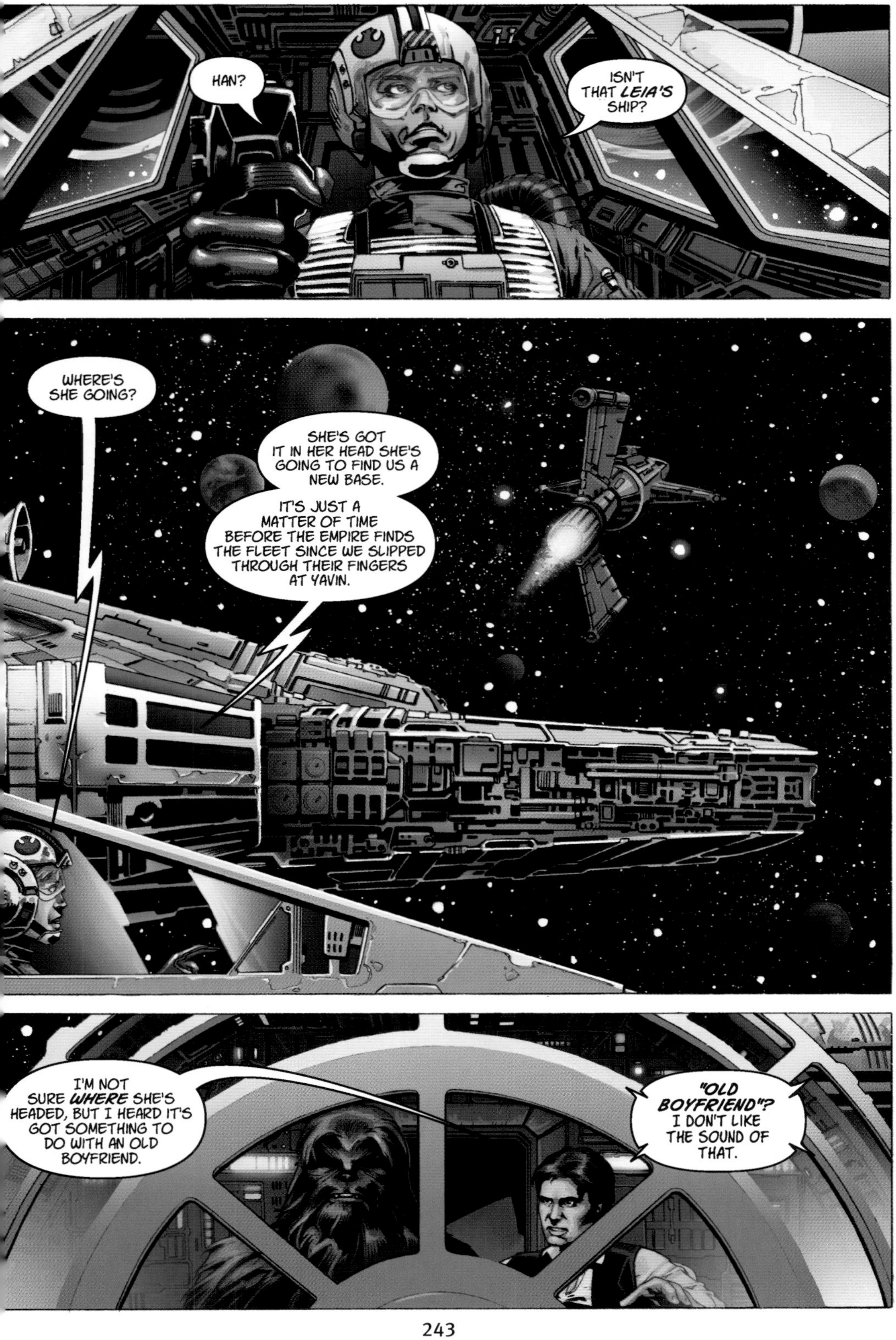
HAN?
ISN'T THAT *LEIA'S* SHIP?
WHERE'S SHE GOING?
SHE'S GOT IT IN HER HEAD SHE'S GOING TO FIND US A NEW BASE.
IT'S JUST A MATTER OF TIME BEFORE THE EMPIRE FINDS THE FLEET SINCE WE SLIPPED THROUGH THEIR FINGERS AT YAVIN.
I'M NOT SURE *WHERE* SHE'S HEADED, BUT I HEARD IT'S GOT SOMETHING TO DO WITH AN OLD BOYFRIEND.
"OLD BOYFRIEND"? I DON'T LIKE THE SOUND OF THAT.

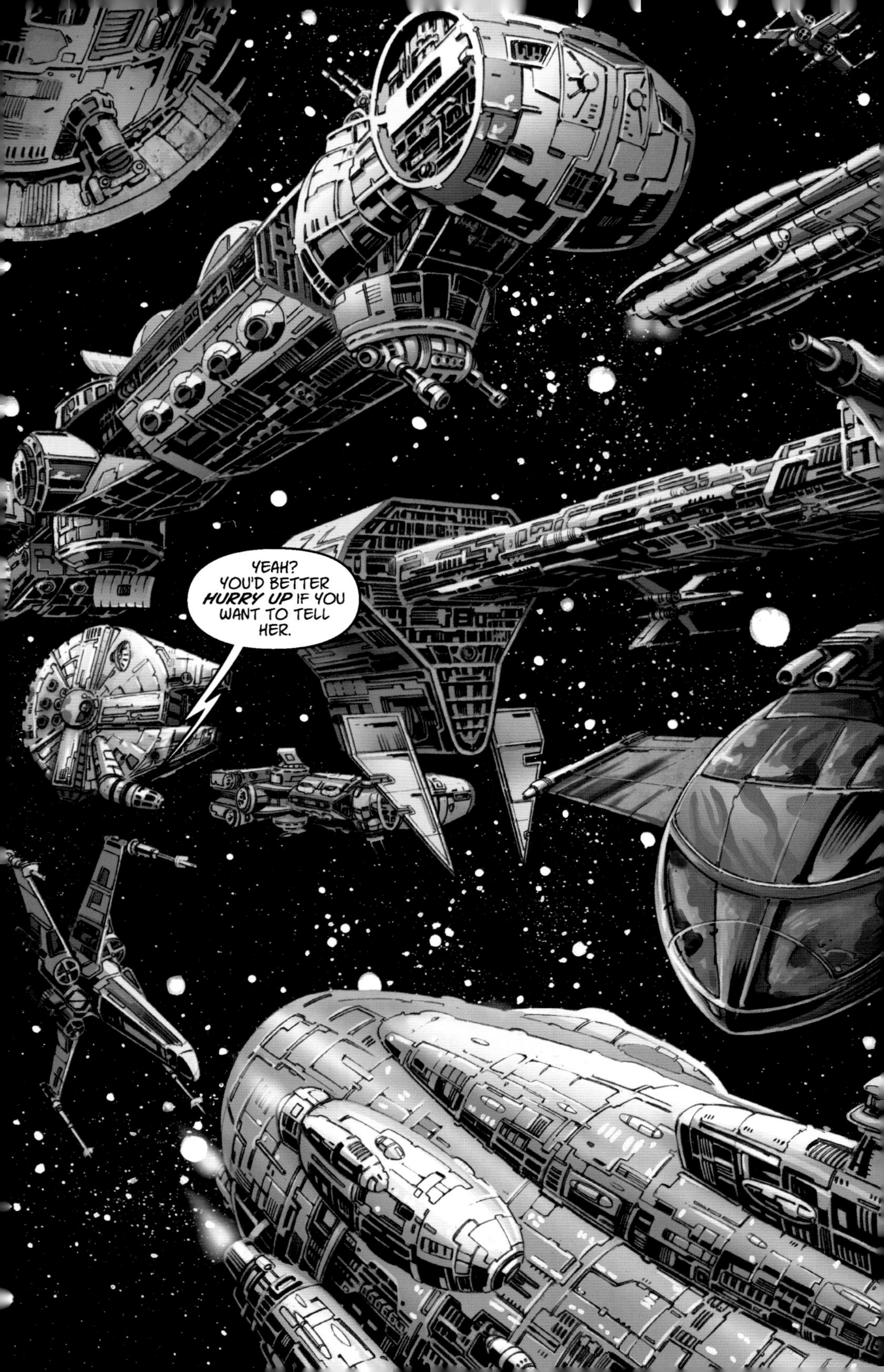
YEAH? YOU'D BETTER HURRY UP IF YOU WANT TO TELL HER.

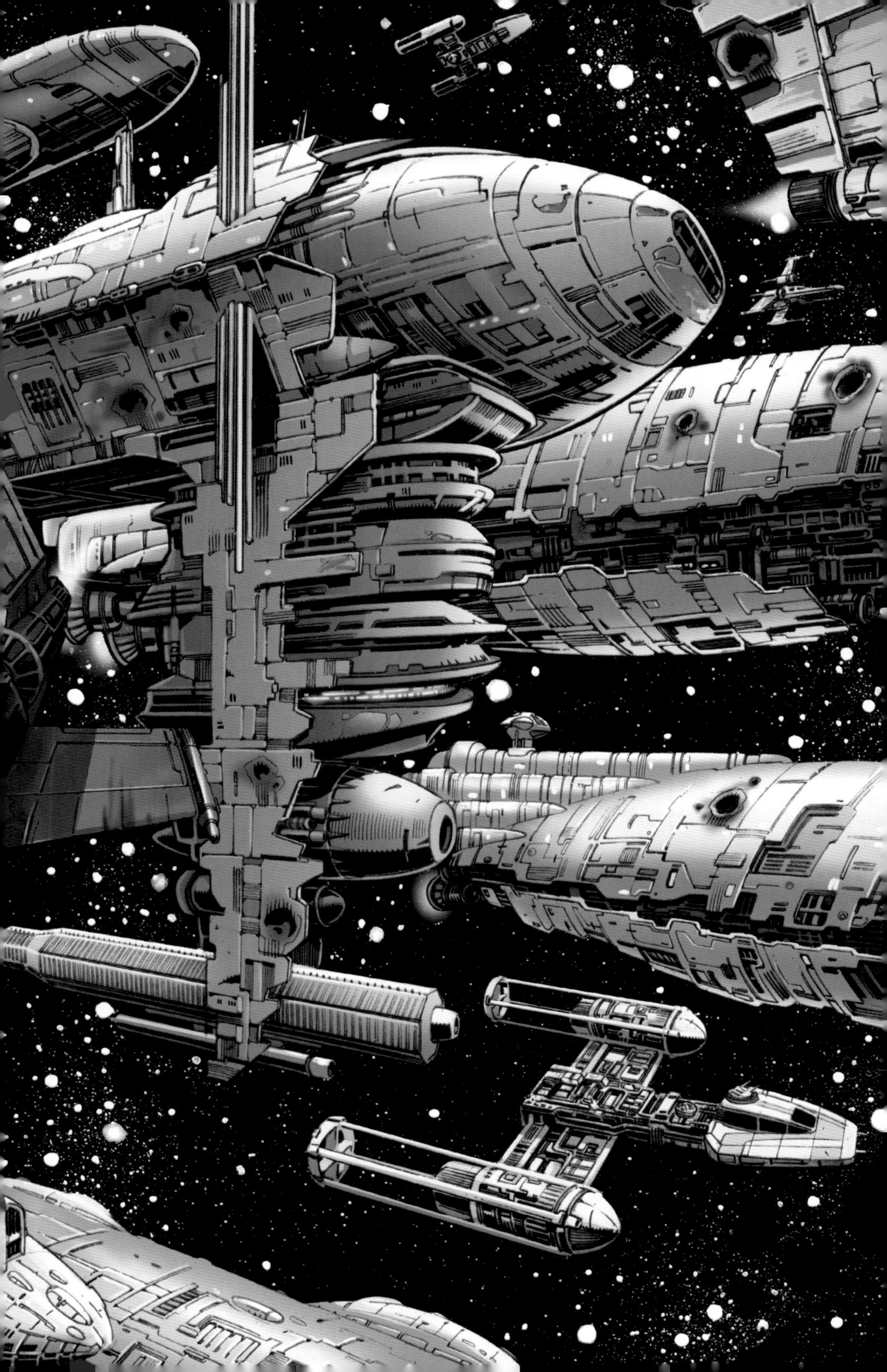

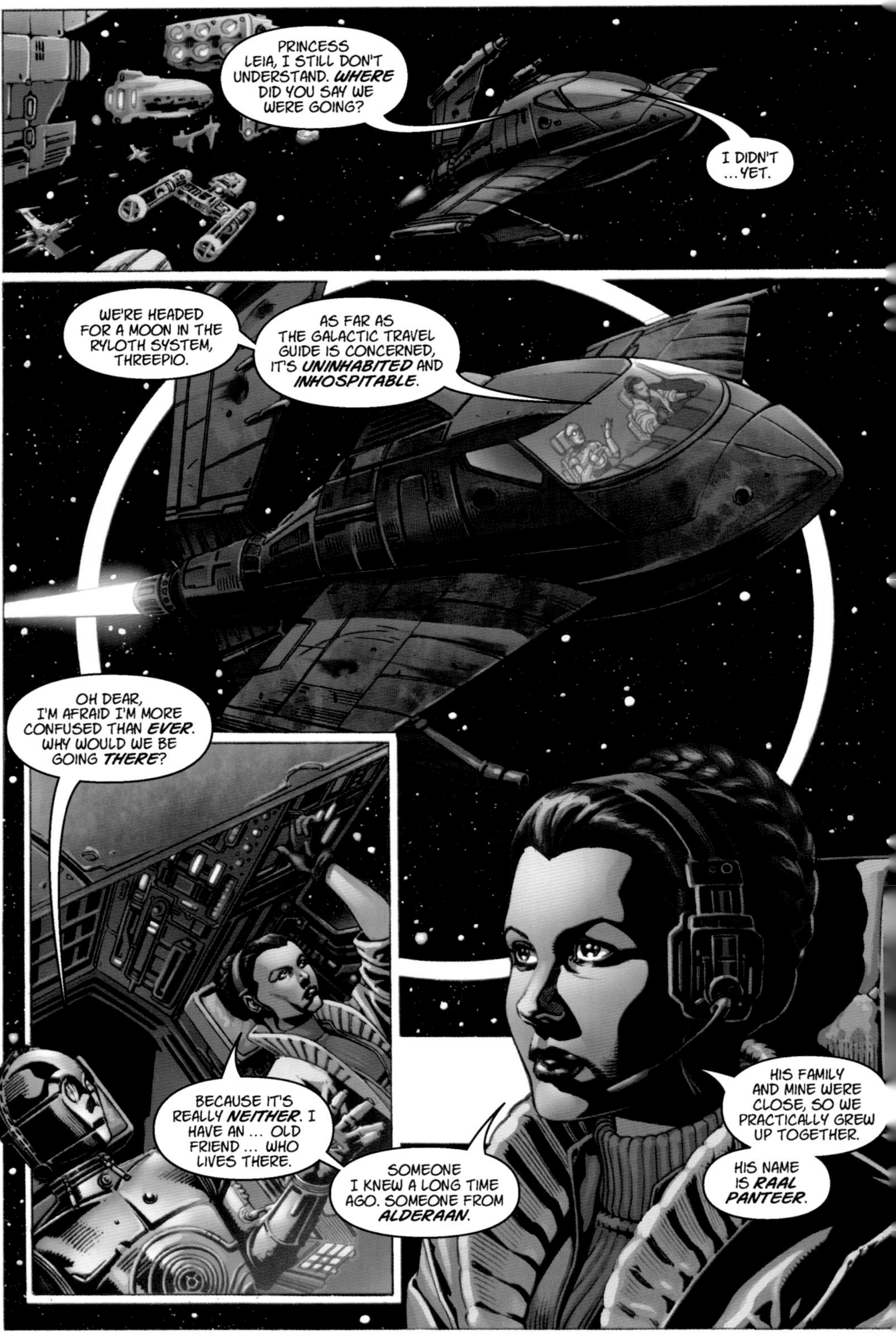
PRINCESS LEIA, I STILL DON'T UNDERSTAND. *WHERE* DID YOU SAY WE WERE GOING?
I DIDN'T ...YET.
WE'RE HEADED FOR A MOON IN THE RYLOTH SYSTEM, THREEPIO.
AS FAR AS THE GALACTIC TRAVEL GUIDE IS CONCERNED, IT'S *UNINHABITED* AND *INHOSPITABLE*.
OH DEAR, I'M AFRAID I'M MORE CONFUSED THAN *EVER*. WHY WOULD WE BE GOING *THERE*?
BECAUSE IT'S REALLY *NEITHER*. I HAVE AN ... OLD FRIEND ... WHO LIVES THERE.
SOMEONE I KNEW A LONG TIME AGO. SOMEONE FROM *ALDERAAN*.
HIS FAMILY AND MINE WERE CLOSE, SO WE PRACTICALLY GREW UP TOGETHER.
HIS NAME IS *RAAL PANTEER*.

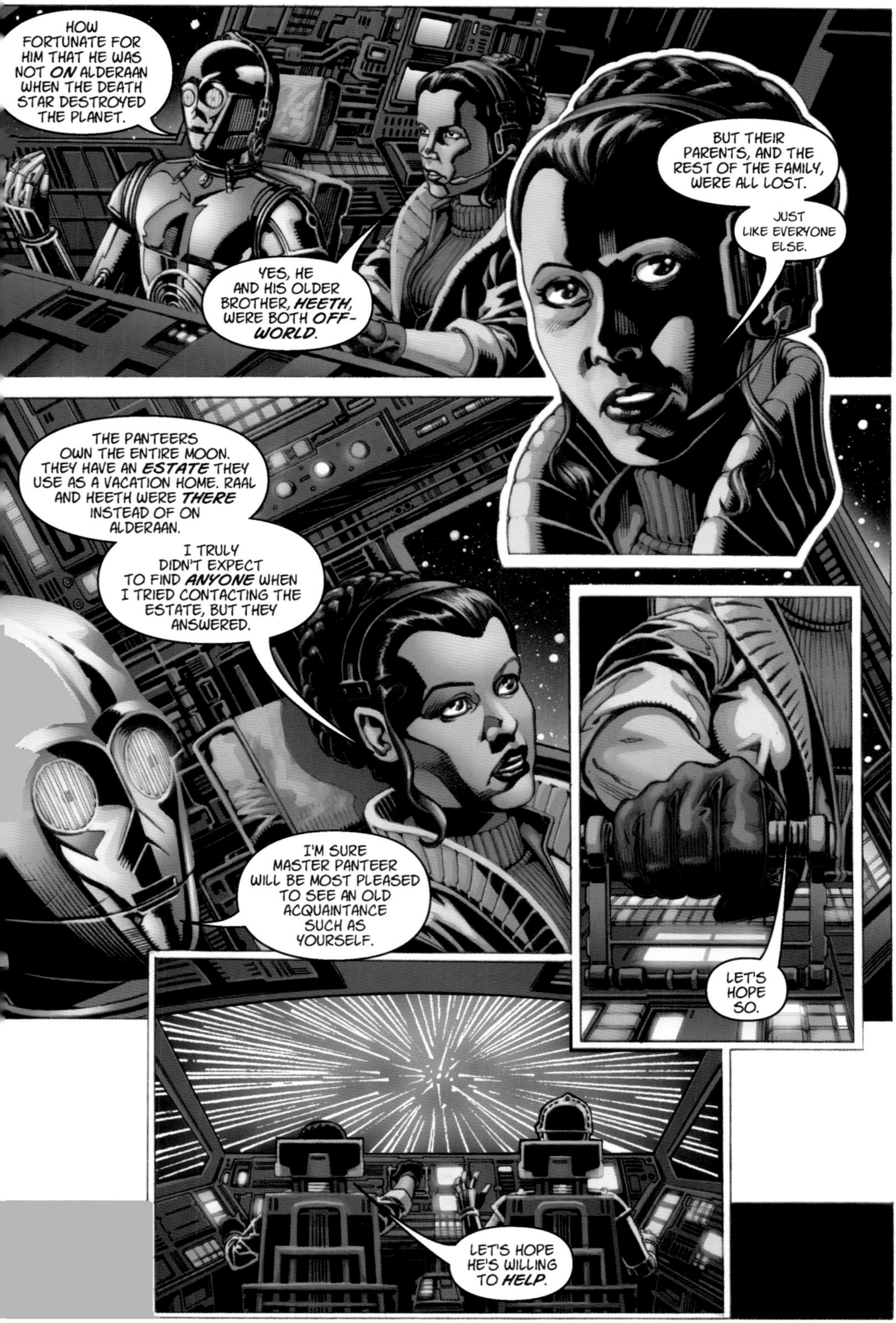
HOW FORTUNATE FOR HIM THAT HE WAS NOT ON ALDERAAN WHEN THE DEATH STAR DESTROYED THE PLANET.
YES, HE AND HIS OLDER BROTHER, HEETH, WERE BOTH OFF-WORLD.
BUT THEIR PARENTS, AND THE REST OF THE FAMILY, WERE ALL LOST.
JUST LIKE EVERYONE ELSE.
THE PANTEERS OWN THE ENTIRE MOON. THEY HAVE AN ESTATE THEY USE AS A VACATION HOME. RAAL AND HEETH WERE THERE INSTEAD OF ON ALDERAAN.
I TRULY DIDN'T EXPECT TO FIND ANYONE WHEN I TRIED CONTACTING THE ESTATE, BUT THEY ANSWERED.
I'M SURE MASTER PANTEER WILL BE MOST PLEASED TO SEE AN OLD ACQUAINTANCE SUCH AS YOURSELF.
LET'S HOPE SO.
LET'S HOPE HE'S WILLING TO HELP.

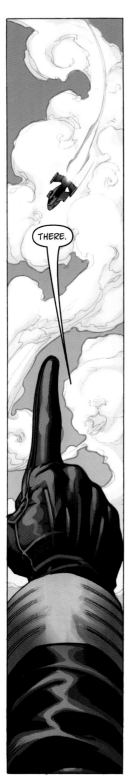

THERE.

HOW IS IT THAT YOUR EYES ARE *STILL* SHARPER THAN MINE?

DO YOU THINK SHE'S *CHANGED* MUCH?

IN MY EXPERIENCE ... *EVERYONE* DOES, TO ONE DEGREE OR ANOTHER.

WELCOME TO THE PANTEER ESTATE, PRINCESS.

NALLEN?

YES. I WAS HERE SERVING MASTERS RAAL AND HEETH WHEN THE TRAGEDY OCCURRED. IF YOU'LL FORGIVE MY FAMILIARITY, I SHOULD LIKE TO SAY IT'S MOST PLEASING TO SEE YOU AGAIN. WE ARE *ALL* BETTER FOR YOUR PRESENCE HERE.

I'M PLEASED TO SEE *YOU* AS WELL. I DON'T KNOW WHY, BUT I NEVER THOUGHT THAT YOU'D BE HERE TOO.

LEIA!

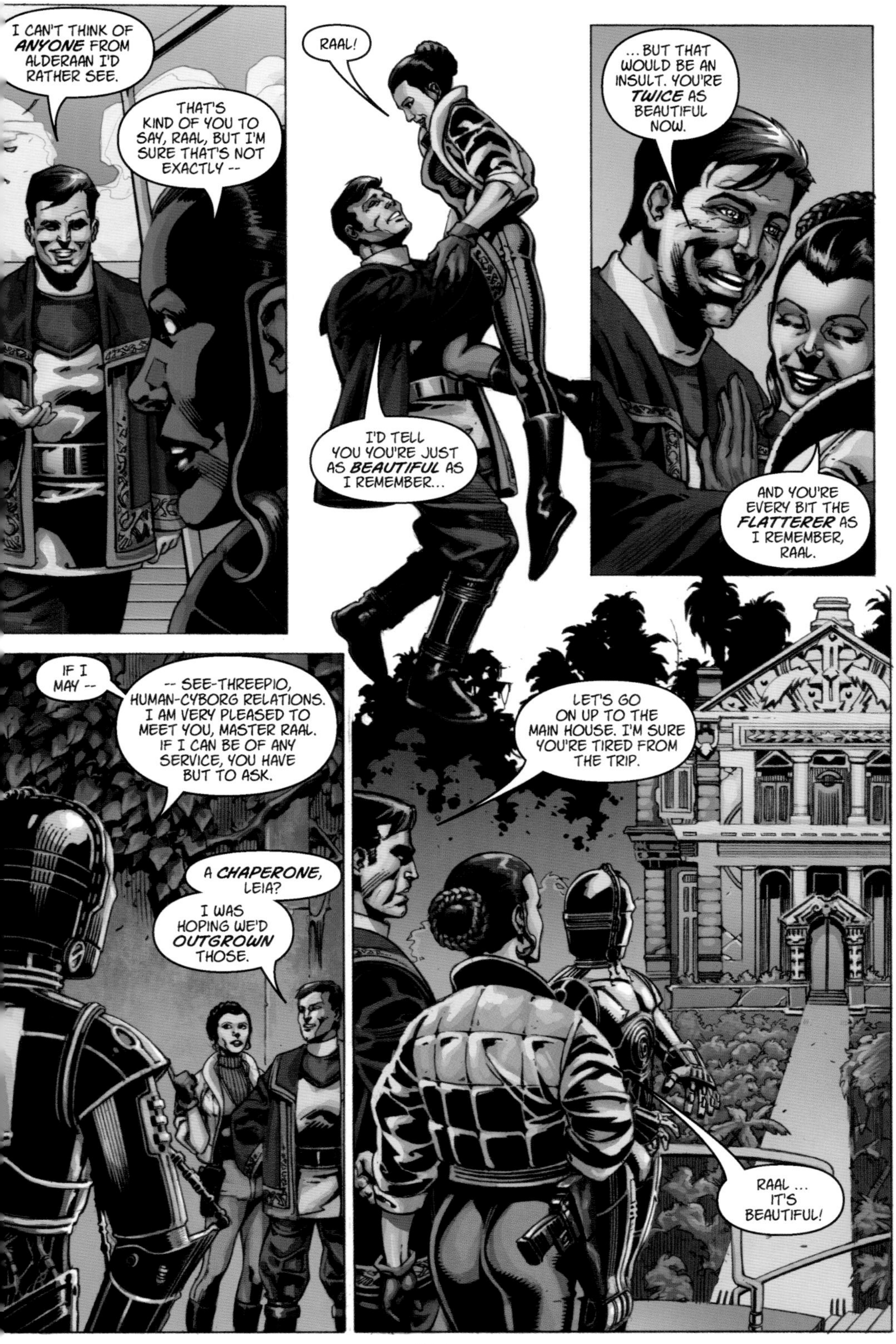

I CAN'T THINK OF ANYONE FROM ALDERAAN I'D RATHER SEE.
THAT'S KIND OF YOU TO SAY, RAAL, BUT I'M SURE THAT'S NOT EXACTLY --
RAAL!
I'D TELL YOU YOU'RE JUST AS BEAUTIFUL AS I REMEMBER...
... BUT THAT WOULD BE AN INSULT. YOU'RE TWICE AS BEAUTIFUL NOW.
AND YOU'RE EVERY BIT THE FLATTERER AS I REMEMBER, RAAL.
IF I MAY --
-- SEE-THREEPIO, HUMAN-CYBORG RELATIONS. I AM VERY PLEASED TO MEET YOU, MASTER RAAL. IF I CAN BE OF ANY SERVICE, YOU HAVE BUT TO ASK.
A CHAPERONE, LEIA?
I WAS HOPING WE'D OUTGROWN THOSE.
LET'S GO ON UP TO THE MAIN HOUSE. I'M SURE YOU'RE TIRED FROM THE TRIP.
RAAL ... IT'S BEAUTIFUL!

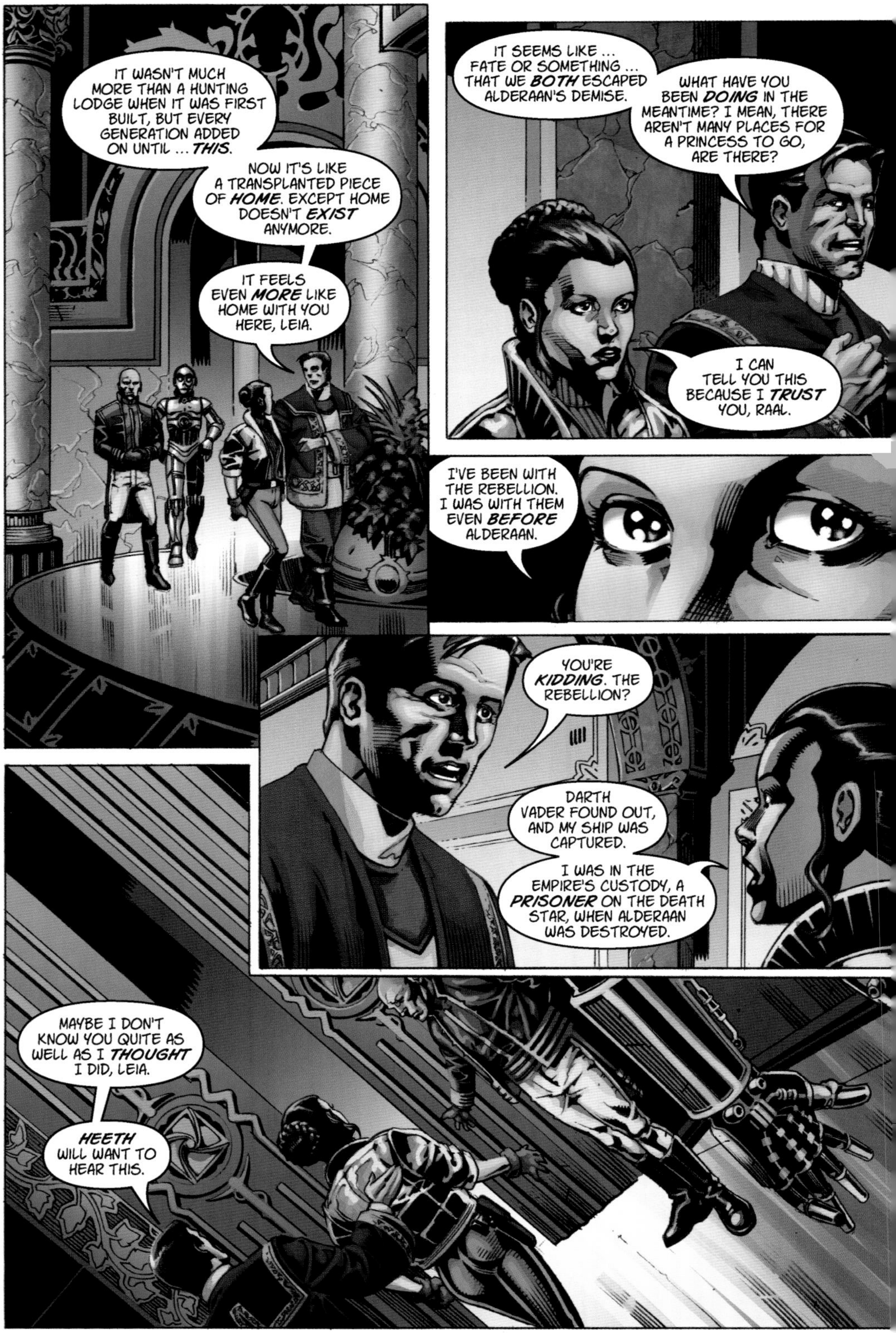
IT WASN'T MUCH MORE THAN A HUNTING LODGE WHEN IT WAS FIRST BUILT, BUT EVERY GENERATION ADDED ON UNTIL ... THIS.
NOW IT'S LIKE A TRANSPLANTED PIECE OF HOME. EXCEPT HOME DOESN'T EXIST ANYMORE.
IT FEELS EVEN MORE LIKE HOME WITH YOU HERE, LEIA.
IT SEEMS LIKE ... FATE OR SOMETHING ... THAT WE BOTH ESCAPED ALDERAAN'S DEMISE.
WHAT HAVE YOU BEEN DOING IN THE MEANTIME? I MEAN, THERE AREN'T MANY PLACES FOR A PRINCESS TO GO, ARE THERE?
I CAN TELL YOU THIS BECAUSE I TRUST YOU, RAAL.
I'VE BEEN WITH THE REBELLION. I WAS WITH THEM EVEN BEFORE ALDERAAN.
YOU'RE KIDDING. THE REBELLION?
DARTH VADER FOUND OUT, AND MY SHIP WAS CAPTURED.
I WAS IN THE EMPIRE'S CUSTODY, A PRISONER ON THE DEATH STAR, WHEN ALDERAAN WAS DESTROYED.
MAYBE I DON'T KNOW YOU QUITE AS WELL AS I THOUGHT I DID, LEIA.
HEETH WILL WANT TO HEAR THIS.

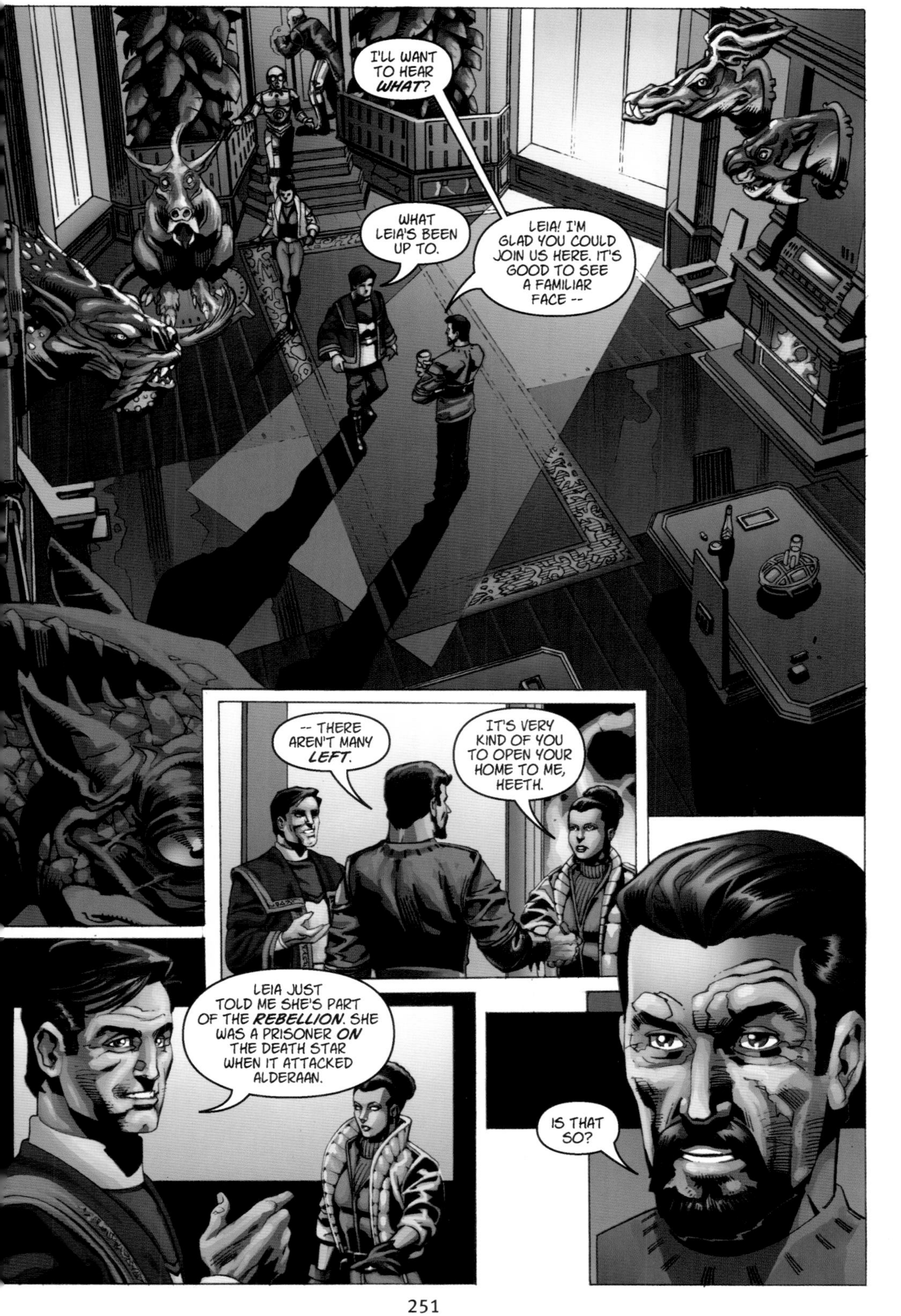
I'LL WANT TO HEAR WHAT?
WHAT LEIA'S BEEN UP TO.
LEIA! I'M GLAD YOU COULD JOIN US HERE. IT'S GOOD TO SEE A FAMILIAR FACE --
-- THERE AREN'T MANY LEFT.
IT'S VERY KIND OF YOU TO OPEN YOUR HOME TO ME, HEETH.
LEIA JUST TOLD ME SHE'S PART OF THE REBELLION. SHE WAS A PRISONER ON THE DEATH STAR WHEN IT ATTACKED ALDERAAN.
IS THAT SO?

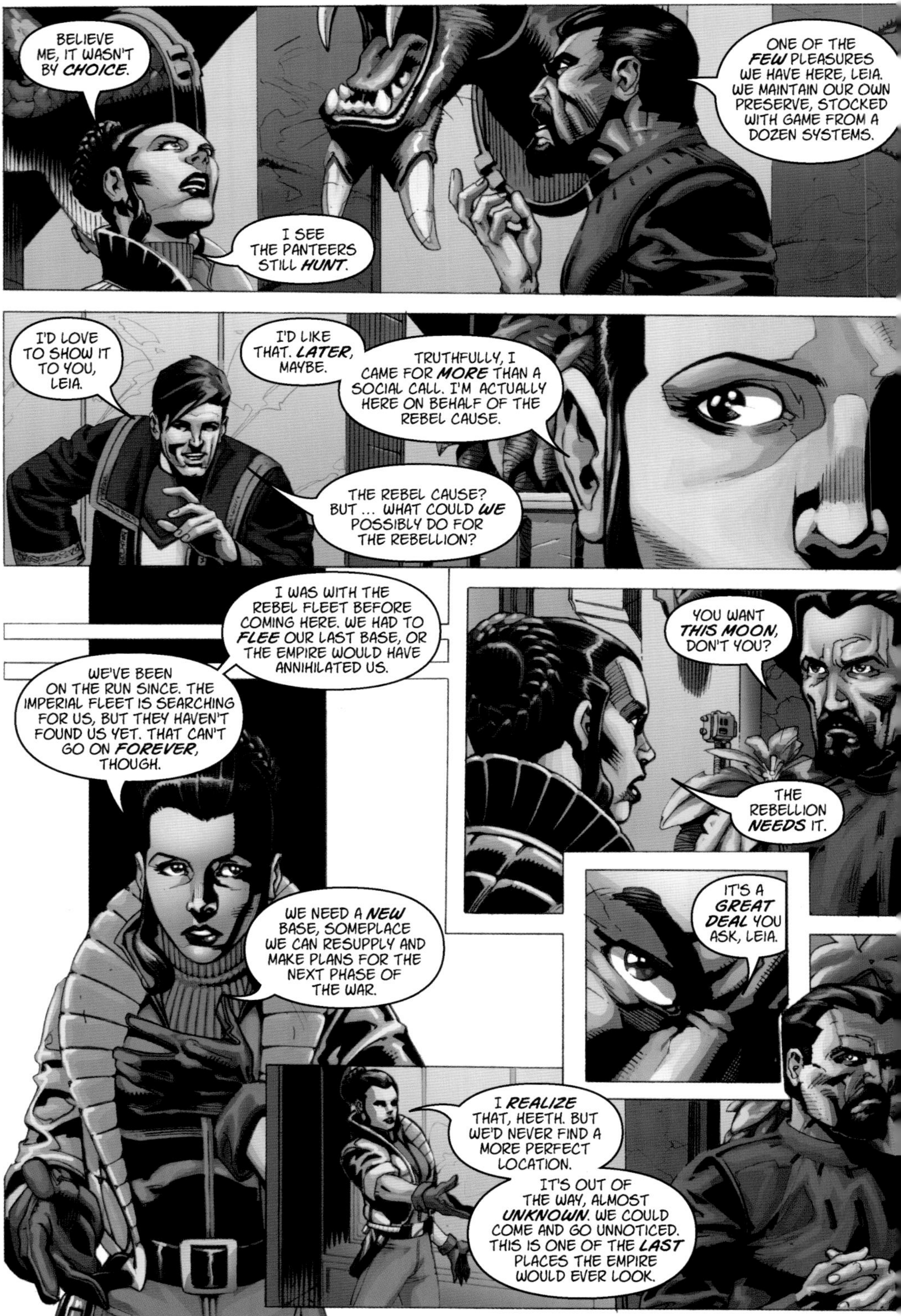
BELIEVE ME, IT WASN'T BY CHOICE.
ONE OF THE FEW PLEASURES WE HAVE HERE, LEIA. WE MAINTAIN OUR OWN PRESERVE, STOCKED WITH GAME FROM A DOZEN SYSTEMS.
I SEE THE PANTEERS STILL HUNT.
I'D LOVE TO SHOW IT TO YOU, LEIA.
I'D LIKE THAT. LATER, MAYBE.
TRUTHFULLY, I CAME FOR MORE THAN A SOCIAL CALL. I'M ACTUALLY HERE ON BEHALF OF THE REBEL CAUSE.
THE REBEL CAUSE? BUT ... WHAT COULD WE POSSIBLY DO FOR THE REBELLION?
I WAS WITH THE REBEL FLEET BEFORE COMING HERE. WE HAD TO FLEE OUR LAST BASE, OR THE EMPIRE WOULD HAVE ANNIHILATED US.
WE'VE BEEN ON THE RUN SINCE. THE IMPERIAL FLEET IS SEARCHING FOR US, BUT THEY HAVEN'T FOUND US YET. THAT CAN'T GO ON FOREVER, THOUGH.
WE NEED A NEW BASE, SOMEPLACE WE CAN RESUPPLY AND MAKE PLANS FOR THE NEXT PHASE OF THE WAR.
YOU WANT THIS MOON, DON'T YOU?
THE REBELLION NEEDS IT.
IT'S A GREAT DEAL YOU ASK, LEIA.
I REALIZE THAT, HEETH. BUT WE'D NEVER FIND A MORE PERFECT LOCATION.
IT'S OUT OF THE WAY, ALMOST UNKNOWN. WE COULD COME AND GO UNNOTICED. THIS IS ONE OF THE LAST PLACES THE EMPIRE WOULD EVER LOOK.

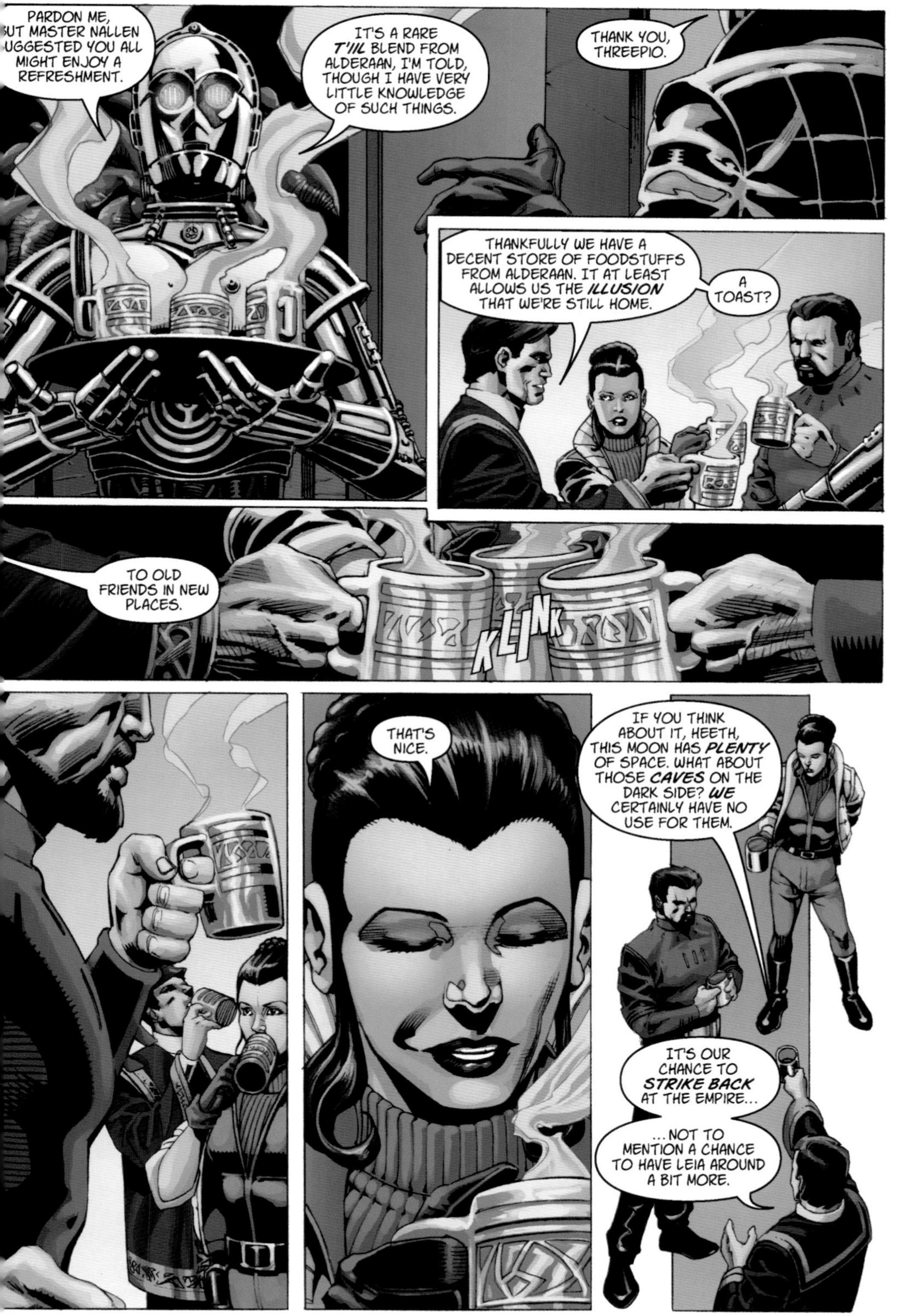
PARDON ME, BUT MASTER NALLEN SUGGESTED YOU ALL MIGHT ENJOY A REFRESHMENT.
IT'S A RARE T'IIL BLEND FROM ALDERAAN, I'M TOLD, THOUGH I HAVE VERY LITTLE KNOWLEDGE OF SUCH THINGS.
THANK YOU, THREEPIO.
THANKFULLY WE HAVE A DECENT STORE OF FOODSTUFFS FROM ALDERAAN. IT AT LEAST ALLOWS US THE ILLUSION THAT WE'RE STILL HOME.
A TOAST?
TO OLD FRIENDS IN NEW PLACES.
KLINK
THAT'S NICE.
IF YOU THINK ABOUT IT, HEETH, THIS MOON HAS PLENTY OF SPACE. WHAT ABOUT THOSE CAVES ON THE DARK SIDE? WE CERTAINLY HAVE NO USE FOR THEM.
IT'S OUR CHANCE TO STRIKE BACK AT THE EMPIRE...
...NOT TO MENTION A CHANCE TO HAVE LEIA AROUND A BIT MORE.

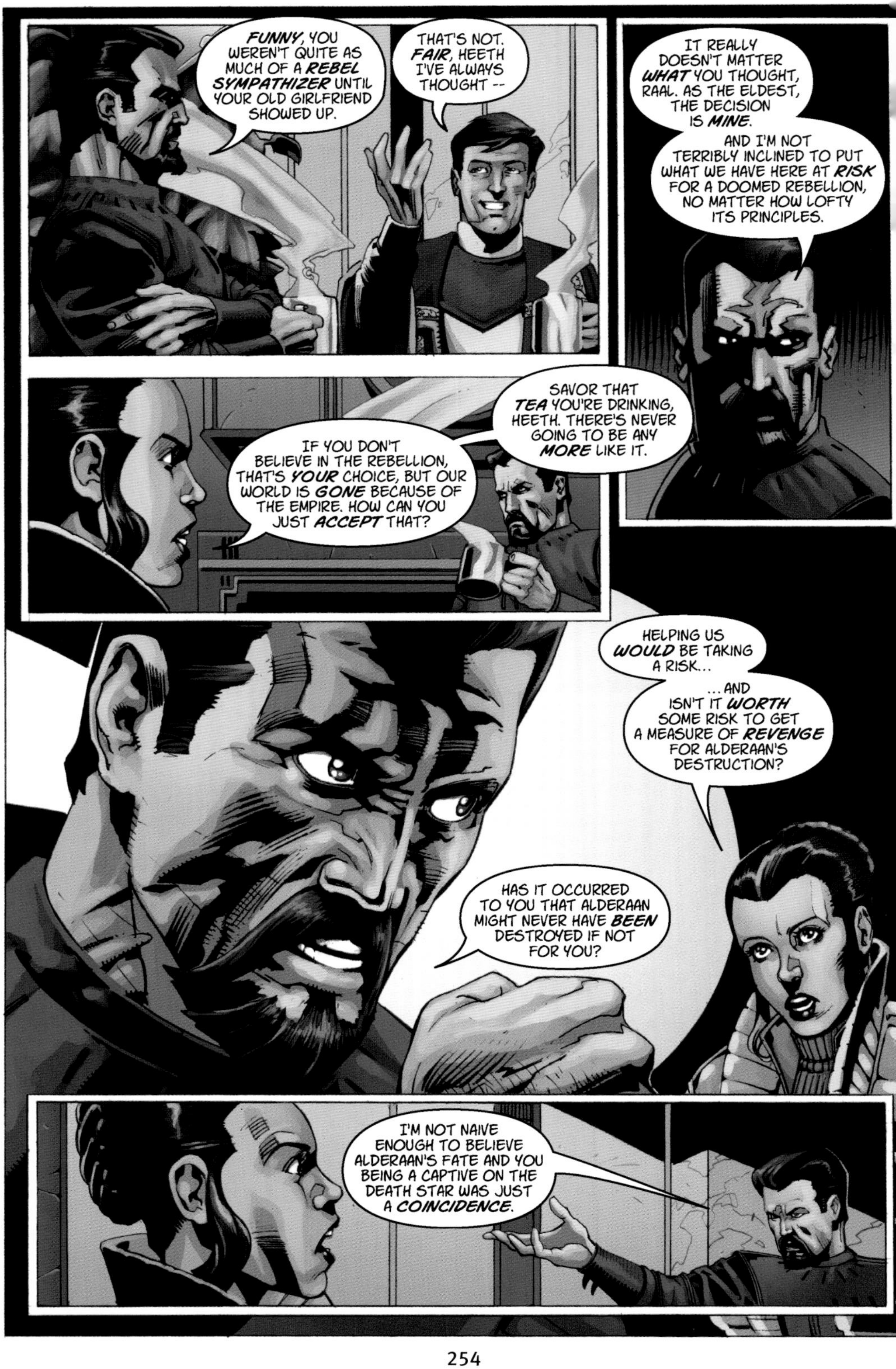
FUNNY, YOU WEREN'T QUITE AS MUCH OF A REBEL SYMPATHIZER UNTIL YOUR OLD GIRLFRIEND SHOWED UP.
THAT'S NOT. FAIR, HEETH I'VE ALWAYS THOUGHT --
IT REALLY DOESN'T MATTER WHAT YOU THOUGHT, RAAL. AS THE ELDEST, THE DECISION IS MINE.
AND I'M NOT TERRIBLY INCLINED TO PUT WHAT WE HAVE HERE AT RISK FOR A DOOMED REBELLION, NO MATTER HOW LOFTY ITS PRINCIPLES.
IF YOU DON'T BELIEVE IN THE REBELLION, THAT'S YOUR CHOICE, BUT OUR WORLD IS GONE BECAUSE OF THE EMPIRE. HOW CAN YOU JUST ACCEPT THAT?
SAVOR THAT TEA YOU'RE DRINKING, HEETH. THERE'S NEVER GOING TO BE ANY MORE LIKE IT.
HELPING US WOULD BE TAKING A RISK...
...AND ISN'T IT WORTH SOME RISK TO GET A MEASURE OF REVENGE FOR ALDERAAN'S DESTRUCTION?
HAS IT OCCURRED TO YOU THAT ALDERAAN MIGHT NEVER HAVE BEEN DESTROYED IF NOT FOR YOU?
I'M NOT NAIVE ENOUGH TO BELIEVE ALDERAAN'S FATE AND YOU BEING A CAPTIVE ON THE DEATH STAR WAS JUST A COINCIDENCE.

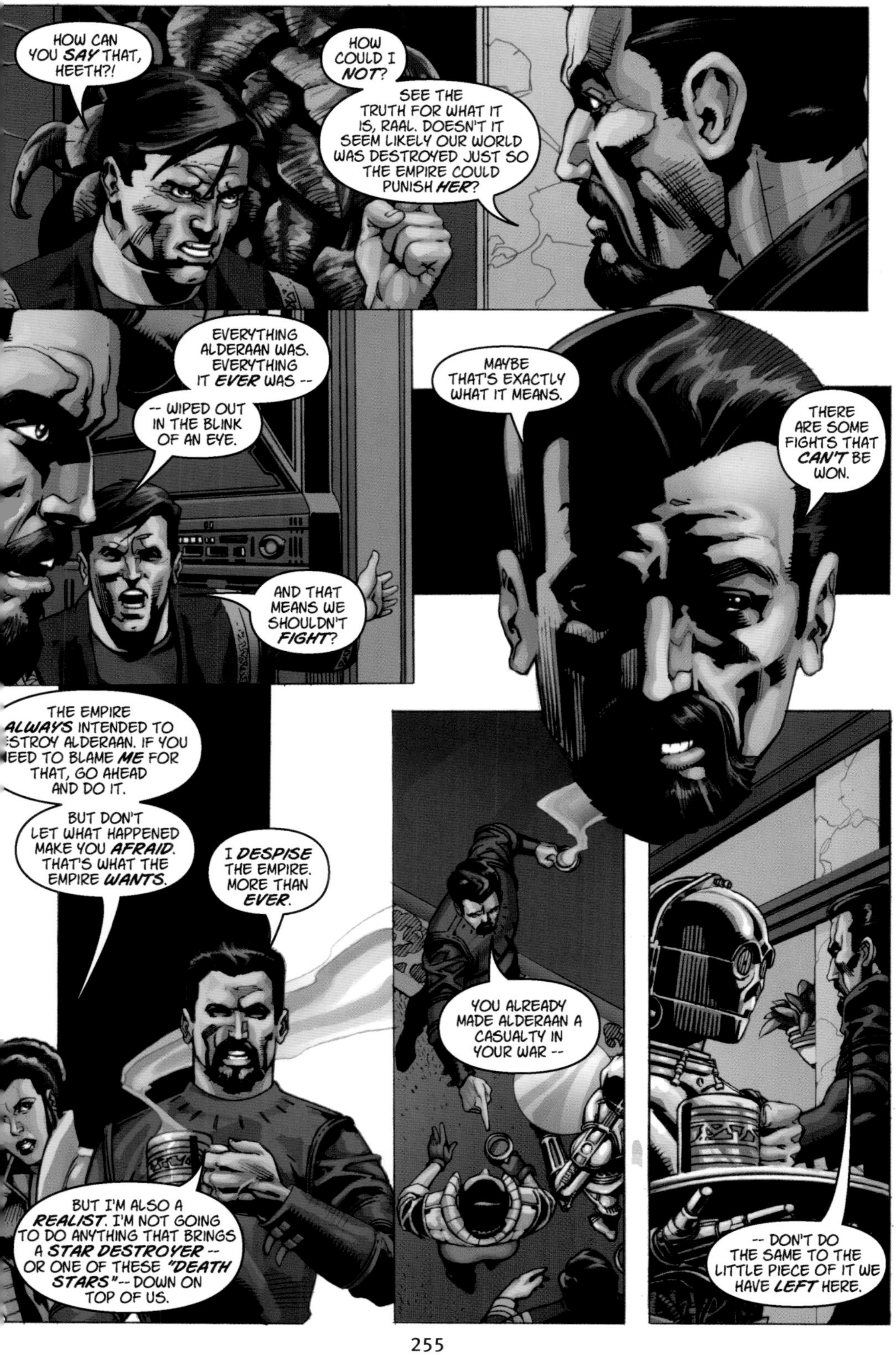
HOW CAN YOU SAY THAT, HEETH?!
HOW COULD I NOT?
SEE THE TRUTH FOR WHAT IT IS, RAAL. DOESN'T IT SEEM LIKELY OUR WORLD WAS DESTROYED JUST SO THE EMPIRE COULD PUNISH HER?
EVERYTHING ALDERAAN WAS. EVERYTHING IT EVER WAS --
-- WIPED OUT IN THE BLINK OF AN EYE.
AND THAT MEANS WE SHOULDN'T FIGHT?
MAYBE THAT'S EXACTLY WHAT IT MEANS.
THERE ARE SOME FIGHTS THAT CAN'T BE WON.
THE EMPIRE ALWAYS INTENDED TO ESTROY ALDERAAN. IF YOU EED TO BLAME ME FOR THAT, GO AHEAD AND DO IT.
BUT DON'T LET WHAT HAPPENED MAKE YOU AFRAID. THAT'S WHAT THE EMPIRE WANTS.
I DESPISE THE EMPIRE. MORE THAN EVER.
BUT I'M ALSO A REALIST. I'M NOT GOING TO DO ANYTHING THAT BRINGS A STAR DESTROYER -- OR ONE OF THESE "DEATH STARS"-- DOWN ON TOP OF US.
YOU ALREADY MADE ALDERAAN A CASUALTY IN YOUR WAR --
-- DON'T DO THE SAME TO THE LITTLE PIECE OF IT WE HAVE LEFT HERE.

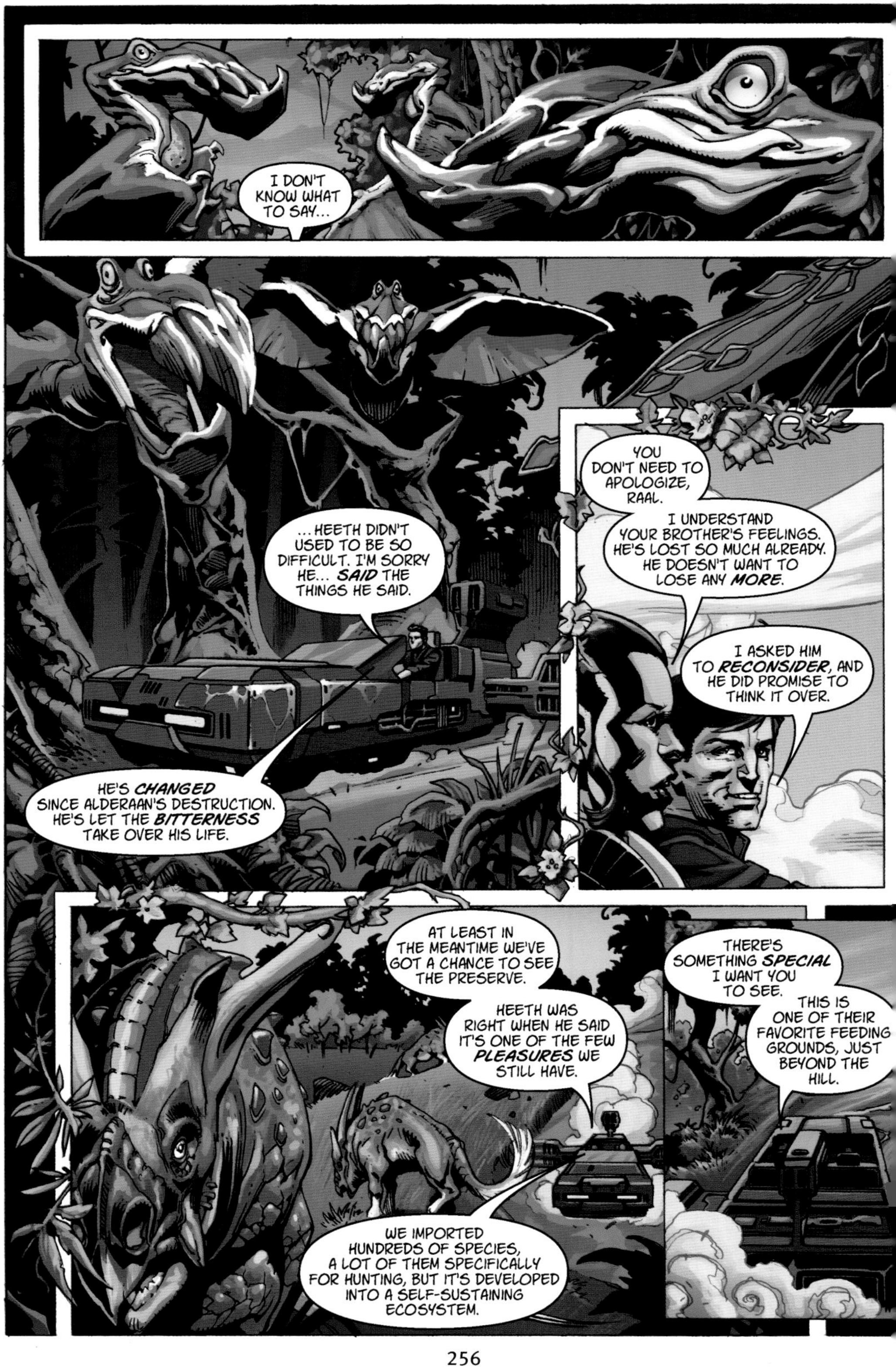

I DON'T KNOW WHAT TO SAY...
...HEETH DIDN'T USED TO BE SO DIFFICULT. I'M SORRY HE... SAID THE THINGS HE SAID.
HE'S CHANGED SINCE ALDERAAN'S DESTRUCTION. HE'S LET THE BITTERNESS TAKE OVER HIS LIFE.
YOU DON'T NEED TO APOLOGIZE, RAAL.
I UNDERSTAND YOUR BROTHER'S FEELINGS. HE'S LOST SO MUCH ALREADY. HE DOESN'T WANT TO LOSE ANY MORE.
I ASKED HIM TO RECONSIDER, AND HE DID PROMISE TO THINK IT OVER.
AT LEAST IN THE MEANTIME WE'VE GOT A CHANCE TO SEE THE PRESERVE.
HEETH WAS RIGHT WHEN HE SAID IT'S ONE OF THE FEW PLEASURES WE STILL HAVE.
WE IMPORTED HUNDREDS OF SPECIES, A LOT OF THEM SPECIFICALLY FOR HUNTING, BUT IT'S DEVELOPED INTO A SELF-SUSTAINING ECOSYSTEM.
THERE'S SOMETHING SPECIAL I WANT YOU TO SEE.
THIS IS ONE OF THEIR FAVORITE FEEDING GROUNDS, JUST BEYOND THE HILL.

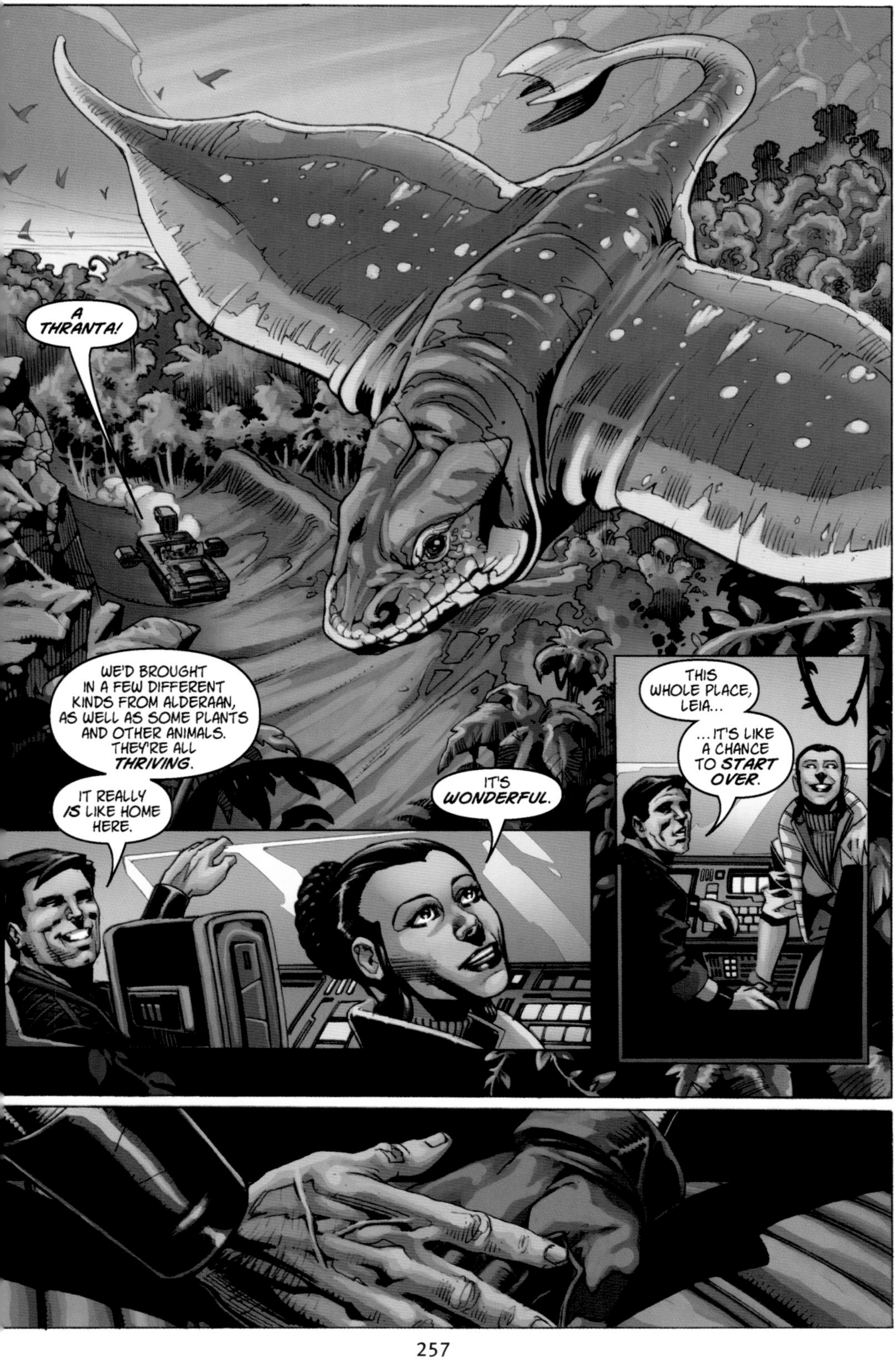
A THRANTA!
WE'D BROUGHT IN A FEW DIFFERENT KINDS FROM ALDERAAN, AS WELL AS SOME PLANTS AND OTHER ANIMALS. THEY'RE ALL THRIVING.
IT REALLY IS LIKE HOME HERE.
IT'S WONDERFUL.
THIS WHOLE PLACE, LEIA...
...IT'S LIKE A CHANCE TO START OVER.

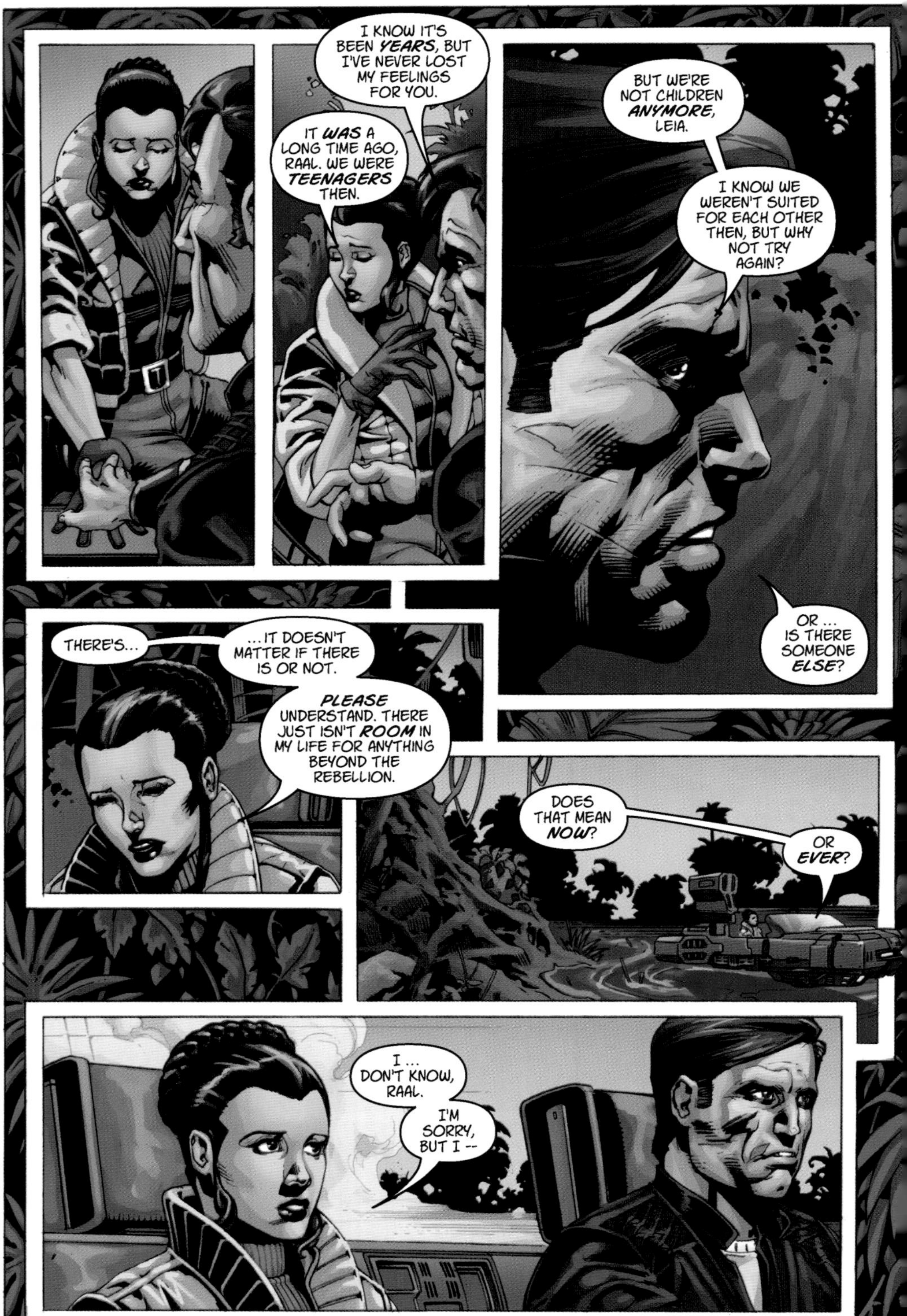
I KNOW IT'S BEEN YEARS, BUT I'VE NEVER LOST MY FEELINGS FOR YOU.
IT WAS A LONG TIME AGO, RAAL. WE WERE TEENAGERS THEN.
BUT WE'RE NOT CHILDREN ANYMORE, LEIA.
I KNOW WE WEREN'T SUITED FOR EACH OTHER THEN, BUT WHY NOT TRY AGAIN?
OR ... IS THERE SOMEONE ELSE?
THERE'S...
...IT DOESN'T MATTER IF THERE IS OR NOT.
PLEASE UNDERSTAND. THERE JUST ISN'T ROOM IN MY LIFE FOR ANYTHING BEYOND THE REBELLION.
DOES THAT MEAN NOW?
OR EVER?
I ... DON'T KNOW, RAAL.
I'M SORRY, BUT I --

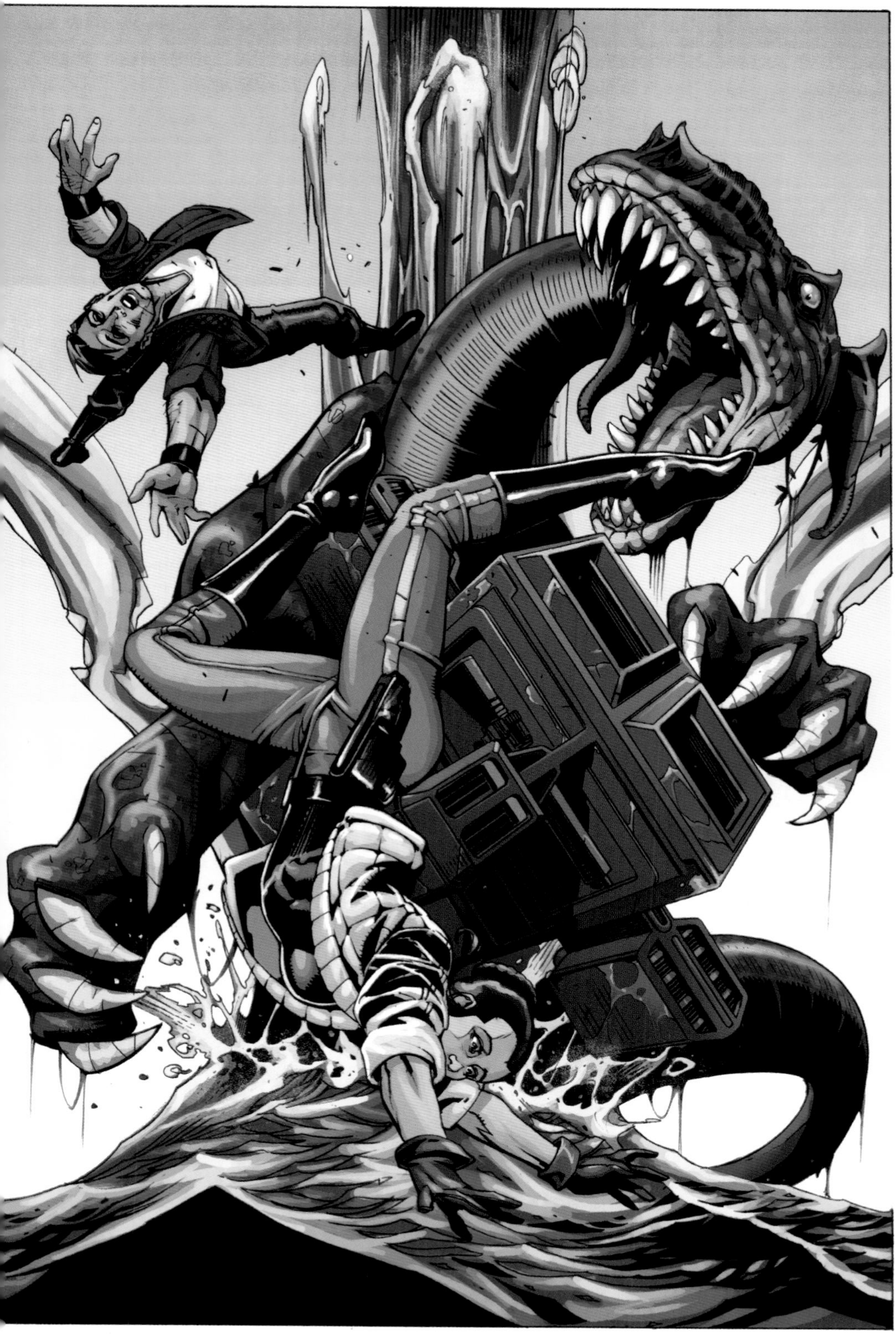

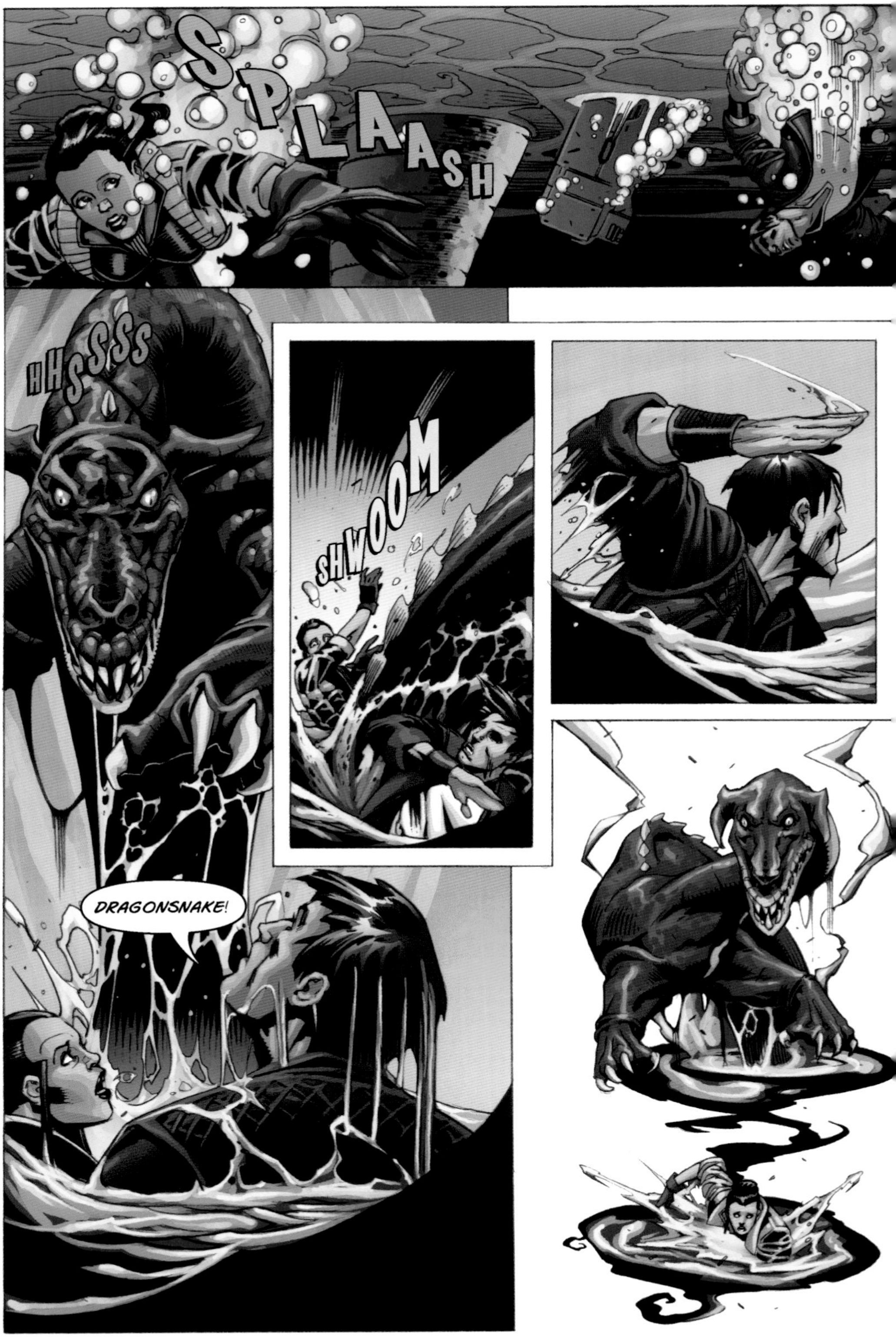
SPLAASH
HHSSSS
SHWOOM
DRAGONSNAKE!

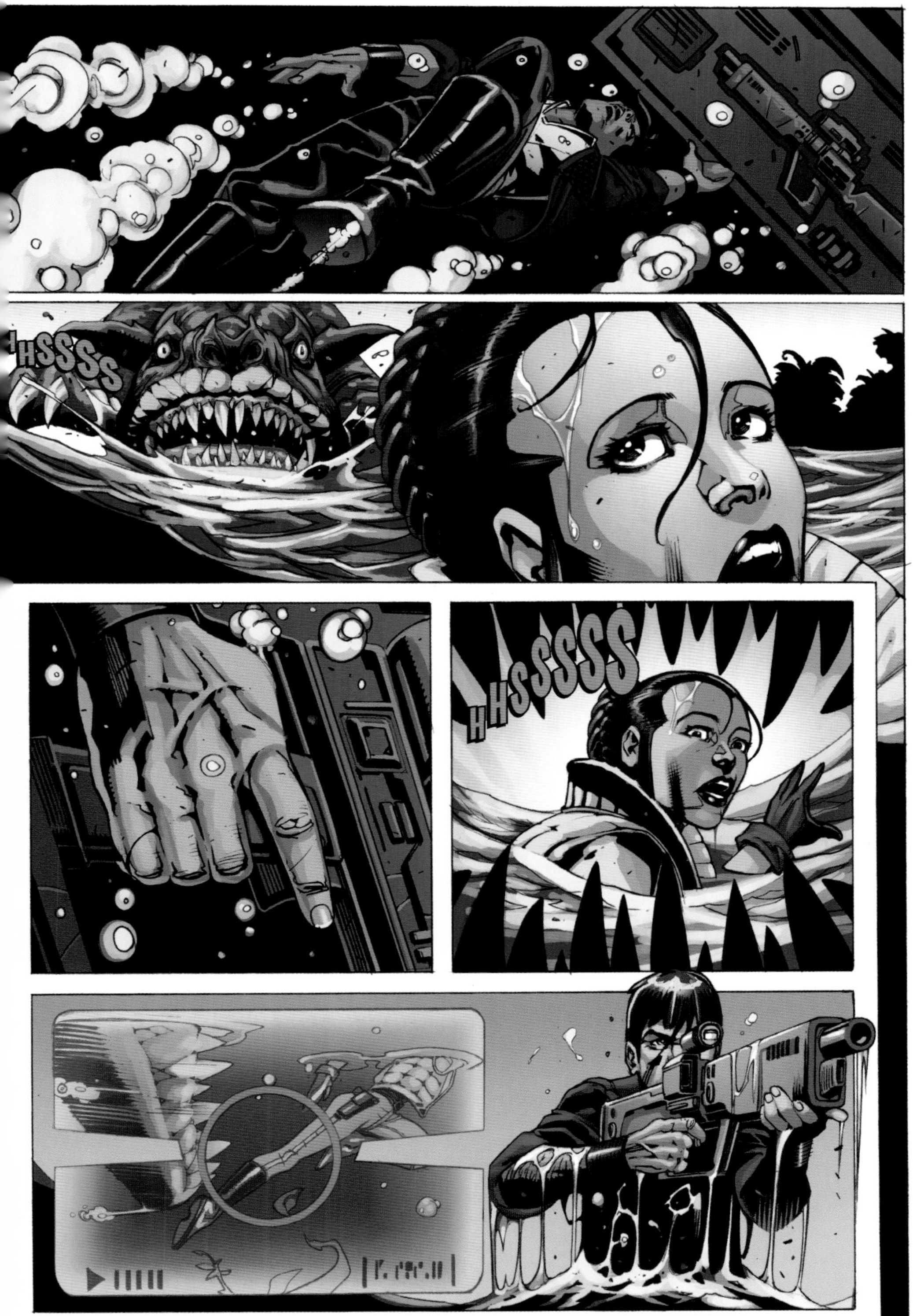
HHSSSS
HHSSSSS

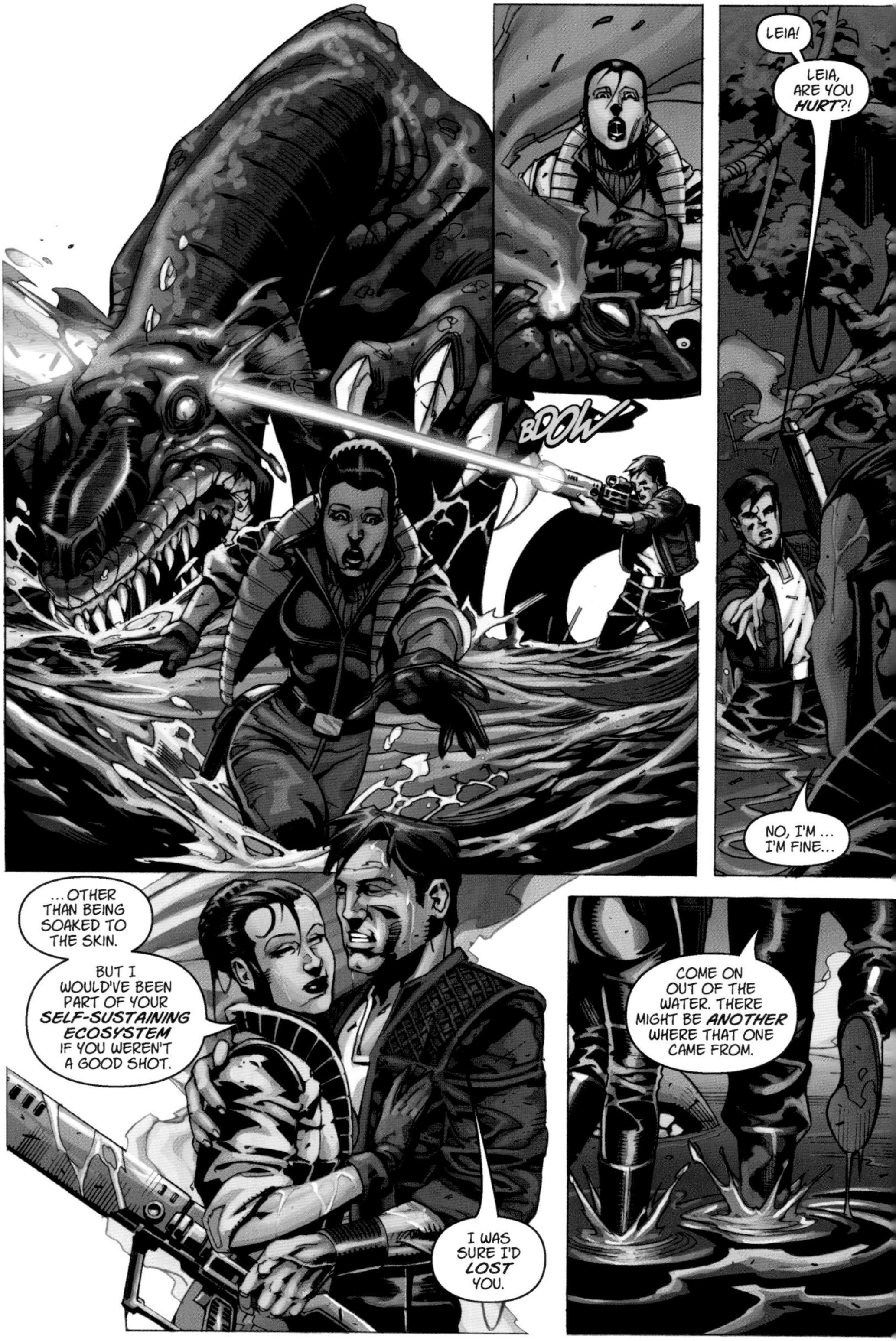
BDOW
LEIA!
LEIA, ARE YOU *HURT*?!
NO, I'M ... I'M FINE...
...OTHER THAN BEING SOAKED TO THE SKIN.
BUT I WOULD'VE BEEN PART OF YOUR ***SELF-SUSTAINING ECOSYSTEM*** IF YOU WEREN'T A GOOD SHOT.
I WAS SURE I'D *LOST* YOU.
COME ON OUT OF THE WATER. THERE MIGHT BE ***ANOTHER*** WHERE THAT ONE CAME FROM.

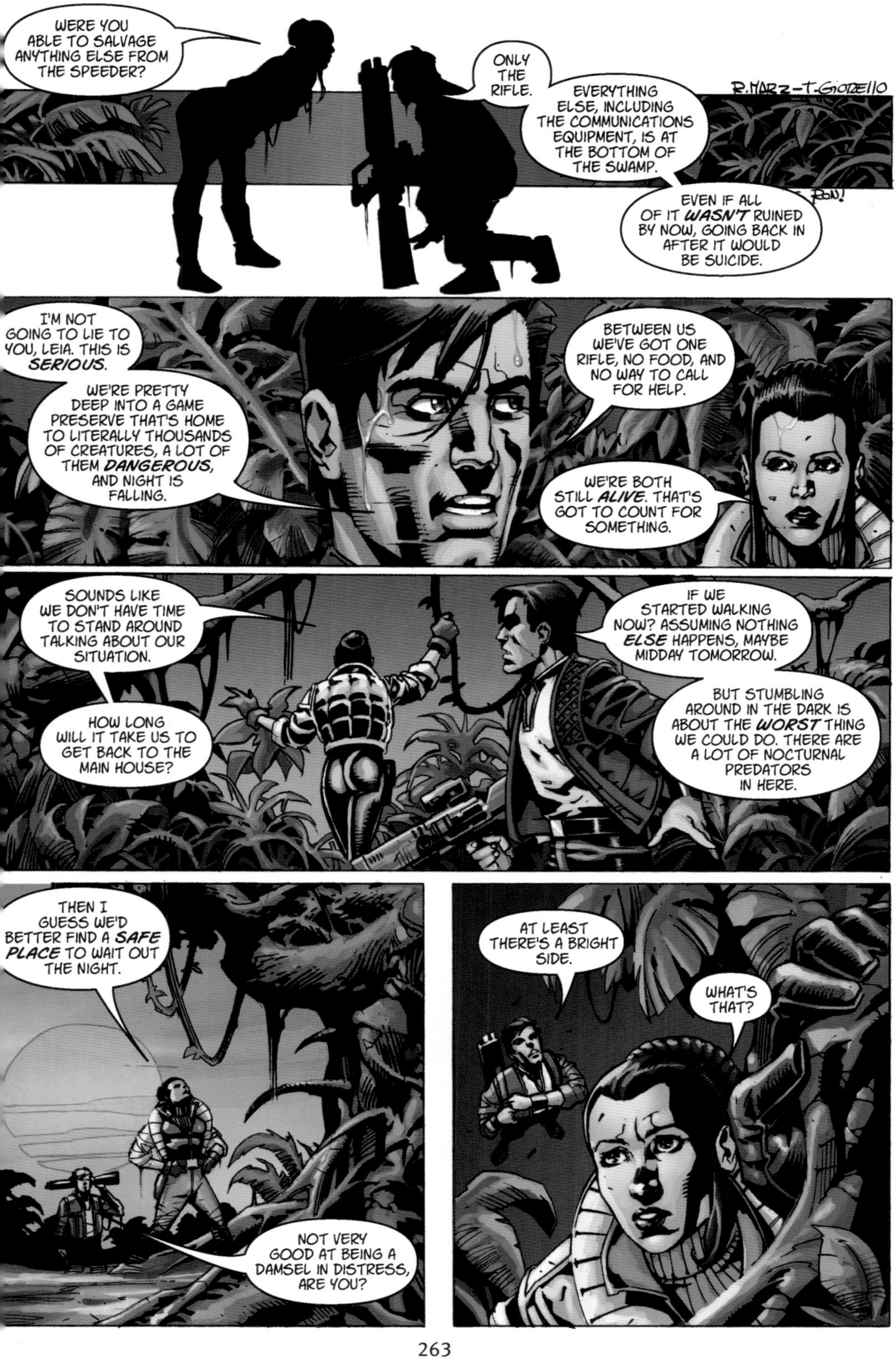
WERE YOU ABLE TO SALVAGE ANYTHING ELSE FROM THE SPEEDER?
ONLY THE RIFLE.
R.MARZ—T.GIORELLO
EVERYTHING ELSE, INCLUDING THE COMMUNICATIONS EQUIPMENT, IS AT THE BOTTOM OF THE SWAMP.
EVEN IF ALL OF IT WASN'T RUINED BY NOW, GOING BACK IN AFTER IT WOULD BE SUICIDE.
I'M NOT GOING TO LIE TO YOU, LEIA. THIS IS SERIOUS.
WE'RE PRETTY DEEP INTO A GAME PRESERVE THAT'S HOME TO LITERALLY THOUSANDS OF CREATURES, A LOT OF THEM DANGEROUS, AND NIGHT IS FALLING.
BETWEEN US WE'VE GOT ONE RIFLE, NO FOOD, AND NO WAY TO CALL FOR HELP.
WE'RE BOTH STILL ALIVE. THAT'S GOT TO COUNT FOR SOMETHING.
SOUNDS LIKE WE DON'T HAVE TIME TO STAND AROUND TALKING ABOUT OUR SITUATION.
HOW LONG WILL IT TAKE US TO GET BACK TO THE MAIN HOUSE?
IF WE STARTED WALKING NOW? ASSUMING NOTHING ELSE HAPPENS, MAYBE MIDDAY TOMORROW.
BUT STUMBLING AROUND IN THE DARK IS ABOUT THE WORST THING WE COULD DO. THERE ARE A LOT OF NOCTURNAL PREDATORS IN HERE.
THEN I GUESS WE'D BETTER FIND A SAFE PLACE TO WAIT OUT THE NIGHT.
NOT VERY GOOD AT BEING A DAMSEL IN DISTRESS, ARE YOU?
AT LEAST THERE'S A BRIGHT SIDE.
WHAT'S THAT?

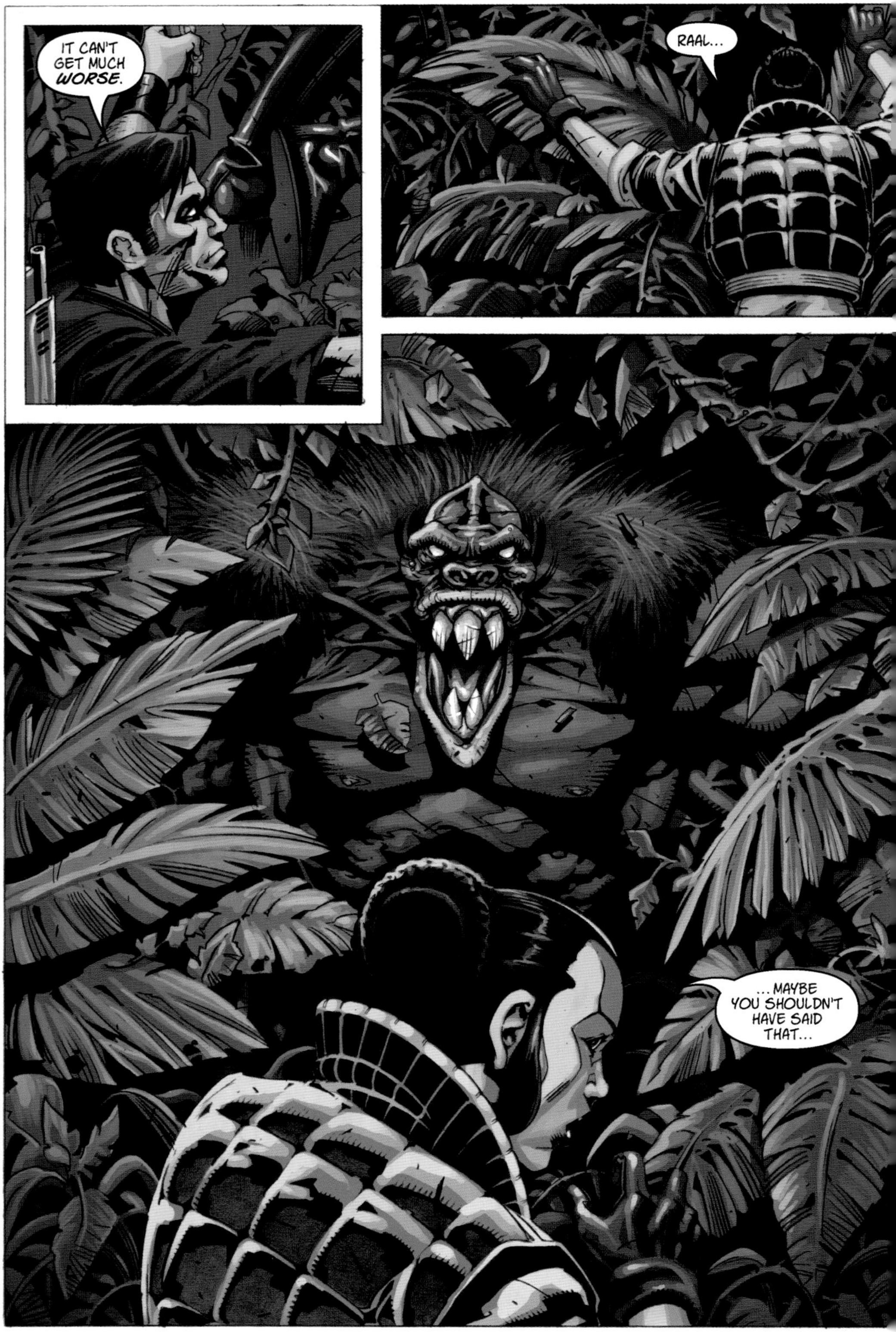
IT CAN'T GET MUCH *WORSE*.
RAAL...
...MAYBE YOU SHOULDN'T HAVE SAID THAT...

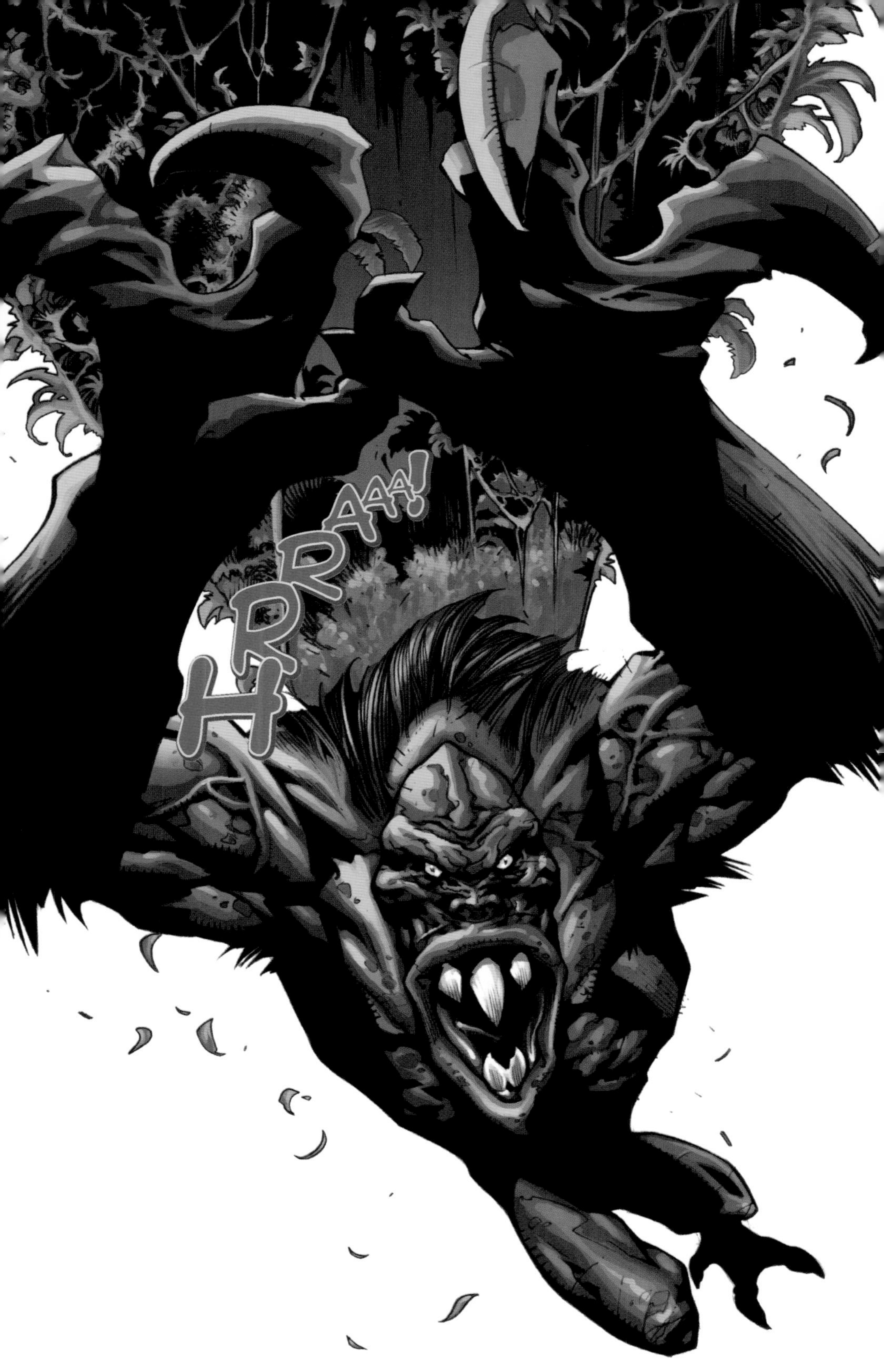
HRRAAA!

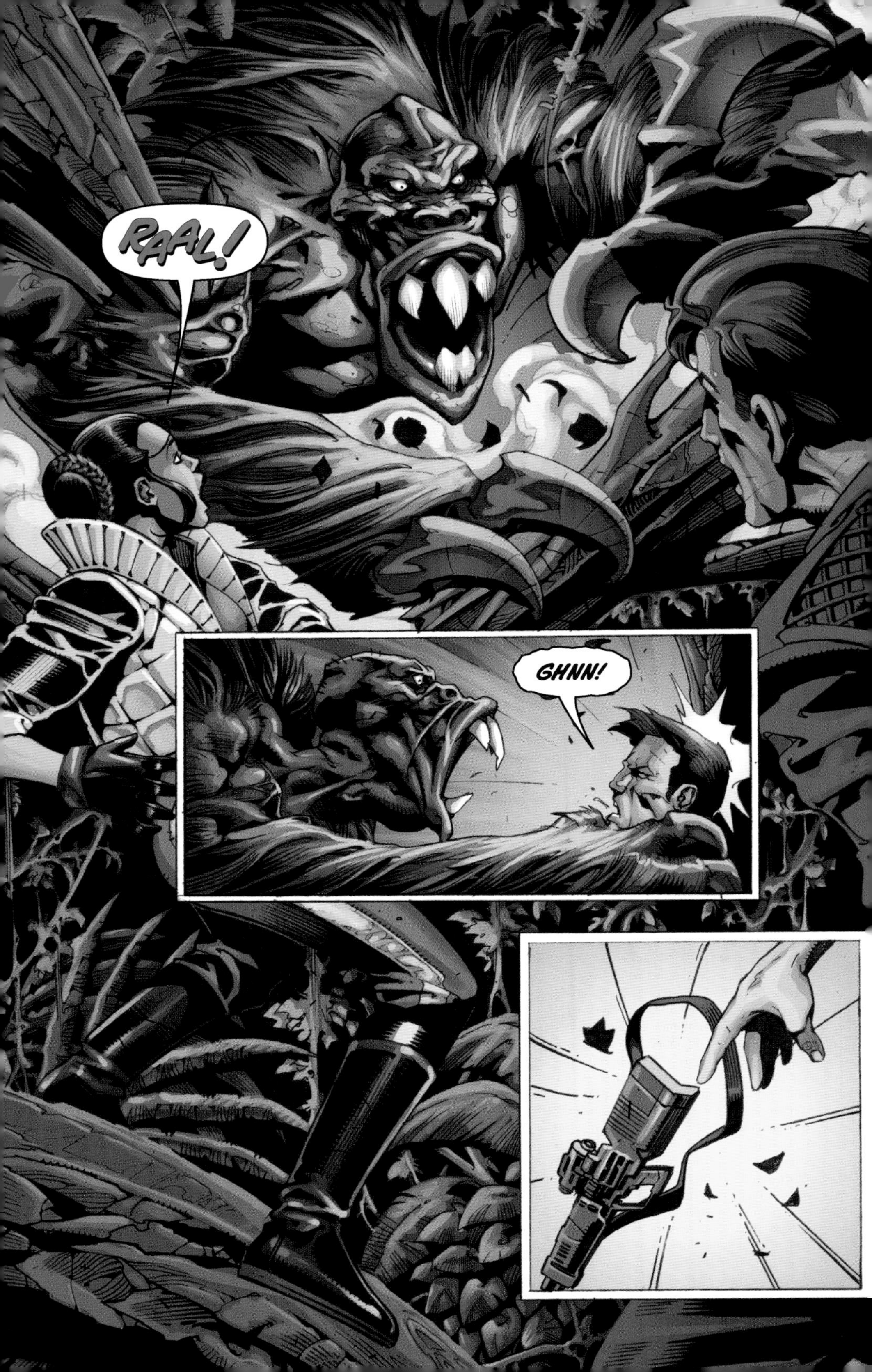
RAAL!
GHNN!

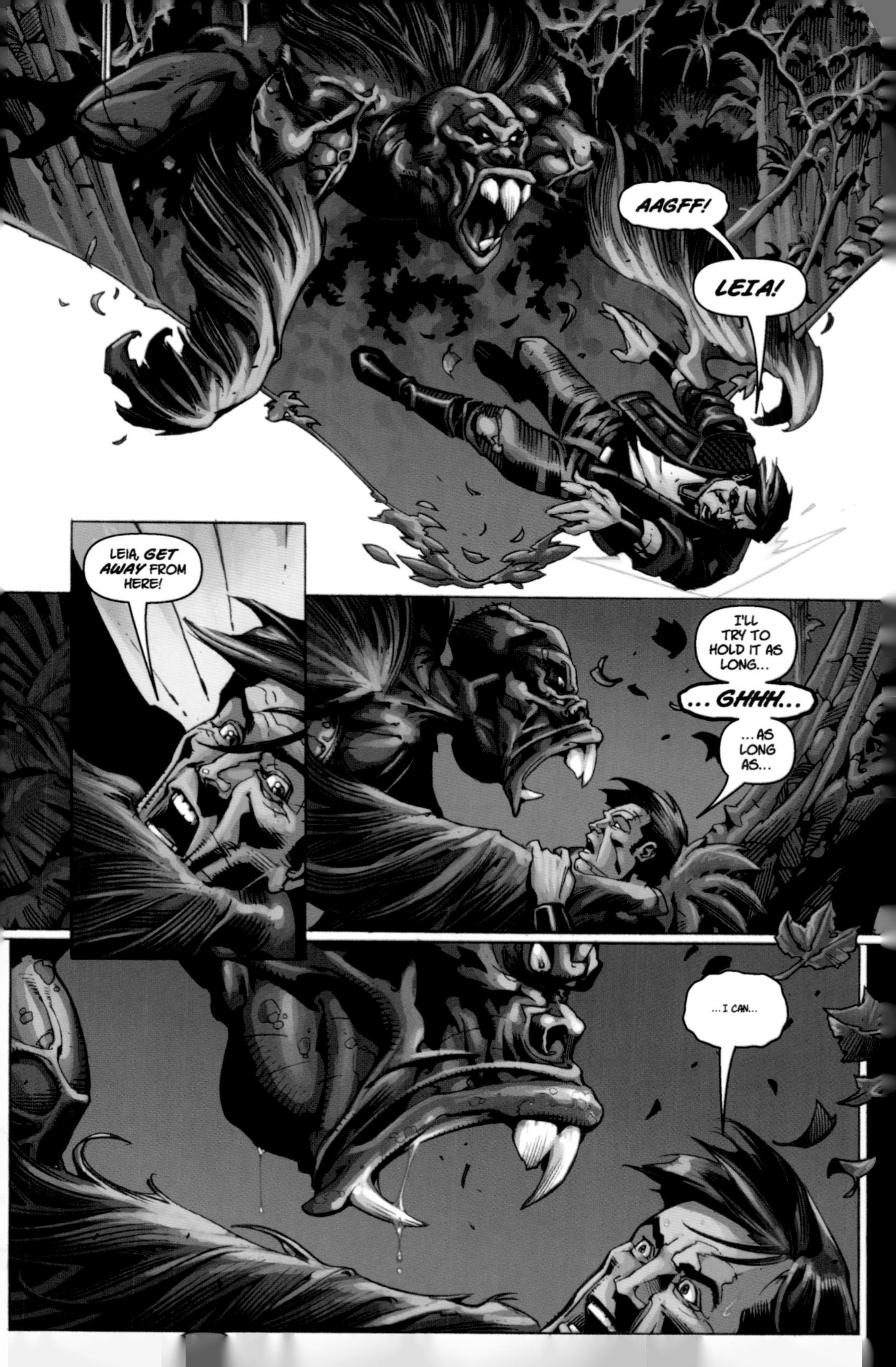
AAGFF!
LEIA!
LEIA, GET AWAY FROM HERE!
I'LL TRY TO HOLD IT AS LONG...
...GHHH...
...AS LONG AS...
...I CAN...

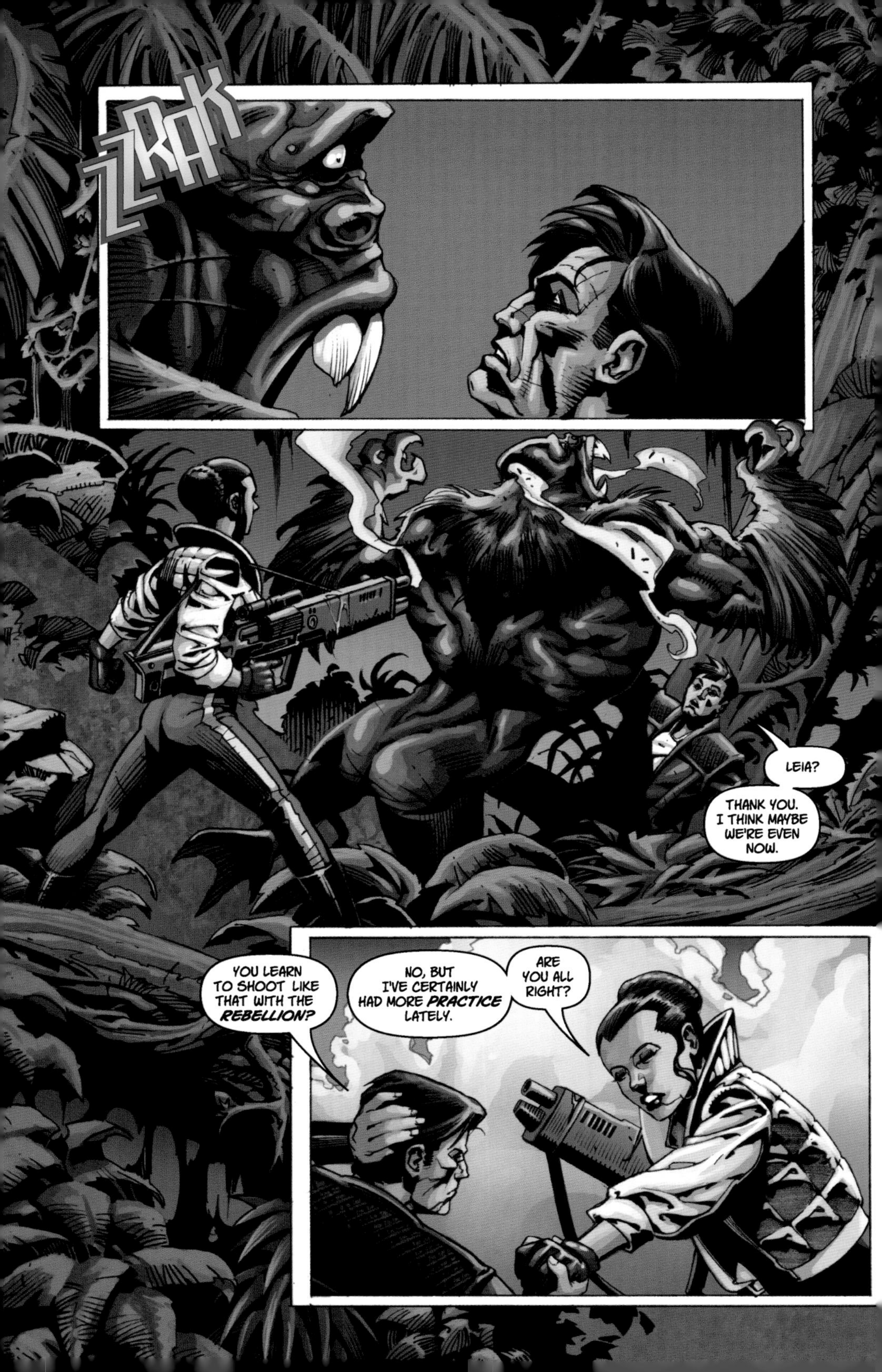
ZZRAK
LEIA?
THANK YOU. I THINK MAYBE WE'RE EVEN NOW.
ARE YOU ALL RIGHT?
NO, BUT I'VE CERTAINLY HAD MORE *PRACTICE* LATELY.
YOU LEARN TO SHOOT LIKE THAT WITH THE *REBELLION?*

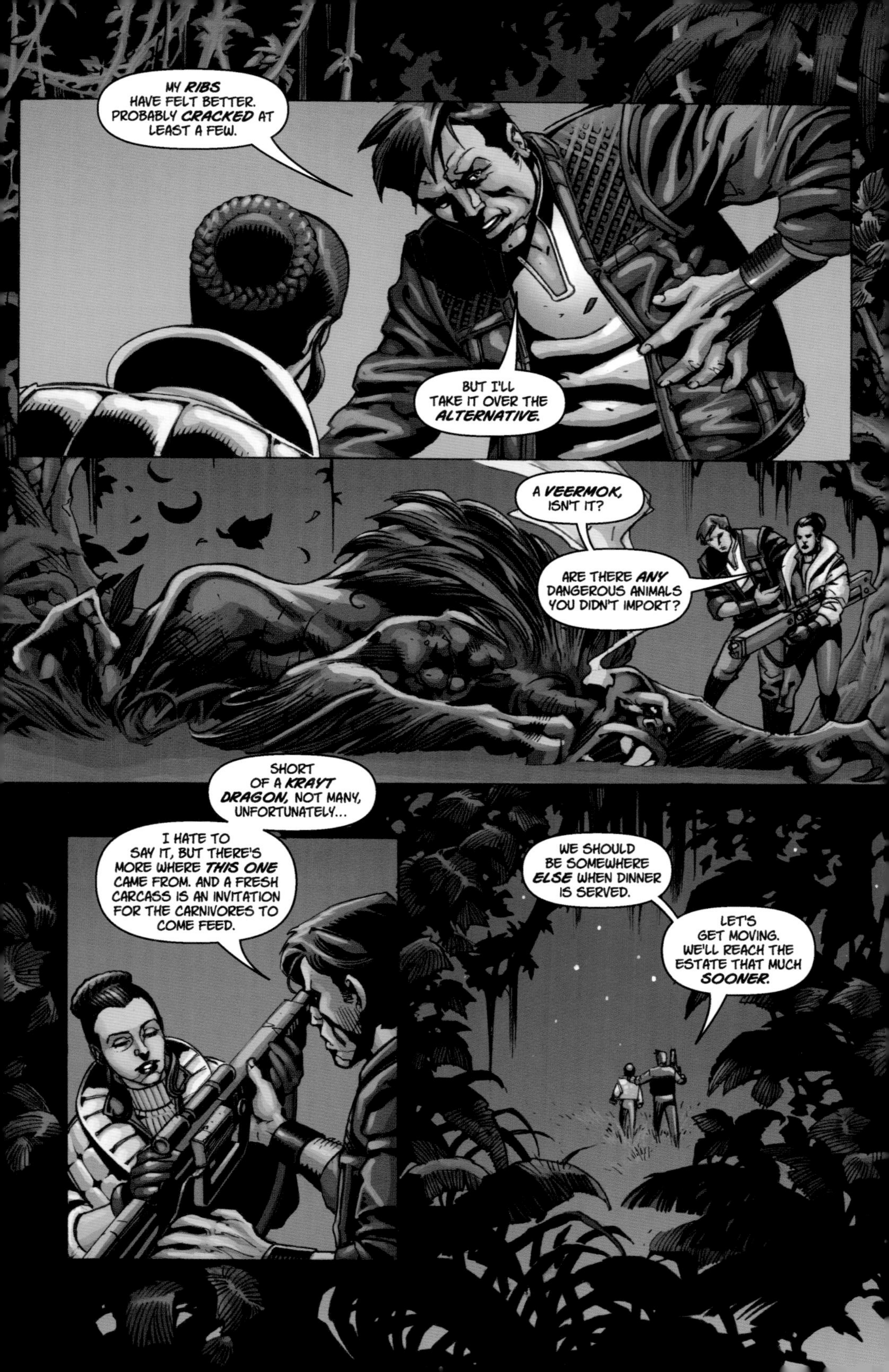
MY RIBS HAVE FELT BETTER. PROBABLY CRACKED AT LEAST A FEW.
BUT I'LL TAKE IT OVER THE ALTERNATIVE.
A VEERMOK, ISN'T IT?
ARE THERE ANY DANGEROUS ANIMALS YOU DIDN'T IMPORT?
SHORT OF A KRAYT DRAGON, NOT MANY, UNFORTUNATELY...
I HATE TO SAY IT, BUT THERE'S MORE WHERE THIS ONE CAME FROM. AND A FRESH CARCASS IS AN INVITATION FOR THE CARNIVORES TO COME FEED.
WE SHOULD BE SOMEWHERE ELSE WHEN DINNER IS SERVED.
LET'S GET MOVING. WE'LL REACH THE ESTATE THAT MUCH SOONER.

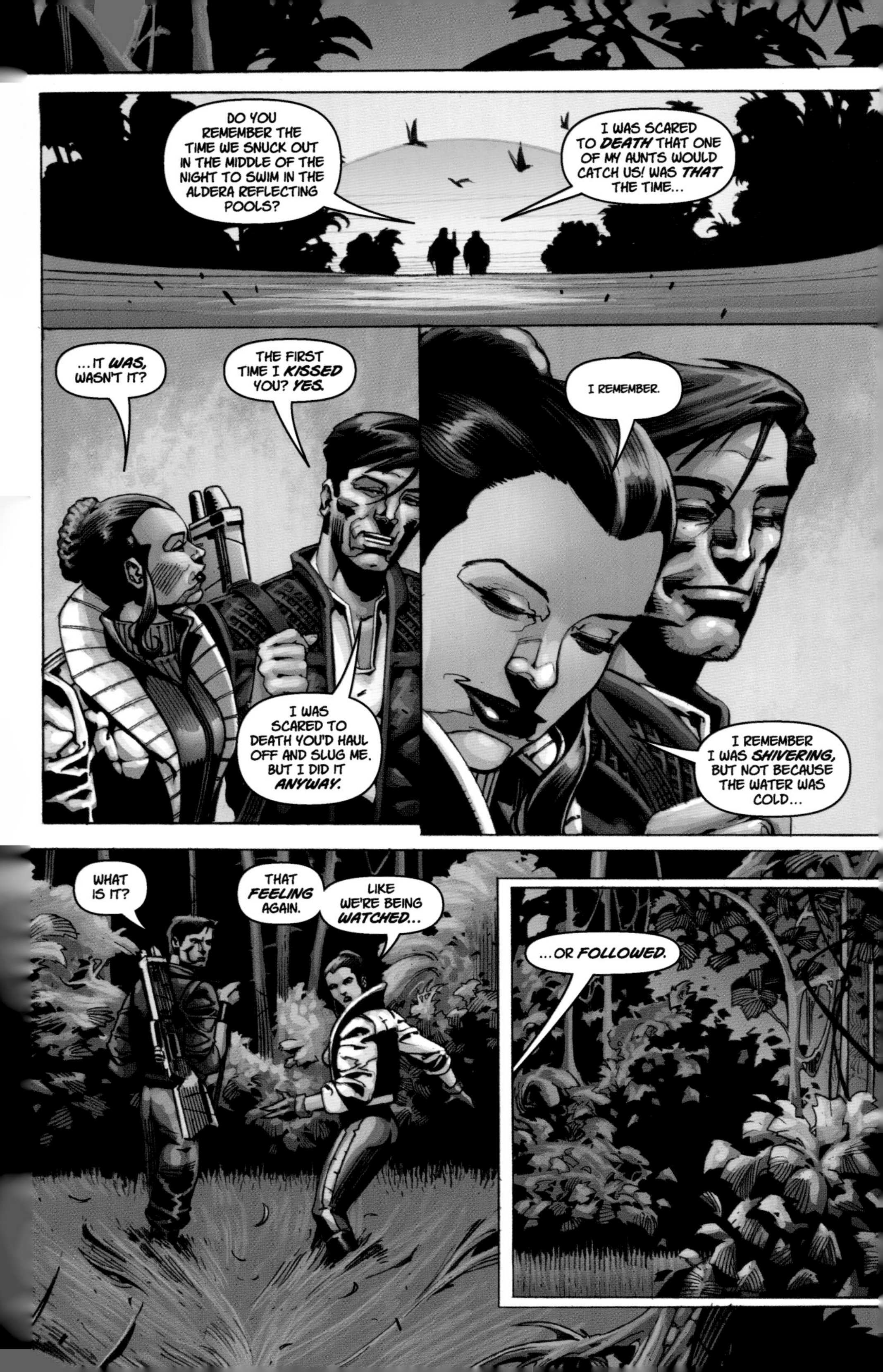

DO YOU REMEMBER THE TIME WE SNUCK OUT IN THE MIDDLE OF THE NIGHT TO SWIM IN THE ALDERA REFLECTING POOLS?
I WAS SCARED TO *DEATH* THAT ONE OF MY AUNTS WOULD CATCH US! WAS *THAT* THE TIME...
...IT *WAS*, WASN'T IT?
THE FIRST TIME I *KISSED* YOU? *YES*.
I WAS SCARED TO DEATH YOU'D HAUL OFF AND SLUG ME. BUT I DID IT *ANYWAY*.
I REMEMBER.
I REMEMBER I WAS *SHIVERING*, BUT NOT BECAUSE THE WATER WAS COLD...
WHAT IS IT?
THAT *FEELING* AGAIN.
LIKE WE'RE BEING *WATCHED*...
...OR *FOLLOWED*.

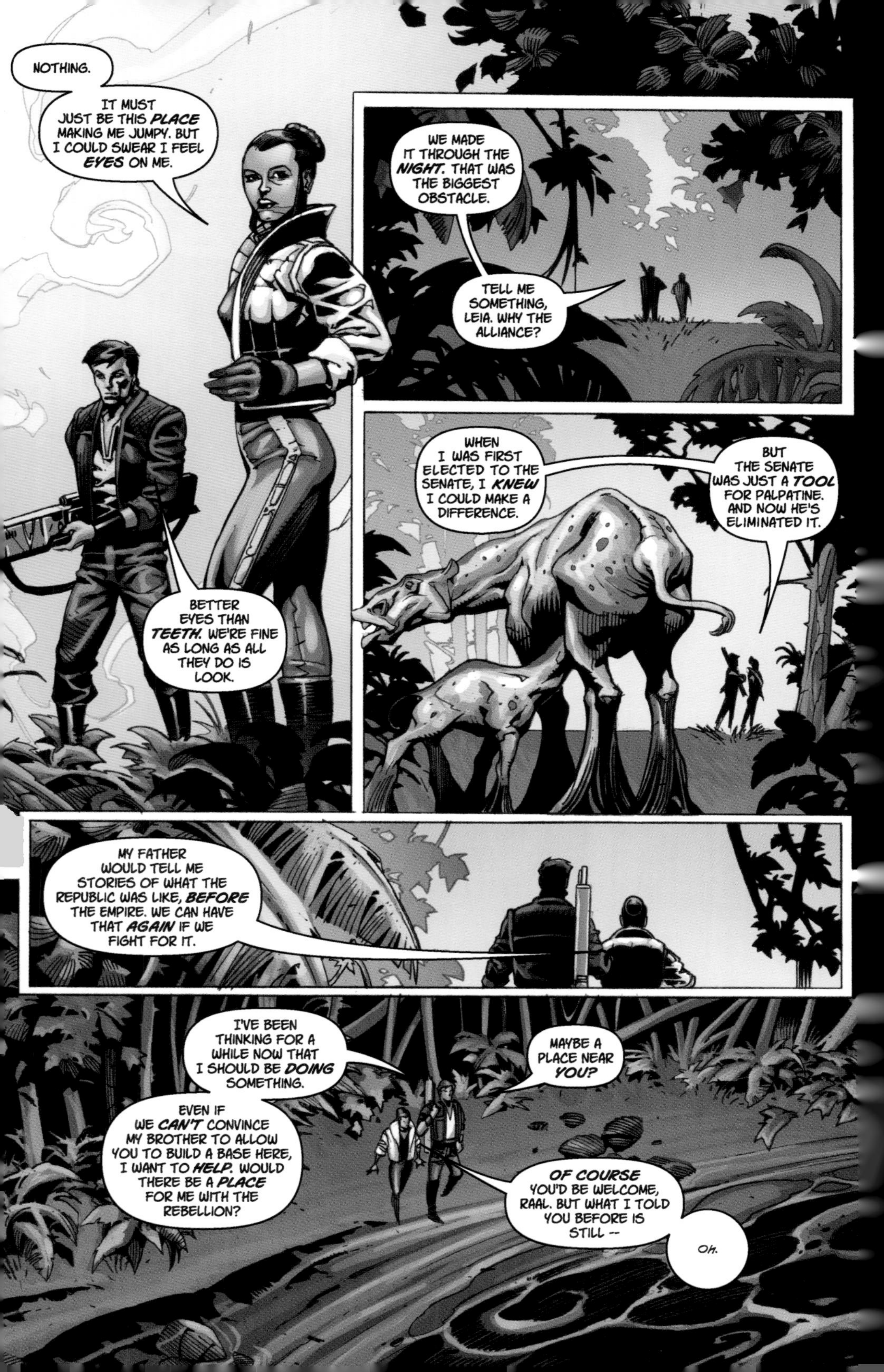
NOTHING.
IT MUST JUST BE THIS *PLACE* MAKING ME JUMPY. BUT I COULD SWEAR I FEEL *EYES* ON ME.
BETTER EYES THAN *TEETH.* WE'RE FINE AS LONG AS ALL THEY DO IS LOOK.
WE MADE IT THROUGH THE *NIGHT*. THAT WAS THE BIGGEST OBSTACLE.
TELL ME SOMETHING, LEIA. WHY THE ALLIANCE?
WHEN I WAS FIRST ELECTED TO THE SENATE, I *KNEW* I COULD MAKE A DIFFERENCE.
BUT THE SENATE WAS JUST A *TOOL* FOR PALPATINE. AND NOW HE'S ELIMINATED IT.
MY FATHER WOULD TELL ME STORIES OF WHAT THE REPUBLIC WAS LIKE, *BEFORE* THE EMPIRE. WE CAN HAVE THAT *AGAIN* IF WE FIGHT FOR IT.
I'VE BEEN THINKING FOR A WHILE NOW THAT I SHOULD BE *DOING* SOMETHING.
EVEN IF WE *CAN'T* CONVINCE MY BROTHER TO ALLOW YOU TO BUILD A BASE HERE, I WANT TO *HELP*. WOULD THERE BE A *PLACE* FOR ME WITH THE REBELLION?
MAYBE A PLACE NEAR *YOU?*
OF COURSE YOU'D BE WELCOME, RAAL. BUT WHAT I TOLD YOU BEFORE IS STILL --
Oh.

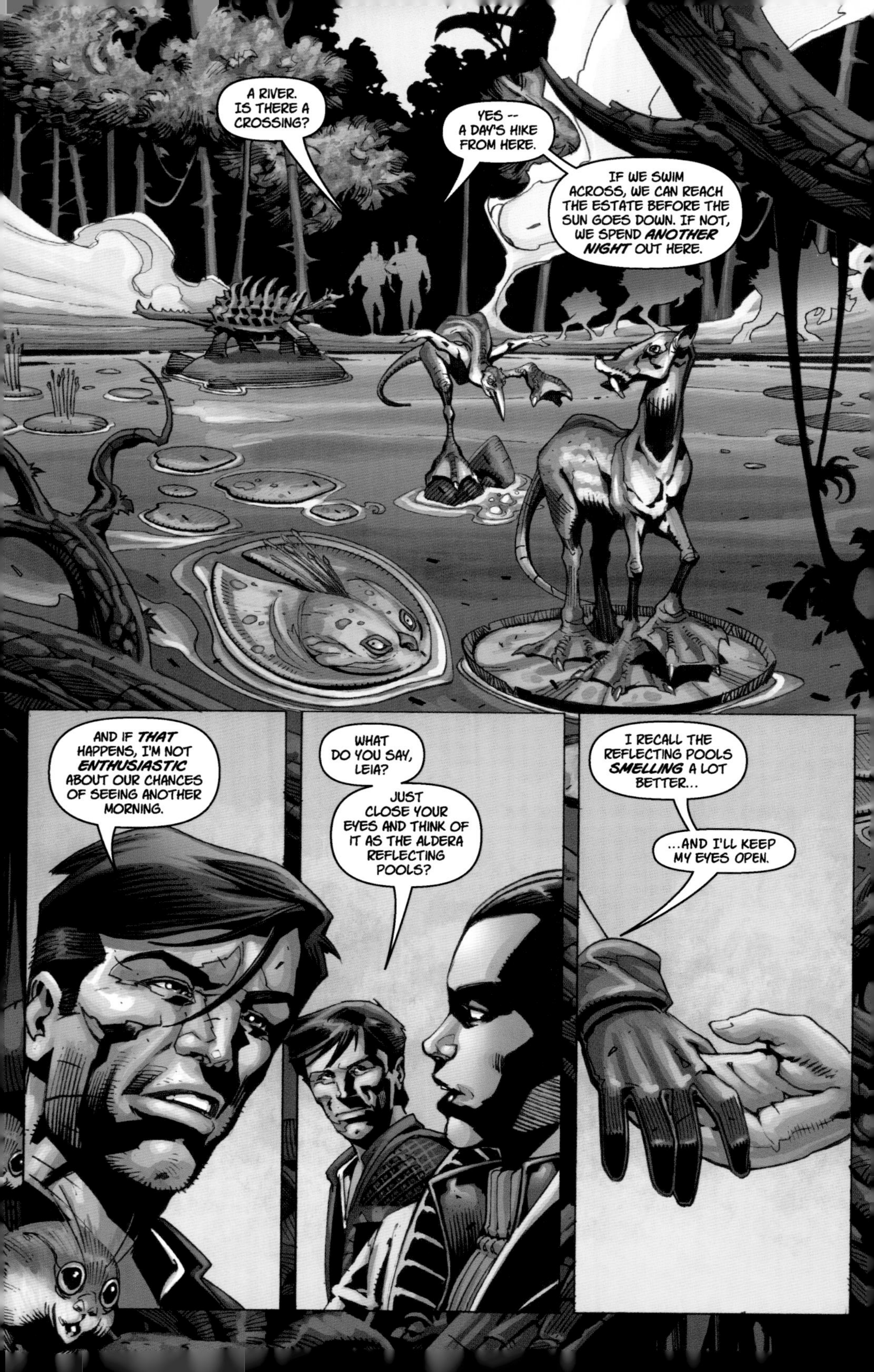
A RIVER. IS THERE A CROSSING?
YES -- A DAY'S HIKE FROM HERE.
IF WE SWIM ACROSS, WE CAN REACH THE ESTATE BEFORE THE SUN GOES DOWN. IF NOT, WE SPEND ANOTHER NIGHT OUT HERE.
AND IF THAT HAPPENS, I'M NOT ENTHUSIASTIC ABOUT OUR CHANCES OF SEEING ANOTHER MORNING.
WHAT DO YOU SAY, LEIA?
JUST CLOSE YOUR EYES AND THINK OF IT AS THE ALDERA REFLECTING POOLS?
I RECALL THE REFLECTING POOLS SMELLING A LOT BETTER...
...AND I'LL KEEP MY EYES OPEN.

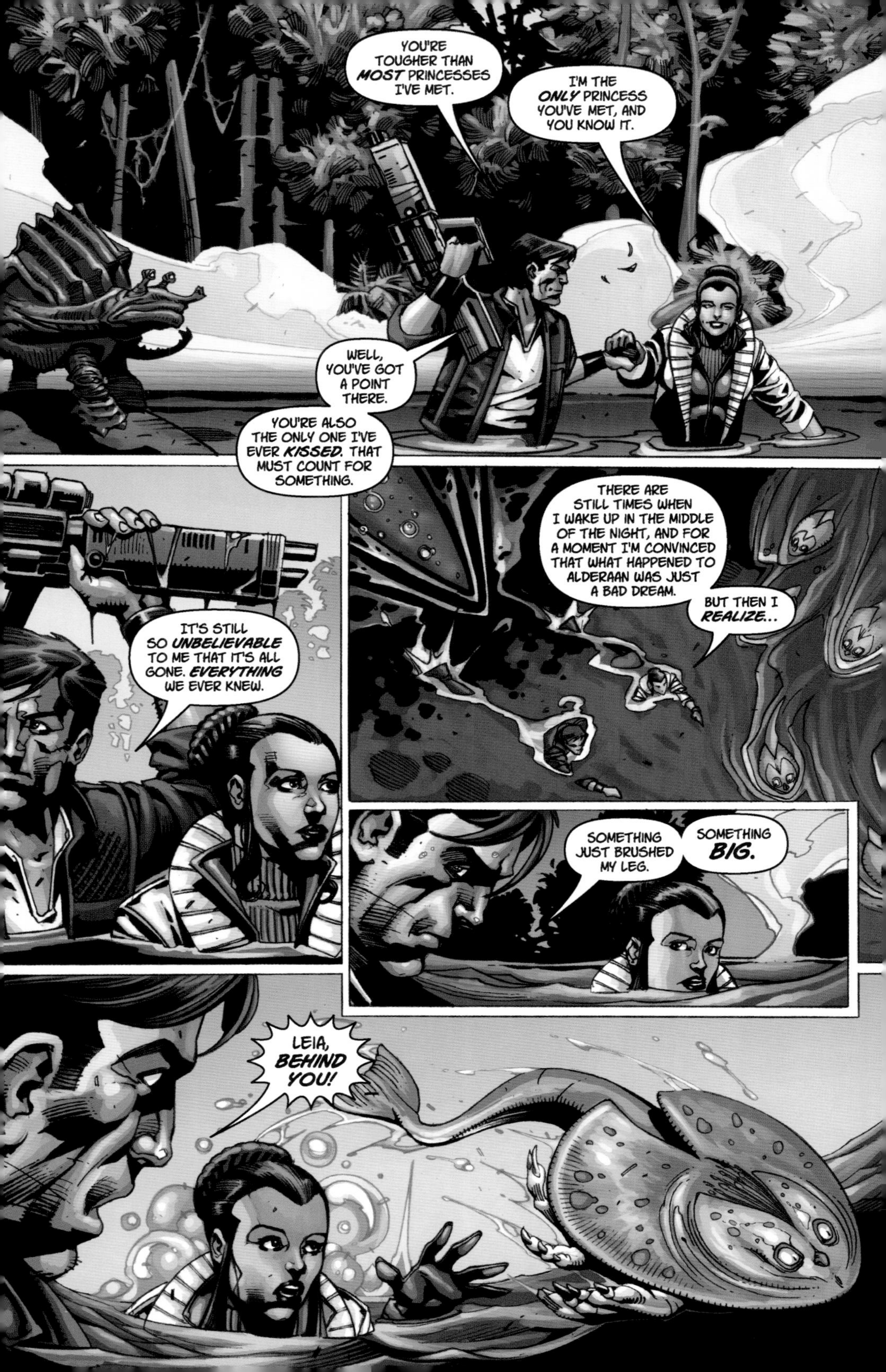
YOU'RE TOUGHER THAN MOST PRINCESSES I'VE MET.
I'M THE ONLY PRINCESS YOU'VE MET, AND YOU KNOW IT.
WELL, YOU'VE GOT A POINT THERE.
YOU'RE ALSO THE ONLY ONE I'VE EVER KISSED. THAT MUST COUNT FOR SOMETHING.
IT'S STILL SO UNBELIEVABLE TO ME THAT IT'S ALL GONE. EVERYTHING WE EVER KNEW.
THERE ARE STILL TIMES WHEN I WAKE UP IN THE MIDDLE OF THE NIGHT, AND FOR A MOMENT I'M CONVINCED THAT WHAT HAPPENED TO ALDERAAN WAS JUST A BAD DREAM.
BUT THEN I REALIZE...
SOMETHING JUST BRUSHED MY LEG.
SOMETHING BIG.
LEIA, BEHIND YOU!

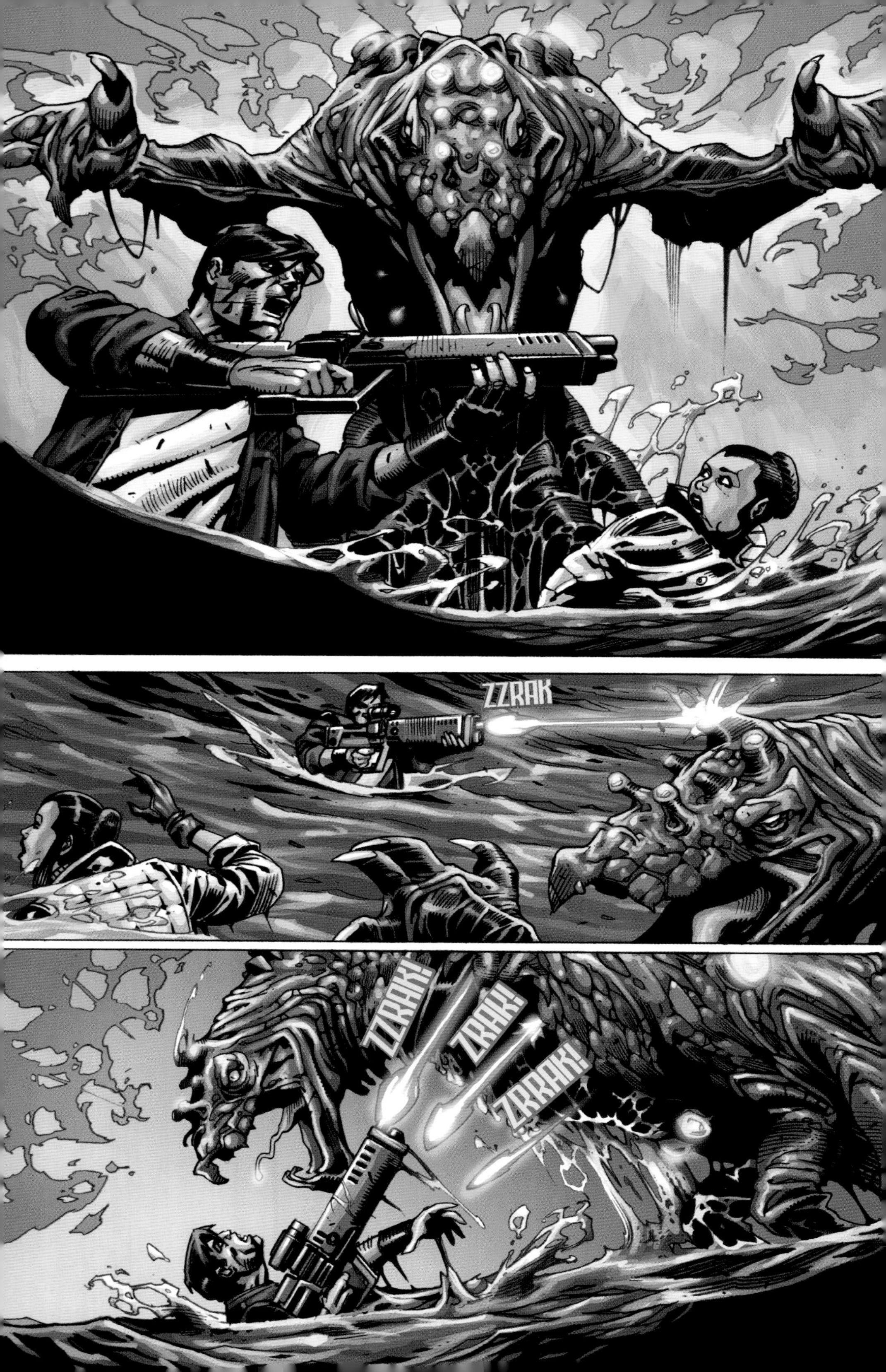
ZZRAK
ZZRAK!
ZRAK!
ZRRAK!

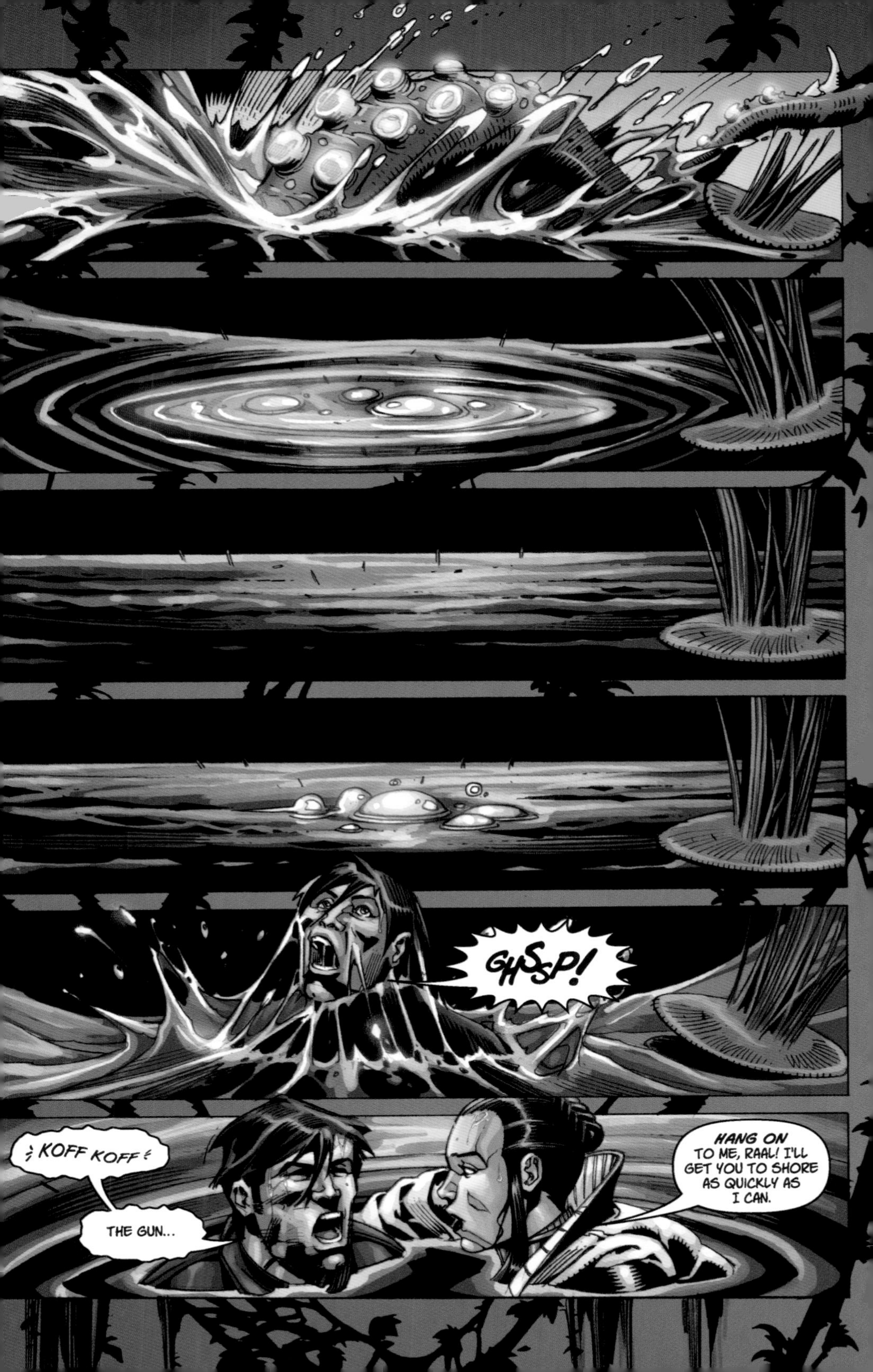
GHSSP!
KOFF KOFF
THE GUN...
HANG ON TO ME, RAAL! I'LL GET YOU TO SHORE AS QUICKLY AS I CAN.

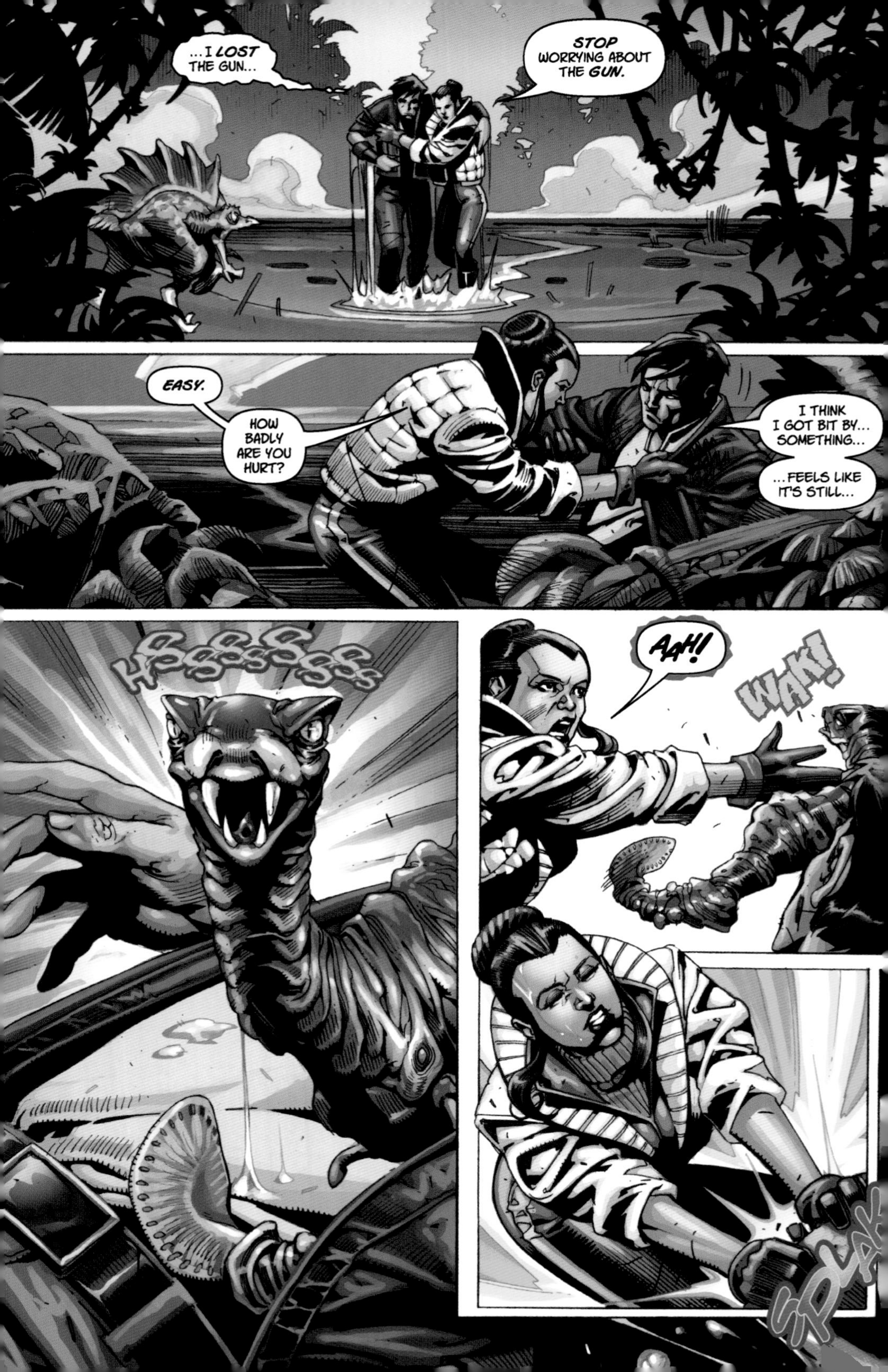
...I LOST THE GUN...
STOP WORRYING ABOUT THE GUN.
EASY.
HOW BADLY ARE YOU HURT?
I THINK I GOT BIT BY... SOMETHING...
...FEELS LIKE IT'S STILL...
HSSSSSSS
AAH!
WAK!
SPLAK

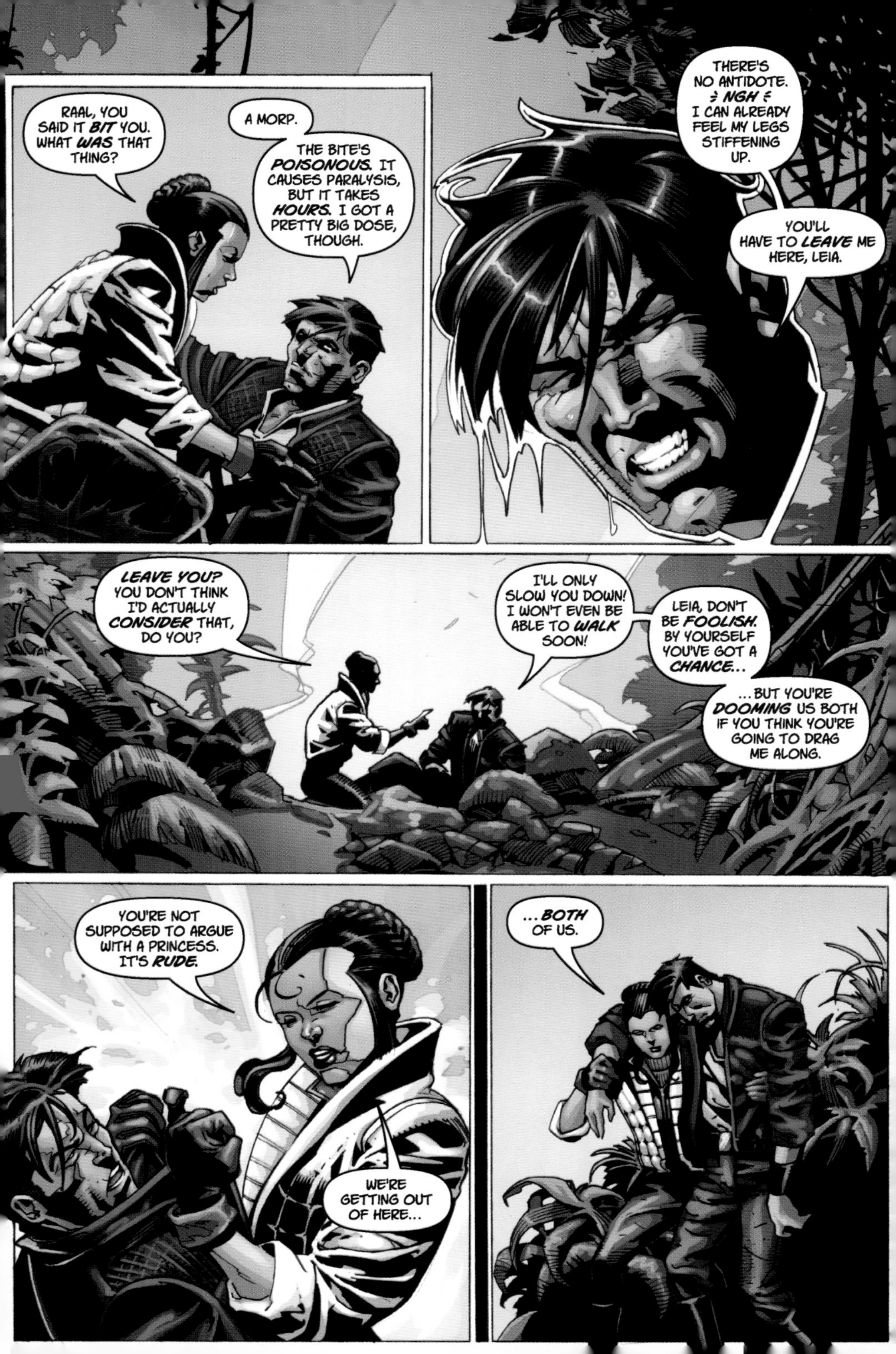

RAAL, YOU SAID IT BIT YOU. WHAT WAS THAT THING?
A MORP.
THE BITE'S POISONOUS. IT CAUSES PARALYSIS, BUT IT TAKES HOURS. I GOT A PRETTY BIG DOSE, THOUGH.
THERE'S NO ANTIDOTE. NGH I CAN ALREADY FEEL MY LEGS STIFFENING UP.
YOU'LL HAVE TO LEAVE ME HERE, LEIA.
LEAVE YOU? YOU DON'T THINK I'D ACTUALLY CONSIDER THAT, DO YOU?
I'LL ONLY SLOW YOU DOWN! I WON'T EVEN BE ABLE TO WALK SOON!
LEIA, DON'T BE FOOLISH. BY YOURSELF YOU'VE GOT A CHANCE...
...BUT YOU'RE DOOMING US BOTH IF YOU THINK YOU'RE GOING TO DRAG ME ALONG.
YOU'RE NOT SUPPOSED TO ARGUE WITH A PRINCESS. IT'S RUDE.
WE'RE GETTING OUT OF HERE...
...BOTH OF US.

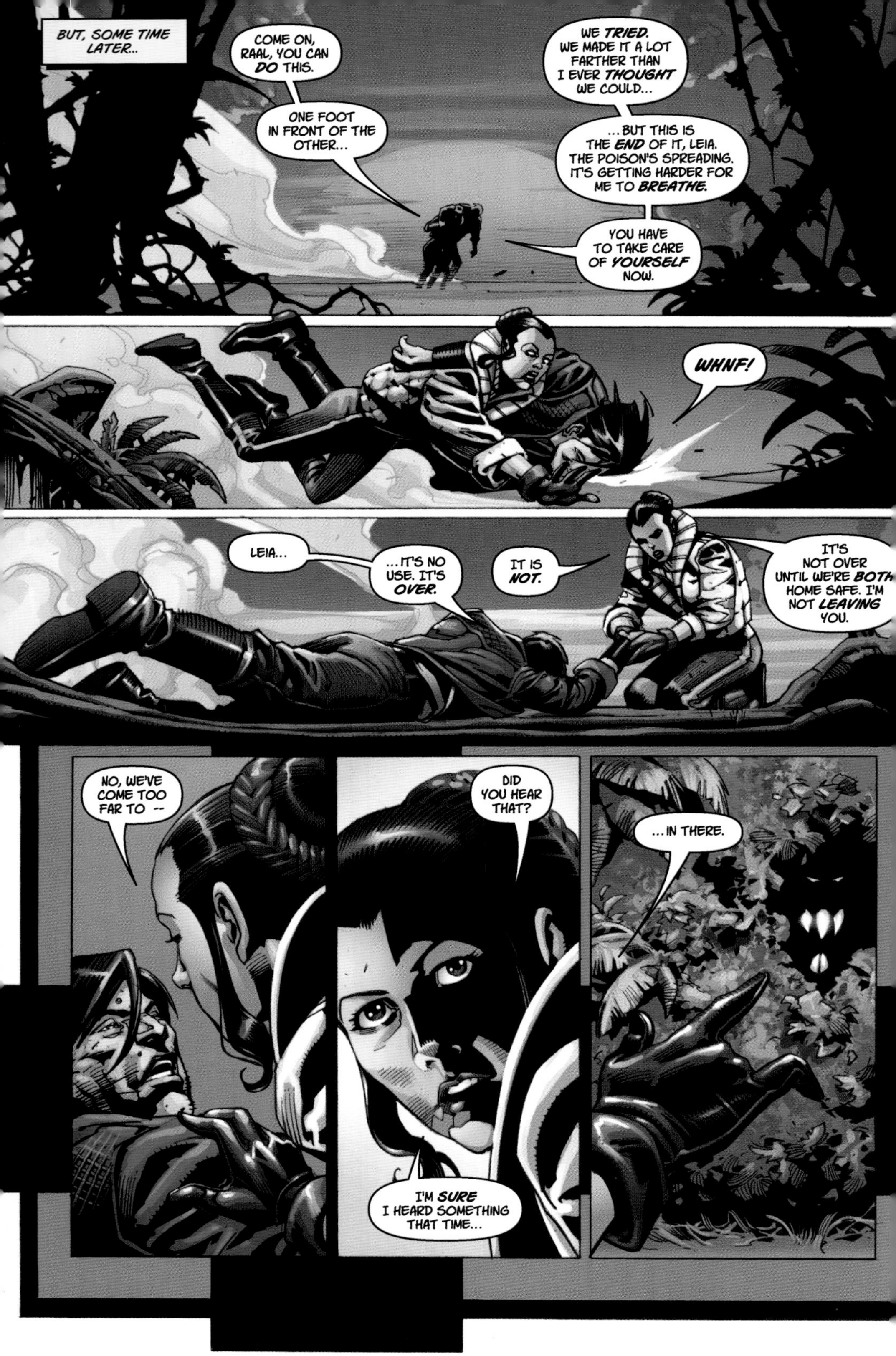
BUT, SOME TIME LATER...
COME ON, RAAL, YOU CAN DO THIS.
ONE FOOT IN FRONT OF THE OTHER...
WE TRIED. WE MADE IT A LOT FARTHER THAN I EVER THOUGHT WE COULD...
...BUT THIS IS THE END OF IT, LEIA. THE POISON'S SPREADING. IT'S GETTING HARDER FOR ME TO BREATHE.
YOU HAVE TO TAKE CARE OF YOURSELF NOW.
WHNF!
LEIA...
...IT'S NO USE. IT'S OVER.
IT IS NOT.
IT'S NOT OVER UNTIL WE'RE BOTH HOME SAFE. I'M NOT LEAVING YOU.
NO, WE'VE COME TOO FAR TO --
DID YOU HEAR THAT?
I'M SURE I HEARD SOMETHING THAT TIME...
...IN THERE.

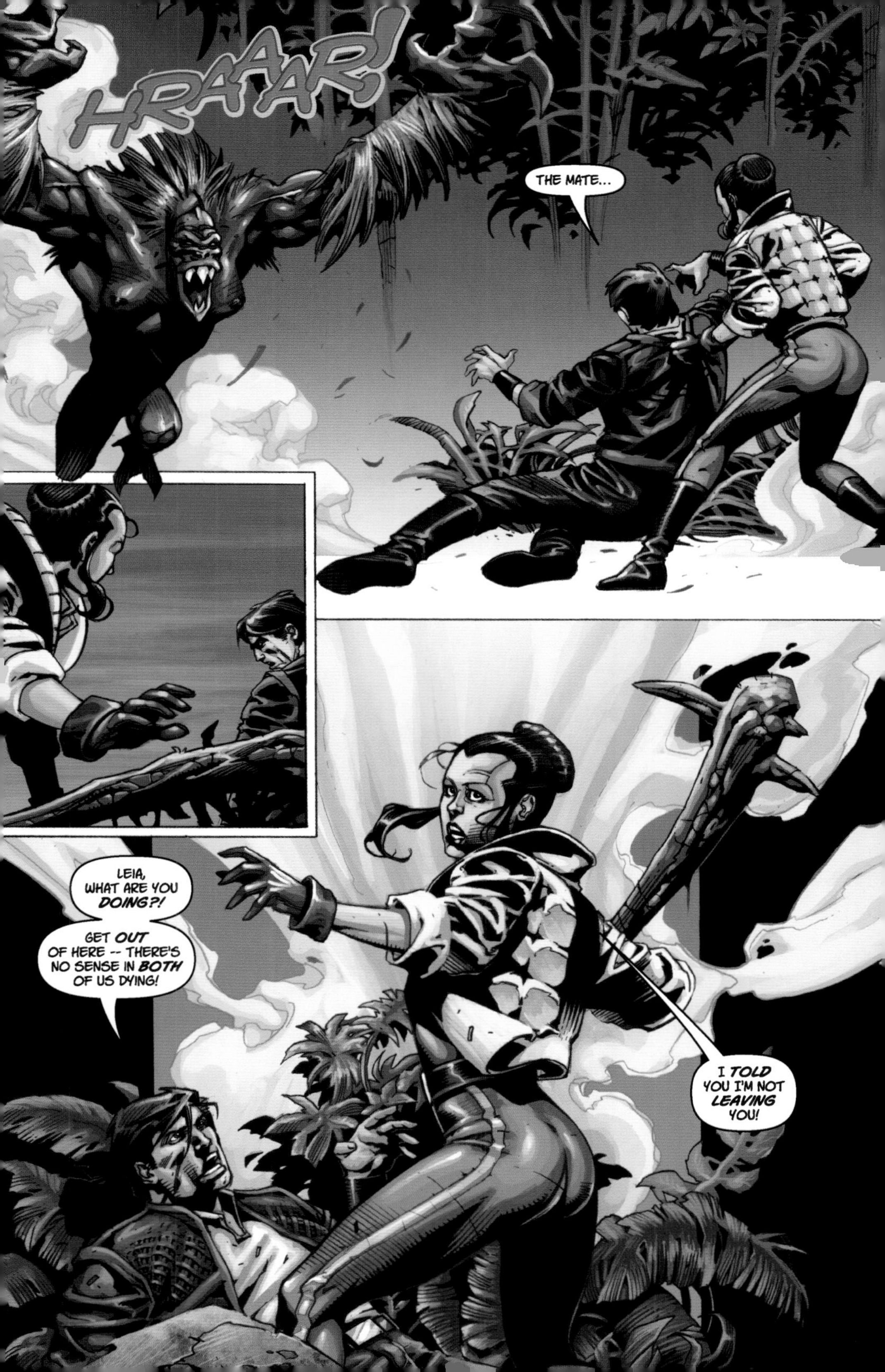
HRAAAR!
THE MATE...
LEIA, WHAT ARE YOU DOING?!
GET OUT OF HERE -- THERE'S NO SENSE IN BOTH OF US DYING!
I TOLD YOU I'M NOT LEAVING YOU!

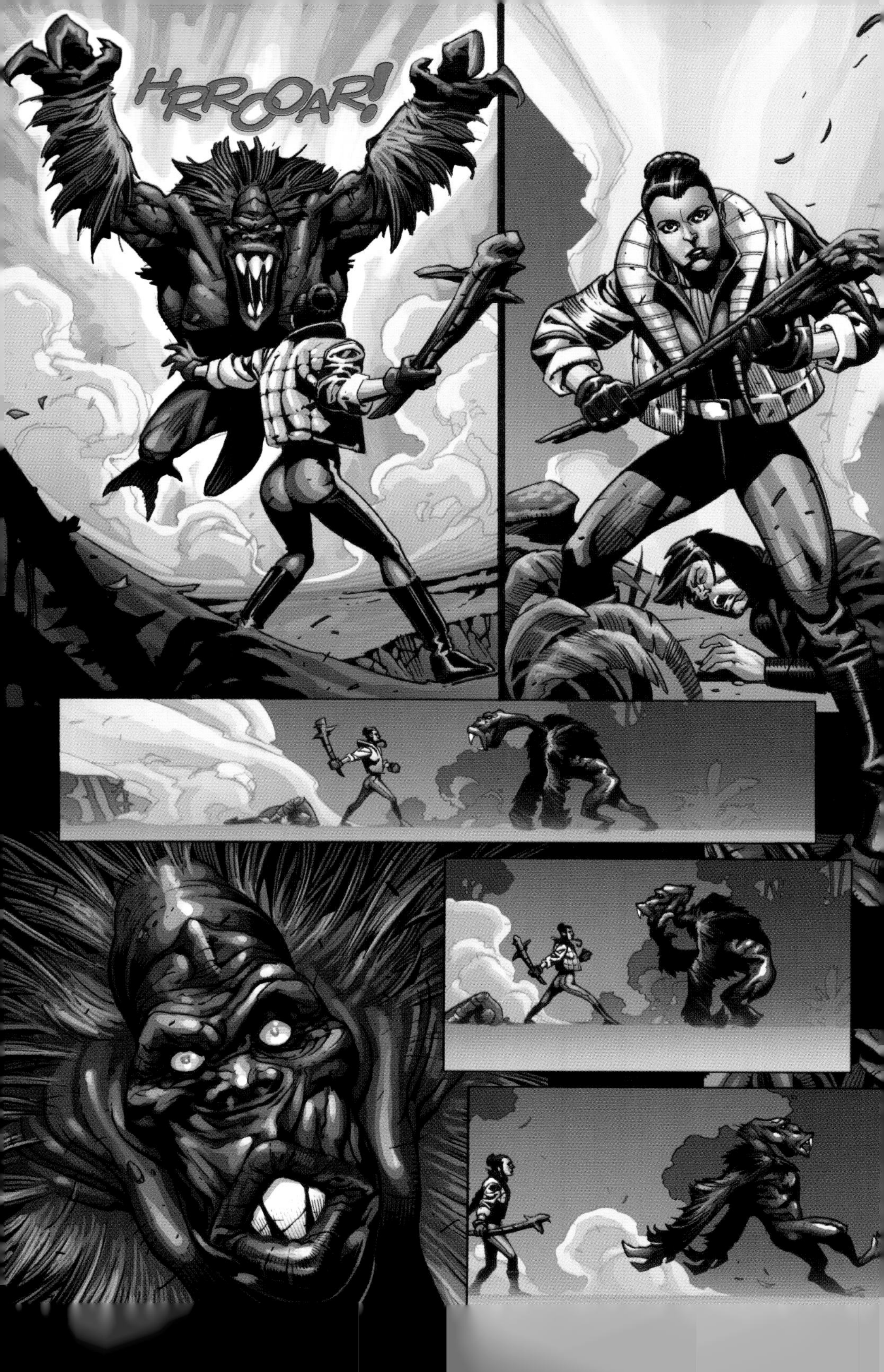
HRRROOAR!

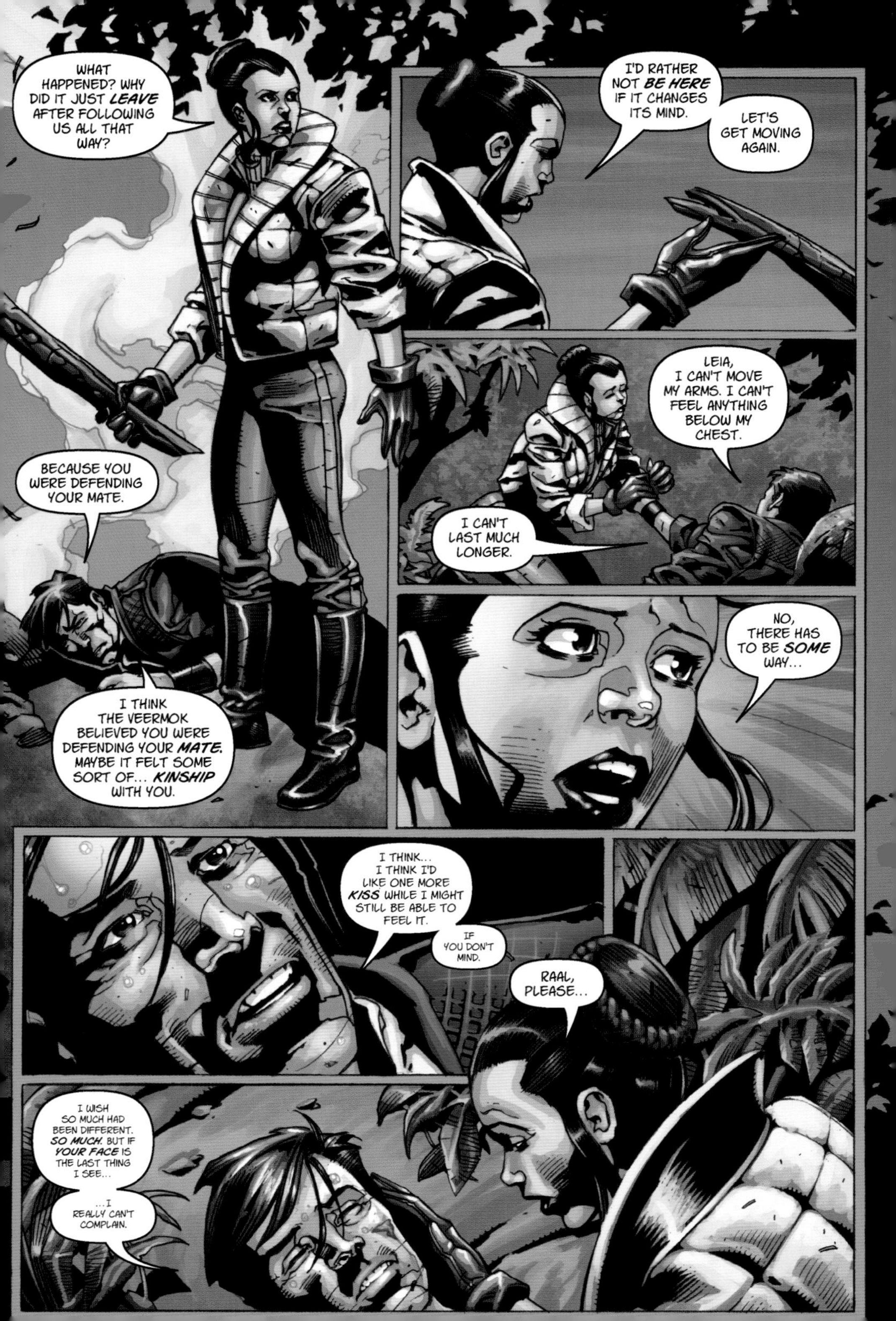

WHAT HAPPENED? WHY DID IT JUST *LEAVE* AFTER FOLLOWING US ALL THAT WAY?
BECAUSE YOU WERE DEFENDING YOUR MATE.
I THINK THE VEERMOK BELIEVED YOU WERE DEFENDING YOUR *MATE*. MAYBE IT FELT SOME SORT OF... *KINSHIP* WITH YOU.
I'D RATHER NOT *BE HERE* IF IT CHANGES ITS MIND.
LET'S GET MOVING AGAIN.
LEIA, I CAN'T MOVE MY ARMS. I CAN'T FEEL ANYTHING BELOW MY CHEST.
I CAN'T LAST MUCH LONGER.
NO, THERE HAS TO BE *SOME* WAY...
I THINK... I THINK I'D LIKE ONE MORE *KISS* WHILE I MIGHT STILL BE ABLE TO FEEL IT.
IF YOU DON'T MIND.
RAAL, PLEASE...
I WISH SO MUCH HAD BEEN DIFFERENT. *SO MUCH*. BUT IF *YOUR FACE* IS THE LAST THING I SEE...
...I REALLY CAN'T COMPLAIN.

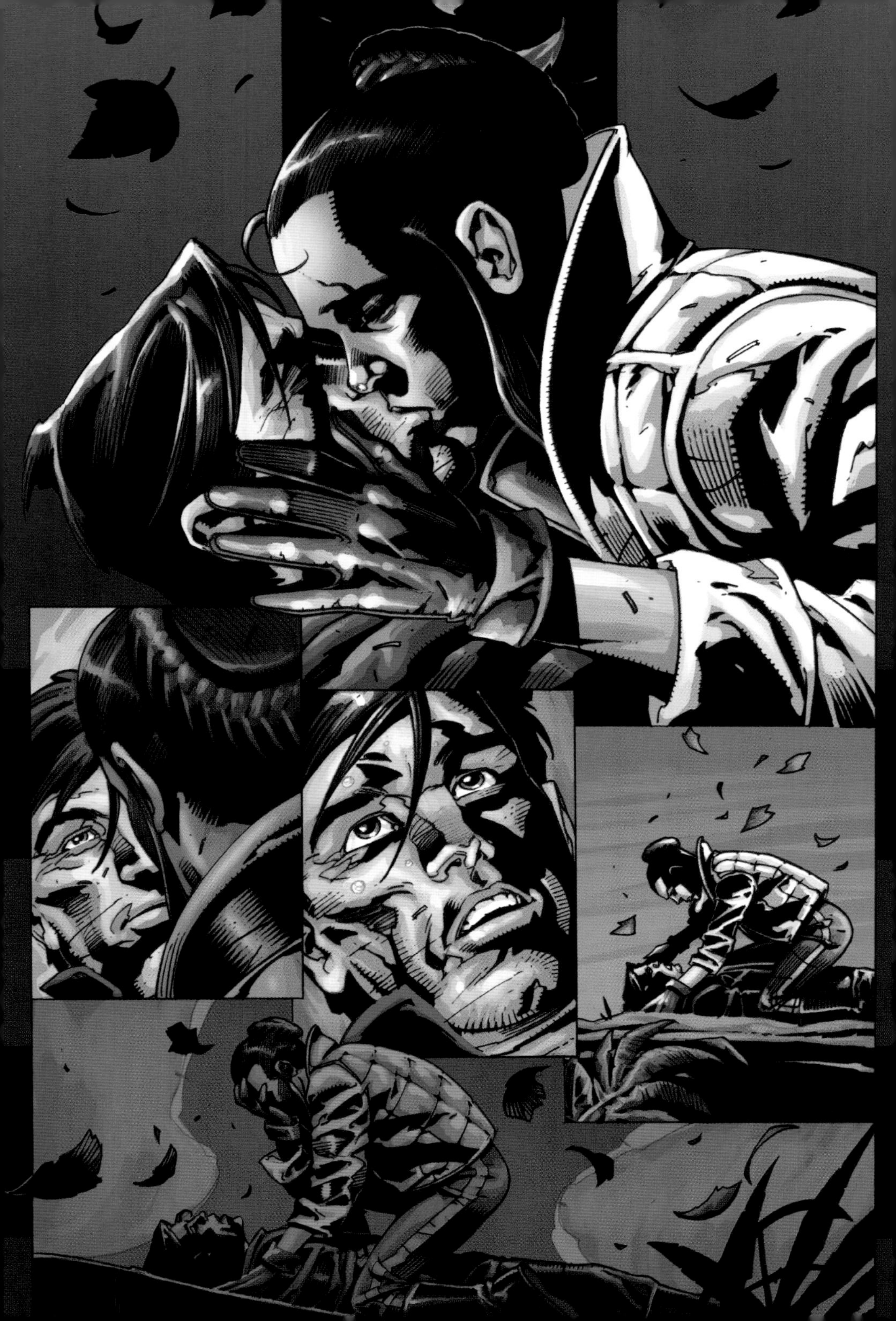

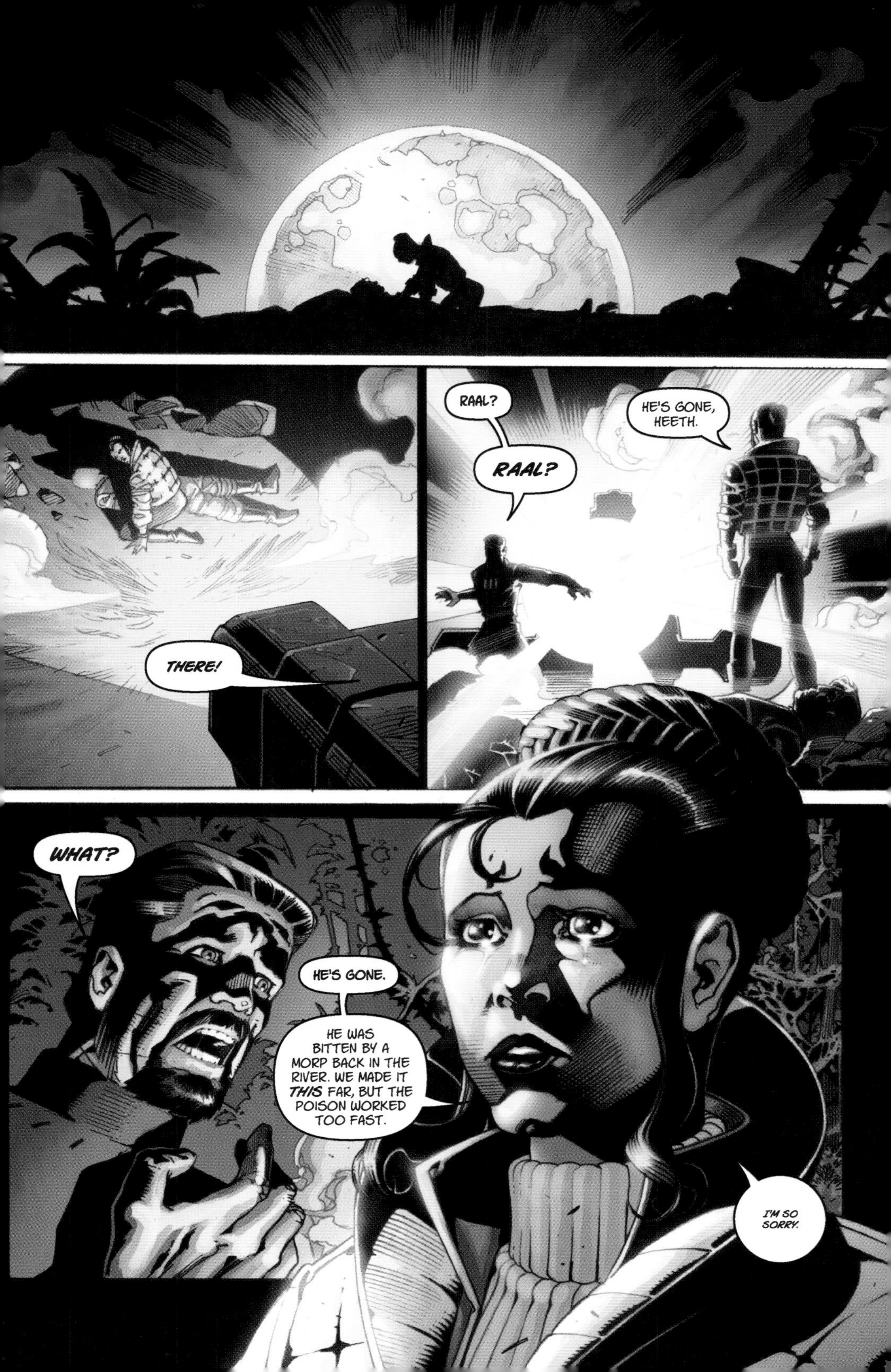
THERE!
RAAL?
RAAL?
HE'S GONE, HEETH.
WHAT?
HE'S GONE.
HE WAS BITTEN BY A MORP BACK IN THE RIVER. WE MADE IT THIS FAR, BUT THE POISON WORKED TOO FAST.
I'M SO SORRY.

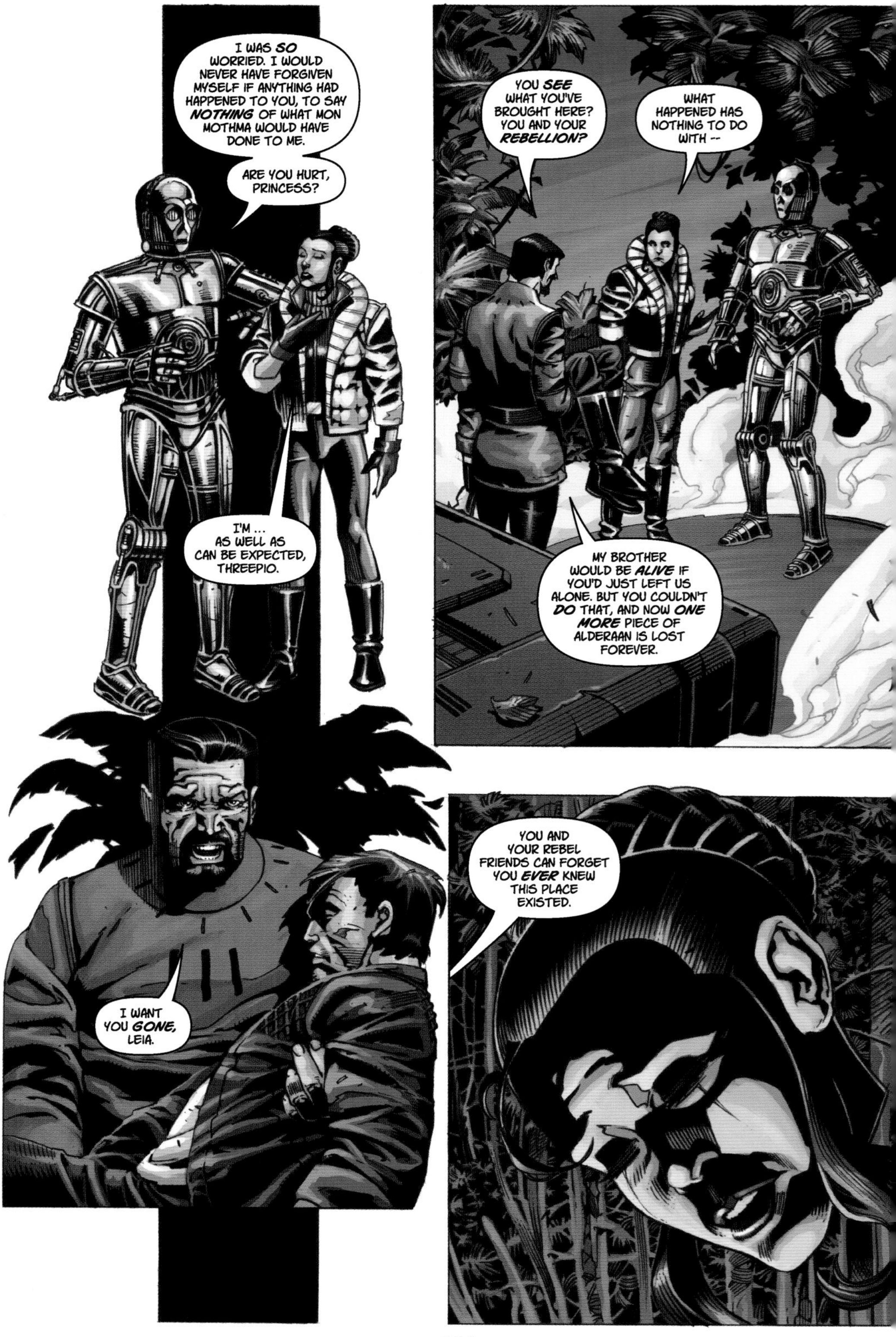
I WAS SO WORRIED. I WOULD NEVER HAVE FORGIVEN MYSELF IF ANYTHING HAD HAPPENED TO YOU, TO SAY NOTHING OF WHAT MON MOTHMA WOULD HAVE DONE TO ME.
ARE YOU HURT, PRINCESS?
I'M ... AS WELL AS CAN BE EXPECTED, THREEPIO.
YOU SEE WHAT YOU'VE BROUGHT HERE? YOU AND YOUR REBELLION?
WHAT HAPPENED HAS NOTHING TO DO WITH --
MY BROTHER WOULD BE ALIVE IF YOU'D JUST LEFT US ALONE. BUT YOU COULDN'T DO THAT, AND NOW ONE MORE PIECE OF ALDERAAN IS LOST FOREVER.
I WANT YOU GONE, LEIA.
YOU AND YOUR REBEL FRIENDS CAN FORGET YOU EVER KNEW THIS PLACE EXISTED.

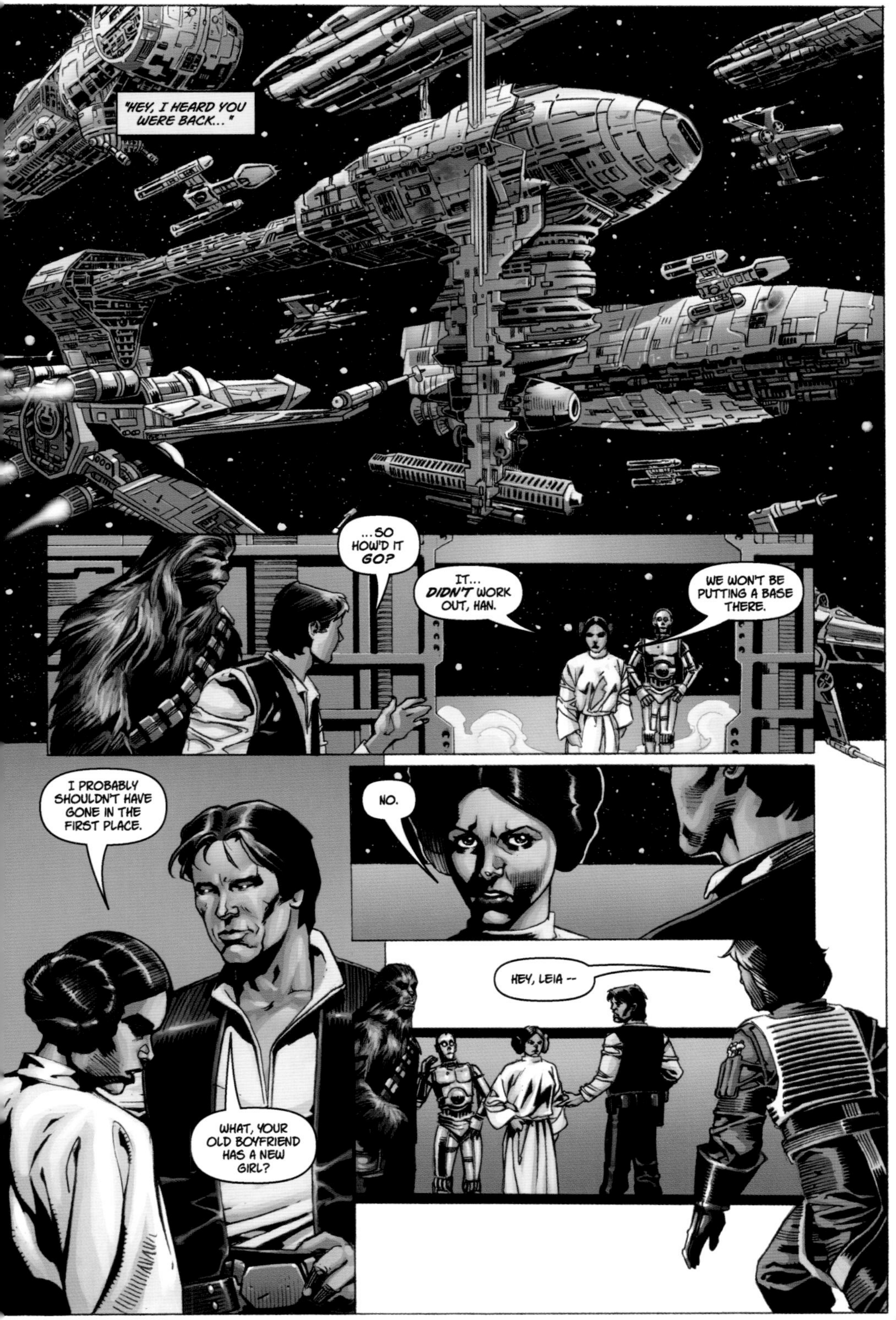
"HEY, I HEARD YOU WERE BACK..."
...SO HOW'D IT GO?
IT... DIDN'T WORK OUT, HAN.
WE WON'T BE PUTTING A BASE THERE.
I PROBABLY SHOULDN'T HAVE GONE IN THE FIRST PLACE.
WHAT, YOUR OLD BOYFRIEND HAS A NEW GIRL?
NO.
HEY, LEIA --

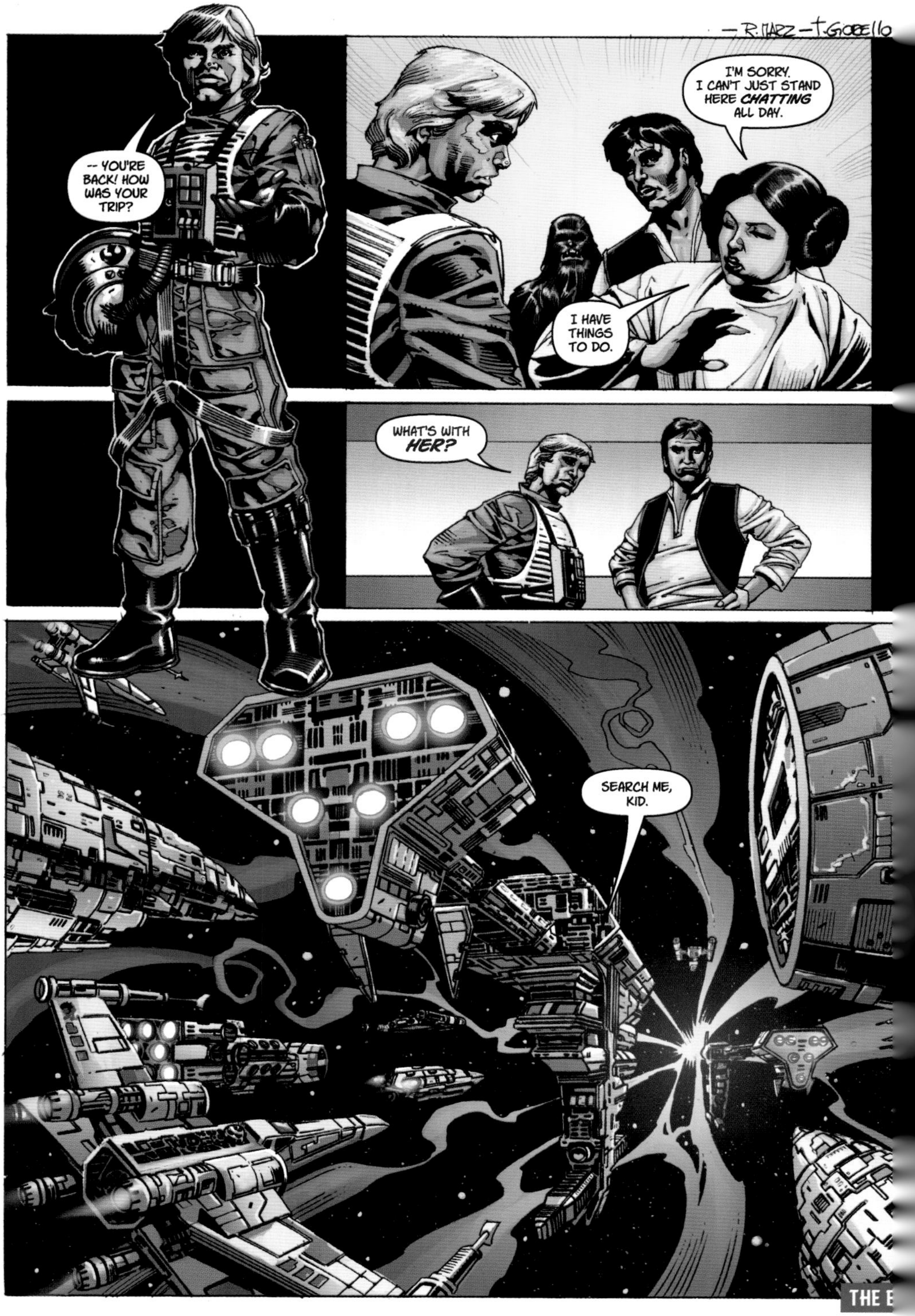
-- YOU'RE BACK! HOW WAS YOUR TRIP?
I'M SORRY. I CAN'T JUST STAND HERE CHATTING ALL DAY.
I HAVE THINGS TO DO.
WHAT'S WITH HER?
SEARCH ME, KID.
THE E

Target: Vader | Illustration by Douglas Wheatley

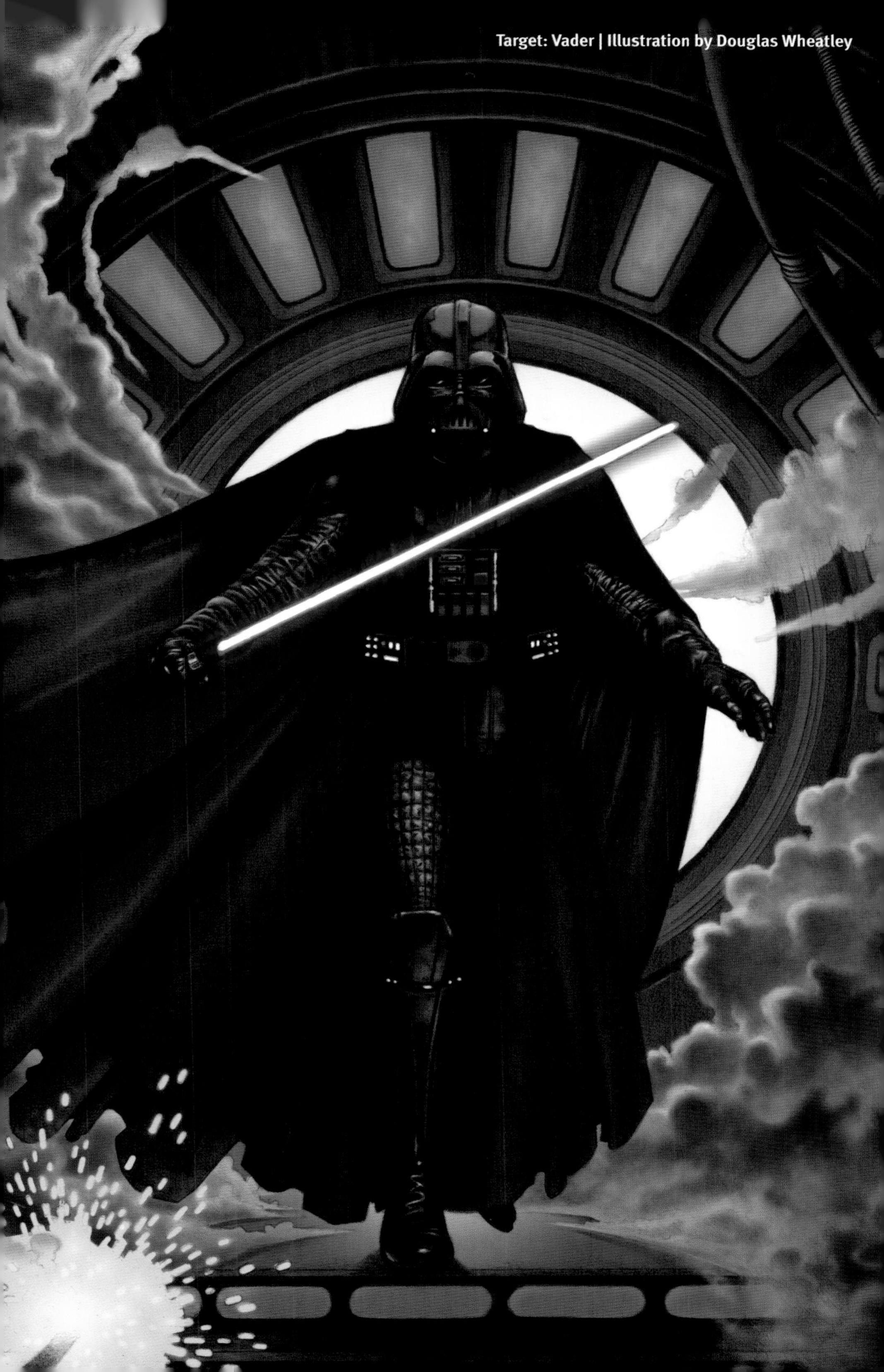

APPROXIMATELY SIX MONTHS AFTER THE BATTLE
OF YAVIN . . .

script by Ron Marz
pencils by Brian Ching
colors by Brad Anderson
lettering by Sno Cone Studios

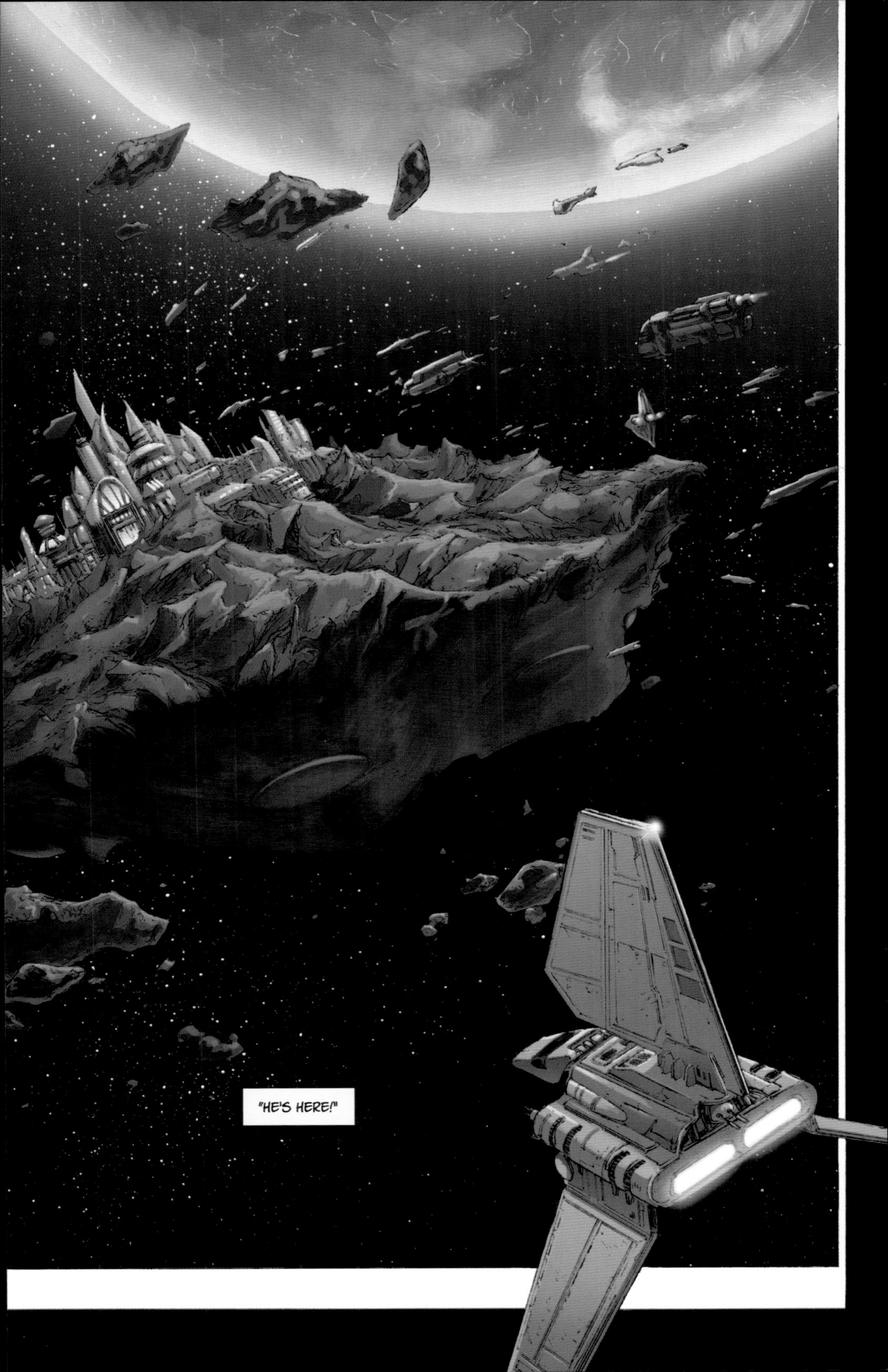
"HE'S HERE!"

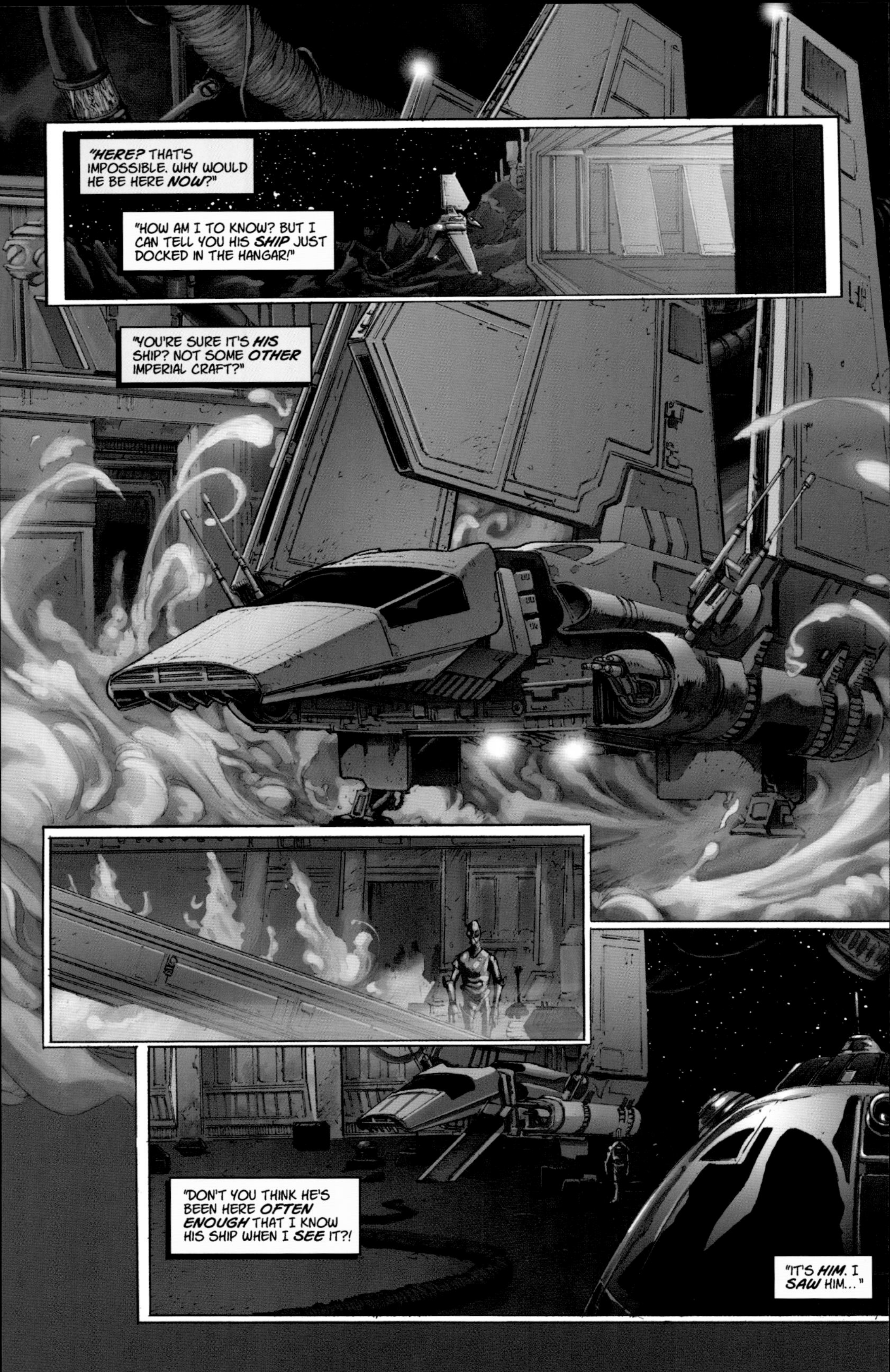
"HERE? THAT'S IMPOSSIBLE. WHY WOULD HE BE HERE NOW?"
"HOW AM I TO KNOW? BUT I CAN TELL YOU HIS SHIP JUST DOCKED IN THE HANGAR!"
"YOU'RE SURE IT'S HIS SHIP? NOT SOME OTHER IMPERIAL CRAFT?"
"DON'T YOU THINK HE'S BEEN HERE OFTEN ENOUGH THAT I KNOW HIS SHIP WHEN I SEE IT?!
"IT'S HIM. I SAW HIM..."

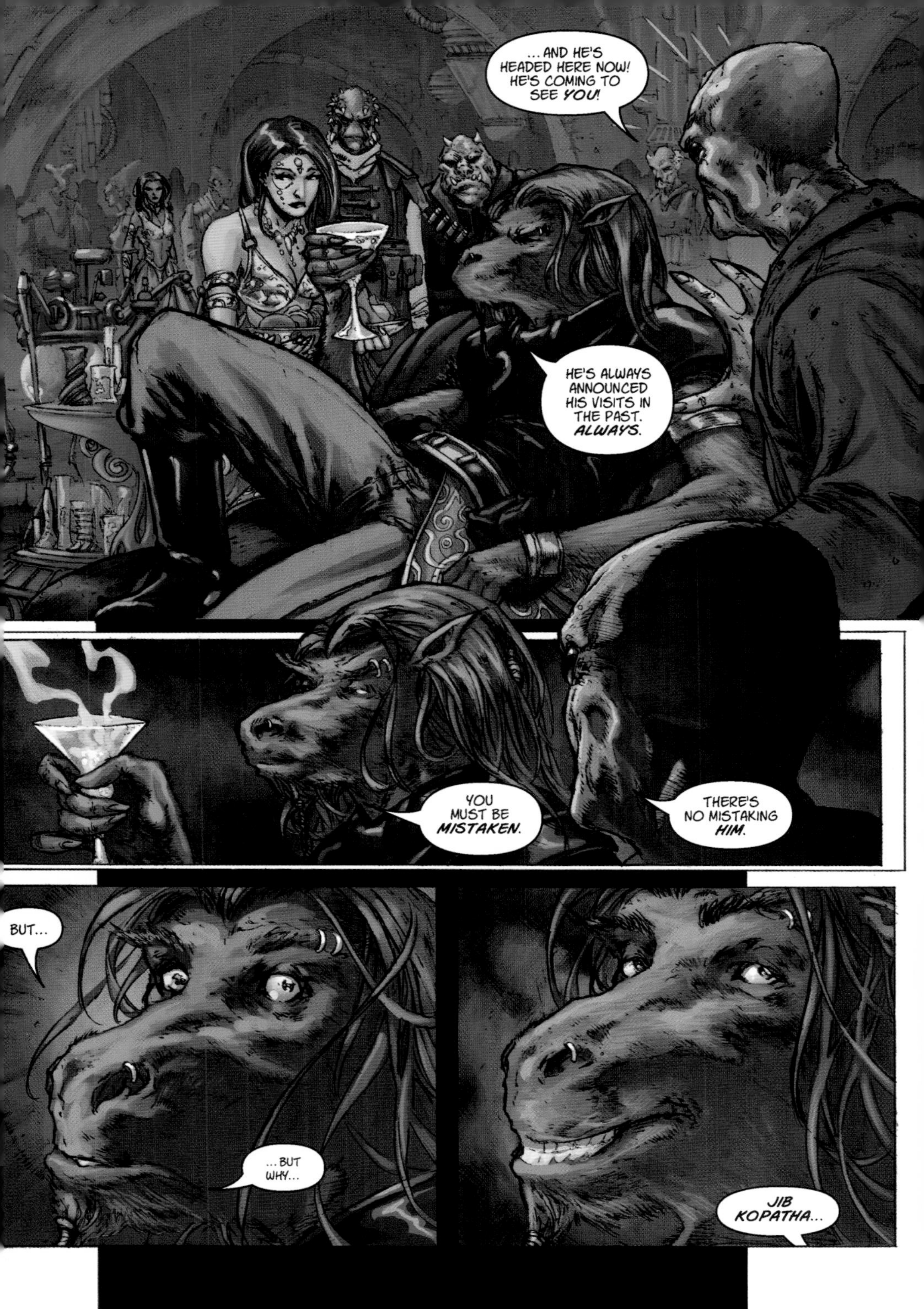
...AND HE'S HEADED HERE NOW! HE'S COMING TO SEE YOU!
HE'S ALWAYS ANNOUNCED HIS VISITS IN THE PAST. ALWAYS.
YOU MUST BE MISTAKEN.
THERE'S NO MISTAKING HIM.
BUT...
...BUT WHY...
JIB KOPATHA...

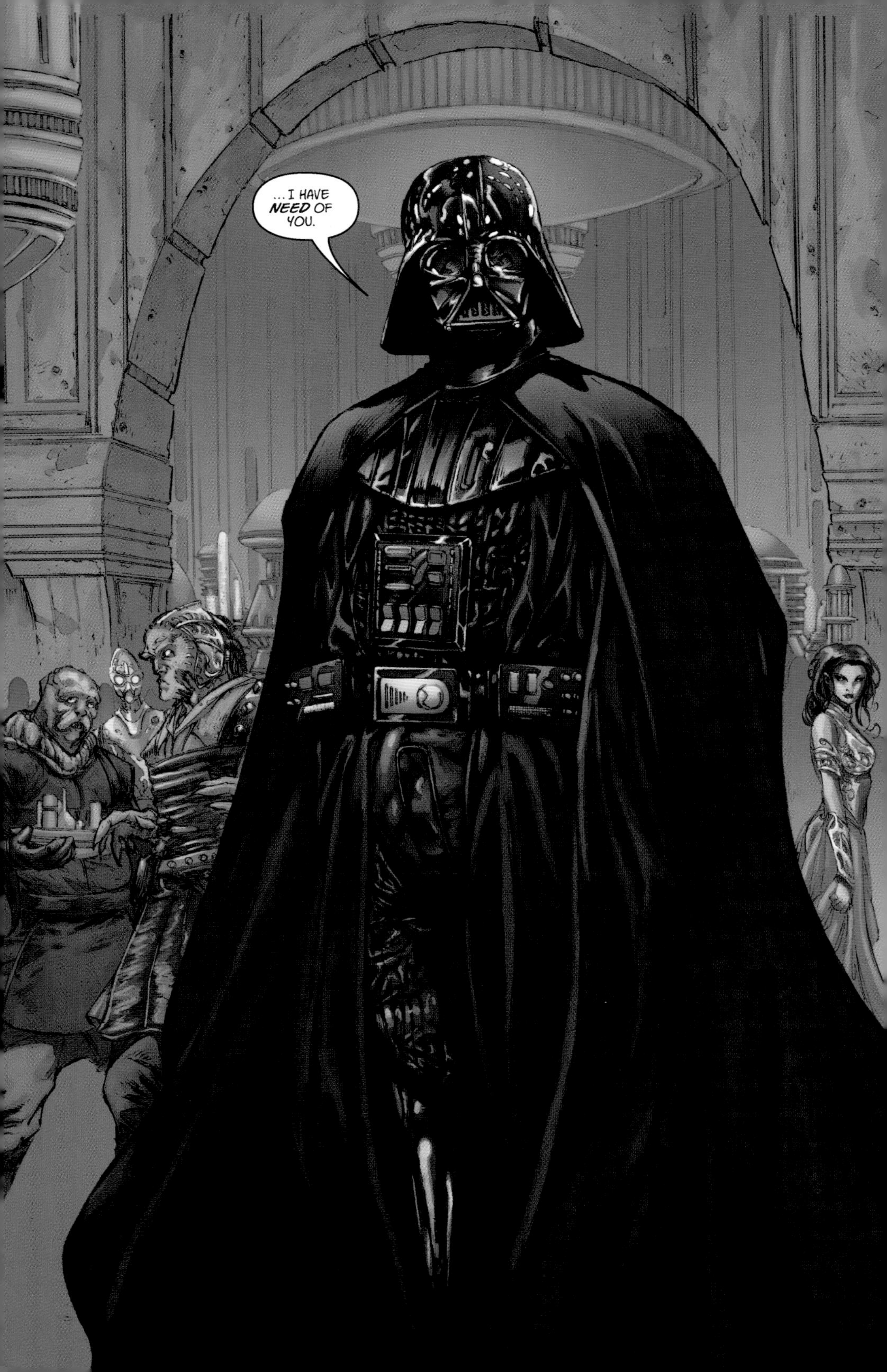
...I HAVE NEED OF YOU.

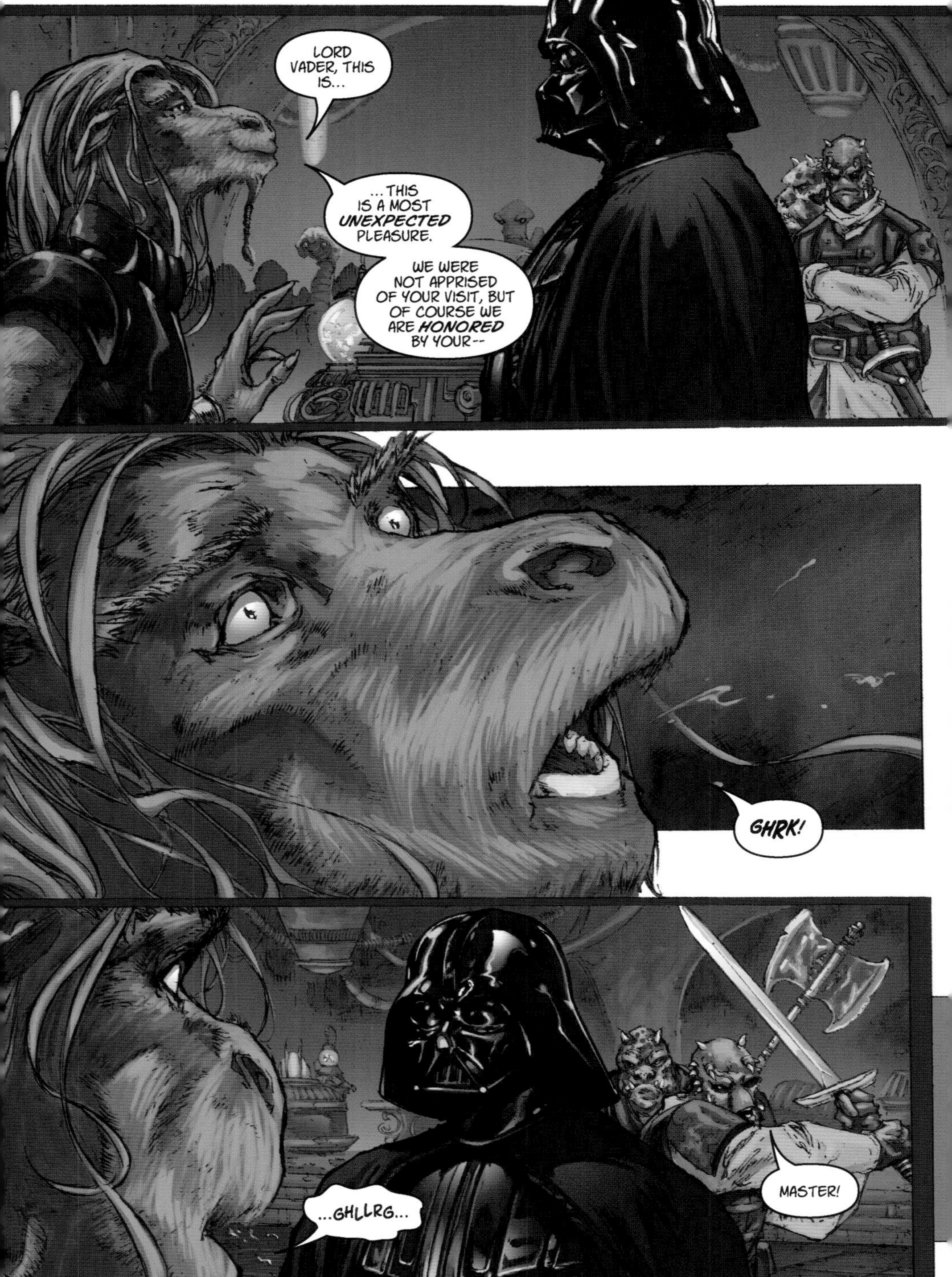
LORD VADER, THIS IS...
...THIS IS A MOST **UNEXPECTED** PLEASURE.
WE WERE NOT APPRISED OF YOUR VISIT, BUT OF COURSE WE ARE **HONORED** BY YOUR--
GHRK!
...GHLLRG...
MASTER!

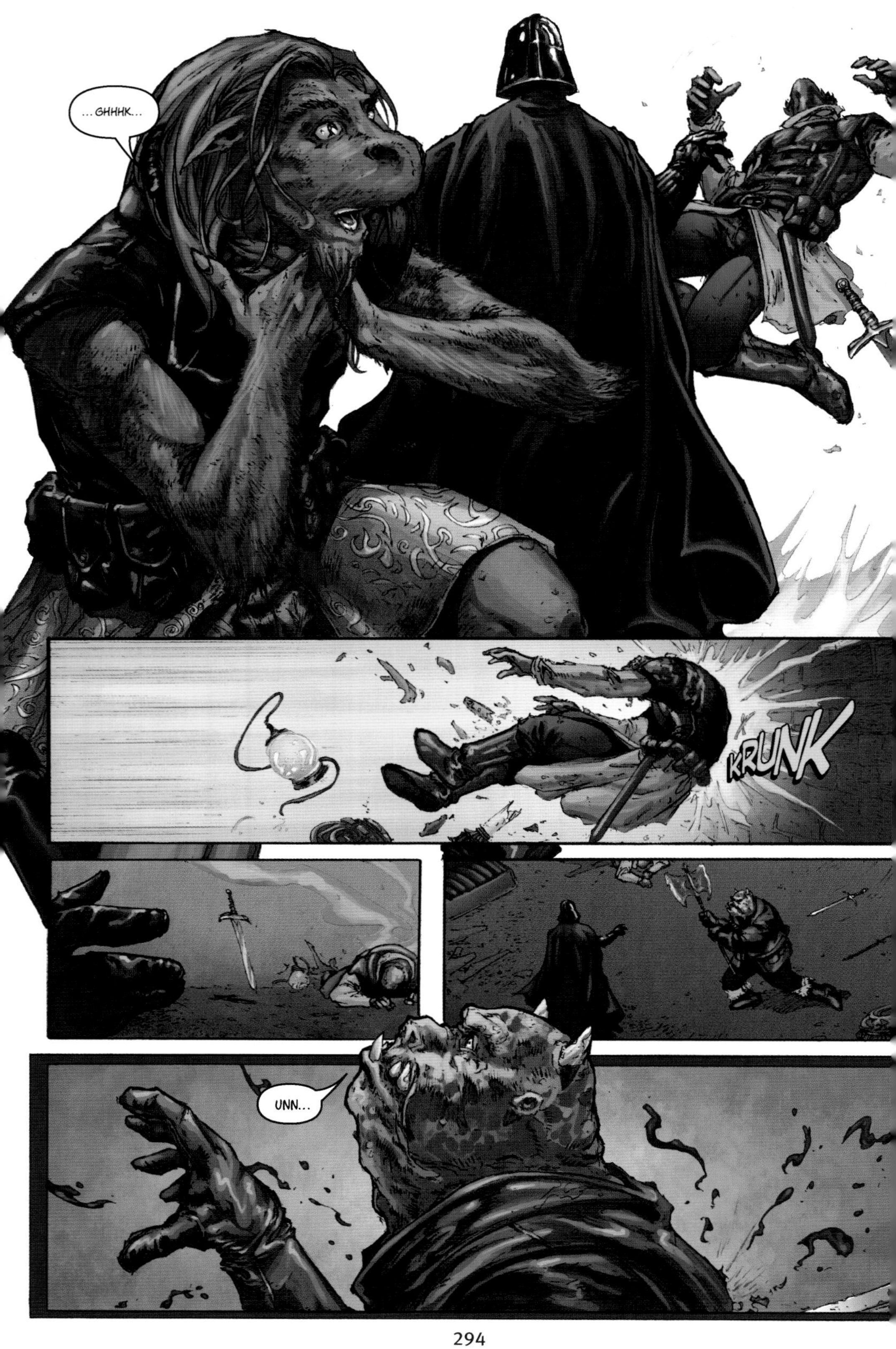

...GHHHK...
KRUNK
UNN...

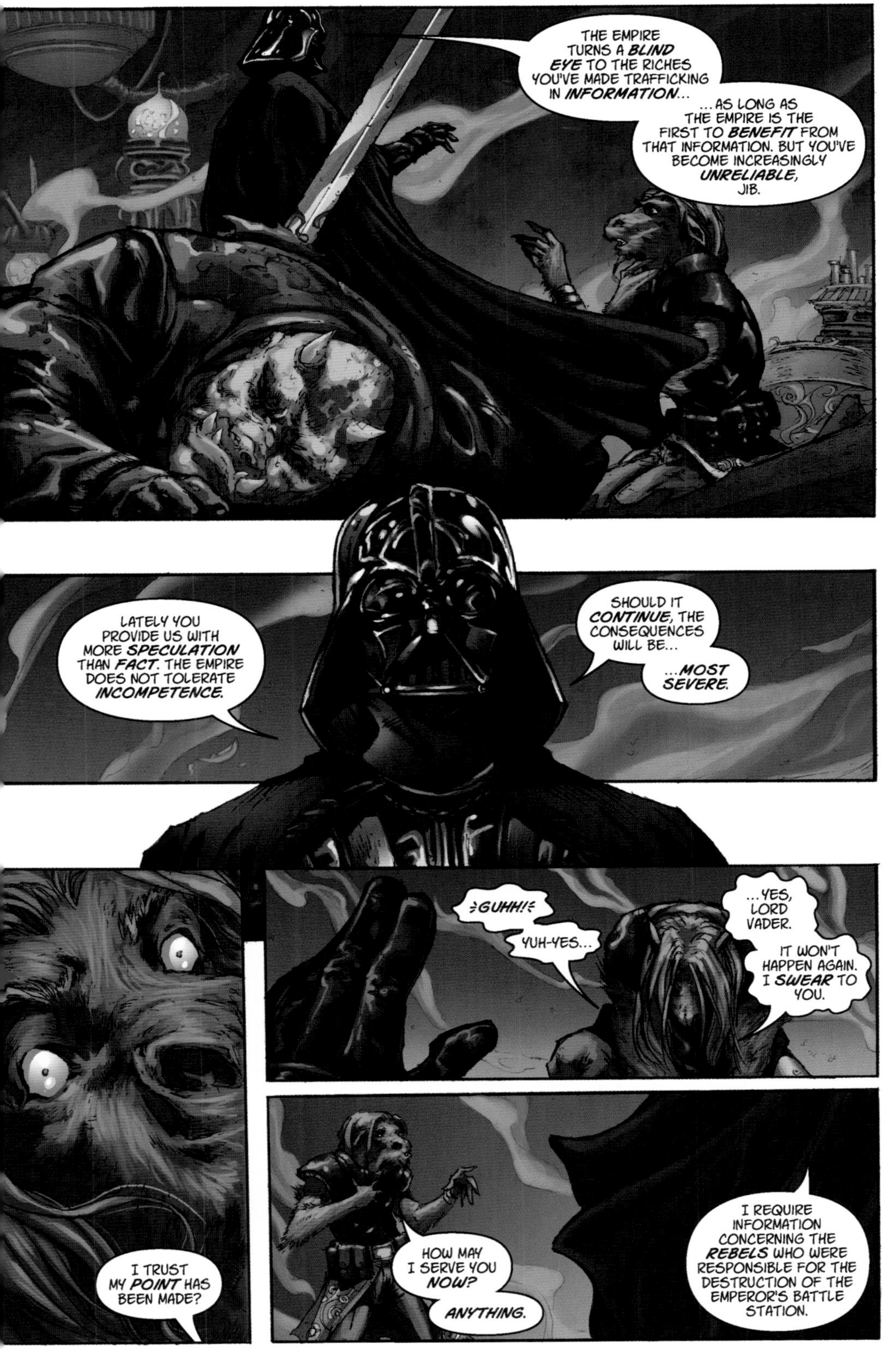
THE EMPIRE TURNS A BLIND EYE TO THE RICHES YOU'VE MADE TRAFFICKING IN INFORMATION...
...AS LONG AS THE EMPIRE IS THE FIRST TO BENEFIT FROM THAT INFORMATION. BUT YOU'VE BECOME INCREASINGLY UNRELIABLE, JIB.
LATELY YOU PROVIDE US WITH MORE SPECULATION THAN FACT. THE EMPIRE DOES NOT TOLERATE INCOMPETENCE.
SHOULD IT CONTINUE, THE CONSEQUENCES WILL BE...
...MOST SEVERE.
I TRUST MY POINT HAS BEEN MADE?
GUHH!
YUH-YES...
...YES, LORD VADER.
IT WON'T HAPPEN AGAIN. I SWEAR TO YOU.
HOW MAY I SERVE YOU NOW?
ANYTHING.
I REQUIRE INFORMATION CONCERNING THE REBELS WHO WERE RESPONSIBLE FOR THE DESTRUCTION OF THE EMPEROR'S BATTLE STATION.

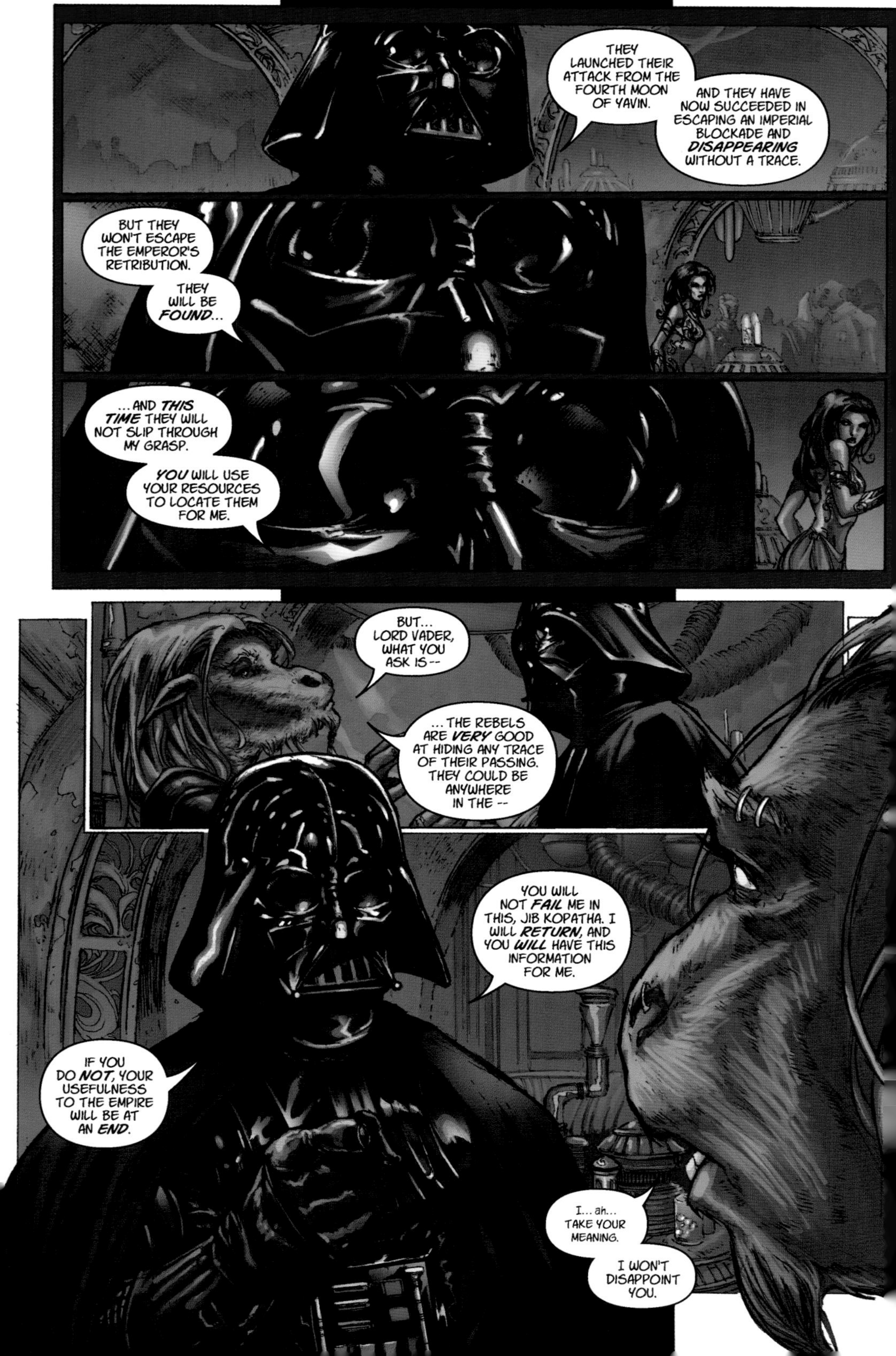
THEY LAUNCHED THEIR ATTACK FROM THE FOURTH MOON OF YAVIN.
AND THEY HAVE NOW SUCCEEDED IN ESCAPING AN IMPERIAL BLOCKADE AND *DISAPPEARING* WITHOUT A TRACE.
BUT THEY WON'T ESCAPE THE EMPEROR'S RETRIBUTION.
THEY WILL BE *FOUND*...
...AND *THIS TIME* THEY WILL NOT SLIP THROUGH MY GRASP.
YOU WILL USE YOUR RESOURCES TO LOCATE THEM FOR ME.
BUT... LORD VADER, WHAT YOU ASK IS--
...THE REBELS ARE *VERY* GOOD AT HIDING ANY TRACE OF THEIR PASSING. THEY COULD BE ANYWHERE IN THE--
YOU WILL NOT *FAIL* ME IN THIS, JIB KOPATHA. I WILL *RETURN*, AND YOU *WILL* HAVE THIS INFORMATION FOR ME.
IF YOU DO *NOT*, YOUR USEFULNESS TO THE EMPIRE WILL BE AT AN *END*.
I... ah... TAKE YOUR MEANING.
I WON'T DISAPPOINT YOU.

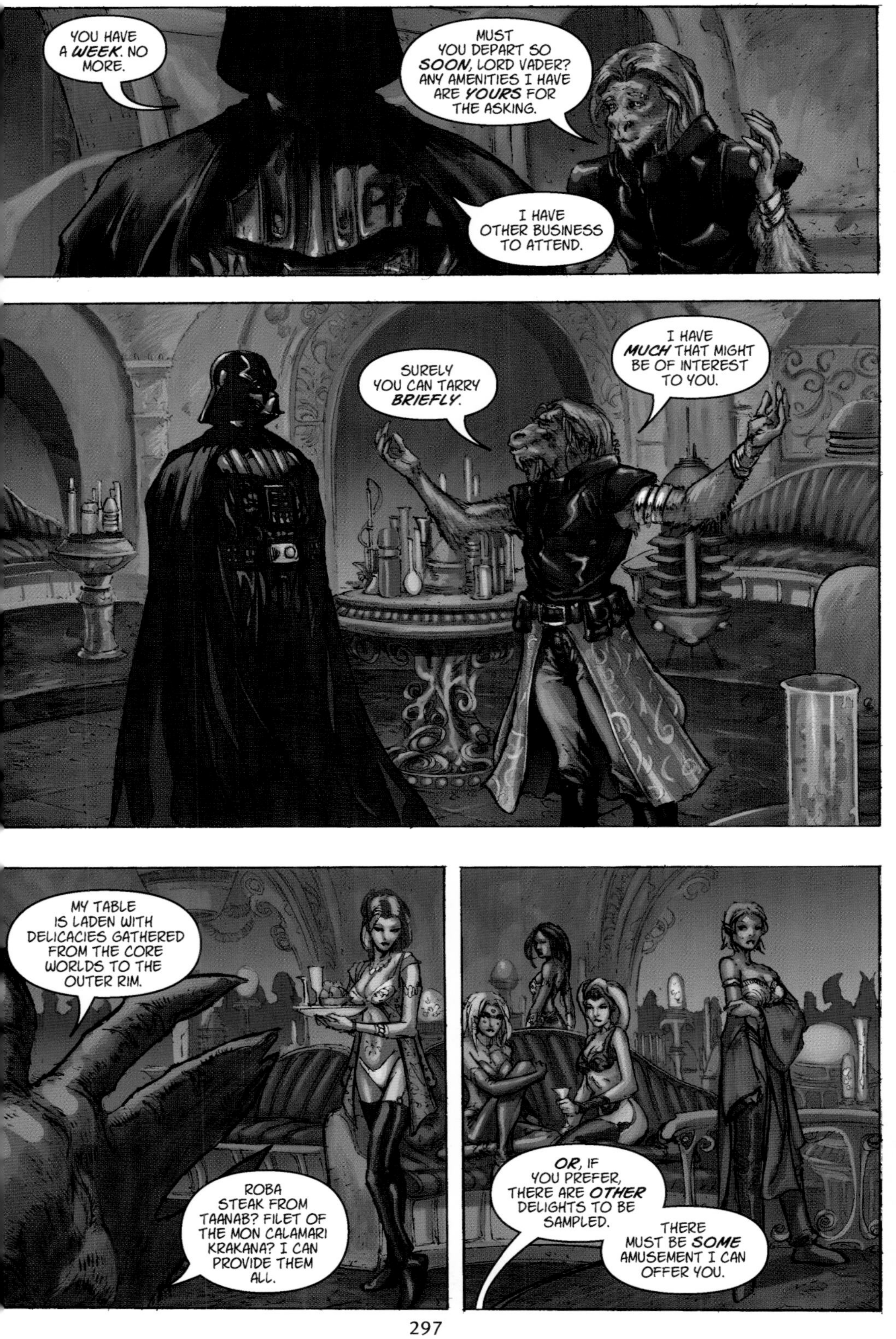
YOU HAVE A WEEK. NO MORE.
MUST YOU DEPART SO SOON, LORD VADER? ANY AMENITIES I HAVE ARE YOURS FOR THE ASKING.
I HAVE OTHER BUSINESS TO ATTEND.
SURELY YOU CAN TARRY BRIEFLY.
I HAVE MUCH THAT MIGHT BE OF INTEREST TO YOU.
MY TABLE IS LADEN WITH DELICACIES GATHERED FROM THE CORE WORLDS TO THE OUTER RIM.
ROBA STEAK FROM TAANAB? FILET OF THE MON CALAMARI KRAKANA? I CAN PROVIDE THEM ALL.
OR, IF YOU PREFER, THERE ARE OTHER DELIGHTS TO BE SAMPLED.
THERE MUST BE SOME AMUSEMENT I CAN OFFER YOU.

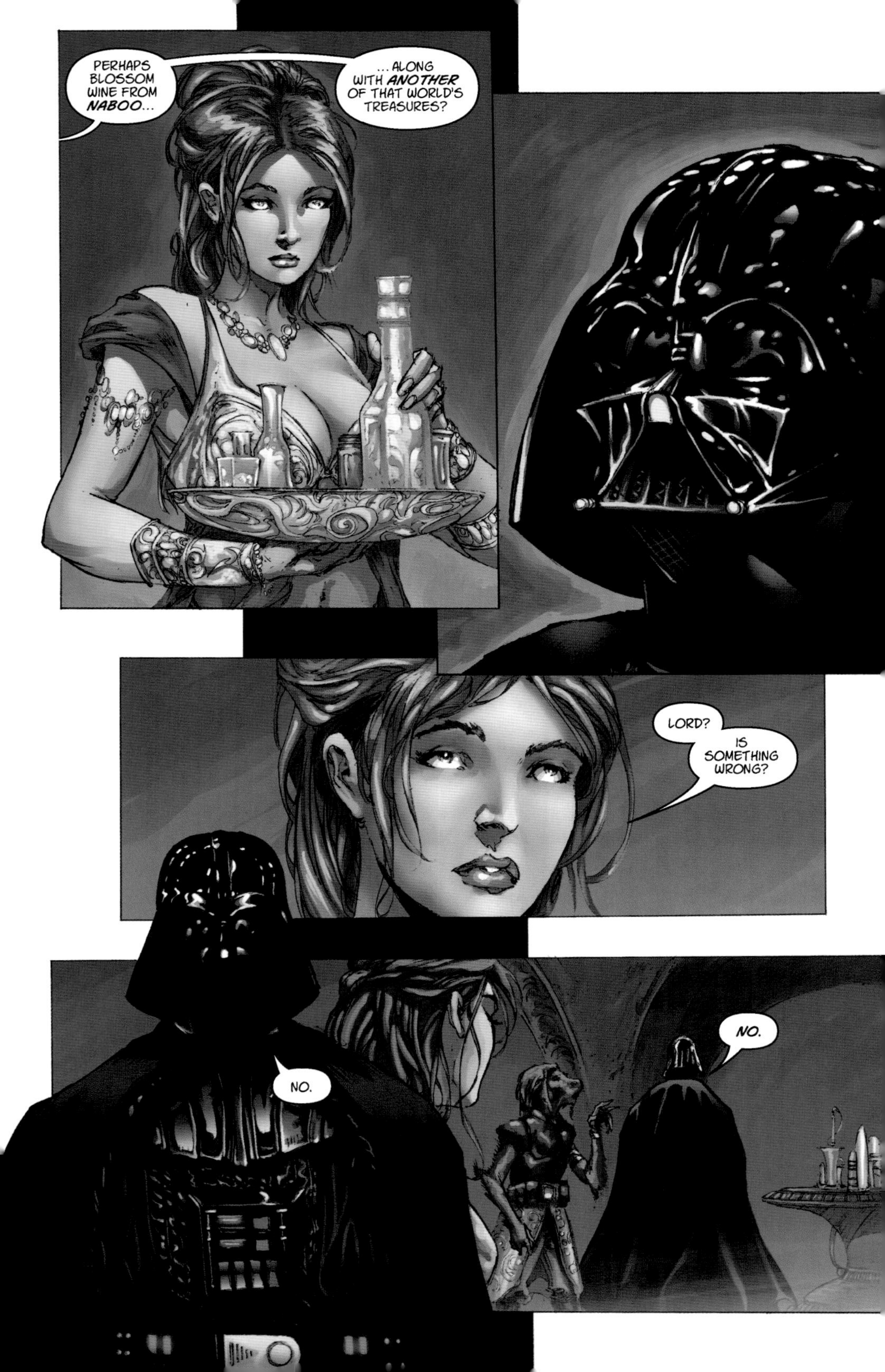
PERHAPS BLOSSOM WINE FROM NABOO...
...ALONG WITH ANOTHER OF THAT WORLD'S TREASURES?
LORD?
IS SOMETHING WRONG?
NO.
NO.

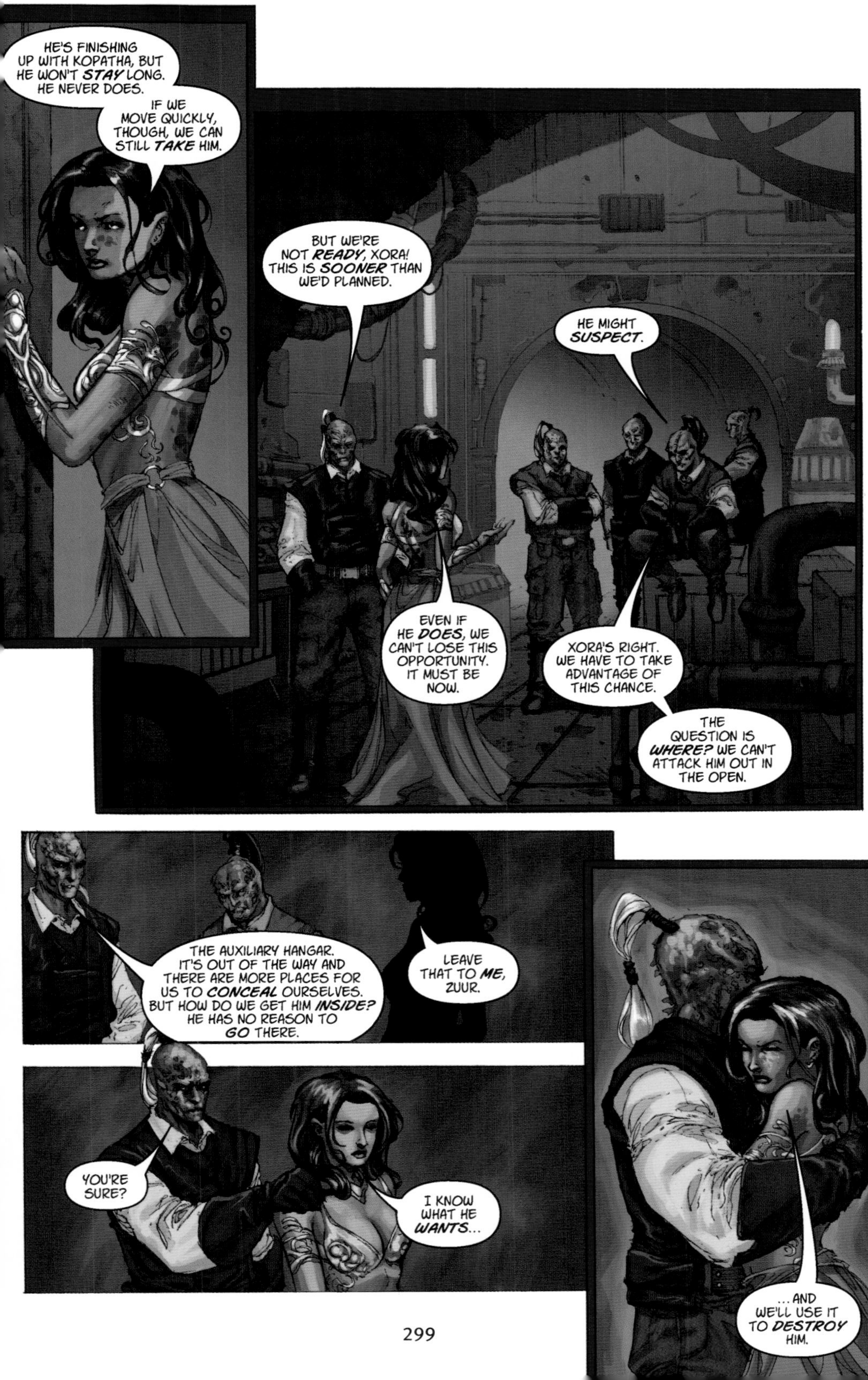
HE'S FINISHING UP WITH KOPATHA, BUT HE WON'T STAY LONG. HE NEVER DOES.
IF WE MOVE QUICKLY, THOUGH, WE CAN STILL TAKE HIM.
BUT WE'RE NOT READY, XORA! THIS IS SOONER THAN WE'D PLANNED.
HE MIGHT SUSPECT.
EVEN IF HE DOES, WE CAN'T LOSE THIS OPPORTUNITY. IT MUST BE NOW.
XORA'S RIGHT. WE HAVE TO TAKE ADVANTAGE OF THIS CHANCE.
THE QUESTION IS WHERE? WE CAN'T ATTACK HIM OUT IN THE OPEN.
THE AUXILIARY HANGAR. IT'S OUT OF THE WAY AND THERE ARE MORE PLACES FOR US TO CONCEAL OURSELVES. BUT HOW DO WE GET HIM INSIDE? HE HAS NO REASON TO GO THERE.
LEAVE THAT TO ME, ZUUR.
YOU'RE SURE?
I KNOW WHAT HE WANTS...
...AND WE'LL USE IT TO DESTROY HIM.

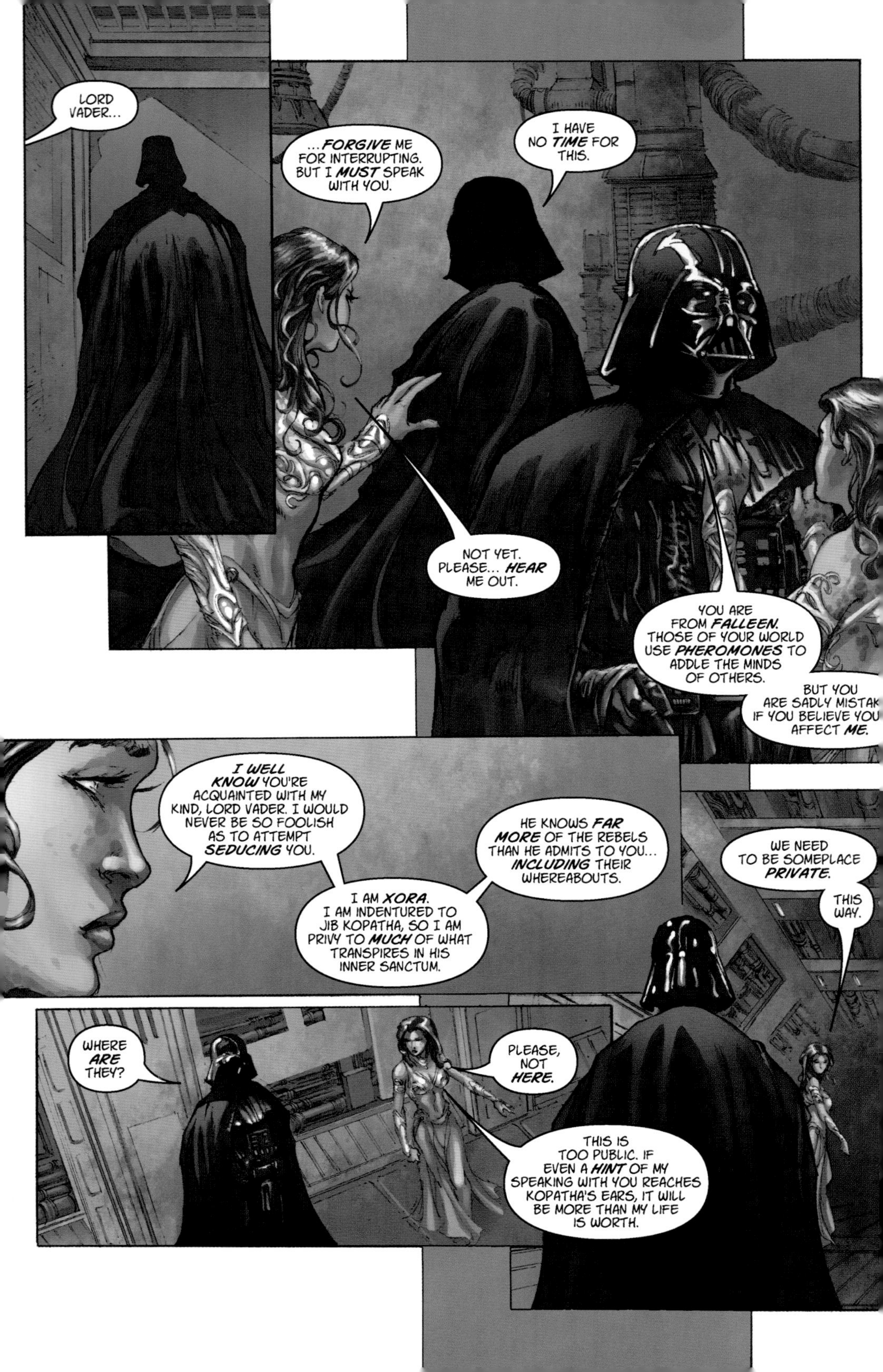
LORD VADER...
...FORGIVE ME FOR INTERRUPTING. BUT I MUST SPEAK WITH YOU.
I HAVE NO TIME FOR THIS.
NOT YET. PLEASE... HEAR ME OUT.
YOU ARE FROM FALLEEN. THOSE OF YOUR WORLD USE PHEROMONES TO ADDLE THE MINDS OF OTHERS.
BUT YOU ARE SADLY MISTAK IF YOU BELIEVE YOU AFFECT ME.
I WELL KNOW YOU'RE ACQUAINTED WITH MY KIND, LORD VADER. I WOULD NEVER BE SO FOOLISH AS TO ATTEMPT SEDUCING YOU.
I AM XORA. I AM INDENTURED TO JIB KOPATHA, SO I AM PRIVY TO MUCH OF WHAT TRANSPIRES IN HIS INNER SANCTUM.
HE KNOWS FAR MORE OF THE REBELS THAN HE ADMITS TO YOU... INCLUDING THEIR WHEREABOUTS.
WE NEED TO BE SOMEPLACE PRIVATE.
THIS WAY.
WHERE ARE THEY?
PLEASE, NOT HERE.
THIS IS TOO PUBLIC. IF EVEN A HINT OF MY SPEAKING WITH YOU REACHES KOPATHA'S EARS, IT WILL BE MORE THAN MY LIFE IS WORTH.

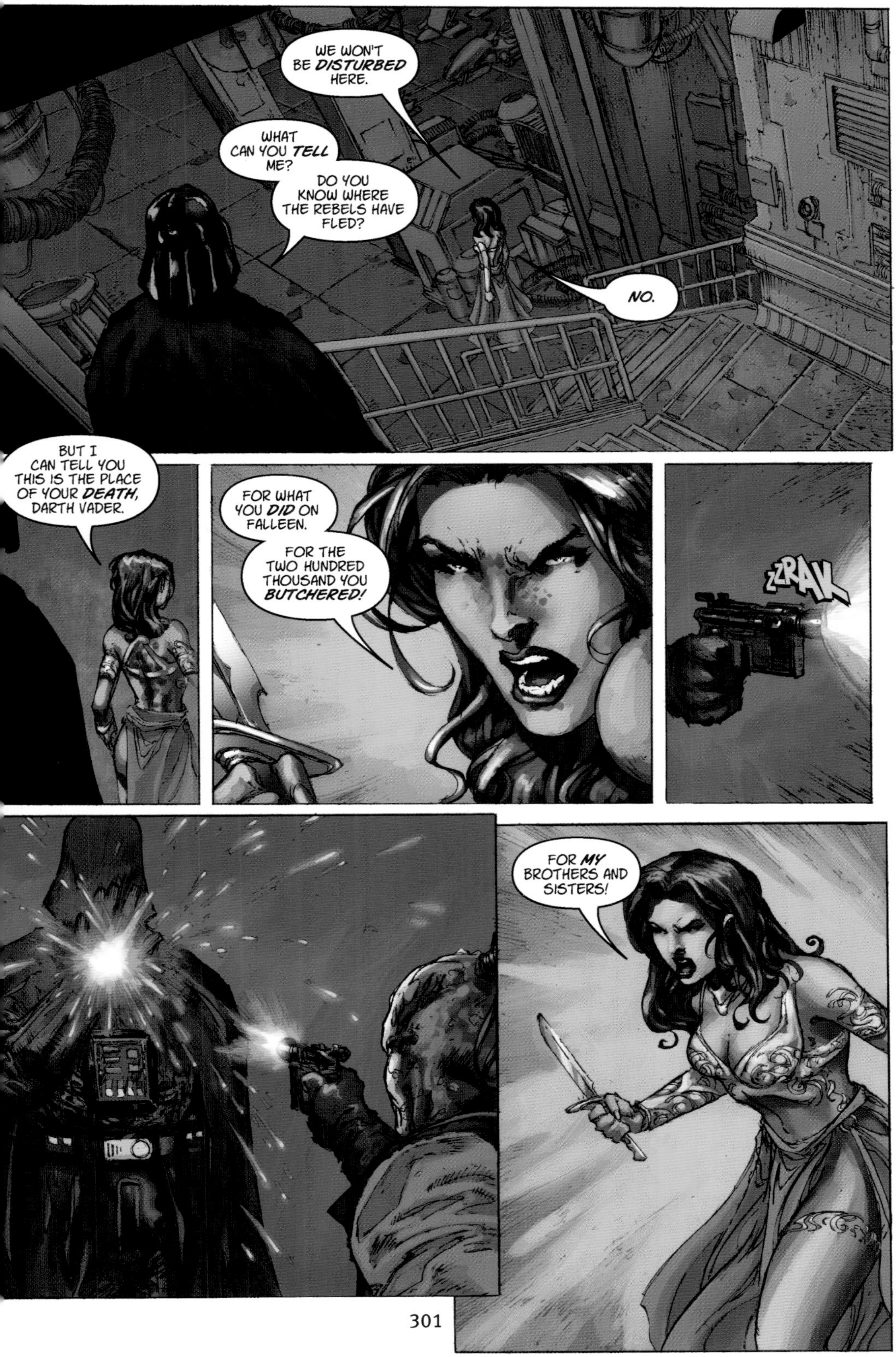
WE WON'T BE DISTURBED HERE.
WHAT CAN YOU TELL ME?
DO YOU KNOW WHERE THE REBELS HAVE FLED?
NO.
BUT I CAN TELL YOU THIS IS THE PLACE OF YOUR DEATH, DARTH VADER.
FOR WHAT YOU DID ON FALLEEN.
FOR THE TWO HUNDRED THOUSAND YOU BUTCHERED!
ZZRAK
FOR MY BROTHERS AND SISTERS!

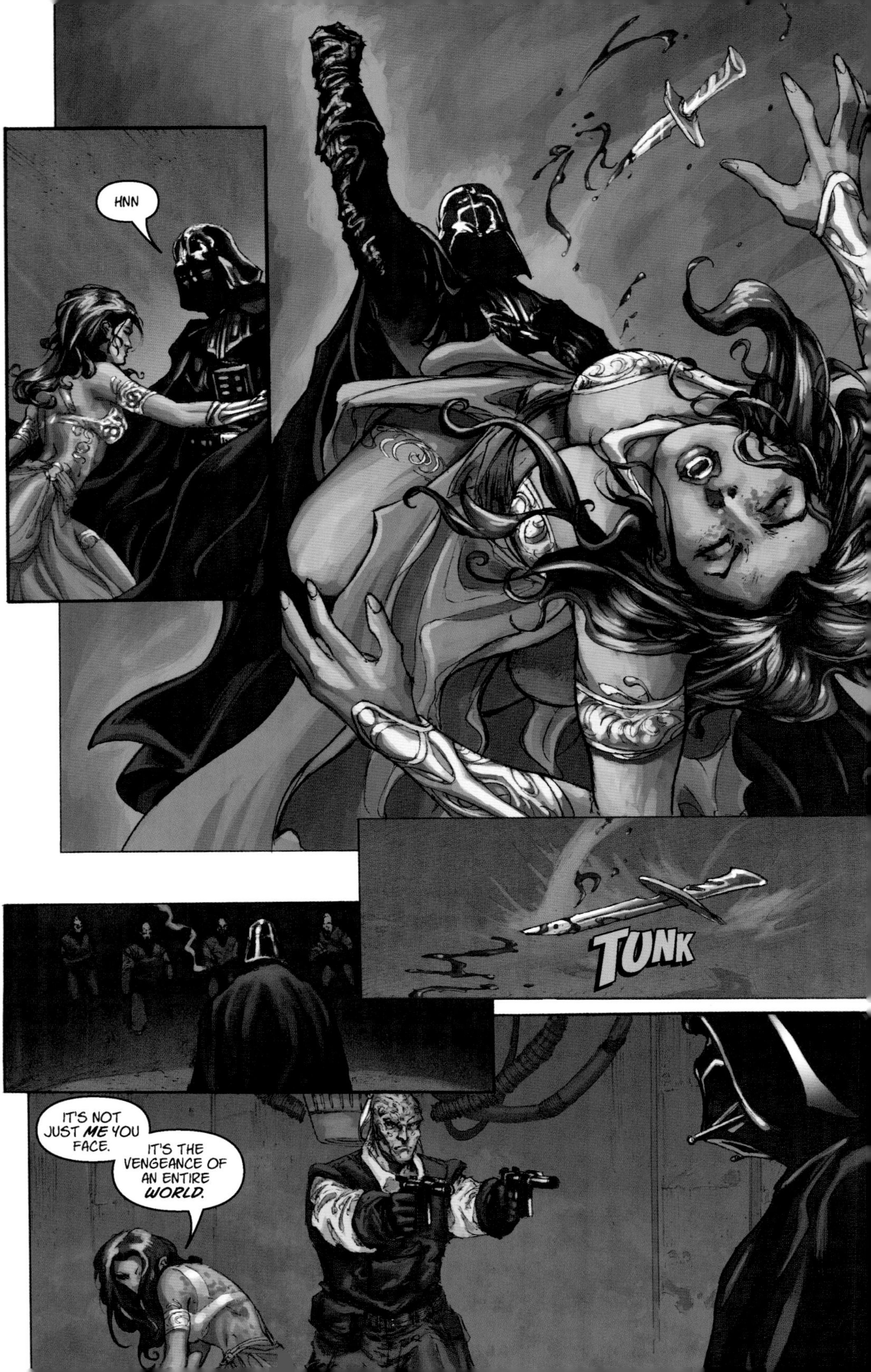
HNN
TUNK
IT'S NOT JUST *ME* YOU FACE.
IT'S THE VENGEANCE OF AN ENTIRE *WORLD*.

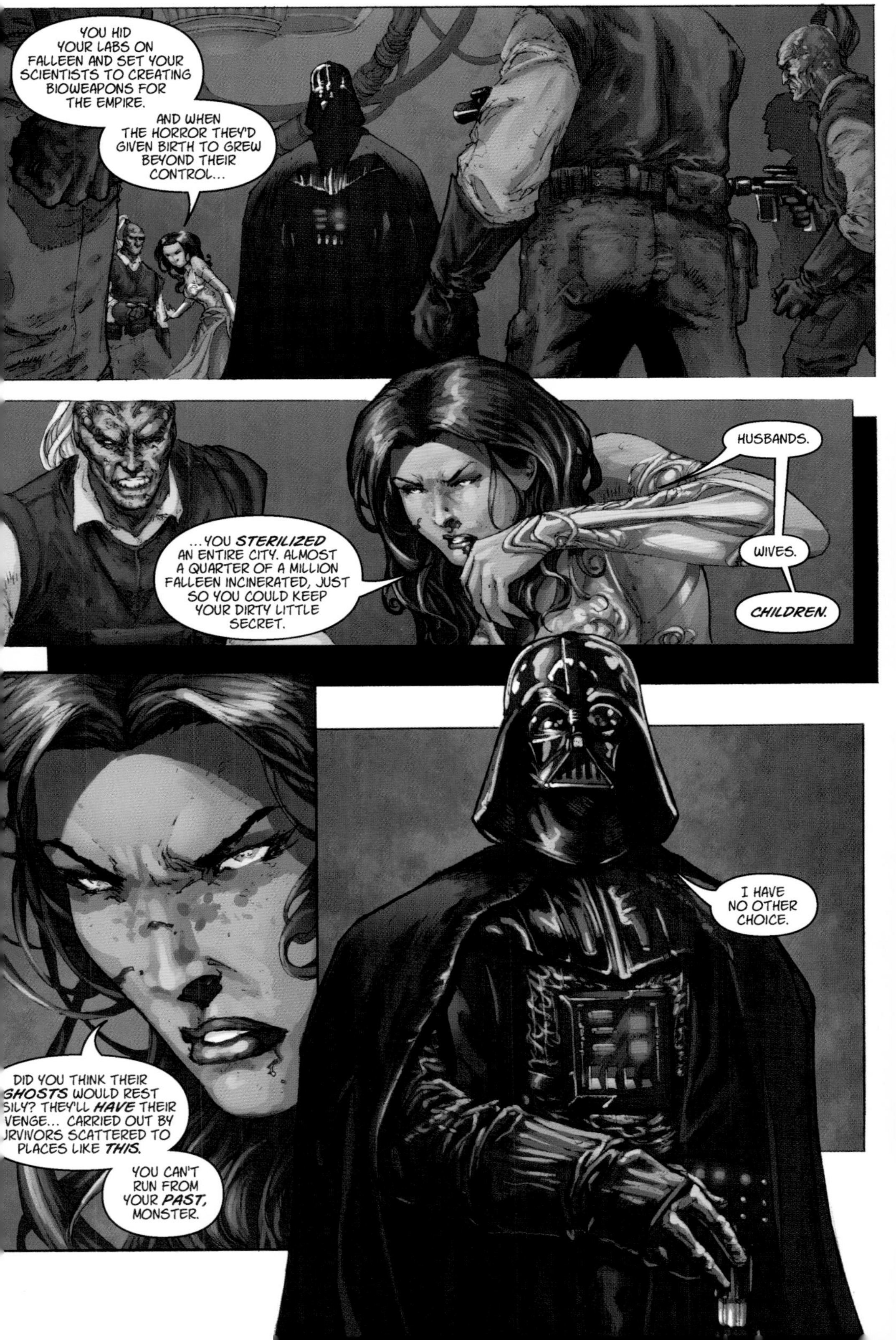
YOU HID YOUR LABS ON FALLEEN AND SET YOUR SCIENTISTS TO CREATING BIOWEAPONS FOR THE EMPIRE.
AND WHEN THE HORROR THEY'D GIVEN BIRTH TO GREW BEYOND THEIR CONTROL...
...YOU STERILIZED AN ENTIRE CITY. ALMOST A QUARTER OF A MILLION FALLEEN INCINERATED, JUST SO YOU COULD KEEP YOUR DIRTY LITTLE SECRET.
HUSBANDS.
WIVES.
CHILDREN.
I HAVE NO OTHER CHOICE.
DID YOU THINK THEIR GHOSTS WOULD REST SILY? THEY'LL HAVE THEIR VENGE... CARRIED OUT BY RVIVORS SCATTERED TO PLACES LIKE THIS.
YOU CAN'T RUN FROM YOUR PAST, MONSTER.

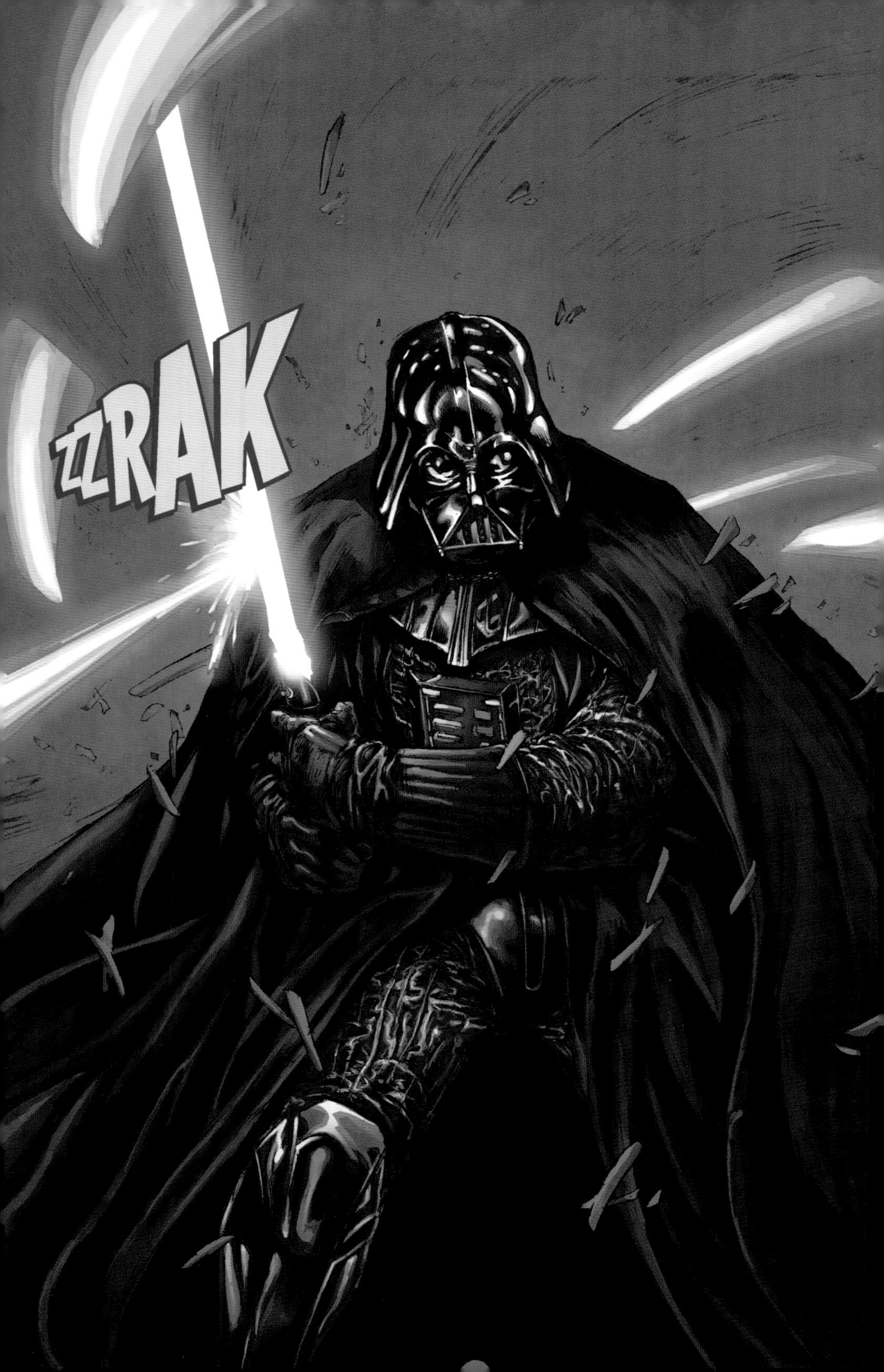
ZZRAK

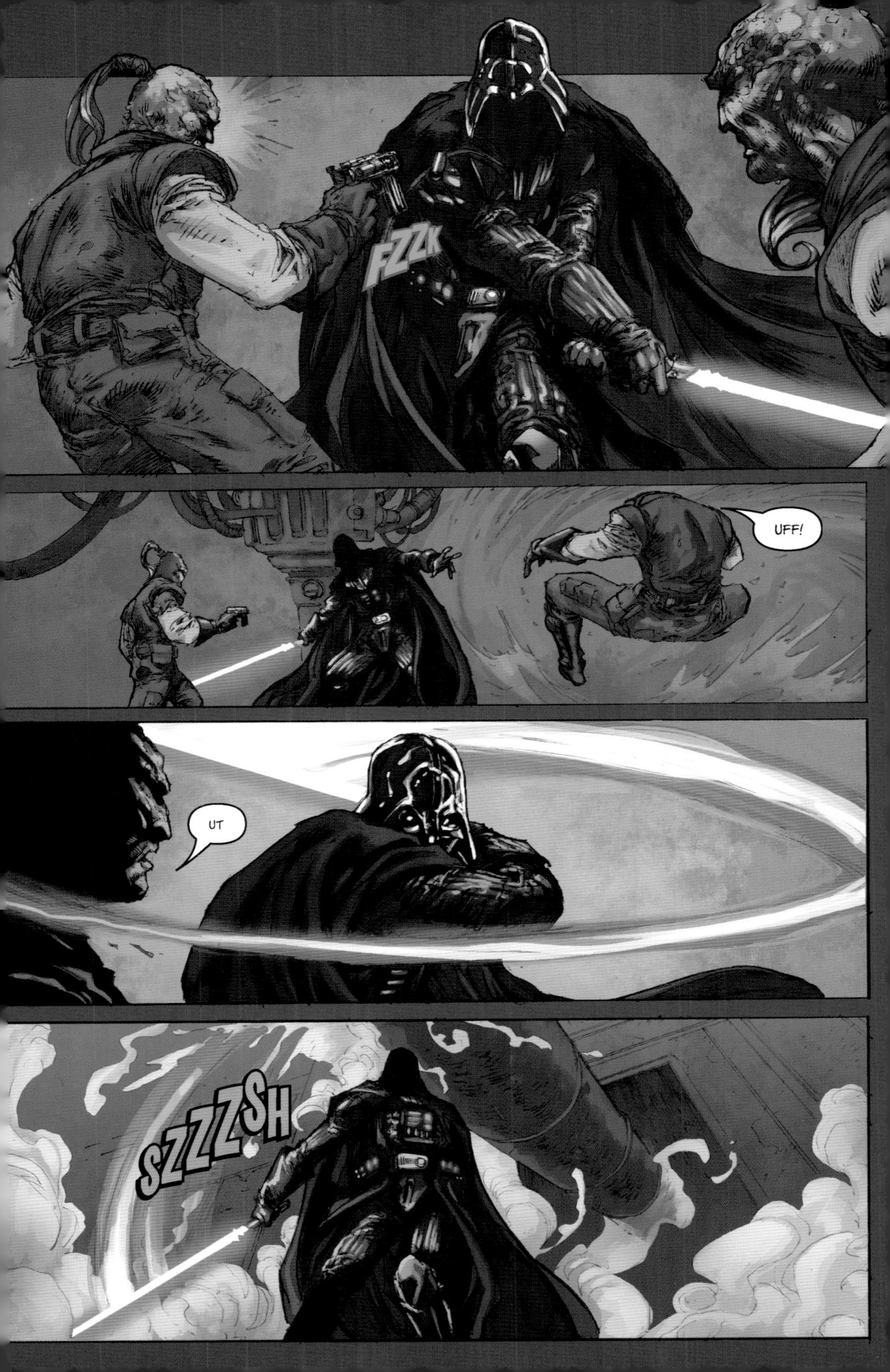
FZZK
UFF!
UT
SZZZSH

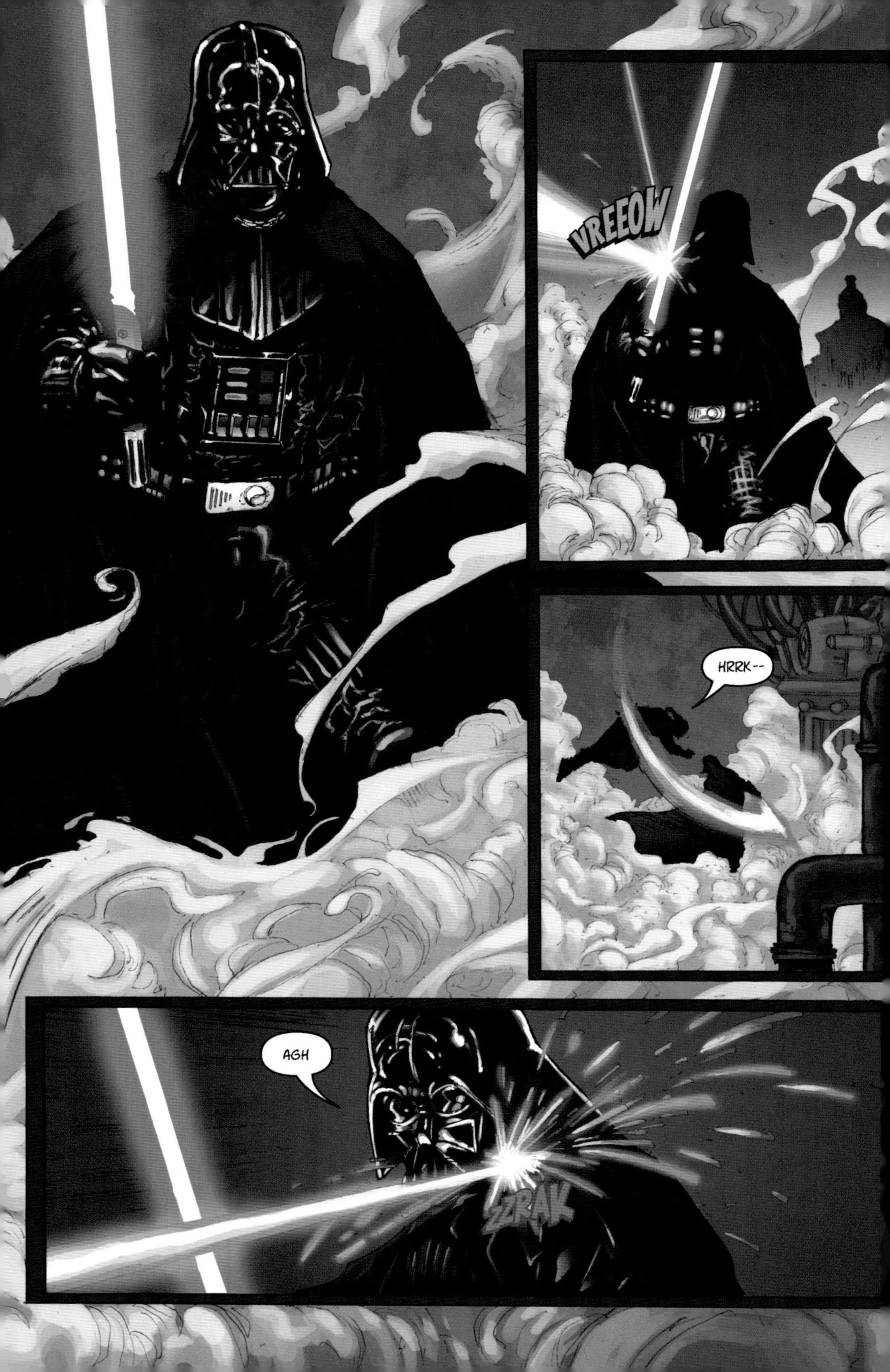
VREEOW
HRRK--
AGH
SZRAK

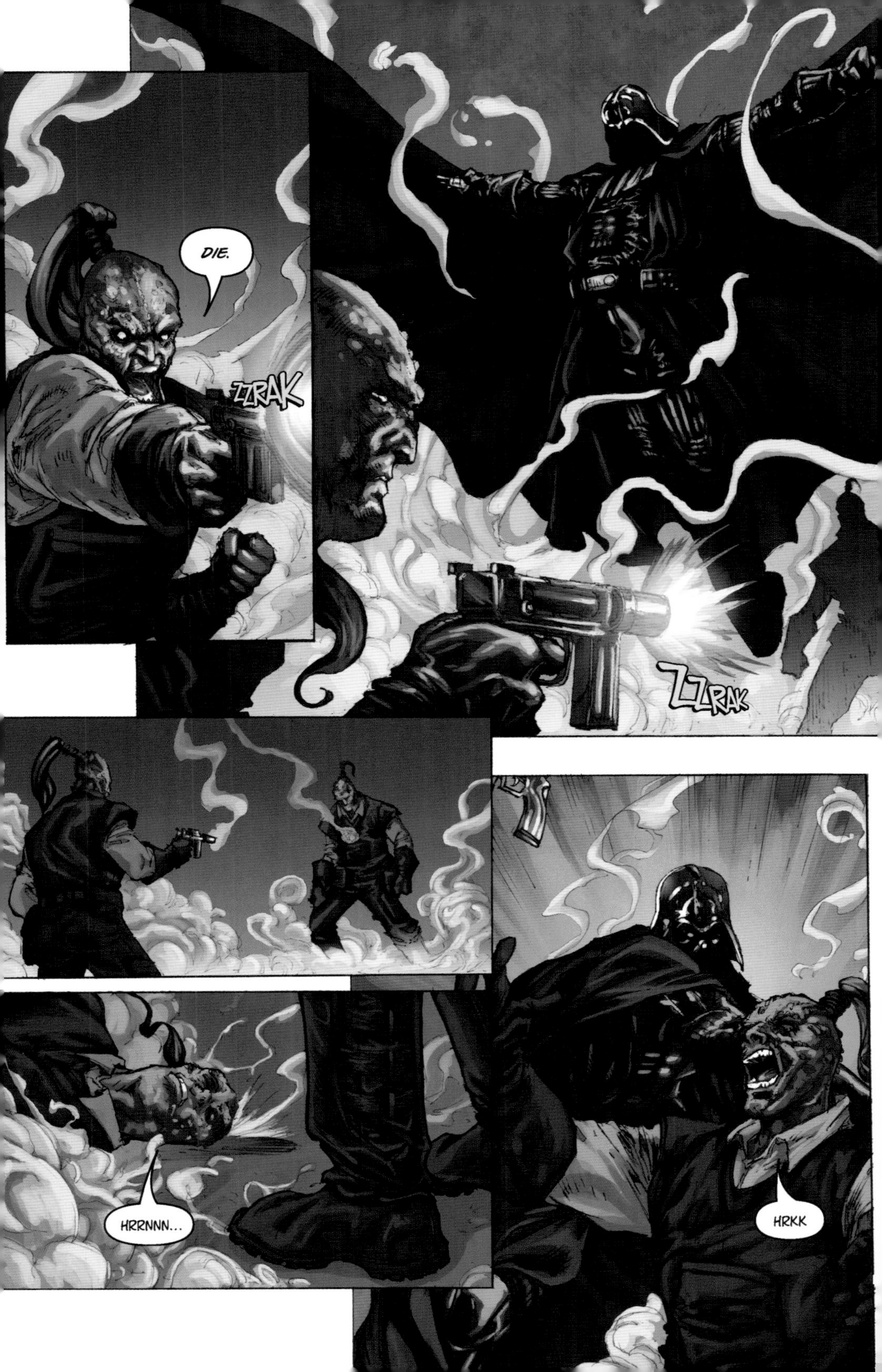
DIE.
ZZRAK
ZZRAK
HRRNNN...
HRKK

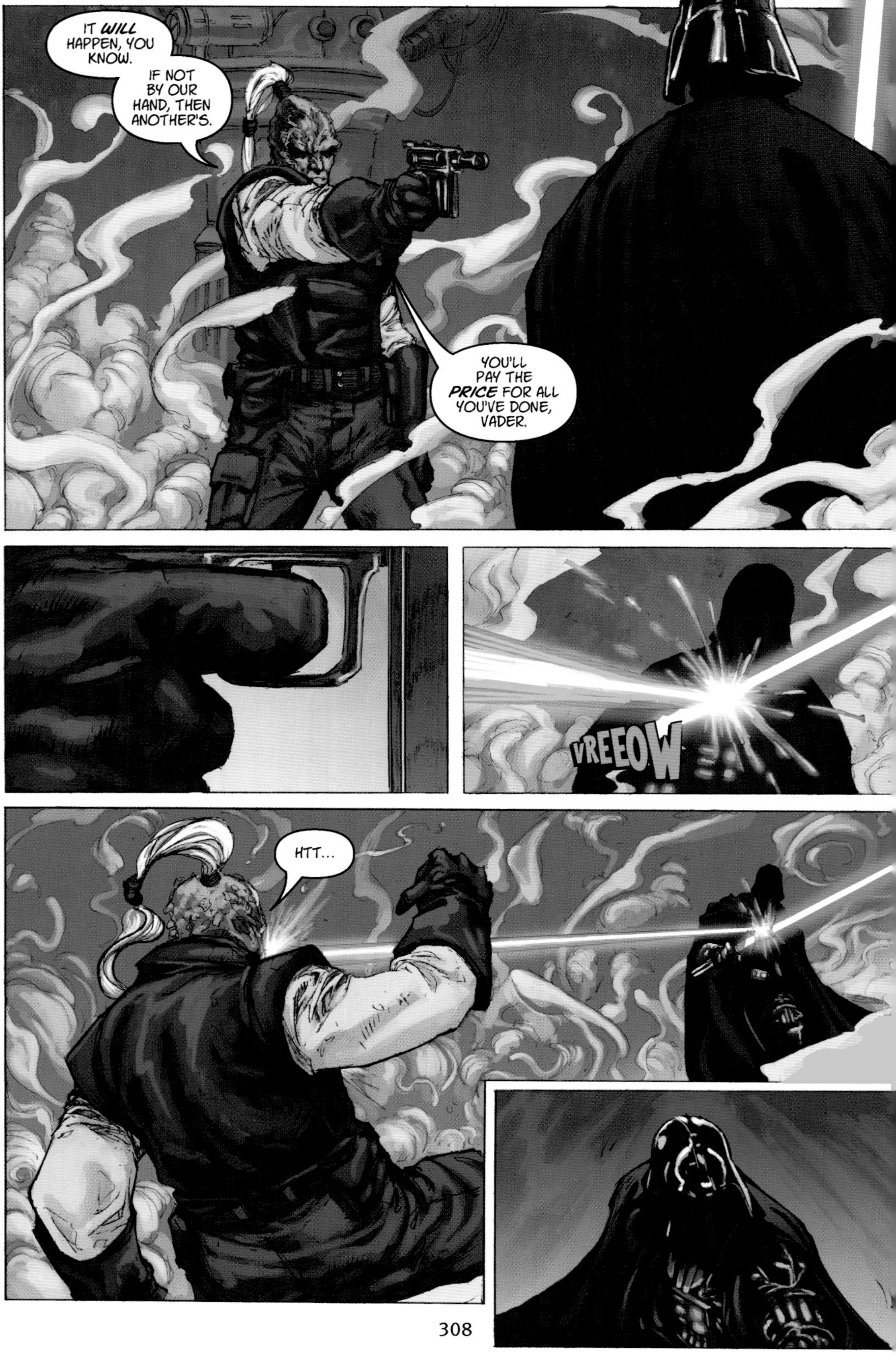

IT WILL HAPPEN, YOU KNOW.
IF NOT BY OUR HAND, THEN ANOTHER'S.
YOU'LL PAY THE PRICE FOR ALL YOU'VE DONE, VADER.
VREEOW
HTT...

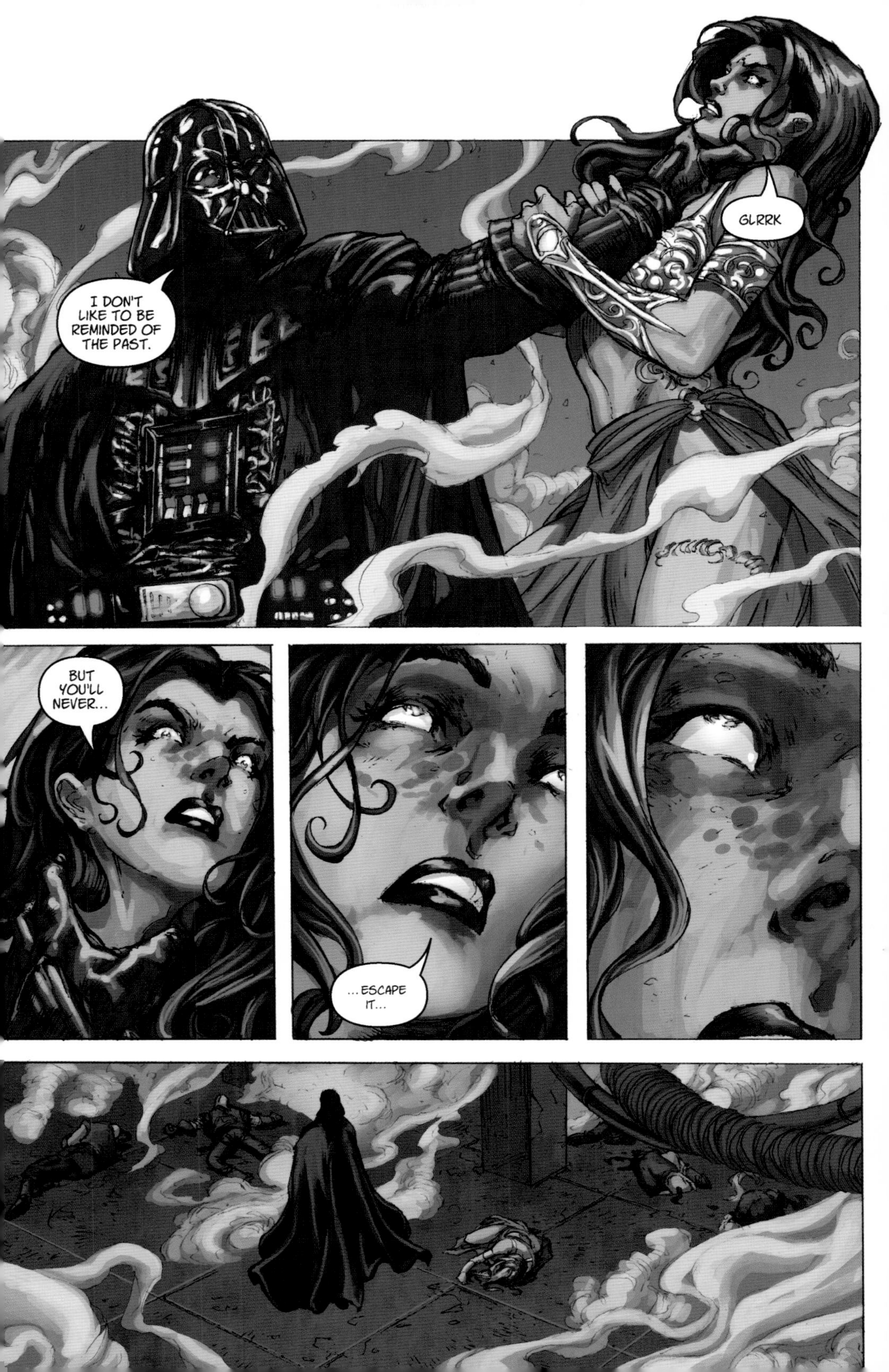
GLRRK
I DON'T LIKE TO BE REMINDED OF THE PAST.
BUT YOU'LL NEVER...
...ESCAPE IT...

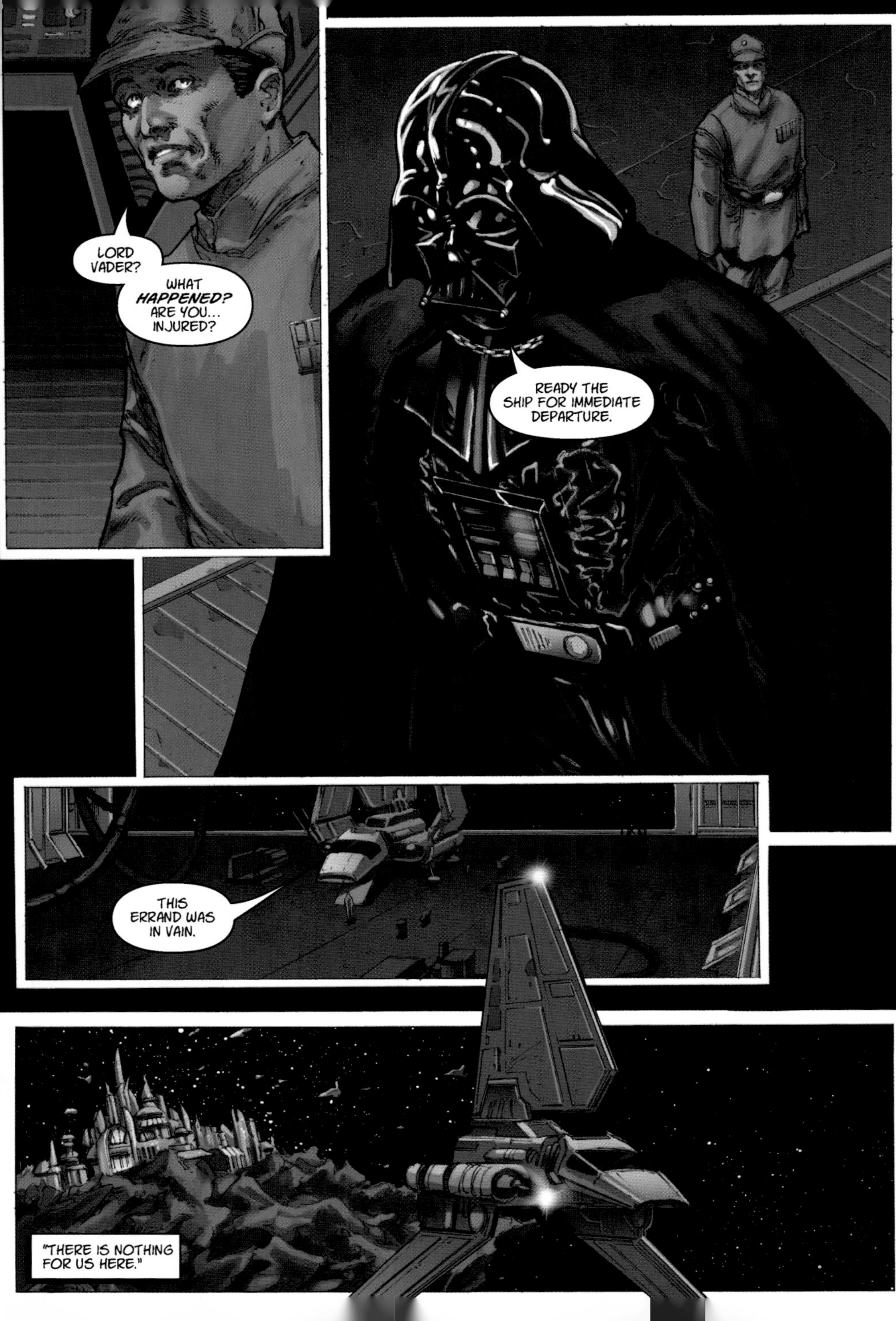
LORD VADER?
WHAT HAPPENED? ARE YOU... INJURED?
READY THE SHIP FOR IMMEDIATE DEPARTURE.
THIS ERRAND WAS IN VAIN.
"THERE IS NOTHING FOR US HERE."

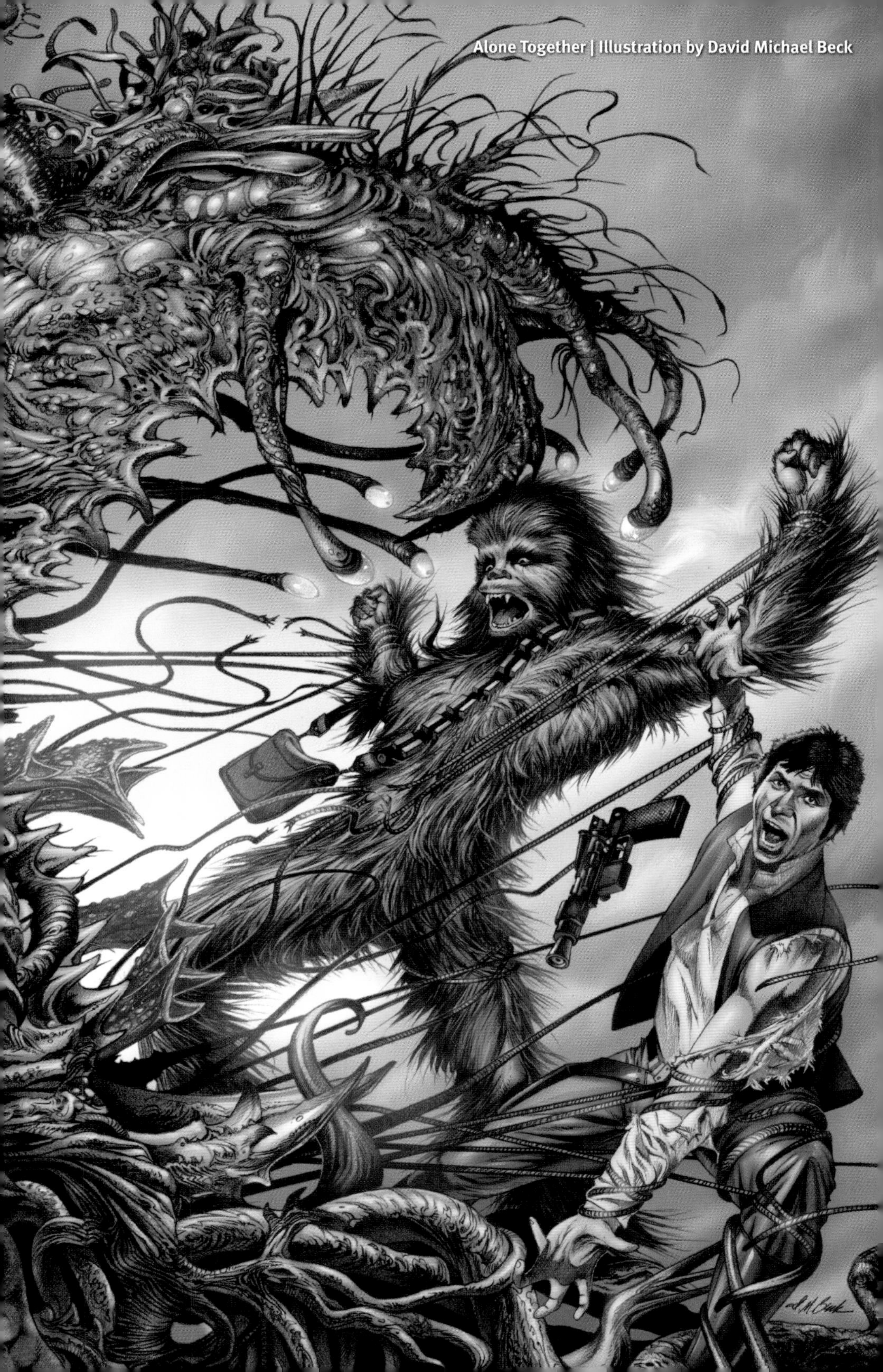

Alone Together | Illustration by David Michael Beck

APPROXIMATELY SIX MONTHS AFTER THE BATTLE
OF YAVIN . . .

script by Welles Hartley
pencils by Adriana Melo
colors by Michael Atiyeh
lettering by Michael David Thomas

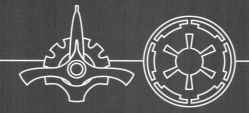

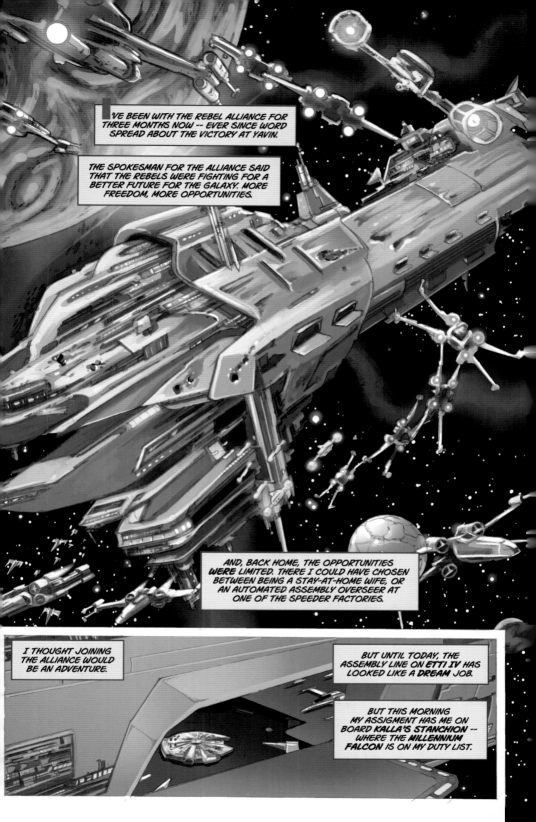

I'VE BEEN WITH THE REBEL ALLIANCE FOR THREE MONTHS NOW -- EVER SINCE WORD SPREAD ABOUT THE VICTORY AT YAVIN.

THE SPOKESMAN FOR THE ALLIANCE SAID THAT THE REBELS WERE FIGHTING FOR A BETTER FUTURE FOR THE GALAXY. MORE FREEDOM, MORE OPPORTUNITIES.

AND, BACK HOME, THE OPPORTUNITIES WERE LIMITED. THERE I COULD HAVE CHOSEN BETWEEN BEING A STAY-AT-HOME WIFE, OR AN AUTOMATED ASSEMBLY OVERSEER AT ONE OF THE SPEEDER FACTORIES.

I THOUGHT JOINING THE ALLIANCE WOULD BE AN ADVENTURE.

BUT UNTIL TODAY, THE ASSEMBLY LINE ON *ETTI IV* HAS LOOKED LIKE A *DREAM JOB.*

BUT THIS MORNING MY ASSIGMENT HAS ME ON BOARD *KALLA'S STANCHION* -- WHERE THE *MILLENNIUM FALCON* IS ON MY DUTY LIST.

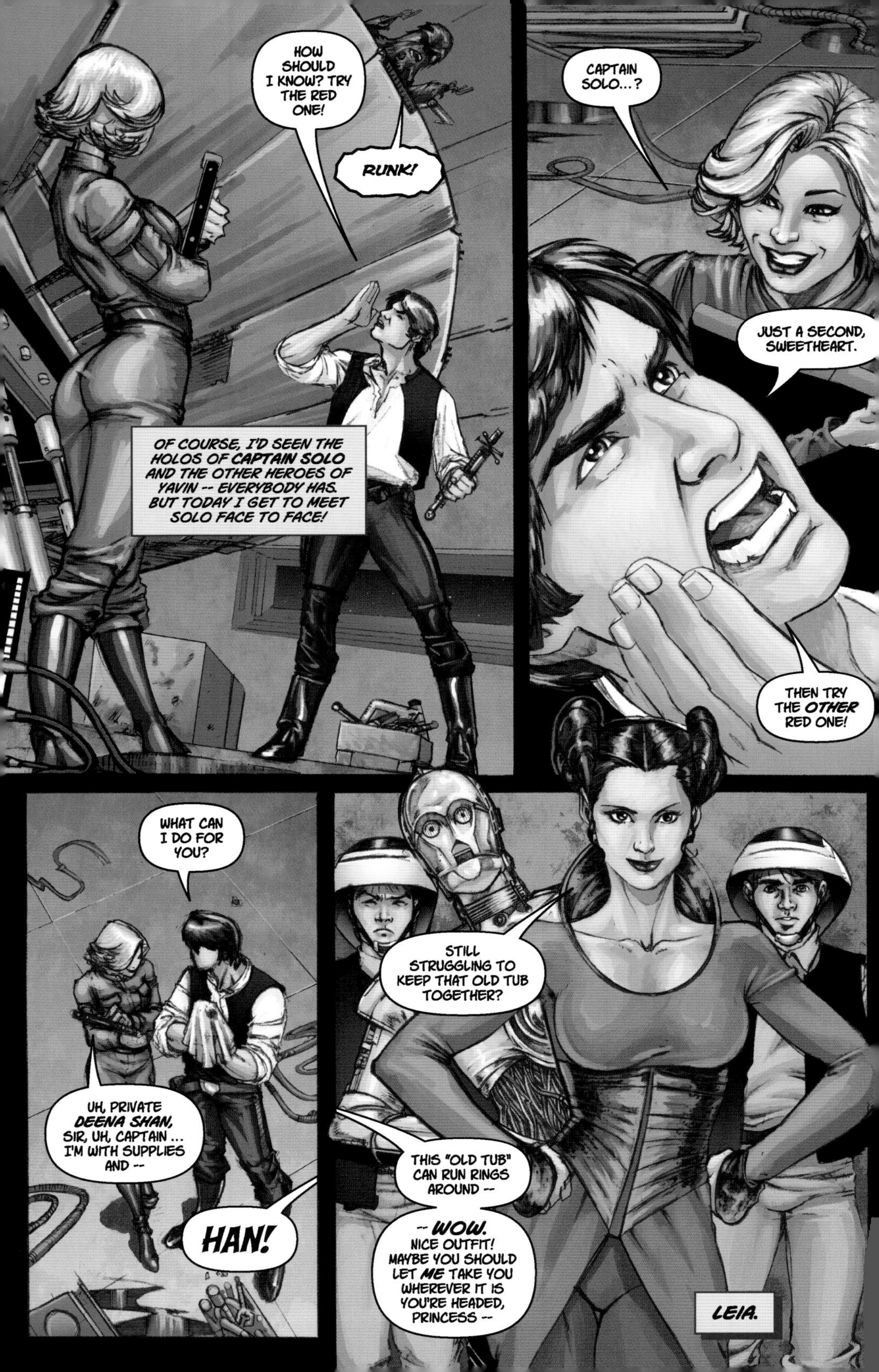
HOW SHOULD I KNOW? TRY THE RED ONE!
RUNK!
OF COURSE, I'D SEEN THE HOLOS OF CAPTAIN SOLO AND THE OTHER HEROES OF YAVIN -- EVERYBODY HAS. BUT TODAY I GET TO MEET SOLO FACE TO FACE!
CAPTAIN SOLO...?
JUST A SECOND, SWEETHEART.
THEN TRY THE OTHER RED ONE!
WHAT CAN I DO FOR YOU?
UH, PRIVATE DEENA SHAN, SIR, UH, CAPTAIN ... I'M WITH SUPPLIES AND --
HAN!
STILL STRUGGLING TO KEEP THAT OLD TUB TOGETHER?
THIS "OLD TUB" CAN RUN RINGS AROUND --
-- WOW. NICE OUTFIT! MAYBE YOU SHOULD LET ME TAKE YOU WHEREVER IT IS YOU'RE HEADED, PRINCESS --
LEIA.

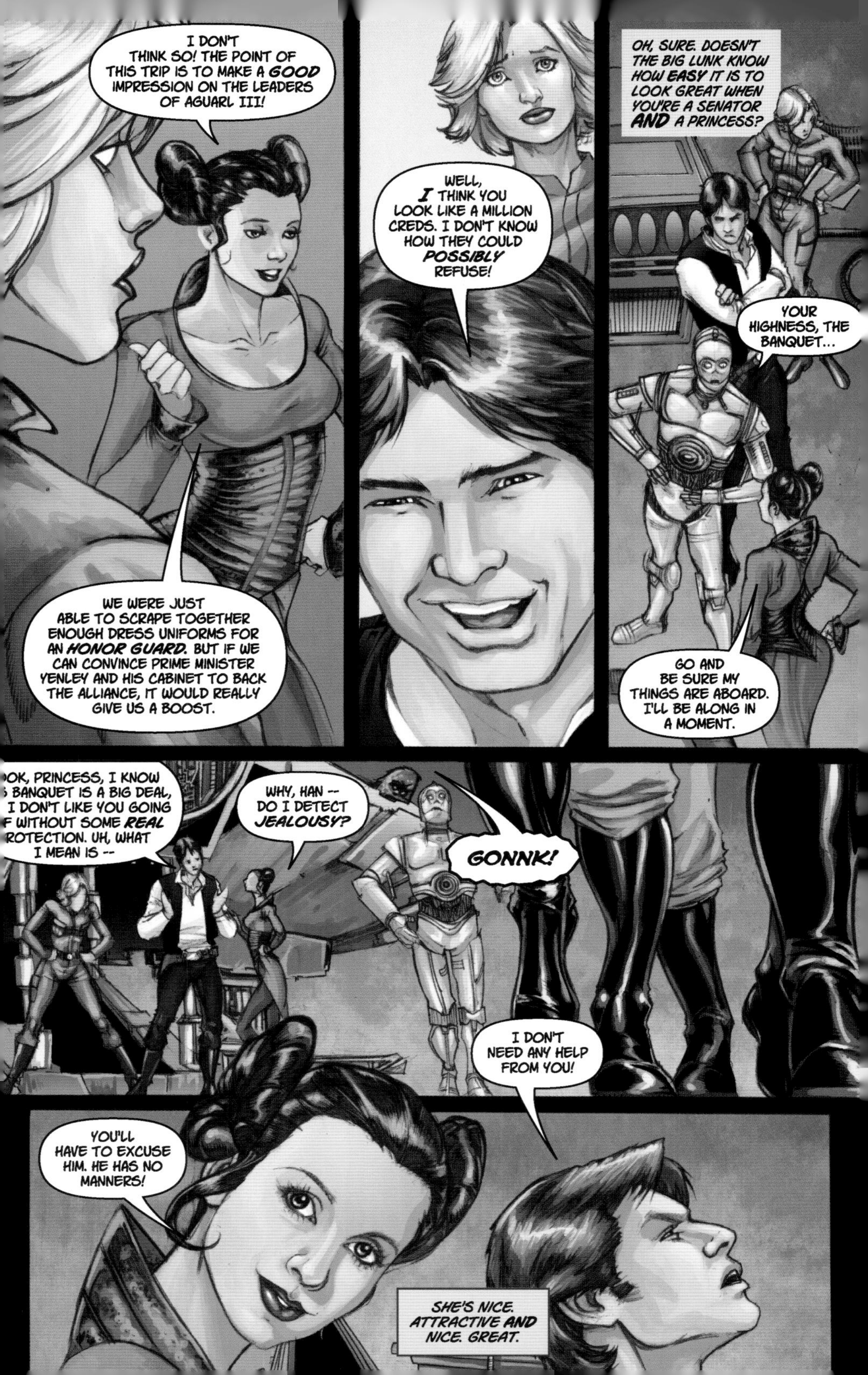
I DON'T THINK SO! THE POINT OF THIS TRIP IS TO MAKE A GOOD IMPRESSION ON THE LEADERS OF AGUARL III!
WE WERE JUST ABLE TO SCRAPE TOGETHER ENOUGH DRESS UNIFORMS FOR AN HONOR GUARD. BUT IF WE CAN CONVINCE PRIME MINISTER YENLEY AND HIS CABINET TO BACK THE ALLIANCE, IT WOULD REALLY GIVE US A BOOST.
WELL, I THINK YOU LOOK LIKE A MILLION CREDS. I DON'T KNOW HOW THEY COULD POSSIBLY REFUSE!
OH, SURE. DOESN'T THE BIG LUNK KNOW HOW EASY IT IS TO LOOK GREAT WHEN YOU'RE A SENATOR AND A PRINCESS?
YOUR HIGHNESS, THE BANQUET...
GO AND BE SURE MY THINGS ARE ABOARD. I'LL BE ALONG IN A MOMENT.
OOK, PRINCESS, I KNOW S BANQUET IS A BIG DEAL, I DON'T LIKE YOU GOING F WITHOUT SOME REAL ROTECTION. UH, WHAT I MEAN IS --
WHY, HAN -- DO I DETECT JEALOUSY?
GONNK!
I DON'T NEED ANY HELP FROM YOU!
YOU'LL HAVE TO EXCUSE HIM. HE HAS NO MANNERS!
SHE'S NICE. ATTRACTIVE AND NICE. GREAT.

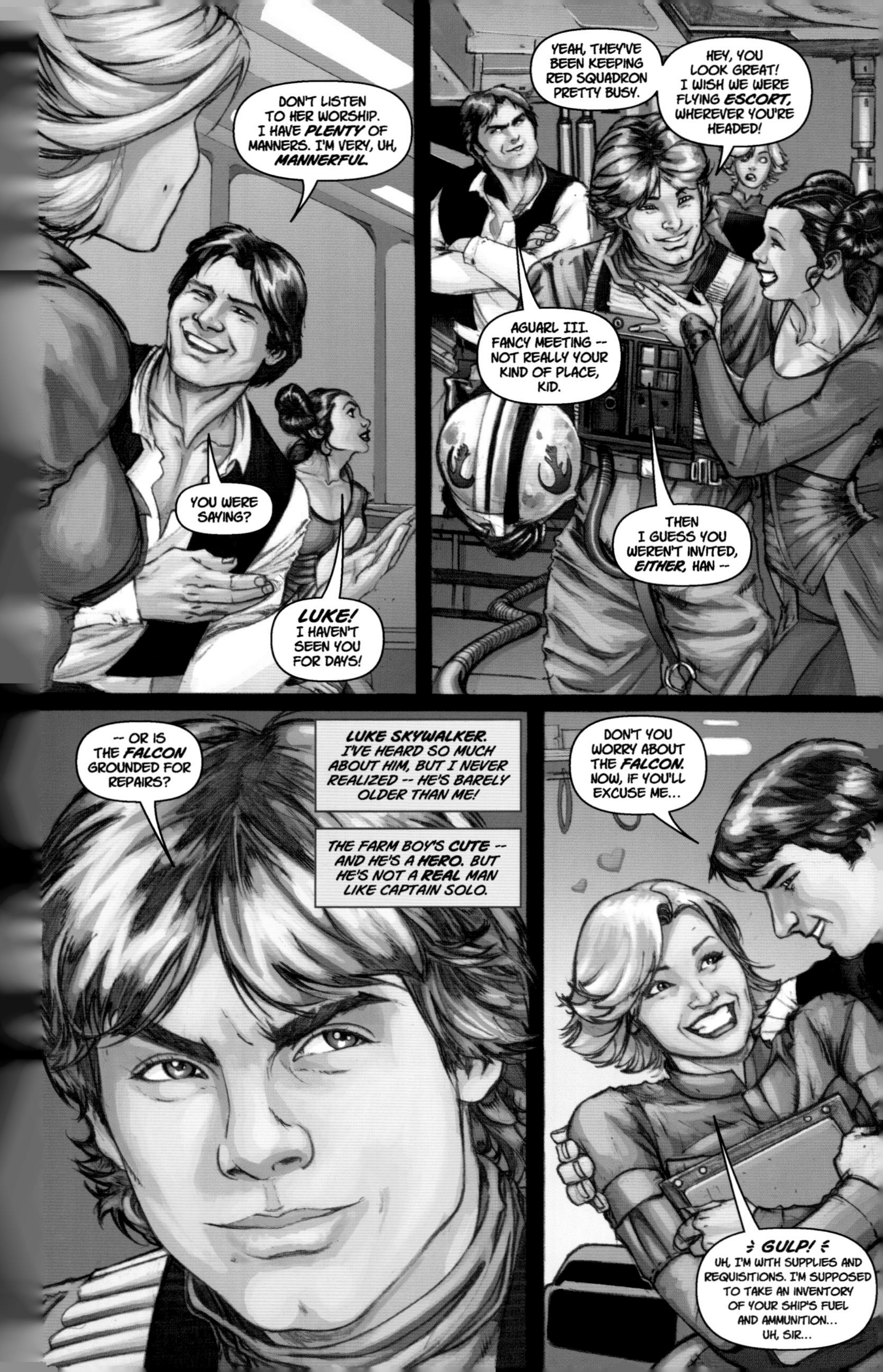
DON'T LISTEN TO HER WORSHIP. I HAVE PLENTY OF MANNERS. I'M VERY, UH, MANNERFUL.
YOU WERE SAYING?
LUKE! I HAVEN'T SEEN YOU FOR DAYS!
YEAH, THEY'VE BEEN KEEPING RED SQUADRON PRETTY BUSY.
HEY, YOU LOOK GREAT! I WISH WE WERE FLYING ESCORT, WHEREVER YOU'RE HEADED!
AGUARL III. FANCY MEETING -- NOT REALLY YOUR KIND OF PLACE, KID.
THEN I GUESS YOU WEREN'T INVITED, EITHER, HAN --
-- OR IS THE FALCON GROUNDED FOR REPAIRS?
LUKE SKYWALKER. I'VE HEARD SO MUCH ABOUT HIM, BUT I NEVER REALIZED -- HE'S BARELY OLDER THAN ME!
THE FARM BOY'S CUTE -- AND HE'S A HERO. BUT HE'S NOT A REAL MAN LIKE CAPTAIN SOLO.
DON'T YOU WORRY ABOUT THE FALCON. NOW, IF YOU'LL EXCUSE ME...
GULP! UH, I'M WITH SUPPLIES AND REQUISITIONS. I'M SUPPOSED TO TAKE AN INVENTORY OF YOUR SHIP'S FUEL AND AMMUNITION... UH, SIR...

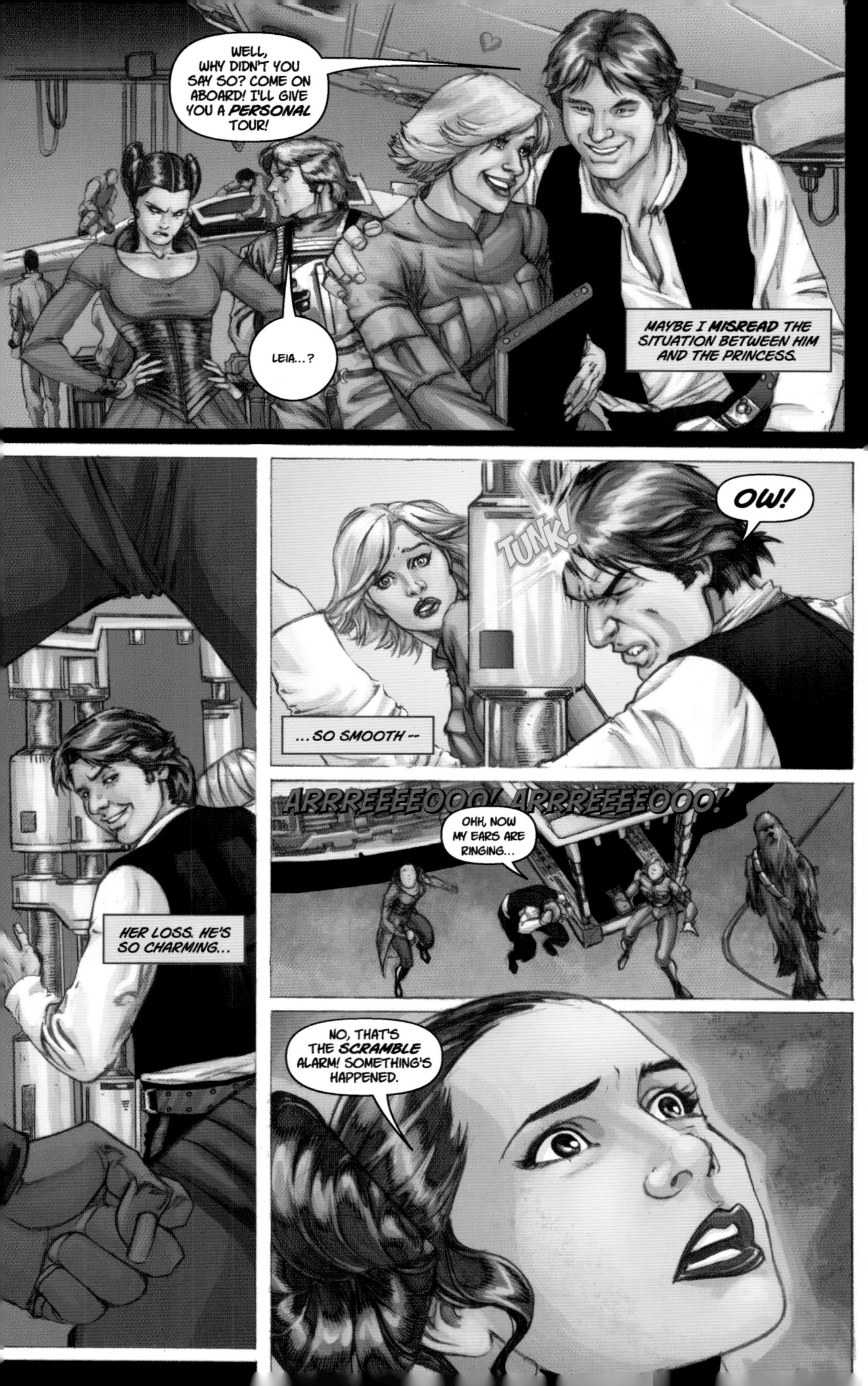
WELL, WHY DIDN'T YOU SAY SO? COME ON ABOARD! I'LL GIVE YOU A PERSONAL TOUR!
LEIA...?
MAYBE I MISREAD THE SITUATION BETWEEN HIM AND THE PRINCESS.
HER LOSS. HE'S SO CHARMING...
...SO SMOOTH --
TUNK!
OW!
ARRREEEEOOO! ARRREEEEOOO!
OHH, NOW MY EARS ARE RINGING...
NO, THAT'S THE SCRAMBLE ALARM! SOMETHING'S HAPPENED.

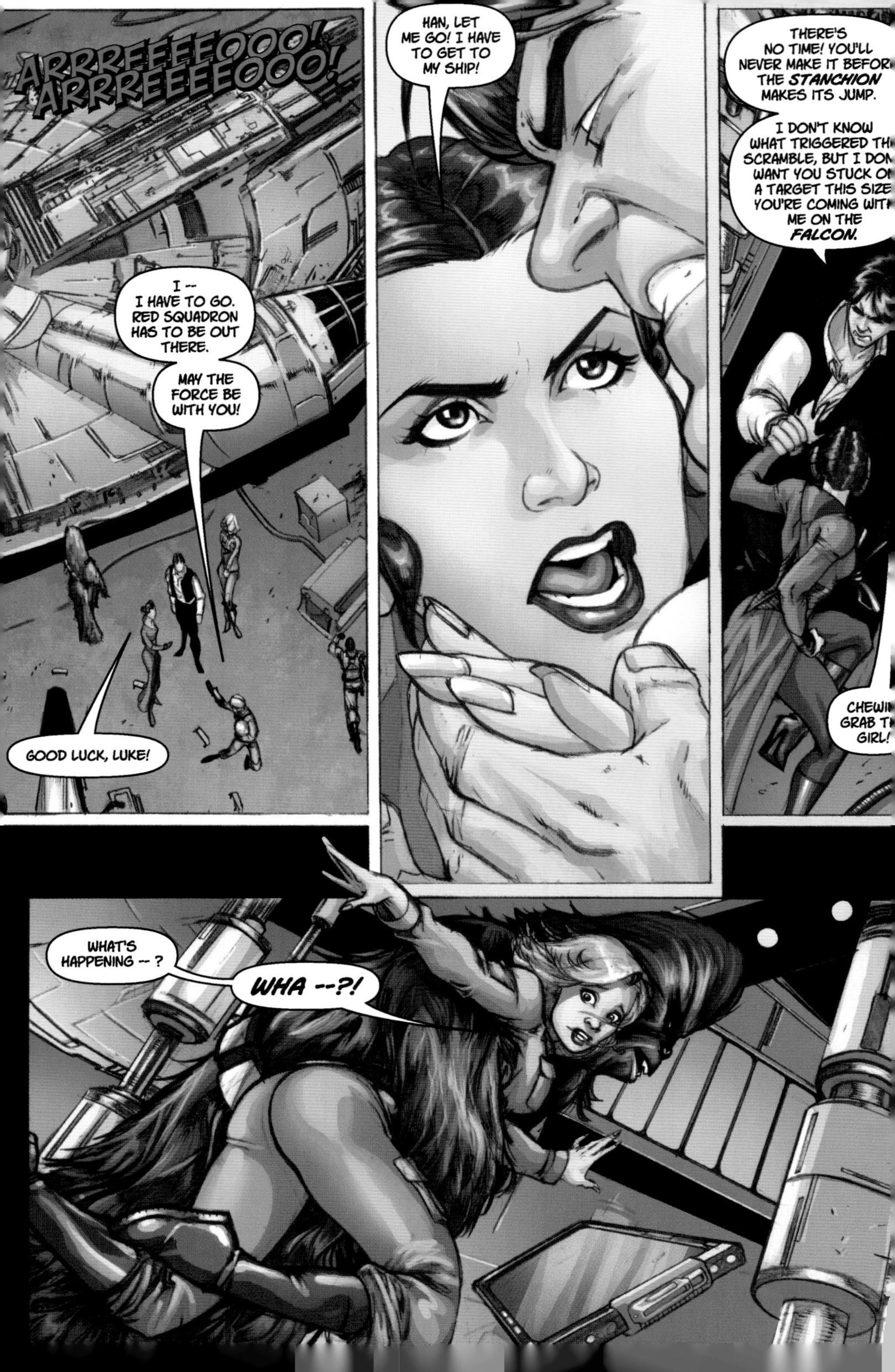

ARRRFEEEFOOO! ARRRREEEEOOO!
I -- I HAVE TO GO. RED SQUADRON HAS TO BE OUT THERE.
MAY THE FORCE BE WITH YOU!
GOOD LUCK, LUKE!
HAN, LET ME GO! I HAVE TO GET TO MY SHIP!
THERE'S NO TIME! YOU'LL NEVER MAKE IT BEFOR THE STANCHION MAKES ITS JUMP.
I DON'T KNOW WHAT TRIGGERED TH SCRAMBLE, BUT I DON WANT YOU STUCK ON A TARGET THIS SIZE YOU'RE COMING WIT ME ON THE FALCON.
CHEWI GRAB T GIRL!
WHAT'S HAPPENING -- ?
WHA --?!

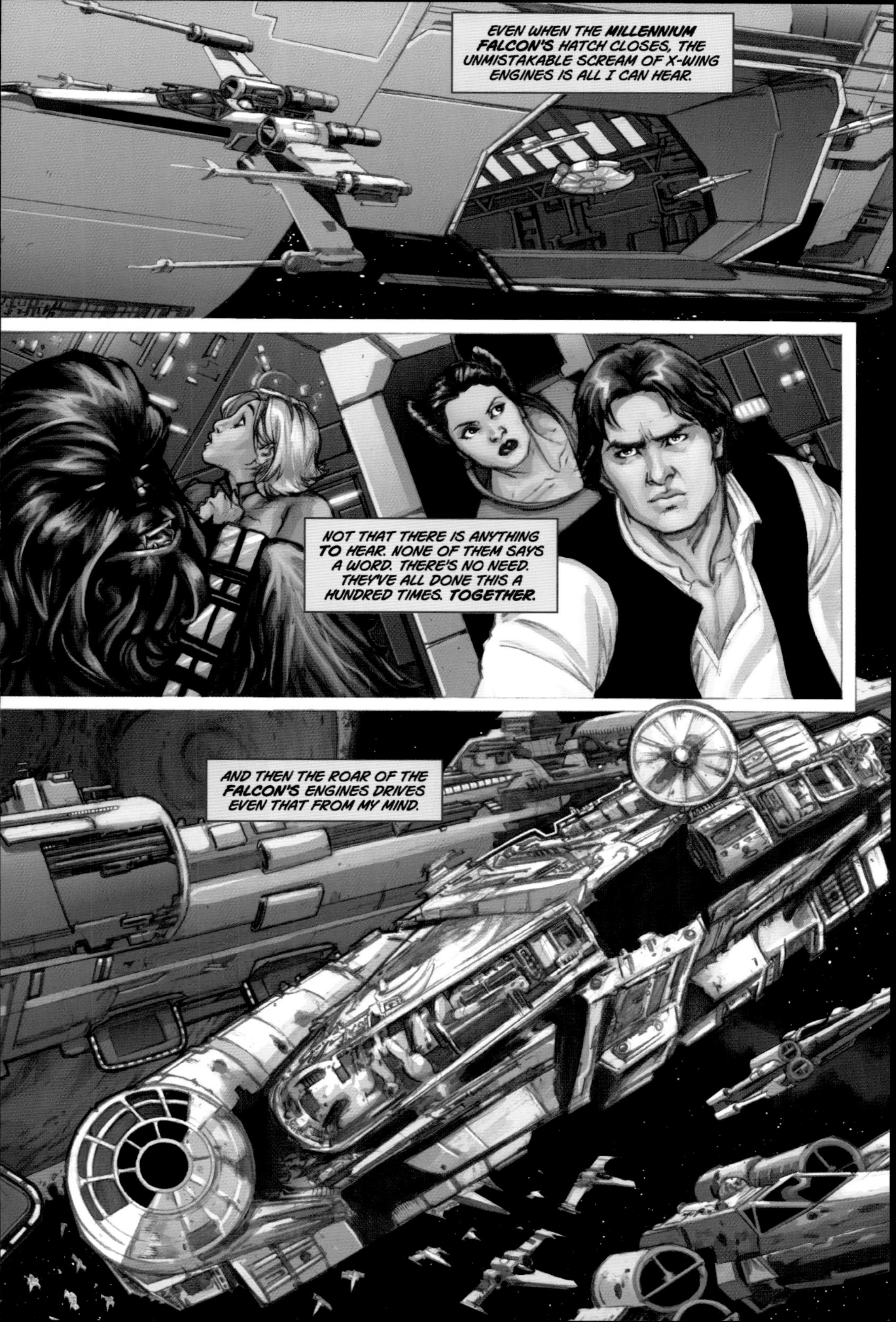
EVEN WHEN THE **MILLENNIUM FALCON'S** HATCH CLOSES, THE UNMISTAKABLE SCREAM OF X-WING ENGINES IS ALL I CAN HEAR.
NOT THAT THERE IS ANYTHING **TO** HEAR. NONE OF THEM SAYS A WORD. THERE'S NO NEED. THEY'VE ALL DONE THIS A HUNDRED TIMES. **TOGETHER.**
AND THEN THE ROAR OF THE **FALCON'S** ENGINES DRIVES EVEN THAT FROM MY MIND.

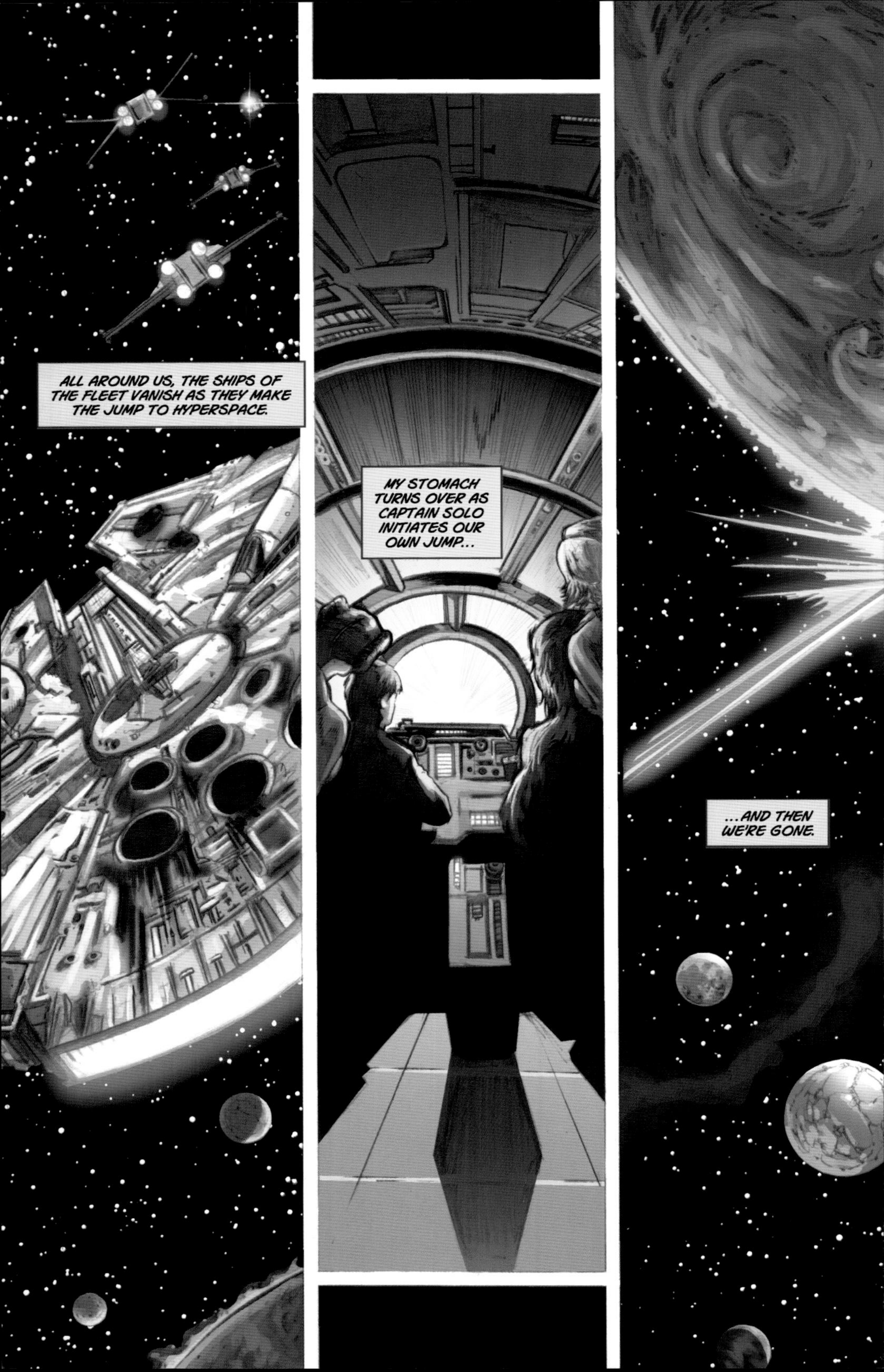
ALL AROUND US, THE SHIPS OF THE FLEET VANISH AS THEY MAKE THE JUMP TO HYPERSPACE.
MY STOMACH TURNS OVER AS CAPTAIN SOLO INITIATES OUR OWN JUMP...
...AND THEN WE'RE GONE.

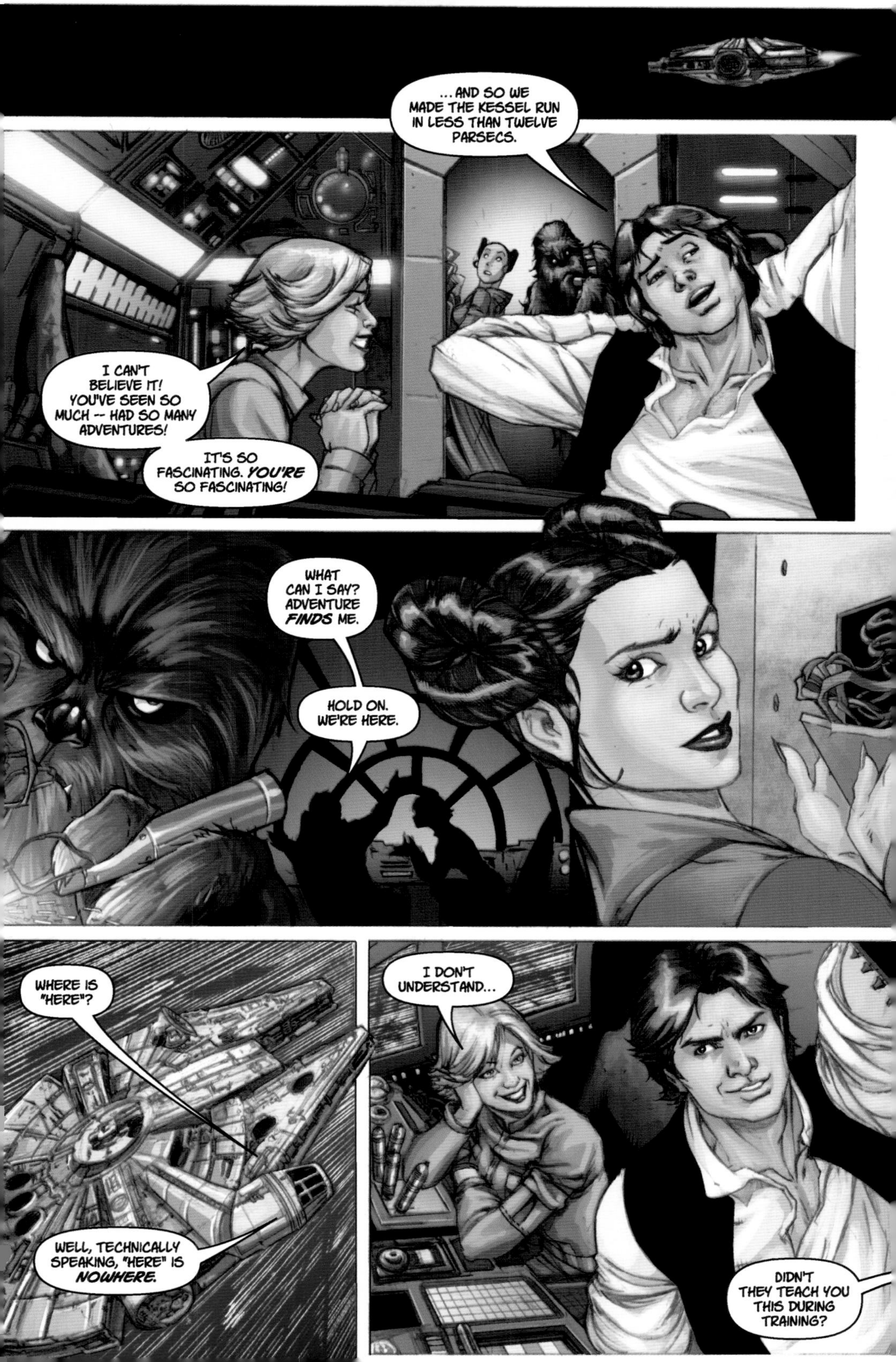
...AND SO WE MADE THE KESSEL RUN IN LESS THAN TWELVE PARSECS.
I CAN'T BELIEVE IT! YOU'VE SEEN SO MUCH -- HAD SO MANY ADVENTURES!
IT'S SO FASCINATING. *YOU'RE* SO FASCINATING!
WHAT CAN I SAY? ADVENTURE *FINDS* ME.
HOLD ON. WE'RE HERE.
WHERE IS "HERE"?
WELL, TECHNICALLY SPEAKING, "HERE" IS *NOWHERE*.
I DON'T UNDERSTAND...
DIDN'T THEY TEACH YOU THIS DURING TRAINING?

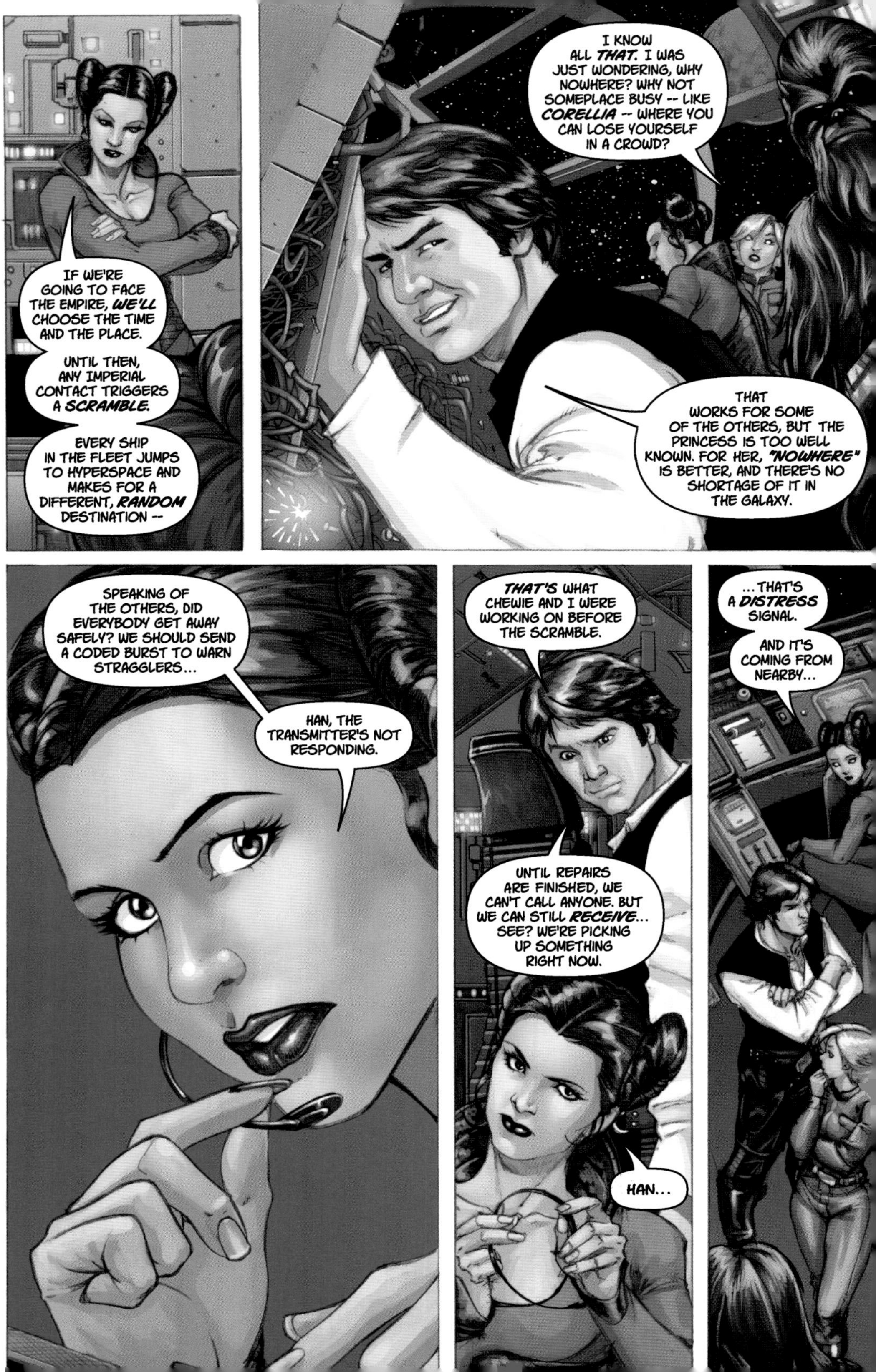
IF WE'RE GOING TO FACE THE EMPIRE, *WE'LL* CHOOSE THE TIME AND THE PLACE.
UNTIL THEN, ANY IMPERIAL CONTACT TRIGGERS A *SCRAMBLE*.
EVERY SHIP IN THE FLEET JUMPS TO HYPERSPACE AND MAKES FOR A DIFFERENT, *RANDOM* DESTINATION --
I KNOW ALL *THAT*. I WAS JUST WONDERING, WHY NOWHERE? WHY NOT SOMEPLACE BUSY -- LIKE *CORELLIA* -- WHERE YOU CAN LOSE YOURSELF IN A CROWD?
THAT WORKS FOR SOME OF THE OTHERS, BUT THE PRINCESS IS TOO WELL KNOWN. FOR HER, *"NOWHERE"* IS BETTER, AND THERE'S NO SHORTAGE OF IT IN THE GALAXY.
SPEAKING OF THE OTHERS, DID EVERYBODY GET AWAY SAFELY? WE SHOULD SEND A CODED BURST TO WARN STRAGGLERS...
HAN, THE TRANSMITTER'S NOT RESPONDING.
THAT'S WHAT CHEWIE AND I WERE WORKING ON BEFORE THE SCRAMBLE.
UNTIL REPAIRS ARE FINISHED, WE CAN'T CALL ANYONE. BUT WE CAN STILL *RECEIVE*... SEE? WE'RE PICKING UP SOMETHING RIGHT NOW.
HAN...
...THAT'S A *DISTRESS* SIGNAL.
AND IT'S COMING FROM NEARBY...

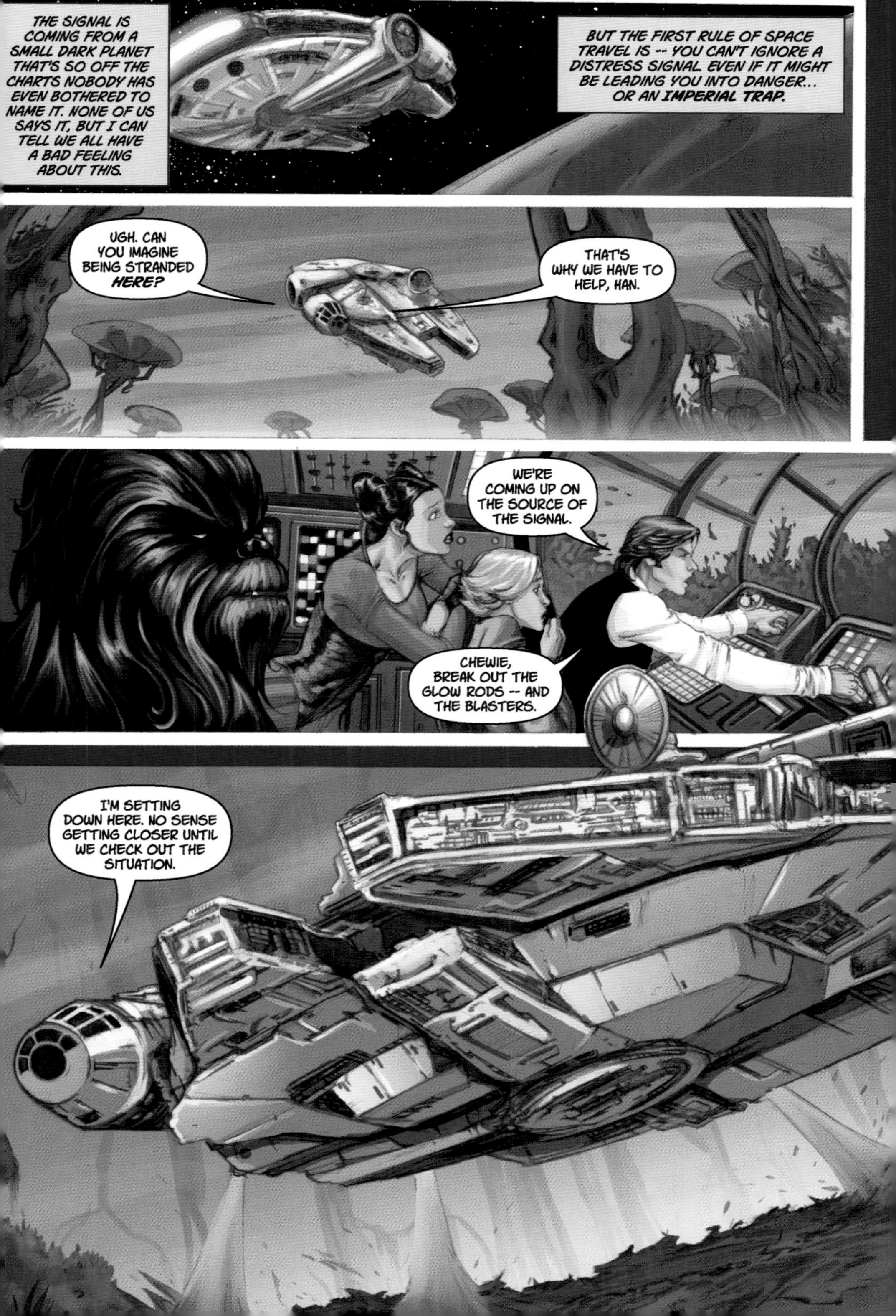
THE SIGNAL IS COMING FROM A SMALL DARK PLANET THAT'S SO OFF THE CHARTS NOBODY HAS EVEN BOTHERED TO NAME IT. NONE OF US SAYS IT, BUT I CAN TELL WE ALL HAVE A BAD FEELING ABOUT THIS.
BUT THE FIRST RULE OF SPACE TRAVEL IS -- YOU CAN'T IGNORE A DISTRESS SIGNAL. EVEN IF IT MIGHT BE LEADING YOU INTO DANGER... OR AN IMPERIAL TRAP.
UGH. CAN YOU IMAGINE BEING STRANDED HERE?
THAT'S WHY WE HAVE TO HELP, HAN.
WE'RE COMING UP ON THE SOURCE OF THE SIGNAL.
CHEWIE, BREAK OUT THE GLOW RODS -- AND THE BLASTERS.
I'M SETTING DOWN HERE. NO SENSE GETTING CLOSER UNTIL WE CHECK OUT THE SITUATION.

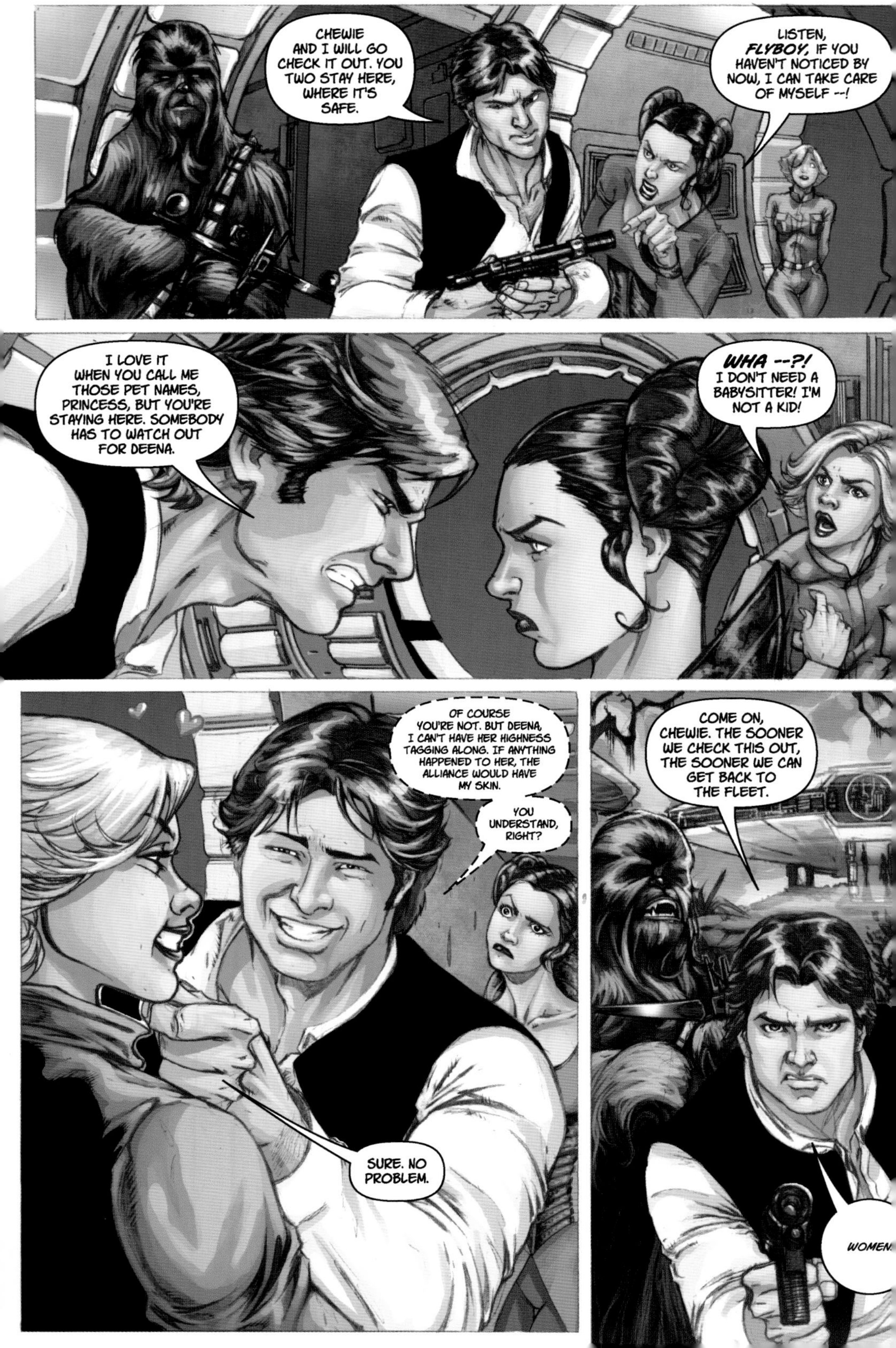
CHEWIE AND I WILL GO CHECK IT OUT. YOU TWO STAY HERE, WHERE IT'S SAFE.
LISTEN, *FLYBOY,* IF YOU HAVEN'T NOTICED BY NOW, I CAN TAKE CARE OF MYSELF --!
I LOVE IT WHEN YOU CALL ME THOSE PET NAMES, PRINCESS, BUT YOU'RE STAYING HERE. SOMEBODY HAS TO WATCH OUT FOR DEENA.
WHA --?! I DON'T NEED A BABYSITTER! I'M NOT A KID!
OF COURSE YOU'RE NOT. BUT DEENA, I CAN'T HAVE HER HIGHNESS TAGGING ALONG. IF ANYTHING HAPPENED TO HER, THE ALLIANCE WOULD HAVE MY SKIN.
YOU UNDERSTAND, RIGHT?
SURE. NO PROBLEM.
COME ON, CHEWIE. THE SOONER WE CHECK THIS OUT, THE SOONER WE CAN GET BACK TO THE FLEET.
WOMEN.

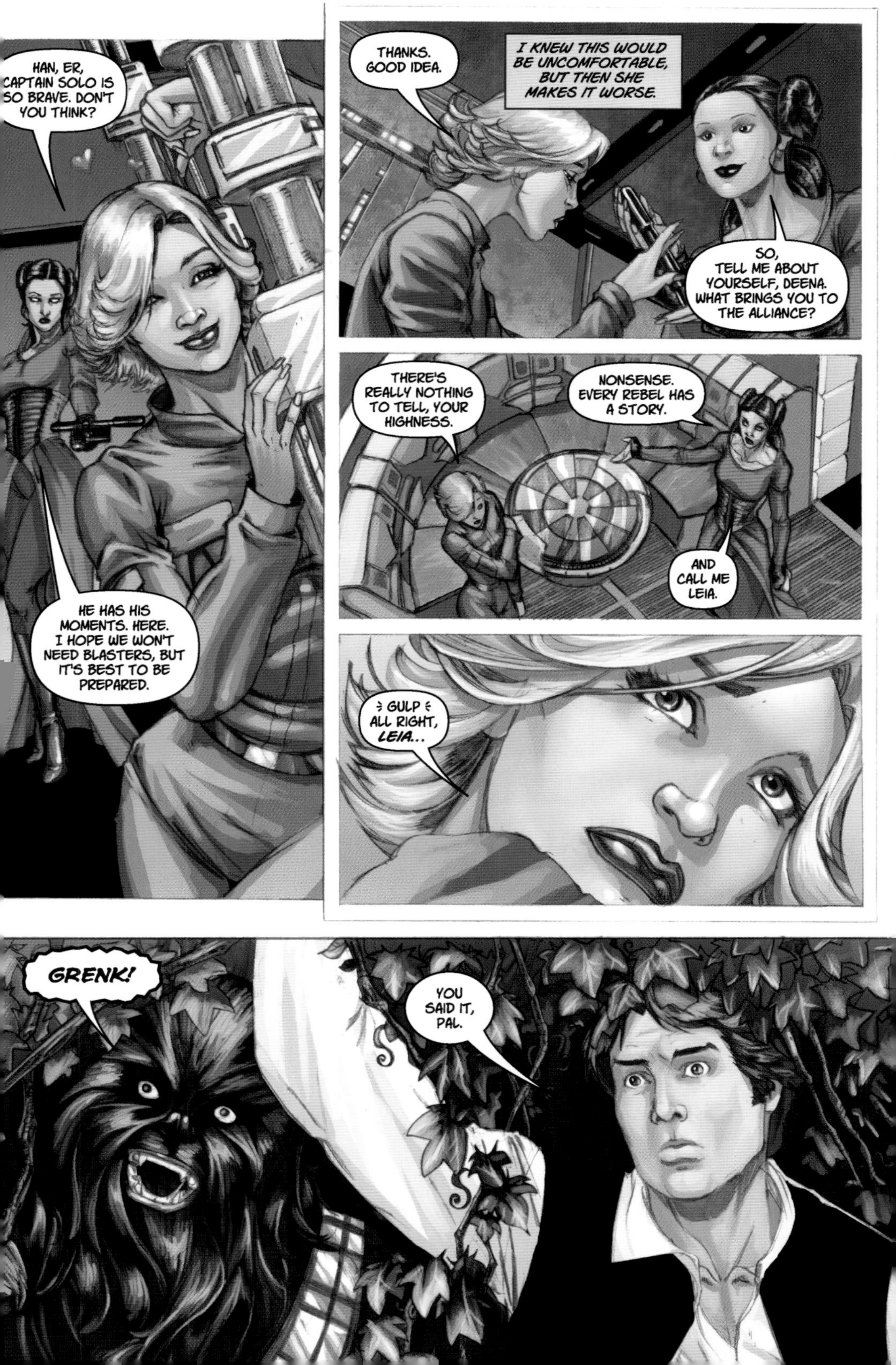
HAN, ER, CAPTAIN SOLO IS SO BRAVE. DON'T YOU THINK?
HE HAS HIS MOMENTS. HERE. I HOPE WE WON'T NEED BLASTERS, BUT IT'S BEST TO BE PREPARED.
THANKS. GOOD IDEA.
I KNEW THIS WOULD BE UNCOMFORTABLE, BUT THEN SHE MAKES IT WORSE.
SO, TELL ME ABOUT YOURSELF, DEENA. WHAT BRINGS YOU TO THE ALLIANCE?
THERE'S REALLY NOTHING TO TELL, YOUR HIGHNESS.
NONSENSE. EVERY REBEL HAS A STORY.
AND CALL ME LEIA.
GULP
ALL RIGHT, LEIA...
GRENK!
YOU SAID IT, PAL.

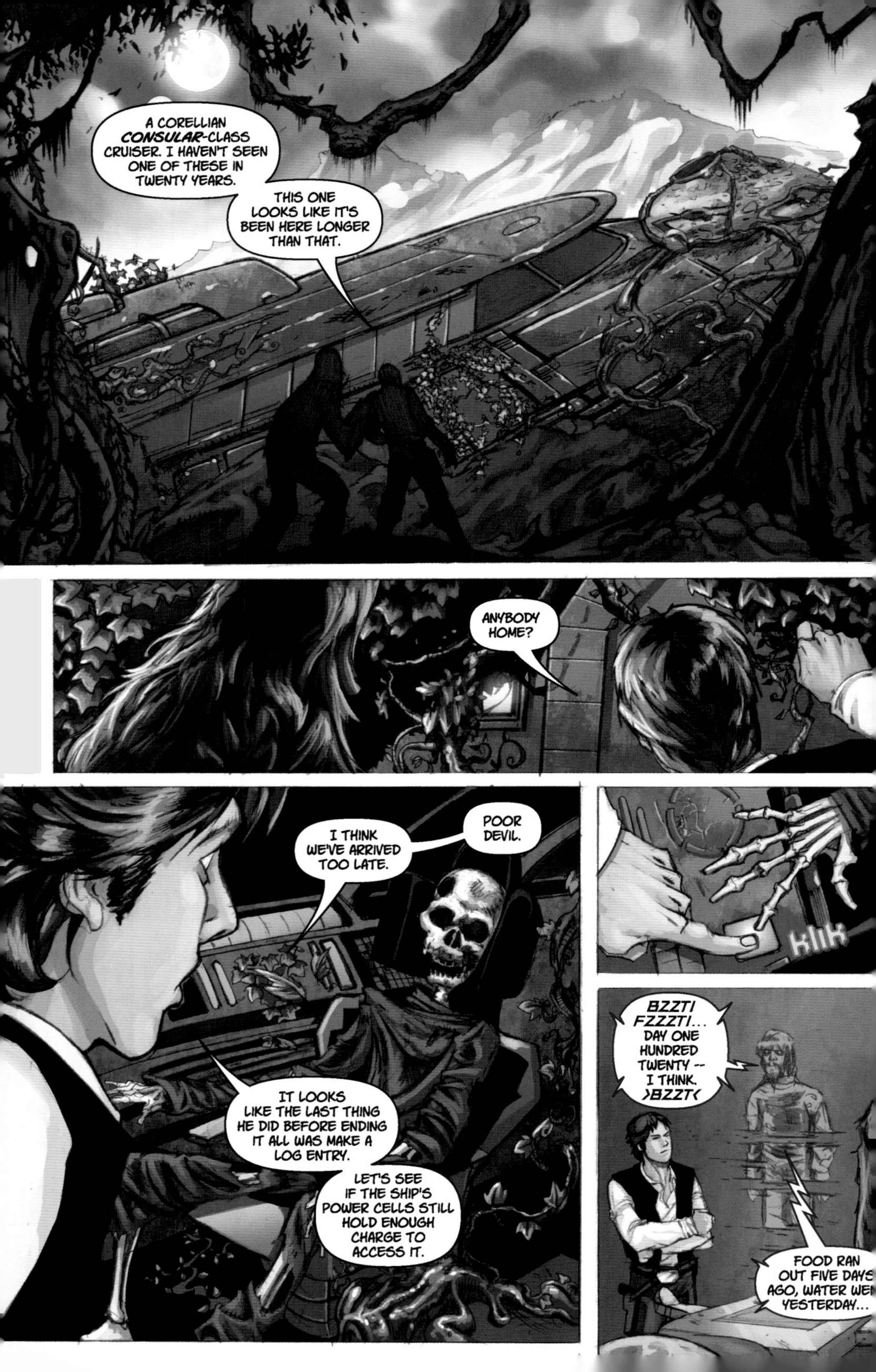

A CORELLIAN *CONSULAR*-CLASS CRUISER. I HAVEN'T SEEN ONE OF THESE IN TWENTY YEARS.
THIS ONE LOOKS LIKE IT'S BEEN HERE LONGER THAN THAT.
ANYBODY HOME?
I THINK WE'VE ARRIVED TOO LATE.
POOR DEVIL.
IT LOOKS LIKE THE LAST THING HE DID BEFORE ENDING IT ALL WAS MAKE A LOG ENTRY.
LET'S SEE IF THE SHIP'S POWER CELLS STILL HOLD ENOUGH CHARGE TO ACCESS IT.
klik
BZZT! FZZZT!... DAY ONE HUNDRED TWENTY -- I THINK. BZZT
FOOD RAN OUT FIVE DAYS AGO, WATER WE YESTERDAY...

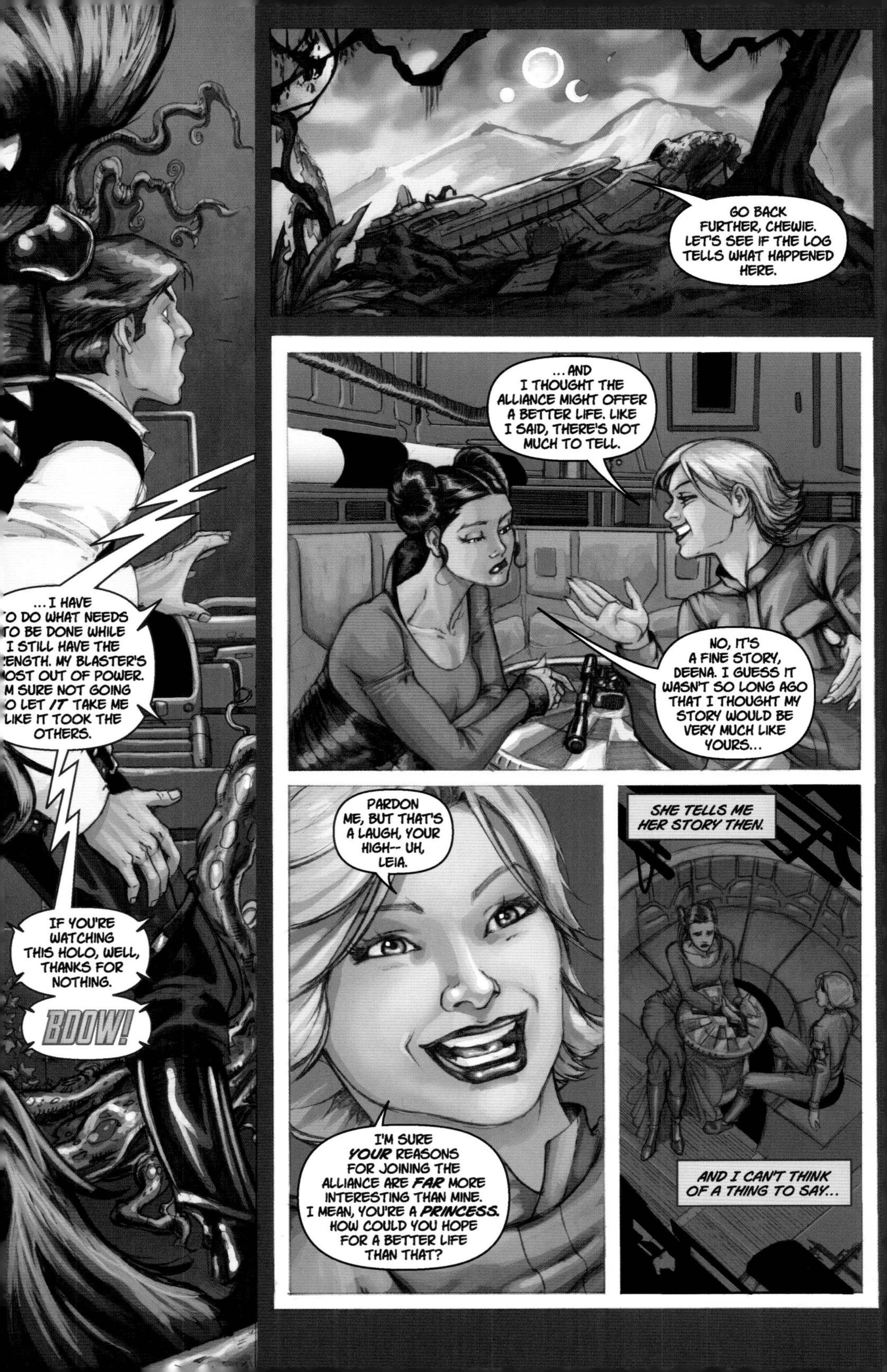
...I HAVE
O DO WHAT NEEDS
TO BE DONE WHILE
I STILL HAVE THE
ENGTH. MY BLASTER'S
OST OUT OF POWER.
M SURE NOT GOING
O LET IT TAKE ME
LIKE IT TOOK THE
OTHERS.
IF YOU'RE WATCHING THIS HOLO, WELL, THANKS FOR NOTHING.
BDOW!
GO BACK FURTHER, CHEWIE. LET'S SEE IF THE LOG TELLS WHAT HAPPENED HERE.
...AND I THOUGHT THE ALLIANCE MIGHT OFFER A BETTER LIFE. LIKE I SAID, THERE'S NOT MUCH TO TELL.
NO, IT'S A FINE STORY, DEENA. I GUESS IT WASN'T SO LONG AGO THAT I THOUGHT MY STORY WOULD BE VERY MUCH LIKE YOURS...
PARDON ME, BUT THAT'S A LAUGH, YOUR HIGH-- UH, LEIA.
I'M SURE YOUR REASONS FOR JOINING THE ALLIANCE ARE FAR MORE INTERESTING THAN MINE. I MEAN, YOU'RE A PRINCESS. HOW COULD YOU HOPE FOR A BETTER LIFE THAN THAT?
SHE TELLS ME HER STORY THEN.
AND I CAN'T THINK OF A THING TO SAY...

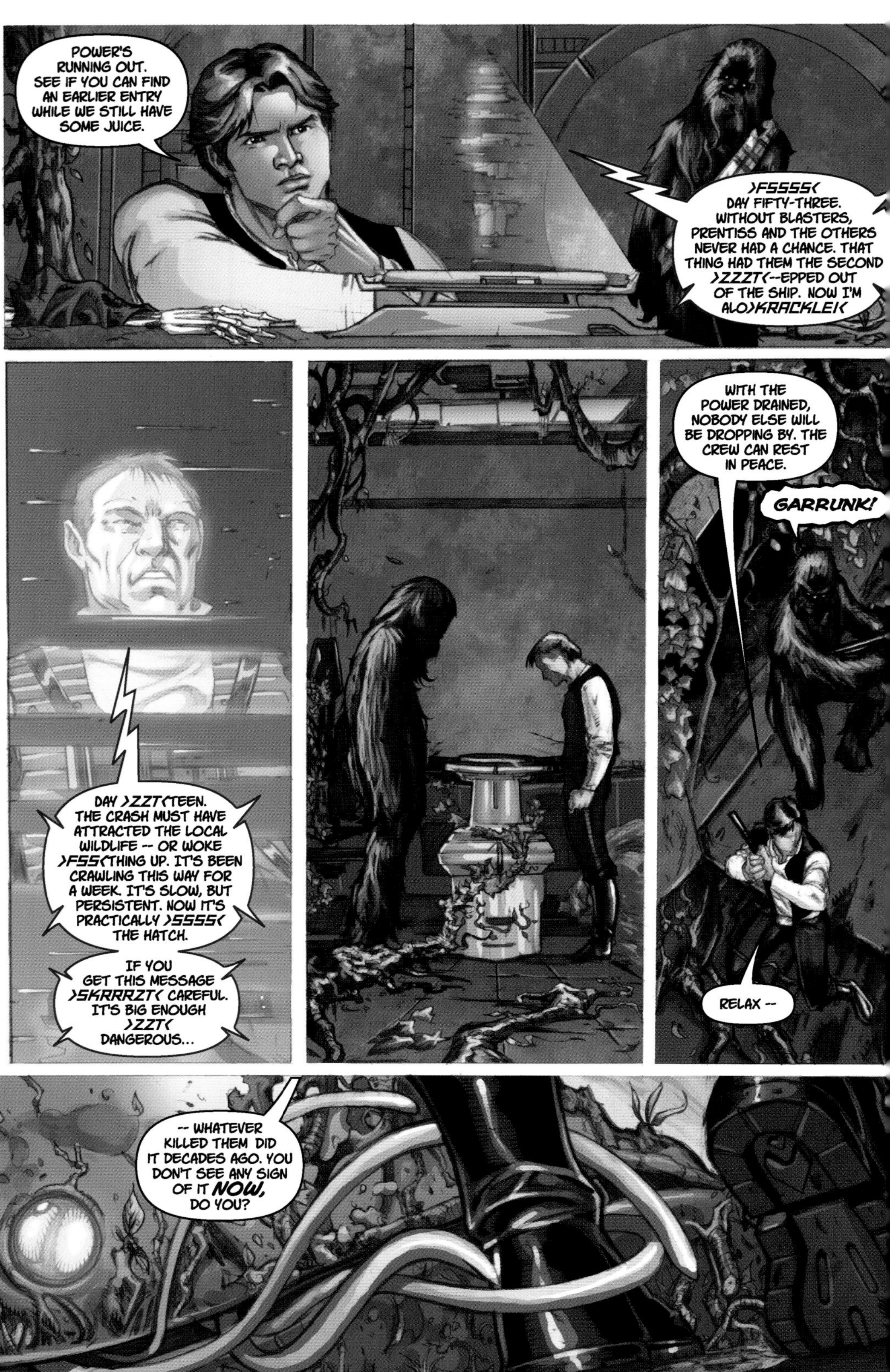
POWER'S RUNNING OUT. SEE IF YOU CAN FIND AN EARLIER ENTRY WHILE WE STILL HAVE SOME JUICE.
>FSSSS< DAY FIFTY-THREE. WITHOUT BLASTERS, PRENTISS AND THE OTHERS NEVER HAD A CHANCE. THAT THING HAD THEM THE SECOND >ZZZT<--EPPED OUT OF THE SHIP. NOW I'M ALO>KRACKLE!<
DAY >ZZT<TEEN. THE CRASH MUST HAVE ATTRACTED THE LOCAL WILDLIFE -- OR WOKE >FSS<THING UP. IT'S BEEN CRAWLING THIS WAY FOR A WEEK. IT'S SLOW, BUT PERSISTENT. NOW IT'S PRACTICALLY >SSSS< THE HATCH.
IF YOU GET THIS MESSAGE >SKRRRZT< CAREFUL. IT'S BIG ENOUGH >ZZT< DANGEROUS...
WITH THE POWER DRAINED, NOBODY ELSE WILL BE DROPPING BY. THE CREW CAN REST IN PEACE.
GARRUNK!
RELAX --
-- WHATEVER KILLED THEM DID IT DECADES AGO. YOU DON'T SEE ANY SIGN OF IT NOW, DO YOU?

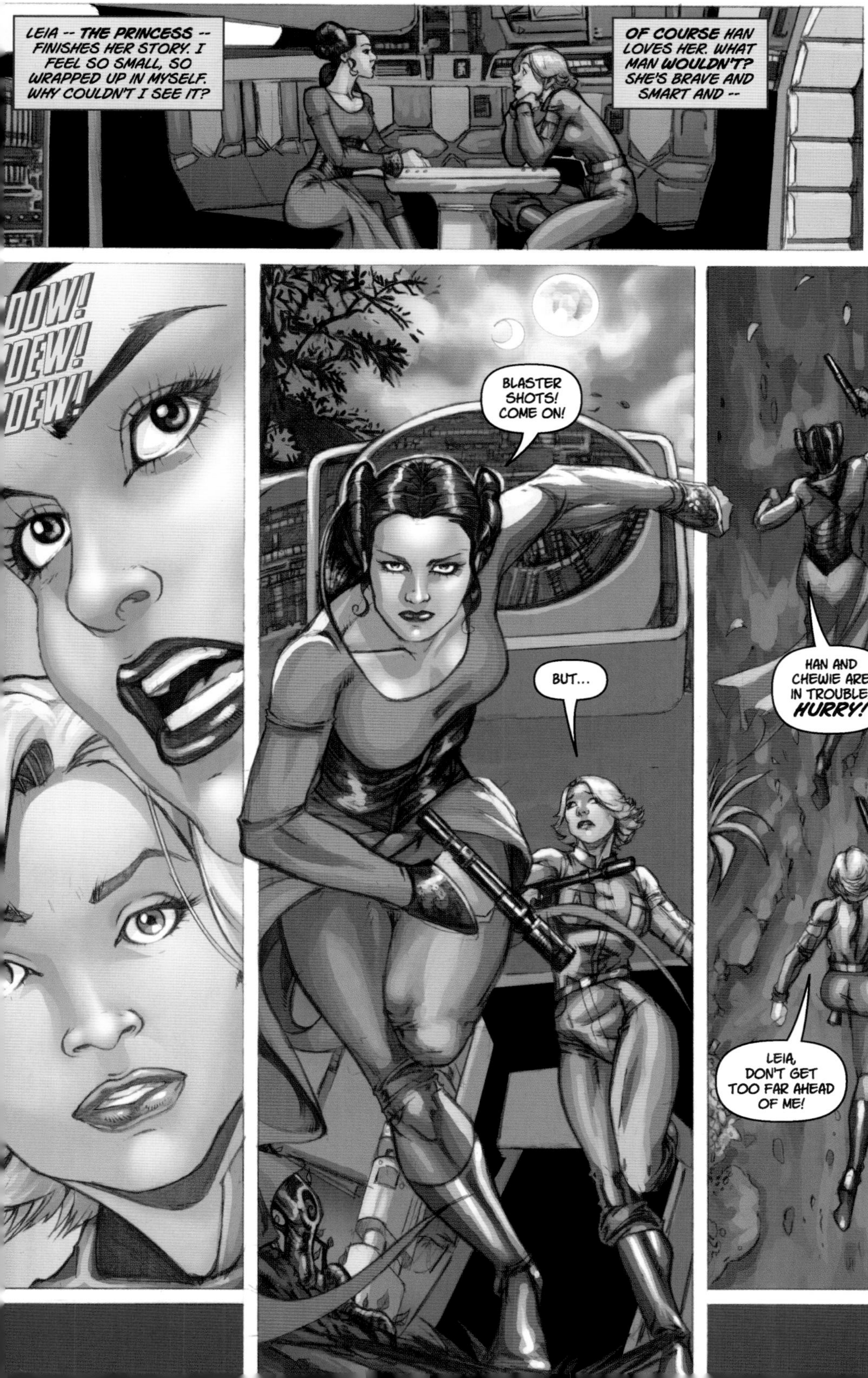
LEIA -- THE PRINCESS -- FINISHES HER STORY. I FEEL SO SMALL, SO WRAPPED UP IN MYSELF. WHY COULDN'T I SEE IT?
OF COURSE HAN LOVES HER. WHAT MAN WOULDN'T? SHE'S BRAVE AND SMART AND --
BLASTER SHOTS! COME ON!
BUT...
HAN AND CHEWIE ARE IN TROUBLE! HURRY!
LEIA, DON'T GET TOO FAR AHEAD OF ME!

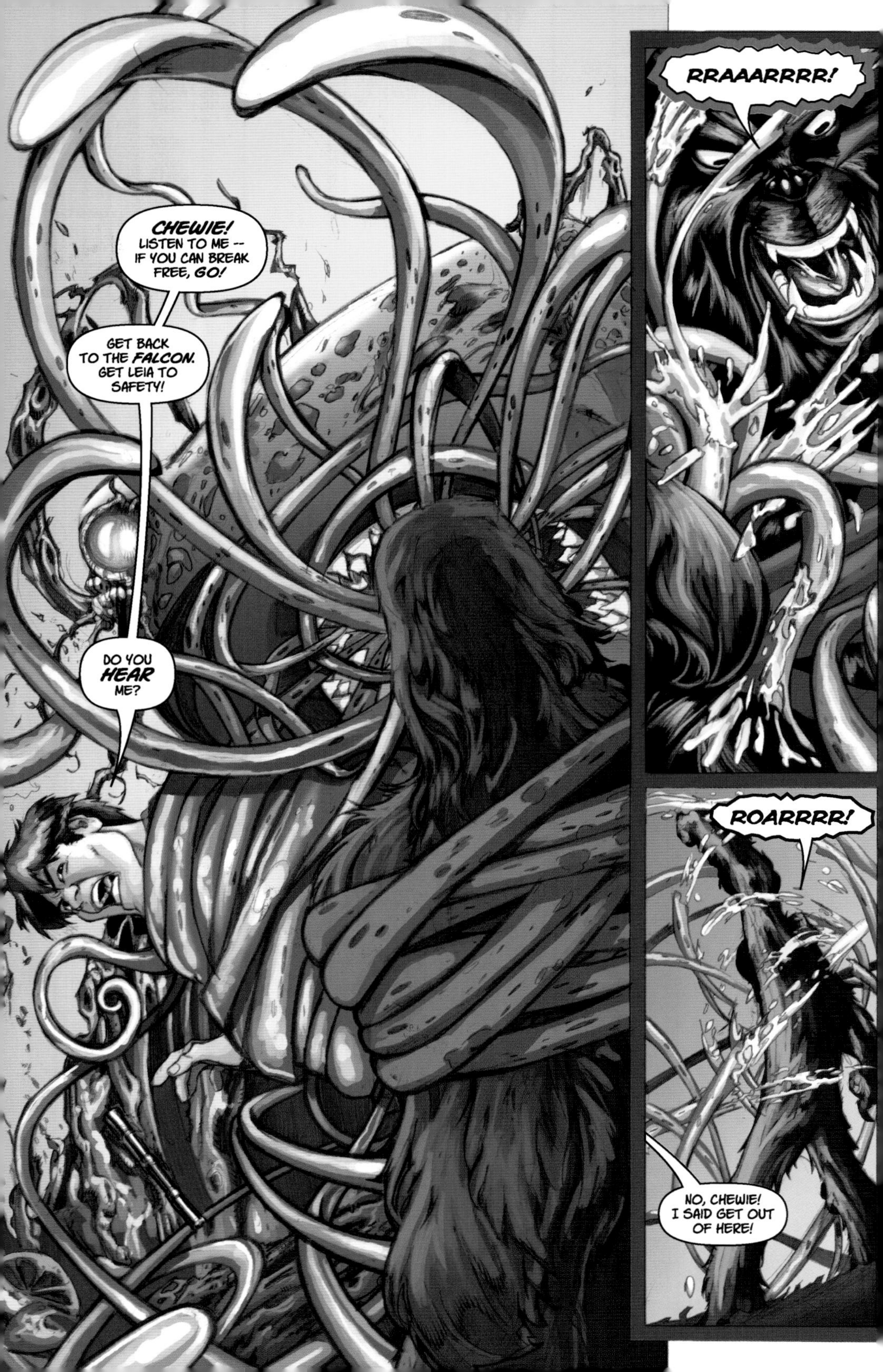
CHEWIE! LISTEN TO ME -- IF YOU CAN BREAK FREE, GO!
GET BACK TO THE FALCON. GET LEIA TO SAFETY!
DO YOU HEAR ME?
RRAAARRRR!
ROARRRR!
NO, CHEWIE! I SAID GET OUT OF HERE!

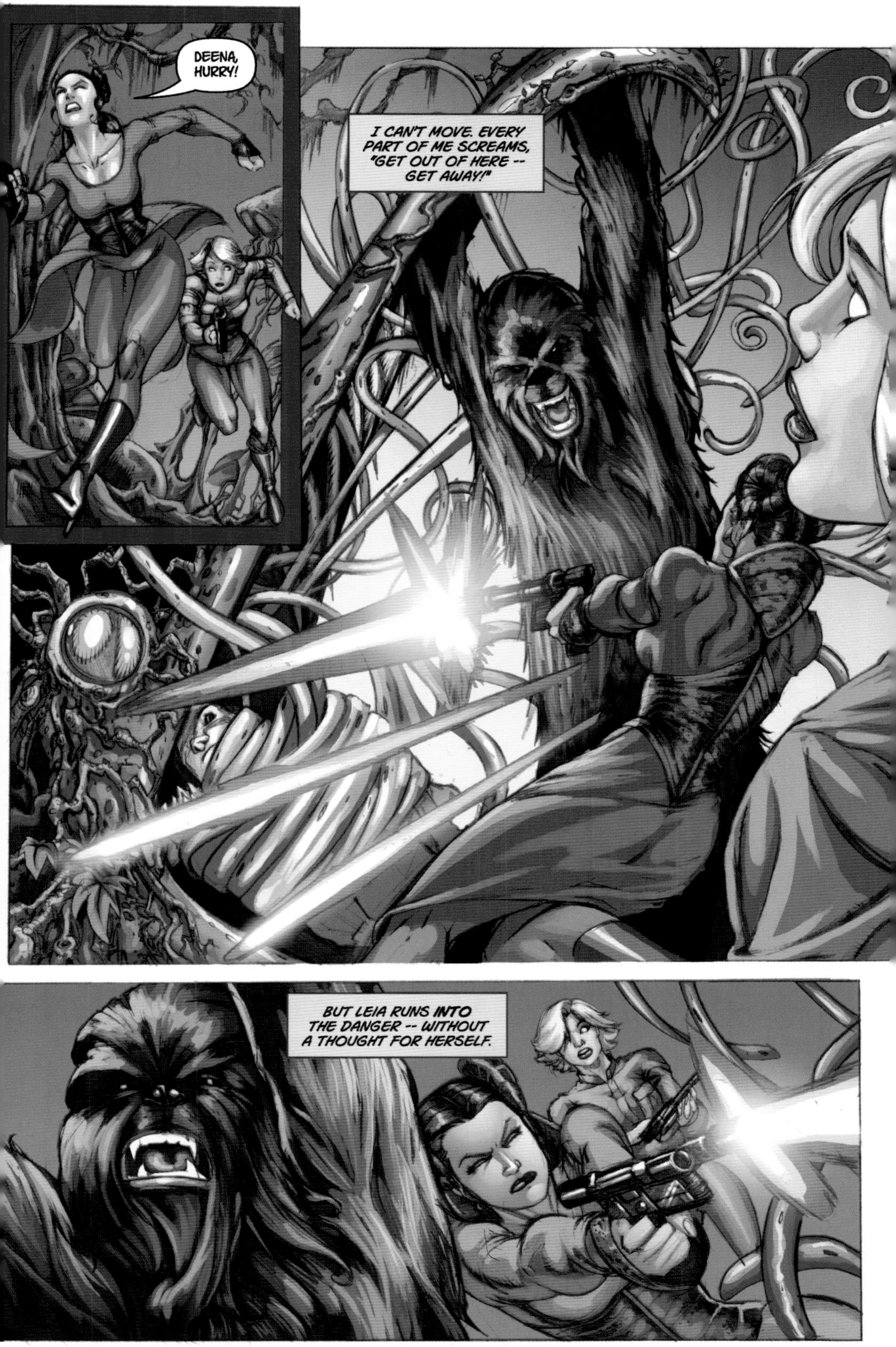
DEENA, HURRY!
I CAN'T MOVE. EVERY PART OF ME SCREAMS, "GET OUT OF HERE -- GET AWAY!"
BUT LEIA RUNS INTO THE DANGER -- WITHOUT A THOUGHT FOR HERSELF.

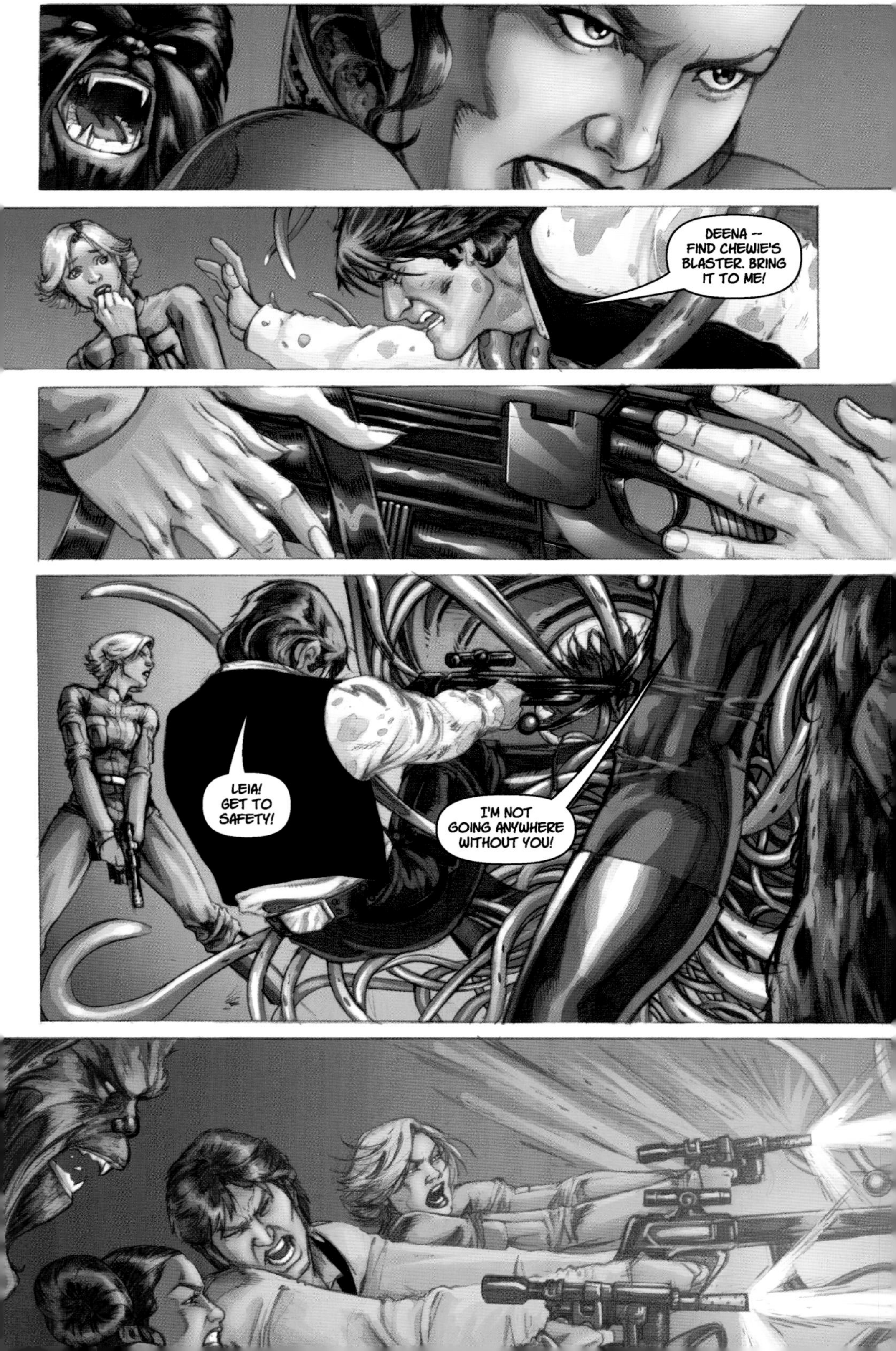
DEENA -- FIND CHEWIE'S BLASTER. BRING IT TO ME!
LEIA! GET TO SAFETY!
I'M NOT GOING ANYWHERE WITHOUT YOU!

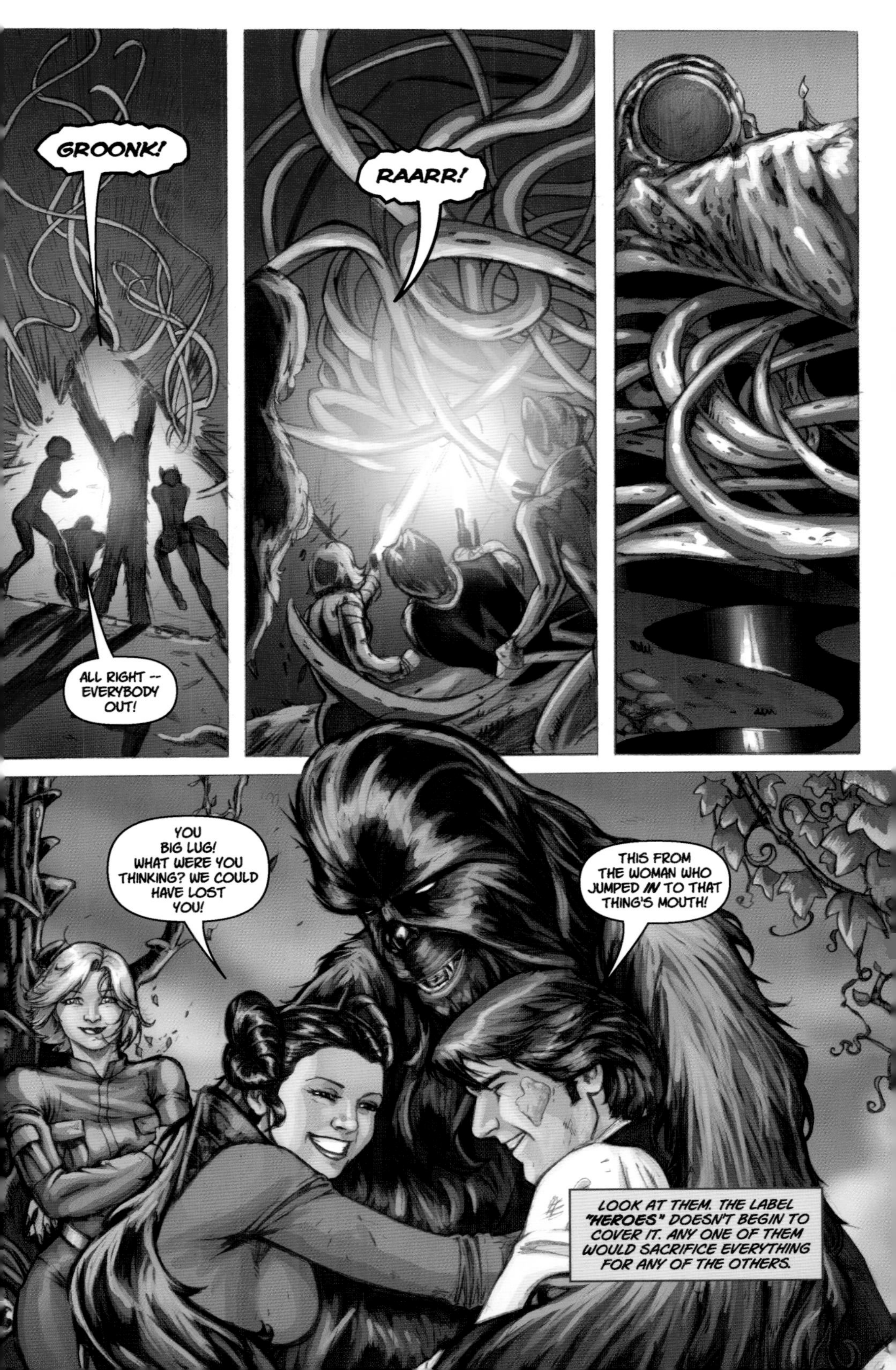
GROONK!
ALL RIGHT -- EVERYBODY OUT!
RAARR!
YOU BIG LUG! WHAT WERE YOU THINKING? WE COULD HAVE LOST YOU!
THIS FROM THE WOMAN WHO JUMPED *IN* TO THAT THING'S MOUTH!
LOOK AT THEM. THE LABEL "HEROES" DOESN'T BEGIN TO COVER IT. ANY ONE OF THEM WOULD SACRIFICE EVERYTHING FOR ANY OF THE OTHERS.

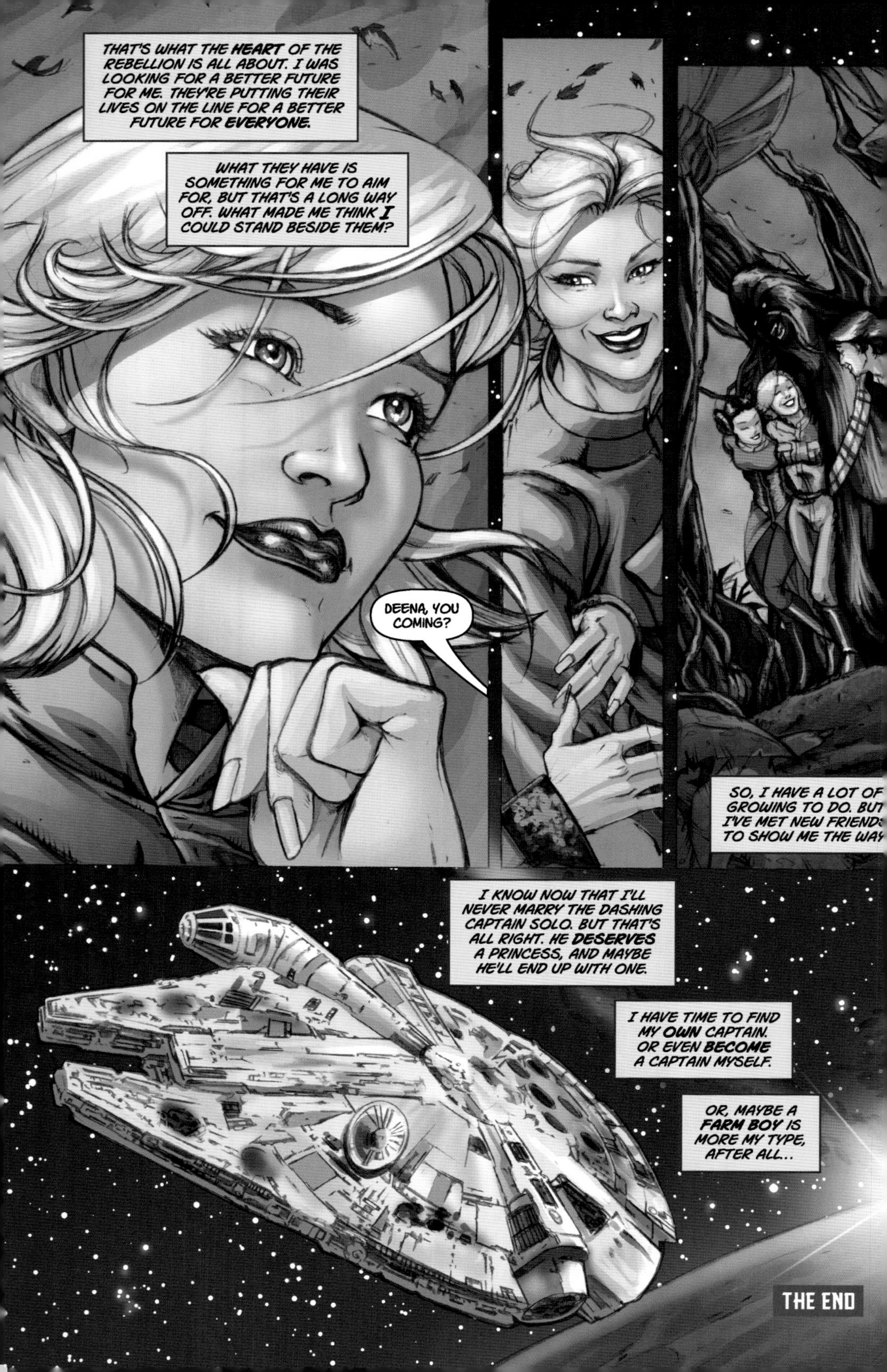
THAT'S WHAT THE HEART OF THE REBELLION IS ALL ABOUT. I WAS LOOKING FOR A BETTER FUTURE FOR ME. THEY'RE PUTTING THEIR LIVES ON THE LINE FOR A BETTER FUTURE FOR EVERYONE.
WHAT THEY HAVE IS SOMETHING FOR ME TO AIM FOR, BUT THAT'S A LONG WAY OFF. WHAT MADE ME THINK I COULD STAND BESIDE THEM?
DEENA, YOU COMING?
SO, I HAVE A LOT OF GROWING TO DO. BUT I'VE MET NEW FRIENDS TO SHOW ME THE WAY
I KNOW NOW THAT I'LL NEVER MARRY THE DASHING CAPTAIN SOLO. BUT THAT'S ALL RIGHT. HE DESERVES A PRINCESS, AND MAYBE HE'LL END UP WITH ONE.
I HAVE TIME TO FIND MY OWN CAPTAIN. OR EVEN BECOME A CAPTAIN MYSELF.
OR, MAYBE A FARM BOY IS MORE MY TYPE, AFTER ALL...
THE END

Idiot's Array | Illustration by Jeff Johnson, colored by Brad Anderson

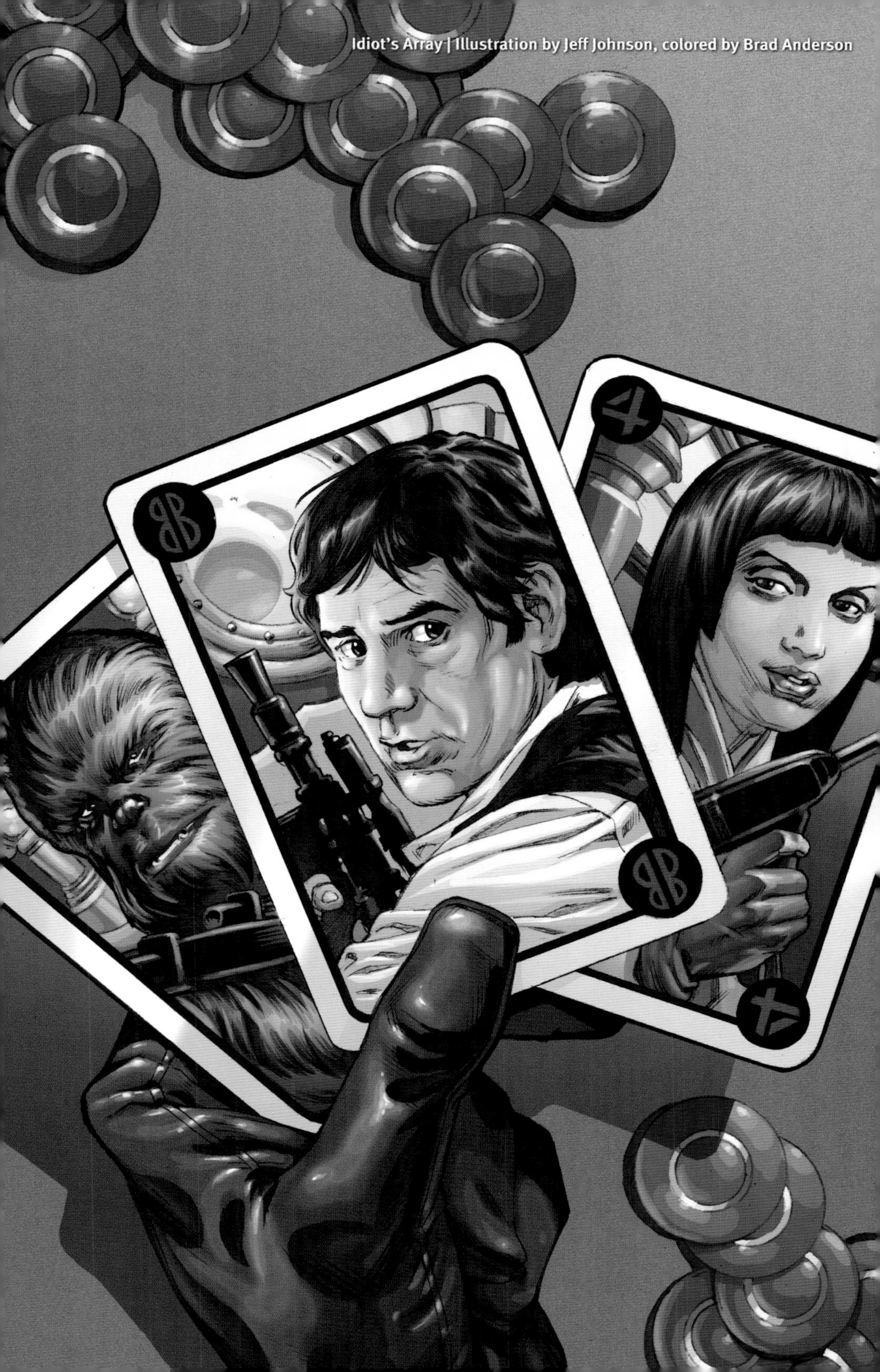

APPROXIMATELY SIX MONTHS AFTER THE BATTLE
OF YAVIN . . .

script by Ron Marz
art by Jeff Johnson and Joe Corroney
colors by Michael Atiyeh
lettering by Michael David Thomas

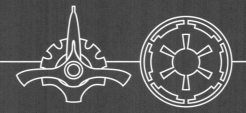

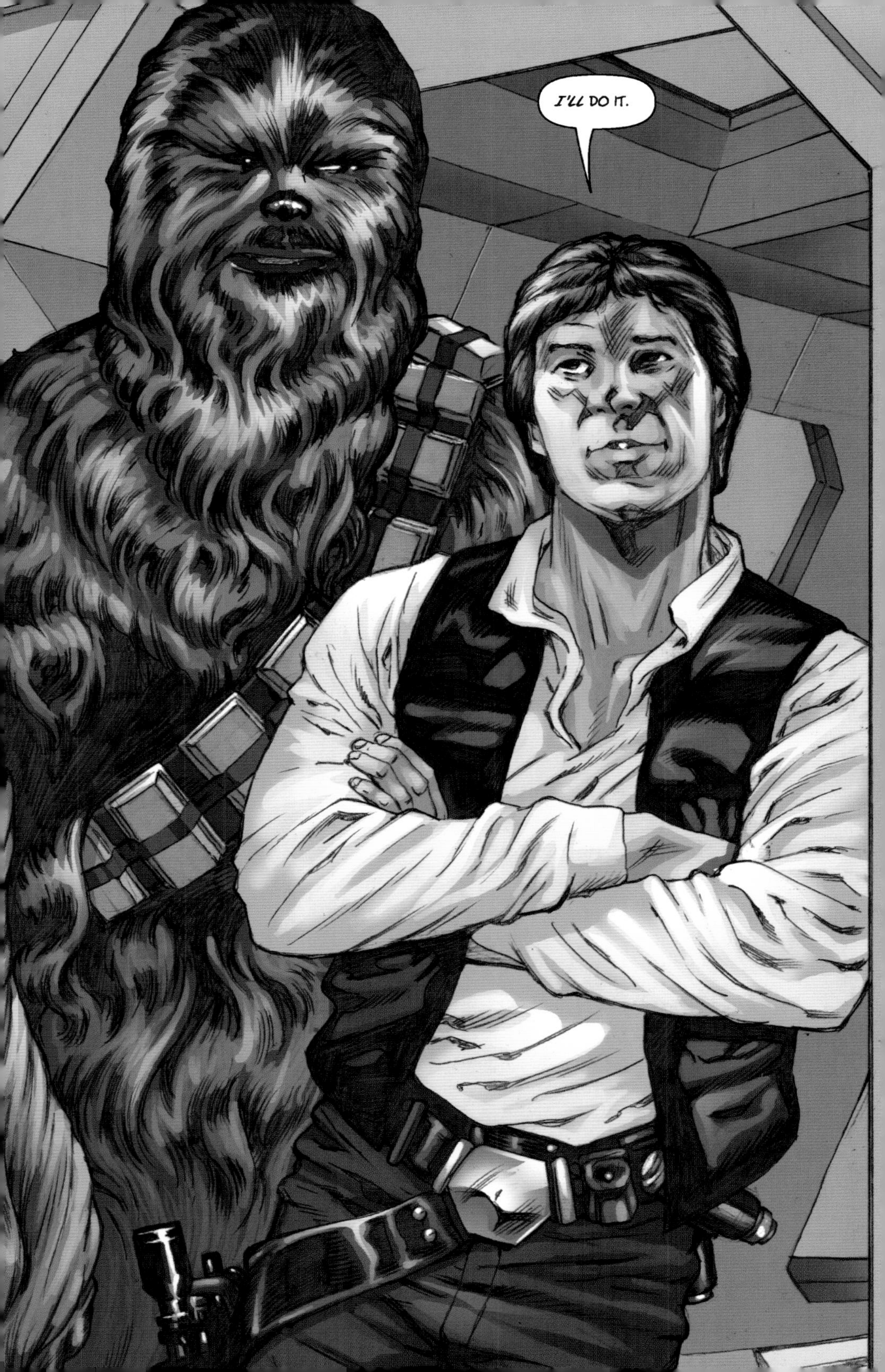
I'LL DO IT.

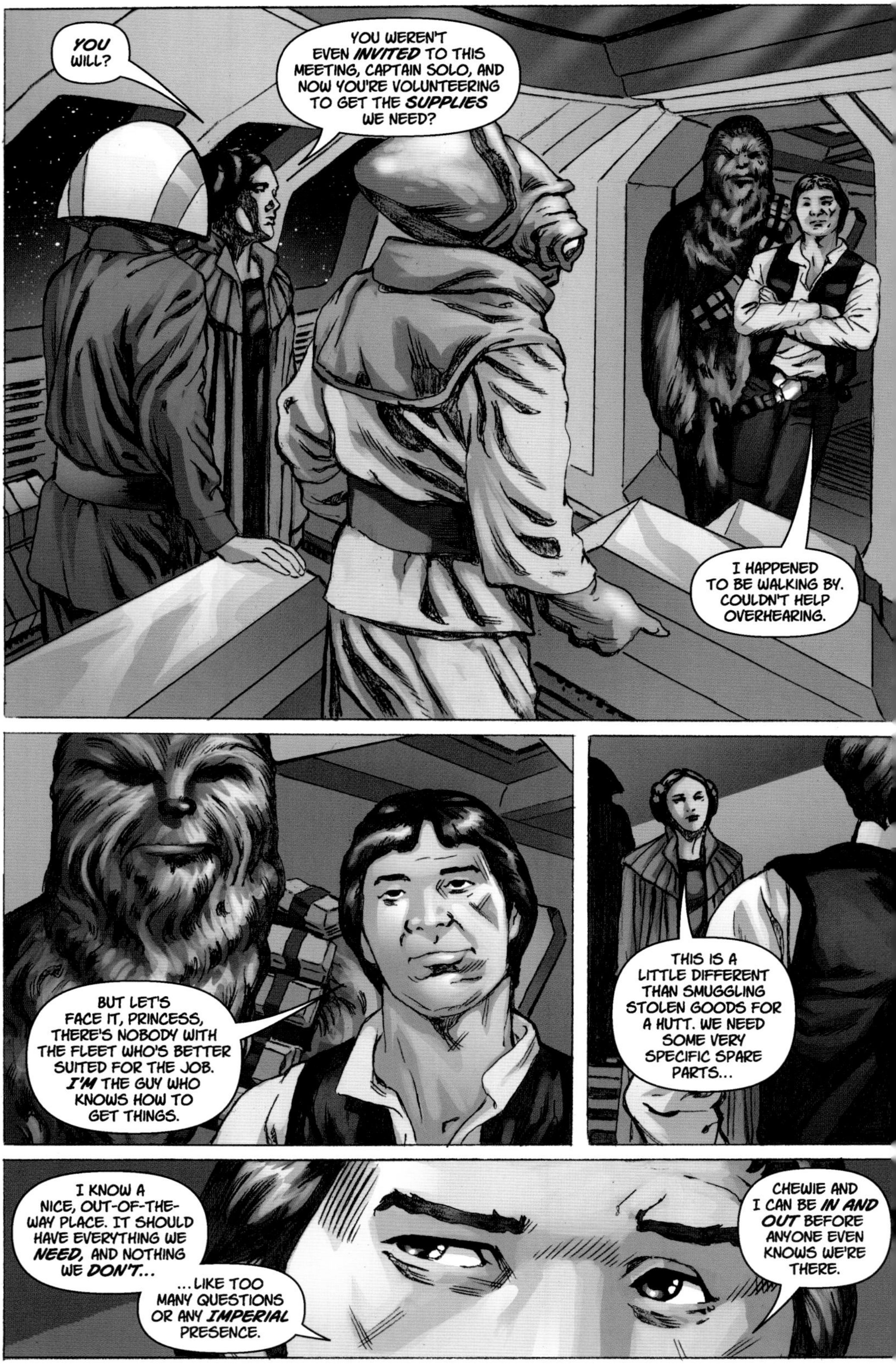
YOU WILL?
YOU WEREN'T EVEN INVITED TO THIS MEETING, CAPTAIN SOLO, AND NOW YOU'RE VOLUNTEERING TO GET THE SUPPLIES WE NEED?
I HAPPENED TO BE WALKING BY. COULDN'T HELP OVERHEARING.
BUT LET'S FACE IT, PRINCESS, THERE'S NOBODY WITH THE FLEET WHO'S BETTER SUITED FOR THE JOB. I'M THE GUY WHO KNOWS HOW TO GET THINGS.
THIS IS A LITTLE DIFFERENT THAN SMUGGLING STOLEN GOODS FOR A HUTT. WE NEED SOME VERY SPECIFIC SPARE PARTS...
I KNOW A NICE, OUT-OF-THE-WAY PLACE. IT SHOULD HAVE EVERYTHING WE NEED, AND NOTHING WE DON'T...
...LIKE TOO MANY QUESTIONS OR ANY IMPERIAL PRESENCE.
CHEWIE AND I CAN BE IN AND OUT BEFORE ANYONE EVEN KNOWS WE'RE THERE.

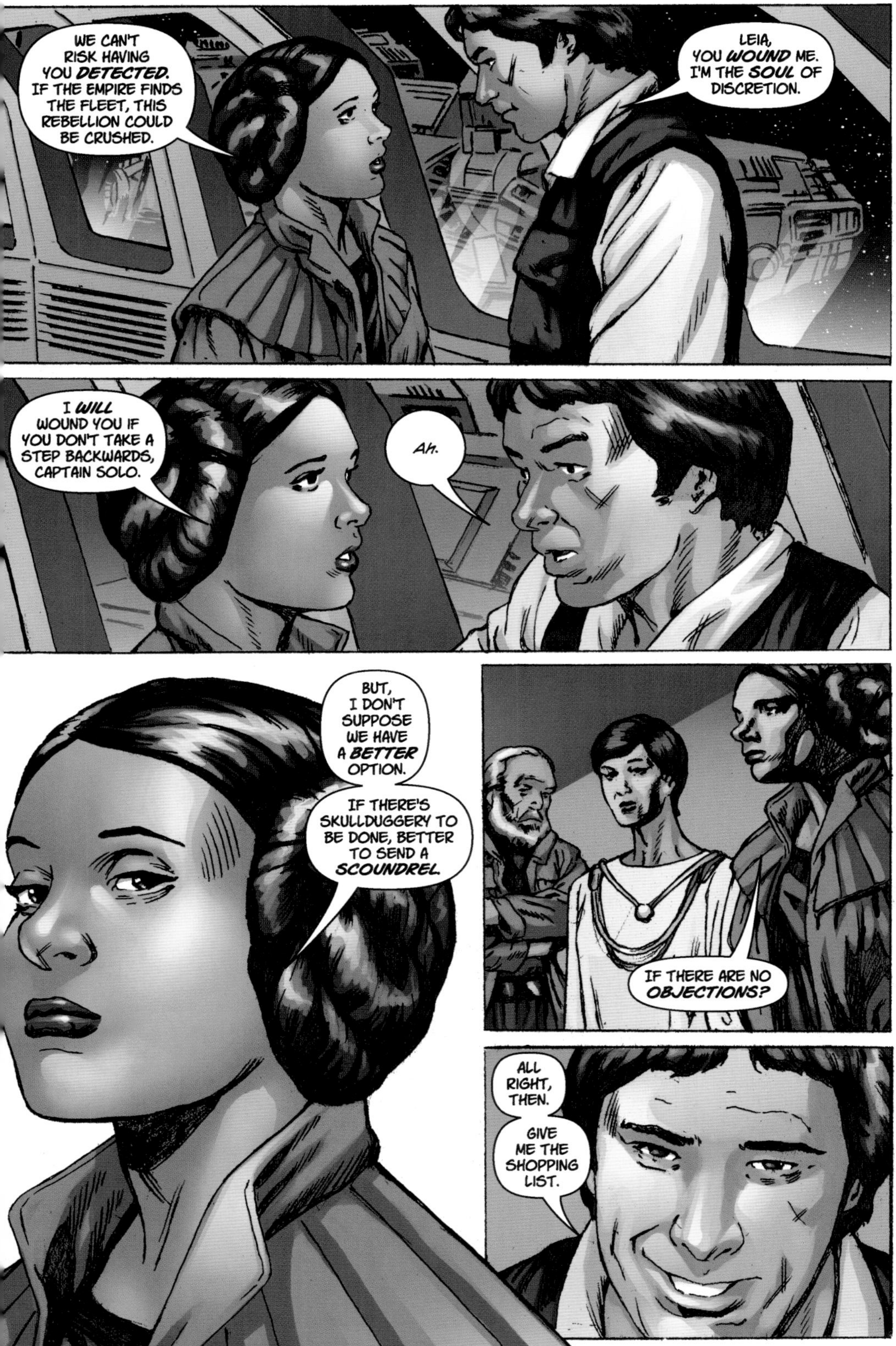
WE CAN'T RISK HAVING YOU DETECTED. IF THE EMPIRE FINDS THE FLEET, THIS REBELLION COULD BE CRUSHED.
LEIA, YOU WOUND ME. I'M THE SOUL OF DISCRETION.
I WILL WOUND YOU IF YOU DON'T TAKE A STEP BACKWARDS, CAPTAIN SOLO.
Ah.
BUT, I DON'T SUPPOSE WE HAVE A BETTER OPTION.
IF THERE'S SKULLDUGGERY TO BE DONE, BETTER TO SEND A SCOUNDREL.
IF THERE ARE NO OBJECTIONS?
ALL RIGHT, THEN.
GIVE ME THE SHOPPING LIST.

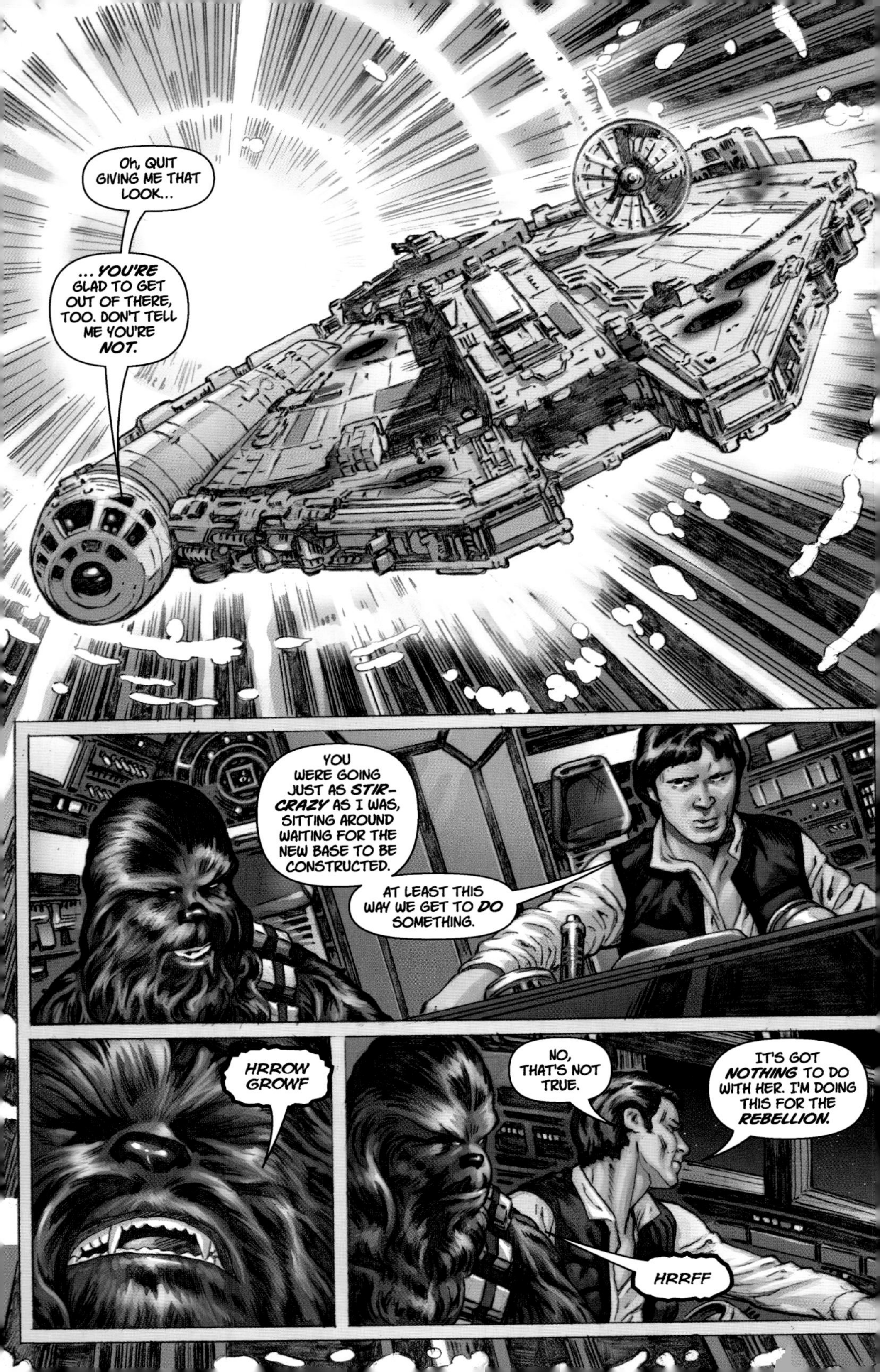
Oh, QUIT GIVING ME THAT LOOK...
...YOU'RE GLAD TO GET OUT OF THERE, TOO. DON'T TELL ME YOU'RE NOT.
YOU WERE GOING JUST AS STIR-CRAZY AS I WAS, SITTING AROUND WAITING FOR THE NEW BASE TO BE CONSTRUCTED.
AT LEAST THIS WAY WE GET TO DO SOMETHING.
HRROW GROWF
NO, THAT'S NOT TRUE.
IT'S GOT NOTHING TO DO WITH HER. I'M DOING THIS FOR THE REBELLION.
HRRFF

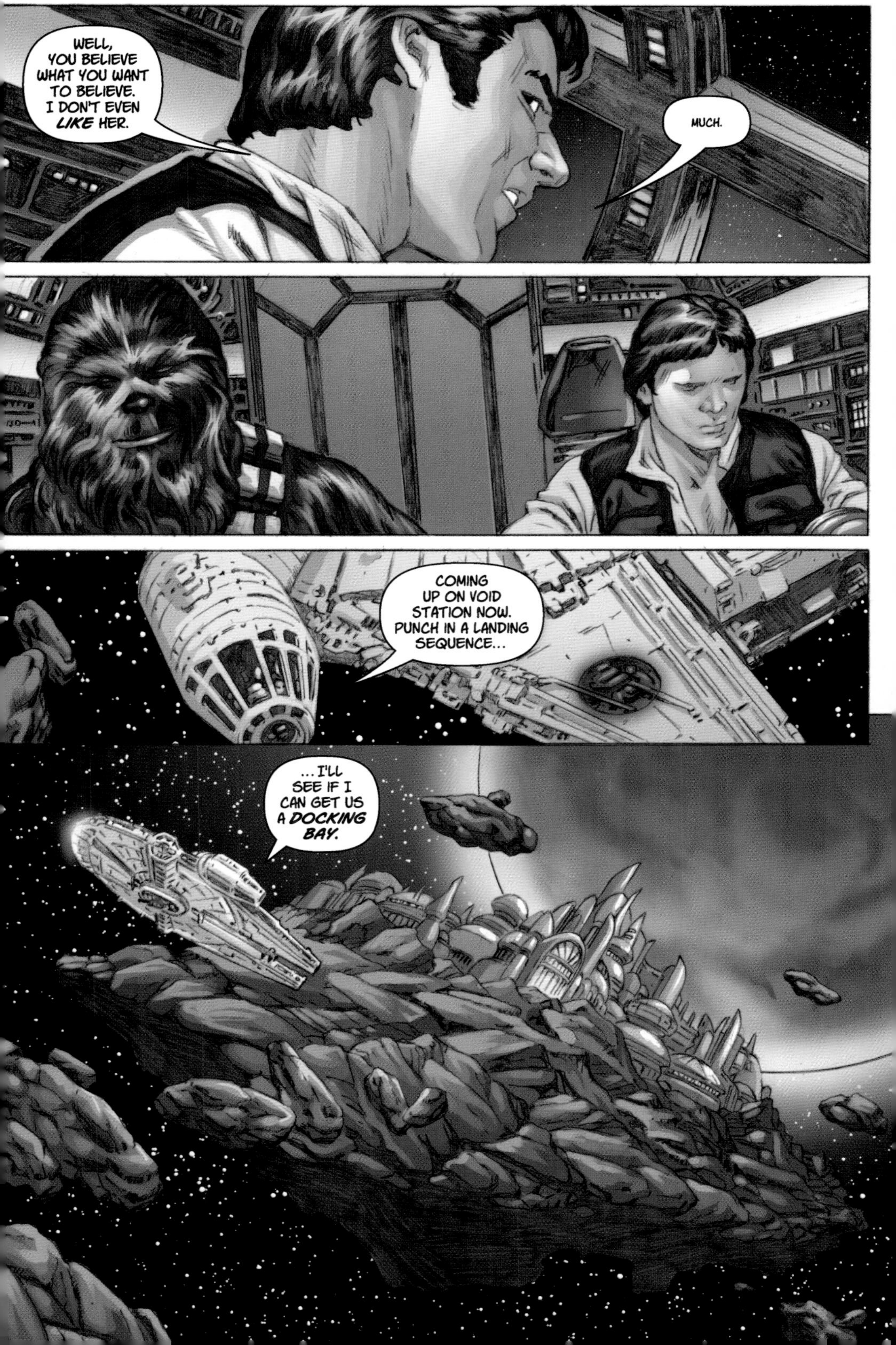
WELL, YOU BELIEVE WHAT YOU WANT TO BELIEVE. I DON'T EVEN *LIKE* HER.
MUCH.
COMING UP ON VOID STATION NOW. PUNCH IN A LANDING SEQUENCE...
...I'LL SEE IF I CAN GET US A *DOCKING BAY.*

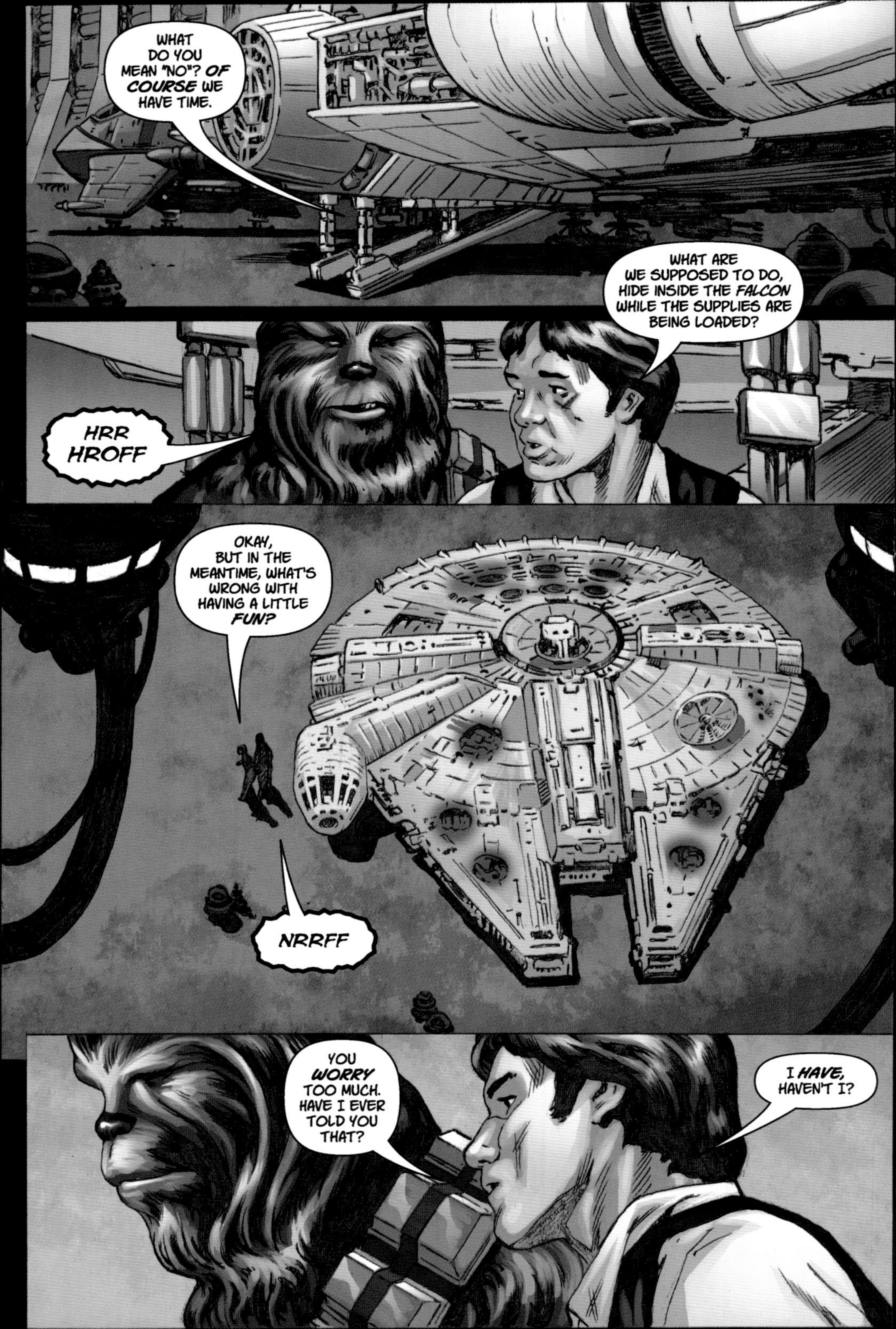
WHAT DO YOU MEAN "NO"? OF COURSE WE HAVE TIME.
WHAT ARE WE SUPPOSED TO DO, HIDE INSIDE THE FALCON WHILE THE SUPPLIES ARE BEING LOADED?
HRR HROFF
OKAY, BUT IN THE MEANTIME, WHAT'S WRONG WITH HAVING A LITTLE FUN?
NRRFF
YOU WORRY TOO MUCH. HAVE I EVER TOLD YOU THAT?
I HAVE, HAVEN'T I?

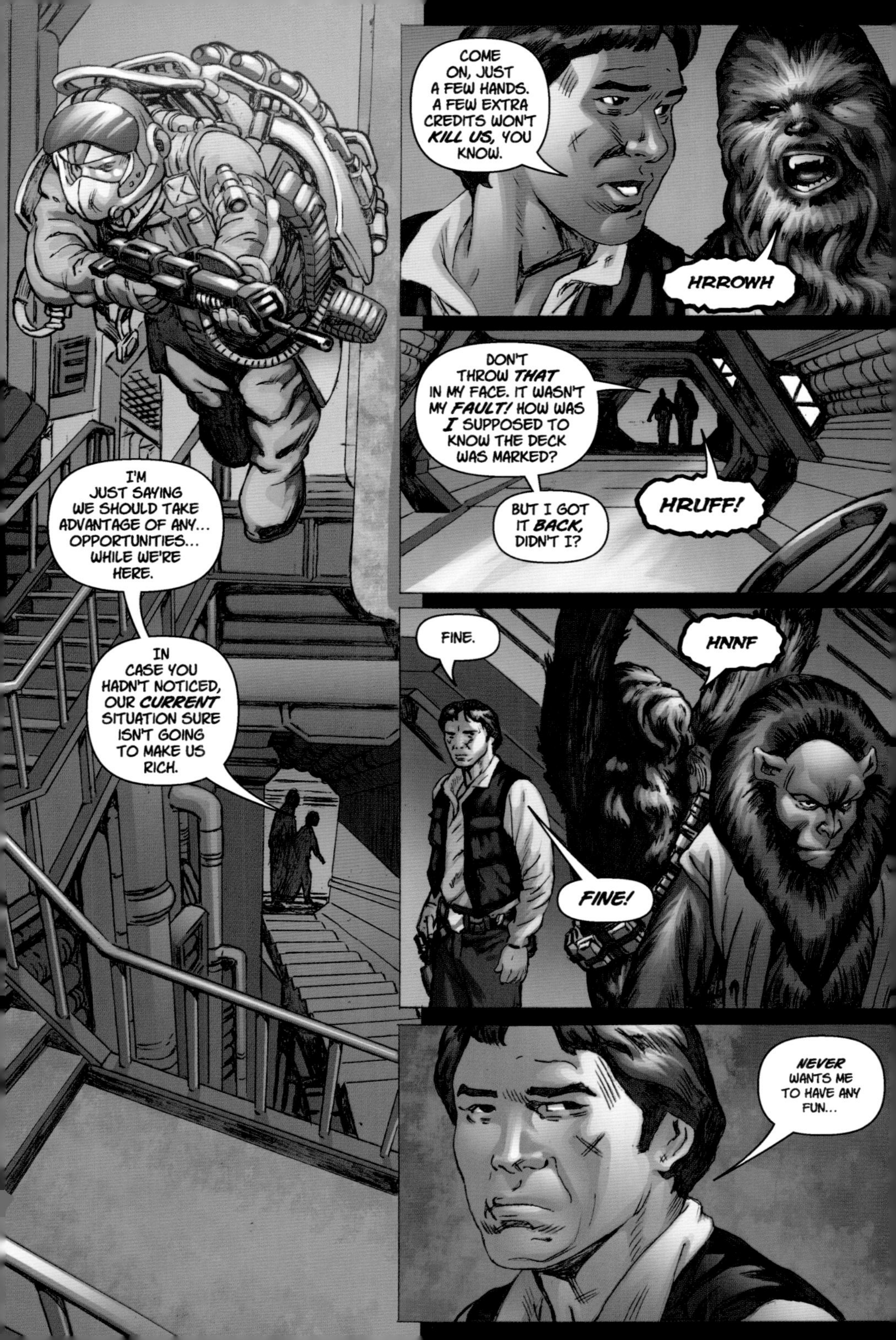

I'M JUST SAYING WE SHOULD TAKE ADVANTAGE OF ANY... OPPORTUNITIES... WHILE WE'RE HERE.
IN CASE YOU HADN'T NOTICED, OUR *CURRENT* SITUATION SURE ISN'T GOING TO MAKE US RICH.
COME ON, JUST A FEW HANDS. A FEW EXTRA CREDITS WON'T *KILL US,* YOU KNOW.
HRROWH
DON'T THROW *THAT* IN MY FACE. IT WASN'T MY *FAULT!* HOW WAS *I* SUPPOSED TO KNOW THE DECK WAS MARKED?
BUT I GOT IT *BACK,* DIDN'T I?
HRUFF!
FINE.
HNNF
FINE!
NEVER WANTS ME TO HAVE ANY FUN...

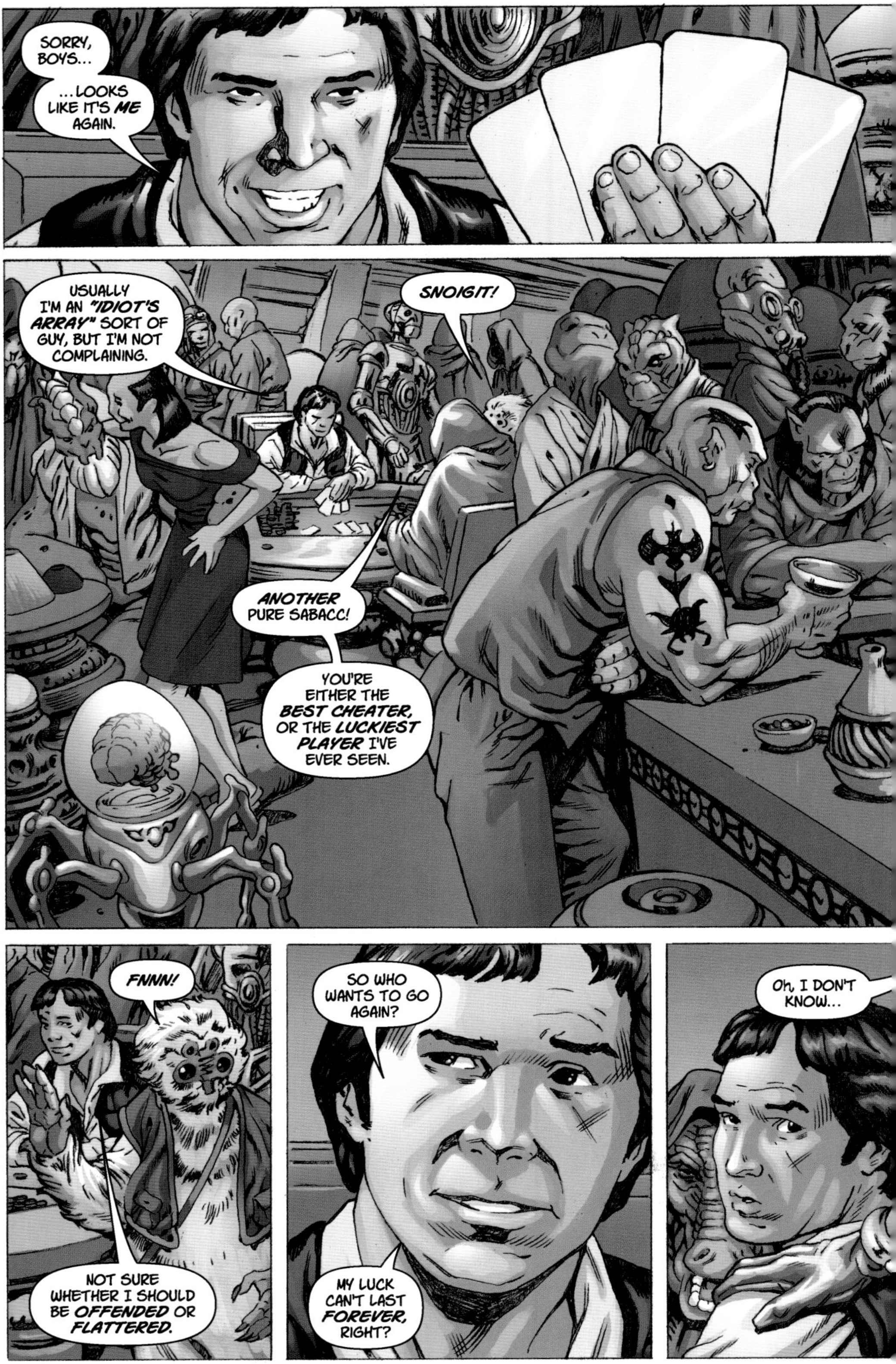
SORRY, BOYS...
...LOOKS LIKE IT'S *ME* AGAIN.
USUALLY I'M AN *"IDIOT'S ARRAY"* SORT OF GUY, BUT I'M NOT COMPLAINING.
SNOIGIT!
ANOTHER PURE SABACC!
YOU'RE EITHER THE *BEST CHEATER*, OR THE *LUCKIEST PLAYER* I'VE EVER SEEN.
FNNN!
NOT SURE WHETHER I SHOULD BE *OFFENDED* OR *FLATTERED*.
SO WHO WANTS TO GO AGAIN?
MY LUCK CAN'T LAST *FOREVER*, RIGHT?
OH, I DON'T KNOW...

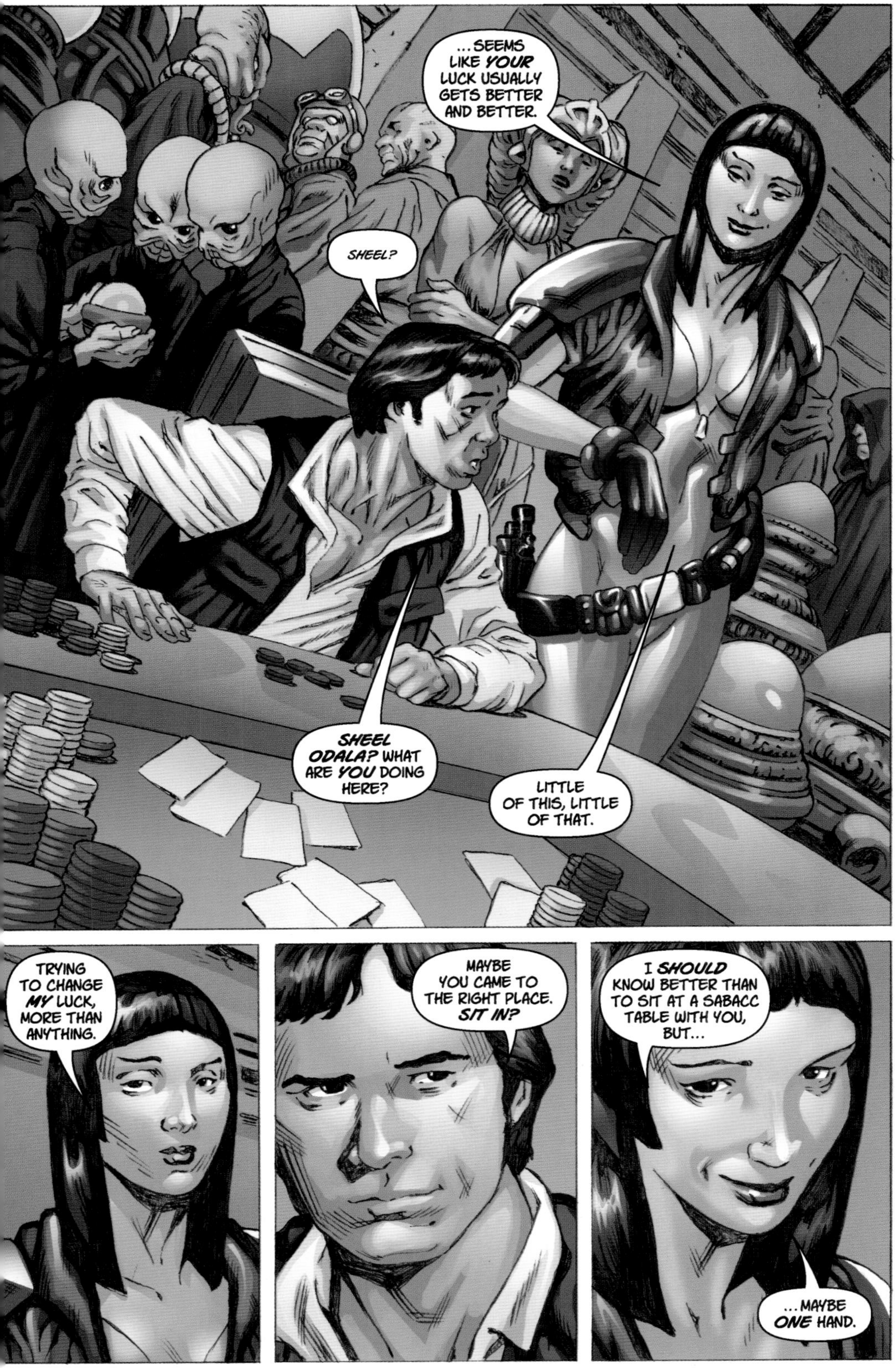
...SEEMS LIKE *YOUR* LUCK USUALLY GETS BETTER AND BETTER.
SHEEL?
SHEEL ODALA? WHAT ARE *YOU* DOING HERE?
LITTLE OF THIS, LITTLE OF THAT.
TRYING TO CHANGE *MY* LUCK, MORE THAN ANYTHING.
MAYBE YOU CAME TO THE RIGHT PLACE. *SIT IN?*
I *SHOULD* KNOW BETTER THAN TO SIT AT A SABACC TABLE WITH YOU, BUT...
...MAYBE *ONE* HAND.

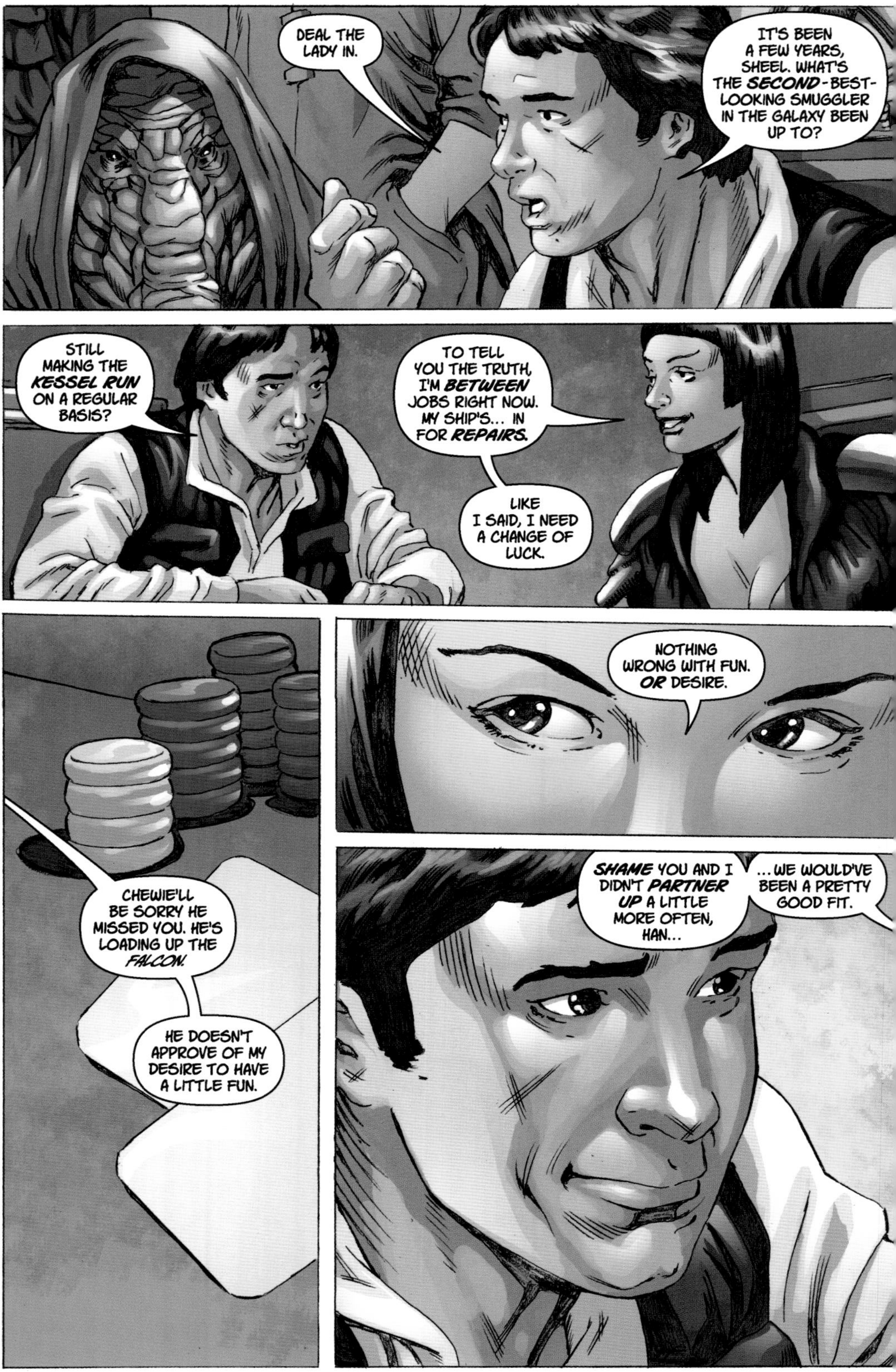
DEAL THE LADY IN.
IT'S BEEN A FEW YEARS, SHEEL. WHAT'S THE *SECOND*-BEST-LOOKING SMUGGLER IN THE GALAXY BEEN UP TO?
STILL MAKING THE *KESSEL RUN* ON A REGULAR BASIS?
TO TELL YOU THE TRUTH, I'M *BETWEEN* JOBS RIGHT NOW. MY SHIP'S... IN FOR *REPAIRS*.
LIKE I SAID, I NEED A CHANGE OF LUCK.
CHEWIE'LL BE SORRY HE MISSED YOU. HE'S LOADING UP THE *FALCON*.
HE DOESN'T APPROVE OF MY DESIRE TO HAVE A LITTLE FUN.
NOTHING WRONG WITH FUN. *OR* DESIRE.
SHAME YOU AND I DIDN'T *PARTNER UP* A LITTLE MORE OFTEN, HAN...
...WE WOULD'VE BEEN A PRETTY GOOD FIT.

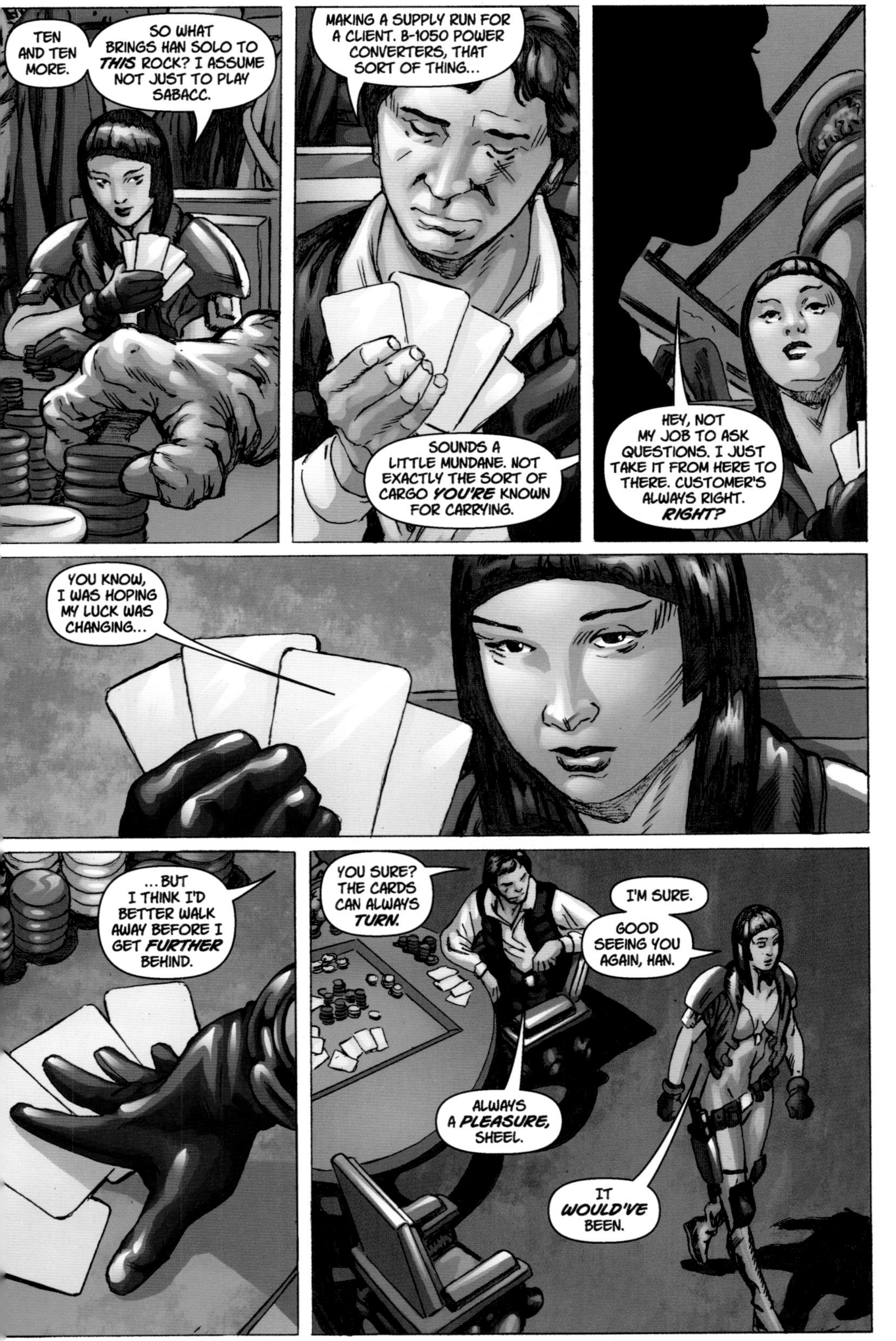
TEN AND TEN MORE.
SO WHAT BRINGS HAN SOLO TO *THIS* ROCK? I ASSUME NOT JUST TO PLAY SABACC.
MAKING A SUPPLY RUN FOR A CLIENT. B-1050 POWER CONVERTERS, THAT SORT OF THING...
SOUNDS A LITTLE MUNDANE. NOT EXACTLY THE SORT OF CARGO *YOU'RE* KNOWN FOR CARRYING.
HEY, NOT MY JOB TO ASK QUESTIONS. I JUST TAKE IT FROM HERE TO THERE. CUSTOMER'S ALWAYS RIGHT. ***RIGHT?***
YOU KNOW, I WAS HOPING MY LUCK WAS CHANGING...
...BUT I THINK I'D BETTER WALK AWAY BEFORE I GET *FURTHER* BEHIND.
YOU SURE? THE CARDS CAN ALWAYS *TURN.*
I'M SURE.
GOOD SEEING YOU AGAIN, HAN.
ALWAYS A *PLEASURE,* SHEEL.
IT *WOULD'VE* BEEN.

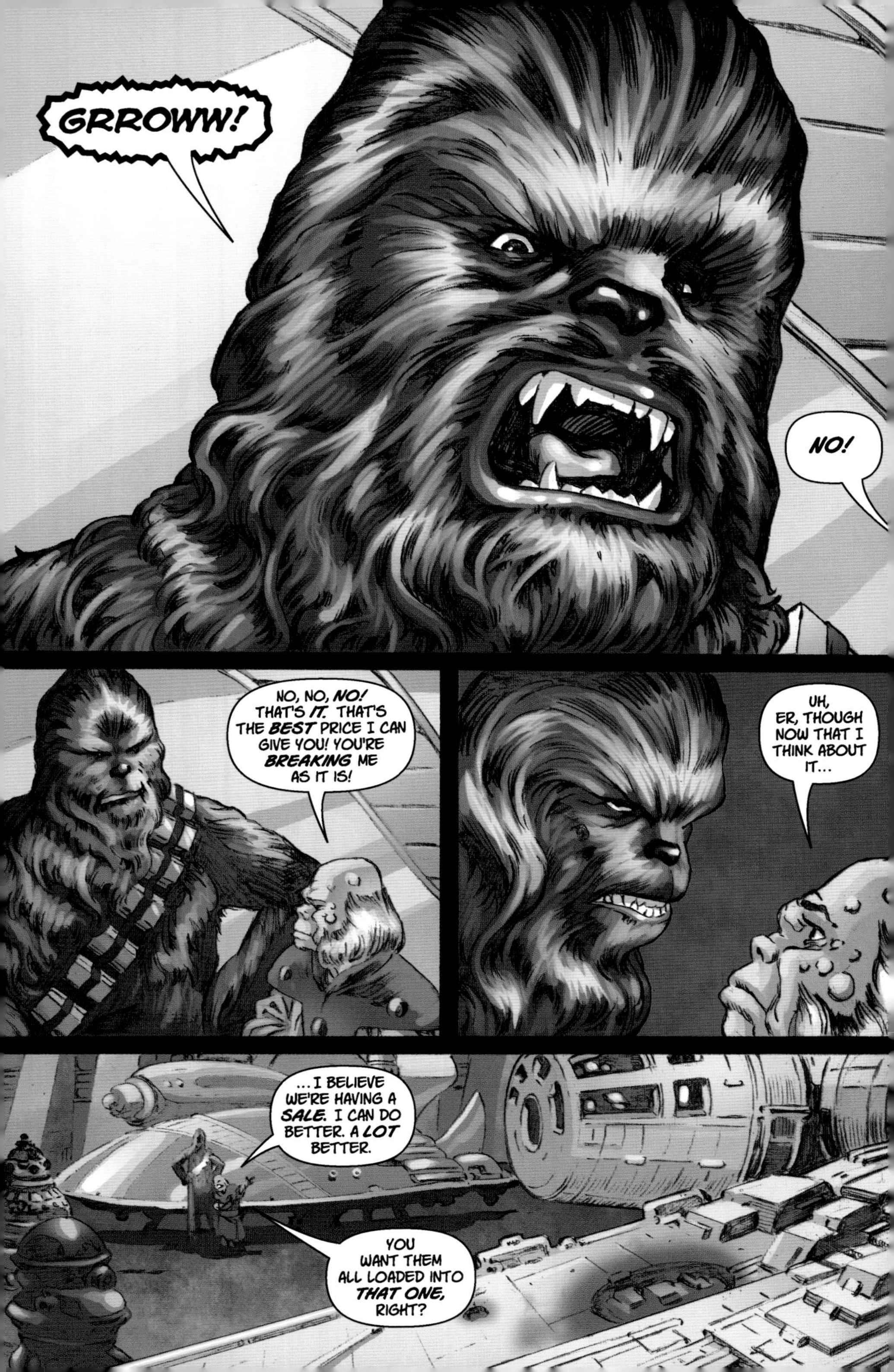
GRROWW!
NO!
NO, NO, NO! THAT'S IT. THAT'S THE BEST PRICE I CAN GIVE YOU! YOU'RE BREAKING ME AS IT IS!
UH, ER, THOUGH NOW THAT I THINK ABOUT IT...
...I BELIEVE WE'RE HAVING A SALE. I CAN DO BETTER. A LOT BETTER.
YOU WANT THEM ALL LOADED INTO THAT ONE, RIGHT?

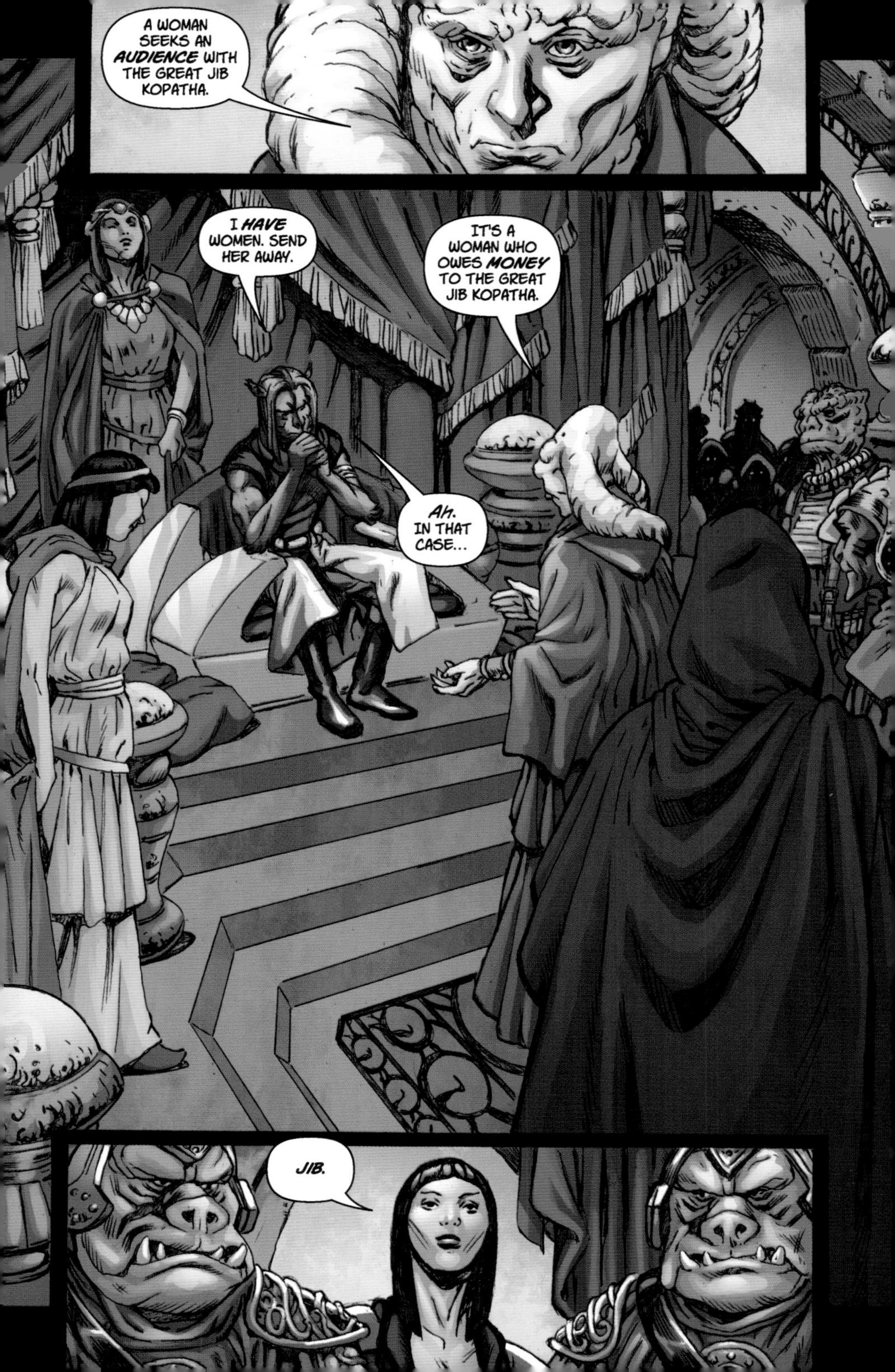
A WOMAN SEEKS AN AUDIENCE WITH THE GREAT JIB KOPATHA.
I HAVE WOMEN. SEND HER AWAY.
IT'S A WOMAN WHO OWES MONEY TO THE GREAT JIB KOPATHA.
Ah. IN THAT CASE...
JIB.

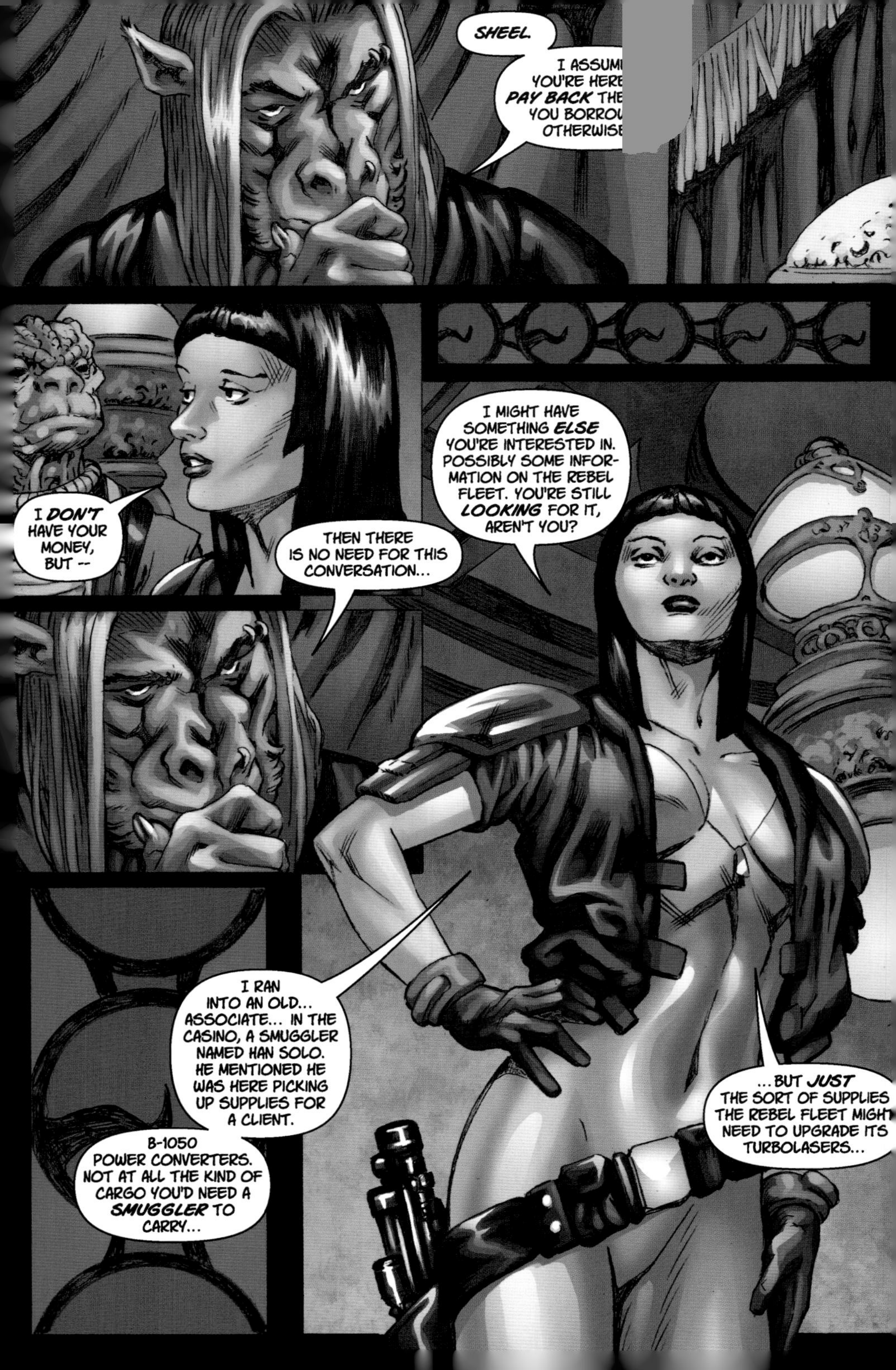
SHEEL.
I ASSUME YOU'RE HERE PAY BACK THE YOU BORROW OTHERWISE
I DON'T HAVE YOUR MONEY, BUT --
THEN THERE IS NO NEED FOR THIS CONVERSATION...
I MIGHT HAVE SOMETHING ELSE YOU'RE INTERESTED IN. POSSIBLY SOME INFORMATION ON THE REBEL FLEET. YOU'RE STILL LOOKING FOR IT, AREN'T YOU?
I RAN INTO AN OLD... ASSOCIATE... IN THE CASINO, A SMUGGLER NAMED HAN SOLO. HE MENTIONED HE WAS HERE PICKING UP SUPPLIES FOR A CLIENT.
B-1050 POWER CONVERTERS. NOT AT ALL THE KIND OF CARGO YOU'D NEED A SMUGGLER TO CARRY...
...BUT JUST THE SORT OF SUPPLIES THE REBEL FLEET MIGHT NEED TO UPGRADE ITS TURBOLASERS...

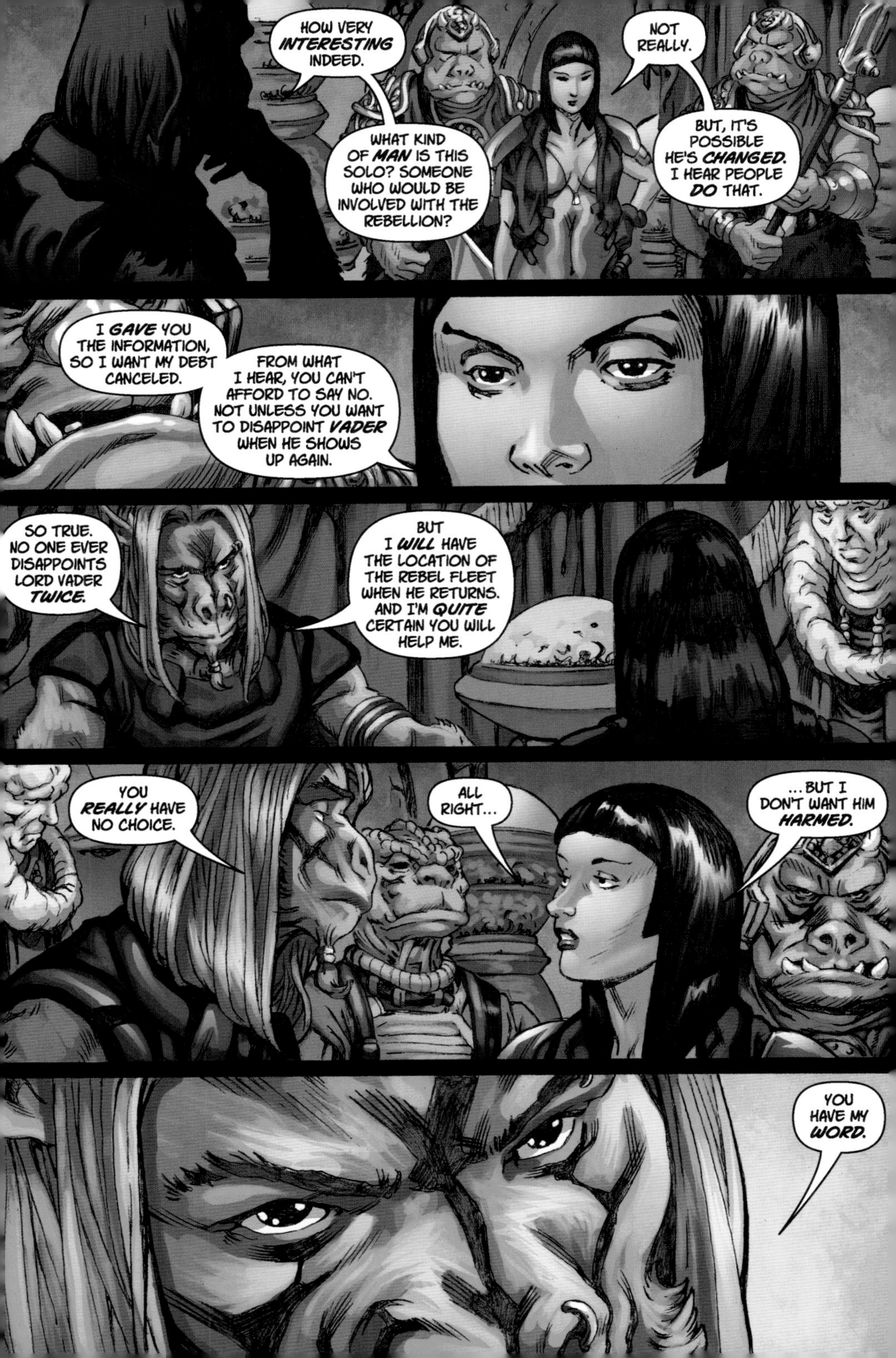
HOW VERY INTERESTING INDEED.
WHAT KIND OF MAN IS THIS SOLO? SOMEONE WHO WOULD BE INVOLVED WITH THE REBELLION?
NOT REALLY.
BUT, IT'S POSSIBLE HE'S CHANGED. I HEAR PEOPLE DO THAT.
I GAVE YOU THE INFORMATION, SO I WANT MY DEBT CANCELED.
FROM WHAT I HEAR, YOU CAN'T AFFORD TO SAY NO. NOT UNLESS YOU WANT TO DISAPPOINT VADER WHEN HE SHOWS UP AGAIN.
SO TRUE. NO ONE EVER DISAPPOINTS LORD VADER TWICE.
BUT I WILL HAVE THE LOCATION OF THE REBEL FLEET WHEN HE RETURNS. AND I'M QUITE CERTAIN YOU WILL HELP ME.
YOU REALLY HAVE NO CHOICE.
ALL RIGHT...
...BUT I DON'T WANT HIM HARMED.
YOU HAVE MY WORD.

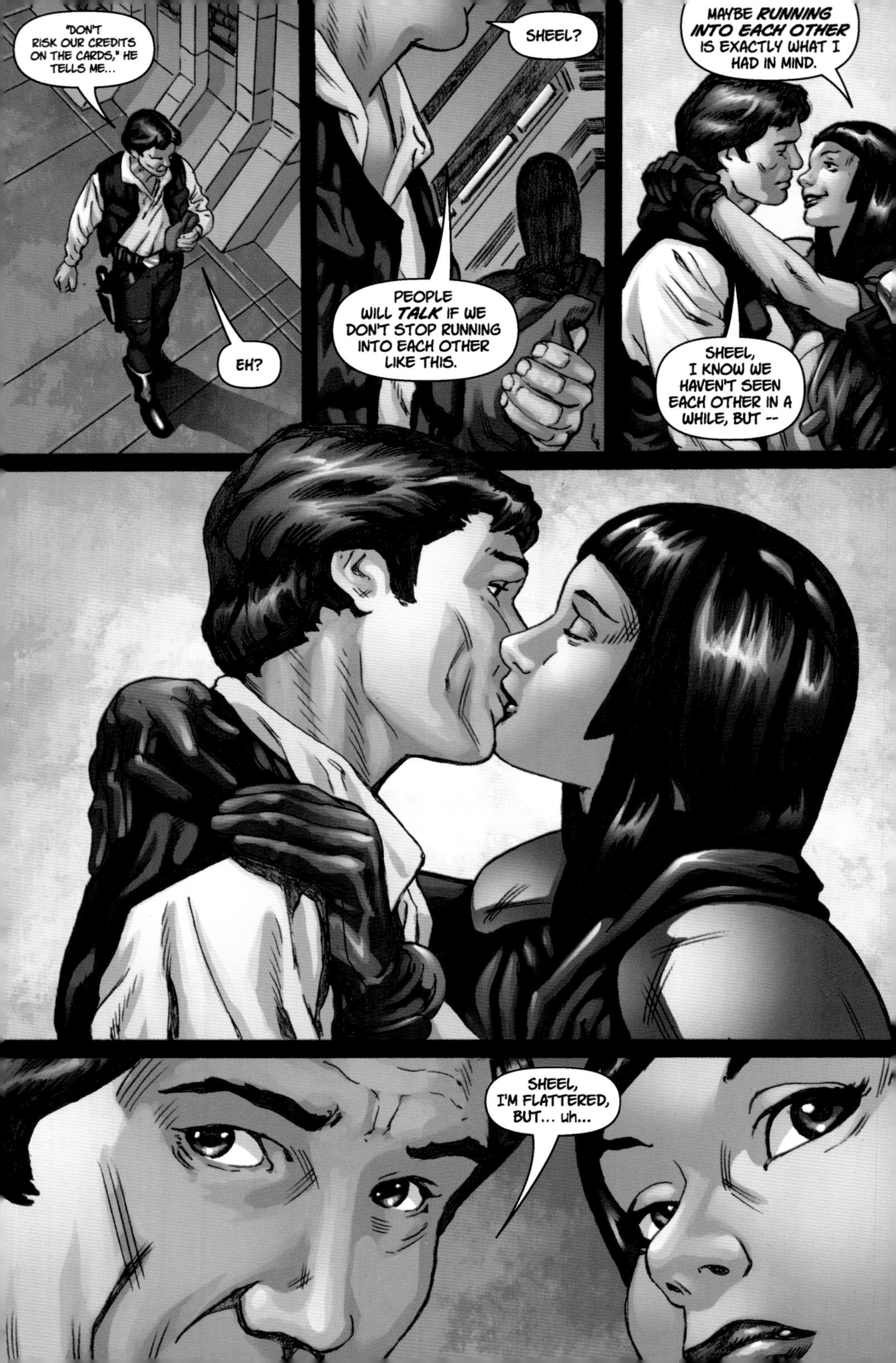
"DON'T RISK OUR CREDITS ON THE CARDS," HE TELLS ME...
EH?
SHEEL?
PEOPLE WILL *TALK* IF WE DON'T STOP RUNNING INTO EACH OTHER LIKE THIS.
MAYBE ***RUNNING INTO EACH OTHER*** IS EXACTLY WHAT I HAD IN MIND.
SHEEL, I KNOW WE HAVEN'T SEEN EACH OTHER IN A WHILE, BUT --
SHEEL, I'M FLATTERED, BUT... uh...

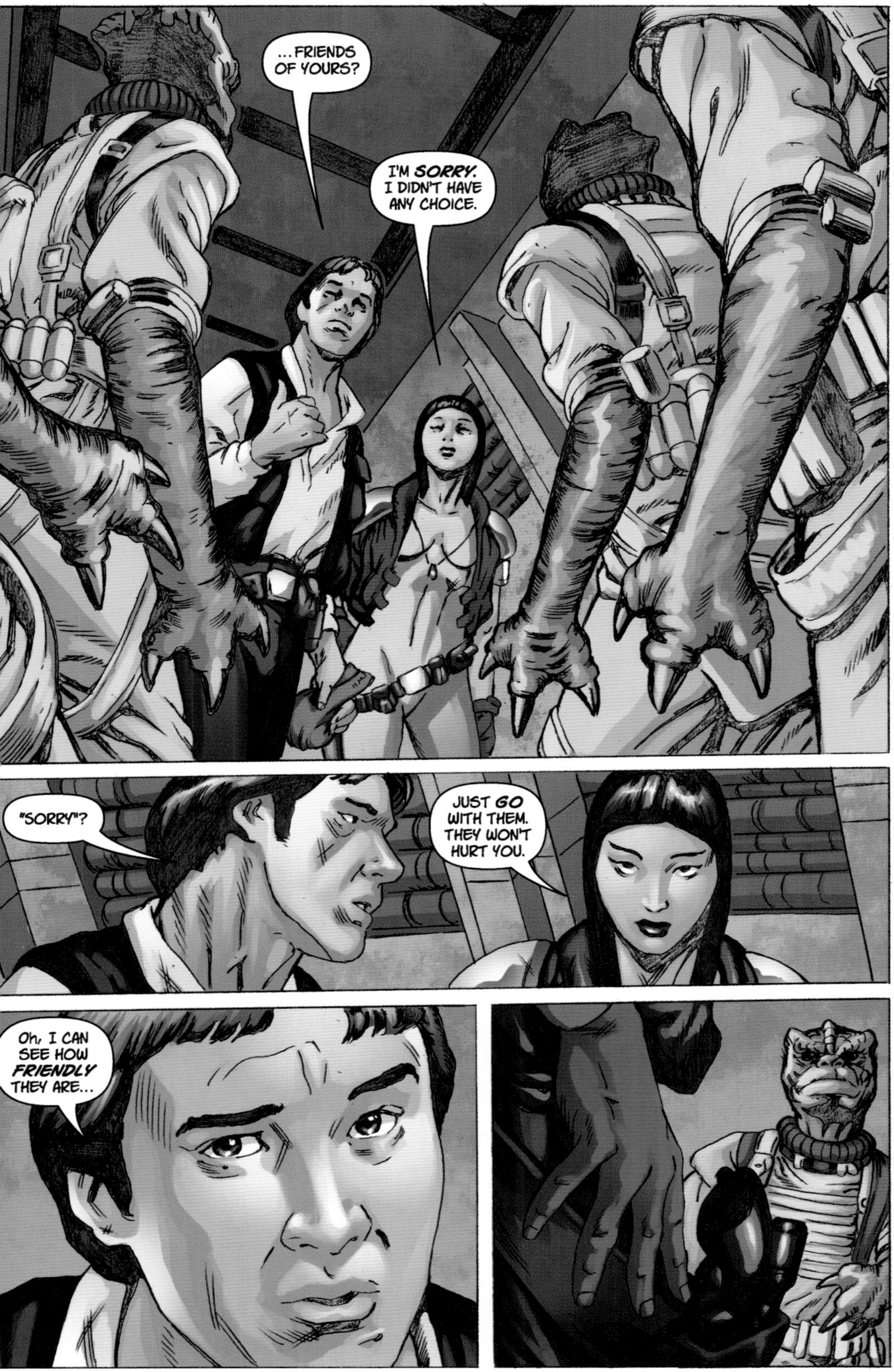
...FRIENDS OF YOURS?
I'M SORRY. I DIDN'T HAVE ANY CHOICE.
"SORRY"?
JUST GO WITH THEM. THEY WON'T HURT YOU.
Oh, I CAN SEE HOW FRIENDLY THEY ARE...

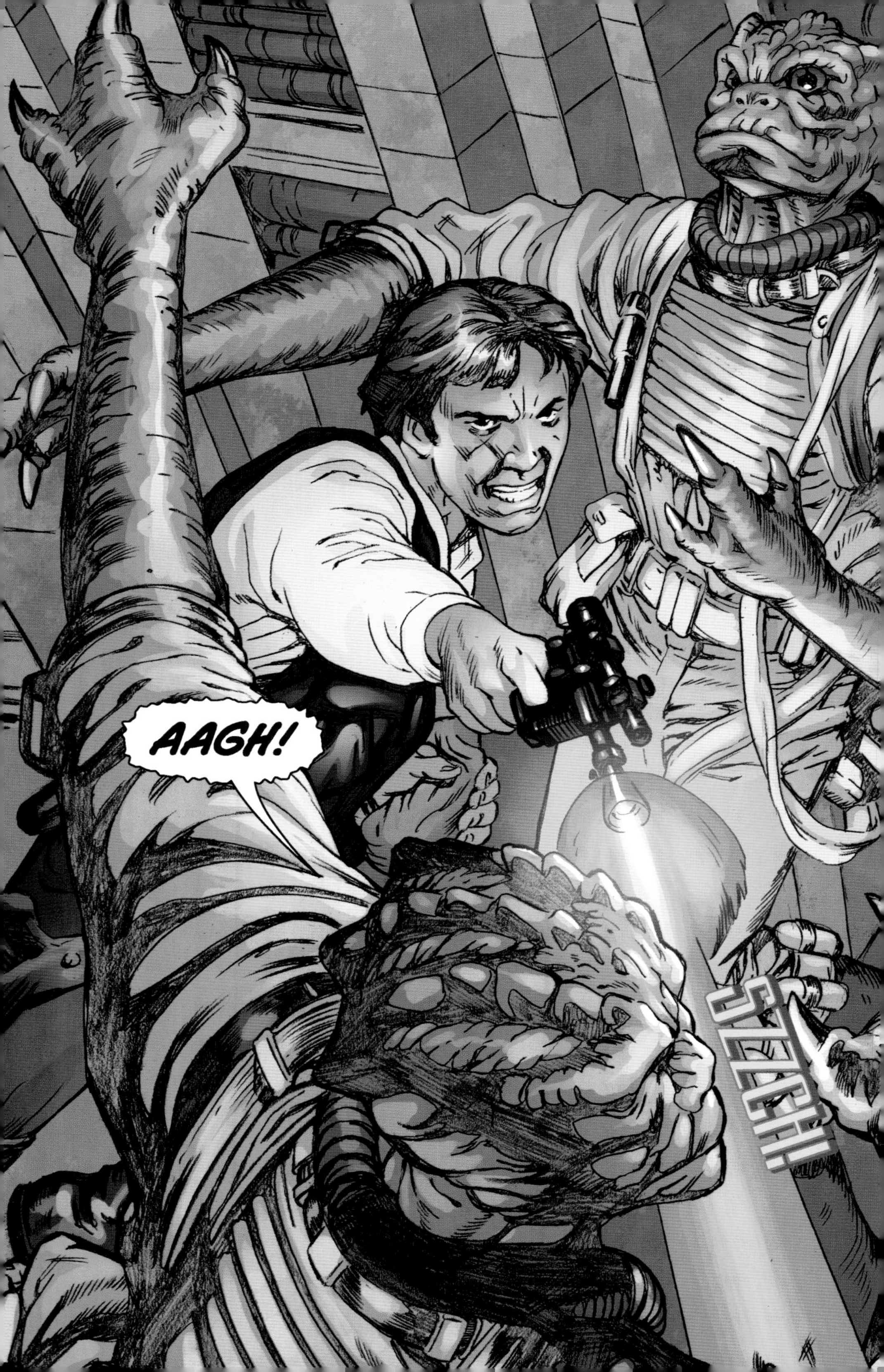
AAGH!
SZZCH!

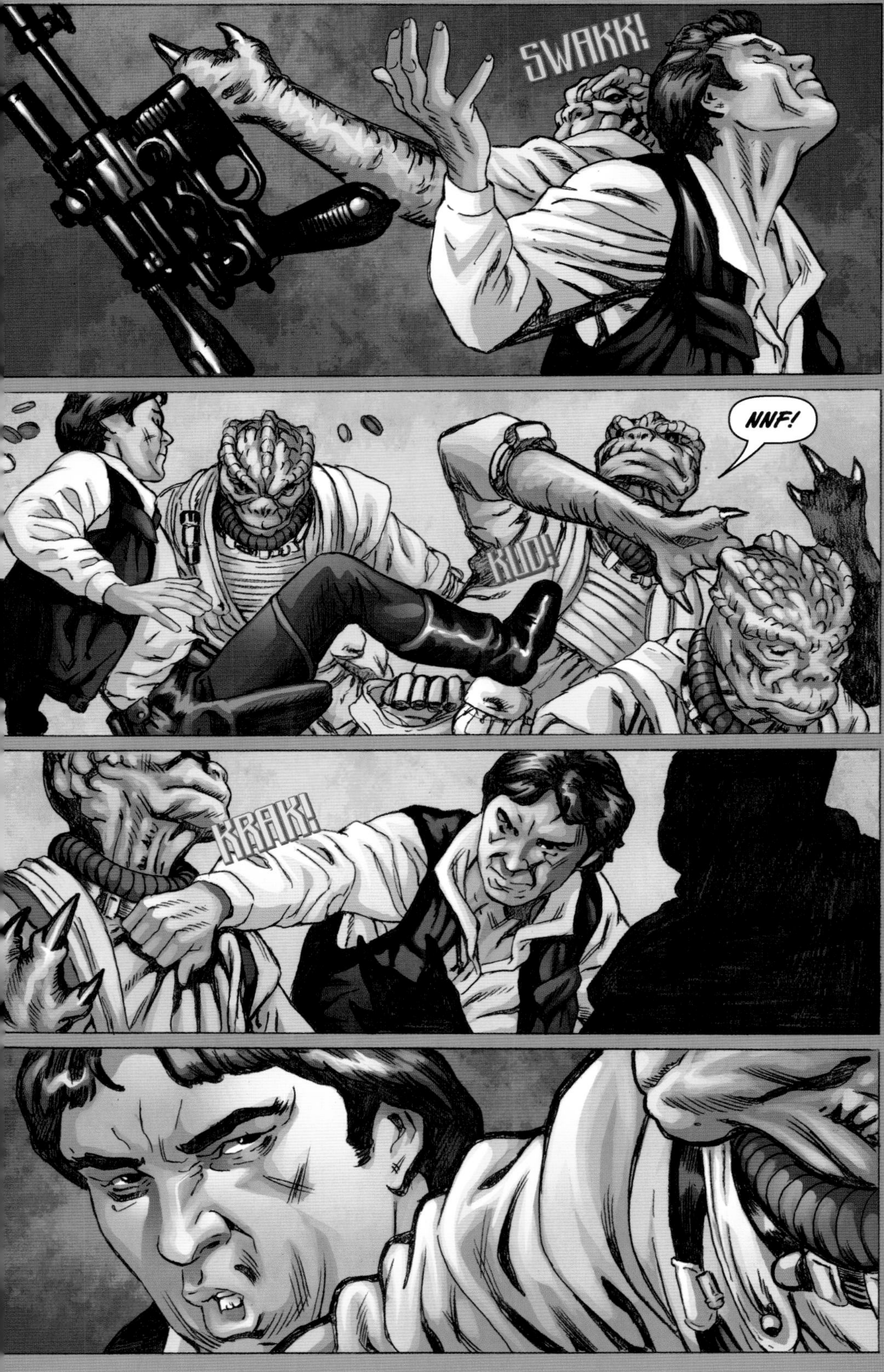
SWAKK!
NNF!
KUD!
KRAK!

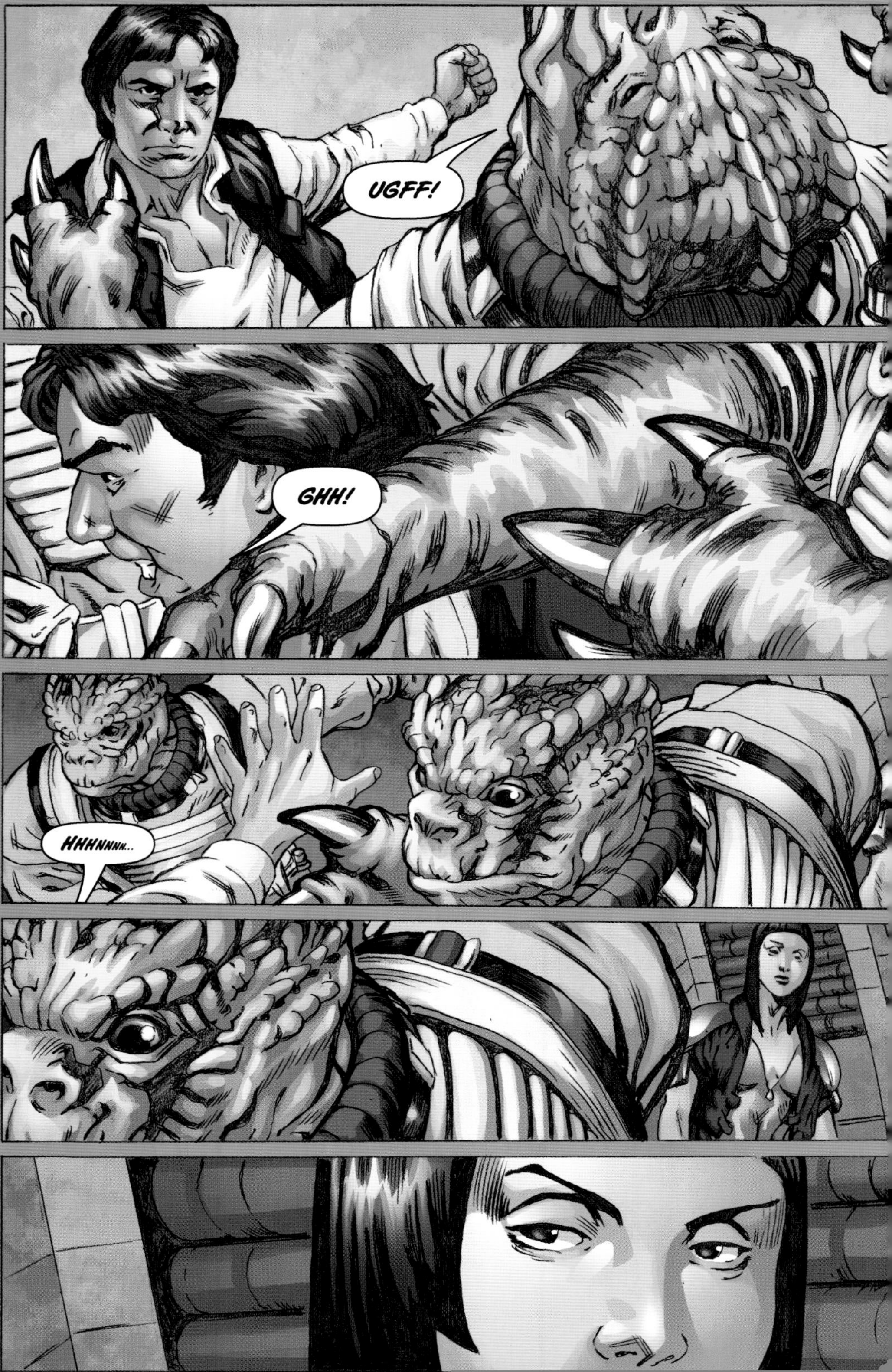
UGFF!
GHH!
HHHNNNN...

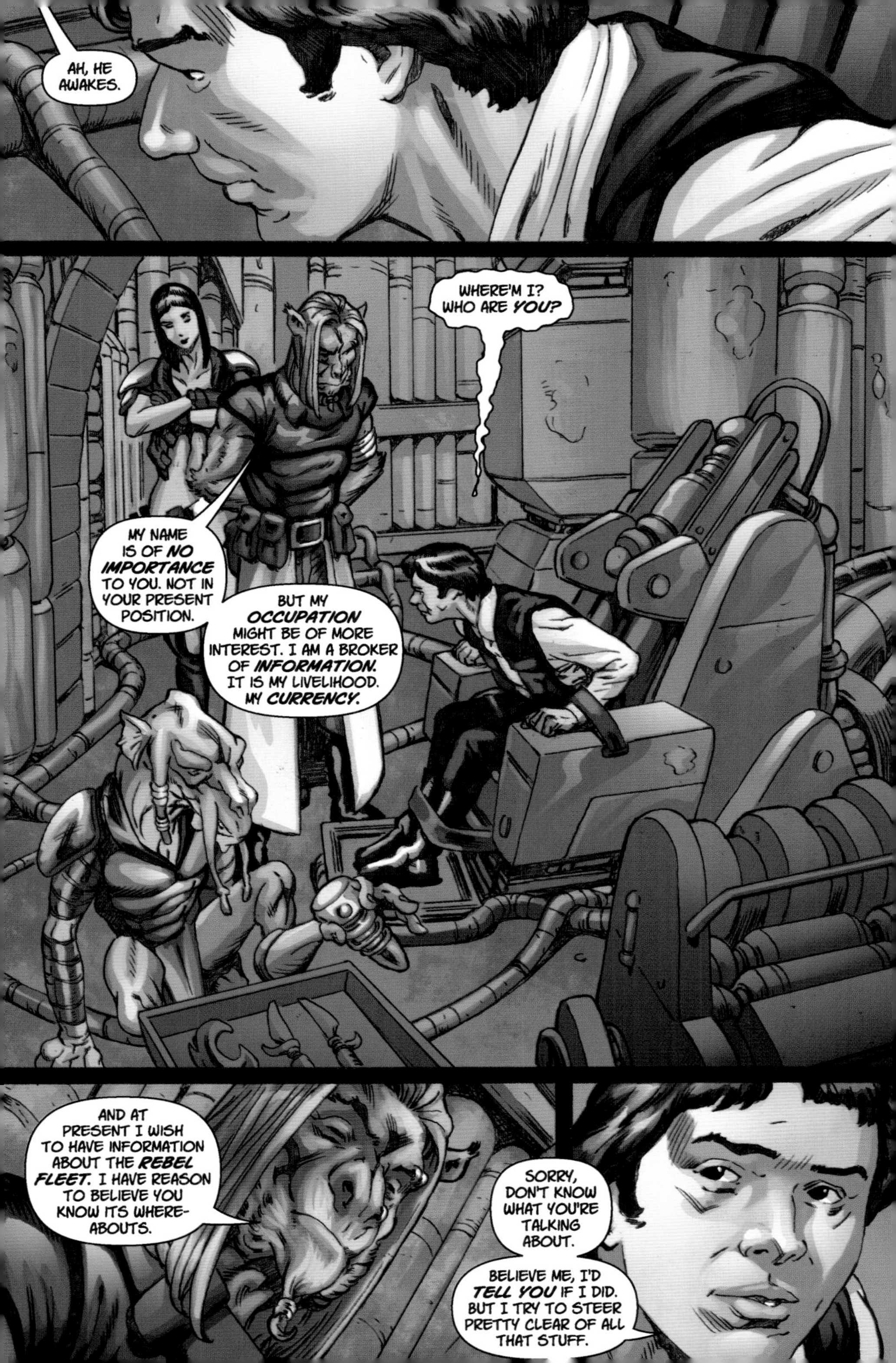
AH, HE AWAKES.
WHERE'M I? WHO ARE *YOU?*
MY NAME IS OF ***NO IMPORTANCE*** TO YOU. NOT IN YOUR PRESENT POSITION.
BUT MY ***OCCUPATION*** MIGHT BE OF MORE INTEREST. I AM A BROKER OF ***INFORMATION.*** IT IS MY LIVELIHOOD. MY ***CURRENCY.***
AND AT PRESENT I WISH TO HAVE INFORMATION ABOUT THE ***REBEL FLEET.*** I HAVE REASON TO BELIEVE YOU KNOW ITS WHERE-ABOUTS.
SORRY, DON'T KNOW WHAT YOU'RE TALKING ABOUT.
BELIEVE ME, I'D ***TELL YOU*** IF I DID. BUT I TRY TO STEER PRETTY CLEAR OF ALL THAT STUFF.

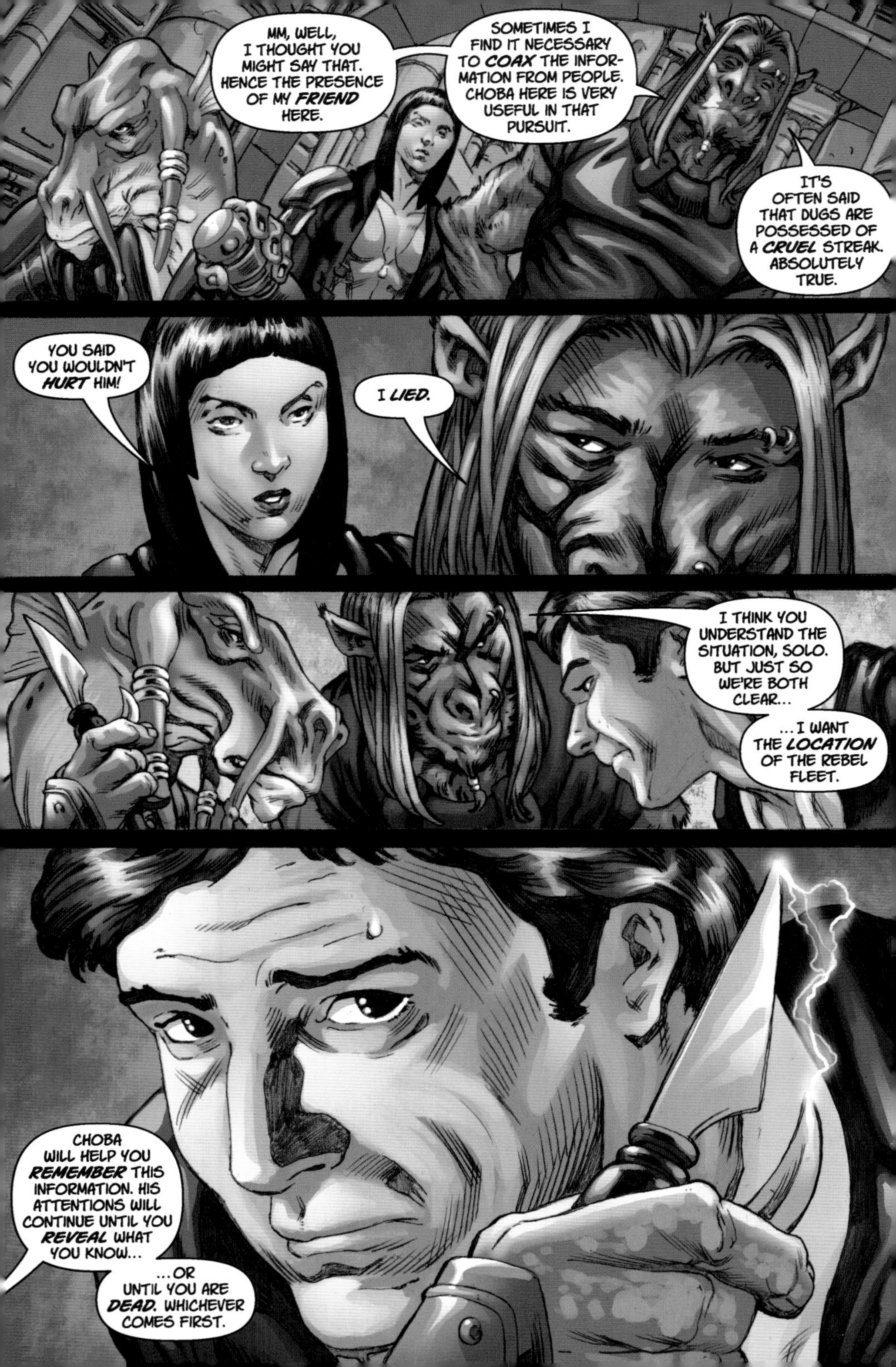
MM, WELL, I THOUGHT YOU MIGHT SAY THAT. HENCE THE PRESENCE OF MY *FRIEND* HERE.
SOMETIMES I FIND IT NECESSARY TO *COAX* THE INFORMATION FROM PEOPLE. CHOBA HERE IS VERY USEFUL IN THAT PURSUIT.
IT'S OFTEN SAID THAT DUGS ARE POSSESSED OF A *CRUEL* STREAK. ABSOLUTELY TRUE.
YOU SAID YOU WOULDN'T *HURT* HIM!
I *LIED*.
I THINK YOU UNDERSTAND THE SITUATION, SOLO. BUT JUST SO WE'RE BOTH CLEAR...
...I WANT THE *LOCATION* OF THE REBEL FLEET.
CHOBA WILL HELP YOU *REMEMBER* THIS INFORMATION. HIS ATTENTIONS WILL CONTINUE UNTIL YOU *REVEAL* WHAT YOU KNOW...
...OR UNTIL YOU ARE *DEAD*. WHICHEVER COMES FIRST.

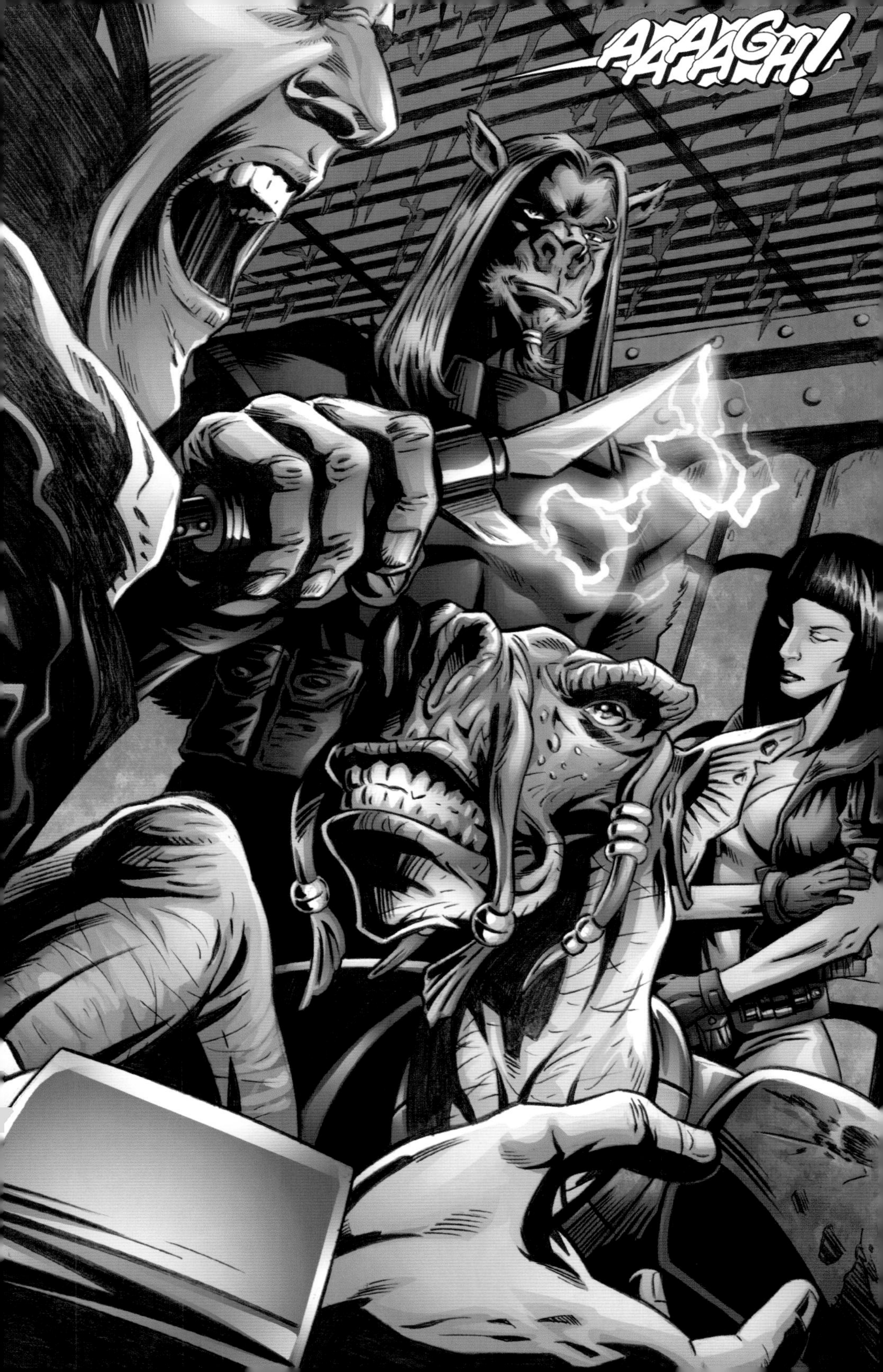
AAAAGH!

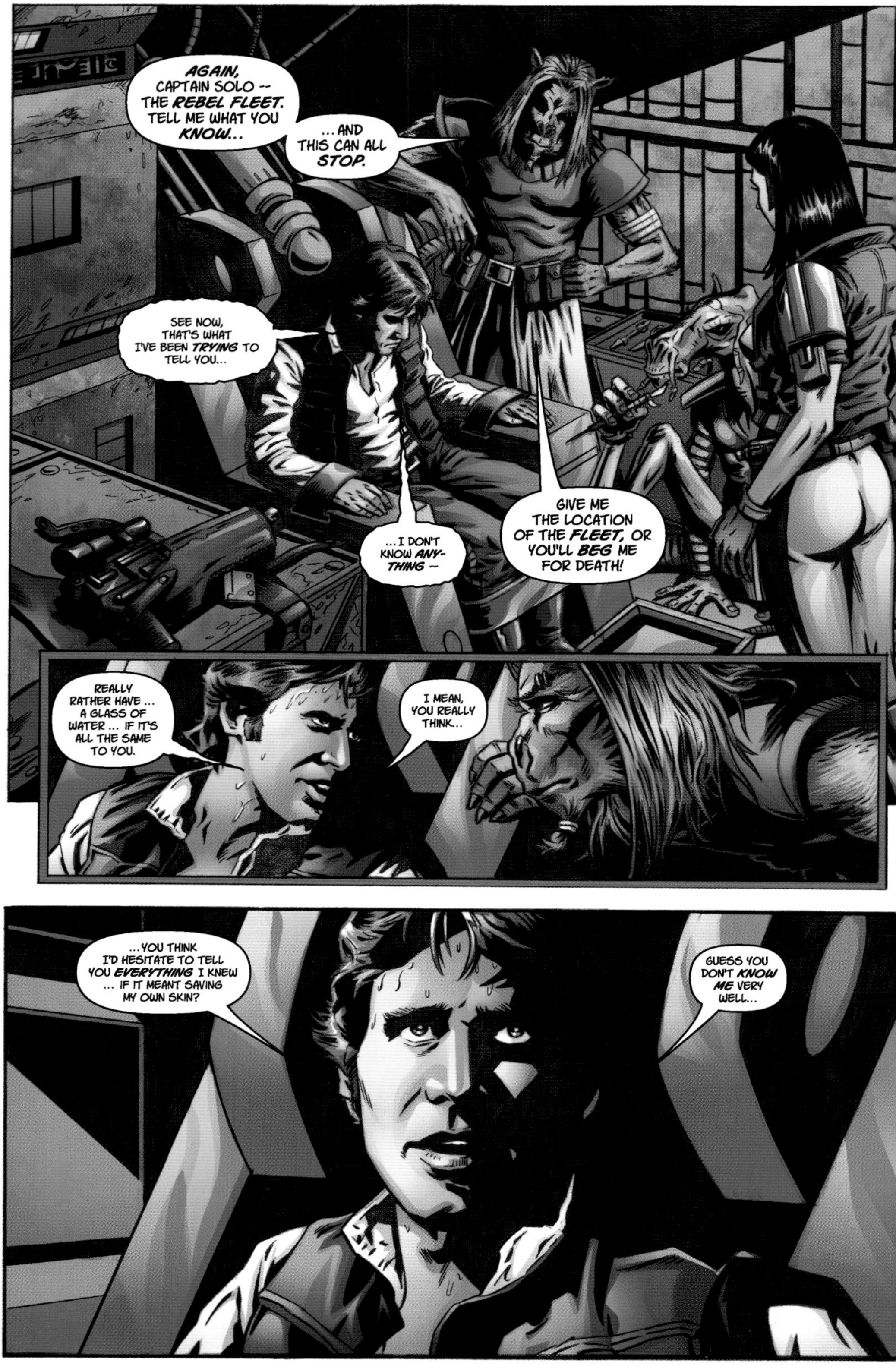
AGAIN, CAPTAIN SOLO -- THE REBEL FLEET. TELL ME WHAT YOU KNOW...
...AND THIS CAN ALL STOP.
SEE NOW, THAT'S WHAT I'VE BEEN TRYING TO TELL YOU...
...I DON'T KNOW ANY-THING --
GIVE ME THE LOCATION OF THE FLEET, OR YOU'LL BEG ME FOR DEATH!
REALLY RATHER HAVE ... A GLASS OF WATER ... IF IT'S ALL THE SAME TO YOU.
I MEAN, YOU REALLY THINK...
...YOU THINK I'D HESITATE TO TELL YOU EVERYTHING I KNEW ... IF IT MEANT SAVING MY OWN SKIN?
GUESS YOU DON'T KNOW ME VERY WELL...

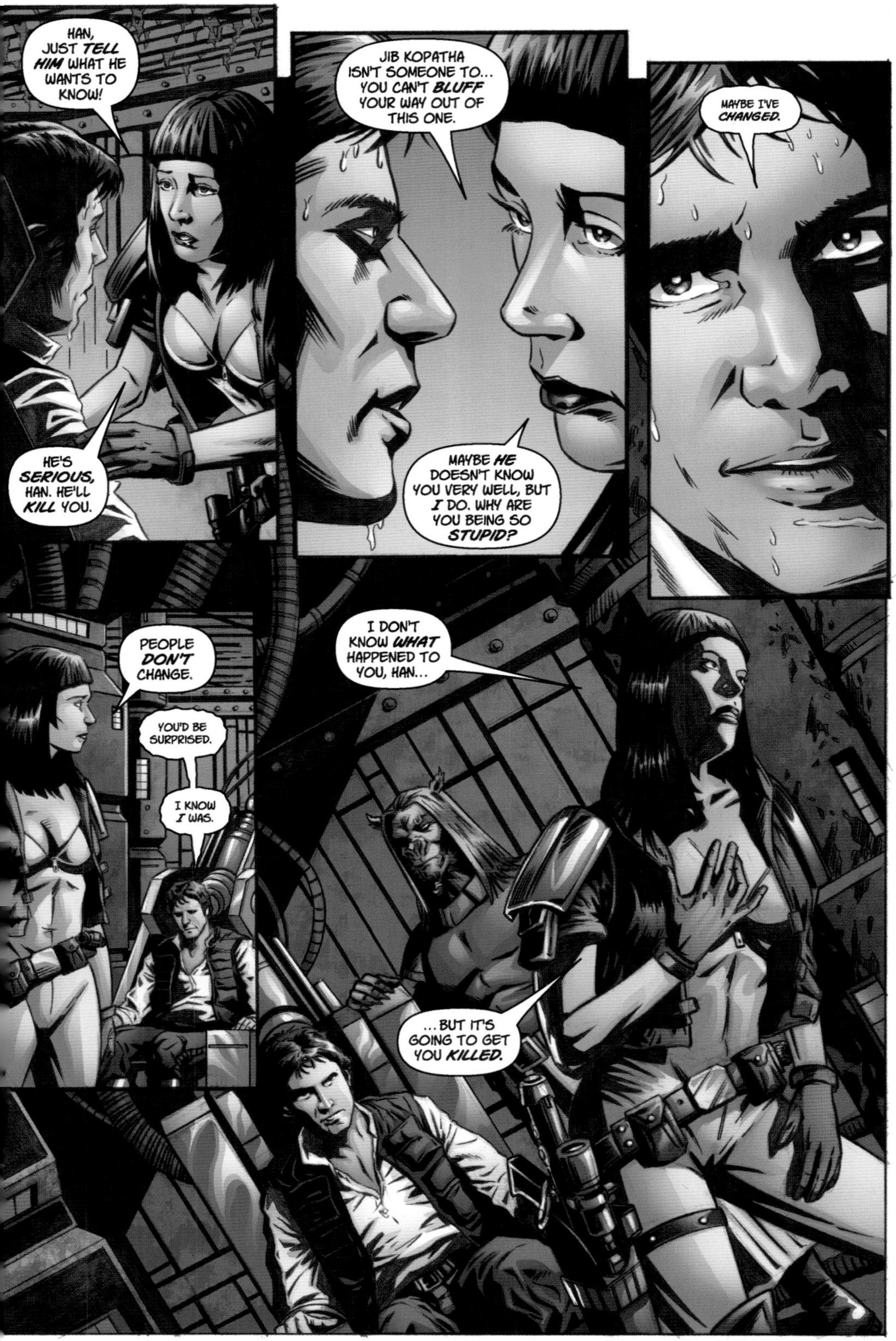
HAN, JUST TELL HIM WHAT HE WANTS TO KNOW!
HE'S SERIOUS, HAN. HE'LL KILL YOU.
JIB KOPATHA ISN'T SOMEONE TO... YOU CAN'T BLUFF YOUR WAY OUT OF THIS ONE.
MAYBE HE DOESN'T KNOW YOU VERY WELL, BUT I DO. WHY ARE YOU BEING SO STUPID?
MAYBE I'VE CHANGED.
PEOPLE DON'T CHANGE.
YOU'D BE SURPRISED.
I KNOW I WAS.
I DON'T KNOW WHAT HAPPENED TO YOU, HAN...
...BUT IT'S GOING TO GET YOU KILLED.

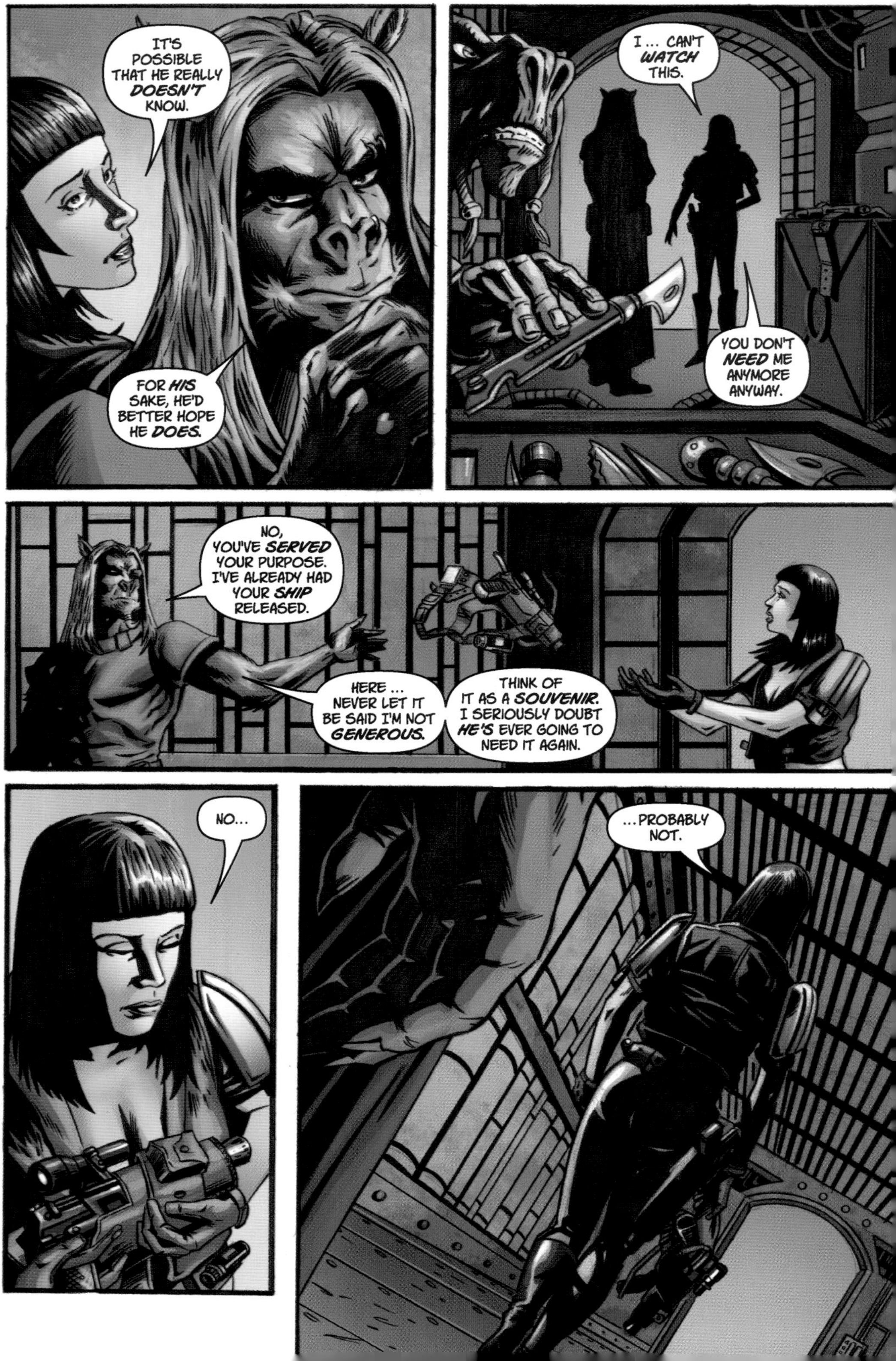

IT'S POSSIBLE THAT HE REALLY DOESN'T KNOW.
FOR HIS SAKE, HE'D BETTER HOPE HE DOES.
I ... CAN'T WATCH THIS.
YOU DON'T NEED ME ANYMORE ANYWAY.
NO, YOU'VE SERVED YOUR PURPOSE. I'VE ALREADY HAD YOUR SHIP RELEASED.
HERE ... NEVER LET IT BE SAID I'M NOT GENEROUS.
THINK OF IT AS A SOUVENIR. I SERIOUSLY DOUBT HE'S EVER GOING TO NEED IT AGAIN.
NO...
...PROBABLY NOT.

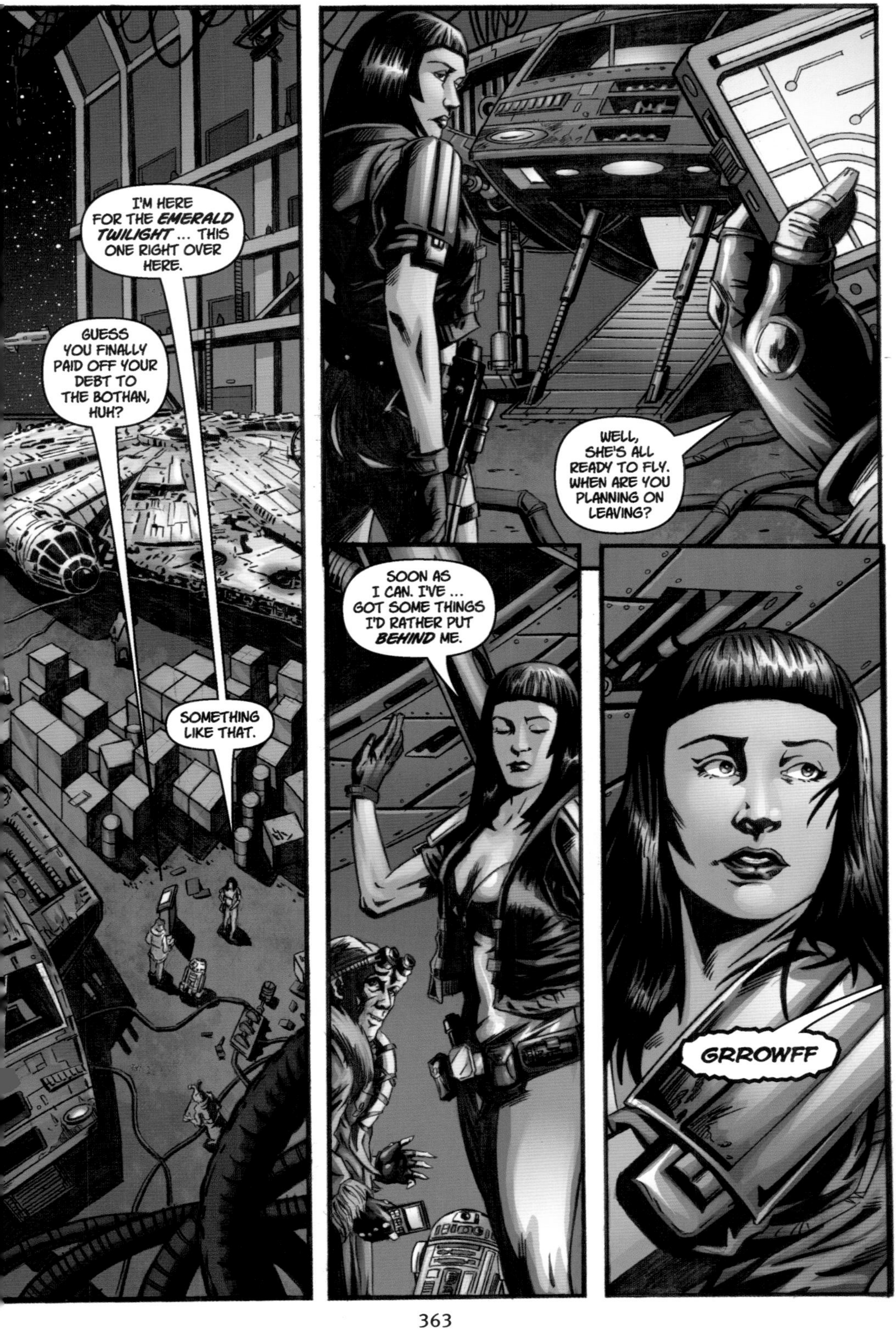
I'M HERE FOR THE EMERALD TWILIGHT ... THIS ONE RIGHT OVER HERE.
GUESS YOU FINALLY PAID OFF YOUR DEBT TO THE BOTHAN, HUH?
SOMETHING LIKE THAT.
WELL, SHE'S ALL READY TO FLY. WHEN ARE YOU PLANNING ON LEAVING?
SOON AS I CAN. I'VE ... GOT SOME THINGS I'D RATHER PUT BEHIND ME.
GRROWFF

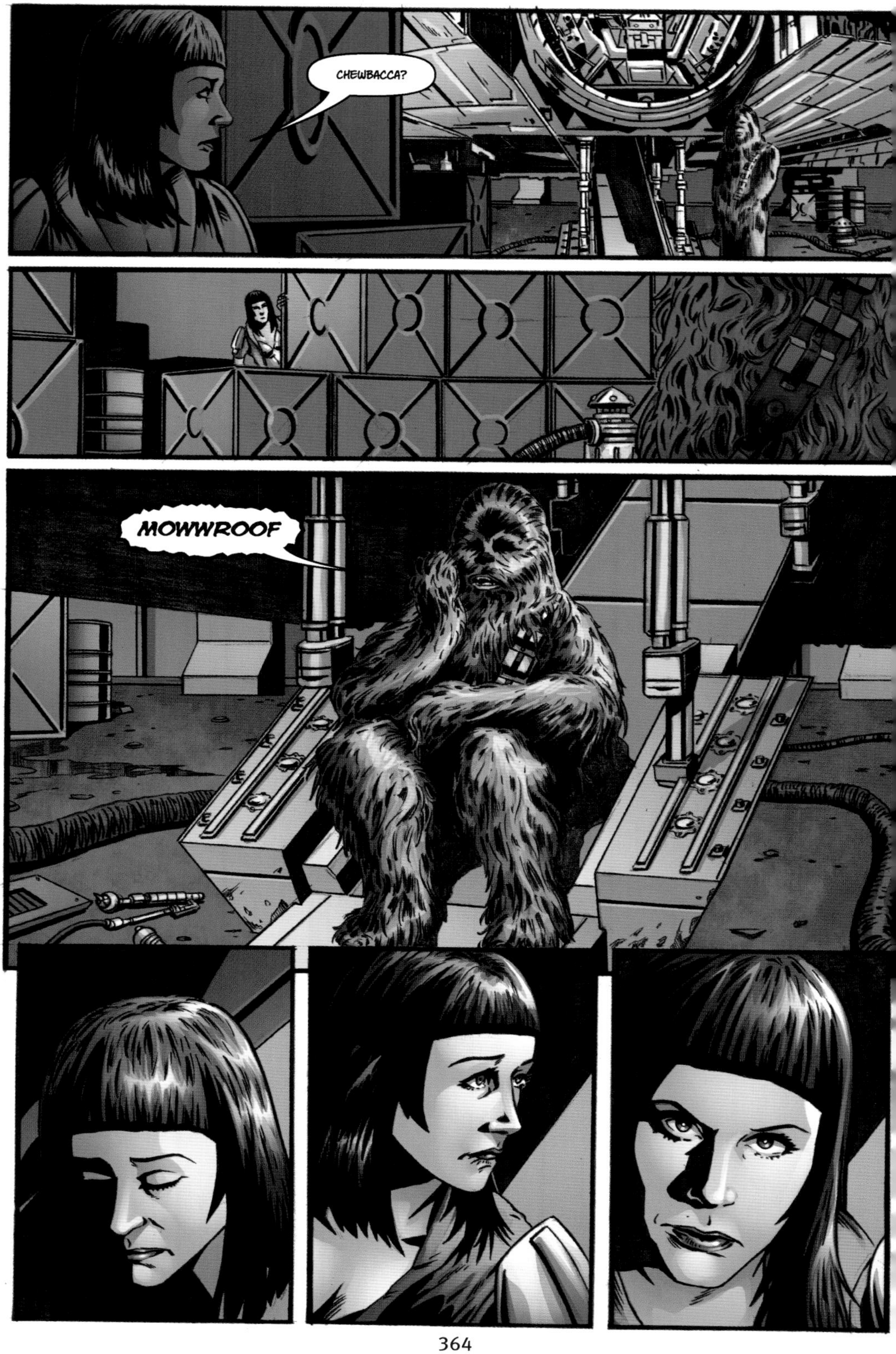
CHEWBACCA?
MOWWROOF

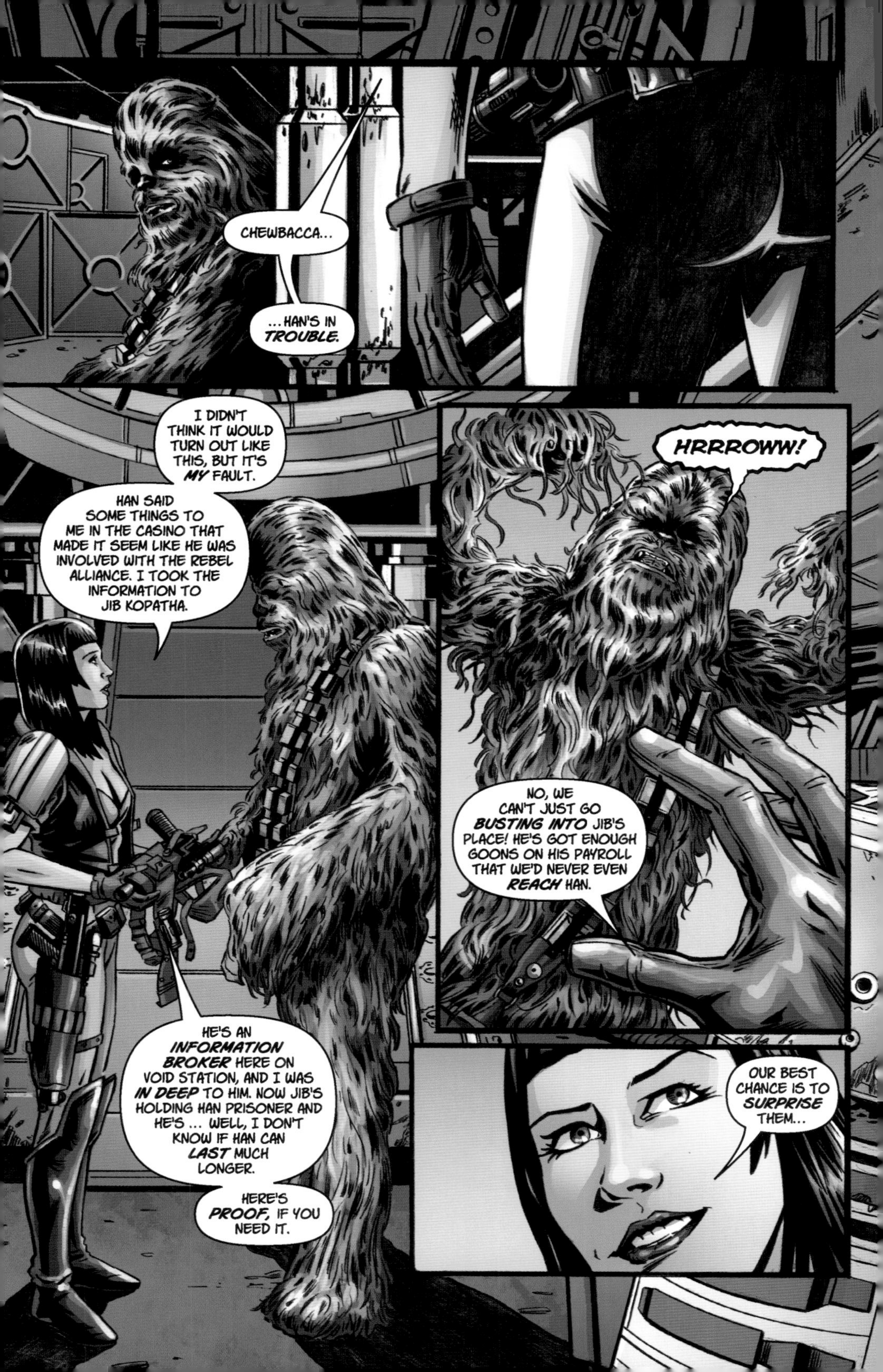
CHEWBACCA...
...HAN'S IN TROUBLE.
I DIDN'T THINK IT WOULD TURN OUT LIKE THIS, BUT IT'S MY FAULT.
HAN SAID SOME THINGS TO ME IN THE CASINO THAT MADE IT SEEM LIKE HE WAS INVOLVED WITH THE REBEL ALLIANCE. I TOOK THE INFORMATION TO JIB KOPATHA.
HE'S AN INFORMATION BROKER HERE ON VOID STATION, AND I WAS IN DEEP TO HIM. NOW JIB'S HOLDING HAN PRISONER AND HE'S ... WELL, I DON'T KNOW IF HAN CAN LAST MUCH LONGER.
HERE'S PROOF, IF YOU NEED IT.
HRRROWW!
NO, WE CAN'T JUST GO BUSTING INTO JIB'S PLACE! HE'S GOT ENOUGH GOONS ON HIS PAYROLL THAT WE'D NEVER EVEN REACH HAN.
OUR BEST CHANCE IS TO SURPRISE THEM...

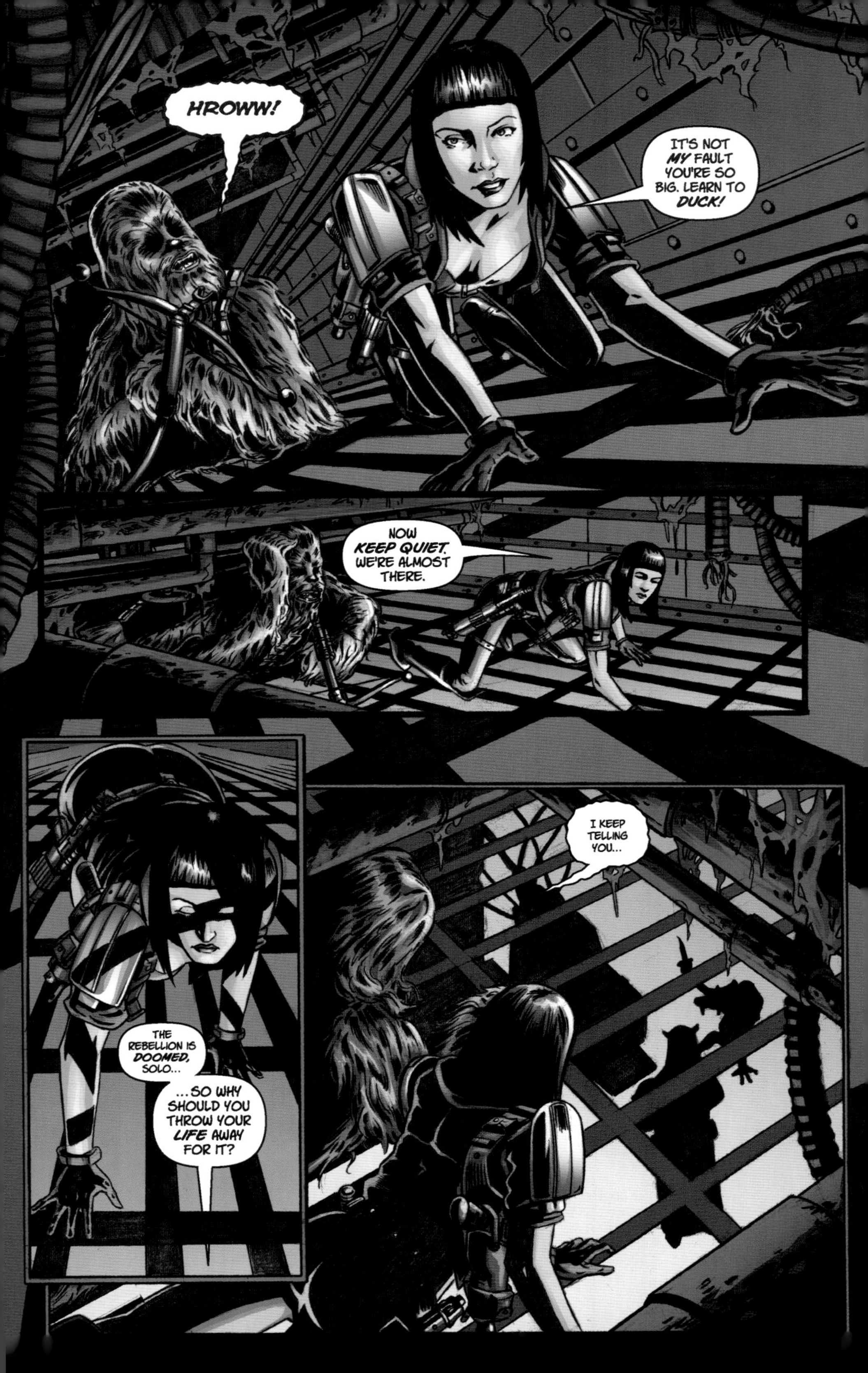
HROWW!
IT'S NOT MY FAULT YOU'RE SO BIG. LEARN TO DUCK!
NOW KEEP QUIET. WE'RE ALMOST THERE.
THE REBELLION IS DOOMED, SOLO...
...SO WHY SHOULD YOU THROW YOUR LIFE AWAY FOR IT?
I KEEP TELLING YOU...

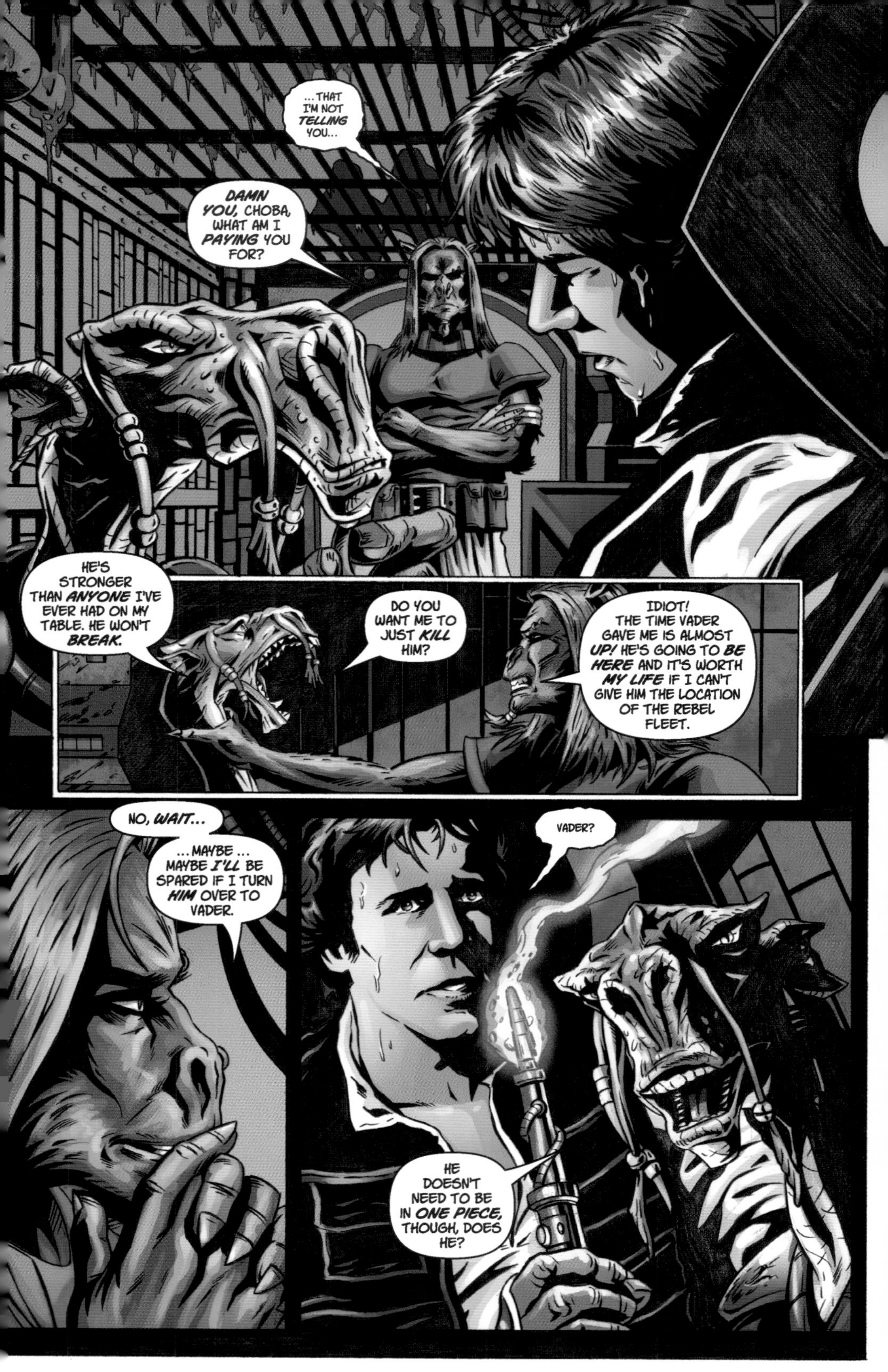
...THAT I'M NOT *TELLING* YOU...
DAMN YOU, CHOBA, WHAT AM I *PAYING* YOU FOR?
HE'S STRONGER THAN *ANYONE* I'VE EVER HAD ON MY TABLE. HE WON'T *BREAK.*
DO YOU WANT ME TO JUST *KILL* HIM?
IDIOT! THE TIME VADER GAVE ME IS ALMOST *UP!* HE'S GOING TO *BE HERE* AND IT'S WORTH *MY LIFE* IF I CAN'T GIVE HIM THE LOCATION OF THE REBEL FLEET.
NO, *WAIT*...
...MAYBE... MAYBE *I'LL* BE SPARED IF I TURN *HIM* OVER TO VADER.
VADER?
HE DOESN'T NEED TO BE IN *ONE PIECE,* THOUGH, DOES HE?

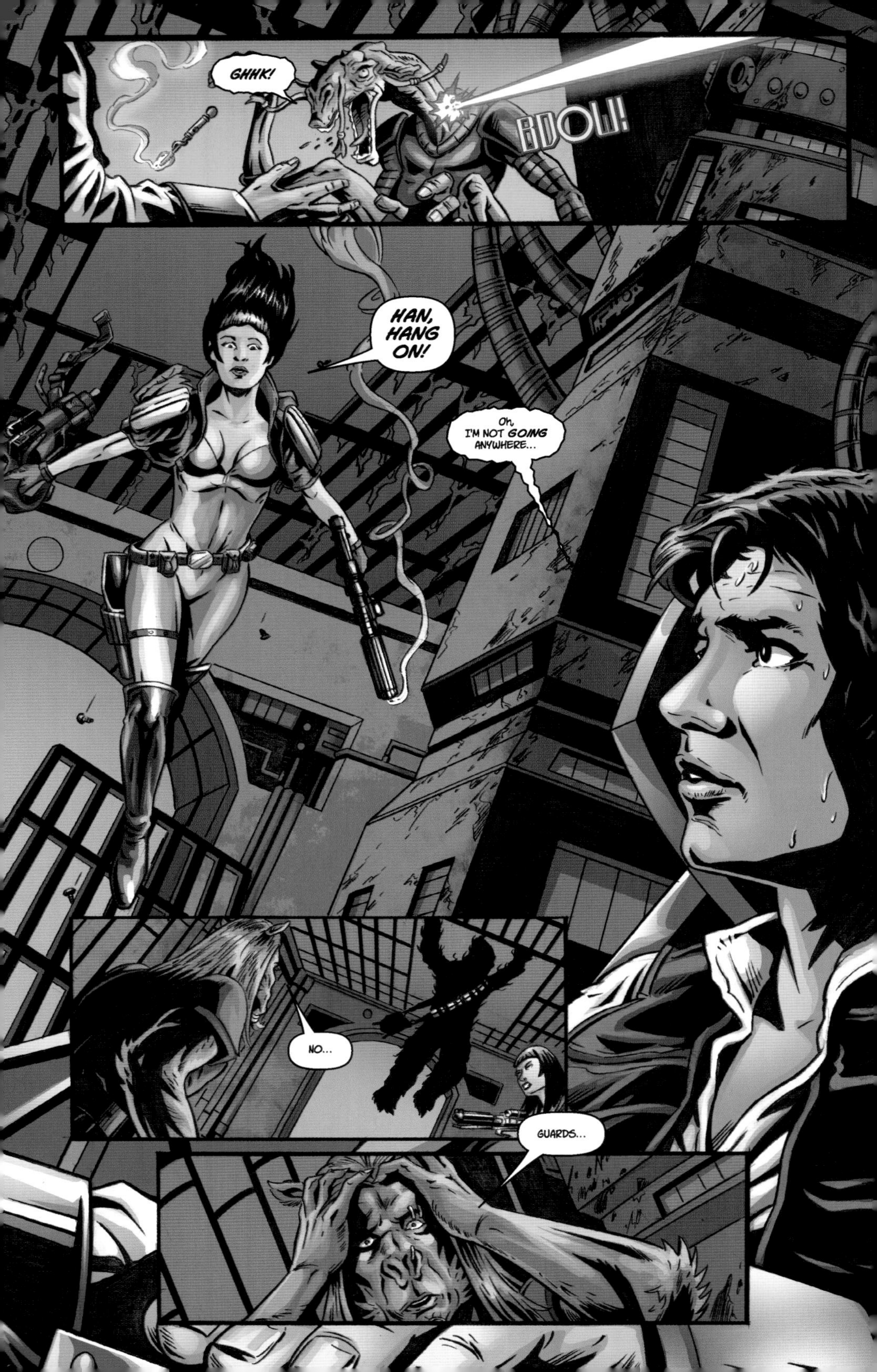
GHHK!
BDOW!
HAN, HANG ON!
Oh, I'M NOT GOING ANYWHERE...
NO...
GUARDS...

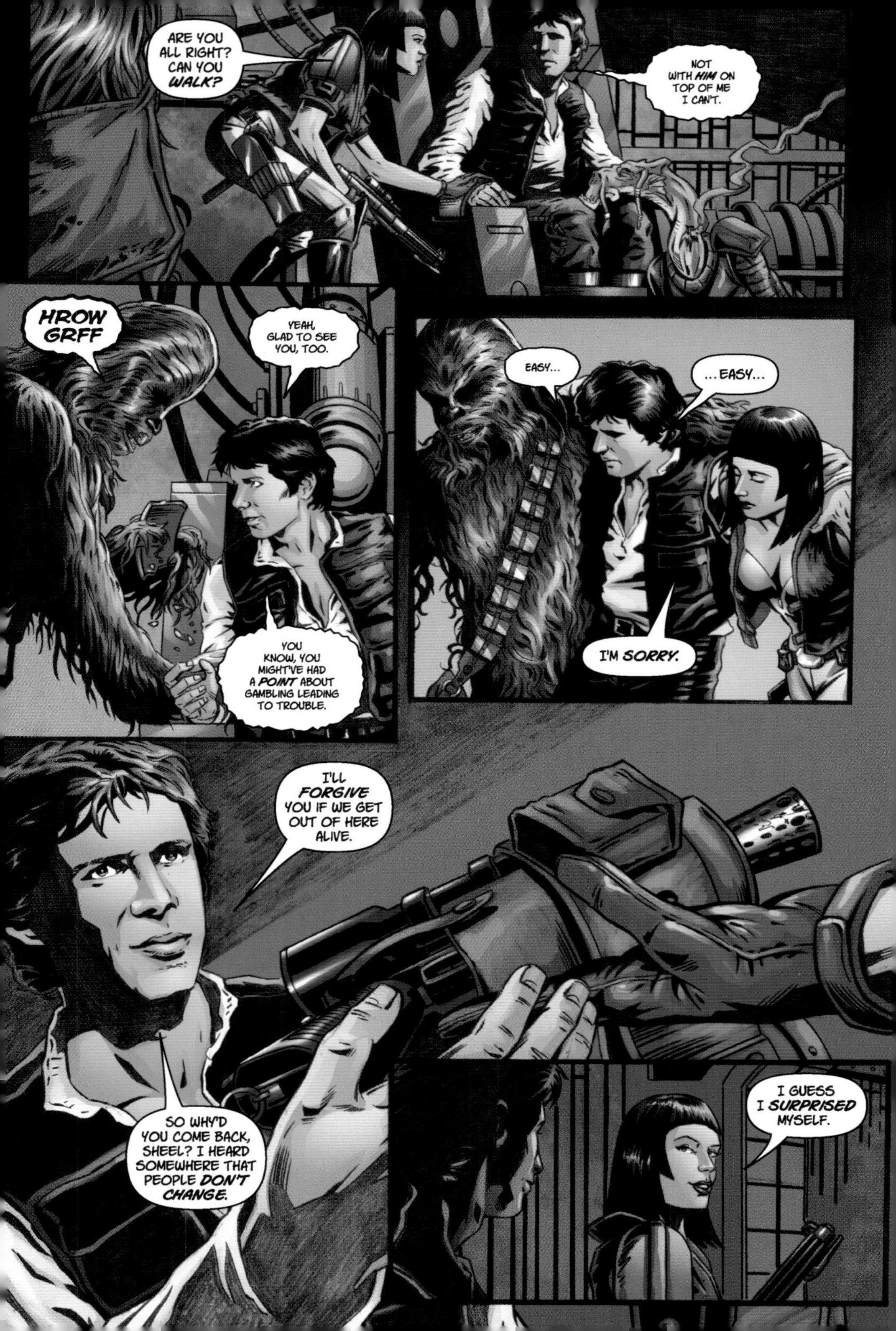
ARE YOU ALL RIGHT? CAN YOU WALK?
NOT WITH HIM ON TOP OF ME I CAN'T.
HROW GRFF
YEAH, GLAD TO SEE YOU, TOO.
YOU KNOW, YOU MIGHT'VE HAD A POINT ABOUT GAMBLING LEADING TO TROUBLE.
EASY...
...EASY...
I'M SORRY.
I'LL FORGIVE YOU IF WE GET OUT OF HERE ALIVE.
SO WHY'D YOU COME BACK, SHEEL? I HEARD SOMEWHERE THAT PEOPLE DON'T CHANGE.
I GUESS I SURPRISED MYSELF.

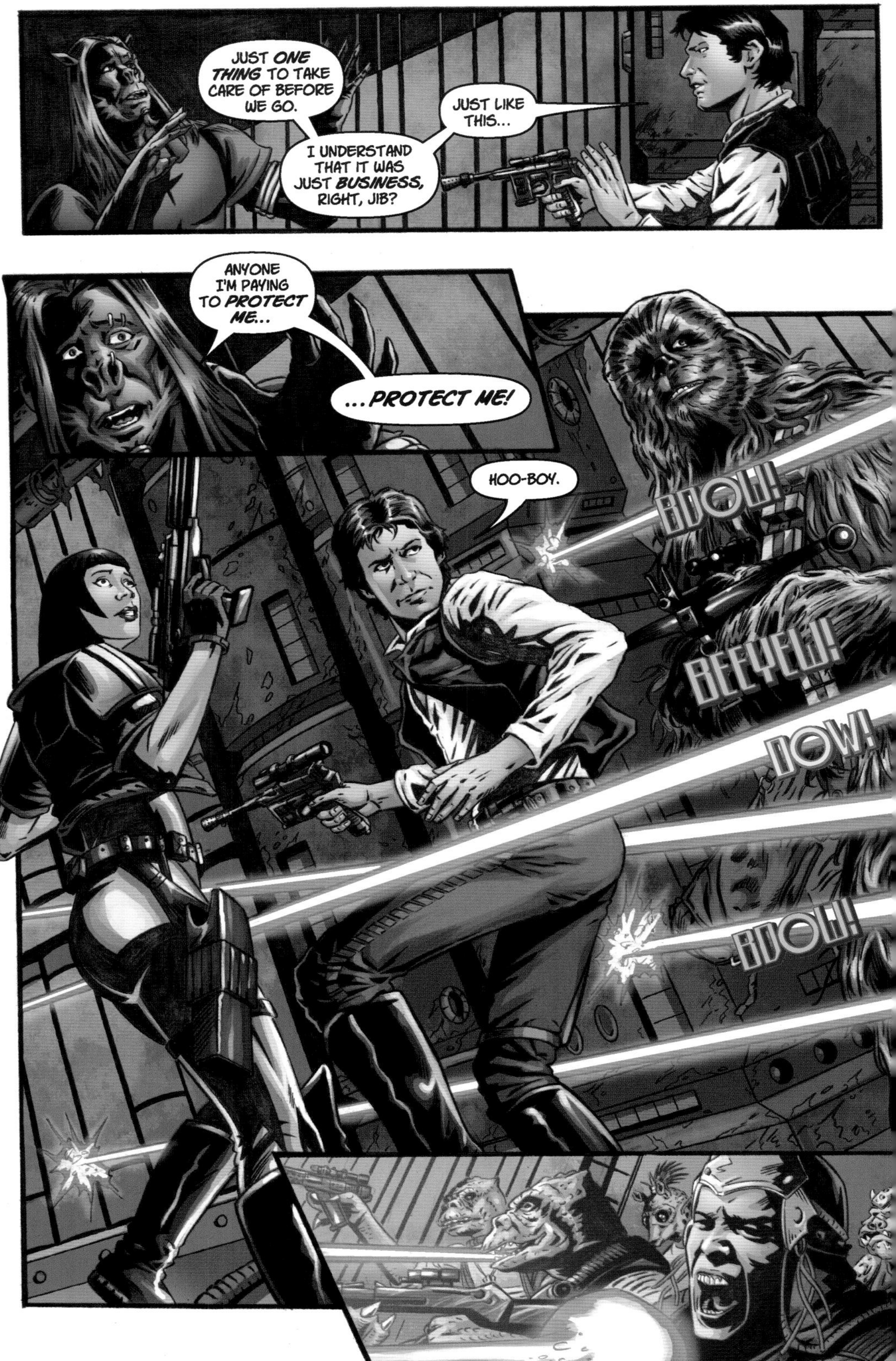
JUST ONE THING TO TAKE CARE OF BEFORE WE GO.
I UNDERSTAND THAT IT WAS JUST BUSINESS, RIGHT, JIB?
JUST LIKE THIS...
ANYONE I'M PAYING TO PROTECT ME...
...PROTECT ME!
HOO-BOY.
BDOW!
BEEYEW!
DOW!
BDOW!

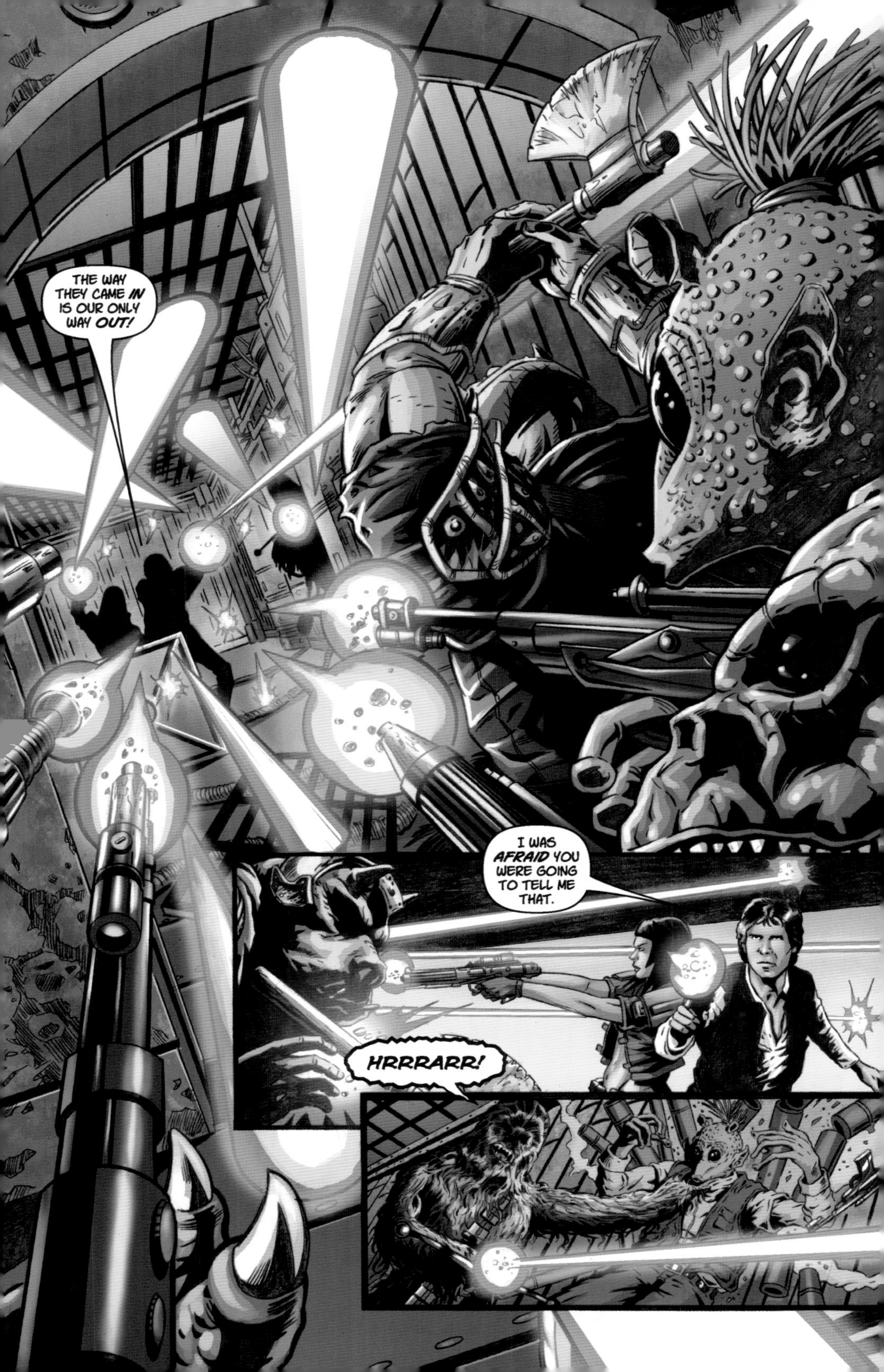
THE WAY THEY CAME IN IS OUR ONLY WAY OUT!
I WAS AFRAID YOU WERE GOING TO TELL ME THAT.
HRRRARR!

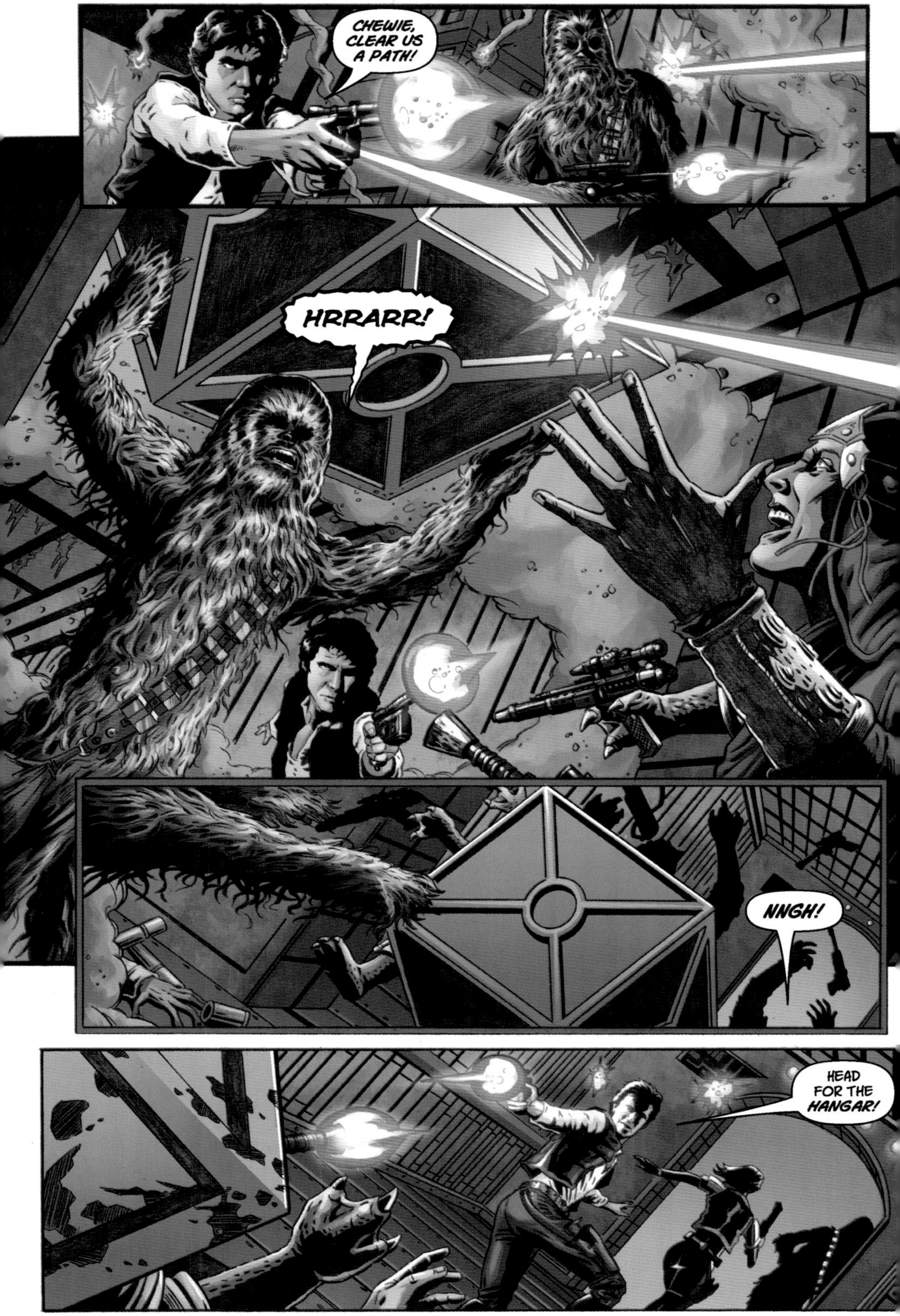
CHEWIE, CLEAR US A PATH!
HRRARR!
NNGH!
HEAD FOR THE HANGAR!

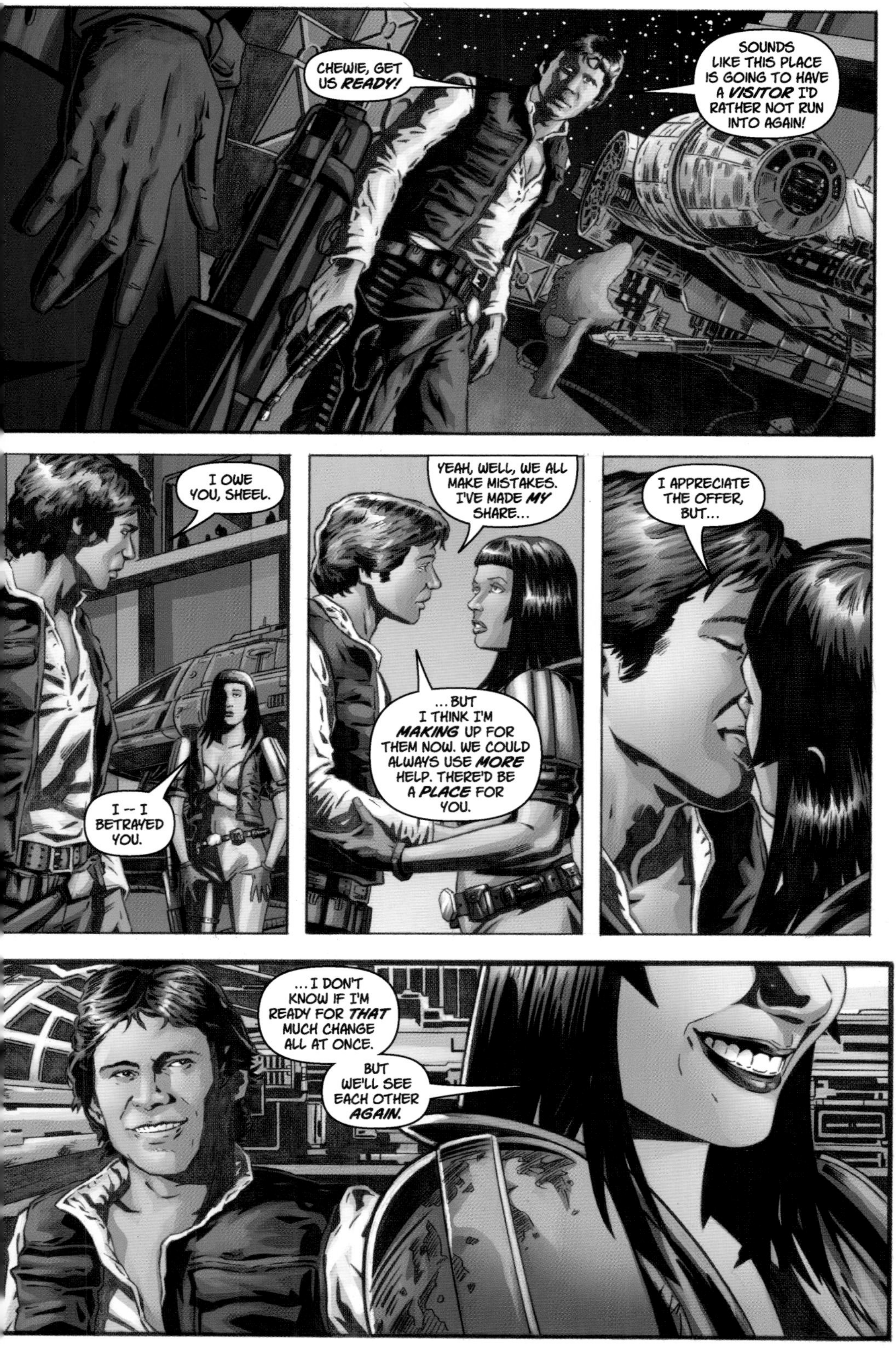
CHEWIE, GET US READY!
SOUNDS LIKE THIS PLACE IS GOING TO HAVE A VISITOR I'D RATHER NOT RUN INTO AGAIN!
I OWE YOU, SHEEL.
I -- I BETRAYED YOU.
YEAH, WELL, WE ALL MAKE MISTAKES. I'VE MADE MY SHARE...
...BUT I THINK I'M MAKING UP FOR THEM NOW. WE COULD ALWAYS USE MORE HELP. THERE'D BE A PLACE FOR YOU.
I APPRECIATE THE OFFER, BUT...
...I DON'T KNOW IF I'M READY FOR THAT MUCH CHANGE ALL AT ONCE.
BUT WE'LL SEE EACH OTHER AGAIN.

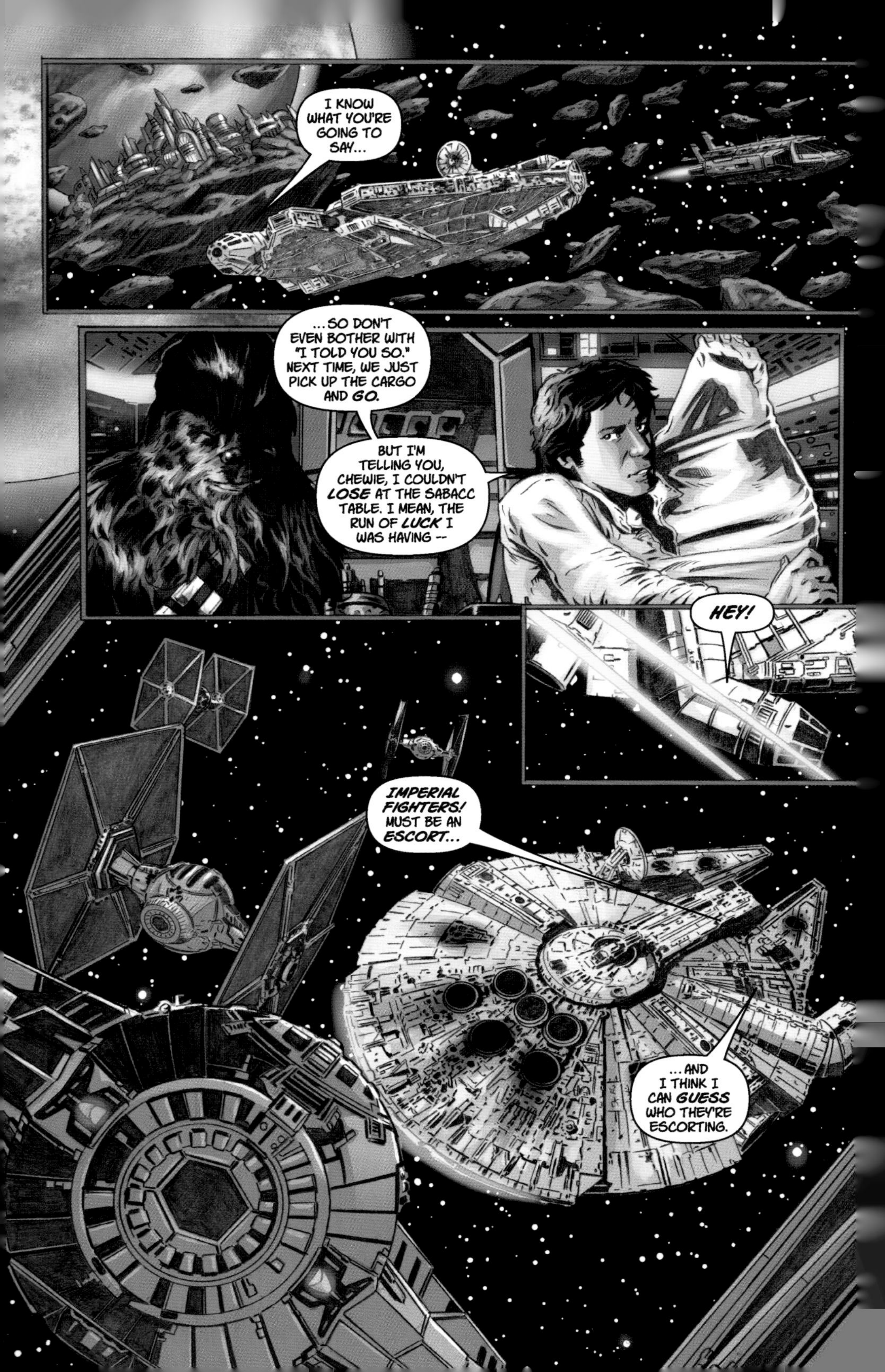
I KNOW WHAT YOU'RE GOING TO SAY...
...SO DON'T EVEN BOTHER WITH "I TOLD YOU SO." NEXT TIME, WE JUST PICK UP THE CARGO AND GO.
BUT I'M TELLING YOU, CHEWIE, I COULDN'T LOSE AT THE SABACC TABLE. I MEAN, THE RUN OF LUCK I WAS HAVING --
HEY!
IMPERIAL FIGHTERS! MUST BE AN ESCORT...
...AND I THINK I CAN GUESS WHO THEY'RE ESCORTING.

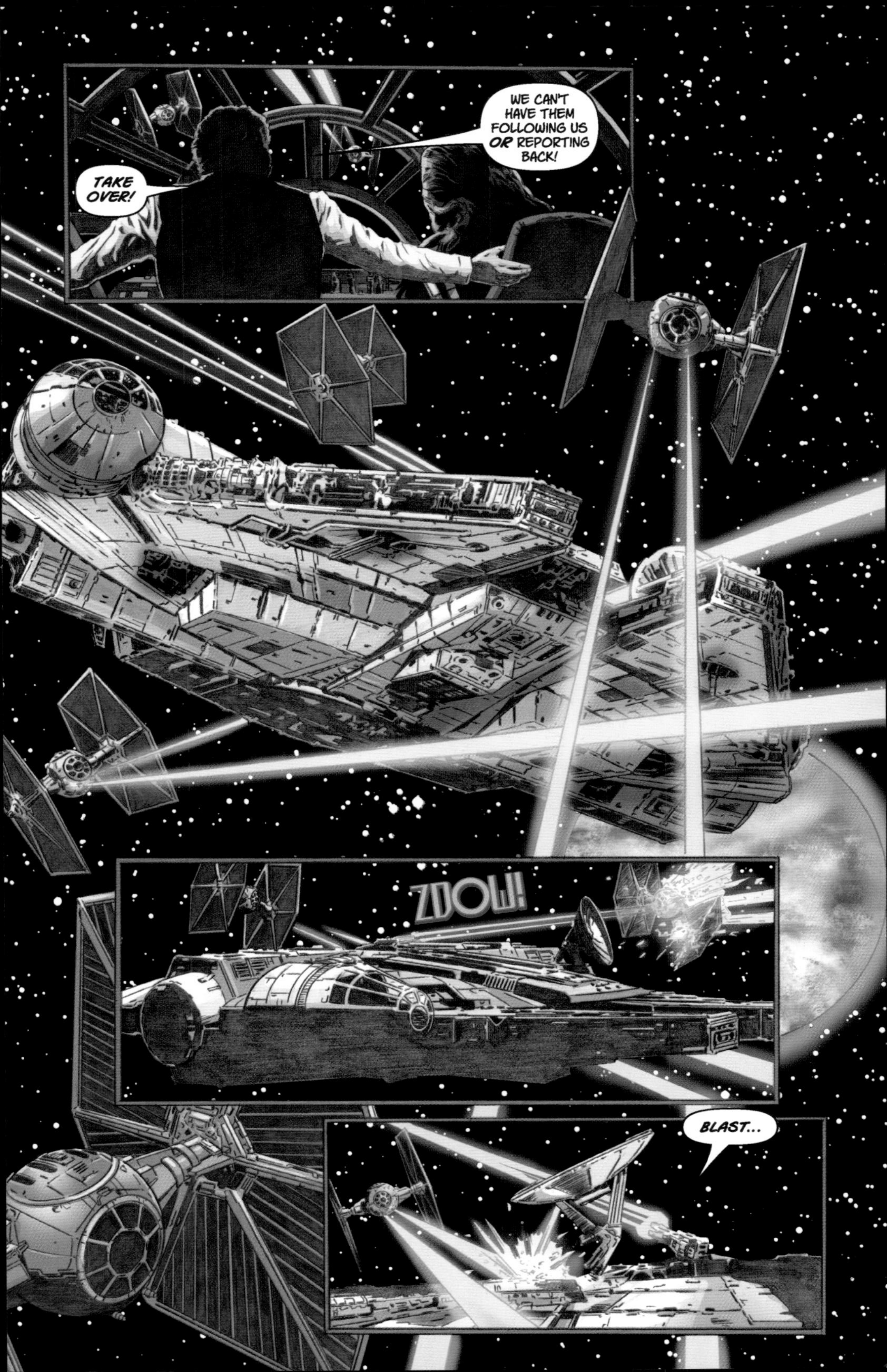
TAKE OVER!
WE CAN'T HAVE THEM FOLLOWING US OR REPORTING BACK!
ZDOW!
BLAST...

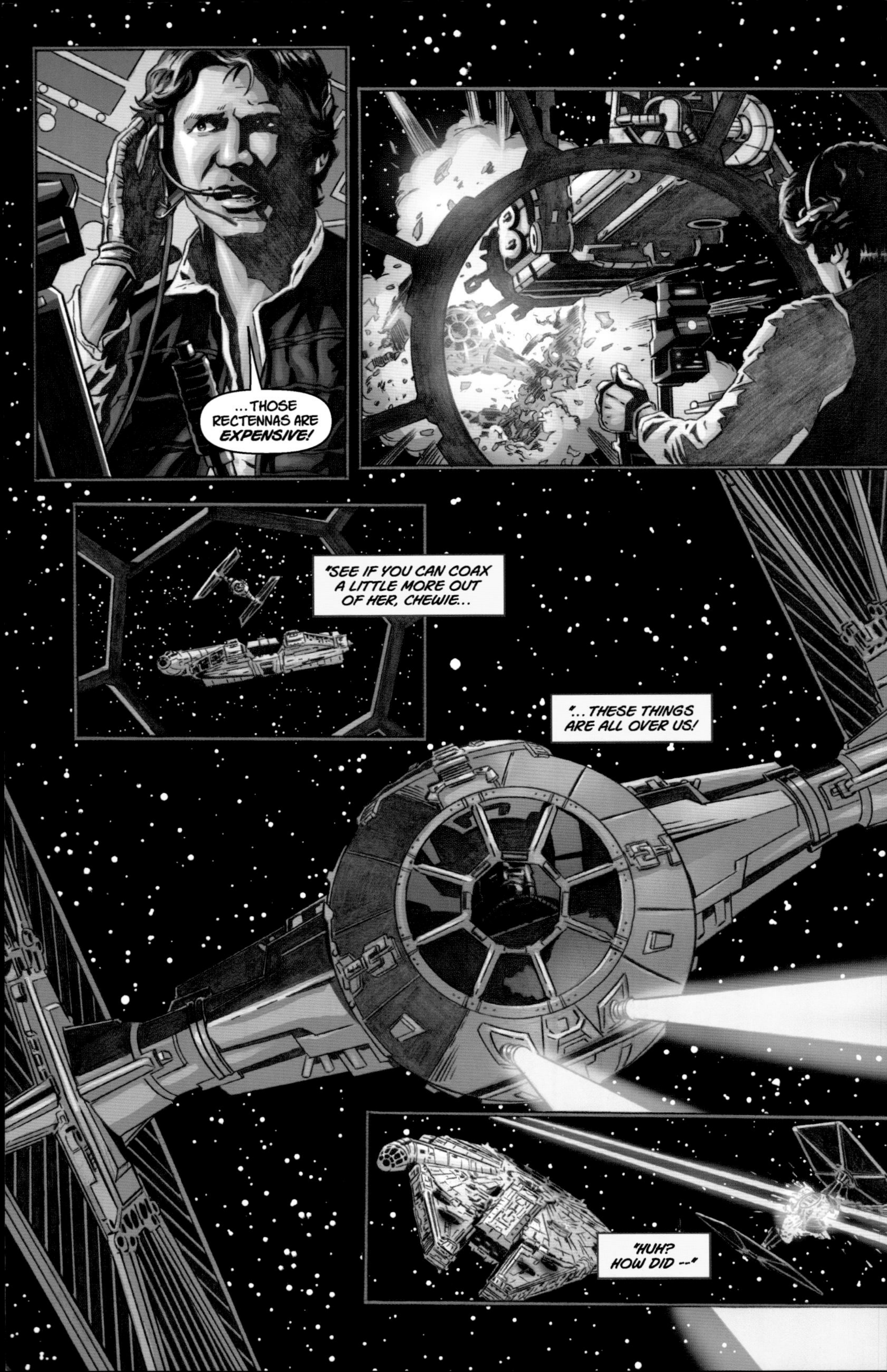
...THOSE RECTENNAS ARE EXPENSIVE!
"SEE IF YOU CAN COAX A LITTLE MORE OUT OF HER, CHEWIE...
"...THESE THINGS ARE ALL OVER US!
"HUH? HOW DID --"

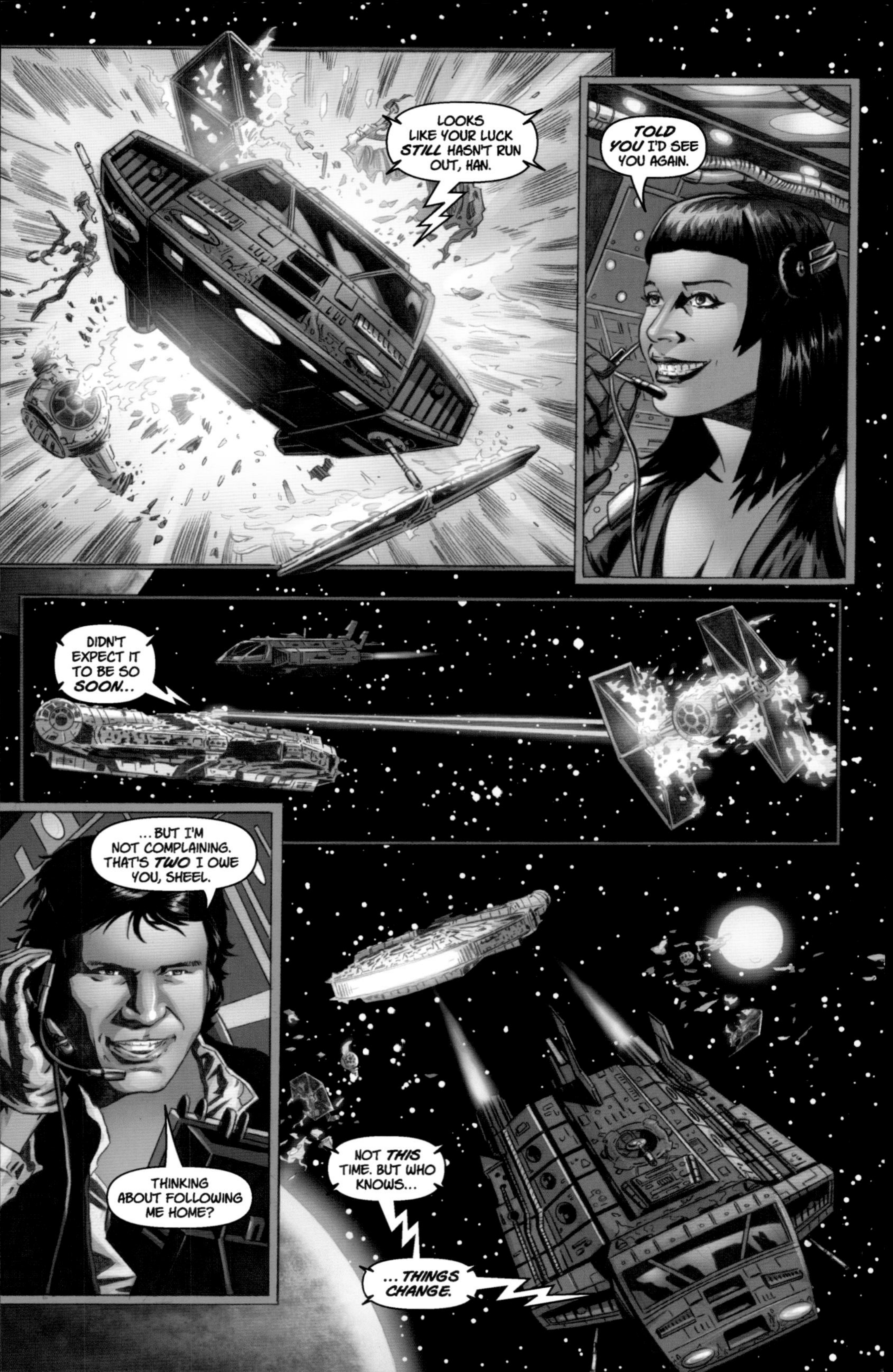
LOOKS LIKE YOUR LUCK STILL HASN'T RUN OUT, HAN.
TOLD YOU I'D SEE YOU AGAIN.
DIDN'T EXPECT IT TO BE SO SOON...
...BUT I'M NOT COMPLAINING. THAT'S TWO I OWE YOU, SHEEL.
THINKING ABOUT FOLLOWING ME HOME?
NOT THIS TIME. BUT WHO KNOWS...
...THINGS CHANGE.

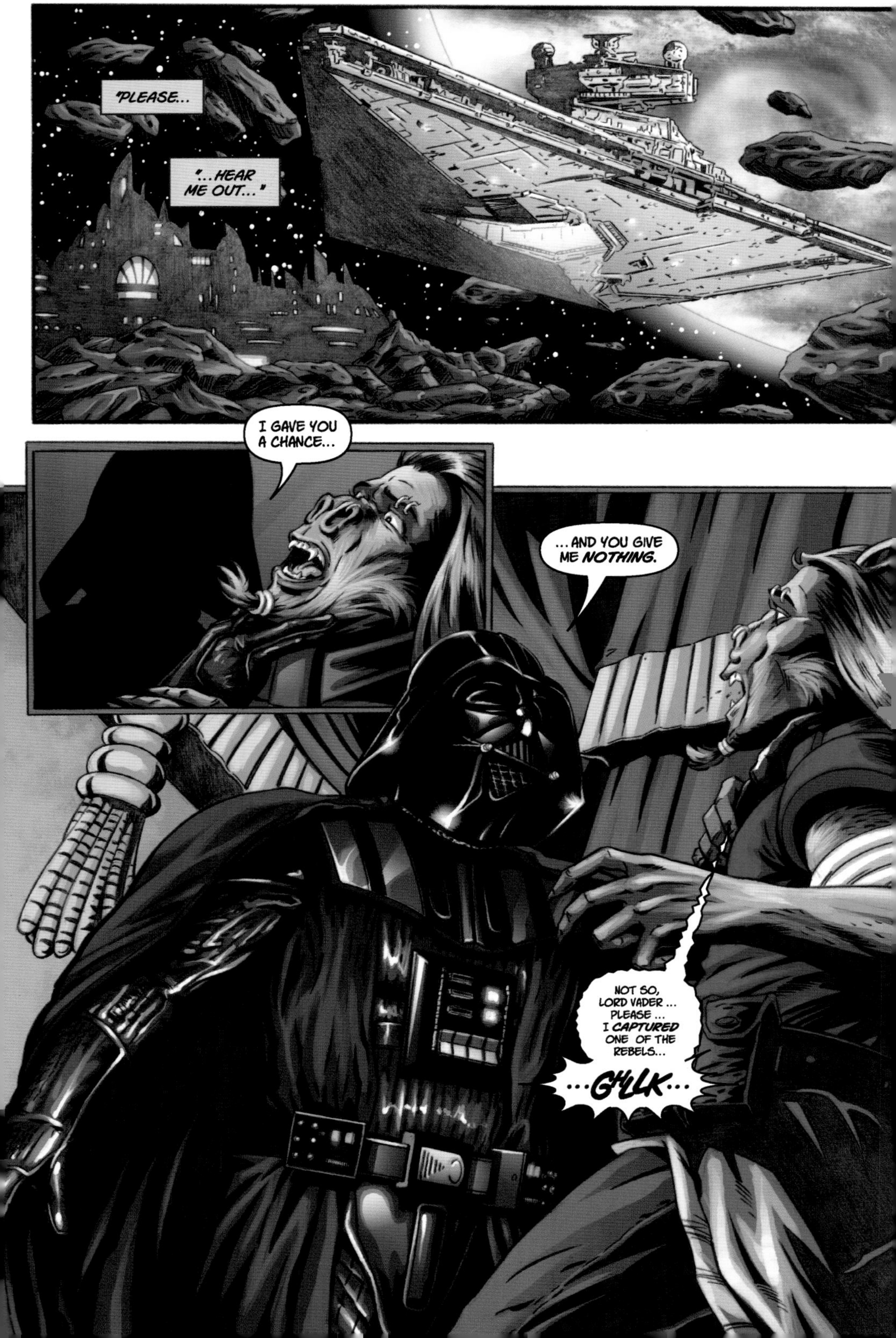
"PLEASE...
"...HEAR ME OUT..."
I GAVE YOU A CHANCE...
...AND YOU GIVE ME *NOTHING*.
NOT SO, LORD VADER ... PLEASE ... I *CAPTURED* ONE OF THE REBELS...
...GHLLK...

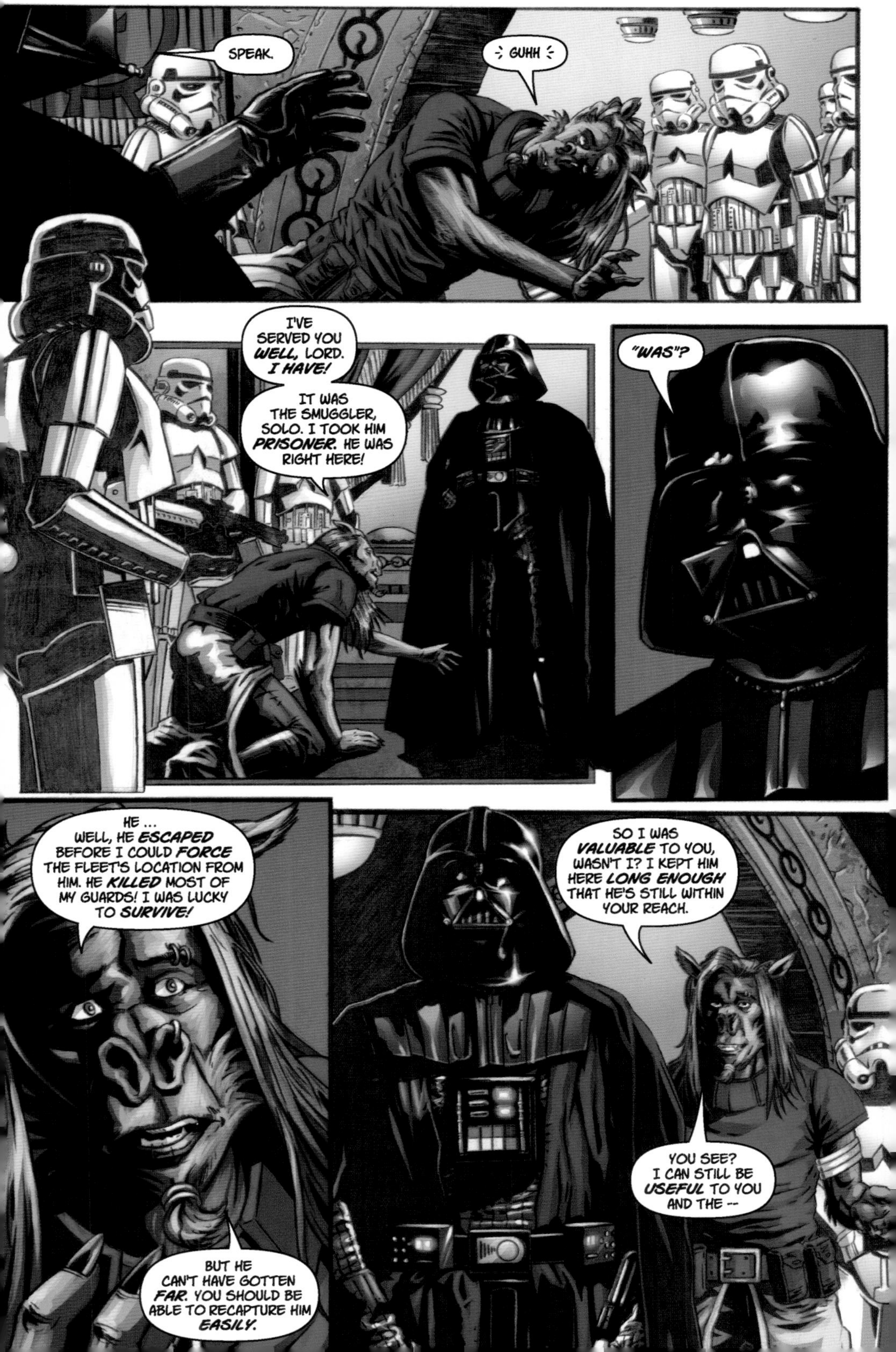

SPEAK.
GUHH
I'VE SERVED YOU WELL, LORD. I HAVE!
IT WAS THE SMUGGLER, SOLO. I TOOK HIM PRISONER. HE WAS RIGHT HERE!
"WAS"?
HE ... WELL, HE ESCAPED BEFORE I COULD FORCE THE FLEET'S LOCATION FROM HIM. HE KILLED MOST OF MY GUARDS! I WAS LUCKY TO SURVIVE!
BUT HE CAN'T HAVE GOTTEN FAR. YOU SHOULD BE ABLE TO RECAPTURE HIM EASILY.
SO I WAS VALUABLE TO YOU, WASN'T I? I KEPT HIM HERE LONG ENOUGH THAT HE'S STILL WITHIN YOUR REACH.
YOU SEE? I CAN STILL BE USEFUL TO YOU AND THE --

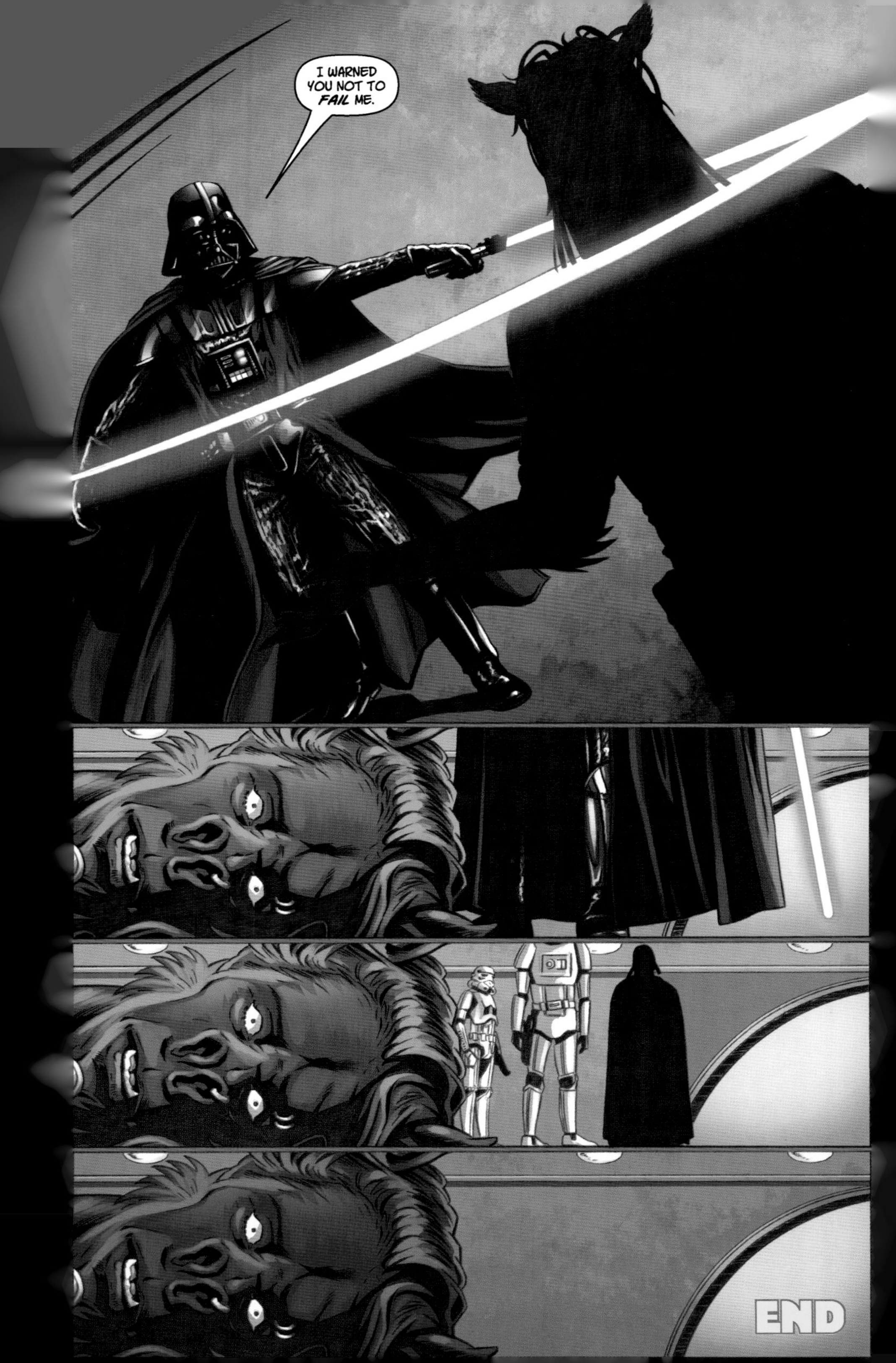
I WARNED YOU NOT TO FAIL ME.
END

The Price of Power | Illustration by Joe Corroney, colored by Dan Jackson

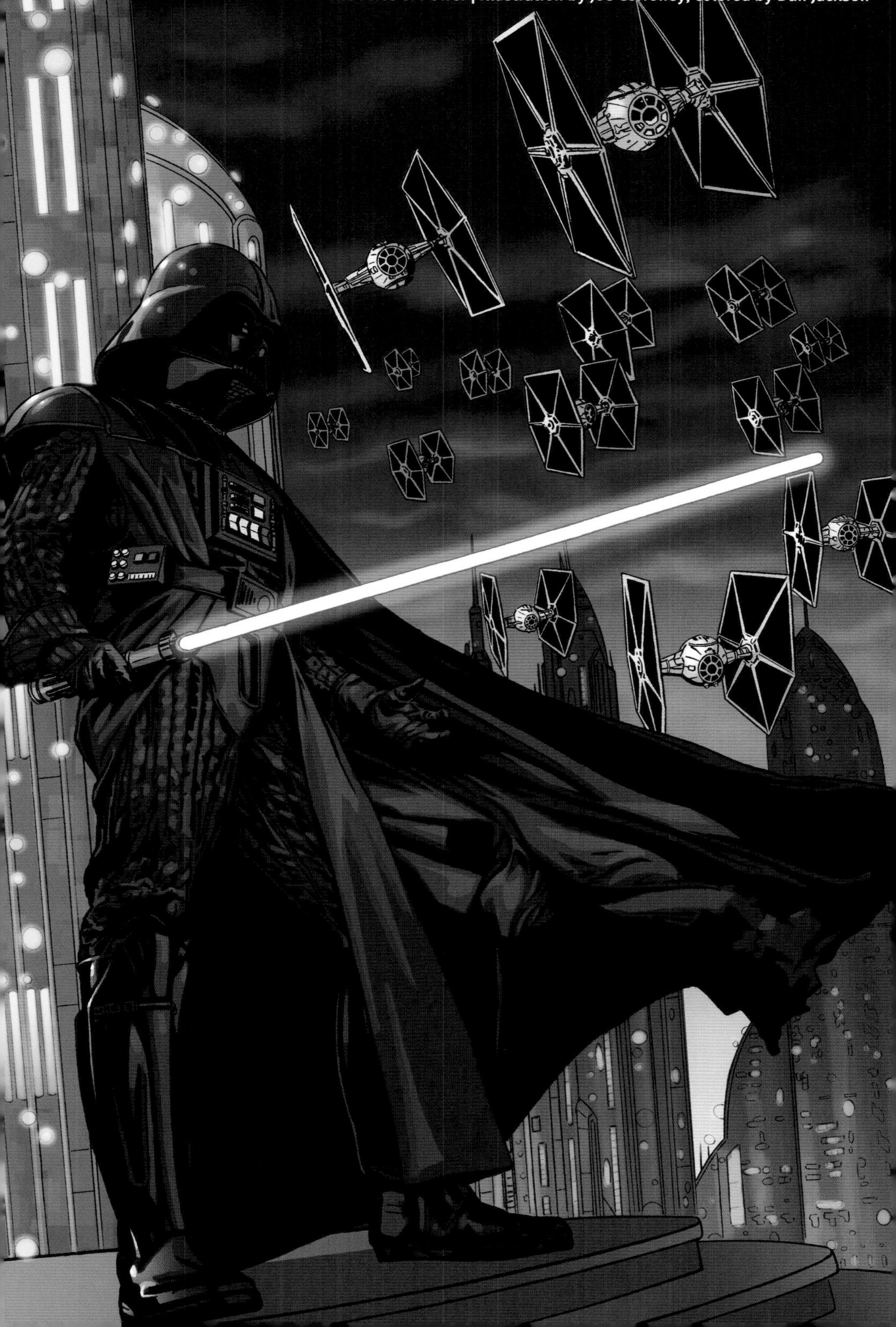

APPROXIMATELY EIGHT MONTHS AFTER THE BATTLE
OF YAVIN . . .

script by Scott Allie
art by Joe Corroney
colors by Michael Atiyeh
lettering by Michael David Thomas

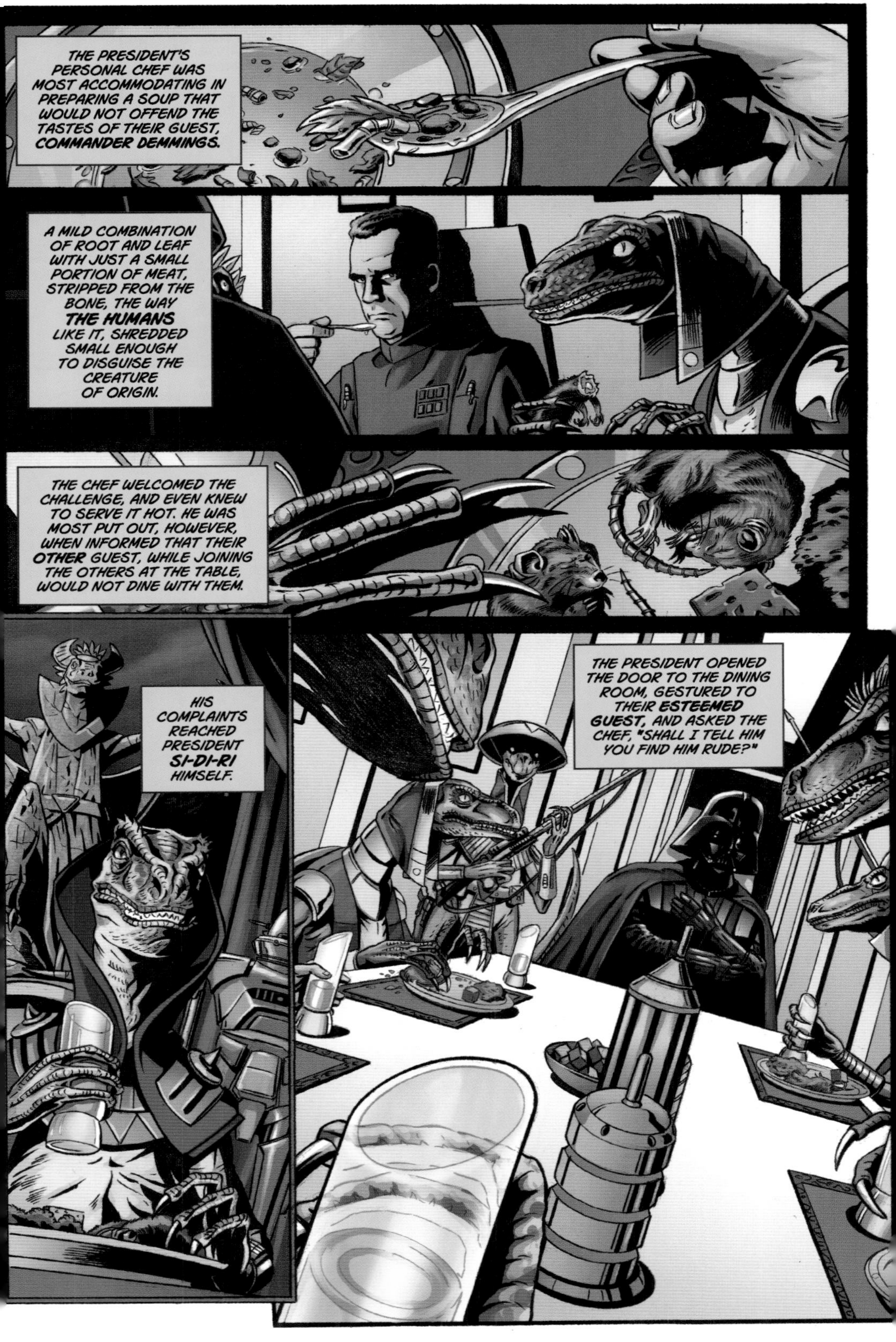
THE PRESIDENT'S PERSONAL CHEF WAS MOST ACCOMMODATING IN PREPARING A SOUP THAT WOULD NOT OFFEND THE TASTES OF THEIR GUEST, COMMANDER DEMMINGS.
A MILD COMBINATION OF ROOT AND LEAF WITH JUST A SMALL PORTION OF MEAT, STRIPPED FROM THE BONE, THE WAY THE HUMANS LIKE IT, SHREDDED SMALL ENOUGH TO DISGUISE THE CREATURE OF ORIGIN.
THE CHEF WELCOMED THE CHALLENGE, AND EVEN KNEW TO SERVE IT HOT. HE WAS MOST PUT OUT, HOWEVER, WHEN INFORMED THAT THEIR OTHER GUEST, WHILE JOINING THE OTHERS AT THE TABLE, WOULD NOT DINE WITH THEM.
HIS COMPLAINTS REACHED PRESIDENT SI-DI-RI HIMSELF.
THE PRESIDENT OPENED THE DOOR TO THE DINING ROOM, GESTURED TO THEIR ESTEEMED GUEST, AND ASKED THE CHEF, "SHALL I TELL HIM YOU FIND HIM RUDE?"

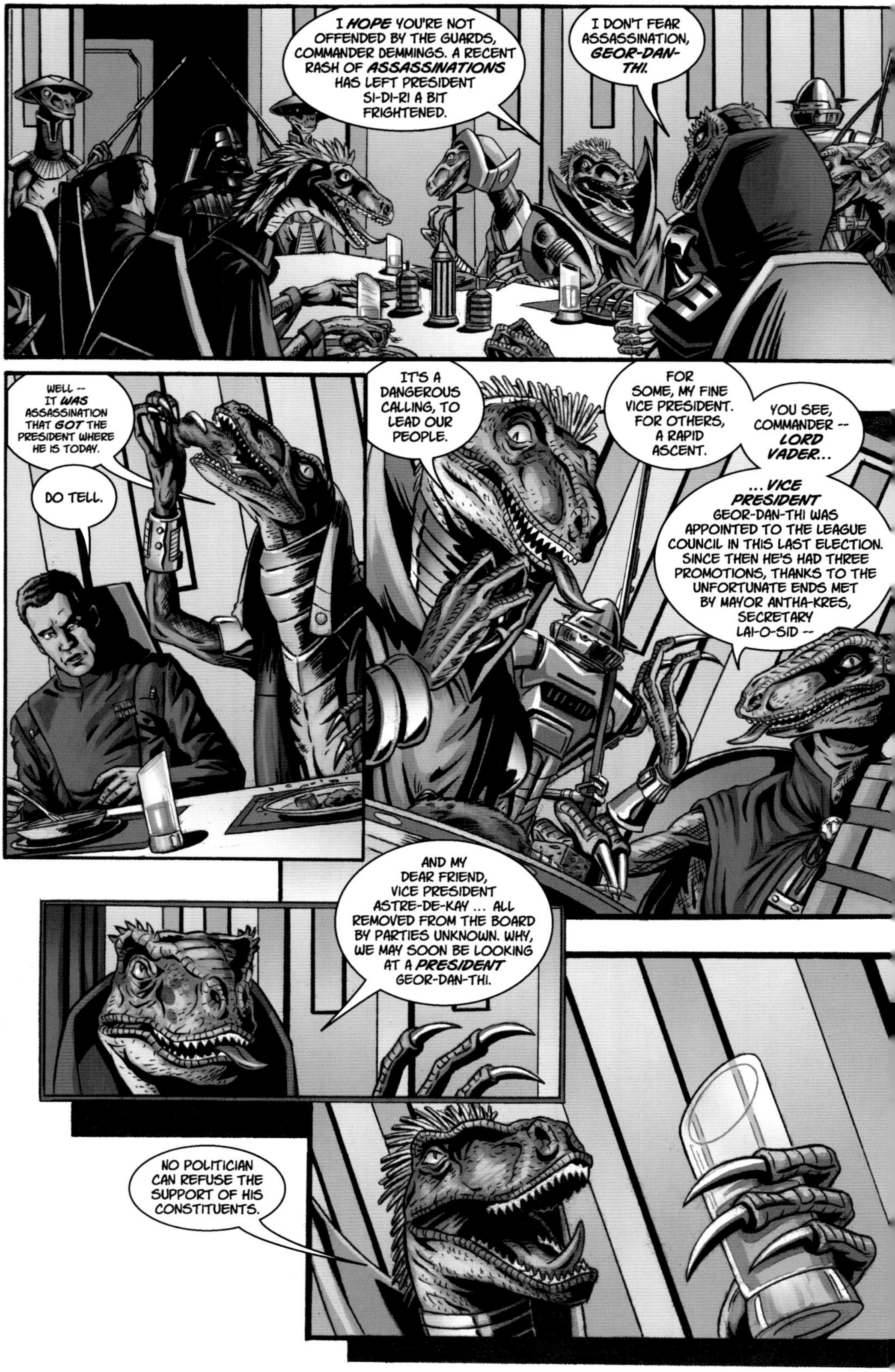
I HOPE YOU'RE NOT OFFENDED BY THE GUARDS, COMMANDER DEMMINGS. A RECENT RASH OF ASSASSINATIONS HAS LEFT PRESIDENT SI-DI-RI A BIT FRIGHTENED.
I DON'T FEAR ASSASSINATION, GEOR-DAN-THI.
WELL -- IT WAS ASSASSINATION THAT GOT THE PRESIDENT WHERE HE IS TODAY.
DO TELL.
IT'S A DANGEROUS CALLING, TO LEAD OUR PEOPLE.
FOR SOME, MY FINE VICE PRESIDENT. FOR OTHERS, A RAPID ASCENT.
YOU SEE, COMMANDER -- LORD VADER...
...VICE PRESIDENT GEOR-DAN-THI WAS APPOINTED TO THE LEAGUE COUNCIL IN THIS LAST ELECTION. SINCE THEN HE'S HAD THREE PROMOTIONS, THANKS TO THE UNFORTUNATE ENDS MET BY MAYOR ANTHA-KRES, SECRETARY LAI-O-SID --
AND MY DEAR FRIEND, VICE PRESIDENT ASTRE-DE-KAY ... ALL REMOVED FROM THE BOARD BY PARTIES UNKNOWN. WHY, WE MAY SOON BE LOOKING AT A PRESIDENT GEOR-DAN-THI.
NO POLITICIAN CAN REFUSE THE SUPPORT OF HIS CONSTITUENTS.

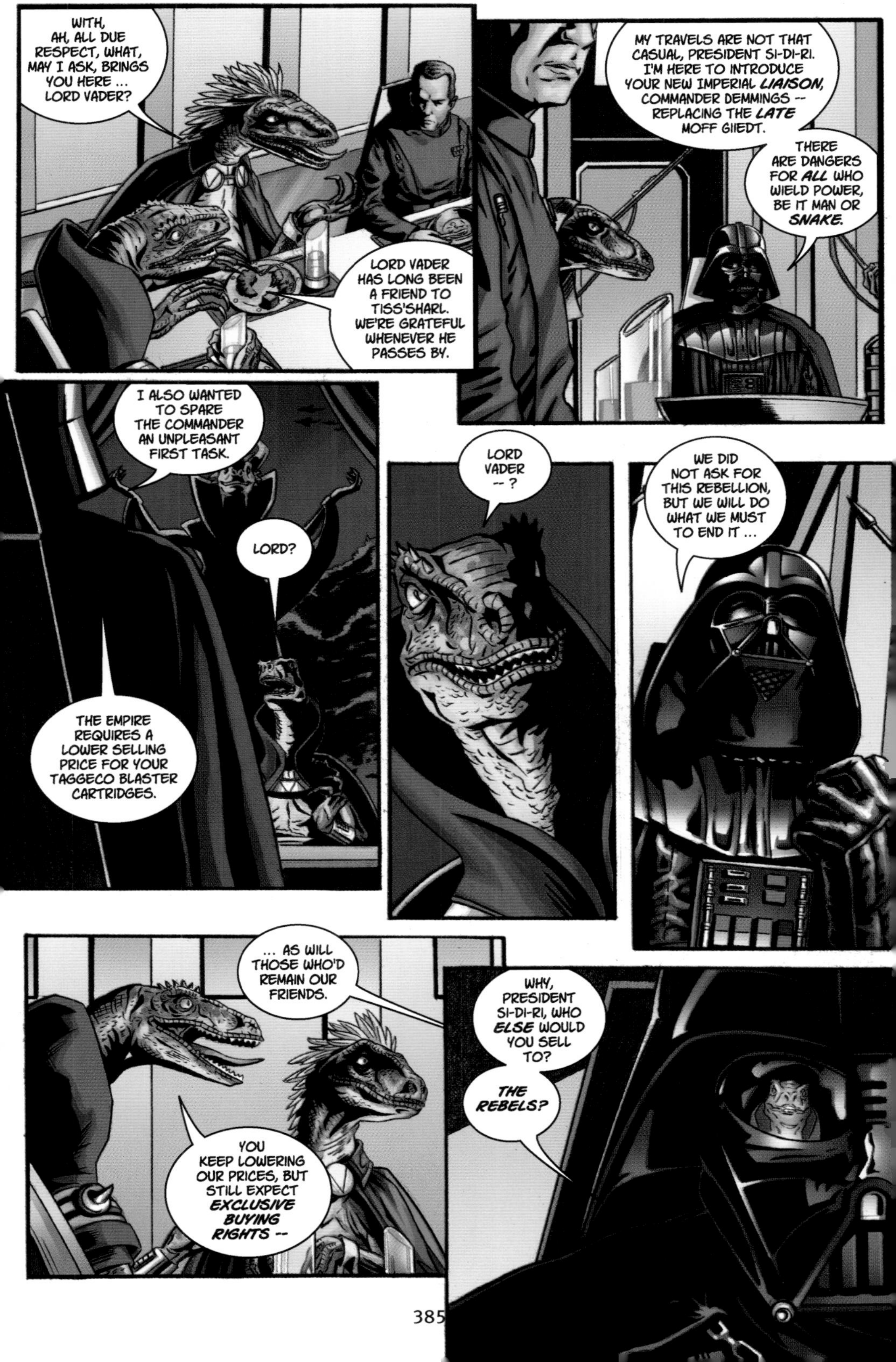
WITH, AH, ALL DUE RESPECT, WHAT, MAY I ASK, BRINGS YOU HERE ... LORD VADER?
LORD VADER HAS LONG BEEN A FRIEND TO TISS'SHARL. WE'RE GRATEFUL WHENEVER HE PASSES BY.
MY TRAVELS ARE NOT THAT CASUAL, PRESIDENT SI-DI-RI. I'M HERE TO INTRODUCE YOUR NEW IMPERIAL LIAISON, COMMANDER DEMMINGS -- REPLACING THE LATE MOFF GIIEDT.
THERE ARE DANGERS FOR ALL WHO WIELD POWER, BE IT MAN OR SNAKE.
I ALSO WANTED TO SPARE THE COMMANDER AN UNPLEASANT FIRST TASK.
LORD?
THE EMPIRE REQUIRES A LOWER SELLING PRICE FOR YOUR TAGGECO BLASTER CARTRIDGES.
LORD VADER -- ?
WE DID NOT ASK FOR THIS REBELLION, BUT WE WILL DO WHAT WE MUST TO END IT ...
... AS WILL THOSE WHO'D REMAIN OUR FRIENDS.
YOU KEEP LOWERING OUR PRICES, BUT STILL EXPECT EXCLUSIVE BUYING RIGHTS --
WHY, PRESIDENT SI-DI-RI, WHO ELSE WOULD YOU SELL TO?
THE REBELS?

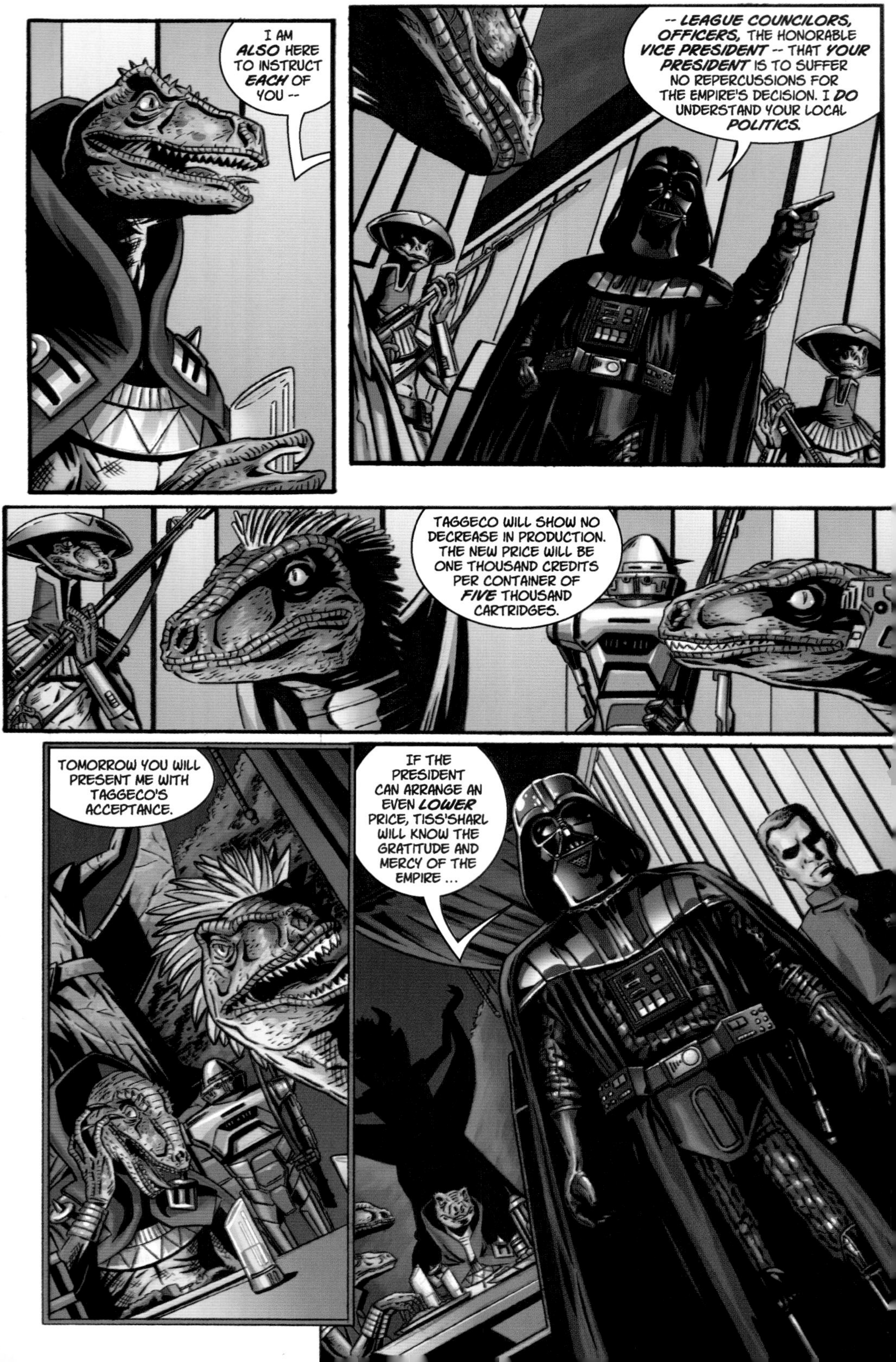
I AM ALSO HERE TO INSTRUCT EACH OF YOU --
-- LEAGUE COUNCILORS, OFFICERS, THE HONORABLE VICE PRESIDENT -- THAT YOUR PRESIDENT IS TO SUFFER NO REPERCUSSIONS FOR THE EMPIRE'S DECISION. I DO UNDERSTAND YOUR LOCAL POLITICS.
TAGGECO WILL SHOW NO DECREASE IN PRODUCTION. THE NEW PRICE WILL BE ONE THOUSAND CREDITS PER CONTAINER OF FIVE THOUSAND CARTRIDGES.
TOMORROW YOU WILL PRESENT ME WITH TAGGECO'S ACCEPTANCE.
IF THE PRESIDENT CAN ARRANGE AN EVEN LOWER PRICE, TISS'SHARL WILL KNOW THE GRATITUDE AND MERCY OF THE EMPIRE ...

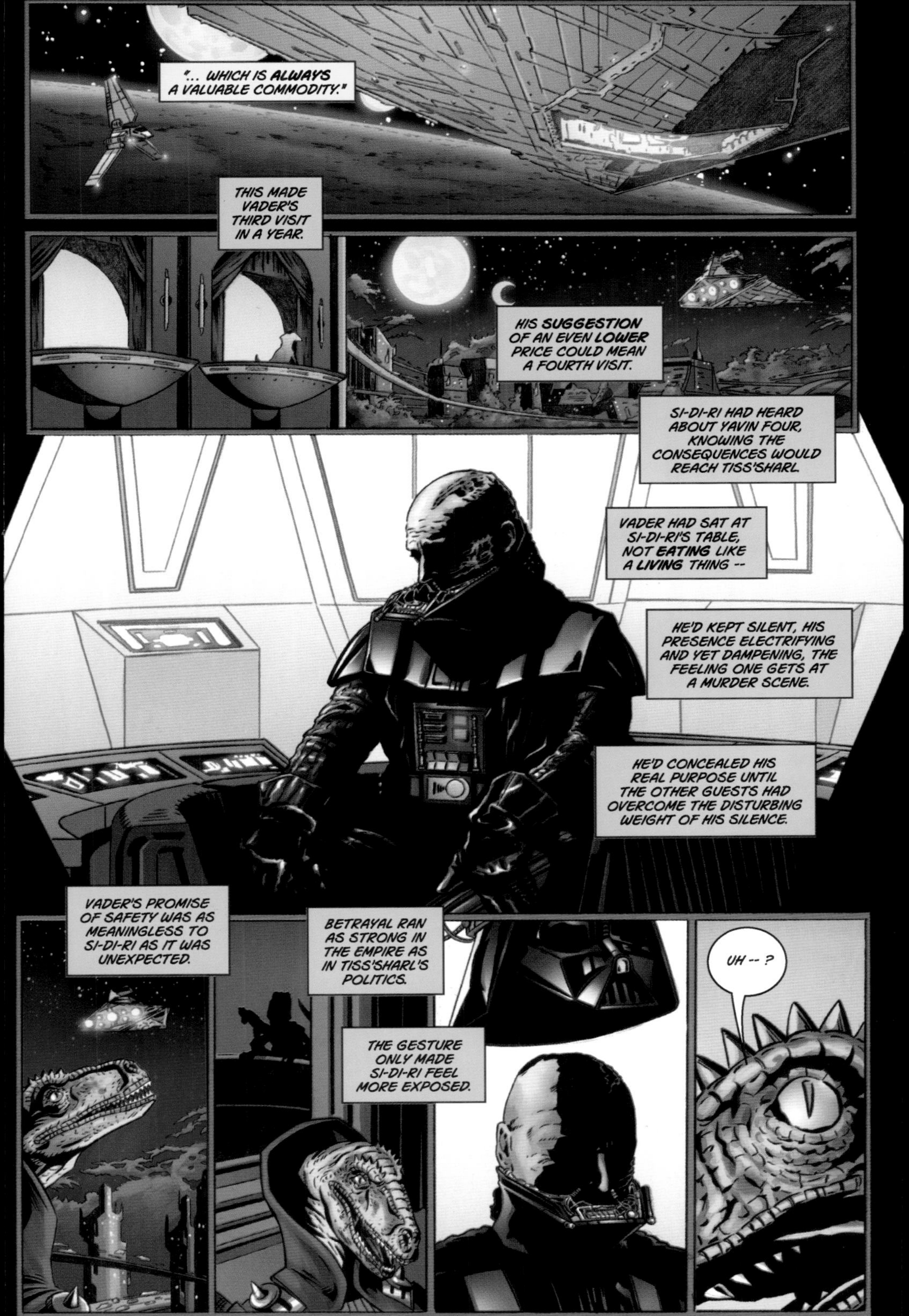
"... WHICH IS ALWAYS A VALUABLE COMMODITY."
THIS MADE VADER'S THIRD VISIT IN A YEAR.
HIS SUGGESTION OF AN EVEN LOWER PRICE COULD MEAN A FOURTH VISIT.
SI-DI-RI HAD HEARD ABOUT YAVIN FOUR, KNOWING THE CONSEQUENCES WOULD REACH TISS'SHARL.
VADER HAD SAT AT SI-DI-RI'S TABLE, NOT EATING LIKE A LIVING THING --
HE'D KEPT SILENT, HIS PRESENCE ELECTRIFYING AND YET DAMPENING, THE FEELING ONE GETS AT A MURDER SCENE.
HE'D CONCEALED HIS REAL PURPOSE UNTIL THE OTHER GUESTS HAD OVERCOME THE DISTURBING WEIGHT OF HIS SILENCE.
VADER'S PROMISE OF SAFETY WAS AS MEANINGLESS TO SI-DI-RI AS IT WAS UNEXPECTED.
BETRAYAL RAN AS STRONG IN THE EMPIRE AS IN TISS'SHARL'S POLITICS.
THE GESTURE ONLY MADE SI-DI-RI FEEL MORE EXPOSED.
UH -- ?

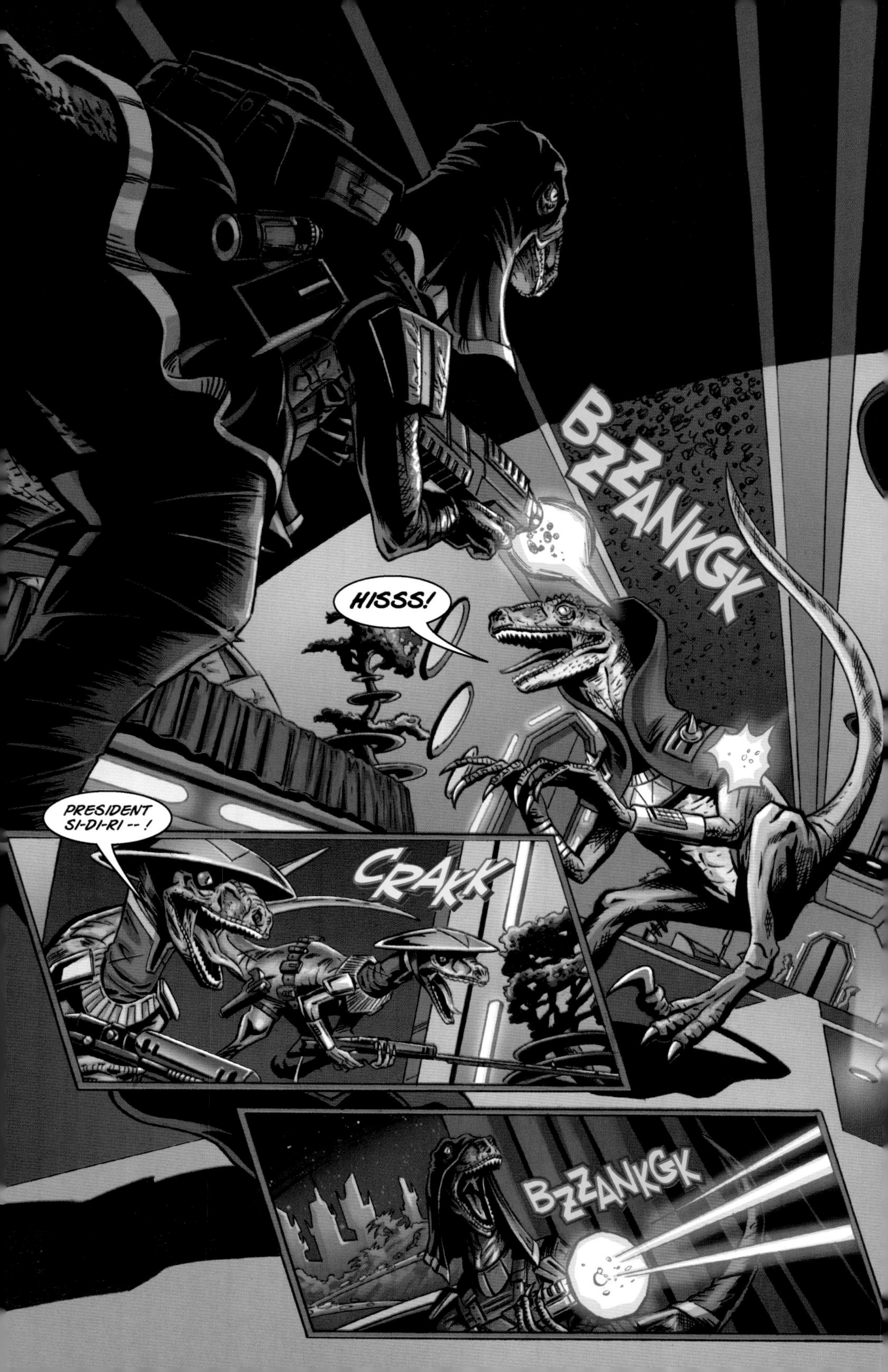
BZZANKGK
HISSS!
PRESIDENT SI-DI-RI -- !
CRAKK
BZZANKGK

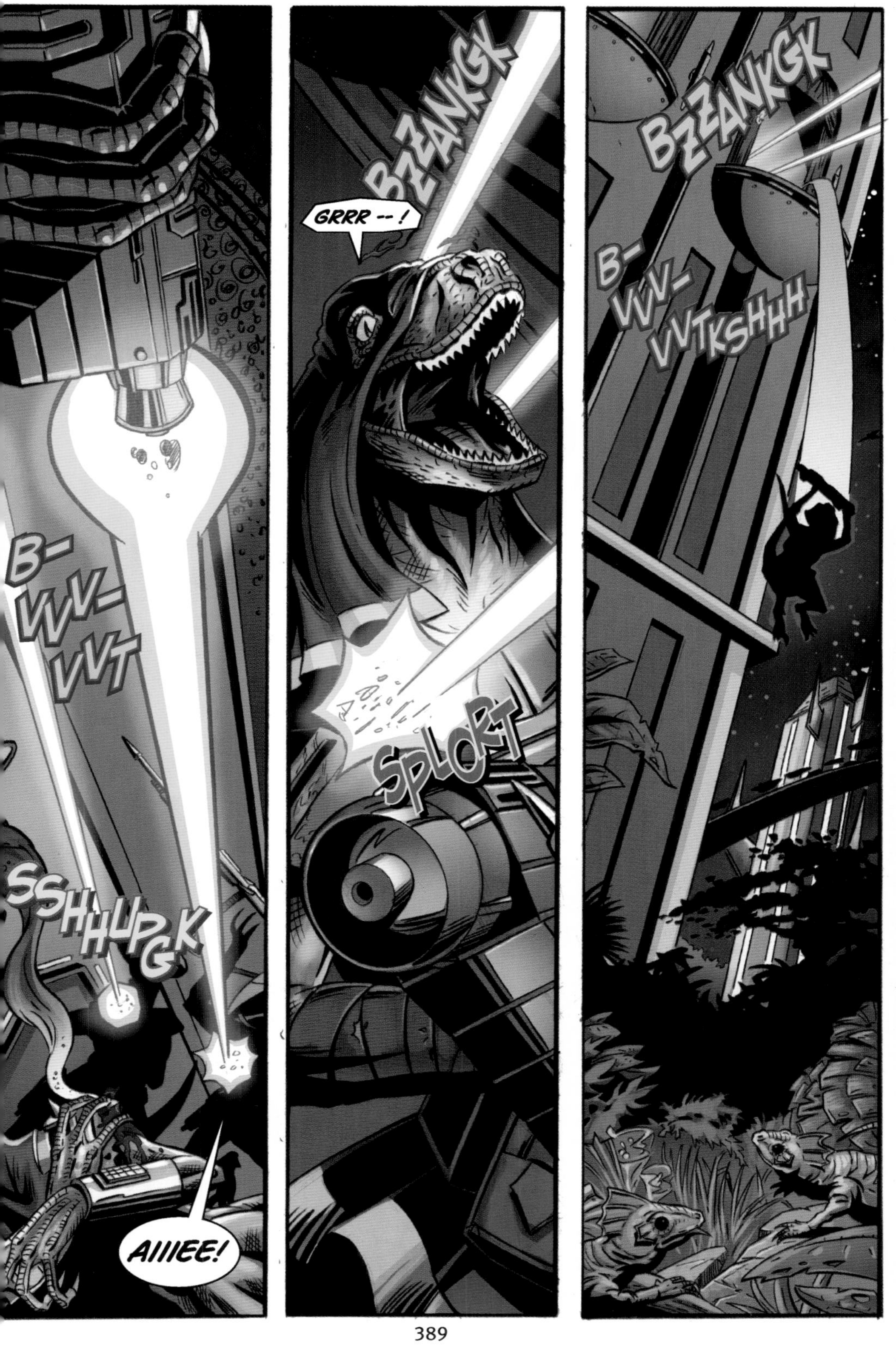

B-VVVV-VVT
SSHHUPGK
AIIIEE!
BZZANKGK
GRRR -- !
SPLORT
BZZANKGK
B-VVV-VVTKSHHH

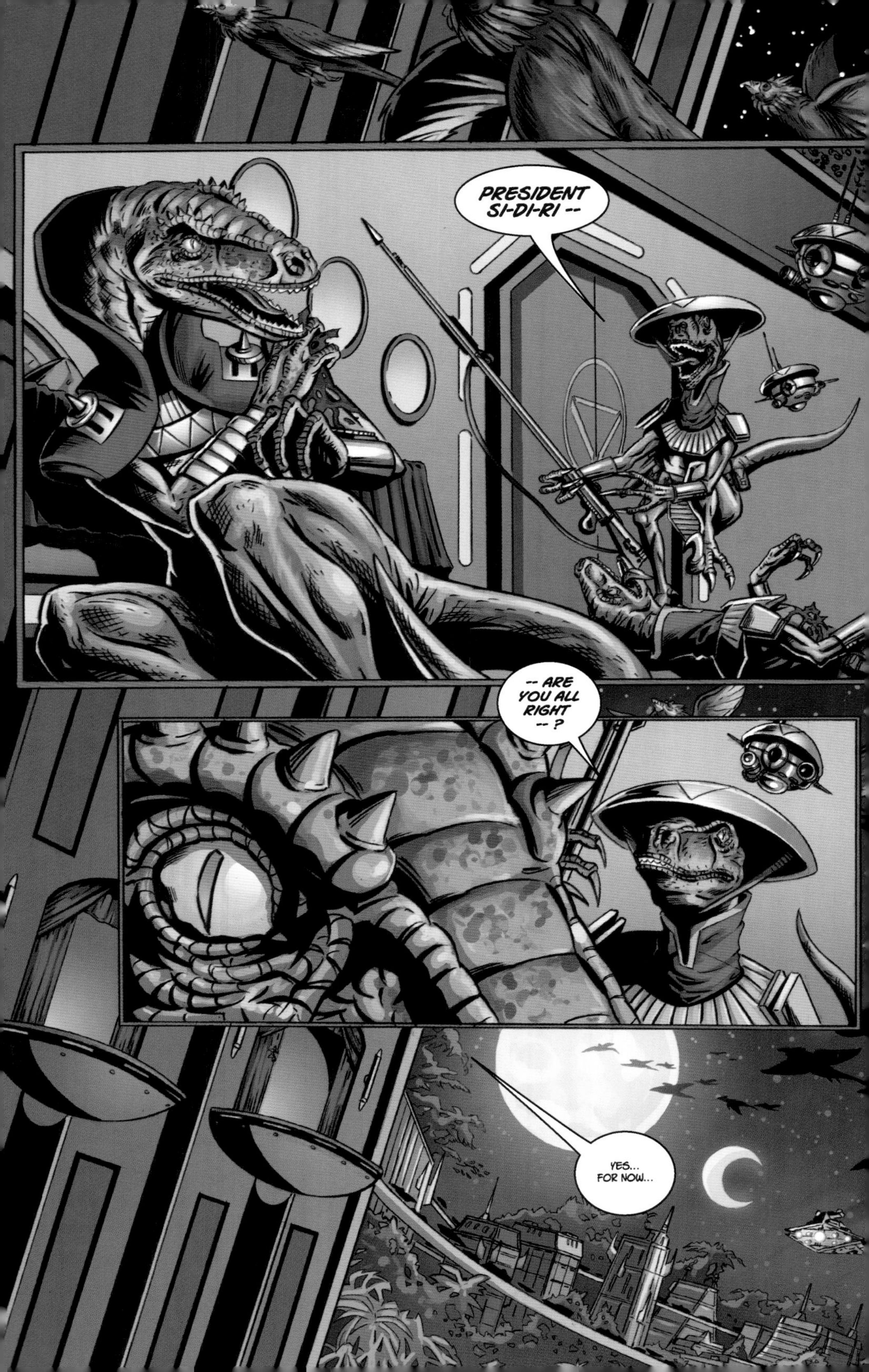
PRESIDENT SI-DI-RI --
-- ARE YOU ALL RIGHT -- ?
YES... FOR NOW...

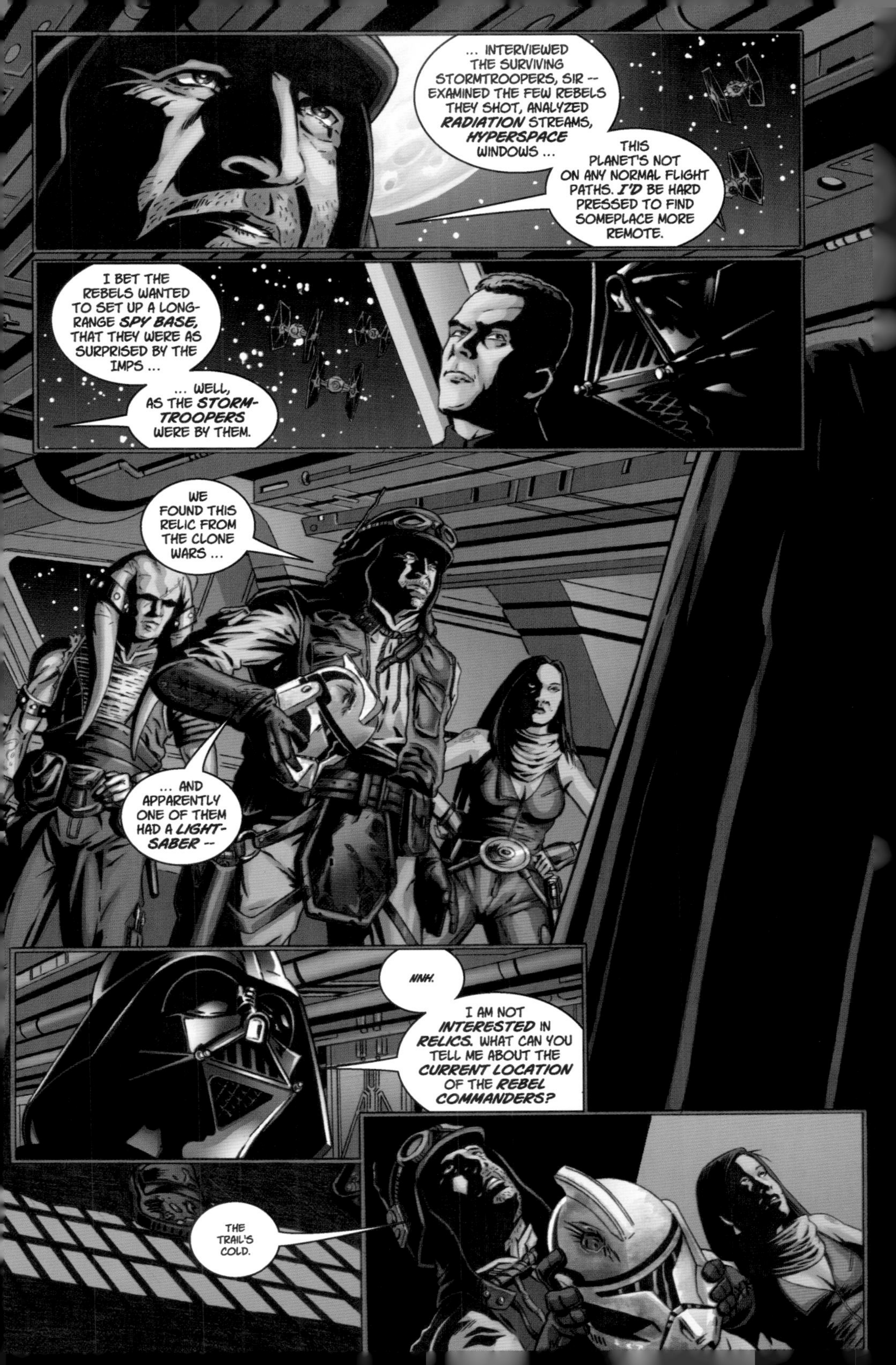
... INTERVIEWED THE SURVIVING STORMTROOPERS, SIR -- EXAMINED THE FEW REBELS THEY SHOT, ANALYZED RADIATION STREAMS, HYPERSPACE WINDOWS ...
THIS PLANET'S NOT ON ANY NORMAL FLIGHT PATHS. I'D BE HARD PRESSED TO FIND SOMEPLACE MORE REMOTE.
I BET THE REBELS WANTED TO SET UP A LONG-RANGE SPY BASE, THAT THEY WERE AS SURPRISED BY THE IMPS ...
... WELL, AS THE STORM-TROOPERS WERE BY THEM.
WE FOUND THIS RELIC FROM THE CLONE WARS ...
... AND APPARENTLY ONE OF THEM HAD A LIGHT-SABER --
NNH.
I AM NOT INTERESTED IN RELICS. WHAT CAN YOU TELL ME ABOUT THE CURRENT LOCATION OF THE REBEL COMMANDERS?
THE TRAIL'S COLD.

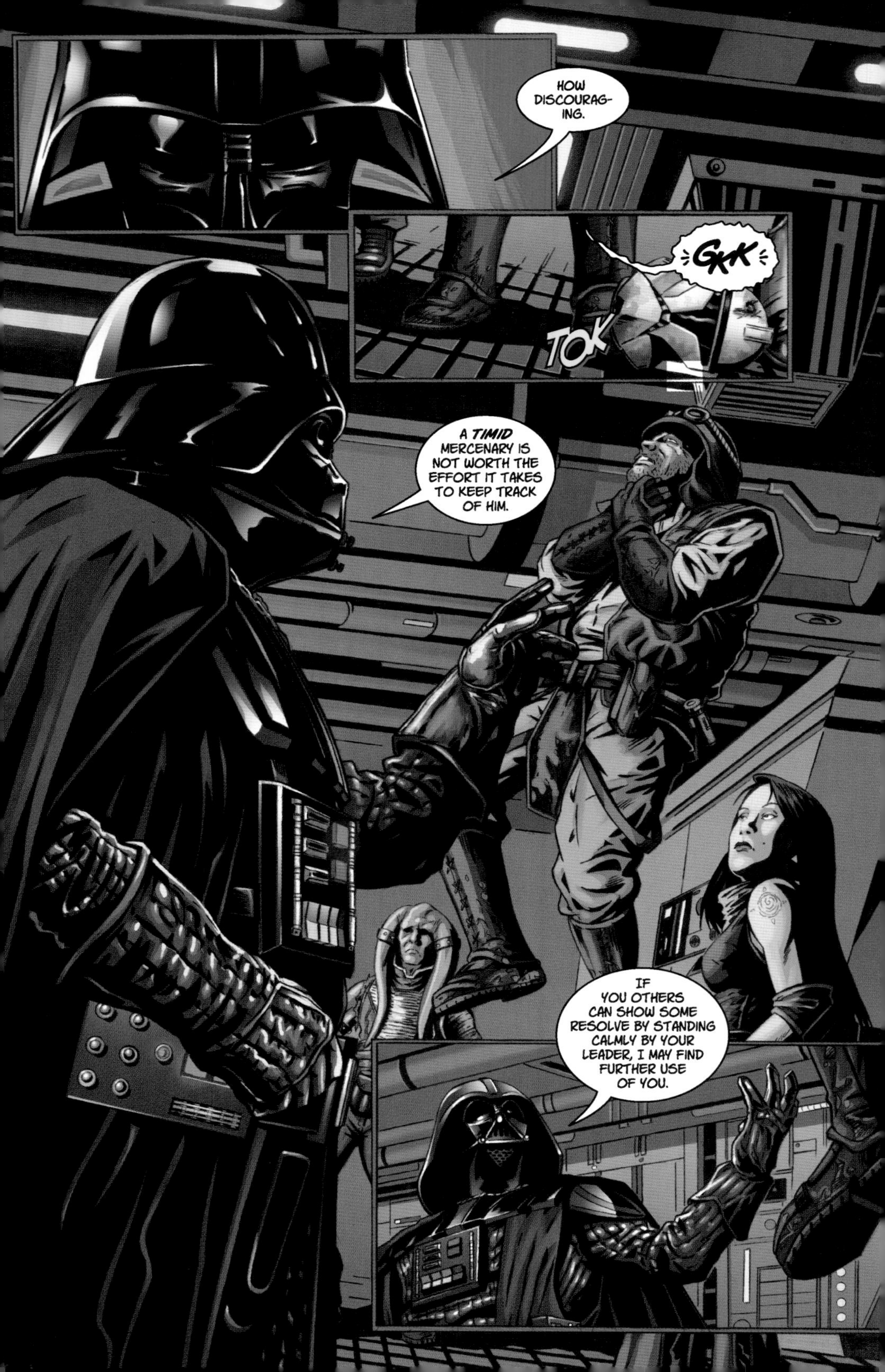
HOW DISCOURAG-ING.
GKK
TOK
A TIMID MERCENARY IS NOT WORTH THE EFFORT IT TAKES TO KEEP TRACK OF HIM.
IF YOU OTHERS CAN SHOW SOME RESOLVE BY STANDING CALMLY BY YOUR LEADER, I MAY FIND FURTHER USE OF YOU.

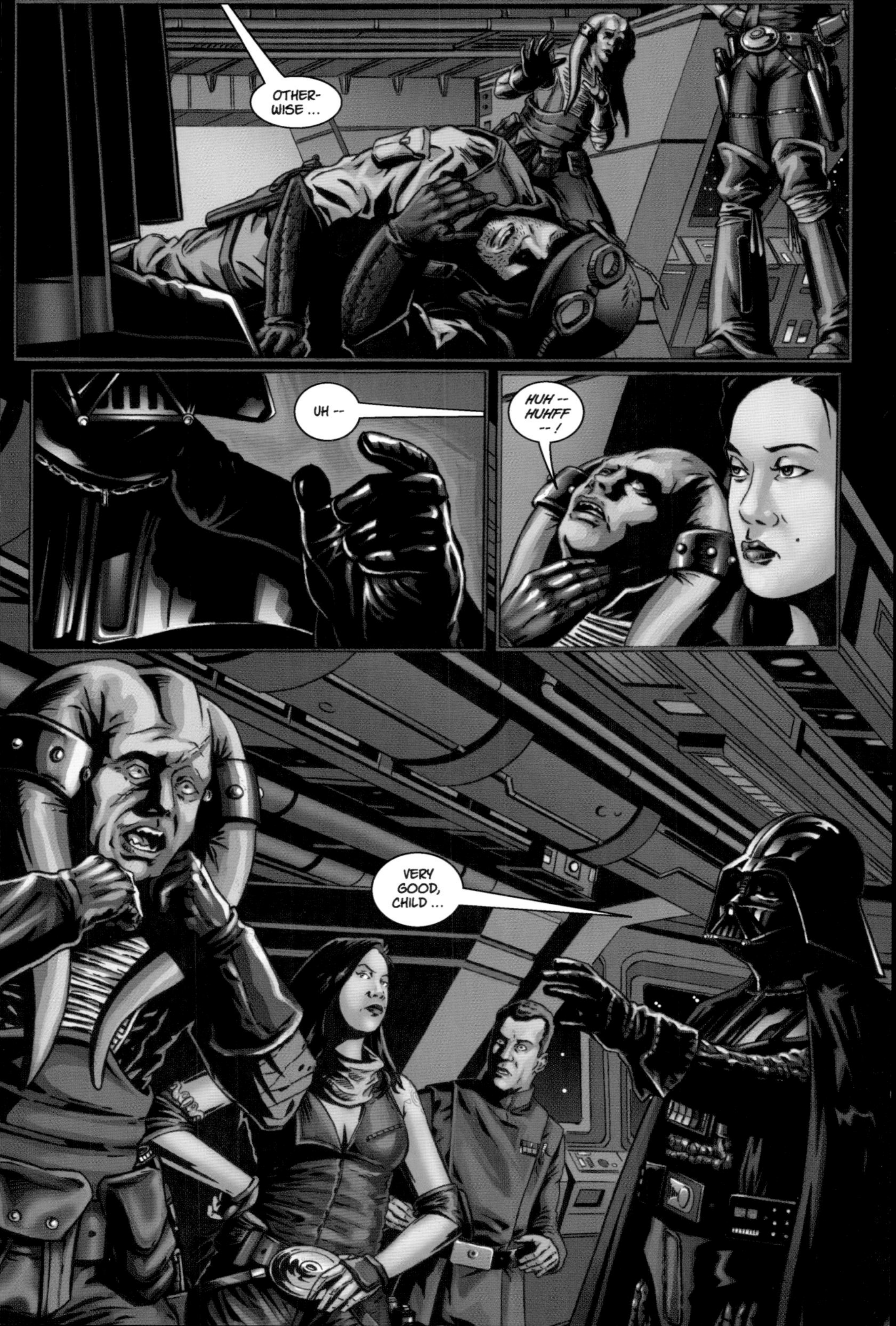
OTHER-
WISE ...
UH --
HUH --
HUHFF
-- !
VERY
GOOD,
CHILD ...

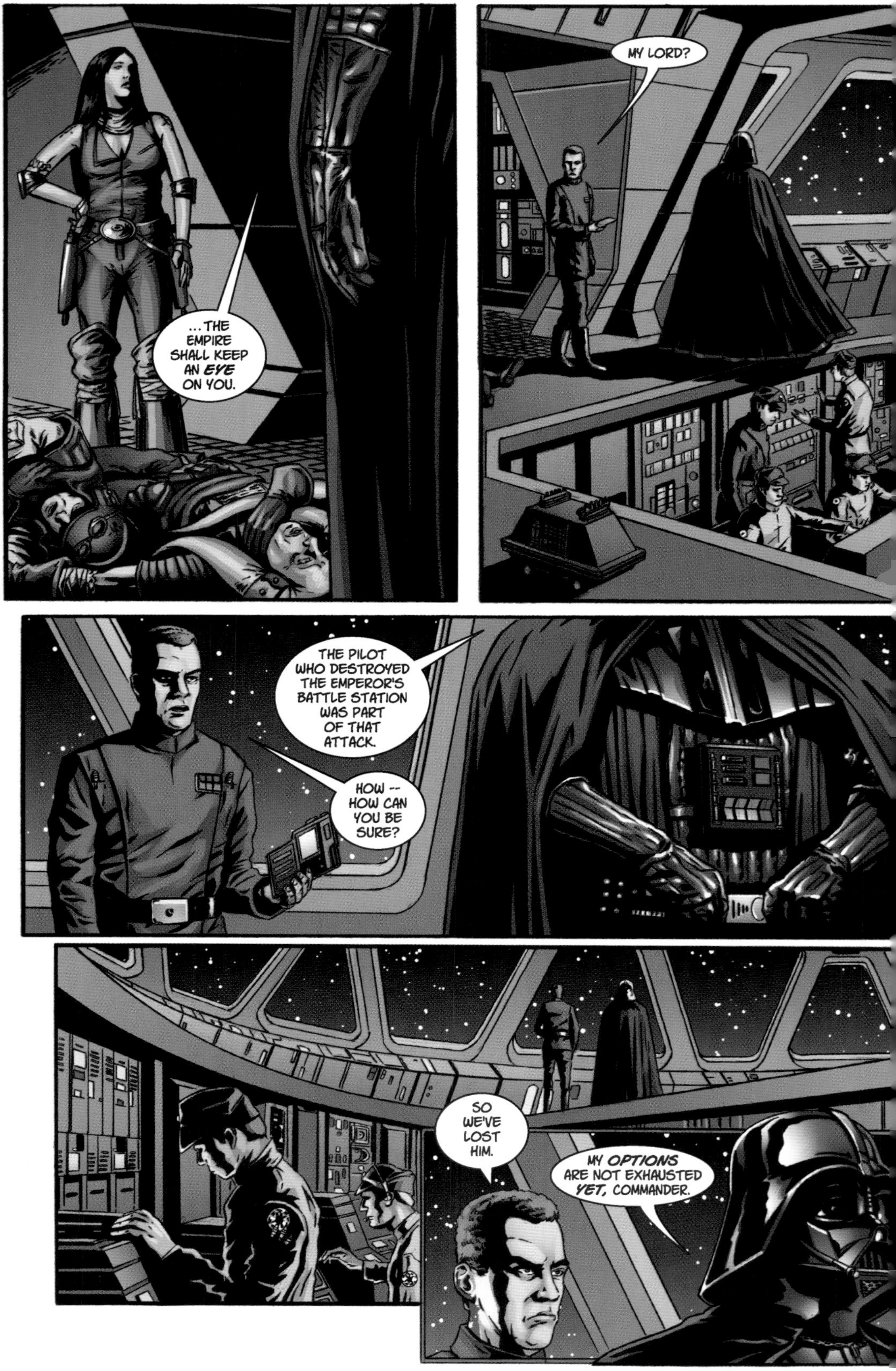
...THE EMPIRE SHALL KEEP AN EYE ON YOU.
MY LORD?
THE PILOT WHO DESTROYED THE EMPEROR'S BATTLE STATION WAS PART OF THAT ATTACK.
HOW -- HOW CAN YOU BE SURE?
SO WE'VE LOST HIM.
MY OPTIONS ARE NOT EXHAUSTED YET, COMMANDER.

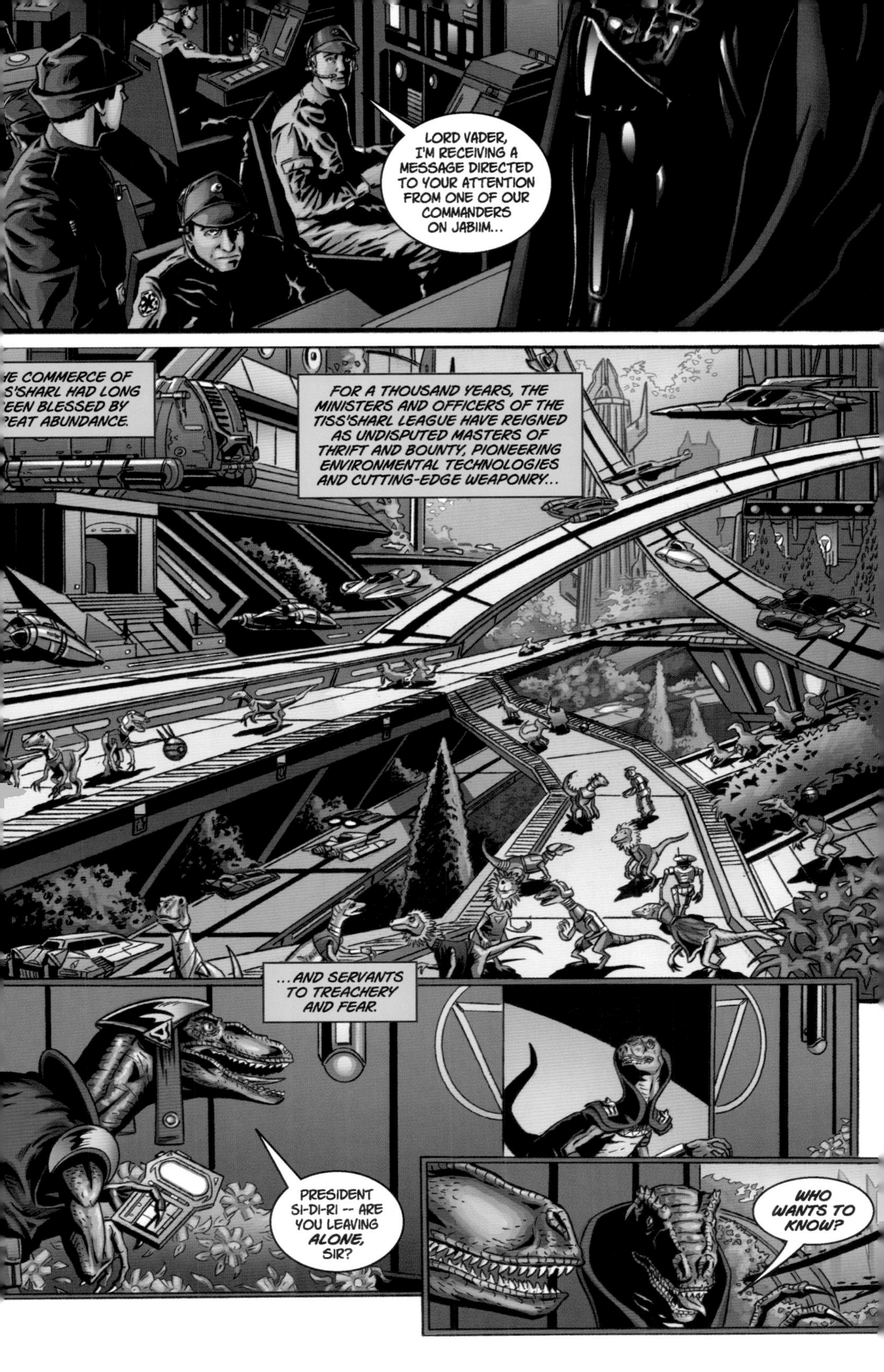

LORD VADER, I'M RECEIVING A MESSAGE DIRECTED TO YOUR ATTENTION FROM ONE OF OUR COMMANDERS ON JABIIM...
HE COMMERCE OF ISS'SHARL HAD LONG EEN BLESSED BY PEAT ABUNDANCE.
FOR A THOUSAND YEARS, THE MINISTERS AND OFFICERS OF THE TISS'SHARL LEAGUE HAVE REIGNED AS UNDISPUTED MASTERS OF THRIFT AND BOUNTY, PIONEERING ENVIRONMENTAL TECHNOLOGIES AND CUTTING-EDGE WEAPONRY...
...AND SERVANTS TO TREACHERY AND FEAR.
PRESIDENT SI-DI-RI -- ARE YOU LEAVING *ALONE*, SIR?
WHO WANTS TO KNOW?

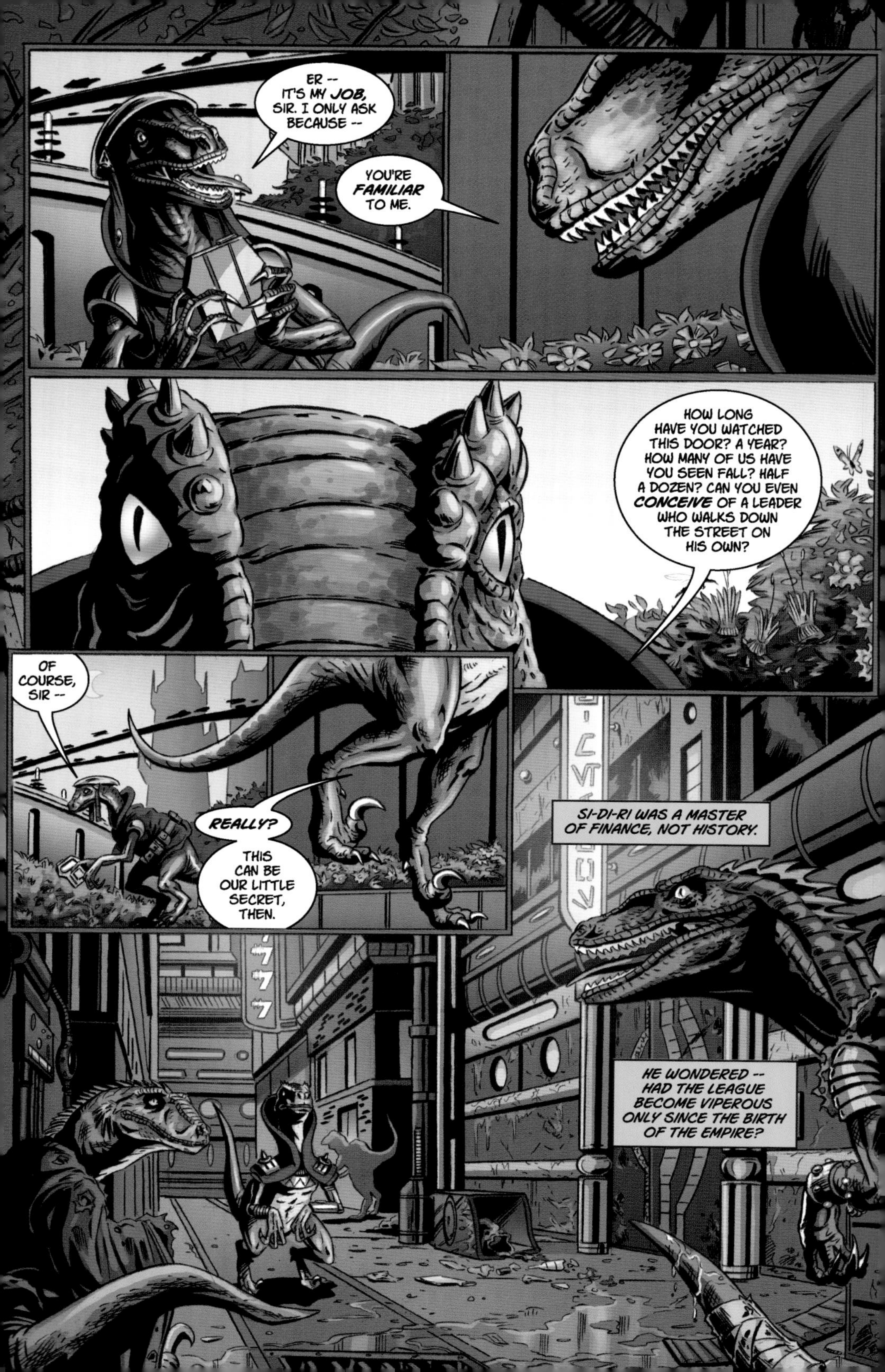
ER -- IT'S MY JOB, SIR. I ONLY ASK BECAUSE --
YOU'RE FAMILIAR TO ME.
HOW LONG HAVE YOU WATCHED THIS DOOR? A YEAR? HOW MANY OF US HAVE YOU SEEN FALL? HALF A DOZEN? CAN YOU EVEN CONCEIVE OF A LEADER WHO WALKS DOWN THE STREET ON HIS OWN?
OF COURSE, SIR --
REALLY?
THIS CAN BE OUR LITTLE SECRET, THEN.
SI-DI-RI WAS A MASTER OF FINANCE, NOT HISTORY.
HE WONDERED -- HAD THE LEAGUE BECOME VIPEROUS ONLY SINCE THE BIRTH OF THE EMPIRE?

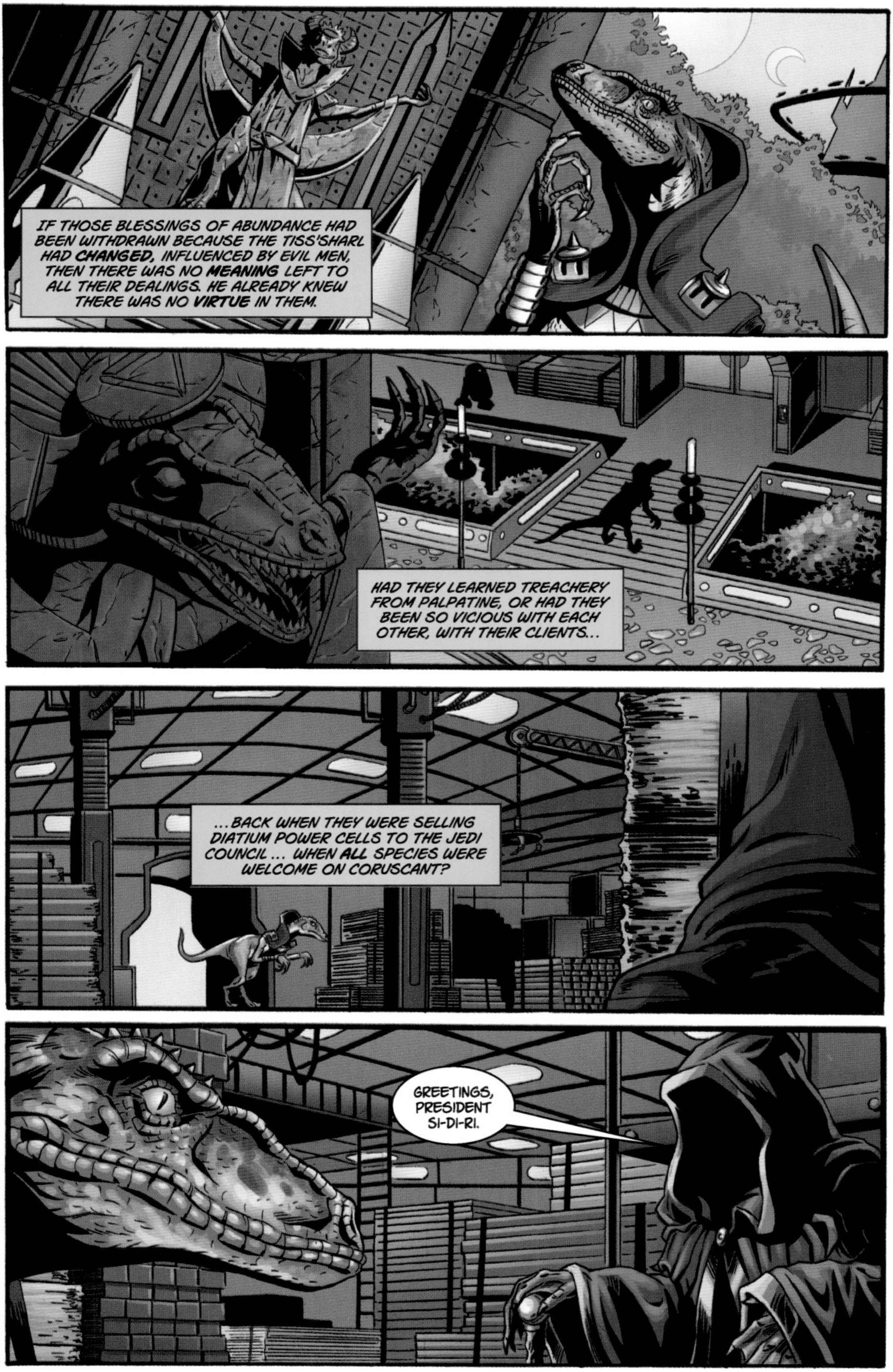
IF THOSE BLESSINGS OF ABUNDANCE HAD BEEN WITHDRAWN BECAUSE THE TISS'SHARL HAD **CHANGED**, INFLUENCED BY EVIL MEN, THEN THERE WAS NO **MEANING** LEFT TO ALL THEIR DEALINGS. HE ALREADY KNEW THERE WAS NO **VIRTUE** IN THEM.
HAD THEY LEARNED TREACHERY FROM PALPATINE, OR HAD THEY BEEN SO VICIOUS WITH EACH OTHER, WITH THEIR CLIENTS...
...BACK WHEN THEY WERE SELLING DIATIUM POWER CELLS TO THE JEDI COUNCIL... WHEN **ALL** SPECIES WERE WELCOME ON CORUSCANT?
GREETINGS, PRESIDENT SI-DI-RI.

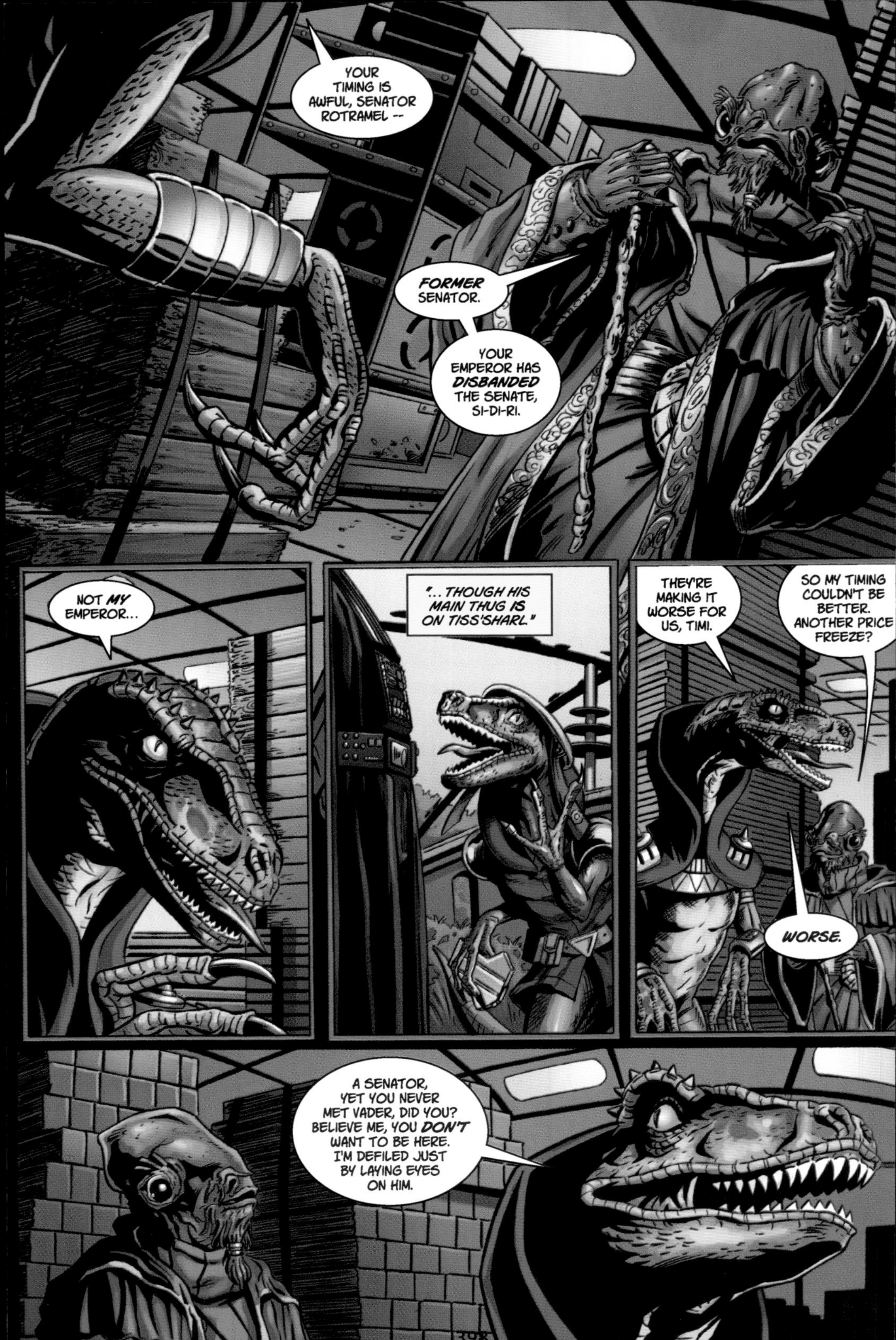
YOUR TIMING IS AWFUL, SENATOR ROTRAMEL --
FORMER SENATOR.
YOUR EMPEROR HAS DISBANDED THE SENATE, SI-DI-RI.
NOT MY EMPEROR...
"...THOUGH HIS MAIN THUG IS ON TISS'SHARL."
THEY'RE MAKING IT WORSE FOR US, TIMI.
SO MY TIMING COULDN'T BE BETTER. ANOTHER PRICE FREEZE?
WORSE.
A SENATOR, YET YOU NEVER MET VADER, DID YOU? BELIEVE ME, YOU DON'T WANT TO BE HERE. I'M DEFILED JUST BY LAYING EYES ON HIM.

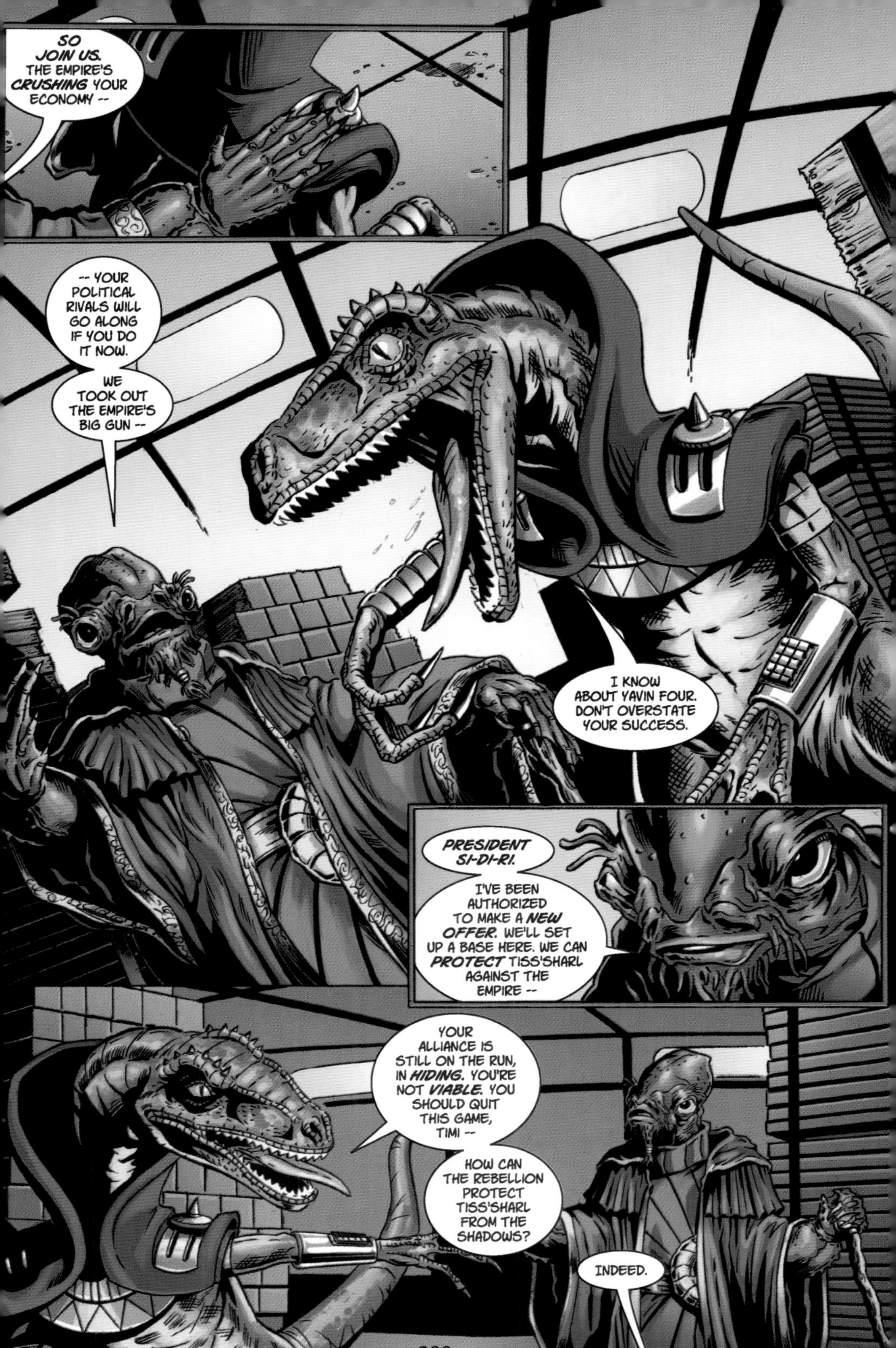

SO JOIN US. THE EMPIRE'S CRUSHING YOUR ECONOMY --
-- YOUR POLITICAL RIVALS WILL GO ALONG IF YOU DO IT NOW.
WE TOOK OUT THE EMPIRE'S BIG GUN --
I KNOW ABOUT YAVIN FOUR. DON'T OVERSTATE YOUR SUCCESS.
PRESIDENT SI-DI-RI.
I'VE BEEN AUTHORIZED TO MAKE A NEW OFFER. WE'LL SET UP A BASE HERE. WE CAN PROTECT TISS'SHARL AGAINST THE EMPIRE --
YOUR ALLIANCE IS STILL ON THE RUN, IN HIDING. YOU'RE NOT VIABLE. YOU SHOULD QUIT THIS GAME, TIMI --
HOW CAN THE REBELLION PROTECT TISS'SHARL FROM THE SHADOWS?
INDEED.

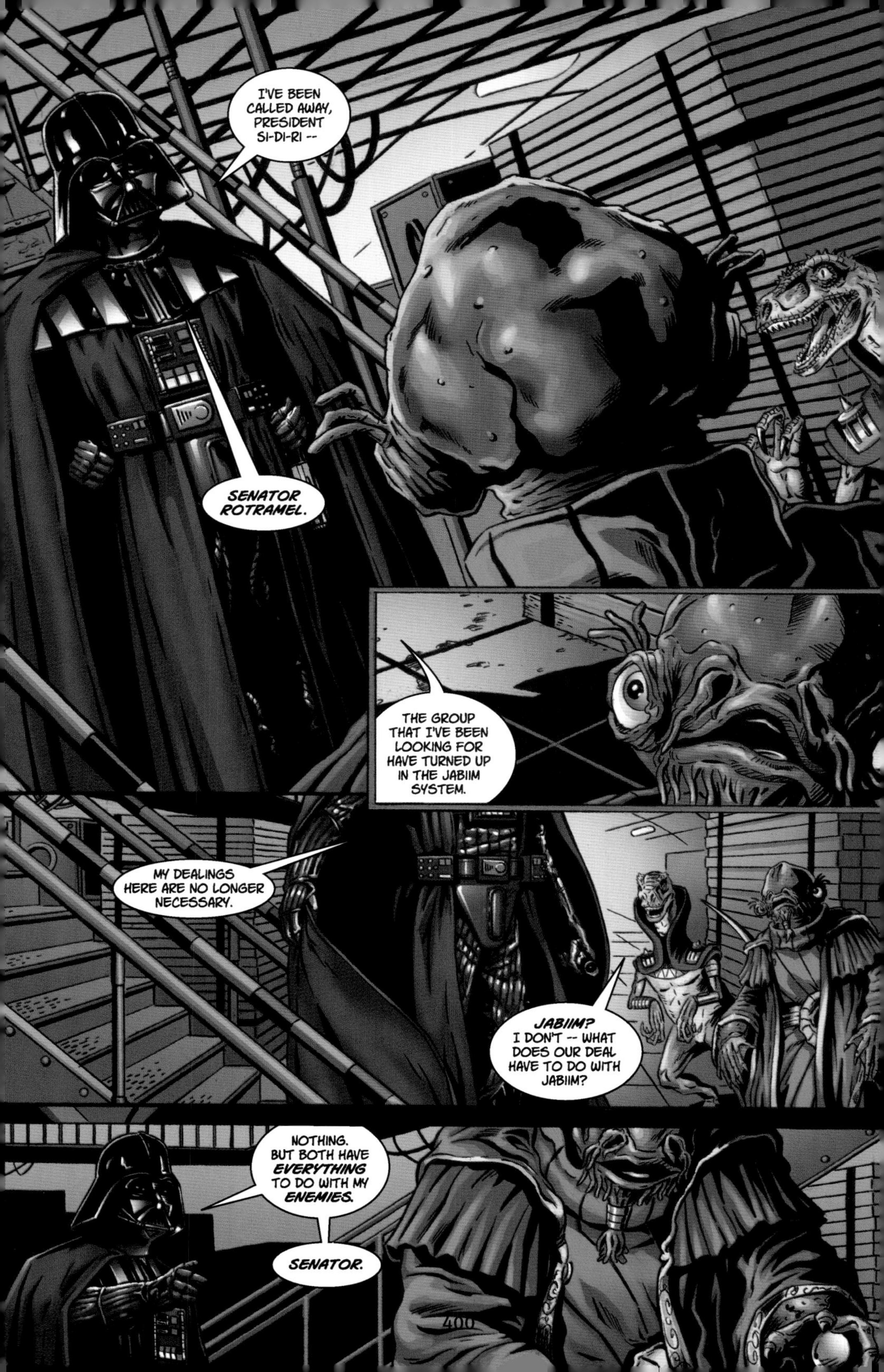
I'VE BEEN CALLED AWAY, PRESIDENT SI-DI-RI --
SENATOR ROTRAMEL.
THE GROUP THAT I'VE BEEN LOOKING FOR HAVE TURNED UP IN THE JABIIM SYSTEM.
MY DEALINGS HERE ARE NO LONGER NECESSARY.
JABIIM? I DON'T -- WHAT DOES OUR DEAL HAVE TO DO WITH JABIIM?
NOTHING. BUT BOTH HAVE EVERYTHING TO DO WITH MY ENEMIES.
SENATOR.

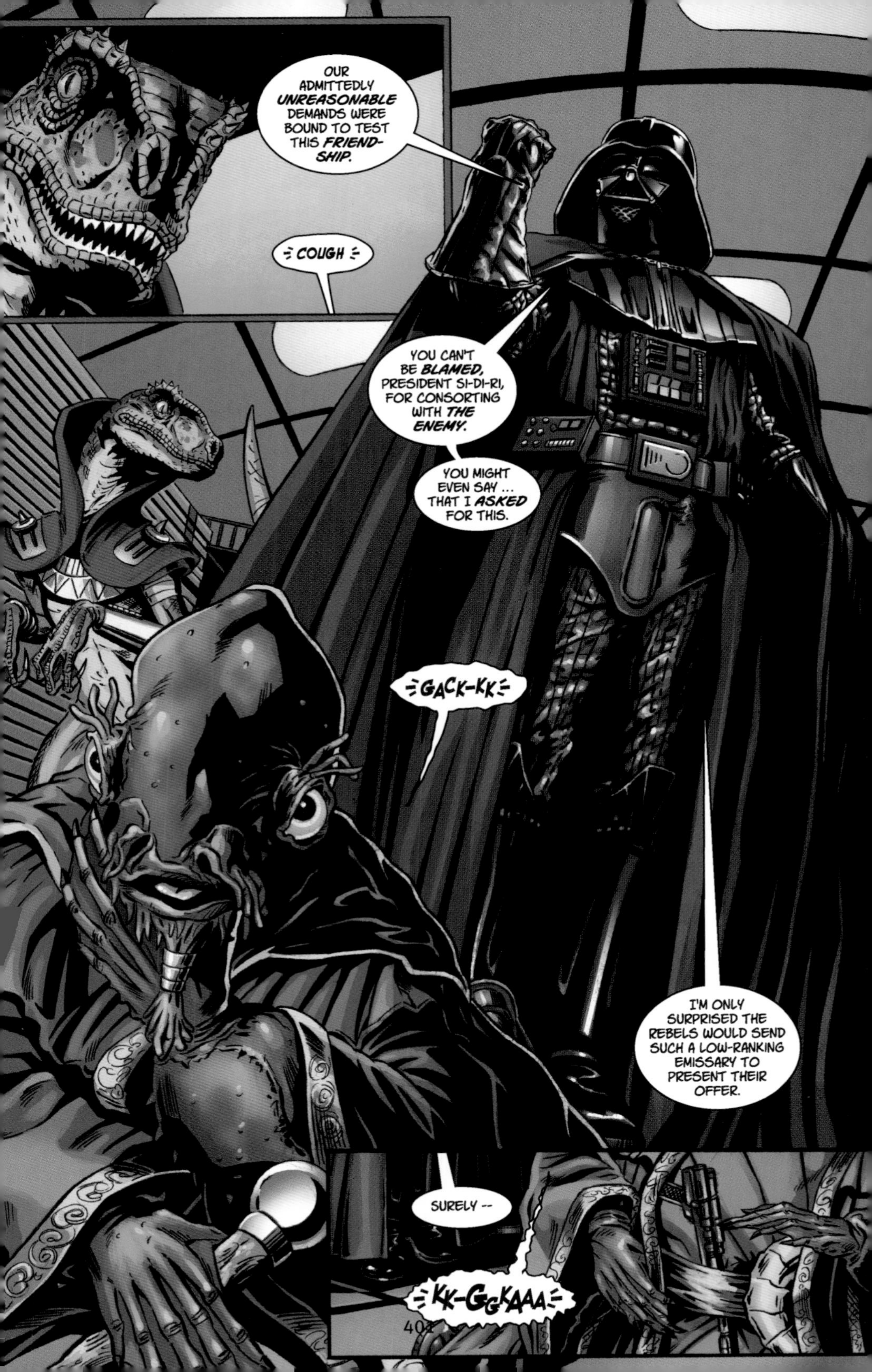
OUR ADMITTEDLY UNREASONABLE DEMANDS WERE BOUND TO TEST THIS FRIEND-SHIP.
COUGH
YOU CAN'T BE BLAMED, PRESIDENT SI-DI-RI, FOR CONSORTING WITH THE ENEMY.
YOU MIGHT EVEN SAY ... THAT I ASKED FOR THIS.
GACK-KK
I'M ONLY SURPRISED THE REBELS WOULD SEND SUCH A LOW-RANKING EMISSARY TO PRESENT THEIR OFFER.
SURELY --
KK-GGKAAA

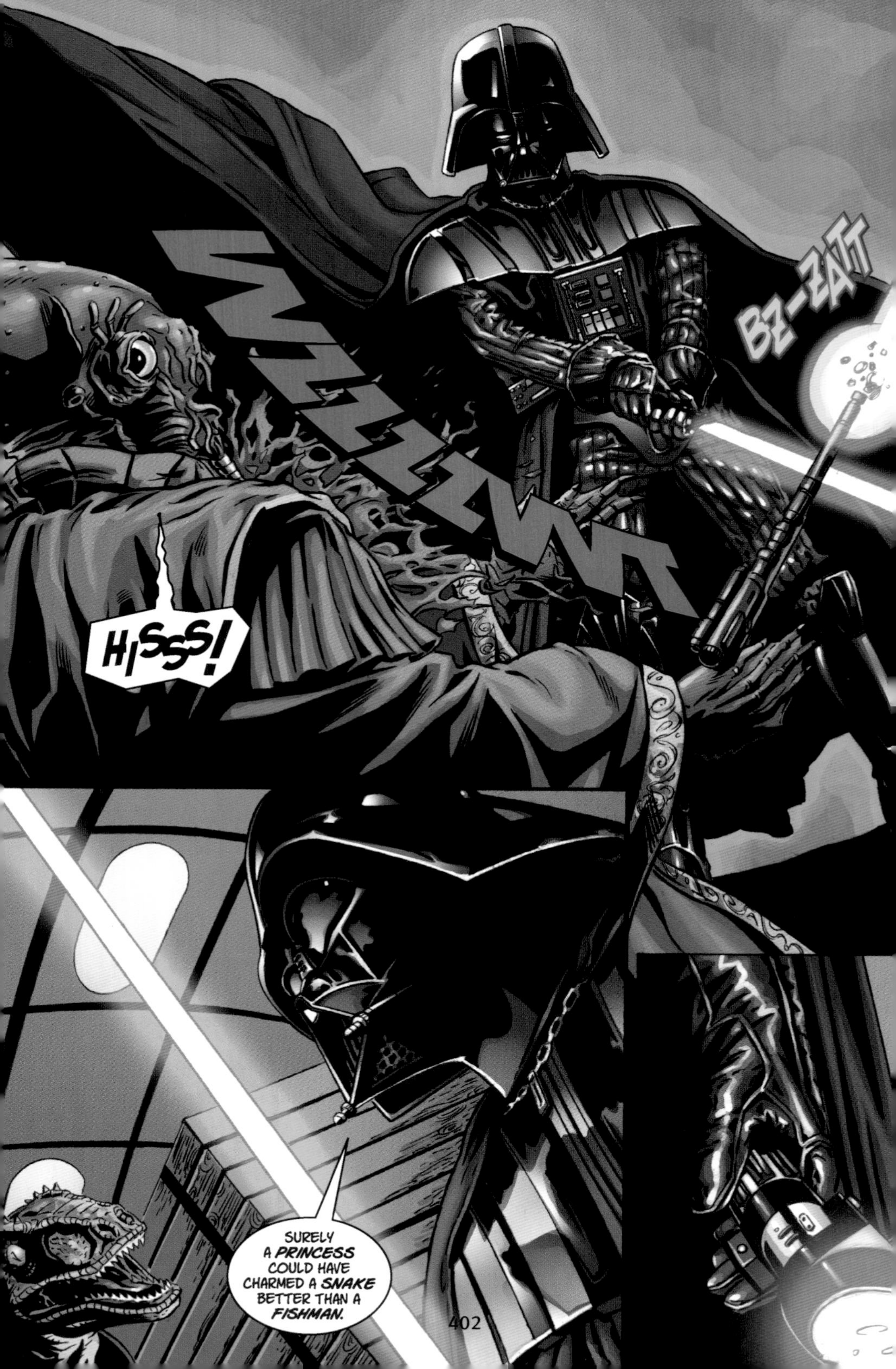

BZ-ZATT
HISSS!
SURELY A PRINCESS COULD HAVE CHARMED A SNAKE BETTER THAN A FISHMAN.

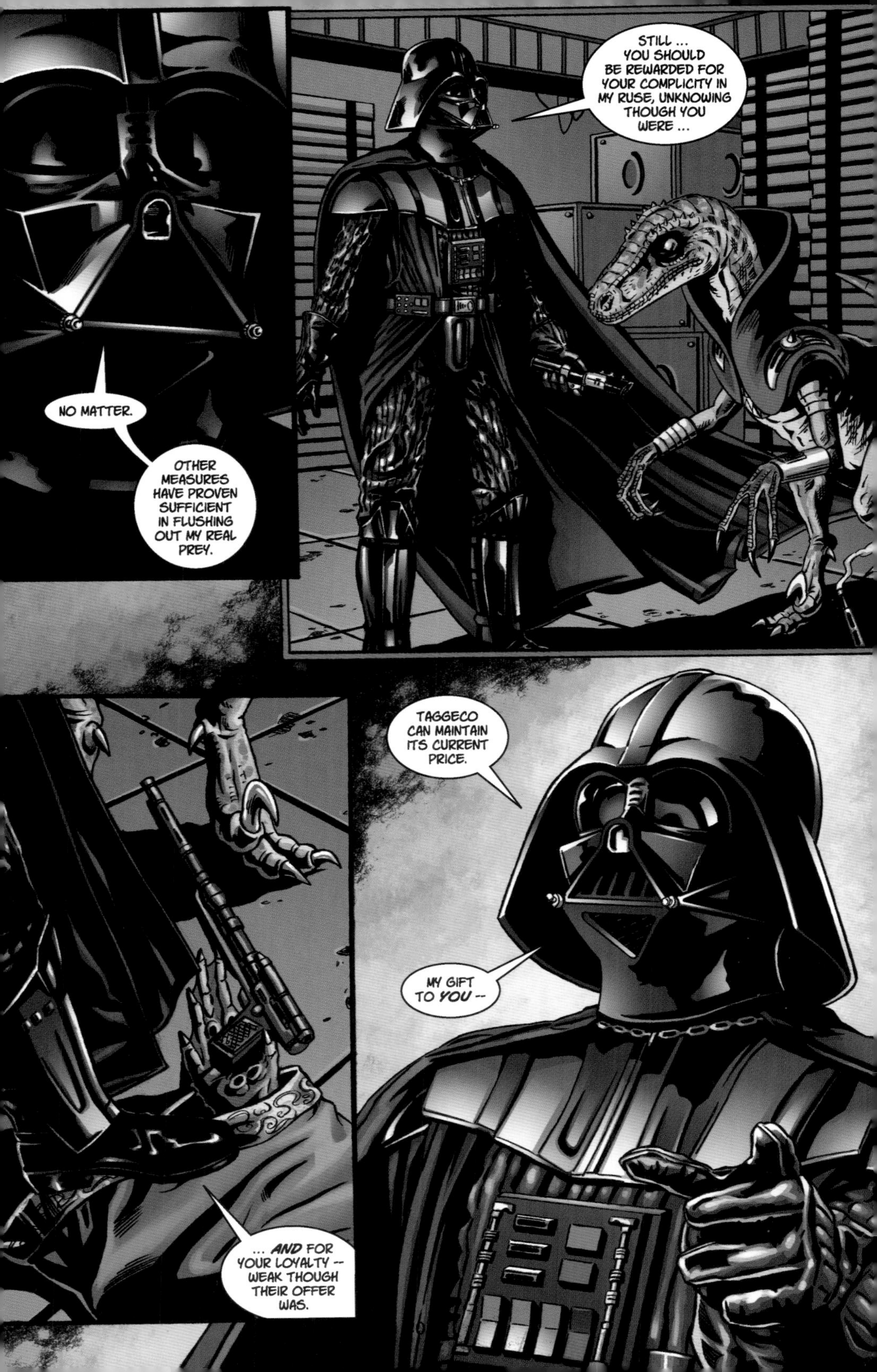

NO MATTER.
OTHER MEASURES HAVE PROVEN SUFFICIENT IN FLUSHING OUT MY REAL PREY.
STILL ... YOU SHOULD BE REWARDED FOR YOUR COMPLICITY IN MY RUSE, UNKNOWING THOUGH YOU WERE ...
TAGGECO CAN MAINTAIN ITS CURRENT PRICE.
MY GIFT TO *YOU* --
... *AND* FOR YOUR LOYALTY -- WEAK THOUGH THEIR OFFER WAS.

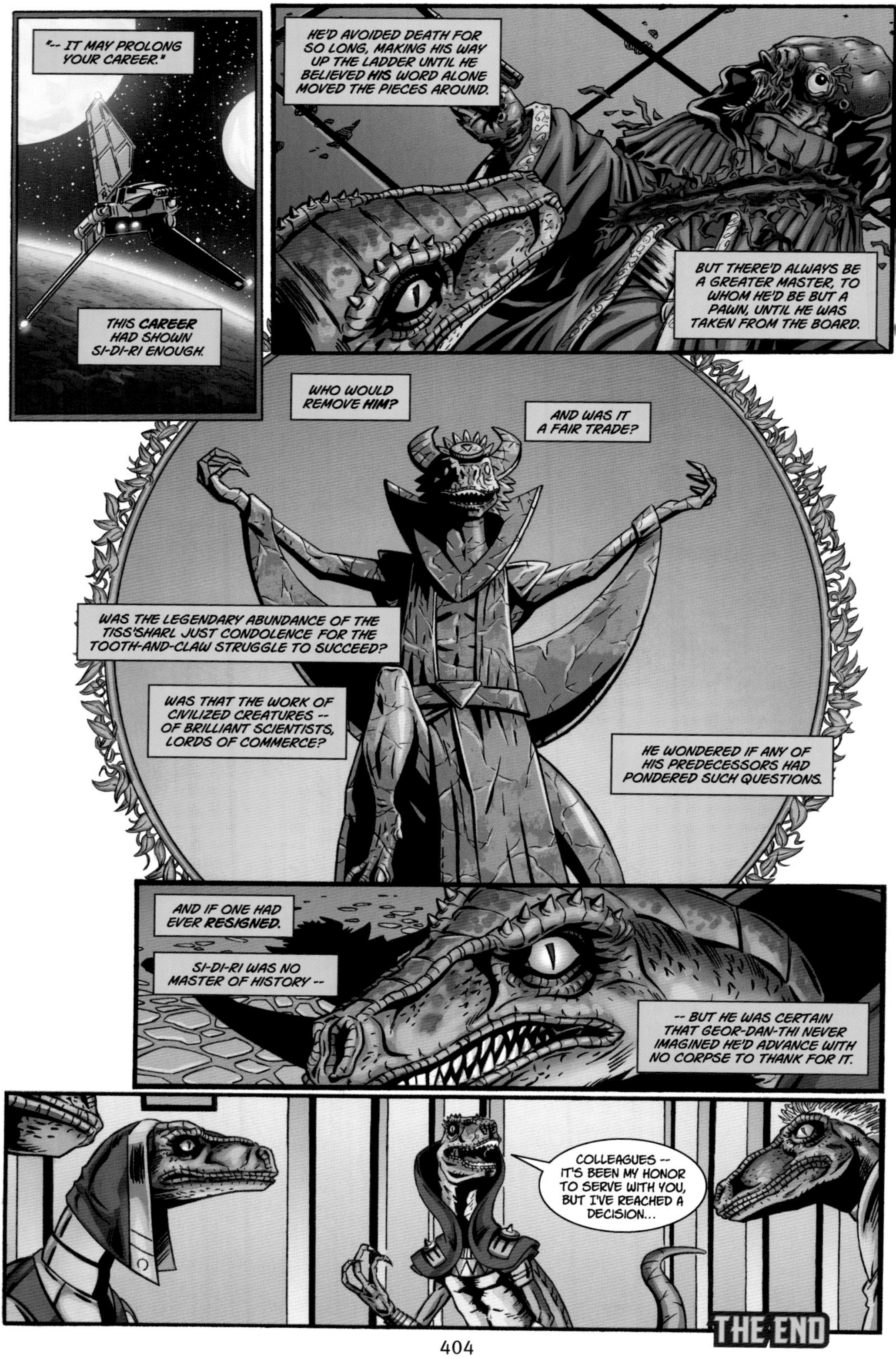
"-- IT MAY PROLONG YOUR CAREER."
THIS CAREER HAD SHOWN SI-DI-RI ENOUGH.
HE'D AVOIDED DEATH FOR SO LONG, MAKING HIS WAY UP THE LADDER UNTIL HE BELIEVED HIS WORD ALONE MOVED THE PIECES AROUND.
BUT THERE'D ALWAYS BE A GREATER MASTER, TO WHOM HE'D BE BUT A PAWN, UNTIL HE WAS TAKEN FROM THE BOARD.
WHO WOULD REMOVE HIM?
AND WAS IT A FAIR TRADE?
WAS THE LEGENDARY ABUNDANCE OF THE TISS'SHARL JUST CONDOLENCE FOR THE TOOTH-AND-CLAW STRUGGLE TO SUCCEED?
WAS THAT THE WORK OF CIVILIZED CREATURES -- OF BRILLIANT SCIENTISTS, LORDS OF COMMERCE?
HE WONDERED IF ANY OF HIS PREDECESSORS HAD PONDERED SUCH QUESTIONS.
AND IF ONE HAD EVER RESIGNED.
SI-DI-RI WAS NO MASTER OF HISTORY --
-- BUT HE WAS CERTAIN THAT GEOR-DAN-THI NEVER IMAGINED HE'D ADVANCE WITH NO CORPSE TO THANK FOR IT.
COLLEAGUES -- IT'S BEEN MY HONOR TO SERVE WITH YOU, BUT I'VE REACHED A DECISION...
THE END

A Word about the Omnibus Collections

Dark Horse Comics' *Star Wars* omnibus collections were created as a way to showcase actual novel-length stories or series, and to provide homes for "orphaned" series, single-issue stories, and short stories that would otherwise never be collected.

STAR WARS GRAPHIC NOVEL TIMELINE (IN YEARS

Omnibus: Tales of the Jedi—5,000–3,986 BSW4

Knights of the Old Republic (9 volumes)—3,964 BSW4

The Old Republic—3653,3678 BSW4

Jedi vs. Sith—1,000 BSW4

Omnibus: Rise of the Sith—33 BSW4

Episode I: The Phantom Menace—32 BSW4

Omnibus: Emissaries and Assassins—32 BSW4

Bounty Hunters—31 BSW4

Omnibus: Quinlan Vos – Jedi in Darkness—31–28 BSW4

Omnibus: Menace Revealed—31–22 BSW4

Honor and Duty—24 BSW4

Episode II: Attack of the Clones—22 BSW4

Clone Wars (9 volumes)—22–19 BSW4

Clone Wars Adventures (10 volumes)—22–19 BSW4

The Clone Wars (7 volumes)—22–19 BSW4

General Grievous—20 BSW4

Episode III: Revenge of the Sith—19 BSW4

Dark Times (4 volumes)—19 BSW4

Omnibus: Droids—3 BSW4

Omnibus: Boba Fett—3–1 BSW4, 0–10 ASW4

The Force Unleashed—2 BSW4

Adventures (4 volumes)—1–0 BSW4, 0–3 ASW4

Episode IV: A New Hope—SW4

Classic Star Wars—0–3 ASW4

A Long Time Ago… (7 volumes)—0–4 ASW4

Empire (6 volumes)—0 ASW4

Rebellion (3 volumes)—0 ASW4

Omnibus: Early Victories—0–1 ASW4

Jabba the Hutt: The Art of the Deal—1 ASW4

Episode V: The Empire Strikes Back—3 ASW4

Omnibus: Shadows of the Empire—3.5–4.5 ASW4

Episode VI: Return of the Jedi—4 ASW4

Omnibus: X-Wing Rogue Squadron—4–5 ASW4

The Thrawn Trilogy—9 ASW4

Dark Empire—10 ASW4

Crimson Empire—11 ASW4

Jedi Academy: Leviathan—13 ASW4

Union—20 ASW4

Chewbacca—25 ASW4

Invasion—25 ASW4

Legacy (10 volumes)—130 ASW4

Old Republic Era
25,000 – 1000 years before
Star Wars: A New Hope

Rise of the Empire Era
1000 – 0 years before
Star Wars: A New Hope

Rebellion Era
0 – 5 years after
Star Wars: A New Hope

New Republic Era
5 – 25 years after
Star Wars: A New Hope

New Jedi Order Era
25+ years after
Star Wars: A New Hope

Legacy Era
130+ years after
Star Wars: A New Hope

Infinities
Does not apply to timeline

Sergio Aragonés Stomps Star Wars
Star Wars Tales
Star Wars Infinities
Tag and Bink
Star Wars Visionaries

BSW4 = before *Episode IV: A New Hope*. ASW4 = after *Episode IV: A New Hope*.

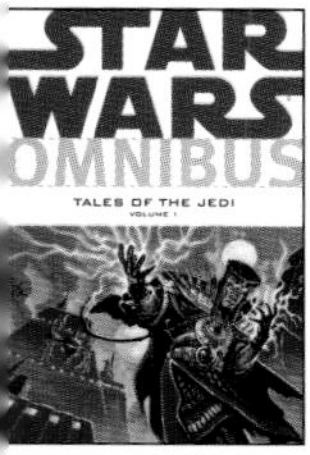
STAR WARS
OMNIBUS
TALES OF THE JEDI

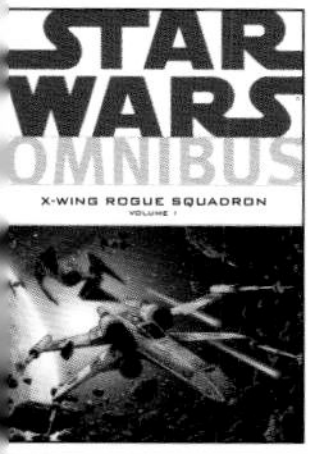
STAR WARS
OMNIBUS
X-WING ROGUE SQUADRON

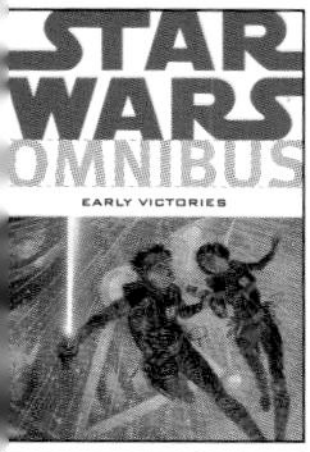
STAR WARS
OMNIBUS
EARLY VICTORIES

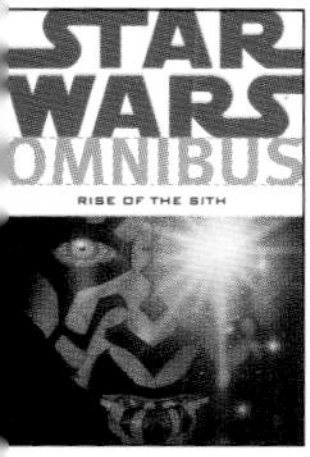
STAR WARS
OMNIBUS
RISE OF THE SITH

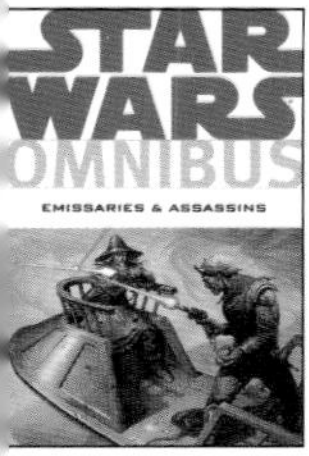
STAR WARS
OMNIBUS
EMISSARIES & ASSASSINS

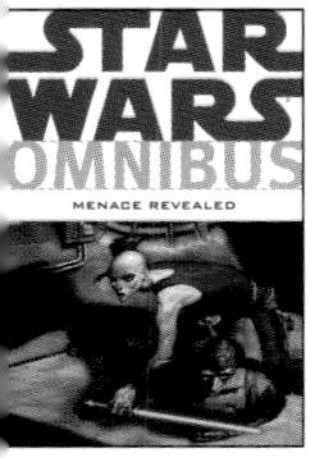
STAR WARS
OMNIBUS
MENACE REVEALED

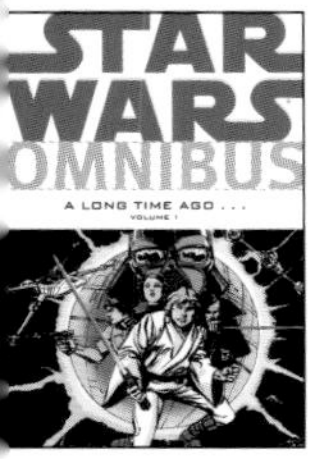
STAR WARS
OMNIBUS
A LONG TIME AGO . . .

STAR WARS OMNIBUS COLLECTIONS

STAR WARS: TALES OF THE JEDI

Including the *Tales of the Jedi* stories "The Golden Age of the Sith," "The Freedon Nadd Uprising," and "Knights of the Old Republic," these huge omnibus editions are the ultimate introduction to the ancient history of the *Star Wars* universe!

Volume 1 ISBN 978-1-59307-830-0 | $24.99 Volume 2 ISBN 978-1-59307-911-6 | $24.99

STAR WARS: X-WING ROGUE SQUADRON

The greatest starfighters of the Rebel Alliance become the defenders of a new Republic in this massive collection of stories featuring Wedge Antilles, hero of the Battle of Endor, and his team of ace pilots known throughout the galaxy as Rogue Squadron.

Volume 1 ISBN 978-1-59307-572-9 | $24.99 Volume 2 ISBN 978-1-59307-619-1 | $24.99

Volume 3 ISBN 978-1-59307-776-1 | $24.99

STAR WARS: BOBA FETT

Boba Fett, the most feared, most respected, and most loved bounty hunter in the galaxy, now has all of his comics stories collected into one massive volume!

ISBN 978-1-59582-418-9 | $24.99

STAR WARS: EARLY VICTORIES

Following the destruction of the first Death Star, Luke Skywalker is the new, unexpected hero of the Rebellion. But the galaxy hasn't been saved yet–Luke and Princess Leia find there are many more battles to be fought against the Empire and Darth Vader!

ISBN 978-1-59582-172-0 | $24.99

STAR WARS: RISE OF THE SITH

Before the name of Skywalker–or Vader–achieved fame across the galaxy, the Jedi Knights had long preserved peace and justice . . . as well as preventing the return of the Sith. These thrilling tales illustrate the events leading up to *The Phantom Menace*.

ISBN 978-1-59582-228-4 | $24.99

STAR WARS: EMISSARIES AND ASSASSINS

Discover more stories featuring Anakin Skywalker, Amidala, Obi-Wan, and Qui-Gon set during the time of Episode I: *The Phantom Menace* in this mega collection!

ISBN 978-1-59582-229-1 | $24.99

STAR WARS: MENACE REVEALED

This is our largest omnibus of never-before-collected and out-of-print *Star Wars* stories. Included here are one-shot adventures, short story arcs, specialty issues, and early Dark Horse Extra comic strips! All of these tales take place after Episode I: *The Phantom Menace*, and lead up to Episode II: *Attack of the Clones*.

ISBN 978-1-59582-273-4 | $24.99

STAR WARS: SHADOWS OF THE EMPIRE

Featuring all your favorite characters from the *Star Wars* trilogy—Luke Skywalker, Princess Leia, and Han Solo—this volume includes stories written by acclaimed novelists Timothy Zahn and Steve Perry!

ISBN 978-1-59582-434-9 | $24.99

STAR WARS: A LONG TIME AGO. . . .

Star Wars: A Long Time Ago. . . . omnibus volumes feature classic *Star Wars* stories not seen in over twenty years! Originally printed by Marvel Comics, these stories have been recolored and are sure to please *Star Wars* fans both new and old.

Volume 1: ISBN 978-1-59582-486-8 | $24.99 Volume 2: ISBN 978-1-59582-554-4 | $24.99

Volume 3: ISBN 978-1-59582-639-8 | $24.99

AVAILABLE AT YOUR LOCAL COMICS SHOP OR BOOKSTORE!

To find a comics shop in your area, call 1-888-266-4226

For more information or to order direct: • On the web: darkhorse.com • E-mail: mailorder@darkhorse.com • Phone: 1-800-862-0052 Mon.–Fri. 9 AM to 5 PM Pacific Time

STAR WARS®
LEGACY

More than one hundred years have passed since the events in *Return of the Jedi* and the days of the New Jedi Order. There is new evil gripping the galaxy, shattering a resurgent Empire, and seeking to destroy the last of the Jedi. Even as their power is failing, the Jedi hold onto one final hope . . . the last remaining heir to the Skywalker legacy.

AVAILABLE AT YOUR LOCAL COMICS SHOP OR BOOKSTORE